# DRAMA
*for Students*

# *Advisors*

**Jayne M. Burton** is a teacher of AP English Language and Composition and an adjunct professor for Northwest Vista College in San Antonio, TX.

**Klaudia Janek** is the school librarian at the International Academy in Bloomfield Hills, Michigan. She holds an MLIS degree from Wayne State University, a teaching degree from Rio Salado College, and a Bachelor of Arts degree in international relations from Saint Joseph's College. She is the IB Extended Essay Coordinator at her school. She is an IB workshop leader for International Baccalaureate North America, leading teacher training for IB school librarians and extended essay coordinators. She is currently the Michigan Association for Media in Education President-elect and a Region 3 affiliate representative for AASL.

**Greg Bartley** is a PhD student in Curriculum and Instruction at the University of Wisconsin-Madison. Previously, he taught high school English and journalism for seven years in Ohio and Virginia. Greg holds an MAEd in English Education from Wake Forest University and a BS in Secondary Integrated Language Arts Education from Miami University.

**Susan Quinn** is an eighth grade honors and traditional English teacher for the Grosse Pointe Public Schools in Michigan. She holds a BA in English and Education from Albion College and a Master's degree in Teaching Special Education from Oakland University.

# DRAMA
## *for Students*

Presenting Analysis, Context, and Criticism
on Commonly Studied Dramas

## VOLUME 35

*Kristen A. Dorsch, Project Editor*

*Foreword by Carole L. Hamilton*

**GALE**
A Cengage Company

Farmington Hills, Mich • San Francisco • New York • Waterville, Maine
Meriden, Conn • Mason, Ohio • Chicago

**Drama for Students, Volume 35**

Project Editor: Kristen A. Dorsch

Rights Acquisition and Management:
Ashley Maynard, Carissa Poweleit

Composition: Evi Abou-El-Seoud

Manufacturing: Rita Wimberley

Imaging: John Watkins

For product information and technology assistance, contact us at
**Gale Customer Support, 1-800-877-4253.**
For permission to use material from this text or product,
submit all requests online at **www.cengage.com/permissions.**
Further permissions questions can be emailed to
**permissionrequest@cengage.com**

*Gale*
27500 Drake Rd.
Farmington Hills, MI, 48331-3535

ISBN-13: 978-1-4103-2833-5
ISSN 1094-9232

This title is also available as an e-book.
ISBN-13: 978-1-4103-2835-9
Contact your Gale, A Cengage Company sales representative for ordering information.

# Table of Contents

Style . . . . . . . . . 36
Historical Context . . . . . . . . 36
Critical Overview. . . . . . . . 38
Criticism. . . . . . . . . 39
Sources . . . . . . . . . 45
Further Reading . . . . . . . . 45
Suggested Search Terms . . . . . . 46

**THE GOSPEL AT COLONUS**

*(by Lee Breuer)* . . . . . . . . . 47
Author Biography . . . . . . . 48
Plot Summary. . . . . . . . . 49
Characters . . . . . . . . . 51
Themes . . . . . . . . . 53
Style . . . . . . . . . 55
Historical Context . . . . . . . 56
Critical Overview. . . . . . . . 59
Criticism. . . . . . . . . 60
Sources . . . . . . . . . 67
Further Reading . . . . . . . 68
Suggested Search Terms . . . . . . 68

**THE KILLER**

*(by Eugène Ionesco)* . . . . . . . . . 69
Author Biography . . . . . . . 70
Plot Summary. . . . . . . . . 70
Characters . . . . . . . . . 74
Themes . . . . . . . . . 77
Style . . . . . . . . . 80
Historical Context . . . . . . . 81
Critical Overview. . . . . . . . 83
Criticism. . . . . . . . . 84
Sources . . . . . . . . . 89
Further Reading . . . . . . . 89
Suggested Search Terms . . . . . . 90

**A MAN FOR ALL SEASONS**

Plot Summary. . . . . . . . . 91
Characters . . . . . . . . . 95
Themes . . . . . . . . . 96
Style . . . . . . . . . 98
Cultural Context . . . . . . . 98
Critical Overview. . . . . . . 100
Criticism. . . . . . . . . 101
Sources . . . . . . . . . 104
Further Reading . . . . . . . 105
Suggested Search Terms . . . . . 105

**NIGHT OF JANUARY 16TH**

*(by Ayn Rand)* . . . . . . . . 106
Author Biography . . . . . . . 106
Plot Summary. . . . . . . . . 108
Characters . . . . . . . . . 111
Themes . . . . . . . . . 113

Style . . . . . . . . . 116
Historical Context . . . . . . . 117
Critical Overview. . . . . . . 118
Criticism. . . . . . . . . 119
Sources . . . . . . . . . 129
Further Reading . . . . . . . 130
Suggested Search Terms . . . . . 130

**SEVEN GUITARS**

*(by August Wilson)* . . . . . . . 131
Author Biography . . . . . . . 132
Plot Summary. . . . . . . . . 133
Characters . . . . . . . . . 135
Themes . . . . . . . . . 138
Style . . . . . . . . . 140
Historical Context . . . . . . . 141
Critical Overview. . . . . . . 143
Criticism. . . . . . . . . 143
Sources . . . . . . . . . 157
Further Reading . . . . . . . 158
Suggested Search Terms . . . . . 158

**TRIBES**

*(by Nina Raine)* . . . . . . . . 159
Author Biography . . . . . . . 159
Plot Summary. . . . . . . . . 160
Characters . . . . . . . . . 163
Themes . . . . . . . . . 164
Style . . . . . . . . . 167
Historical Context . . . . . . . 167
Critical Overview. . . . . . . 168
Criticism. . . . . . . . . 169
Sources . . . . . . . . . 176
Further Reading . . . . . . . 177
Suggested Search Terms . . . . . 177

**UNE TEMPÊTE**

*(by Aimé Césaire)* . . . . . . . 178
Author Biography . . . . . . . 178
Plot Summary. . . . . . . . . 179
Characters . . . . . . . . . 182
Themes . . . . . . . . . 184
Style . . . . . . . . . 185
Historical Context . . . . . . . 186
Critical Overview. . . . . . . 187
Criticism. . . . . . . . . 189
Sources . . . . . . . . . 200
Further Reading . . . . . . . 200
Suggested Search Terms . . . . . 200

**A VIEW FROM THE BRIDGE**

*(by Arthur Miller)* . . . . . . . 201
Author Biography . . . . . . . 202
Plot Summary. . . . . . . . . 203

# *The Study of Drama*

We study drama in order to learn what meaning others have made of life, to comprehend what it takes to produce a work of art, and to glean some understanding of ourselves. Drama produces in a separate, aesthetic world, a moment of being for the audience to experience, while maintaining the detachment of a reflective observer.

Drama is a representational art, a visible and audible narrative presenting virtual, fictional characters within a virtual, fictional universe. Dramatic realizations may pretend to approximate reality or else stubbornly defy, distort, and deform reality into an artistic statement. From this separate universe that is obviously not "real life" we expect a valid reflection upon reality, yet drama never is mistaken for reality—the methods of theater are integral to its form and meaning. Theater is art, and art's appeal lies in its ability both to approximate life and to depart from it. For in intruding its distorted version of life into our consciousness, art gives us a new perspective and appreciation of life and reality. Although all aesthetic experiences perform this service, theater does it most effectively by creating a separate, cohesive universe that freely acknowledges its status as an art form.

And what is the purpose of the aesthetic universe of drama? The potential answers to such a question are nearly as many and varied as there are plays written, performed, and enjoyed. Dramatic texts can be problems posed, answers asserted, or moments portrayed. Dramas (tragedies as well as comedies) may serve strictly "to ease the anguish of a torturing hour" (as stated in William Shakespeare's *A Midsummer Night's Dream*)—to divert and entertain—or aspire to move the viewer to action with social issues. Whether to entertain or to instruct, affirm or influence, pacify or shock, dramatic art wraps us in the spell of its imaginary world for the length of the work and then dispenses us back to the real world, entertained, purged, as Aristotle said, of pity and fear, and edified—or at least weary enough to sleep peacefully.

It is commonly thought that theater, being an art of performance, must be experienced—seen—in order to be appreciated fully. However, to view a production of a dramatic text is to be limited to a single interpretation of that text—all other interpretations are for the moment closed off, inaccessible. In the process of producing a play, the director, stage designer, and performers interpret and transform the script into a work of art that always departs in some measure from the author's original conception. Novelist and critic Umberto Eco, in his *The Role of the Reader: Explorations in the Semiotics of Texts* (Indiana University Press, 1979), explained, "In short, we can say that every performance offers us a complete and satisfying version of the work, but at the same time makes it incomplete for us, because it cannot simultaneously give all the other artistic solutions which the work may admit."

Thus Laurence Olivier's coldly formal and neurotic film presentation of Shakespeare's *Hamlet* (in which he played the title character as well as directed) shows marked differences from subsequent adaptations. While Olivier's Hamlet is clearly entangled in a Freudian relationship with his mother Gertrude, he would be incapable of shushing her with the impassioned kiss that Mel Gibson's mercurial Hamlet (in director Franco Zeffirelli's 1990 film) does. Although each of performances rings true to Shakespeare's text, each is also a mutually exclusive work of art. Also important to consider are the time periods in which each of these films was produced: Olivier made his film in 1948, a time in which overt references to sexuality (especially incest) were frowned upon. Gibson and Zeffirelli made their film in a culture more relaxed and comfortable with these issues. Just as actors and directors can influence the presentation of drama, so too can the time period of the production affect what the audience will see.

A play script is an open text from which an infinity of specific realizations may be derived. Dramatic scripts that are more open to interpretive creativity (such as those of Ntozake Shange and Tomson Highway) actually require the creative improvisation of the production troupe in order to complete the text. Even the most prescriptive scripts (those of Neil Simon, Lillian Hellman, and Robert Bolt, for example), can never fully control the actualization of live performance, and circumstantial events, including the attitude and receptivity of the audience, make every performance a unique event. Thus, while it is important to view a production of a dramatic piece, if one wants to understand a drama fully it is equally important to read the original dramatic text.

The reader of a dramatic text or script is not limited by either the specific interpretation of a given production or by the unstoppable action of a moving spectacle. The reader of a dramatic text may discover the nuances of the play's language, structure, and events at their own pace. Yet studied alone, the author's blueprint for artistic production does not tell the whole story of a play's life and significance. One also needs to assess the play's critical reviews to discover how it resonated to cultural themes at the time of its debut and how the shifting tides of cultural interest have revised its interpretation and impact on audiences. And to do this, one needs to know a little about the culture of the times which produced the play as well as the author who penned it.

*Drama for Students* supplies this material in a useful compendium for the student of dramatic theater. Covering a range of dramatic works that span from 442 BCE to the 1990s, this book focuses on significant theatrical works whose themes and form transcend the uncertainty of dramatic fads. These are plays that have proven to be both memorable and teachable. *Drama for Students* seeks to enhance appreciation of these dramatic texts by providing scholarly materials written with the secondary and college/university student in mind. It provides for each play a concise summary of the plot and characters as well as a detailed explanation of its themes. In addition, background material on the historical context of the play, its critical reception, and the author's life help the student to understand the work's position in the chronicle of dramatic history. For each play entry a new work of scholarly criticism is also included, as well as segments of other significant critical works for handy reference. A thorough bibliography provides a starting point for further research.

This series offers comprehensive educational resources for students of drama. *Drama for Students* is a vital book for dramatic interpretation and a valuable addition to any reference library.

## Sources

Eco, Umberto, *The Role of the Reader: Explorations in the Semiotics of Texts*, Indiana University Press, 1979.

*Carole L. Hamilton*
*Author and Instructor of English at Cary Academy, Cary, North Carolina*

# Introduction

## Purpose of the Book

The purpose of *Drama for Students* (*DfS*) is to provide readers with a guide to understanding, enjoying, and studying dramas by giving them easy access to information about the work. Part of Gale's "For Students" literature line, *DfS* is specifically designed to meet the curricular needs of high school and undergraduate college students and their teachers, as well as the interests of general readers and researchers considering specific plays. While each volume contains entries on "classic" dramas frequently studied in classrooms, there are also entries containing hard-to-find information on contemporary plays, including works by multicultural, international, and women playwrights. Entries profiling film versions of plays not only diversify the study of drama but support alternate learning styles, media literacy, and film studies curricula as well.

The information covered in each entry includes an introduction to the play and the work's author; a plot summary, to help readers unravel and understand the events in a drama; descriptions of important characters, including explanation of a given character's role in the drama as well as discussion about that character's relationship to other characters in the play; analysis of important themes in the drama; and an explanation of important literary techniques and movements as they are demonstrated in the play.

In addition to this material, which helps the readers analyze the play itself, students are also provided with important information on the literary and historical background informing each work. This includes a historical context essay, a box comparing the time or place the drama was written to modern Western culture, a critical essay, and excerpts from critical essays on the play. A unique feature of *DfS* is a specially commissioned critical essay on each drama, targeted toward the student reader.

The "literature to film" entries on plays vary slightly in form, providing background on film technique and comparison to the original, literary version of the work. These entries open with an introduction to the film, which leads directly into the plot summary. The summary highlights plot changes from the play, key cinematic moments, and/or examples of key film techniques. As in standard entries, there are character profiles (noting omissions or additions, and identifying the actors), analysis of themes and how they are illustrated in the film, and an explanation of the cinematic style and structure of the film. A cultural context section notes any time period or setting differences from that of the original work, as well as cultural differences between the time in which the original work was written and the time in which the film adaptation was made. A film entry concludes with a critical overview and critical essays on the film.

To further help today's student in studying and enjoying each play or film, information on audiobooks and other media adaptations is provided (if available), as well as suggestions for works of fiction, nonfiction, or film on similar themes and topics. Classroom aids include ideas for research papers and lists of critical and reference sources that provide additional material on each drama. Film entries also highlight signature film techniques demonstrated, as well as suggesting media literacy activities and prompts to use during or after viewing a film.

## Selection Criteria

The titles for each volume of *DfS* are selected by surveying numerous sources on notable literary works and analyzing course curricula for various schools, school districts, and states. Some of the sources surveyed include: high school and undergraduate literature anthologies and textbooks; lists of award-winners, and recommended titles, including the Young Adult Library Services Association (YALSA) list of best books for young adults. Films are selected both for the literary importance of the original work and the merits of the adaptation (including official awards and widespread public recognition).

Input solicited from our expert advisory board—consisting of educators and librarians—guides us to maintain a mix of "classic" and contemporary literary works, a mix of challenging and engaging works (including genre titles that are commonly studied) appropriate for different age levels, and a mix of international, multicultural and women authors. These advisors also consult on each volume's entry list, advising on which titles are most studied, most appropriate, and meet the broadest interests across secondary (grades 7–12) curricula and undergraduate literature studies.

## How Each Entry Is Organized

Each entry, or chapter, in *DfS* focuses on one play. Each entry heading lists the full name of the play, the author's name, and the date of the play's publication. The following elements are contained in each entry:

**Introduction:** a brief overview of the drama which provides information about its first appearance, its literary standing, any controversies surrounding the work, and major conflicts or themes within the work. Film entries identify the original play and provide understanding of the film's reception and reputation, along with that of the director.

**Author Biography:** in play entries, this section includes basic facts about the author's life, and focuses on events and times in the author's life that inspired the drama in question.

**Plot Summary:** a description of the major events in the play. Subheads demarcate the play's various acts or scenes. Plot summaries of films are used to uncover plot differences from the original play, and to note the use of certain film angles or techniques.

**Characters:** an alphabetical listing of major characters in the play. Each character name is followed by a brief to an extensive description of the character's role in the play, as well as discussion of the character's actions, relationships, and possible motivation. In film entries, omissions or changes to the cast of characters of the film adaptation are mentioned here, and the actors' names—and any awards they may have received—are also included.

Characters are listed alphabetically by last name. If a character is unnamed—for instance, the Stage Manager in *Our Town*—the character is listed as "The Stage Manager" and alphabetized as "Stage Manager." If a character's first name is the only one given, the name will appear alphabetically by the first name. Variant names are also included for each character. Thus, the nickname "Babe" would head the listing for a character in *Crimes of the Heart,* but below that listing would be her less-mentioned married name "Rebecca Botrelle."

**Themes:** a thorough overview of how the major topics, themes, and issues are addressed within the play. Each theme discussed appears in a separate subhead. While the key themes often remain the same or similar when a play is adapted into a film, film entries demonstrate how the themes are conveyed cinematically, along with any changes in the portrayal of the themes.

**Style:** this section addresses important style elements of the drama, such as setting, point of view, and narration; important literary devices used, such as imagery, foreshadowing, symbolism; and, if applicable, genres to which the work might have belonged, such as Gothicism or Romanticism. Literary terms are explained within the entry, but can also be found in the Glossary. Film entries cover how the director conveyed the meaning, message, and mood of the work using film in comparison to the author's use of language, literary device, etc., in the original work.

**Historical Context:** in play entries, this section outlines the social, political, and cultural climate in which the author lived and the play was created. This section may include descriptions of related historical events, pertinent aspects of daily life in the culture, and the artistic and literary sensibilities of the time in which the work was written. If the play is a historical work, information regarding the time in which the play is set is also included. Each section is broken down with helpful subheads. Film entries contain a similar Cultural Context section, because the film adaptation might explore an entirely different time period or culture than the original work, and may also be influenced by the traditions and views of a time period much different than that of the original author.

**Critical Overview:** this section provides background on the critical reputation of the play or film, including bannings or any other public controversies surrounding the work. For older plays, this section includes a history of how the drama or film was first received and how perceptions of it may have changed over the years; for more recent plays, direct quotes from early reviews may also be included.

**Criticism:** an essay commissioned by *DfS* which specifically deals with the play or film and is written specifically for the student audience, as well as excerpts from previously published criticism on the work (if available).

**Sources:** an alphabetical list of critical material used in compiling the entry, with full bibliographical information.

**Further Reading:** an alphabetical list of other critical sources which may prove useful for the student. It includes full bibliographical information and a brief annotation.

**Suggested Search Terms:** a list of search terms and phrases to jumpstart students' further information seeking. Terms include not just titles and author names but also terms and topics related to the historical and literary context of the works.

In addition, each entry contains the following highlighted sections, set apart from the main text as sidebars:

**Media Adaptations:** if available, a list of audiobooks and important film and television adaptations of the play, including source information. The list may also include such variations on the work as musical adaptations and other stage interpretations.

**Topics for Further Study:** a list of potential study questions or research topics dealing with the play. This section includes questions related to other disciplines the student may be studying, such as American history, world history, science, math, government, business, geography, economics, psychology, etc.

**Compare and Contrast:** an "at-a-glance" comparison of the cultural and historical differences between the author's time and culture and late twentieth century or early twenty-first century Western culture. This box includes pertinent parallels between the major scientific, political, and cultural movements of the time or place the drama was written, the time or place the play was set (if a historical work), and modern Western culture. Works written after 1990 may not have this box.

**What Do I Read Next?:** a list of works that might give a reader points of entry into a classic work (e.g., YA or multicultural titles) and/or complement the featured play or serve as a contrast to it. This includes works by the same author and others, works from various genres, YA works, and works from various cultures and eras.

The film entries provide sidebars more targeted to the study of film, including:

**Film Technique:** a listing and explanation of four to six key techniques used in the film, including shot styles, use of transitions, lighting, sound or music, etc.

**Read, Watch, Write:** media literacy prompts and/or suggestions for viewing log prompts.

**What Do I See Next?:** a list of films based on the same or similar works or of films similar in directing style, technique, etc.

## *Other Features*

*DfS* includes "The Study of Drama," a foreword by Carole Hamilton, an educator and author who specializes in dramatic works. This essay examines the basis for drama in societies and what drives people to study such work. The essay also discusses how *DfS* can help teachers

show students how to enrich their own reading/
viewing experiences.

A Cumulative Author/Title Index lists the
authors and titles covered in each volume of the
*DfS* series.

A Cumulative Nationality/Ethnicity Index
breaks down the authors and titles covered in
each volume of the *DfS* series by nationality and
ethnicity.

A Subject/Theme Index, specific to each
volume, provides easy reference for users who
may be studying a particular subject or theme
rather than a single work. Significant subjects
from events to broad themes are included.

Each entry may include illustrations,
including photo of the author, stills from stage
productions, and stills from film adaptations, if
available.

## *Citing* Drama for Students

When writing papers, students who quote
directly from any volume of *DfS* may use the
following general forms. These examples are
based on MLA style; teachers may request that
students adhere to a different style, so the following examples may be adapted as needed.

When citing text from *DfS* that is not attributed to a particular author (i.e., the Themes, Style,
Historical Context sections, etc.), the following
format should be used in the bibliography section:

> "Candida." *Drama for Students*. Ed. Sara
> Constantakis. Vol. 30. Detroit: Gale, Cengage
> Learning, 2013. 1–27. Print.

When quoting the specially commissioned
essay from *DfS* (usually the first piece under

the "Criticism" subhead), the following format
should be used:

> O'Neal, Michael J. Critical Essay on *Candida*.
> *Drama for Students*. Ed. Sara Constantakis.
> Vol. 30. Detroit: Gale, Cengage Learning,
> 2013. 12–15. Print.

When quoting a journal or newspaper essay
that is reprinted in a volume of *DfS*, the following form may be used:

> Lazenby, Walter. "Love and 'Vitality' in *Candida*."
> *Modern Drama* 20.1 (1977): 1–19. Rpt. in
> *Drama for Students*. Ed. Sara Constantakis.
> Vol. 30. Detroit: Gale, Cengage Learning,
> 2013. 18–22. Print.

When quoting material reprinted from a
book that appears in a volume of *DfS*, the following form may be used:

> Phelps, William Lyon. "George Bernard Shaw."
> *Essays on Modern Dramatists*. New York:
> Macmillan, 1921. 67–98. Rpt. in *Drama for
> Students*. Ed. Sara Constantakis. Vol. 30.
> Detroit: Gale, Cengage Learning, 2013. 26. Print.

## *We Welcome Your Suggestions*

The editorial staff of *Drama for Students* welcomes
your comments and ideas. Readers who wish to
suggest dramas to appear in future volumes, or
who have other suggestions, are cordially invited
to contact the editor. You may contact the editor
via e-mail at: **ForStudentsEditors@cengage.com.**
Or write to the editor at:

Editor, *Drama for Students*

Gale

27500 Drake Road

Farmington Hills, MI 48331-3535

# Literary Chronology

**1890:** Agatha Christie is born on September 15 in Torquay, Devon, England.

**1905:** Ayn Rand is born on February 2 in St. Petersburg, Russia.

**1909:** Eugène Ionesco is born on November 13 in Slatina, Romania.

**1913:** Aimé Césaire is born on June 25 in Basse-Pointe, Martinique.

**1915:** Arthur Miller is born on October 17 in New York, New York.

**1924:** Robert Bolt is born on August 15 near Manchester, England.

**1928:** Edward Albee is born on March 12 in Washington, DC.

**1933:** The play *Night of January 16th* is produced.

**1937:** Lee Breuer is born on February 6 in Philadelphia, Pennsylvania.

**1945:** August Wilson is born on April 27 in Pittsburgh, Pennsylvania.

**1949:** Arthur Miller is awarded the Pulitzer Prize for Drama for *Death of a Salesman*.

**1953:** Milcha Sanchez-Scott is born in Bali, Indonesia.

**1953:** The play *Witness for the Prosecution* is produced.

**1955:** The play *A View from the Bridge* is produced.

**1959:** The play *The Killer* is produced.

**1960:** The play *A Man for All Seasons* is produced.

**1962:** The play *Who's Afraid of Virginia Woolf?* is produced.

**1966:** The film *Who's Afraid of Virginia Woolf?* is released.

**1966:** The film *A Man for All Seasons* is released.

**1967:** Elizabeth Taylor is awarded the Academy Award for Best Actress for *Who's Afraid of Virginia Woolf?*

**1967:** Sandy Dennis is awarded the Academy Award for Best Actress in a Supporting Role for *Who's Afraid of Virginia Woolf?*

**1967:** Richard Sylbert and George James Hopkins are awarded the Academy Award for Best Art Direction in Black and White for *Who's Afraid of Virginia Woolf?*

**1967:** Haskel Wexler is awarded the Academy Award for Best Cinematography in Black and White for *Who's Afraid of Virginia Woolf?*

**1967:** Irene Sharaff is awarded the Academy Award for Best Costume Design in Black and White for *Who's Afraid of Virginia Woolf?*

**1969:** The play *A Tempest* is published in French as *Une Tempête*. It is published in English in 1975 as *A Tempest*.

**1974:** Sarah Ruhl is born on January 24 in Wilmette, Illinois.

**1975:** Nina Raine is born in Oxford, England.

**1976:** Agatha Christie dies of natural causes on January 12 in Winterbrook, Cholsey, England.

**1982:** Ayn Rand dies of pneumonia on March 6 in New York, New York.

**1983:** The play *The Gospel at Colonus* is produced.

**1984:** The play *Dog Lady* is produced.

**1987:** August Wilson is awarded the Pulitzer Prize for Drama for *Fences*.

**1987:** August Wilson is awarded the Tony Award for Best Play for *Fences*.

**1990:** August Wilson is awarded the Pulitzer Prize for Drama for *The Piano Lesson*.

**1994:** Eugène Ionesco dies of undisclosed causes on March 28 in Paris, France.

**1995:** Robert Bolt dies after a long illness brought on by heart attack and stroke on February 20 near Petersfield, England.

**1995:** The play *Seven Guitars* is produced.

**2004:** The play *The Clean House* is produced.

**2005:** Arthur Miller dies of congestive heart failure on February 10 in Roxbury, Connecticut.

**2005:** August Wilson dies of liver cancer on October 2 in Seattle, Washington.

**2008:** Aimé Césaire dies of heart failure on April 17 in Fort-de-France, Martinique.

**2010:** The play *Tribes* is produced.

**2016:** Edward Albee dies after an illness on September 16 in Montauk, New York.

**2017:** August Wilson's *Jitney* wins the Tony Award for Best Revival of a Play.

# Acknowledgments

The editors wish to thank the copyright holders of the excerpted criticism included in this volume and the permissions managers of many book and magazine publishing companies for assisting us in securing reproduction rights. We are also grateful to the staffs of the Detroit Public Library, the Library of Congress, the University of Detroit Mercy Library, Wayne State University Purdy/ Kresge Library Complex, and the University of Michigan Libraries for making their resources available to us. Following is a list of the copyright holders who have granted us permission to reproduce material in this volume of DfS. Every effort has been made to trace copyright, but if omissions have been made, please let us know.

**COPYRIGHTED EXCERPTS IN _DfS_, VOLUME 35, WERE REPRODUCED FROM THE FOLLOWING PERIODICALS:**

Bouknight, Jon, and Milcha Sanchez-Scott. "Language as a Cure: An Interview with Milcha Sanchez-Scott." **Latin America Theatre Review**, March-May 1990. Copyright © 1990 _Latin America Theatre Review._—McCulloh, T. H. "Rand's 'Night of January 16th' Has a Good Day in Court." _Los Angeles Times_, January 25, 1995. Courtesy of _Los Angeles Times._—McNully, Charles. "'Tribes' Will Be Heard—and Felt." **Los Angeles Times**, March 11, 2013. Copyright © 2013 _Los Angeles Times._—Miller, Deb. "Review of 'Witness for the Prosecution' at Bristol Riverside Theatre." **DC Metro Theater Arts**, May 12, 2017. Courtesy of _DC Metro Theater Arts._—Raine, Nina. "The King and I." **London Evening Standard**, June 19, 2009. Copyright © 2009 _London Evening Standard._—Shirley, Don. "Machismo Plucked Bare as 'Roosters' Takes Flight." **Los Angeles Times**, June 21, 1988. Copyright © 1988 _Los Angeles Times._—Vogel, Paula, and Sarah Ruhl. "Sarah Ruhl." **BOMB Magazine**, March-May 2007. Copyright © 2007 _BOMB Magazine._—White, Andrew. "WSC Avant Bard's 'The Gospel at Colonus' a Brilliant Revival." **Broadway World**, March 10, 2017. Copyright © 2017 _Broadway World_.

**COPYRIGHTED EXCERPTS IN _DfS_, VOLUME 35, WERE REPRODUCED FROM THE FOLLOWING BOOKS:**

Al-Shamma, James. "Joke as Incarnation in 'The Clean House.'" **Sarah Ruhl: A Critical Study of the Plays**. McFarland & Company, Inc., 2011. Copyright © 2011 McFarland & Company, Inc.— Blackman, Maurice. "Intercultural Framing in Aimé Césaire's 'Une Tempête.'" **The Play within the Play: The Performance of Meta-Theatre and Self-Reflection**. Eds. Gerhard Fischer and Bernhard Greiner. Editions Rodopi, 2007. Copyright © 2007 Editions Rodopi.—Bonds, Ellen. "World War II History/history: Essential Contexts in 'Seven Guitars.'" **August Wilson's Pittsburgh Cycle: Critical Perspectives on the Plays**. Ed. Sandra G. Shannon. McFarland & Company, Inc., 2016. Copyright © 2016

McFarland & Company, Inc.—Epstein, Arthur D. "A Look at 'A View from the Bridge.'" *Critical Essays on Arthur Miller*. Ed. James J. Martine. G. K. Hall, 1979. Copyright © 1979 Cengage Learning.—Griffin, Alice. "'A View from the Bridge.'" *Understanding Arthur Miller*. University of South Carolina Press, 1996. Copyright © 1996 University of South Carolina Press.—Lewis, Allan. "'Amédée' and 'The Killer.'" *Ionesco*. Twayne Publishers, 1972. Courtesy of Twayne Publishers.—Marshall, Peter. "Saints and Cinemas: 'A Man for All Seasons.'" *Tudors and Stuarts on Film: Historical Perspectives*. Eds. Susan Doran and Thomas S. Freeman. Palgrave Macmillan, 2009. Courtesy of Palgrave Macmillan.—Ojo-Ade, Femi. "'Une Tempête': The Dilemma of the African Diaspora." *Aimé Césaire's African Theater: Of Poets, Prophets, and Politicians*. Africa World Press, 2010. Copyright © 2010 Africa World Press.—Pronko, Leonard Cabell. "Eugène Ionesco: From 'The Bald Soprano' to 'The Chairs'—'Victims of Duty', 'The New Occupant' and 'Amédée'—'The Killer' and 'Rhinoceros.'" *Avant-Garde: The Experimental Theater in France*. University of California Press, 1963. Courtesy of University of California Press.— Rand, Ayn. "Esthetics, Art, and Artists." *Ayn Rand Answers: The Best of Her Q&A*. New American Library, 2005. Copyright © 2005 New American Library.—Rix, Lucy. "Maintaining the State of Emergence/y: Aimé Césaire's 'Une Tempête.'" *The Tempest and Its Travels*. Eds. Peter Hulme and William H. Sherman. Reaktion Books, 2000. Copyright © 2000 Reaktion Books.—Rosen, Carol, and August Wilson. "August Wilson: Bard of the Blues." *Conversations with August Wilson*. Eds. Jackson R. Bryer and Mary C. Hartig. University Press of Mississippi, 2006. Copyright © 2006 University Press of Mississippi.—Roudané, Matthew C. "The Characters." *Who's Afraid of Virginia Woolf?: Necessary Fictions, Terrifying Realities*. Twayne Publishers, 1990. Copyright © 1990 Cengage Learning.—Walker, Jeff. "The Cult While the Guru Lived." *The Ayn Rand Cult*. Open Court Publishing Company, 1999. Copyright © 1999 Open Court Publishing Company.—Wetmore, Jr., Kevin J. "Ancient Plays in a New World: Multicultural Currents." *Black Dionysus: Greek Tragedy and African American Theatre*. McFarland & Company, Inc., 2003. Copyright © 2003 McFarland & Company, Inc.—Wolfe, Peter. "All Right with Whom?" *August Wilson*. Twayne Publishers, 1999. Copyright © 1999 Cengage Learning.

# Contributors

**Susan K. Andersen:** Andersen holds a PhD in literature and is a creative writer and former teacher. Entry on *The Clean House*. Original essay on *The Clean House*.

**Bryan Aubrey:** Aubrey holds a PhD in English. Entry on *Une Tempête*. Original essay on *Une Tempête*.

**Charlotte M. Freeman:** Freeman is a writer and editor who lives in Montana. Entry on *The Killer*. Original essay on *The Killer*.

**Kristen Sarlin Greenberg:** Greenberg is a freelance writer and editor with a background in literature and philosophy. Entry on *A Man for All Seasons*. Original essay on *A Man for All Seasons*.

**Michael Allen Holmes:** Holmes is a writer with existential interests. Entries on *The Gospel at Colonus* and *A View from the Bridge*. Original essays on *The Gospel at Colonus* and *A View from the Bridge*.

**David Kelly:** Kelly is an author and a teacher of creative writing. Entry on *Witness for the Prosecution*. Original essay on *Witness for the Prosecution*.

**Amy L. Miller:** Miller is a graduate of the University of Cincinnati. Entry on *Dog Lady*. Original essay on *Dog Lady*.

**Jeffrey Eugene Palmer:** Palmer is a scholar, freelance writer, and teacher of high-school English. Entry on *Tribes*. Original essay on *Tribes*.

**April Paris:** Paris is a freelance writer with a degree in classical literature and a background in academic writing. Entry on *Who's Afraid of Virginia Woolf?* Original essay on *Who's Afraid of Virginia Woolf?*

**William Rosencrans:** Rosencrans is a writer and copy editor. Entry on *Seven Guitars*. Original essay on *Seven Guitars*.

**Bradley A. Skeen:** Skeen is a classicist. Entry on *Night of January 16th*. Original essay on *Night of January 16th*.

# *The Clean House*

## SARAH RUHL

## 2004

Sarah Ruhl has dominated American stages in the twenty-first century. *The Clean House* (2004), a Pulitzer finalist, has remained one of her most frequently staged plays. The play has realistic elements—such as dealing with cancer, divorce, and death—interposed with the fantastic time, space, and imagery of magical realism. Characters eat apples on a balcony and throw the cores into the sea, but they land in the living room of another character. In this world of magical thinking, a joke can kill, and cleaning house can save one's sanity. Ruhl investigates the deeper reaches of love and grief but with a humorous touch. The spare dialogue cuts to the core issues with directness and clarity as the characters put their hearts on the line.

Ruhl's fame right out of graduate school, along with her continuing list of hit dramas on a variety of imaginative topics, speaks of her mentoring at an early age by the Piven Theatre in Chicago and feminist playwright Paula Vogel, her professor at Brown. Ruhl has a grounding in the literary classics, having adapted Virginia Woolf and Anton Chekhov for the stage. She prefers a theater of poetry and symbolism to a drama of psychological realism. Her understanding of the power of drama is deep, and she gathers techniques from many traditional and ethnic sources, such as using puppets or untranslated languages.

*The Clean House* begins with an untranslated joke in Portuguese from the Brazilian

*Sarah Ruhl* (© WENN Ltd | Alamy Stock Photo)

maid, Matilde, who tells jokes because she is in mourning. She has a lot to teach her boss, Lane, a doctor who thinks she knows everything until her husband falls in love with another woman. The play is a ritual for grief and loss that allows the audience to participate, but within Ruhl's characteristic mood of lightness and humor that leads to acceptance. The characters move from isolation to community and learn to forgive and let go of control.

## AUTHOR BIOGRAPHY

Ruhl was born on January 24, 1974, to Kathy Kehoe Ruhl and Patrick Ruhl in Wilmette, Illinois. Sarah's mother was a high school teacher. Her father marketed toys before he died of cancer when Ruhl was twenty, a deep crisis in her life as she began writing plays. He loved language and history, taking Sarah and her sister, Kate, to the pancake house once a week to learn special vocabulary words. Sarah was raised as a Catholic but left the church as a teenager because of what she felt was its bias against women. She is deeply influenced by the church's rituals, however, in her idea of theater.

Kathy directed high school plays and acted in community theater, taking Sarah with her to rehearsals, so that she grew up in the theater. Kathy also worked in alternative theater in Chicago. Even as a child, Sarah took classes at the Piven Theatre Workshop in Evanston, Illinois, with her mother. The Piven Workshop teaches improvisational skills using myth, folktales, and fairy tales focusing on transformation, one of Ruhl's main themes. The exercises help the actors to live in the moment, also a characteristic of Ruhl's plays, and there are no props, only language, to tell the story. The Piven Workshop also helped Ruhl to develop *The Clean House*.

Ruhl wrote whimsical stories as a child about vegetables and landmasses getting married. She first thought she would be a poet. She wrote poems and studied English at Brown University, spending her junior year abroad at Oxford. After graduation in 1997, she taught English in Providence, Rhode Island, at Wheaton College, before returning to Chicago to write the adaptation of *Orlando* for Piven. Ruhl then continued her studies at Brown, earning a master of fine arts degree in playwriting in 2001 under her mentor, Pulitzer Prize–winning playwright Paula Vogel.

Ruhl married Anthony Charuvastra, a child psychiatrist, in 2005. They had a daughter, Anna, in 2006 and twins in 2010. Ruhl was upset when she had to move to Los Angeles, where her husband did his medical residency, but it turned to her advantage as she became well known through regional theater on the West Coast before returning to New York.

After an initial period when no one was interested in her plays, Ruhl became successful in having her work constantly performed while still in her thirties. Using techniques like magic realism, puppets, and nonlinear structure, she deals with issues of gender, race, class, sexuality, politics, religion, cultural differences, and art. Her plays include *Melancholy Play: A Contemporary Farce* (2002), *Eurydice* (2003), *Passion Play* (2003), *Orlando* (2003), *The Clean House* (2004), *Demeter in the City* (2006), *Dead Man's Cell Phone* (2007), *In the Next Room (or the Vibrator Play)* (2009), *Stage Kiss* (2011), *Dear Elizabeth* (2012), *The Oldest Boy* (2014), *For*

*Peter Pan on Her 70th Birthday* (2017), and *How to Transcend a Happy Marriage* (2017). In 2004, she won the Susan Smith Blackburn Award of $10,000. She was also awarded the MacArthur Foundation "genius grant" of half a million dollars in 2006 and the Steinberg Distinguished Playwright Prize in 2016. The recipient of dozens of other awards, she has also been a Pulitzer finalist twice.

## PLOT SUMMARY

The play happens in a living room in Connecticut, not a physical place but a metaphysical one, according to the stage directions. It is near a city and the sea. The living room is white with an overlooking balcony. Some scenes have subtitles, and some do not. Some productions display these subtitles to the audience. There is double casting, with Charles and Ana also playing Matilde's parents.

### *Act 1*

#### SCENE 1: MATILDE

Matilde, a young Brazilian maid, tells a joke in Portuguese to the audience and then exits.

#### SCENE 2: LANE

Lane, a middle-aged doctor, addresses the audience, explaining it has been a hard time because her cleaning lady from Brazil is depressed and has stopped cleaning her house. She took Matilde to the hospital for medication, but she still will not work. Lane is upset, believing that a woman who has been to medical school should not have to clean her own house.

#### SCENE 3: VIRGINIA

Lane's middle-aged sister, Virginia, addresses the audience, saying that it does not make sense to give up the privilege of cleaning your own house, because then you do not know if any progress is being made. If she did not have her cleaning to do in the day, she would have too much leisure time. Her sister is a doctor at an important hospital, but all hospitals are places to put dead bodies. She apologizes for being morbid.

#### SCENE 4: MATILDE

Matilde addresses the audience, telling the story of her parents. Her father was the funniest man in Brazil and would not marry until the age of sixty-three because he did not want to marry

# MEDIA ADAPTATIONS

- In an article called "Is Theater Helpful? (Or Some Things I Learned from Rehearsing *The Oldest Boy*)," Ruhl tells of her involvement with the Buddhist community as she rehearsed her play. The piece was posted at HowlRound.com, a resource created by and for the theater community (http://howl round.com/is-theatre-helpful-or-some-things-i-learned-from-rehearsing-the-oldest-boy).

- In an interview at Lincoln Center Theater, Ruhl talks about staging *The Clean House* there. She also mentions some of her favorite plays. A recording of the interview can be viewed on YouTube (https://www.youtube.com/watch?v=brr2sxSIooA).

- Ruhl talks about creating "poor theater" without using much money or scenery in "Playwright Conversations," produced by Samuel French and available on YouTube (https://www.youtube.com/watch?v=Zvgm 4eXP0wg).

a woman who was not equally witty. He admitted that Matilde's mother was funnier than he was. They laughed all day, even when they made love. Matilde wears black because she is in mourning for her parents. Her mother died laughing at a joke her father worked on for a whole year as a present for their anniversary. He was so upset at her death, he shot himself. Then Matilde came to America.

#### SCENE 5: LANE AND MATILDE

Matilde is looking out the window when Lane enters, asking her to clean the bathroom. Although Matilde agrees, she does not move. Lane scolds a silent Matilde. When Lane asks what Matilde did before coming to the United States, she explains that she was a student of humor. Now that her parents are dead, there is no one to laugh at her jokes.

Lane explains that Matilde's personal life is not relevant to her job of cleaning the house.

She does not like to have to push the maid into cleaning. Matilde responds to Lane's emotion, telling Lane she should give her orders as she orders the nurses at the hospital. Lane orders Matilde to polish the silver, and Matilde complies, at least until Lane exits.

## SCENE 6: MATILDE

Matilde stops polishing and addresses the audience, imagining a scene with her parents. A couple appears and begins to dance in clumsy fashion as Matilde narrates the scene. They dance, laugh, and kiss.

## SCENE 7: VIRGINIA AND MATILDE

The doorbell rings, and Matilde's parents leave, blowing kisses. Virginia comes in. Matilde knows who she is and introduces herself as Ma-chil-gee, the maid, giving the correct Brazilian pronunciation. Virginia pronounces it as *Matilda*. Virginia asks Matilde to sit on the couch for a chat. Matilde admits she does not like to clean houses. Virginia says she likes to clean because it clears her mind. Matilde says it is different to clean someone else's house for money. She gets mad about it and then cannot think of funny jokes.

While Matilde fetches coffee, Virginia tests the dust in Lane's house by wiping her finger on a table. She proposes to Matilde that she secretly clean Lane's house because she does not have enough to do. Since age twenty-two, Virginia has been in a downward spiral in her life. She wanted to be a writer but had nothing to say. Now she cleans. Matilde agrees to let Virginia clean Lane's house because she wants her to be happy.

## SCENE 8: LANE AND MATILDE

Lane enters and exclaims at the house's cleanliness. Matilde is reading the funny papers. Lane assumes the medication is helping, but when Lane leaves, Matilde throws the medication in the garbage.

## SCENE 9: MATILDE

Matilde explains to the audience the magic of the perfect joke. She imagines a scene with her parents sitting at a cafe. Her mother tells a dirty joke, and her father laughs so hard he bangs the table with his knees. She spits out her coffee. Matilde is a little girl and cannot understand the joke. She asks her parents what is so funny. Her mother says she will get it when she is thirty. Matilde is almost thirty but will never know that joke.

## SCENE 10: VIRGINIA AND MATILDE

The next day, Virginia folds laundry while Matilde watches. They are happy. Matilde wants to tell a joke, but Virginia does not want to hear it because she does not like to laugh out loud. Her husband says she sounds as if she is wheezing. Matilde wants to know if she likes her husband, and Virginia compares him to a piece of furniture. Matilde asks if he makes her laugh, and Virginia says no. Matilde claims that laughing makes you clean.

As Virginia folds the clothes, she finds a pair of black women's underpants with her brother-in-law's underwear. Virginia and Matilde stare at each other. Virginia remarks the black pants are too sexy to belong to Lane.

## SCENE 11: LANE AND VIRGINIA HAVE COFFEE

Lane and Virginia are having coffee in the living room. Virginia compliments the house being so clean. She asks Lane about her husband, Charles. Lane says he is fine, though they hardly see each other. Lane calls for Matilde to clear the cups. Matilde winks at Virginia and leaves. Lane apologizes for not introducing Matilde to Virginia and then wonders if it is proper etiquette to introduce the maid.

Virginia says somewhat sarcastically that it must make her uncomfortable to have someone else cleaning up after her. However, Lane does not feel guilty for having a maid because she herself works hard at her job all day. She makes a dig at her sister in this speech because she does not have a job. The stage directions remark that for a moment the two sisters are as children again, mad at each other. Lane tries to make up by saying that she should have her sister and husband over for dinner, but she has been so busy.

## SCENE 12: LANE AND MATILDE

It is night, and Matilde is sitting in the living room in the dark trying to think of the perfect joke. Lane comes in, turns on the light, and asks Matilde what she is doing. Matilde says she almost had a joke, and now it is gone. Lane asks if Charles is home. Matilde says no, and he did not call. Lane says he is probably sleeping at the hospital. When Lane and Charles were younger, they communicated by paging each other at the hospital to say good night. They do not need that now they are older and understand one another. Lane exits as Matilde continues to think of the perfect joke in the dark.

**SCENE 13: VIRGINIA AND MATILDE. THEN LANE.**

The next day, Virginia is ironing while Matilde describes how jokes have rhythms. She is creating one with six beats. Virginia did not know jokes had this kind of rhythm, but Matilde makes a joke out of explaining her problem is timing by coming in at the wrong time with the punch line. Virginia does not laugh. Matilde is afraid of finding a perfect joke because it might kill her.

Virginia finds some red underwear, and she and Matilde wonder where Charles is having his affair: in the house or in the park? Perhaps some nurse is walking around in the hospital without underwear.

Lane comes in and asks Virginia what she is doing there. In turn, Virginia asks why Lane is not at work. Lane claims she is going to shoot herself, goes to the kitchen, and wounds her hand on a can opener trying to make a martini. She admits to Virginia that Charles has fallen in love with one of his patients. Lane is particularly surprised because the other woman is older than she is. Lane has never been jealous because she believes no other woman is her equal as a doctor loved by her patients, but Charles apparently wanted a housewife.

Lane figures out that Virginia has been cleaning the house. Angry, Lane fires Matilde, though she offers to buy Matilde a plane ticket home. Matilde would rather move to New York to become a comedian.

Lane does not understand why Virginia cleaned her house, but she does not like her looking through her things. Virginia explains that she has a boring life and would like to take care of her sister, though Lane thinks she does not need anyone to take care of her. Matilde says good-bye and exits.

**SCENE 14: LANE. THEN MATILDE. THEN VIRGINIA.**

Lane relates to the audience her fantasy of Charles and his new wife, Ana. The couple appears. (They are the same actors who play Matilde's parents.) Lane narrates as Charles undresses Ana and kisses different parts of her body, like a sacred ritual. While they are doing this, Matilde enters with her suitcase and asks who the people are. Lane explains that it is her husband and his lover, but it is only her imagination.

Matilde tries to cheer Lane up with a joke in Portuguese. Lane tries to laugh but cries. She keeps crying and laughing. Virginia enters to announce Charles's arrival with a beautiful woman. Charles calls out Lane's name as the stage blacks out for intermission.

## Act 2

**SCENE 1: CHARLES PERFORMS SURGERY ON THE WOMAN HE LOVES**

For this scene, the white living room is transformed into a hospital set. Ana is lying under a sheet while music plays, and Charles performs surgery on her as an act of love. The stage directions suggest that Ana and Charles sing a love duet in Latin. After the surgery, Charles removes the sheet, revealing Ana wearing a nice dress.

**SCENE 2: ANA**

Ana tells the audience that she has avoided doctors her whole life, finding them cold. Nevertheless, once she met Charles, it was instant love. She thinks he left his soul inside her when he did the surgery.

**SCENE 3: CHARLES**

Charles explains that he is not a man who falls in love easily. He met his wife at age twenty-two when life was simple. Once he met Ana, he learned how inspiring true love can be.

**SCENE 4: CHARLES AND ANA**

Charles and Ana have their conference as doctor and patient. He informs her she has breast cancer while she fights tears. He tells her she will need some time to adjust, but she insists that he cut off the breast the very next day. He promises to keep her alive. They understand they are falling in love and kiss.

**SCENE 5: LANE, VIRGINIA, MATILDE, CHARLES, AND ANA**

In the white living room, Charles introduces Ana to Lane, and the two women shake hands. Then Virginia is introduced. Matilde remarks to Ana that she looks like her mother. Lane introduces Matilde as the maid, who was fired that morning. Meanwhile, Ana, who is from Argentina, talks with Matilde in Spanish and Portuguese. They laugh and enjoy each other. Lane wants everyone to leave, but Virginia invites them to sit. Virginia takes orders for coffee, though Lane would prefer alcohol.

Ana tells Lane her story. She is not really a home-wrecker. She had been married to an alcoholic geologist and did not want to have children with him. He died. Her heart was broken, and she thought she would never love again. She did not want to go with Charles, a married man, until he told her about a Jewish law that allows one to leave one's spouse if one finds one's *bashert*, or soul mate. Lane points out that Charles is not Jewish. He heard about it on a radio show, and he feels it is a metaphysical law you cannot break. Ana, who is Jewish, explains that God picks your soul mate when you are in the womb. This is why she and Charles do not feel guilty.

Lane drinks and makes sarcastic replies. Suddenly, Matilde asks if anyone would like to hear a joke. Ana says yes, so Matilde says it in Portuguese, and Ana laughs, but everyone else is silent. Ana says that she would like to hire Matilde to clean their house now because Charles likes things to be clean.

Lane is upset that Charles and Ana are taking everything away from her at once. Virginia objects to Matilde leaving because she thinks of her as a sister. Lane says she needs Matilde. Ana tries to get Matilde to come with her by saying she will need to hear one joke a day. Matilde is conciliatory, saying she will split her time.

Charles and Ana leave to go apple picking, asking if anyone else would like to come. Everyone wants to go except Lane, who begins a sarcastic speech. Ana, Charles, and Matilde exit, but Virginia stays with her sister. At first, Lane resists Virginia's sympathy but finally accepts it.

**SCENE 6: ANA'S BALCONY**

Ana and Matilde are on Ana's balcony overlooking the sea, also right over Lane's living room. They are surrounded by apples. They eat apples and throw them into the sea, which is Lane's living room. Matilde is happy because she has made up eighty-four jokes in Ana's house. Matilde plans to become a comedian someday after making up the perfect joke, though she is afraid the perfect joke will kill her, because her mother died laughing.

Charles comes in and kisses Ana all over. Ana gives the best apple to Charles. He picks up Ana and carries her into the bedroom.

Matilde tells the audience the perfect joke comes by accident, and once you hear it, you never want to hear it again.

**SCENE 7: MATILDE, VIRGINIA, AND LANE**

Virginia happily cleans Lane's house, while Lane is in pajamas, shuffling cards. Lane calls to

Matilde on the balcony telling her it is her turn to deal. Matilde enters the living room. Virginia offers to sew a slipcover for Lane's couch because it is dirty, and Lane accepts. Above on the balcony, Ana and Charles dance slowly. Lane asks about Charles and Ana. Matilde confirms that they are in love and reveals that Charles does not go to the hospital, because he stays in bed all day with Ana, who is dying. Matilde describes how Ana and Charles fought over her refusal to take medicine or go to the hospital.

**SCENE 8: CHARLES AND ANA TRY TO READ ONE ANOTHER'S MINDS**

Ana is in a bathrobe on the balcony with Charles. They try to guess each other's thoughts, thinking of numbers and colors and trying to guess one another's choice. Charles explains that Houdini and his wife practiced reading each other's minds in case one of them died, so they could still communicate. He tries to persuade Ana to go to the hospital, but she goes for a swim instead. Charles takes off his clothes and throws them in Lane's living room, as if he is getting ready to follow Ana.

In her living room, Lane finds Charles's sweater. Matilde leans over the balcony and says she has made up the perfect joke!

**SCENE 9: LANE AND VIRGINIA. THEN MATILDE.**

Lane sits holding Charles's sweater. Virginia enters, vacuuming the rug. Lane throws a tantrum, swearing that she never wants anything to be clean again. The two sisters fight. Virginia accuses Lane of lacking compassion, while Ana has plenty of compassion. Lane exits.

Ana is on her balcony listening to an opera recording. While she does this, Virginia accidentally spills dirt from a plant on the rug of Lane's living room, and she begins to make a big mess while the music plays. Matilde comes in and asks what Virginia is doing. Lane then enters and sees the mess. Virginia offers to clean it up, but Matilde announces that Ana is very sick.

Charles has gone away to Alaska to find the bark of a yew tree to save Ana. Lane explains that yew bark is made into the cancer drug Taxol. Charles wants to plant the tree in the garden so Ana can smell it since she will not go to the hospital. Virginia thinks this is a beautiful love story, but Lane thinks Charles is selfish to leave Ana while she is dying.

Matilde wonders if there are doctors who make house calls. Matilde and Virginia look at Lane. Lane refuses at first to consider it. In the background, Charles is seen in a parka looking for a tree.

### SCENE 10: LANE MAKES A HOUSE CALL TO HER HUSBAND'S SOUL MATE

Lane listens to Ana's heart on her balcony, with a stethoscope, asking questions about her pain and breathing. Ana says to Lane that she must hate her, but Lane says she is just a doctor at the moment. Lane says Ana should go to the hospital for tests, but she understands that Ana does not want to go. Ana asks if Lane thinks she is crazy. When Lane does not answer, she goes to get her iced tea. When she gets back, Lane is standing on the balcony weeping. She gives a broken speech: she does not hate Ana, but she sees that Ana has something that she does not have. Ana glows; she could be anyone's soul mate because she has that certain something. Charles also glows now, and he never looked at Lane like that.

Ana asks how Lane and Charles fell in love. Lane tells the story of how she met Charles in medical school. They fell in love over a dead body as partners in an anatomy class. Lane and Ana look at each other as an act of forgiveness. Ana offers Lane an apple. Charles is seen walking across the stage with an ax. It is snowing on the balcony.

### SCENE 11: LANE CALLS VIRGINIA

Lane explains to Virginia on the phone that Ana is coming to live with her because she will not go to a hospital. She asks Virginia to come too to look after her during the day with Matilde. Virginia says she now has a job as a clerk at a grocery store. She enjoys the work and the solidarity with the other workers. Though Lane accuses Virginia of lying about her job, she agrees to help with Ana.

### SCENE 12: ANA AND VIRGINIA. THEN MATILDE. THEN LANE.

Ana's possessions are in Lane's living room—her apples, fishbowl, and suitcase. Virginia is preparing food for Ana and listening as Ana explains she does not like medical language, as though she has a relationship with cancer. She does not want a relationship with a disease. It is better to have a relationship with death, because that is important. She eats the casserole Virginia

has fixed for her and thanks her. Virginia is visibly moved because someone thanked her.

Matilde enters with a telegram from Charles for Ana. In the distance, Charles is seen in his parka. It snows in the living room. He has found the tree but cannot take it on the plane, so he will have to learn to fly. He asks her to wait for him. Ana mentions she wishes he would be her nurse but instead he wants to explore. Lane enters. Virginia says she made ice cream and asks who wants some. Lane sees that Ana's fish is still alive in the fishbowl. The women all eat ice cream from the same container and compliment Virginia. Ana is cold, so Lane and Virginia exit to find her a blanket.

Ana tells Matilde her bones hurt. She asks Matilde to tell her a joke that will kill her, as her father killed her mother with a joke. Matilde suggests waiting for Charles to return, but Ana fears she will lose her courage if she waits. Matilde promises to do it the following day. Everyone says good night, but Lane sits up with Ana while she sleeps.

### SCENE 13: MATILDE TELLS ANA A JOKE

Lane, Virginia, and Matilde are around Ana, who bids them good-bye. Ana asks Lane to take care of Charles, knowing that she still loves him. Virginia cries. Ana does not like her tears and asks for the joke.

Ana wants to die standing up, and she tells Lane and Virginia to leave so they will not die. They exit. The lights change, and there is music. Matilde whispers the joke to Ana. A subtitle on stage says to the audience: *The Funniest Joke in the World.* Ana laughs and laughs and then collapses. Matilde begins to wail, and Virginia and Lane return. Lane does not know what to do because she works in a hospital where someone else always cleans up. Matilde gives instructions about closing the eyes and washing the body. Virginia says a prayer.

Charles pounds on the door and calls Ana's name. Lane lets Charles in. He is carrying a big tree. He sees it is too late. Lane kisses Charles on the forehead, and he goes to Ana and collapses over her body as the lights focus on Matilde.

### SCENE 14: MATILDE

Matilde speaks to the audience. Ana and Charles become Matilde's mother and father. Matilde says that her mother is about to give birth to her, but the hospital is too far away.

She lies down under a tree while her husband tells her a joke. She laughed so hard that Matilde was born laughing. She looks at her parents, and they look at her. Matilde thinks heaven is full of jokes that cannot be translated, but everyone is laughing.

## CHARACTERS

### Ana

Ana is a middle-aged Argentine woman with breast cancer. She is charismatic and charming. She is older than Lane, and in act 1, the actress playing Ana doubles as Matilde's mother. She seems to be quite sexy, even with a mastectomy, because Charles wants only to kiss her and stay in bed with her all day. Ana embraces life and accepts death, rejecting the civilized institutions that put up screens so people do not deal with death directly. She refuses a hospital and drugs, showing her bravery and strong character. She looks wistfully out to sea in a dramatic pose, and yet she makes everyone around her want to live life to the fullest.

Ana is a peacemaker. Even though she steals Lane's husband and maid, she reconciles everyone into a friendly and intimate group. Before she dies, she makes sure that Lane will take Charles back. Ana is capable of standing up for herself, as when she and Charles actually have a physical fight over whether she will go to the hospital. She is sad when he is not with her at the end, but she does not try to stop Charles from going to Alaska on his own quest.

### Charles

Charles is Lane's husband, a doctor in his fifties, compassionate and caring. He wears a white coat and sings while performing a mastectomy on Ana. He is direct and childlike, believing that because Ana is his soul mate, he has a right to leave Lane without guilt. Once he meets Ana, he wants to fulfill all his desires immediately, such as to go apple picking or visit Machu Picchu. He appears to love Ana sincerely and is not put off by her loss of a breast. She is older than his wife. Charles is distraught when Ana's cancer comes back and she will not go to the hospital. He does a lot of bargaining with death, in order to avoid watching Ana die.

### Lane

Lane is a doctor in her fifties. She wears white and has a white house. Lane is proud of her profession. She believes her life is perfect. Because she is confident of her own perfection as a doctor beloved by her patients, she has never been jealous of another woman. She lists her own good traits: she is poised, athletic, still attractive, and a good conversationalist. However, Lane also has faults. She is class conscious, believing she deserves to have someone else clean her house. She has a certain arrogance; for example, she does not truly see Virginia or Matilde as her equals and does not bother to pronounce Matilde's name correctly until she has been humbled. Lane begins to change when her husband leaves her. At first angry and sarcastic, she eventually becomes more accepting and loving as she cares for the dying Ana in an unselfish act. She also learns to appreciate her sister and Matilde.

### Matilde

Matilde (pronounced "Ma-chil-gee" in Portuguese) is Lane's cleaning lady, a woman from Brazil in her twenties. She wears black because she is in mourning for her parents. She likes to tell jokes, especially in Portuguese, and does it deadpan. Matilde is not able to hide the fact that though she is a cleaning lady, she hates to clean. She considers herself an artist, a comedian, forced to clean for the money. When Lane is not looking, Matilde stops cleaning and composes jokes. Even when Lane has her medicated for depression, Matilde will not clean. She joins Virginia's conspiracy to let the sister clean the house and pretend she is doing it.

Matilde is not intimidated by anything, determined to lead her own life. She misses her parents because they are the only other funny people she knew. They all laughed at each other's jokes. Now Matilde, once the third funniest in the family, is the first and only. She imagines scenes with her parents dancing or telling each other jokes and laments that she can never hear those jokes. She was marginal to their partnership. She has absorbed her mother's wisdom and passes it on to the other characters, serving as a sort of witness or chorus to the action.

Matilde and Lane are in opposition in the beginning but come closer together during Ana's death. Matilde is the one who can tell the perfect joke that will kill Ana at the right moment.

She also teaches Lane how to attend to a dead person at home, doing the last rites.

## Matilde's Parents

Matilde's parents are already dead when the play opens, but she sees them in fantasies (played by the actors who play Charles and Ana). They were very funny and married late because they did not want to live with someone who was not funny. Her father waited to find his match in wit and did not marry until age sixty-three, when he met Matilde's mother. He later told his daughter that her mother was even funnier than he was. They were always laughing. In fact, her mother died laughing when her father took a year to compose a joke for their anniversary. It was so funny, it killed her because she could not stop laughing. He was so depressed that he committed suicide. This has left Matilde with both a love of humor and fear that it will kill her.

## Virginia

Virginia is Lane's sister. Sometimes when they disagree they feel as if they are little girls again. Virginia is well educated but does not have a profession. She studied Greek literature and went to Greece to see the ruins, wanting to write about them, but found she had nothing to say. Her life has been going downhill since the age of twenty-two, when she discovered this. She has never done what she wanted to do, and now she is too old to change. She cleans house all day to have something to do, so she will not kill herself. Her husband is like a piece of furniture to her. Virginia persuades Matilde to let her clean Lane's house secretly. As she folds underwear, she discovers Ana's underwear in with Charles's and figures out that he is having an affair. Virginia is so starved for human company, she makes friends first with Matilde and then with Ana. She thinks her sister is cold-hearted when Lane accuses her of not having a job, as though she is not worth anything. When Lane changes in the second half of the play the two sisters become friends again.

## THEMES

### Love

*The Clean House* shows domestic conflicts but centers on love and caring. One variety of love depicted is family love. Matilde, the Brazilian maid, was loved by her parents and misses them since their death. She has vivid fantasies of her parents dancing or telling jokes, and she immediately takes to Ana because she reminds her of her mother. Matilde's parents were devoted to one another and showed it by telling jokes. Matilde carries on the family legacy with pride, trying to use humor for good. Matilde is warm and compassionate to others. She gives understanding and companionship to Virginia and administers euthanasia to Ana at her request with a joke.

The play also features romantic love. Charles believes that Ana is his *bashert*, or soul mate, and that it is his duty to be with her no matter what. Charles and Ana display a touching and unusual love story. They are middle-aged and fall in love during Ana's mastectomy, with Charles the surgeon who cuts off her breast. Far from being repulsed by Ana's changed body, he smothers her with kisses and stays in bed with her all day, neglecting his job. He goes on a journey to Alaska for her to find a healing tree.

Lane is represented as cold in the beginning, concerned only with her hospital work. Her marriage is loveless. By contrast, Charles is passionate with Ana, and Lane is in shock that her orderly life is falling apart. However, she eventually rises to the occasion, agreeing to treat Ana, her husband's mistress, and even letting her move into the house and caring for her as she dies. Lane lets go of her jealousy, recognizing Ana's great charisma, and lets herself love Ana and then her sister, Virginia, with whom there had been rivalry. Virginia herself is in a boring marriage, and she longs for a life purpose and someone to care for. She loves her sister and eventually persuades Lane to let her be a support and comfort to her. Finally, Lane accepts Charles back after Ana's death.

### Death

Many of Ruhl's plays deal with death and mourning, such as *Eurydice*, written for her father. Ruhl's father died of cancer as Ana does in *The Clean House*. Like Matilde, Ruhl's father cracked jokes constantly. Ruhl was moved by his sense of humor as he was dying. His jokes helped the family to deal with their loss. Matilde also deals with her grief for her parents' deaths by making up jokes, even though the situation was quite tragic: her father was so grief stricken over her mother's death, he committed suicide.

# TOPICS FOR FURTHER STUDY

- Ruhl is interested in traditional and ethnic forms of drama. In a comparative theater project, have each person in a group present a description of traditional ethnic theater styles, along with slides and an excerpt from a play from that culture. Examples would be kabuki theater from Japan, Indonesian puppet theater, or a play like fifth-century *Shakuntala* by the Indian playwright, Kālidāsa. Along with these traditional styles, other reports could cover contemporary ethnic playwrights, such as African Americans Lorraine Hansberry and Amiri Baraka; Chicanos Lynne Alvarez and Luis Valdez; Native Americans Linda Hogan and E. Donald Two-Rivers; or Asian Americans Frank Chin and Wakako Yamauchi.

- Discuss Ana's reasons for refusing cancer treatment. What are the choices a cancer patient has in terms of modern medicine (hospital and hospice), alternative medicine, and letting nature take its course? Evaluate each option, using both the evidence in the play and your personal experience of illness with family or friends. Even if you do not agree with Ana's choice, write a short paper explaining what you think were her reasons and whether a person should have rights about their own death. Refer to the characters and lines in the play as part of your answer.

- With a group, pick some of the most moving scenes of *The Clean House* and do a reading of them aloud. Discuss Ruhl's method of characterization. Are the characters mostly good or bad? Are they in conflict? Do they argue about their ideas or cooperate? What do you think she is trying to show about human nature? Which characters are most attractive to you and why? Take one character and write up a character study based on the lines from the play and also what is not stated directly but hinted.

- Use the theater and acting exercises that Ruhl grew up with by consulting *In the Studio with Joyce Piven: Theatre Games, Story Theatre and Text Work for Actors* (Performance Books, 2012). Locate exercises that may have led to characters, themes, and incidents in *The Clean House*, a play that was partly developed in Piven's workshop. Try these exercises with some of your classmates.

- Read a young-adult novel centered on teens dealing with a mother with cancer. One choice is Patrick Ness's *A Monster Calls* (2011), which is about a British boy who is visited by a storytelling monster while his mother is dying. Alternatively, you might pick Alice Kuipers's *Life on the Refrigerator Door* (2007), which portrays a daughter who exchanges notes on the refrigerator with her mother, who has breast cancer. Write a short review of your novel as if you were going to publish it on a blog that reviews young-adult fiction. Look up examples to see what a good review should contain. For instance, it should include the author, the title, an overview of the characters and their situation, and the author's theme or main point. End with your evaluation and give quotes to back up your opinion. Post it online and allow your classmates to comment.

---

In addition, Ana is dying, and her death changes everyone else in the play. Matilde is able to have a relationship with Ana as a mother surrogate and be the one to administer the fatal joke. Ana rouses Virginia to claim her own life and dignity, challenging Lane's notion that she is nothing because she does not have a profession. Virginia's addiction to cleaning is a sort of ritual mourning about her life. She had planned on becoming a scholar, but it did not happen.

She has no child, no life, and no meaningful relationship with her husband.

Ana is accepting and does not make others feel guilty. Virginia feels happy and stimulated by Ana. Though Ana seems to embody an almost visible life force, she chooses death with dignity rather than go to the hospital or take drugs. She says she prefers a relationship to death to a relationship with a disease. She teaches the others what it is to live and to die.

Charles, however, is in denial. When he cannot persuade Ana to go to the hospital, he runs off to Alaska to find the yew tree rather than watch her die. She had wanted him to be there, but he could not face it. Lane is used to dealing with death in the hospital and having someone else clean up the dead body. Matilde shows her how to close Ana's eyes and wash the body, dealing with death at home, as it used to be done. All the characters come together and become close through Ana's death.

### Community
The characters begin the play with a number of monologues, addressing the audience rather than one another. They are alone on stage with their own internal dramas. Gradually, they have dialogue about mundane things, and as the play progresses, they begin to confess feelings to one another. Virginia and Matilde, as the marginal people in Lane's house, bond and tell stories.

The low point for Lane is when she finds out her husband is having an affair. Virginia and Matilde find out first by folding the laundry together, but they do not tell Lane. Lane wakes up to the fact that she has lost her sister, Virginia, to Matilde, who is now her buddy. She has lost her husband to Ana. Ana and Charles even take Matilde as their maid. Lane feels alone and rejects Virginia's sympathy. Everyone else seems happy with the new arrangement, and all decide to go apple picking together. Lane cannot understand what has happened or why Charles prefers Ana, a dying woman, to her, with her impeccable reputation as a doctor. Lane begins to reverse this trend of isolation when she goes beyond jealousy to treat Ana's illness. Soon she, like everyone else, is attracted to Ana and brings her home.

Ana's dying creates a new community of the four women: Matilde, Virginia, Lane, and Ana. Charles as the man then becomes the marginal figure in the new group. The women bond in sympathy and love, eating ice cream together and sharing Ana's last days, while Charles tries

to solve the problem; he goes on an action quest instead of being part of the intimacy offered by Ana's illness. By the end of the play, there is only cooperation and understanding, and Lane even accepts Charles back.

### Rituals
Ruhl's plays often deal with the human rituals that help people to transform or to cope with life and death. There are many traumas in life, and *The Clean House* discusses how people negotiate challenges. Two rituals in the play, jokes and cleaning, are metaphors for rituals that come from the subconscious need to respond to life in a positive or accepted way.

Virginia's obsession with cleaning obviously characterizes a person in deep depression. She can find no way forward in life and has no interest in anything or connection with other people. Lane is too busy for her. Her husband is too boring. If she did not clean, she would commit suicide, she jokes. Because she finishes her house by three o'clock in the afternoon, she needs more work and offers to clean Lane's house secretly. This also becomes a ritual of caring for her sister after the revelation about Charles's adultery. Lane pushes Virginia aside as a nonperson and does not accept her offers of help. As Lane becomes aware of what she has done, she lets Virginia care for her and clean the house.

For Lane, cleaning is also a ritual but in a different way. It confirms her status. Her life has been orderly, as indicated by her spotless white living room. She will not clean for herself, however, believing she is above doing her own cleaning. Instead, she pays a servant to clean. In a defiant act to reclaim her own life, Virginia throws dirt on Lane's rug and makes a mess, feeling suddenly liberated. She no longer has to identify herself with the cleaning ritual. The living room goes from spotless in act 1 to messy in act 2 as Ana moves in with her things as she dies.

Jokes are also used as a ritual in this play, and Matilde is the priestess or shaman who performs this magic. She learned it from her parents, who knew jokes so potent they could kill. Jokes function in Matilde's family as important rites of passage, accompanying her parents' marriage, her own birth, her mother's death. Throughout the entire play, Matilde searches for the perfect joke, and when she finds it, she tells it to Ana to end her painful life. Matilde says a perfect joke can be told only once, and so it is her gift to Ana, easing her transition into death.

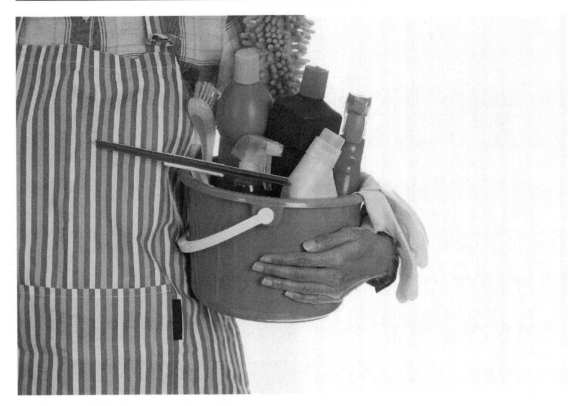

*Matilde, whose lines are in both Portuguese and English, is a housemaid who hates cleaning* (© Chutima
Chaochaiya / Shutterstock.com)

## STYLE

### Plot Structure

Ruhl bases her stories on transformations. These
are not the kinds of transformations in an Aristotelian plot, which has a rising action leading to
a climax, but rather the transformations in fantasy, fairy tale, and myth. Ruhl's transformations happen all throughout her plays. There is
not one central revelation, but rather poetic wisdom in many moments. Her characters have one
foot in common life and one foot in a more primal
space, where they confront the big challenges of
life: love, death, loss, and happiness.

Ruhl says this play is set in Connecticut, but
in a metaphysical rather than a physical state. By
this, she means that she is interested in deeper
philosophical aspects of human life. In some
ways, *The Clean House* is like a dance, with characters moving apart and together in different
moods and responses. Matilde seems to be a cat-
alyst whose presence changes the dance and the
partners in it. Ruhl prefers nonlinear storytelling
with short scenes or vignettes that allow the

audience to feel emotion and experience the characters' revelations in the moment. It is as if each
scene is for its own sake, not necessarily trying to
lead up to something else.

### Defamiliarization

Defamiliarization is a technique made famous
by the playwright Bertolt Brecht. He wanted
people to see topics in a fresh light, so he viewed
them with distance or objectivity. He did not
want the audience to get lost in the illusion of
the story, so he called attention to the theatricality of the play. Ruhl makes use of this sort of
defamiliarization by breaking the fourth wall,
the illusion that we are just looking in on the
characters' story through one wall of a room, as
represented by the stage. She has her characters
address the audience directly.

In *The Clean House*, Ruhl breaks boundaries immediately by opening with Matilde's telling a joke in Portuguese. Ruhl has explained that
she wanted to see how much humor could be
conveyed without the meaning of the words.
The audience should be able to tell the speech is

a joke and feel something from it. As Matilde explains to Virginia, a joke has a certain structure or rhythm, an emotional tone, and a timing like music. Another technique to break the realist illusion is the overlapping space of Ana's balcony and Lane's living room. Items thrown off the balcony are picked up by Lane, visually demonstrating how she is affected by what is going on with her husband and his lover. It is as if they are in her living room.

### Double Casting

Ruhl double-casts characters in her plays. In *The Clean House*, Charles and Ana also double as Matilde's parents in her fantasy. This repetition has thematic resonance in that Charles and Ana become surrogate parental figures for Matilde. This double casting highlights the archetypal nature of character rather than individual characters.

### Myth and Magic Realism

Ruhl's plays are non-naturalistic; they are symbolic and archetypal rather than about everyday reality. She draws from ancient myths such as that of Eurydice in her play by that name and from Christianity, as she uses Ana as an Eve figure. She uses magic realism to tell a story, a style first made popular in Latin American fiction in the 1960s but now used by many postmodern authors and playwrights, such as Tony Kushner in *Angels in America* (1991) and José Rivera in *Marisol* (1992). This approach includes magic or the supernatural happening alongside realistic events.

This way of viewing life is found in many traditional cultures, such as the South American countries of Brazil and Argentina, Matilde's and Ana's respective homelands. Matilde is a shamanic character who wields jokes like magic spells and can even kill with them. Ana is a larger-than-life figure whose charisma and association with nature makes her a sort of symbolic nature goddess. She has an abundance of apples with which she feeds and attracts people. She has a fish she has kept alive in a bowl for twelve years, suggesting she has supernatural powers of life and death. Yet she chooses death, and when Ana dies, everyone is transformed.

This play subverts the rational Anglo point of view represented by the doctors, Charles and Lane. Lane condescends to the Latina Matilde and Ana at first, feeling superior. She yields to their magical world, however, when she runs

into grief. Ruhl uses surreal scenes to get the audience to feel this alternative viewpoint, such as Ana and Matilde's eating apples and throwing them over the balcony into the sea, which turns out to be Lane's living room. Lane sees apple cores dumped on her rug, a funny symbol of her missing out on the forbidden fun of Charles's alternative family.

### Lyric Language

Ruhl began as a poet. As she wrote plays, she envisioned them as three-dimensional poems with people acting out the images. The imagery of apples and snow associated with Ana and the advance of her cancer says without words what the characters are going through. The apples are the happiness they share; the snow comes down in the living room as Ana is sick and Charles tramps through Alaska to find a yew tree to save her. Ruhl plays on words, such as having Matilde misunderstand yew tree as "you tree." Ruhl also uses the postmodern or absurdist technique of making metaphors literal, such as Matilde's mother dying of laughter.

Ruhl avoids long exposition or backstory or psychological analysis, preferring brief poetic exchanges between characters. She is thinking of Greek drama with its rhythm of ritual and poetry and its addressing metaphysical matters—life, death, fate, and the gods. Some of the scenes involve the characters imagining, as when Matilde imagines her parents dancing, and Lane imagines the love ritual of Charles and Ana. They narrate their visions to the audience as they are acted out.

### Lightness

Victor Shklovsky (1893–1984), the Russian formalist, influenced both Ruhl's mentor, Paula Vogel, and Ruhl herself. He expounds on the virtues of defamiliarization and insists that artists do not have to copy reality. Ruhl also frequently mentions as an influence Italo Calvino (1923–1985), the Italian fabulist. Calvino introduces the quality of "lightness" in the art of the future in *Six Memos for the Next Millennium* (1993). Ruhl injects a lightness into her work because she is an idealist and optimist. Even serious topics such as cancer, death, and loss are treated with humor and some detachment. Philosophically, she believes theater should allow an acceptance of life through irony, insight, and humor. In *The Clean House*, the characters are dealing with heavy life burdens: divorce, death, cancer, separation, isolation, lack of self-esteem, and grief, but there is humor and a rising up to meet these fates with dignity in a ritual or magic way rather than a strictly realistic way, allowing the audience distance and contemplation.

## HISTORICAL CONTEXT

### *Stages of Mourning*

Many psychologists have written books about the process of mourning happening in stages. The stages overlap and are given various names but are about letting go. Ruhl provides her own vision of grief, based on her life experience of having two grandmothers and a father die of cancer. She began as a successful playwright with *Eurydice*, a play about death and the underworld in memory of her father.

Ruhl portrays different stages or types of grief in *The Clean House*. Denial and shock are typically a first response of finding out about a major loss, such as death of a loved one, one's own imminent death, or a divorce. The loss is unthinkable, and the person is unable to accept that it is real. Matilde's father, for instance, kills himself when he accidentally is responsible for his wife's death with a perfect joke, so that she laughs herself to death. His response indicates the guilt that often accompanies mourning. Lane exhibits denial and shock when she first learns her husband has left her. She tries to explain that she has never imagined a rival because she thought she was perfect. Why would Charles leave her for a breast cancer patient?

Another response of a mourning person is anger at the loss. Lane cuts her hand on a can opener while trying to make a martini, as though to punish someone. She is sarcastic to Charles and Ana. Charles, on the other hand, tries the strategy of control or bargaining, another stage of mourning, when Ana decides to die instead of continuing cancer treatments. He wants Ana to learn mind reading, so they can communicate after her death. He sets out on a quest to Alaska, thinking that will postpone Ana's death. None of this works, because she is dead when he returns.

Another response to grief is depression, which may prolong mourning and make it hard for the person to heal. Matilde represents this aspect of grief, for she wears black and is depressed, still mourning and missing her parents.

She fantasizes about them. A final stage of grief is acceptance, when the person lets go and finally acknowledges the loss and moves on. This is represented in the last scene when the mourners gather around Ana's body to wash it and pray. Her death has the positive outcome of bringing people together into a new community as they work out their loss together.

### *Joke Theory*

Jokes are potent in *The Clean House*. As with her exploration of grief, Ruhl examines different ideas of humor and jokes in her play as a way to deal with grief. In terms of social relations, joking can be used to make the teller feel superior while belittling someone. Humor is a form of political or class power when it is derived from scorn or ridicule. Lane's sarcasm might fit into this category, because she clearly feels superior to others and puts them down with her catty remarks, feeling self-righteous in the beginning of the play. Matilde uses a stereotype for telling a joke when she makes a remark that Argentinian men think too highly of themselves.

Sigmund Freud had a psychological explanation of jokes as a sort of relief of psychic tension. A joke is like dream work, allowing pressures in the unconscious to work out in a substitute form. Virginia tells such a joke in her opening monologue when she explains how boring her life is: if she did not clean house, she might kill herself; then she says she is only joking and laughs. The joke allows her to express forbidden feeling. Sexual jokes also fulfill repressed feelings. Matilde tells dirty jokes in Portuguese, claiming her parents told each other dirty jokes when she was too little to understand. Her exclusion from their laughter was based on an exclusion from their sexual bond. Another type of joke is based on incongruity, when something clashes with expectations. The punch line suddenly shifts us somewhere else, and we laugh.

Finally, Matilde explains to the audience and the other characters her deeper theory of jokes as cleansing and healing. One must laugh to clean out the dirt from inside. She implies a further metaphysical definition of a perfect joke because life, love, and death are like dirty jokes: they are a messy and unexpected feature of human life. Her mother died laughing, and Matilde sends Ana off in a similar manner, by killing her with a joke. She is the high priestess of jokes, using them ritually to cleanse or cause a transition. Her mother taught

# COMPARE
# &
# CONTRAST

- **2004:** A lumpectomy and radiation are often just as effective as a mastectomy in treating breast cancer, explaining why Charles in *The Clean House* is surprised Ana chooses the more radical treatment.

  **Today:** More tailored and personal treatments for breast cancer are available because of greater accuracy of classification of cancer subtypes and genetic testing to predict how a person will react to different treatments.

- **2004:** Domestic workers from third world countries are frequently underpaid women and often illegal immigrants who have no rights.

**Today:** The International Labor Organization in Geneva has ratified the Convention Concerning Decent Work for Domestic Workers, C189, outlining basic rights and fair pay, to help immigrant workers.

- **2004:** Humor is a feminist tool in the hands of a few well-known and gifted comedians like Lily Tomlin.

  **Today:** The number of women comedians expands in many venues, including writing, producing, TV sitcoms, stand-up comedy, and political shows, with such figures as Ellen DeGeneres, Samantha Bee, Tina Fey, and Latina comedians Cristela Alonzo and Grace Parra.

---

her that to tell a good joke you have to think your problems are small compared to the world's. She means that joking lessens the burdens and leads to balance. Her mother also tells her that if more women knew jokes, there would be justice in the world.

Jokes deliver truths. A good joke does not always make one laugh, however. Matilde tells a joke to Lane that makes her cry and laugh at the same time in a moment of catharsis. The catharsis, or release, is not always predictable. Jokes are a two-edged sword. They can make you forget and remember your life at the same time, Matilde explains: the paradox of the perfect joke. This indicates that a joke is a kind of awareness about the human condition. It has a ritual and almost religious significance in the play; it cleanses, forgives, and shifts towards acceptance.

## Theater as Catharsis

Ruhl mentions in a 2009 article for *American Theatre* that she would like to see theater shift towards a kind of community-cleansing ritual. This is in keeping with feminist ideas of theater as building or serving community but also looks back historically to classic and various ethnic ideas of theater.

Ruhl prefers the Roman author Ovid's model of transformation for her plots rather than the classical idea of the arc of action described by the Greek philosopher Aristotle (384–322 BCE).

Aristotle, in his *Poetics* (ca. 335 BCE) defined the plot line of tragedy that became the norm for Western plays in general. The acts unfold in rising and sequential action to a climax where everything is most complex. Then the knot is undone during the falling action as the resolution is presented. Each play presents only one clear rising and falling action, which has to take place within twenty-four hours, centered on an important character in the process of making a moral choice. The unities of time, place, and action have to be observed.

Ovid (43 BCE–17 or 18 CE) is best known for his *Metamorphoses* (9 CE), a verse narrative containing Greek and Roman myths of humans in transformation, as when Daphne becomes a tree to avoid the advances of Apollo, Philomela becomes a nightingale, and Midas changes everything to gold with his touch. Similarly, Ruhl wants to see characters in constant transformation, rather than in one big crisis of action precipitated by a single character, as in Aristotle's philosophy.

---

*Ana and Matilde bond over picking and eating apples* (© Natalya Bidyukova / Shutterstock.com)

While Ruhl rejects the classical shape of plot for a more mythic kind of storytelling that is magic and nonlinear, involving the interactions of many characters spread through time and overlapping spaces (for example, Ana's balcony overlooking Lane's living room), she admires the Greek idea of group catharsis through audience participation in the play. Aristotle defined *catharsis* as a shift in the audience triggered by pity and fear as they witness the story of another, usually one falling through pride. Greek theater originated in religious festivals to Dionysus, god of wine and ecstasy. The festival was held outdoors in Athens in March. It included singing and dancing and speaking, something of a cross between opera and drama.

Ruhl prefers theater as Dionysian in its tragicomic emotions rather than rational and realistic. Greek actors wore masks, wigs, and elaborate costumes, including high boots to make them larger than life. Ruhl also uses these techniques, such as masks, puppets, stilts, ropes to make the characters fly, and dancing or songs to make the story more mythic and not realistic. Charles and Ana sing an operatic duet as he removes her breast in the operating room. Ruhl

breaks the fourth wall so characters can address the audience, thus making them part of the play.

The Greek chorus was a group of twelve to fifteen actors who spoke or sang the poetic commentaries between scenes. They represented the populace and gave background information on the author's themes. Ruhl works with a chorus in some plays, such as the Chorus of Stones in *Eurydice*. Matilde functions as a sort of chorus in *The Clean House*. Ruhl's characters are archetypal, like those in myth and fairy tale, and not realistic in terms of having a whole individual backstory and psychological motivation. What Ruhl takes from both Greek drama and Ovid is the poetry and mythic tale. Her dialogue, as in Greek plays, is spare and poetic. She wants to move the audience's soul, not make them think.

## CRITICAL OVERVIEW

Ruhl began to be noticed right out of Brown's theater master's program, where she worked with Paula Vogel, a Pulitzer Prize–winning playwright. *Euridyce* was Ruhl's first national hit, in

2003. In a review of *Eurydice* for the *New Yorker*, John Lahr praises Ruhl for her "luminous" retelling of the Greek myth from the wife's point of view:

> Watching it, we enter a singular, surreal world, as lush and limpid as a dream—an anxiety dream of love and loss—where both author and audience swim in the magical, sometimes menacing, and always thrilling flow of the unconscious.

Lahr's article "Surreal Life" for the *New Yorker* calls Ruhl "a fabulist," a writer of moral fables. Lahr describes Ruhl's work as "bold," praising "her nonlinear form of realism," which is "full of astonishments, surprises, and mysteries." Lahr also marvels at Ruhl's gift of instilling "lightness—the distillation of things into a quick, terse, almost innocent directness" in the dialogue of her plays.

The director of the production of *Eurydice* for Artists Repertory Theatre in Portland, Oregon, Randall Stuart, along with scenic designer Michael Olich and costumer Sarah Gahagan, include detailed notes of the production design for Ruhl's play in an article for *American Theatre*. Each production of Ruhl's plays is mounted by local artists and is different, making Ruhl a favorite among stage designers. For this production, Stuart used references to *Alice's Adventures in Wonderland* and Jules Verne's *Twenty Thousand Leagues under the Sea* with cartoons from Winsor McCay's *Little Nemo in Slumberland*. A Verne-like glass column on wheels was made to deliver Orpheus to the underworld. Ruhl has expressed her delight with each unique production of her work.

However, *The Clean House*, which premiered the year after *Euridyce*, has been one of her most commonly performed plays. A short review of the play in *American Theatre* in October 2004 announces that the play won the 2004 Susan Smith Blackburn Prize. The reviewer notes the role of the Brazilian maid in forcing a family to confront its dysfunctions with her jokes and that the play is currently produced in several important venues across the country. In an article for the *Eugene O'Neill Review*, James Al-Shamma also focuses on the character of Matilde, placing her among the famous melancholy characters in theater. Matilde appears as the archetype of the gifted melancholic who is sad because of the impermanence of life. Al-Shamma feels that her parents' deaths removed

the context of her life, and her melancholy seems to endow her at an early age with wisdom.

Overall, critics agree that Ruhl's work is emotionally resonant and extremely innovative. Indeed, in Michael Bloom's review of Ruhl's 2014 book of essays, he describes her as "one of the most original playwrights of our time." *The Clean House*, according to Charles Isherwood of the *New York Times*, shows off her "alchemical imagination," combining "an elaborate joke told in Portuguese" with "consideration of the meaning of dust" and the "trek to Alaska to retrieve a cancer-curing tree," none of which seem like "promising building blocks for a contemporary American stage comedy." However, Isherwood points out how, with Ruhl's remarkable skills, "this strange grab bag of ideas and images, together with some more exotic ingredients, magically coheres to form one of the finest and funniest new plays you're likely to see."

## CRITICISM

### Susan K. Andersen

*Andersen holds a PhD in literature and is a creative writer and former teacher. In the following essay, she investigates* The Clean House *as a ritual of cleansing.*

On one level, Ruhl's play *The Clean House* is a fable about women's work and women's community. On another, deeper level, it is a ritual for grief. A woman dies of breast cancer in the play as Ruhl's two grandmothers had, and her father also died of cancer. Charles and Lane are two doctors who live in a sanitized and sterile world, symbolized by Lane's spotless white living room. They have trouble keeping things clean, however, for they employ Matilde, a Brazilian maid who hates to clean. Virginia, the sister of Lane, jumps in to help, because she has an obsession with cleanliness and cannot find enough work to do in her own house.

This mania for cleaning is a symbol for control, and gradually in the play the clean lives of the characters become messier and messier. Each character must learn to give up cleaning for cleansing, meaning a spiritual purification. Lane and Virginia end by washing the dead body of Ana as a last act of respect to her and an acknowledgment of death and change in their lives that must be lived through but not controlled. The two women who bring about this

EACH CHARACTER MUST LEARN TO

GIVE UP CLEANING FOR CLEANSING, MEANING

A SPIRITUAL PURIFICATION."

metamorphosis in Lane's family are from South America: Matilde from Brazil and Ana from Argentina. Their ways seem disorderly and un-American. Matilde is melancholy and just wants to tell jokes and mourn her parents. Ana, who is in her sixties, has just had a mastectomy but is still seductive enough to steal Charles from Lane. These women have much to teach Lane's family about work and play, about life and death, and about love and loss.

Leslie Atkins Durham, in her book *Women's Voices on American Stages in the Early Twenty-first Century: Sarah Ruhl and Her Contemporaries*, sees Ruhl as a feminist playwright, learning her craft from her staging of Virginia Woolf's *Orlando* in terms of the theme of gender roles in society. Durham explains *The Clean House*, among other things, as a study of women's work. Lane as the doctor is class conscious and looks down on the women who do not have professions, taking on a traditionally male perspective. Matilde is a paid woman of color, Lane's domestic help. Lane tries to drug Matilde, because her job makes her depressed.

Lane sees her sister, Virginia, as a failed professional, for she could not motivate herself to be a cold-blooded scholar, writing about Greek ruins. Virginia also seems to feel she is a failure. Now, she is a bored housewife but mentions that doing housework with Matilde gives her a sense of community, as women in ancient days did their laundry together, gossiping and joking. Making a mess in Lane's living room is Virginia's moment of emotional release from the housekeeper role. The two South American women bring in wild and fresh air. They insist on being themselves. Matilde represents aspects of the feminine as artist and healer. Ana is an archetypal and magical Eve figure. The play shifts all the relationships and ends with a loving and caring women's group.

However, *The Clean House* is more than a feminist study. It opens with a joke told by

Matilde in Portuguese. It is not translated, and in this way Ruhl immediately forces the audience out of its head and into feeling. The actress performs the joke as joke, like music without words that the audience can feel, not understand. Jokes in the play, as critic James Al-Shamma notes in *Sarah Ruhl: A Critical Study of the Plays*, have a ritual function, and Matilde is the shaman who performs this magic. A shaman as healer in traditional cultures facilitates a shift for the community. Matilde's jokes are the deep magic in this play, creating the shifts. Al-Shamma comments that the actual audience of the play experiences these shifts (people are heard crying or laughing), but they are not cued by the dialogue, as in ordinary drama. It is the entire play itself that reenacts a change of perspective. Ruhl sees drama as ideally doing the work of ritual cleansing for a community. In a 2009 interview with *American Theatre*, Ruhl hopes for an almost religious revival of the stage in the next twenty-five years, closer to the Greek understanding of community catharsis.

Lane and Virginia do not understand Matilde's jokes not only because they are in a foreign language but also because they lack humor and what in Ruhl's philosophy is an attitude of lightness or conscious acceptance. Virginia admits she does not laugh because it makes her unattractive, and Lane is far too serious to be interested in Matilde's frivolous pastime. Before Matilde and Ana show up, Lane, Virginia, and Charles—as well as Virginia's husband, according to her accounts—are cold and dried up. Virginia describes her husband as a piece of furniture. She calls him barren, unable to have children. It is probably best not to have children, she concludes, for they would just be kidnapped or destroyed in some way. Life is very dirty and nasty. She has to clean all day to keep from being depressed by her empty life, to avoid committing suicide, she jokes.

Lane thinks she has the perfect life until her husband leaves her. She believes she is attractive, a respected professional, and a good conversationalist. She dresses in white and has a spotless white living room. She does not believe another woman could rival her. Ana, who takes Charles from her, asks how they fell in love, and Lane replies that she and Charles dissected the same cadaver in medical school. They rarely see each other, and Lane hardly ever sees her sister. Lane believes her patients love her, but she is not

# WHAT DO I READ NEXT?

- Jesse Andrews's young-adult novel *Me and Earl and the Dying Girl* (2012) features high school senior Greg and his buddy Earl, amateur filmmakers who make a film about and for their classmate, Rachel, who is dying of leukemia. Greg goes through the stages of grief and mourning for Rachel, even as he learns to be an artist.

- Anton Chekhov's "The Lady with the Dog" is one of his celebrated short stories that Ruhl adapted for the stage. It was published in Russian in 1899 and in English in 1903. It tells of two people, like Charles and Ana, who fall deeply in love outside of the socially accepted boundaries.

- Kelly Corrigan's *The Middle Place* (2008) is a memoir by a newspaper columnist about dealing with her own breast cancer at age thirty-six while having to care for her beloved father with terminal cancer as well. The book is funny, brave, and heart-warming.

- *The Year of Magical Thinking*, by Joan Didion, was published in 2005 and chronicles her year of grief at the sudden death of her husband of forty years while their daughter was in a coma in the hospital, soon to die as well. The book won a National Book Award, and Didion adapted it for Broadway in 2007.

- Barbara Ehrenreich and Arlie Russell Hochschild are editors of *Global Woman: Nannies, Maids, and Sex Workers in the New Economy* (2004), a collection of essays by scholars discussing the mass migration of women from the third world countries to modernized countries to be domestic workers and what this means economically and morally.

- Latina playwright Lisa Loomer's *Living Out* premiered in 2003 and was published in 2005. It details the relationship between an Anglo woman lawyer and her child's nanny, an undocumented immigrant from El Salvador.

- Elliott Oring's book on joke theory, *Joking Asides: The Theory, Analysis, and Aesthetics of Humor* (2016), is written by a folklorist about jokes and their functions. He discusses different theories of humor, including his own idea of incongruity.

- Ruhl's 2007 play, *Dead Man's Cell Phone*, shows how modern technology divides and unites people in strange ways when a woman answers a dead man's phone and gets involved with his family.

- Korean American playwright Diana Son, in her play *Satellites*, first staged in 2006, tells the story of a Korean American wife who hires a Korean nanny for her interracial child. The nanny has racist attitudes towards the child's African American father.

---

an understanding person with heart. Virginia accuses her of having no compassion, while Ana is attractive because she has compassion in abundance. Lane argues that she has given her whole life to taking care of patients in a hospital. What more could be asked of her? She learns, however, by dealing with Ana's death in her home that dying at home and in the hospital are two different things. In the hospital, she has no idea how the nurses clean up a dead body. She does not have to hold the patient's hand or show sympathy.

Charles, Virginia, and Lane all go through transformations in the play, with Matilde and Ana as the catalysts for change. Matilde is the youngest person, under thirty, yet has a spiritual maturity about her. She is dressed in mourning clothes but also attends to what she feels is her gift for comedy, a way to connect to her dead parents, who were the funniest people in Brazil. In fact, her mother died laughing at a fatal joke told by her father. Matilde tells Virginia that a good joke can clean your insides out; without laughing often, one can feel dirty. Matilde alludes to the idea that humor has a cathartic function, removing burdens or at least transforming them. Lane's house may be clean in the literal sense, but it is dirty as far as Matilde is concerned. The perfect joke is like music; it cannot be made to happen: it is a sort of magic that you catch in the air, Matilde explains. She mentions that the perfect joke makes you forget your life but paradoxically .also helps you remember your life. She describes humor as a sort of awareness, acceptance, and a kind of joy and spontaneity obviously missing in Lane's rigid house.

Humor is not just psychologically cleansing but a sort of ritual of transformation in Ruhl's play as well. It shifts the person to another perception, to acceptance, or even to another state of existence. In this way, a joke may cleanse in an unexpected way. It may be so powerful, it could even include death, as when Matilde finds the perfect joke to send Ana out of her pain so she can die. Again, life is messy—not really a clean house. Matilde tells Lane that people imagine those who are in love are happy, but she claims that love is a dirty joke. She alludes to the fact that Ana disrupts Lane's marriage by falling in love with Charles, and Ana causes Charles both joy and pain by giving him brief happiness but then dying of cancer. Matilde is also thinking of her parents, who were in love but died of laughter. The comic and tragic seem inexplicably interwoven. This is illustrated when Matilde tries to help Lane through her grief in divorce by telling a joke. The joke is in Portuguese, again displaying its ritual function rather than its meaning. Lane laughs and cries and laughs and cries. She is undergoing a cleansing, accepting that Charles has left her for another woman.

Lane's transformation is actually quite moving, as she goes through stages of loss and grief. She is persuaded to do a humanitarian act by going to Ana's house to care for her because she will not go to the hospital. While there, Lane admits to Ana that she understands why Charles was attracted to her. Anyone would be in love with Ana, for she positively glows with life and a loving nature. Lane takes on humility and turns in her grief to serve others. She takes responsibility for Ana, bringing her into her home to die. She sets aside her own jealousy and grief to embrace a larger view. Ana is not the enemy; she becomes part of the family.

Charles's transformation is brilliantly portrayed in scenes of comedy and then grief. The confrontation between Charles and his new lover, Ana, and his discarded wife, Lane, is a brief sketch in Ruhl's characteristic style of lightness that suggests the comic and tragic together in the same moment of revelation. Charles and Ana show no guilt for their affair but bounce into the living room in their newfound joy at discovering they are *basherts*, or soul mates. Charles informs his wife that according to Jewish law it is his duty to drop his old wife for his soul mate. He hopes there are no hard feelings. Lane is, of course, furious. This is funny and sad at the same time. Charles's claim to innocence in falling in love with Ana is actually the way it is. This kind of loss of a spouse happens in the same way loss through death happens. It is unexpected, and there is nothing to do about it. Moralizing on it does not change it. Lane must go through loss and grieving and acceptance. Later, Charles has to go through this loss when Ana dies. He tries to bargain with Ana to keep her from dying, by teaching her the mind-reading trick and by making her wait until he goes to Alaska to find the yew tree. In the end, he will have the same kind of loss Lane experienced. He and Lane will be drawn back together again, but with greater understanding.

Ana seems supernatural, almost a goddess in her glow, sexiness, and ability to make others happy. She is frank and not judgmental. Ruhl provides her with fertility symbolism in the form of the ever-present apples: Ana takes Charles and the others apple picking and has abundant apples on her balcony that people eat together. The apple symbol makes her an Eve figure, but there is no guilt or evil attached. Ana has a joy of life. She has kept her pet fish alive in the fishbowl for twelve years, making it seem she has some sort of magic against death. The fish is a symbol of her spirit. At the same time, she seems to be in love with death, embracing it willingly, toting the fishbowl to Lane's living room where she will die. She does not hold back or ask for more time. She does everything fully, including dying. The way Ruhl portrays Ana's death in a sort of primal or ritual way instead of realistically as a cancer victim, makes Ana an archetypal character who teaches the others. Matilde finds in Ana her mother; Charles finds his soul mate; Lane and Virginia find a sister.

Ritual is a force for this transformation of the characters and can be seen in the symbolic acts of eating ice cream together, picking apples,

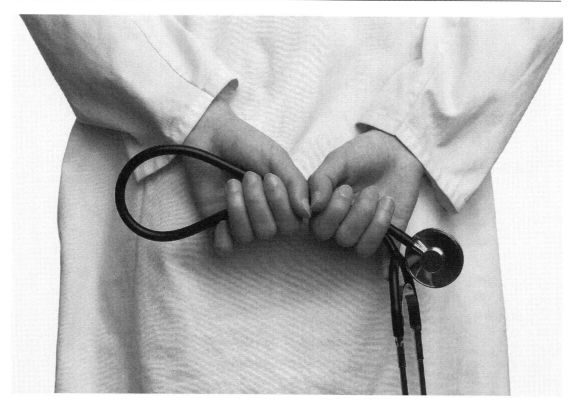

*Matilde convinces Lane to treat Ana, in spite of the fact that Charles abandoned his marriage with Lane for Ana (© LeventeGyori | Shutterstock.com)*

searching for a yew tree, or laughing at jokes. Ruhl looks deeper than the surface. The play takes place in a metaphysical Connecticut, according to the stage directions. Through spare dialogue and few props, Ruhl examines the great human issues, as in a Greek play. The drama leads to a rebalancing of relationships, with the ending note of forgiveness and compassion.

**Source:** Susan K. Andersen, Critical Essay on *The Clean House*, in *Drama for Students*, Gale, Cengage Learning, 2018.

## James Al-Shamma

*In the following excerpt, Al-Shamma discusses the significance of cleaning in Ruhl's play.*

### WALTZING AND CLEANING

...In "*The Baltimore Waltz* and the Plays of My Childhood," included in the collection *The Play That Changed My Life* (2009), Ruhl illuminates her early dramatic influences. As the title of the essay indicates, Paula Vogel's work was primary in this regard. The production to which she refers was a student one at Brown University,

which Ruhl saw at the age of 19 during the time that her father was dying of cancer, accompanied by a friend who had lost her own father to AIDS in the 1980s. The performance devastated both of them. Ruhl lists lessons she may have learned unconsciously that evening, brought to consciousness once she became Vogel's student. Foremost among them is the recognition that Vogel "created a modern architecture for grief," a structure that exposed grief while providing distance from it. Furthermore, she employed lightness in the sense of laughing at the horrible. She ignored the fourth wall, and seamlessly transitioned between modes and styles. She demonstrated both the comforting and alienating aspects of language. She conceptualized theater as "a place for memory, and for ghosts," and defamiliarized the familiar, after the Russian Formalist Victor Shklovsky. She provided a ritual response to death within a culture badly in need of one. She taught Ruhl that theater could give the audience a place to mourn (121-3).

Although the effect of these lessons is apparent throughout Ruhl's work, *The Clean House*

> THE TITLE ALSO SUGGESTS THAT A HOUSE IS NOT NECESSARILY A HOME; ONLY AFTER THE WHITENESS OF CHARLES AND LANE'S DWELLING IS SULLIED DOES IT BECOME ONE."

owes the greatest debt directly to *The Baltimore Waltz*. In Vogel's play, which premiered in 1992, she imagines a trip she might have taken to Europe at her brother Carl's invitation, but which, in real life, she declined, unaware that he was HIV-positive. The invitation came in 1986; Carl passed away in 1988 (Vogel, "Baltimore Waltz," 4). Vogel's play appears to have influenced *The Clean House* not just in sweeping dramaturgical terms, but also in its specific details. Vogel's characters vacation in an imaginary Europe (Vogel, "Baltimore Waltz," 4); Ruhl's inhabit a "metaphysical Connecticut" (Ruhl, "Clean House," 7). Vogel has christened her alter ego Anna after the love interest in *The Third Man*, a film that her play spoofs. Ruhl utilizes the same name, with a Latinized spelling, for her Argentinian Ana. In both works, siblings with a two-year age difference engage in moments of intense rivalry (Vogel, "Baltimore Waltz," 17; Ruhl, "Clean House," 30). Both playwrights overlap locations: in Ruhl, Ana's balcony overlooks Lane's living room; in Vogel, Carl dispassionately analyzes a painting in the Louvre as his sister makes love to a French waiter in their hotel room (Vogel, "Baltimore Waltz," 22-3).

Both plays include references to foreign language, film, and dancing. Ruhl opens with a joke in Portuguese, and Matilde and Ana converse in a mélange of Portuguese, Spanish, and English as they sort apples on the balcony. Linguistic and cultural markers isolate Matilde from the American characters while binding her with the other Latina, Ana. In Vogel, Anna attempts basic travel phrases whereas Carl speaks six European languages fluently (7). In terms of film, Vogel spoofs *The Third Man* (1949) while basing her imaginary Europe upon Hollywood cliché (6), and signaling Carl's homosexuality through a furtive exchange of stuffed rabbits with the mysterious Third Man. In *The Clean*

*House*, when her husband invites her to go apple picking with him and his lover, a distraught Lane lambastes him by referring to an *arrangement* in a foreign film (68). She perhaps alludes to the West German film *The Perfect Arrangement*, released in 1971 with the tagline, "The Triangle That Worked out...Almost" ("The Perfect Arrangement")! As with film, dance assumes greater significance in Vogel than in Ruhl. It serves as the primary metaphor in *The Baltimore Waltz*, as the siblings' trip is framed as an imaginary waltz through Europe. The grotesque dance between Anna and a stiff Carl is followed by an elegant and graceful reprise of loving remembrance. In *The Clean House*, Matilde's parents dance ineptly, inebriated with laughter.

Both works exhibit a distrust of modern medicine. Vogel infects Anna with ATD, or Acquired Toilet Disease, a fictional ailment contracted by sharing the toilet with elementary school students (11). Her doctor's admission that there is no cure and his ridiculous suggestions to avoid spreading the disease lampoon the medical profession's helplessness in the face of AIDS at the time, as well as superstitious fears about its transmission. Modern medicine also proves insufficient in Ruhl. Distrustful of doctors and hospitals in general, Ana declines treatment when her cancer recurs.

Both plays confront death with humor. In the "Playwright's Note" to *The Baltimore Waltz*, Vogel has published a letter from Carl in which he details his last wishes, laced with black humor. A similar sense of humor colors *The Baltimore Waltz*. It lightens the pathos as the brother's health declines, and takes the form of the grotesque when the quack doctor guzzles Anna's urine (51-4) and when Anna waltzes with a stiff, corpse-like Carl (55-6). Ruhl's father's jokes, like Carl's, benefited everyone concerned. Ruhl relates that they put the people around him at ease and demonstrated a heroism and selflessness ("Playwright Sarah Ruhl"), qualities also to be found in Ruhl's Ana. Although the influence of Vogel's play on *The Clean House* runs deep, Ruhl's work nevertheless stands independently as the unique expression of her own creative voice. Ruhl has fully absorbed her mentor's teachings and made them her own.

### "LIKE WATER RUNNING OVER YOUR HAND"

In addition to death and humor, significant themes of *The Clean House* include cleaning, community, and rationality versus emotion. Ruhl intends cleaning to assume a spiritual, cleansing dimension as the play advances into the second act (Wren, 146). In an interview with Pamela Renner, Ruhl remembers a workshop at Brown University with a member of the theater collective DAH from Belgrade, during which it was considered essential to mop the stage beforehand. Ruhl attributes the act of cleaning with the power to imbue both sacred and secular spaces with a spiritual quality. She includes theatrical space in this discussion as both sacred and profane (Renner, 50). Through cleaning, Ruhl also explores class issues and what it means "to be alienated from your own dirt" (qtd. in Weckwerth, 32).

The immigrant Matilde hates her job, and this presents a problem for Lane, who wants her house to be cleaned with minimal supervision on her part. She balks at giving orders to her unmotivated employee; early in the play, she practically begs her to clean the bathroom. Eventually, seeing that Lane is on the verge of tears, Matilde coaches her to order her as if she were a nurse (12). When Lane finally does, Matilde starts polishing silver, a task that she abandons the instant Lane leaves the room (14). Later, when Lane comes home from work to find Matilde sitting in the dark, Matilde insinuates that she has disturbed her concentration and caused her to forget the joke that she was thinking up. Matilde brings their discussion to a close by pretending that she will clean up before she goes to bed, but then turns out the light to sit in the dark (32-3). Matilde throws away her antidepressants (23). She plays the comic, high-status servant rather than the obedient domestic. However, her genuine compassion belies the role, and she comforts Lane when she has trouble supervising her, and again when her husband leaves her.

Lane prefers to maintain class barriers, essentially telling Matilde and Virginia that she would rather not get to know the help too well (13, 45). Lane overlooks Matilde's dislike of cleaning and discounts her emotional life. When Matilde confesses that she is mourning her parents, Lane stresses that cleaning supersedes personal concerns (13). She expresses surprise when Virginia reveals that Matilde, rather than being depressed, simply does not like to clean (42). The intimate nature of their economic relationship only intensifies Lane's discomfort—after all, Matilde literally handles her dirty laundry. Lane attempts to keep Matilde at arm's length even as she grants her access to her underwear drawer.

As much as Matilde hates to clean, Virginia loves to. She enjoys cleaning her own home because, she claims, it both clears her bead and makes her feel clean (18-9). She offers to clean her sister's house because it gives her purpose. Another theme of the play is the attainment of a sense of purpose through appropriate employment. As opposed to Matilde, who would much rather be creating jokes, Virginia derives great pleasure and a sense of accomplishment from cleaning, exulting in the satisfaction of transforming a toilet from a dirty to a clean state (23). Virginia's obsession with cleanliness stems from an impulse to impose order on the world. Her rationalization for not wanting children belies a great fear of losing control: she imagines beautiful children growing up in an ugly world, ultimately left naked in the road, raped and dying, while indifferent strangers pass by (21-2). Her household belongings function as surrogate children, ones that rest safely in their place as she tucks in the silverware (21). She finishes cleaning her own house by midafternoon, and this ritual gives meaning to her life. She half-jokingly credits cleaning with preventing suicide, which might tempt her if her days were free (10). Cleaning grants her a shred of meaning in a life that has "gone downhill" since she reached the age of 22 (22). Unlike Matilde, for whom cleaning is a necessary burden, through it Virginia escapes the curse of abundant leisure time.

In the second act, cleaning assumes a spiritual dimension that is not, however, manifested on the physical plane. On the contrary, the pristine, white living room that contains Lane's ordered, controlled life is incrementally sullied by apple cores, exploding yellow spice, potting soil, and finally Ana's wasted body. Lane only realizes compassion for Ana once she has surrendered to filth. She shouts her newfound affinity for dirt at her sister, wishing her house to be filled with "shiny" cows and dirty, unmatched socks (82). Lane only humbles herself to pay a house call on Ana once her environment reflects her inner turmoil. Through externalizing her pain, she is eventually able to release it and arrive at a state of compassion.

Virginia exuberantly lets go as she contributes to the mess in her sister's living room. After Lane vehemently prohibits her from cleaning anymore, she creates a gigantic mess (84). Making a mess purges pent-up emotion and frees Virginia from her compulsion to clean. Ultimately, the acceptance of chaos and disorder leads to the acceptance of Ana's death. Early in the play, Virginia envisions hospitals as places for storing the waste of dead bodies (10). When Ana's body finally comes to rest in Lane's living room, the ambiance is that of a temple rather than a hospital. The women close Ana's eyes, wash her body, and say a prayer (106-9). Virginia herself weeps her farewell (105). Her acceptance of her own lack of control has facilitated a profound attitudinal shift.

The characters gather around Ana's body as a community. In the first act, Ruhl establishes the isolation of each of the characters. Lane rarely sees her husband and imagines him tied up in surgery all day. She explains to Matilde that they used to keep in touch throughout the day with their beepers, a practice they abandoned as they began to take their relationship for granted (32-3). They have become so disconnected that she is oblivious to his affair, which is a price she pays for not doing her own laundry— she has missed Ana's brightly colored panties cohabiting with her husband's socks. Matilde is isolated in a foreign country, both of her parents recently deceased. More than Matilde, even, Virginia expresses the loneliness and isolation of modern existence. Without employment or community, her life lacks purpose. She considers her husband on par with a piece of furniture, one that should be functional but not too beautiful (25). Although Virginia meets with her sister over coffee, Lane forestalls an attempt to get together for dinner (31). Virginia's relationship with her sister fails to satisfy her social needs.

Only with Matilde is Virginia able to create some sort of meaningful bond. They spend time together as Virginia cleans. Desperate for anyone to talk to, Virginia immediately shares intimate details about her personal life. They chat about the structure of jokes and imagine the details of Charles's suspected affair. Faced with having Matilde hired away from Lane in the second act, Virginia imagines her as a sister during an older time when women gathered in the square to chat and wash clothes. She laments, "Now we are all alone in our separate houses and it is terrible" (65). Lane longs for a simpler, more communal lifestyle.

Another theme is that of head versus heart, or rationality versus emotion and intuition. This theme plays out in the love triangle between Charles, Lane, and Ana. Charles and Lane describe their marriage as built on rationality. They fall in love in anatomy class under distinctly unromantic circumstances, over a cadaver (93). Although Charles and Ana also meet within the medical establishment, their relationship quickly takes an emotional, even irrational turn. They fall in love and "kiss wildly" within a few lines of setting a date for surgery (55), and conceive of themselves as *basherts*, or soulmates. Curiously, Charles expresses this metaphysical dimension in a tone of scientific objectivity, as if it were genetically predetermined (61-2). Charles justifies the disruption of his marriage by ascribing the certainty of the empirical to that which is intangible.

Charles delineates a particular kind of logical justice that brought him and Lane together, as a sort of reward for good behavior (53). For her part, Lane is able to quantify the reasons that Charles should be in love with her as though on a resume (40). Theirs is a marriage based on intellect and respect; in contrast, Charles's affair with Ana stems from a passion rooted in the metaphysical. The whirlwind affair of the heart destroys the respectable marriage of minds. Ultimately, however, with Ana's passing, Lane implicitly reclaims her husband. Ana predicts that she will take care of him because she still loves him (104-5), and Lane tenderly kisses Charles on the forehead when he delivers the tree (108). Rather than a reuniting of minds, however, this plays as an act of compassion and forgiveness. Not only humor, then, but compassion as well tempers the impact of Ana's death, one that the cold logic of medical science is unable to prevent.

The title of the play suggests the term "clean room," which is an environment in which dust and other airborne contaminants are reduced to a minimum to facilitate the production of delicate equipment or the "manipulation of biological materials" ("Clean Room"). A synonym for "clean room" is "white room," and this term seems to have inspired the color scheme of Lane's living room as indicated by the stage directions (8). The sterile setting represents an extreme attempt to maintain control over both the physical and emotional environment at the expense of comfort. The title also suggests that a house is not necessarily a home; only after the whiteness of Charles and Lane's dwelling is sullied does it become one . . . .

**Source:** James Al-Shamma, "Joke as Incarnation in *The Clean House*," in *Sarah Ruhl: A Critical Study of the Plays*, McFarland, 2011, pp. 42–49.

> " I COME INTO THE THEATER WANTING TO FEEL AND THINK AT THE SAME TIME, TO HAVE THE THOUGHT AFFECT THE EMOTION AND THE EMOTION AFFECT THE THOUGHT. THAT IS THE PINNACLE OF A GREAT NIGHT AT THE THEATER."

## Paula Vogel and Sarah Ruhl

*In the following interview excerpt, Ruhl talks about various elements that make a play successful.*

**Sarah Ruhl** The longer I do theater, the more shocked I am that you can get the play's punctuation, the story, the casting, even the director right. Still, you have to deal with variables like: Is this the right audience? Do I have the right month of the year, the right city? Is the right reviewer coming? So much of it is chance in terms of how the aesthetic object is received. Sometimes it makes you just want to write a slim volume of poetry.

*PV The architectural design of the theater will impact the perception and the choices in directing your play. So, yeah, the variables are intense.*

**SR** As my grandmother used to say, "You play the hand you're dealt." In that sense, I love the materiality of the theater; you have a set of material givens and you work with them. For example, the Newhouse Theater is three quarters, and in some ways the intimacy of the audience wrapping around the stage is good for the play, but it's very hard to play a comedy in three quarters. It's hard to have visual surprise. It's hard to do subtitles.

*PV There is a perceptual switching of framing in your plays that is pre-twentieth century. In* Clean House, *or* Passion Play *or* Eurydice, *you can see the structural bones of a different theatrical relationship with the audience, be it medieval, Jacobean, or impressionist.* Clean House *works very well within a proscenium arch, which predates the twentieth century. What's exciting about your work and that of the other rising playwrights in your generation is that there's a reclaiming of theater out of that mishmash of assumptions made about realism. Assumptions that were not even theatrical issues in previous centuries.*

**SR** I think our generation has to look at Freud and Freud's impact, and many of us say, Oh, maybe Freud didn't have it right. Something that he was right about he got from literature: the Oedipal complex, from the Greeks. So maybe we ought to go back to the Greeks instead of back to Freud on the Greeks.

*PV When you put a chorus on stage, as in* Eurydice, *there's a focus on the theatricality. There's no way that you can be in that intimate, fourth-wall realism once that happens. Freud's legacy in America is anti-realism. Think about those extraordinary, wild flourishings of the Provincetown Playhouse that are in conversation with Freud. Your* Melancholy Play *is in conversation with Freud, and yet it does not lead to a surface reality that clings to the Stanislavsky method of performance.*

**SR** For me, it's putting things up against Freud. In *Melancholy Play*, one character is so depressed that she turns into an almond. *(laughter)* It's a more medieval sensibility of the humors, melancholia, black bile and transformation. If you excavate people's subjectivity and how they view the world emotionally, you don't get realism.

*PV Has anything prepared you for this moment in time? The impact of success is actually a shock.*

**SR** Hmm, yes and no. Every production prepares you for the next production, and in that sense it's cumulative. We think: Oh, New York is definitive. In a way, it's just another production of one of my plays in another city. I've worked so much regionally that it gives me less of a sense of living or dying by one interpretation.

*PV Good, because in essence, the vocabulary of the Sarah Ruhl play is formed by layers of production and a national sense of what those plays mean.*

**SR** The New York model is an old one: You premiere in New York, and if it does well, it'll be done regionally. If it tanks, its life is over. Now people are starting to premiere things regionally and build up the momentum and then take it to New York. New York theaters are so scared of the press that fewer risks are being taken.

*PV I think that in New York, we are still experiencing a kind of post-traumatic stress disorder. And it's a stress level for critics and audiences as well as the artist. When you're stressed, you don't want to be told a story that is going to disturb your sleep, or make you think. And theater really is communal; an audience comes into a public space, and then must be open or receptive. It's part of the ritual.*

*SR* I come into the theater wanting to feel and think at the same time, to have the thought affect the emotion and the emotion affect the thought. That is the pinnacle of a great night at the theater.

*PV The shift in your writing embraces the emotional vocabulary of theater, which a lot of plays avoid. We're used to plays that build into their structure a kind of rational mousetrap, but you're exploring emotional resonance without embarrassment. There is an impulse to be ashamed of emotions in theater, which is rather odd because one would think that's why we have theater.*

*SR* I love that term, *rational mousetrap*. Ten years ago, if you were writing, as e. e. cummings would say, about such trite themes as love and death, you were considered a hack. I felt that theater was actually a place where the voice could be attached to emotion. Theater is still a living tradition of speech and emotion. It's something that deeply attracts me.

*PV Now, you've worked in many, many productions with many directors and actors. What are your actors teaching you? What kind of impact does that have on your sense of the characters you're now writing?*

*SR* I've worked with so many actors with different methods and vocabularies. In almost all the productions I've had, it's been the usual mode: You cast the play out of LA and New York, and the actors meet each other on the first day of rehearsal. I've been very pleased and honored and moved by the integrity of all the productions. But I'd like to discover what would happen if I worked with the same actors and designers over and over in a concentrated way. If the actor and I were able to know exactly what we meant if I said, "Give this line a little more space." As opposed to one actor who thinks space is a subtext and another who thinks space is a technical pause.

*PV Have you experienced performances where you think, A: Oh, I never saw it that way; or B: [gasp] That was the image in my head that I'd forgotten?*

*SR* I had a remarkable time going to the Goodman production of *The Clean House*, directed by Jessica Thebus. It was exactly the play and yet more so, because there were

elements I would never have thought of that were so sublime. For instance, there's a scene where Lane, a doctor married to a doctor, imagines her husband kissing the breast of his new lover, who is one of his patients. The stage direction says, "Ana wears a gown. Is it a hospital gown or a ballroom gown?" Well, Marilyn Dodds Frank, who plays Ana, walked out in a renaissance ball gown made of lavender hospital-gown material. It had a train that was about 20 yards long. So she begins walking out in this purple gown, and it just keeps coming and coming and coming. I would never have thought of that. That was a high point of my life really, watching that production and thinking: They really read my mind. Also, the living room was very architectural, spare and abstract. There had been a beautiful skylight in Act One and in the second act it cantilevered down and became the balcony. It was so shocking—you wouldn't think that it could just come out of the air like that. The designer completely understood abstraction and transformation of space.

*PV The production of* Eurydice *at Yale also has a transformation of space. It seems to me your work actually calls that out of designers and directors. Whereas the theater of the rational mousetrap, when it insists that characters change, it means the furniture remains stable.* (laughter) *I get so visually bored when the emotional space doesn't change, that thrill, as you describe it in your article on Maria Irene Fornés, the embrace of the state of being. Where the emotional state changes, but not the psychological character. Some of the descriptions in* Melancholy Play *produce those resonances. Music always does that.*

*SR* If you transform space and atmosphere, you don't have to connect the dots psychologically in a linear way. It reminds me of an essay I've been wanting to write, about the death of combat and duels on stage. We used to go to the theater for bloodlust, to watch people kill each other on Shakespeare's stage and see a good fight. The advent of guns stopped that: You can't really have a good gunfight on stage. We've replaced that physicality with the idea of drama as conflict, with people bickering on stage. I'd rather watch a clash of swords. I mean, an argument, the idea of opposition and dialectic, is very important to me, but the bickering I could do without.

*PV Arnold Aronson blames it all on the introduction of the chair to the stage. Once you put* a chair on the stage, we sit down and have a chat. You know, "Mrs. Tesman, let's have a little chat."

SR Do you ever tell your students to write a play in which there are no chairs?

*PV No, but that's a great idea. I'm going to do that.*

SR I think *Eurydice* has no chairs. Maria Dizzia, who played Eurydice, said when she was scared at one point in the process, "There are no pillars to hide behind." And there are no chairs to sit on.

*PV Your plays challenge actors. They have to get up there and emote. It's about those larger-than-life moments; there's no hiding and you can't work your way up to it in a logical sequence of events. You have to jump in the cold, deep end of the pool.*

SR That's how I experience emotions. They come at you so suddenly sometimes. I watch my daughter, who's in the middle of crying, and then you do a little dance for her and she starts laughing. Not that we're all infants—

*PV Yes, we are. (laughter)*

SR I don't think that our emotions are easily bendable to dramaturgical reason. Emotions can come out of thin air in my work and it can be difficult for actors, especially if their training doesn't allow that.

*PV I think of each production as a Tower of Babel. Everybody comes in with different training, speaking different languages, and you have four weeks to speak the same language. Here's a question for you: How do we get critics or audience members to ask the right questions? Is it simply by writing play after play and creating a body of work that breaks out of the rational mousetrap?*

SR Well, in life, how do we get people to ask the right questions of us? A love interest, for instance. How do you get them to ask you the right question about yourself or about your day? Part of it is training. In Thai marriage vows (my husband is half-Thai), training is one of the precepts. But you don't have breakfast with critics. There's such a gulf between critics and playwrights right now; I know it's necessary for objectivity, but I don't think it's a very good gulf. What do you think?

*PV Well, it's an ongoing debate I've had. I very much respect a lot of the critics' writing. For example, Linda Winer is a passionate, caring critic. The problem revolves around this notion of objectivity. I had a private tour of O'Neill's house when I was visiting the lovely Wendy Goldberg, who is doing an amazing job of turning around the drift of the O'Neill Theater. Upstairs in his study, the curator pointed to a trunk and said, "That was given to the O'Neills as a gift from the critic Brooks Atkinson, before they took their European trip." I felt stabbed through the heart. There was a time in New York when critics and playwrights and actors and directors drank at the same bar, got into their fist fights, had affairs, kissed and made up, stormed at each other, but they did it face-to-face and occasionally, critics would ask to be cast in plays. It was a world that we shared together.*

SR That trunk, and the idea of gift-giving, interests me. What do you do when a critic changes your life for the better? Can you send them a bottle of champagne and a letter thanking them? Charles Isherwood changed my life for the better. I find myself wanting to send him a crate of citrus for the winter months, but I know that I can't; it would compromise his next review of my work. Ben Brantley probably changed your life for the better. But you can't thank them, can you? And when a critic destroys you, there is no recourse. You can't tell them, You destroyed that play. That was seven years of my life. I think in a town like Chicago critics and playwrights are more likely to meet each other, but I could imagine going a lifetime without meeting a critic in New York....

**Source:** Paula Vogel and Sarah Ruhl, "Sarah Ruhl," in *Bomb*, Spring 2007.

# SOURCES

Al-Shamma, James, *Sarah Ruhl: A Critical Study of the Plays*, McFarland, 2011, pp. 1–11, 38–67.

———, "Worshipping the Black Sun: Melancholy in Eugene O'Neill and Sarah Ruhl," in *Eugene O'Neill Review*, No. 35, No. 1, Spring 2014, p. 61.

Bloom, Michael, "Balancing Acts: In a Book of Essays and an Epistolary Play, Sarah Ruhl Makes the Case for Beauty and Repose, Despite Distance and Distraction," in *American Theatre*, October 2014, p. 142.

Durham, Leslie Atkins, *Women's Voices on American Stages in the Early Twenty-first Century: Sarah Ruhl and Her Contemporaries*, Palgrave Macmillan, 2013, pp. 1–29, 53–73.

Isherwood, Charles, "Always Ready with a Joke, If Not a Feather Duster," in *New York Times*, October 31, 2006, http://www.nytimes.com/2006/10/31/theater/reviews/always-ready-with-a-joke-if-not-a-feather-duster.html (accessed August 21, 2017).

Lahr, John, "Gods and Dolls," in *New Yorker*, Vol. 83, No. 18, July 2, 2007, p. 82.

———, "Surreal Life," in *New Yorker*, Vol. 84, No. 5, March 17, 2008, p. 78.

Ruhl, Sarah, *The Clean House and Other Plays*, Theatre Communications Group, 2006.

———, Introduction to *Chekhov's "Three Sisters" and Woolf's "Orlando": Two Renderings for the Stage*, Theatre Communications Group, 2013, pp. ix–xiii.

"Sarah Ruhl," in *American Theatre*, Vol. 21, No. 8, October 2004, p. 104.

"Sarah Ruhl, Playwright, New York City," in *American Theatre*, Vol. 26, No. 4, April 2009, p. 37.

Stuart, Randall, Michael Olich, and Sarah Gahagan, "Eurydice: Artists Repertory Theatre," in *American Theatre*, Vol. 26, No. 8, October 2009, p. 98.

## FURTHER READING

Ovid, *Metamorphoses*, edited and with an introduction by E. J. Kenney, translated by A. D. Melville, Oxford's World Classics, Oxford University Press, 1998.

> Roman poet Ovid wrote on topics of love and mythological transformations in elegiac couplets in this masterpiece from 9 CE. Ruhl is greatly influenced by his storytelling.

Ruhl, Sarah, *100 Essays I Don't Have Time to Write: On Umbrellas and Sword Fights, Parades and Dogs, Fire Alarms, Children, and Theater*, Straus and Giroux, 2014.

> These are very short essays written when Ruhl was a young mother. The book's topics range from the personal to the future possibilities of theater. It was selected by the *New York Times* as one of the hundred most notable books of 2014.

Schmidt, Kerstin, *The Theater of Transformation: Postmodernism in American Drama*, Rodopi, 2005.

> Schmidt teaches American studies and investigates contemporary experimental theater from the 1960s on, including information on texts and performances and issues of gender, class, race, and ethnicity.

Van Erven, Eugene, *Community Theatre: Global Perspectives*, Psychology Press, 2001.

> Van Erven is a lecturer at Utrecht University in the Netherlands. He describes the power of community theater for healing and for political activism around the world, including examples in Los Angeles, Kenya, Australia, the Philippines, and other places. Ruhl has expressed her desire to see theater go in this direction and often references theater practices from other cultures.

Woolf, Virginia, *Orlando: A Biography*, Hogarth Press, 1928.

> Woolf wrote a feminist fantasy on her friend Vita Sackville-West that is a satire on English literature through the centuries, with Sackville-West as an incarnation in each age, sometimes a man and sometimes a woman. Ruhl credits Woolf as a major inspiration and adapted *Orlando* for the stage.

## SUGGESTED SEARCH TERMS

Sarah Ruhl

*The Clean House*

magic realism

defamiliarization AND theater

joke theory

breast cancer treatment

stages of mourning

Paula Vogel

Italo Calvino AND lightness

Victor Shklovsky

# *Dog Lady*

## MILCHA SANCHEZ-SCOTT
## 1984

In Milcha Sanchez-Scott's one-act play *Dog Lady* (1984), a young woman, Rosalinda, dreams of escaping the barrio as she trains for a marathon. When her neighbor, an ineffable but powerful healer, decides to help her, Rosalinda's quest for glory becomes a wild chase as she is given the dog spirit—a benign but chaotic enchantment that makes her run like the wind. Included in the *Best Short Plays of 1986*, *Dog Lady* was first produced at INTAR in New York City, from April 27 to May 27, 1984. With a cast of lovable, funny characters and positive themes, *Dog Lady* encourages its audience to seek the good in others in order to build a stronger community and brighter future. The play appears in *Dog Lady and The Cuban Swimmer*, Dramatists Play Service, 1984.

## AUTHOR BIOGRAPHY

Sanchez-Scott was born in Bali, Indonesia, in 1953, to a Colombian father and Indonesian, Dutch, and Chinese mother. She spent her childhood in Colombia, Mexico, and England, where she was educated at a Catholic girls' school outside of London. The family moved to La Jolla, California, when Sanchez-Scott was fourteen. There, she encountered marked racial prejudice for the first time while waiting for the school bus on her first day when a white boy threw rocks at

*The story is set in a Los Angeles barrio* (© Joseph Sohm / Shutterstock.com)

her and told her to wait at the Mexican bus stop. Because of this incident, her parents enrolled her in an Episcopalian girls' school.

Sanchez-Scott attended the University of San Diego, where she studied literature, theater, and philosophy. After graduation, she worked at an employment agency for household workers in Beverly Hills and as an actress, including roles in the television series *Police Story* and *Starsky and Hutch*. It was while performing in a women's prison that Sanchez-Scott was inspired to write the stories of the struggling immigrant women in her life. Her first play, *Latina*, was produced in Los Angeles in 1980. A critical success, *Latina* launched Sanchez-Scott's career as a playwright.

Susan Lowenberg, the producing director of the new works division of Artists in Prison and Other Places, commissioned Sanchez-Scott to write a second play. The result was *Dog Lady* and *The Cuban Swimmer*, two one-act plays first produced in 1984 by INTAR in New York City and selected for the Theatre Communications Group Plays in Process series. The plays were produced at Rutgers University and in London, England, in 1985. *Dog Lady* went on to be produced by El Teatro Campesino in 1988. Sanchez-Scott was

also invited to Mária Irene Fornés's Hispanic Playwrights-in-Resident Laboratory. She published her most well-known play, *Roosters*, in 1987. It was followed by *Evening Star* in 1988, *Stone Wedding* in 1989, *El Dorado* in 1990, and *Regression 500* in 1992.

Sanchez-Scott's awards include seven Drama-Logue Awards for *Latina*, a Vesta Award for *Dog Lady and The Cuban Swimmer*, Le Compte du Nüoy Foundation Award, and a First Level Award for American Playwriting from the Rockefeller Foundation. She was the Latino Theatre Initiative Playwright Fellow from 1995 to 1996 and was a member of the New Dramatists. As of 2017, she lived in Los Angeles.

## PLOT SUMMARY

### First Day

*Dog Lady* is set in a barrio off the Hollywood freeway in Los Angeles, during the summer. It is early morning on Castro Street, with orange sunlight washing over the stage. Two front lawns sit side by side. One lawn is trimmed and neat, with a sprinkler watering the grass. The other lawn is wild and overgrown with unfamiliar plants. It looks like a jungle. Tires and broken-down objects are scattered everywhere. The sign on the lawn reads "Curandera—Healer." Each house has a mailbox, and the neat house has a jacaranda tree. A man of eighteen or nineteen leans against the fence of the neat house, calling out Rosalinda's name. His name is Raphael, and his eyes smolder beneath the dark felt hat he wears.

When the mailman, Orlando, appears, Raphael runs away. Orlando mutters under his breath about the heat. He shakes his head at the healer sign in the jungle-like lawn. He has no mail for Doña Luisa's mailbox. He moves on to the second mailbox just as Rosalinda comes out of the neat house preparing for a run. She is eighteen years old and very pretty, busy stretching as Orlando warns her not to run in such heat. Rosalinda ignores him, announcing that she is going to win. She gets into starting position, saying that she will run around the world: Africa today, India tomorrow, Rome on Saturday. Orlando calls out: "On your mark. Get set. The whole barrio's behind you.... Go!" She runs off, and Orlando wishes her luck. He leaves the stage.

The sun rises in the sky. Rosalinda's mother, María Pilar Luna, stands on her neat front lawn in a nice, clean housedress and apron. She calls for Rosalinda with no results. On the overgrown lawn, Luisa Ruiz wanders among the plants and rubbish in a dingy, torn white bathrobe. She wears bright red lipstick, and her hair is uncombed. Luisa asks what María is doing. María explains patiently that she is calling for her daughter. Luisa begins to talk about each of the neighborhood dogs and whether they respond to their name or must be called with a whistle. She owns an ultrasonic dog whistle, but another neighbor— Mr. Mura—has complained that it opens his garage door every time she blows it. María tells Luisa that her daughter is not a dog to be whistled for, but Luisa continues to talk about the neighborhood dogs. María calls to the house for Jesse, her younger daughter, to bring her antacid tablets, but Jesse calls back that she cannot find them. Just as María is about to leave to go inside, Luisa grabs her arm and points to a dog in the window of her house. She tells María that the dog is spoiled and lazy, but María counters that the dog is blind and Luisa should take it to the vet.

On the way inside, María passes Jesse and suggests that her late husband might not approve of his daughter's appearance. Jesse asks why she should put herself together if she is not going anywhere. She says that she never goes anywhere and that no one notices her. As she is lamenting this, she moves toward Luisa. Together they describe a small cloud in the sky, drifting aimlessly. But the cloud grows until— Luisa says—it blinds her. Jesse is confused. She thinks the cloud is a metaphor for her life. Luisa is referring to cataracts that cloud her dog's eyes. Luisa has tried to heal the dog with herbs, to no effect. She wanders away just as Raphael reappears. Jesse yells at him that Rosalinda is not interested, that she is going to leave the barrio and see the world. Jesse picks up a rock to throw, and Orlando flees. Jesse shouts after him to stop calling their house and hanging up. Softly she adds that she recognizes his breathing.

### First Night
Night falls. Crickets chirp and dogs howl. A single light is on in the Luna house. Rosalinda steps outside, running in place in a sweatshirt, and pants. She says, "I'm going to run around the world, over oceans and islands and continents. I'm going to jump over the Himalayas, skip the Spanish Steps and dip my toes in the

Blue Nile." She speaks of seeing new things and meeting new people. She introduces herself in different languages to these imaginary peoples: "*Yo soy* Rosalinda. *Je suis* Rosalinda ... *Io sono* Rosalinda. *Jumbo*! Me Rosalinda from America." Jesse appears in the lit-up window with an alarm clock in hand. She warns her sister that she may be mugged, but Rosalinda says she is too fast for that. Jesse asks which way she is going, and Rosalinda replies north—over the top of the North Pole. When Jesse tells her to say hello to the Eskimos, Rosalinda scoffs and tells her to hurry up. After Jesse counts down and Rosalinda runs off, Raphael appears. He throws pebbles at the window, calling Rosalinda's name. Hiding behind a curtain, Jesse pretends to be her sister and answers him.

Raphael says he knows she has other things on her mind with the upcoming race Saturday, but he cannot be ignored any longer: "*Si*, I'm going to declare myself." He reads a poem called "Rosalinda." Jesse throws a shoe at him. Raphael begs Rosy not to be cruel to him. Jesse tells him Rosalinda would never answer to Rosy and that she does not date when she is training. She mocks his declaration of love but stops him as he sulks away to tell him she likes his poem. They tell each other goodnight. Rosalinda arrives home, listing the names of cities with each labored breath. She asks Jesse how she did, but Jesse has lost track of the time. Rosalinda says she will go again, running off as she lists the imaginary cities she is passing once more.

### Second Day
María stands in her yard calling for Rosalinda. Luisa, too, is outside, complaining of the Santa Ana wind. When María worries about Rosalinda, Luisa confuses her for a dog again. María explains that her daughter is training for the Our Lady of a Thousand Sorrows Marathon on Saturday. Father Estefan personally has gone door to door collecting her entrance fee. Luisa is upset that she did not give any money—Father Estefan did not come to her door. While María complains that her husband in heaven has not helped his family by begging God, the saints, and angels for blessings, Luisa is distraught that she has not helped Rosalinda. Rosalinda is a kind and generous girl, Luisa says. She always gives Luisa a free ice cream cone when she visits her at work. María says that without divine help from her father, Rosalinda is forced to run like a dog to succeed. The phrase catches Luisa's attention,

and she continues to repeat it aloud, deep in thought. Jesse comes outside, only to be berated by her mother over her sloppy appearance. She tells Luisa she cannot help it, that her body has a natural slouch. Inside the house, María discovers a stash of snack food under Jesse's bed.

### Second Night

The moon is almost full. There is a low humming in the air. Luisa stands in her doorway in a dark kimono with her hands outstretched. She holds a red flannel cloth over her hands. Raphael spies on the scene from behind the jacaranda tree. When Rosalinda steps outside in her running clothes, Luisa beckons her over slowly, as if hypnotizing her with the flannel cloth. Rosalinda approaches and kneels before Luisa, who gives her a special yu-yu amulet. It is a small red flannel bag filled with herbs and potions that hangs around the neck by a string. As Luisa drapes it around Rosalinda's neck, she speaks in Spanish, calling on the saints. She chants their names, clapping after each one. When she is finished, a dog howls. Raphael leaves the scene. Night becomes day.

### Third Day

On the day of the race, María calls for Rosalinda. When there is no answer, she tells Jesse to go find her. Rosalinda needs to eat a good breakfast and attend a special Mass for runners during which Father Estefan will bless her feet. Jesse leaves. Orlando enters with the mail. He tells María not to worry. The Santa Ana winds are agitating her nerves. As the priest leaves, Jesse returns, shouting for her mother. She has seen Rosalinda with a pair of neighborhood stray dogs. Jesse says that Rosalinda barked at her and ran up to a car and jumped over it. She also bought a pound of meat and bones at the market, even though she is a vegetarian. Jesse could not catch her but saw her running in place at a stoplight with her tongue hanging out and her hands held up in the air like paws. María is livid, explaining to Jesse that Rosalinda will ruin her ovaries running that hard. Jesse is disgusted.

Rosalinda runs past with a pack of dogs, all of them barking. Followed the pack is Mrs. Amador, who tells María that Rosalinda and the dogs have destroyed her rose bed and all of her roses. Rosalinda and the dogs pass again. Jesse, who has followed them, tells the women that Rosalinda was chasing cars down Castro Street. Mrs. Amador says she saw Rosalinda in her garden with wild hair and bared teeth with blood around her mouth. Orlando limps into the scene, his pant leg torn, telling them Rosalinda is responsible. Jesse says that Rosalinda is now catching Frisbee disks in the park. Mrs. Amador says Rosalinda must be on drugs and crazy, but Jesse defends her. Luisa comes outside, calling for her dogs. Raphael runs toward Jesse, shouting about Rosalinda, but when he sees Luisa he points at her, shouting: "She's the one! La Dog Lady! She gave her something. She put a curse on her. She turned her into a dog!"

María demands to know what Luisa has done. Luisa explains that she has given Rosalinda the dog spirit to help her run. She promises it will not hurt Rosalinda, but Mrs. Amador calls it the work of the devil and tells everyone to shield their eyes. Orlando tells her not to talk nonsense, but she reminds him that Father Estefan has told them that Luisa's dog has gone blind because of the herbs she put in its eyes and has urged everyone to avoid her. Raphael pulls a knife on Luisa, telling her to turn Rosalinda back. Orlando tells him to back down, that the Santa Ana winds have made everyone crazy. María acknowledges that Luisa is a powerful woman and asks if she will turn her daughter back. Luisa uses her ultrasonic dog whistle. Mrs. Amador gasps as Mr. Mura's garage door opens by itself. Everyone but Jesse and Luisa cross themselves. Rosalinda arrives, running in place with a Frisbee disk in her mouth and covered in mud and rose petals. She runs off stage, ready for the marathon. The others run after her. Raphael stays behind, realizing that Rosalinda is too much trouble: "She's never home, she's a lot of trouble, running, jumping, barking." Luisa also stays behind, explaining to her two dogs that the race is for Catholic girls only.

### Third Night

Under a full moon, a mariachi band is playing. A party is going on at the Luna house, a banner reads "Rosalinda Number One." Mrs. Amador is alarmed when Rosalinda comes out, but Rosalinda appears to have returned to normal. She has won an all-expenses-paid trip to Rome: "I'm going to see the world.... I'm going to see the universe.... I am going to dance on Venus, Skate on Saturn's rings, dive into the Milky Way and wash my hair with stars." While Rosalinda, María, and Mrs. Amador watch the sky, Orlando and Raphael arrive, wearing suits. Jesse appears in the doorway transformed into a princess. Raphael splits the bouquet in two, giving each sister half. Luisa joins the party, and Orlando asks her to dance with him. Jesse and Rosalinda have a moment alone. Rosalinda promises that no matter what, they will be sisters forever. Jesse asks to see the yu-yu bag. Rosalinda hangs it around Jesse's neck but warns her she will still need to work hard. Jesse stands and begins to walk away down the street toward the moon while her mother calls for her.

## CHARACTERS

### Mrs. Amador

Mrs. Amador is a neighbor of the Luna family. She becomes involved in the play's action after Rosalinda and the dog pack destroy the precious roses in her garden. She is the most easily scandalized of the characters, warning her neighbors that Luisa is dangerous, according to Father Estefan. She is frightened of Rosalinda, even after she returns to her old self.

### Father Estefan

Father Estefan is the neighborhood's priest. He personally goes door to door collecting money for Rosalinda's marathon entrance fee. He believes that Luisa has blinded her dog by rubbing herbs in its eyes and warns the neighborhood to keep their distance from her. He holds a special Mass the day of the race to bless Rosalinda's feet, but caught in Luisa's spell he is unable to attend.

### Jesse Luna

Jesse is Rosalinda's younger sister. Her mother hounds her over her unkempt appearance. Jesse is disillusioned with her life and considers herself invisible. She halfheartedly helps her sister train for the marathon. She chases Raphael from their house, though she harbors a secret crush on him. After Rosalinda becomes subject to Luisa's dog spirit enchantment, Jesse chases her around town, excited by all the action. At the celebration after the race, Jesse is transformed into a beautiful princess. Raphael gives her half of the bouquet he has brought for Rosalinda. The two sisters talk about Rosalinda's bright future, and Rosalinda gives Jesse her amulet. The play ends with Jesse wearing the amulet while walking toward the full moon.

### Juanito Luna

Juanito is María's late husband and Jesse and Rosalinda's father. María frequently addresses him in heaven, particularly to scold him for not using his divine influence to help his family.

### María Pilar Luna

María is Rosalinda and Jesse's mother. Her husband, Juanito, has died, leaving her alone. She takes good care of her daughters, the house, and the yard and is kind to Luisa, though she is frustrated by their circular conversations. María scolds Jesse for her sloppy appearance and worries that Rosalinda will damage her ovaries through running. When she discovers the spell, María is respectful in asking Luisa to reverse it, unlike Mrs. Amador and Raphael. She is ecstatic when Rosalinda wins the marathon.

### Rosalinda Luna

Rosalinda is a runner and the play's protagonist. Her dream is to travel the world, and when she runs, she lists the places she is passing in her imagination. She trains constantly, hoping to escape the barrio through her athletic prowess. Because her family is too poor to purchase the best shoes, she must work harder. She has a job at Dairy Queen, where she gives Luisa free ice cream cones, earning her respect. Luisa gives Rosalinda the dog spirit in a late night ceremony, transforming her. She becomes fast, agile, and tireless, though she retains other, less useful canine traits like a love for getting dirty, tearing up gardens, and catching Frisbee disks. She wins the marathon with Luisa's help and will go on an all-expenses-paid trip to Rome. Her dream has come true, and she sets her sights next on the stars.

### Mr. Mura

Mr. Mura is a neighbor of the Luna family. He asks Luisa not to use her ultrasonic dog whistle because it opens his garage door.

### Orlando

Orlando is the mailman. He blames the strange behavior of the neighbors on the Santa Ana winds. He is excited for the race, cheering Rosalinda on as she trains. An affable and easygoing man, Orlando defends Luisa when Raphael and Mrs. Amador blame her for the spell. At the end of the play, he arrives at the party in a suit and asks Luisa to dance.

### Raphael

Raphael is a lovesick man of eighteen or nineteen who has strikingly dark features. His doomed attempts to woo Rosalinda are mocked by Jesse, who secretly likes him. Raphael is overly dramatic and clueless about the object of his desire. Though he acknowledges that Rosalinda has an important race coming up, he continually appears at the house to bother her. She is rarely home when he visits and seems to not know he exists. Raphael witnesses Luisa's spell and later pulls a knife on her, demanding that she change Rosalinda back.

### Luisa Ruiz

Luisa is the dog lady, a neighborhood healer. She seems to be scatterbrained, frequently misunderstanding the words of the person speaking to her. She is often lost in her own thoughts. She has dogs, including a blind dog that she calls lazy. Father Estefan believes that she has caused the dog to go blind by rubbing herbs in its eyes, but Luisa says she has rubbed herbs on the dog's eyes in an attempt to cure its blindness. Luisa considers Rosalinda a generous woman and a friend. When she discovers she has missed the chance to contribute to Rosalinda's race entry fee, Luisa casts a spell to give her the dog spirit. The neighbors threaten Luisa and call it the devil's work, but Rosalinda is grateful after she wins the marathon.

## THEMES

### Ambition

Rosalinda is driven to train by her powerful ambition to leave the barrio and travel the world. Her ambition is what motivates her to run all day and night to the exclusion of all other activities. Rosalinda has a job at Dairy Queen and an admirer in Raphael, but neither of these is on her mind when she is on stage. Instead, she is single-mindedly focused on her goal. She is always thinking two steps ahead, and it is not winning the marathon or impressing the barrio that captures her imagination but the trip to Rome and the potential to travel even further. Rosalinda's greatest ambition is to leave the barrio, and so life in the barrio—her job, her peers—do not hold her interest. Conversely, the barrio rallies around Rosalinda. Everyone from the mailman to the priest to the neighborhood

## TOPICS FOR FURTHER STUDY

- Read *Any Small Goodness: A Novel of the Barrio*, by Tony Johnston (2001). How is barrio life described in the story? Write an essay in which you compare and contrast barrio life as depicted in *Any Small Goodness* with the barrio of *Dog Lady*. What conclusions about life in the barrio can you draw from these two works?

- Create a blog from Rosalinda's point of view in which you collect photos from each of the places Rosalinda dreams of visiting. Write each entry to reflect Rosalinda's character in style and appearance. Give each photo a short caption in Rosalinda's voice. You may also include articles on travel, running, and barrio life. Blogger.com offers free blog space.

- Create an infographic on the topic of life in the East Los Angeles barrio. You may choose to create a time line of the barrio's history, a graph showing the neighborhood's population growth, or a comparative chart of the barrio's poverty rate versus that of other Los Angeles neighborhoods, such as Beverly Hills or Compton. Choose any topic for your infographic but provide reliable sources for your statistics. Easel.ly offers free infographics.

- Write a scene from the point of view of one of the characters in *Dog Lady* besides Rosalinda. For example, follow Orlando on his mail route, describe Raphael's creative process as he writes his poem for Rosalinda, or show María having a one-sided argument with her husband in heaven as she goes about her household chores. Your scene does not have to be in play form, but you should attempt to closely mimic the character's voice and speech patterns in your own dialogue.

healer wants Rosalinda to succeed. It is not the people of the barrio but the barrio itself—the poverty and lack of opportunity—that Rosalinda wants to outrun. The people of the barrio want

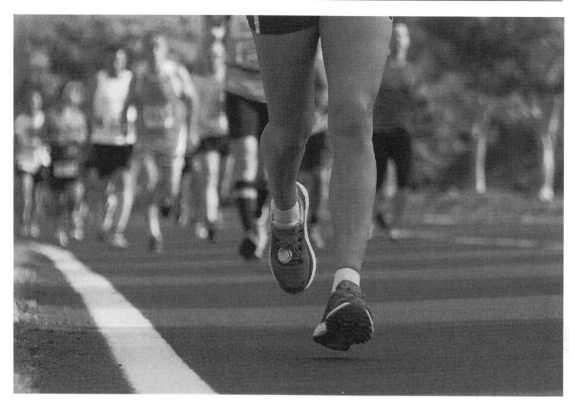

*When Rosalinda competes in the marathon, she does not run in the usual manner* (© Pavel1964 / Shutterstock.com)

what she wants, and they help however they can—cheering, donating money, and getting out of her way.

Rosalinda's ambition is notable for its purity. Her goal is personal, not motivated by resentment or a desire to impress or be acknowledged as the greatest. She is a humble and kind person who dreams of a better life for herself. It is not money or material wealth she desires but new experiences. Her clear-eyed ambition is rewarded by Luisa's spell—a boon Rosalinda earns through her generous spirit. Yet at play's end, Rosalinda recognizes that hard work is necessary with or without magical intervention. She tells her sister as she passes on Luisa's amulet that if she wants to change her life, she must do it herself.

### Generosity

Throughout *Dog Lady* the characters are quick to help one another. A giving nature unites the neighborhood as a counter to the chaos of the Santa Ana winds. If the winds represent the adversity inherent in barrio life, the community's spirit of generosity is the force that stands strong, unbending to that pressure. When Rosalinda and the Luna family cannot afford her entrance fee, Father Estefan personally goes door to door to collect money for her. Everyone gives. When Luisa discovers she has not been asked to contribute, she is horrified and gives a gift of her own, inspired by Rosalinda's acts of generosity toward her. After winning, Rosalinda is most concerned with thanking Luisa for her help. She then gives the yu-yu amulet to her sister and with it the chance to escape life in the barrio.

María works tirelessly to maintain her home and raise her children as a widow. Orlando encourages Rosalinda and defends Luisa from accusations of witchcraft. Even Raphael, comically self-centered in his pursuit of Rosalinda, arrives in the final scene with a gift of flowers: half for Rosalinda and half for her sister. Jesse also sacrifices, staying up late to time her sister's runs. In a play named for an animal known for its generous affection, the characters of *Dog Lady* do not hesitate to support each other.

## Spirituality

Various religions and belief systems converge in the play. Superstition, Catholicism, and folk magic blend in the barrio to create an atmosphere of magic and miracles. Representing superstition is Orlando, who insists that the San Ana winds are putting everyone on edge, causing erratic and inexplicable behavior. Representing Catholicism are the Lunas, Mrs. Amador, and Father Estefan. María argues frequently with her husband in heaven, suggesting that he beg favors from the saints to help his family out of poverty. Father Estefan and Mrs. Amador both disapprove of Luisa. She represents folk magic: Catholicism, holistic healing, and folk religion blended together much like Haitian voodoo. Luisa calls on the Catholic saints in her midnight spell, though her work is denounced as Satanic by Mrs. Amador.

Several miracles take place in the play: the community comes together to produce Rosalinda's entrance fee, Luisa gives Rosalinda the dog spirit, and Jesse is transformed into a princess. Each of these miracles originates from a different source, whether the spirit of giving, Luisa's magic, or Jesse's willingness to change. At no point is one path depicted as greater or better than the other. Instead, the mixed spiritualties of the characters are a reflection of the barrio's diverse heritage and happy amalgam of cultures. Luisa's performance of the powerful dog spirit spell is the spiritual climax of the play, but its results are chaotic and humorous as the characters cope with Rosalinda's less admirable canine attributes.

The play ends with the characters gazing at the sky, emphasizing the deeply personal nature of spiritualism. María sees her husband in the stars. Mrs. Amador sees nothing but nevertheless is afraid. Rosalinda, always the dreamer, sees her future travels—not only in this world but also to other worlds. Jesse walks toward the moon, next in line to find her dream is within reach if she works hard and believes in herself.

# STYLE

## Magical Realism

Magical realism is a style in which fantastic or magical elements coexist and interact with everyday reality. It is traditionally associated with Latin American authors. Often the magical elements in a work of magical realism are an accepted part of life to the characters who witness them. For example, when María hears that Rosalinda is acting like a dog, running in place with her hands in the air like paws, she is more concerned that Rosalinda will damage her ovaries by running too hard. Later, Jesse reports to her mother that Rosalinda is catching Frisbee disks in the park, emphasizing that she is very good at it. In this way the characters in a work of magical realism are more complacent toward the magical elements at work in their lives than might be expected. Although Rosalinda's transformation causes a shock, it does not stop her from running in and winning the marathon. Magical realism is an expression of Latin American identity in which reality is made new again through the lens of fantastic events, leading to unexpected self-discoveries and adventures. Harry J. Elam Jr. writes in *Staging Difference: Cultural Pluralism in American Theatre and Drama*: "Magic realism destabilizes the 'real' of everyday life by interposing the inexplicable and enabling ordinary objects to be perceived with new 'eyes of wonder.'"

## Monologue

A monologue in a drama is a speech given by a single character that reveals that character's innermost thoughts and conflicts. Hamlet's soliloquy ("To be or not to be . . .") speech is a famous example of a dramatic monologue. In *Dog Lady*, Rosalinda delivers a monologue during the First Night scene. Running in place in front of her home, Rosalinda dreams aloud of leaving the barrio and traveling the world. She names landmarks, countries, and cities she cannot wait to see and introduces herself in many languages as she imagines the people she will meet. This is Rosalinda's first significant speech of only a few. Though she is the protagonist of the play, she rarely stands still long enough for dialogue with another character and is frequently offstage while training. Her First Night monologue introduces the audience to Rosalinda's ultimate goal: to use her talent as a runner to escape the barrio life she knows and launch herself eagerly into a world unknown.

# HISTORICAL CONTEXT

## Santa Ana Winds

Santa Ana winds constitute a weather phenomenon that occurs in Southern California and upper Baja California. They happen when air travels from the Great Basin in Nevada, where

# COMPARE
# &
# CONTRAST

- **1984:** It is a common misconception that running damages the ovaries. This unfounded fear leads to women's being barred from some entering sporting events by organizers eager to exclude them on the basis of gender. The International Olympic Committee first allows women to compete in the marathon this year.

  **Today:** In 2010, the International Olympic Committee denies entrance to women ski jumpers, partially on the ground that participating in the sport might damage their reproductive organs. Long acknowledged as a sexist myth, the idea that women cannot compete for this reason is used as an excuse by misogynists who see physical activity and competition as inherently unfeminine and women's only purpose as reproductive.

- **1984:** The *teatro chicano* movement begins to fade along with the Chicano movement to

which it belongs, but the work of Hispanic American theater activists opens up new opportunities in professional theaters across the United States.

  **Today:** El Teatro Campesino celebrates its fiftieth anniversary in 2015. After years of experimentation the theater returns to its origins as a vehicle for positive social change with a focus on environmental causes.

- **1984:** Young athletes hope to escape the barrio through their athletic prowess.

  **Today:** Young minority members living in poverty use sports to improve their circumstances. Involvement in sports keeps youths out of gang life, provides a sense of community, and introduces outside opportunities. Many charities in the United States provide sports equipment to low-income neighborhoods and schools.

---

air pressure is high, toward the Pacific Ocean, where pressure is low. As the air travels, it becomes hot, dry, strong, and fast, rushing from the high altitude of the desert over the mountains and down toward sea level. Named for the Santa Ana Canyon in Southern California, the Santa Ana winds are most common in the fall and can cause wildfires. As the winds dry the vegetation, the brush becomes more susceptible to fire, and if a fire does start, the strong, hot wind feeds and spreads it quickly.

The Santa Ana winds have been assigned many names by the locals who feel their effects, including Red Wind and Devil Wind. Many people, like Orlando in *Dog Lady*, believe the winds cause changes in human behavior, including irritability, tension, and stress. Others compare this belief to the common association of the full moon with madness. Whether fact or myth, the winds feature in many works of literature and in songs set in the region. The winds are powerful enough

to trigger car alarms and uproot trees. Similar conditions occur in western Europe, where the strong, dry wind is called *foehn*, and in the Middle East, where is it known as *khamsin*.

## *Hispanic American Theater in the Southwestern United States*

In 1965, a Hispanic American theater movement was born in the fields of California when an emerging playwright, Luis Valdez, moved from San Francisco to Delano to join the labor leader César Chávez as he fought to unionize the farmworkers there. Valdez founded El Teatro Campesino, a theater troupe whose thematic focus was the poor conditions suffered by field laborers. Part of the larger Chicano movement that saw increased national visibility of issues faced by Chicano Americans, El Teatro Campesino grew and spread. There were troupes on college campuses and in Chicano communities. The founders worked to build a movement in

---

*Rosalinda goes to see a healer in the neighborhood* *(© Elena Ray | Shutterstock.com)*

theater that represented the Chicano experience. They produced plays on the issues faced by Spanish-speaking and bilingual working-class and rural immigrants, migrants, and second-generation Americans. By 1970 that dream was realized in the *teatro chicano*, a wholly Chicano theater style. Across the United States, small troupes formed in schools, communities, churches, and parks. Some presented street performances of *actos*, which were one-act plays, like *Dog Lady*, that focused on Chicano and Hispanic American life.

Through the *teatro chicano*, a Chicano identity was created that empowered individuals and communities that had not yet found recognition in mainstream American culture. At the height of the movement's power in 1976, five *teatro chicano* festivals were held in the summer to celebrate the American bicentennial. Theaters included the Teatro Urbano in Los Angeles, El Teatro de la Gente in San Jose, El Teatro de la Esperanza in Santa Barbara, and El Teatro Desengano del Pueblo in Gary, Indiana. Though

the movement began to fade from prominence in the 1980s, it launched the professional careers of many playwrights, directors, actors, and technicians. In Los Angeles, where Sanchez-Scott's first play was produced in 1980, the theater community included Central and South Americans as well as Chicanos and Mexicans.

## CRITICAL OVERVIEW

*Dog Lady* met with critical and audience approval and was included in the *Best Short Plays of 1986*. Herbert Mitgang writes in his review of *Dog Lady* and its companion piece, *The Cuban Swimmer*: "In both plays, Hispanic-Americans use athletic skills to propel themselves into the mainstream of middle-class life in this country."

Jane T. Peterson and Suzanne Bennett write in *Women Playwrights of Diversity: A Bio-bibliographical Sourcebook*: "Sanchez-Scott's work frequently explores women's experiences in an Hispanic American bicultural context. Her plays are a combination of gritty realism with flights of surrealistic fantasy." Sanchez-Scott was notable in particular for her unique use of English and Spanish and the way in which she used magical realism in her heroine's struggles with poverty, patriarchy, and white American hegemony.

Mel Gussow writes in his review of *Roosters* for the *New York Times*: "Sanchez-Scott has a natural theatrical talent and an ability to ensnare an audience in a tale . . . . The playwright makes the bizarre seem everyday." Her fantastical plays tested the ingenuity of set designers and directors, such as the setting of the open waters of the Gulf of Mexico in *The Cuban Swimmer*.

Critics frequently praised the surprising and deliberately elevated English of Sanchez-Scott's bilingual characters. As Elam writes, Sanchez-Scott uses "a poetic language that approaches more classical notions of the sublime, the drama as the site for exalted language, rather than traditional definitions of realistic dialogue as the discourse of every day life."

The tensions and contradictions within Sanchez-Scott's work—whether between reality and fantasy, individual and community, or English and Spanish—created a dynamic spectacle from which it is hard to look away. In *Necessary Theater: Six Plays about the Chicano Experience*,

Jorge Huerta writes about *Roosters*: "It is a play about survival, told in a poetic style that evokes images of pure beauty and grace, contrasted with the severity of poverty and the desert."

Although their struggles are complex, Sanchez-Scott's characters remain humble, lovable, and eager for progress. Jon Bouknight writes in "Language as a Cure: An Interview with Milcha Sanchez-Scott": "Sanchez-Scott's first play, *Latina*, premiered in Los Angeles in 1980. Since then, her characters in their simple clothes have appeared often, healing with poetry when their world offered no remedies."

## CRITICISM

### Amy L. Miller

*Miller is a graduate of the University of Cincinnati. In the following essay, she discusses individualism, community, and the role of magical realism in Sanchez-Scott's* Dog Lady.

*Dog Lady* is a play about personal spirituality. Each character has beliefs, a personal mythology, and a unique sense of self fed by those beliefs. Their beliefs determine the characters' relationships to the larger barrio community. Some are ostracized for being different, and others benefit from following the herd. In Rosalinda, the barrio recognizes an exceptional individual on whom all may hang their belief systems. Her success becomes the success of the barrio and recognition of the righteousness of their spirituality. Rosalinda, through her trip to Rome, is indirectly associated in the play with the gods of ancient Roman mythology. The barrio is her training ground, but she sets her sights not only on Rome but also on the moon, the stars, and the Milky Way. Escape is a physical exit from the barrio and a spiritual journey to the sky. Rosalinda is a young goddess who must prove herself worthy of her elevated status: she is kind but distant from those around her.

Unconcerned with money, love, and material things, Rosalinda wants to see the world. Her individualism is unique in a strong community, but she is not the only singular figure in the play. By the nature of Sanchez-Scott's magical realism, each of the characters takes on a mythically singular position: the courier, the lover, the mother, the sister, the healer, the priest, and the neighbor. They are simultaneously individualistic and members of the community. Their individual

> THE DREAMS OF THE BARRIO REST ON ROSALINDA'S SHOULDERS, BUT SHE IS MADE WEIGHTLESS BY THE GENEROSITY AND KINDNESS OF THE COMMUNITY TO WHICH SHE BELONGS."

desires complicate the goals of the group, but their loyalty to Rosalinda remains unshaken. The dreams of the barrio rest on Rosalinda's shoulders, but she is made weightless by the generosity and kindness of the community to which she belongs.

C. W. E. Bigsby writes in *Modern American Drama, 1945–2000*: "The theatre is an arena in which societies debate with themselves. It is where the delicate negotiation between the individual and the group finds its natural context." In *Dog Lady*, the negotiation between the individual and the group is a recurring motif. Jesse is scolded for her unfeminine appearance. Rosalinda is a prominent member of a community she wishes to escape. Raphael is aware of the race but puts his own misguided feelings first. Father Estefan encourages the ostracism of Luisa while María, who adores Father Estefan, nevertheless treats Luisa with respect and patience. This and countless other compromises between the desires of the community and the individual pepper the narrative so that the play is full of the wild hopes and deferred dreams of its characters.

Adding to this back-and-forth movement of community negotiation is the immense spiritual depth of the play, which features a powerful spell as its turning point. In the barrio, where Catholicism mixes comfortably with folk magic and superstition, anything is possible. Elam writes: "This cultural environment nurtures miracles and the aesthetic practice of magic realism." The miracle of Rosalinda's transformation is met with a mixture of astonishment, anger, and hilarity. The angriest of all the characters are those who know Rosalinda the least: Mrs. Amador and Raphael. Both find Luisa's actions threatening and sinister and distance themselves from Rosalinda after the spell has been cast, as if she, too, has been tainted by Luisa's witchcraft. They are naturally fearful characters who are cast as the

# WHAT DO I READ NEXT?

- Pam Muñoz Ryan's young-adult novel *Esperanza Rising* (2000) tells the story of a happy girl forced to flee her affluent life in Mexico and become a California migrant farmworker during the Great Depression. Faced with harsh conditions, racism, and cruelty, Esperanza must grow up quickly in order to save her mother and herself from certain doom.

- *El Teatro Campesino: Theater in the Chicano Movement*, by Yolanda Broyles-González (1994), presents the history of El Teatro Campesino using interviews with troupe members to uncover previously unknown stories from the theater's first days and wild success to its disbanding in 1980.

- In Sanchez-Scott's *Roosters* (1998), the tension between Hector and his father, Gallo, who has just been released from prison for manslaughter, boils over as they fight for the future of their prized gamecock. While the women in the family attempt to rise above the fray, the men's battle threatens to engulf the household in a dangerous downward spiral of violent machismo.

- August Wilson's Tony Award– and Pulitzer Prize–winning play *Fences* (1986) explores the shifting dynamics of an African American family on the brink of the 1960s cultural, political, and social upheaval as their patriarch, Troy Maxson, lets his bitterness over a lifetime of racial injustice sour his personal relationships.

- *Beautiful Señoritas & Other Plays* (1991), by the Cuban American playwright Dolores Prida, includes *Beautiful Señoritas*, *Coser y Cantar*, *Savings*, *Pantallas*, and *Botánica*. Known for her humor and warmth, Prida invents lovable and memorable characters.

- Luis Valdez's *Zoot Suit and Other Plays* (1992) collects some of the playwright's most recognized works, including *Zoot Suit*, *Bandido!*, and *I Don't Have to Show You No Stinking Badges*. Valdez was the founder of El Teatro Campesino.

- Cherríe Moraga's *Heroes and Saints and Other Plays* (1994) collects the prominent Chicana feminist author's most celebrated works for the stage, including the award-winning *Heroes and Saints*, *Shadow of a Man*, and *Giving Up the Ghost*.

---

most unsympathetic: Mrs. Amador for her pearl-clutching conservatism and Raphael for his clueless selfishness. On the opposite end of the spectrum are the fearless characters who are hoisted as barrio heroines: Rosalinda and Luisa. Sanchez-Scott has, as Elam writes: "created female characters that magically transcend the real life constraints placed upon them by social codes, domestic and religious patriarchy, and gender roles." Rosalinda, according to the stage directions, is a pretty and feminine young woman. However, the audience is soon introduced to Rosalinda's mother, who criticizes Jesse, her younger daughter, for appearing less than feminine and bemoans Rosalinda's athleticism as potentially damaging to her reproductive future.

Produced in the first year that women were allowed to run in the marathon at the Olympic Games, *Dog Lady*, in presenting an athletic female lead, rejects the long-standing misogynist myth that women cannot compete in sports without sacrificing their femininity. Whether a female athlete is appropriately feminine according to male-created cultural standards of beauty should be dismissed as irrelevant to the woman's athletic prowess. When Raphael decides to give up his pursuit of Rosalinda because of her unfeminine canine behaviors, the audience laughs at his stupidity, not Rosalinda's lack of manners. Rosalinda herself is unconcerned: she is thankful for Luisa's help, not embarrassed by the effects of the spell. She is above the fray because her sights are set on a brighter future.

Luisa, too, represents a culturally transgressive magical woman who is demonized for being different. Her yard, unlike María's, is a tangle of trash and overgrown plants. While María correctly performs her gendered role as a mother and homemaker, Luisa represents the traditional witch: tangled hair, ragged clothes, unmarried, without children, and cast as a danger to the community by the patriarchal figure of Father Estefan. Yet for all her faults, María is always kind to Luisa and acknowledges her power when she asks her respectfully to end the enchantment on Rosalinda. María may be a traditional Catholic mother, but she lives in the barrio, where many cultures and spiritualties not only are present but also interact at all times. Elam writes: "Sanchez-Scott locates the action of her play in the southwest . . . an area where Catholicism has been historically intertwined with indigenous rituals, superstitions and religious and cultural practices. In these spaces miracles are possible."

The stage directions call for an orange hue in the sunlight to represent the Santa Ana winds that so trouble Orlando. He sees the mark of the winds throughout the play—from María's indigestion in the first scene to Rosalinda's attack in which she rips his pant leg with her teeth, spurred on by a dog's natural hatred of the mailman. His devotion to the Santa Ana winds is no more or less real than María's conversations with her husband. She blames her husband for not properly wielding influence in heaven, leaving his wife and children to struggle for every dollar. María and Orlando both nurture a personal spirituality in the play—finding and cataloging evidence that proves their own beliefs, ignoring what does not fit their views. Raphael, too, worships at a personal altar: that of his cherished Rosalinda. It does not seem to matter to him that the object of his devotion seems unaware of his existence. It is the worship of Rosalinda that he loves—he is in love with being in love.

The strongest spiritual devotion in the play may belong to Rosalinda herself. As Peterson and Bennett write: "The romantic young woman sees winning this race and its free trip to Rome as a way of escaping the Los Angeles barrio; she motivates herself by traversing the world in her imagination." Much like Luisa, Rosalinda lives inside her own head. If Luisa's stream-of-consciousness dialogue is difficult for the characters to follow, Rosalinda's is just as unfathomable. She responds in short, blunt sentences to direct questions, spending the rest of

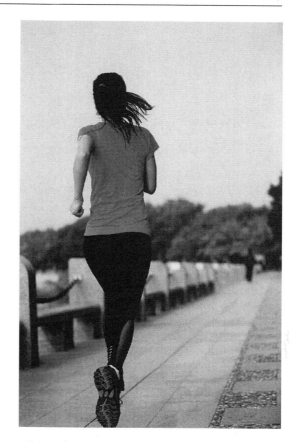

*Although she trains, Rosalinda cannot quite achieve the speed she hopes for* (© lzf | Shutterstock.com)

the time lost in her fantasy. She inhabits a trance-like state, appropriate for a young woman singularly chosen to explore the universe. Luisa frightens others with her detachment from reality, in particular her treatment of her blind dog, but Rosalinda is left alone to her dream. The barrio respects her vision and makes room for it among their countless beliefs. Peterson and Bennett write: "Whether Rosalinda's success can be attributed to hard work, Mexican mojo, or divine guidance, it is apparent that the entire neighborhood is transformed by Rosalinda's winning the race." Each of them sees in Rosalinda's success an affirmation of their own beliefs. As a Catholic, Rosalinda has made her community proud. María sees in her success the hand of her husband. Luisa is embraced by the neighborhood. Jesse is given a glimpse of the moonlit path out of the barrio. Orlando is witness to the wildest wind yet as Rosalinda races by.

Contained within all works of magical realism is a rejection of the nonmagical reality put forth as fact by mainstream art. Elam

"

**AS FOR WHAT I FEEL, I FEEL I'M AN AMERICAN WRITER WHO HAS BEEN INFLUENCED BY THE PLACES I'VE LIVED OR WHERE MY PARENTS WERE BORN."**

writes: "The unexpected, non-realistic conclusions to [the] plays suggest that realism itself is problematic and inadequate to accommodate certain cultural experiences or expressions of the current postmodern condition." What realism is there truly in the story of an athlete who comes from the deepest poverty in the most neglected of neighborhoods to capture the attention of the world? Yet it happens all the time. *Dog Lady* depicts the brute force required to launch a star from the barrio to hang shining in the sky. It is not, to María's great regret, pretty. But Rosalinda makes her dream come true through her willingness to run like a dog.

**Source:** Amy L. Miller, Critical Essay on *Dog Lady*, in *Drama for Students*, Gale, Cengage Learning, 2018.

### Jon Bouknight and Milcha Sanchez-Scott
*In the following interview excerpt, Sanchez-Scott talks about being a minority playwright.*

*. . . You often get asked the question, "Are you a Chicana playwright?" Do these labels get in your way?*

I've just come back from what they call "The Hispanic Playwright's Conference" at South Coast Repertory in Orange County, right outside of Los Angeles. Playwrights, dramaturgs, and producers come from all over to meet, to share their thoughts, to read new plays, and to take a look at these plays and wonder if they can do something with them in their theatres. So it becomes part market and part meeting.

This year a lot of the playwrights were Hispanic in name only. Some of the plays were very wonderful and very beautifully crafted—and the level of craft has certainly gone up—but anybody could have written these plays. In one play, the only thing "Hispanic" was that the mother's name was "Carmen."

Some of the playwrights don't speak Spanish. They've assimilated so much! I thought to myself, "Well, that's one of the wonderful things about America, and it's also one of the bad things about America as a melting pot." That's what we're supposed to do—we're supposed to assimilate. Yet one feels like we've lost a lot of rich ground. Particularly in the Southwest because it's worked into the natural history. So the theatre people from the Southwest were up in arms. They said, "Why are you calling this a Hispanic festival? This isn't about our culture or our people. This is mainstream!"

The term "Hispanic," to me, encompasses everybody that has a history, a background with the Spanish Language. The problem with the label is that "Hispanic" is going to be stretched and stretched to cover a whole range of things—Chicanos in the Southwest, Puerto Ricans in New York, Cubans in Miami—until I don't know what good the label is. I suppose it's very good when you're trying to sell tickets.

As for what I feel, I feel I'm an American writer who has been influenced by the places I've lived or where my parents were born.

*So although it might be easier to get grant money for an "Hispanic play," it becomes limiting?*

I'll tell you what is so limiting by telling you what's so wonderful about doing *Roosters* at the New Mexico Repertory. In every Hispanic theatre, I have felt that sometimes the Hispanic actor that was available at that time was not the actor I needed and we could not go outside the community to get that actor. Maybe a Hispanic actor who was perfect for Gallo was working on a film, but this other Hispanic actor was available. He didn't fit the part really, but he was Hispanic, so I was forced to use him as opposed to an Anglo actor who is a Gallo. So I get punished sometimes as a playwright.

*. . . You mean, in general, that the generations can improve?*

We have to! We're facing such strange dilemmas in environmental issues; we've all been witness to incredible acts of terror; I'm sure our parents have too. I think these lessons have got to serve their purpose. We have to change; we have to become greater, or as great as we can be. This could be the most wonderful world when we get it, but we have to reach.

Though it's a very slow process, I really feel that it's speeding up a bit now. We have all of these people choosing a form of government that is universally held as being democratic. Everybody is breaking the chains to be in that form of government. That helps a great deal in facing our problems, which I see now as global problems as opposed to just national problems. If we're more united, they would become easier to solve. We still have environmental and health issues, you name it, we have all the issues here. *The Architect Piece*—I wanted to stress the environmental more—deals with the rain forest in Brazil.

*I predict a pretty big debate on the issue of machismo, because* Roosters *doesn't seem to give it a favorable verdict.*

But in another sense Chata has a lot of machismo—she's what they call a "macha." And I think of it as a spirit of life. We have a war spirit. I think all human beings do. It's there to give us energy. I think all of our emotions are very useful, and I just think that we need to channel it as opposed to bombing people and working on more nuclear weapons.

It depends a lot on the production, whether you admire the machismo or not. One character says, "We're independent." We all have to hope for that, for being independent.

*So it's no simple theme, like "we must override the machismo."*

You can't be simple about anything in life. Everything's really complicated and yet simple. Like the double helix, the DNA molecule, and how they found out about it—how complicated and how simple and elegant it is at the same time.

*Finally, I'd like to ask you about language. Are you doing anything in particular with the code-switching [between Spanish and English] in* Roosters *or are you just trying to mirror a world that you know?*

No. When I talk to people who speak Spanish in this country, for instance busboys, they—even from the introduction—give their names and say, "A sus ordenes." It's a very typical Spanish introduction—"Awaiting your orders"—which I think is so beautiful. The Spanish they use is so beautiful, so rich, and so high falutin'! Yet at the same time when they speak in English, they sometimes sound very common. How is it that a person who can think in this language that is so beautiful in its structure, will speak English and choose the most common words? I don't know why that is, but the [Spanish] language is taught that way—they use powerful words. I want Chicanos to think they should speak English in the same way they choose to speak Spanish.

I've had people get upset, saying "This isn't realistic, I've never heard a Chicano talk like this," and that sort of thing. Well, no, I never heard a shepherd sound like Shakespeare's either. So if he can do it, why can't we?

*What should the role of theatre—your theatre in particular—be in education?*

I don't see theatre as an entertainment form as much as I see it as a ritualistic form. We can learn by stories and rituals. They move people! I think the theatre should impassion people. Film is so common and can tell a realistic story so much better these days, that theatre has to become something else. And theatre's strength really is that it's personal: people are there, people are alive on stage. With those kinds of strengths it, hopefully, will impassion and empower people.

*What changes do you see happening to theatre that might emphasize the ritual more?*

Well, I don't want to negate entertainment. I think by ritual, we're entertaining. I would have to come up with why people performed rituals: to make themselves feel better, to cast out the darkness. I think there's something very primitive in us that needs ritual. To mark different times, to mark the seasons even, and to teach.

As theatre people, we have to gather, and see where our strengths are. Live theatre becomes very special. If your generation has been raised on film and television—as I have—going to the theatre becomes a participation in community, and that's where its strength is, in that community.

*Does the writing itself have a ritualistic dimension?*

Only habitually. One has one's rituals with writing: paper and pen, you know.

For me, it becomes about language and poetry. Some shamans in Oaxaca believe in the language—what comes from our mouths, the words we choose from our brains—as almost a cure. In that form, writing is a ritual. It lets you uncover problems, lets you heal problems.

*Language is a cure then, certainly for the writer. Is it also a cure for the audience, even the illiterate?*

There are countless people who haven't had the benefits of education. Who plod along and work very, very hard for a living. But I haven't seen a *coarseness* of soul—Do you know what I mean? I mean that their souls, their hearts, their spirits are still incredibly sensitive, as sensitive as somebody who's, say, been reared with a lot of literature. They may not understand, but they feel. They come—open heart and open mind—to the theatre and realize that they're part of this body, they're participating.

A friend of mine who's at The Public [The Public Theatre in New York City] said that she met Mother Teresa when she was in New York and had been so inspired by this woman, that she wanted to follow Mother Teresa to India to help the poor. Mother Teresa said, "well, we may be poor in the material sense, but this country is very hungry in the spiritual sense." She said that my friend's work in literature was the best that she could do for this country.

I feel that that is our job as playwrights, to nurture people . . . .

**Source:** Jon Bouknight and Milcha Sanchez-Scott, "Language as a Cure: An Interview with Milcha Sanchez-Scott," in *Latin America Theatre Review*, Spring 1990, pp. 65–66, 71–73.

### Don Shirley

*In the following excerpt, Shirley praises Sanchez-Scott's use of language.*

A hard-kicking flyer is "the ultimate bird" in the world of cockfighting, we quickly learn in *Roosters* at Los Angeles Theatre Center.

*Roosters* is something of a hard-kicking flyer itself. Playwright Milcha Sanchez-Scott kicks *machismo* around the stage until it hasn't a leg to stand on. Her play also flies, in the sense of ascending. Her language leaps from earthbound conversation into flights of poetic fantasy, and her imagery soars—literally so, at the end of the play, when a character levitates.

The style is "magic realism," and Sanchez-Scott's writing honors both of those words. Magically, roosters become human dancers, and spirits descend through mysterious lighting displays to speak with a teenaged girl. Realistically, an aging whore offers cynical wisecracks that sometimes undercut the most poetic speeches, and the characters enact a parent-child drama that is not unlike the stories told in a hundred other plays.

It's the story of a neglectful father (Pepe Serna), obsessed with his work, and the children who resent him. This particular father is so identified with his work, cockfighting, that his name is Gallot—Spanish for rooster. In case we don't catch the analogy, Sanchez-Scott underlines it in other ways: speaking to a cock, Gallo says, "Papa's got you now." We also hear that fighting cocks kill their young. The analogy would be heavy-handed, and the characters too starkly drawn, in a plain old realistic play. But here they seem more archetypal than stereotyped.

In a *Times* interview, Sanchez-Scott acknowledged that "these people in this play are mythical, archetypal characters." The two women, for example, are "typical Latin role models—(the) mother (Evelina Fernandez) is the long-suffering madonna and (the) aunt (Lupe Ontivero's) is a whore."

The children are somewhat more complex, especially 15-year-old Angela (Victoria Gallegos). She is intellectually precocious, socially slow (she hides under the porch and plays with dolls) and spiritually obsessed (her dolls are saints). She plans to escape her lot by praying for divine intervention.

Her 20-year-old brother, Hector (Fausto Bara), has more concrete plans to escape the drudgery of farm work. He has inherited a prize cock from his grandfather and plans to use its earnings to leave this valley, somewhere in the Southwest, and search for a better tomorrow. But when Papa comes home after seven years in prison, he covets the same cock. A father-son clash, replete with Oedipal echoes, is the result.

Director Jose Luis Valenzuela and an exceptional cast turn this familiar tale into quite a show. Sanchez-Scott wrote some blistering monologues for Hector, expressing his disgust at his present life and his hopes for a better one, and Bara runs with them. Fernandez shines in a scene in which she, too, begins to glimpse a ray of hope on the horizon.

As tough old Aunt Chata, Ontiveros is a hoot through most of the play, her jaw flapping, her flesh protruding anxiously from behind the kimono, slip and pink shoes provided by costumer Tina Navarro. But she doesn't allow the bitterness to get lost in the laughter.

Gallegos has a fine time, juxtaposing Angela's girlish fantasies with her dawning awareness of the world. And E. J. Castillo also gets some laughs as Hector's naive friend Adan. When the opportunity arises, Adan is ready to stand in as Gallo's substitute son, but he never seems like an opportunist.

Serna's Gallo is the most problematic character. He doesn't have the dimension that a great myth would require. He is a rat more than a rooster. While Serna brings a lot of animalistic energy to the role, he hasn't figured out how to make a man out of this man.

But if you look at *Roosters* primarily as the children's story, it offers moments of considerable power. The lighting design, a firestorm of desert colors and dramatic shadows, has a lot to do with this; it's credited to Tinian Alsaker and Douglas D. Smith. Alsaker also created the set, which looks so Sam Shepardian that LATC could save money by doing *Roosters* in repertory with, say, "Curse of the Starving Class."

The design raises questions at the end of the play. Angela's levitation isn't like Mary Martin in *Peter Pan*; she stands on a clearly visible platform which rises from the stage. Was this a mistake, or was it intended? If intended, what was the intent? It's a question that should be asked at one of those post-show symposiums....

**Source:** Don Shirley, "Machismo Plucked Bare as *Roosters* Takes Flight," in *LA Times*, June 21, 1988.

# SOURCES

Arkatov, Janice, "Playwright Enters World of Cockfighting in *Roosters*," in *Los Angeles Times*, June 15, 1988, http://articles.latimes.com/1988-06-15/entertainment/ca-4339_1_roosters (accessed June 22, 2017).

Bigsby, C. W. E., *Modern American Drama, 1945–2000*, Cambridge University Press, 2004, p. 360.

Bouknight, Jon, "Language as a Cure: An Interview with Milcha Sanchez-Scott," in *Latin American Theatre Review*, Spring 1990, Vol. 23, No. 2, pp. 63–74.

Bradford, Wade, "*The Cuban Swimmer*: One Act Drama by Milcha Sanchez-Scott," ThoughtCo, updated June 18, 2017, https://www.thoughtco.com/the-cuban-swimmer-overview-2713479 (accessed June 22, 2017).

Duginski, Paul, "Infographic: Where Do the Santa Ana Winds Come From?," in *Los Angeles Times*, September 26, 2016, http://www.latimes.com/visuals/graphics/la-me-g-santa-ana-winds-listicle-htmlstory.html (accessed June 22, 2017).

Elam, Harry J., Jr., "Of Angels and Transcendence: An Analysis of *Fences* by August Wilson and *Roosters* by Milcha Sanchez-Scott," in *Staging Difference: Cultural Pluralism in American Theatre and Drama*, edited by Marc Maufort, Peter Lang, 1995, pp. 294–99.

Fovell, Robert, "The Santa Ana Winds," UCLA Atmospheric and Oceanic Sciences website, http://people.atmos.ucla.edu/fovell/ASother/mm5/SantaAna/winds.html (accessed June 22, 2017).

Gregory, Ruth, "Reproductive Rights and Athletics: The Curious Tale of Female Ski Jumpers," in *Society Pages*, January 9, 2010, https://thesocietypages.org/sexuality/2010/01/09/reproductive-rights-and-athletics-the-curious-tale-of-female-ski-jumpers (accessed June 22, 2017).

Gussow, Mel, "Stage: *Roosters* at INTAR," in *New York Times*, March 24, 1987.

Huerta, Jorge, "Milcha Sanchez-Scott," in *Necessary Theater: Six Plays about the Chicano Experience*, Arte Publico Press, 1989, 82–84.

Kanellos, Nicolas, "Hispanic Theatre in the United States: Post-War to the Present," in *Latin American Theatre Review*, Spring 1992, pp. 197–209.

"Milcha Sanchez-Scott," IMDb, http://www.imdb.com/name/nm0761085 (accessed June 22, 2017).

Mitgang, Herbert, "Theater: *Dog Lady* and *Swimmer*," in *New York Times*, May 10, 1984, http://www.nytimes.com/1984/05/10/theater/theater-dog-lady-and-swimmer.html (accessed June 22, 2017).

Needham, John, "The Devil Winds Made Me Do It: Santa Anas Are Enough to Make Anyone's Hair Stand on End," in *Los Angeles Times*, March 12, 1988, http://articles.latimes.com/1988-03-12/news/li-942_1_santa-ana-winds (accessed June 22, 2017).

Peterson, Jane T., and Suzanne Bennett, "Milcha Sanchez-Scott," in *Women Playwrights of Diversity: A Bio-bibliographical Sourcebook*, edited by Jane T. Peterson and Suzanne Bennett, Greenwood Press, 1997, pp. 293–96.

"Playwright Milcha Sanchez-Scott to Direct STC Theatre Production of *Roosters*," in *South Texas College News*, January 17, 2014, https://news.southtexascollege.edu/?p=7783 (accessed June 22, 2017).

Sanchez-Scott, Milcha, "Dog Lady," in *Dog Lady and the Cuban Swimmer*, Dramatists Play Service, 1984, pp. 7–30.

Van Erven, Eugene, *Community Theatre: Global Perspectives*, Routledge, 2001, pp. 95–96.

# FURTHER READING

Faris, Wendy B., and Lois Parkinson Zamora, *Magical Realism: Theory, History, Community*, Duke University Press Books, 1995.

This study explores individual works of magical realism and the origins of the genre in the early twentieth century. By expanding the definition of magical realism to include non–Latin American authors, Faris and Zamora consider the universal fascination with the magical, mysterious, and unexplained.

Larson, Catherine, and Margarita Vargas, *Latin American Women Dramatists: Theater, Texts, and Theories*, Indiana University Press, 1999.

In this collection of essays, prominent figures in the study of Latin American literature discuss fifteen works by playwrights from Mexico, Puerto Rico, Brazil, Chile, Argentina, Venezuela, and elsewhere. Each essay includes a biography of the playwright, an overview of her work in the theater, a description of the political or cultural challenges she faced in bringing her work to the stage, and a close reading of the selected work.

Romo, Richardo, *East Los Angeles: History of a Barrio*, University of Texas Press, 1983.

Romo tells the story of the largest Mexican American community in the United States. Facing racism, poverty, segregation, and oppression, the Mexican Americans of East Los Angeles first arrived in the city to work undesirable jobs for low wages. With tenacity and resilience, they survived and thrived, forming a community, identity, and culture of their own.

Sanchez-Scott, Milcha, *The Cuban Swimmer*, in *Dog Lady and the Cuban Swimmer*, Dramatists Play Service, 1984.

In *The Cuban Swimmer*, a young woman races from San Pedro to Catalina Island, followed closely by her family in their sinking boat and monitored by a helicopter. Margarita must ignore the distractions of her family and the commentary of the announcer in her quest to swim her way out of her life of poverty.

## SUGGESTED SEARCH TERMS

Milcha Sanchez-Scott

Milcha Sanchez-Scott AND Dog Lady

Milcha Sanchez-Scott AND American playwrights

magical realism

barrio AND sports

Latina American playwrights

Los Angeles and magical realism

Santa Ana winds

Teatro Chicano

# *The Gospel at Colonus*

**LEE BREUER**

**1989**

One of the most original productions in Broadway history, Lee Breuer's *The Gospel at Colonus* is an adaptation of classical Greek theater set in an African American Pentecostal church service. After studying the drama of ancient Greece in part by visiting the sites where the original plays were staged, Breuer arrived at a full realization of how the Greek theatrical experience, complete with dramatic narrative, moral investigation, effusive music, and choral and audience involvement, was inherently religious, and the modern religious practice that most readily correlates with that ancient theatrical experience is the African American gospel church.

*The Gospel at Colonus*, an oratorio, is adapted from the play *Oedipus at Colonus*, by Sophocles, which was first produced in 405 BCE, the year after the author's death. The tragedy of Oedipus's life, told in Sophocles's more famous *Oedipus the King*—also called *Oedipus Rex*—is well known: by an accident of fate, Oedipus ended up unwittingly killing his father and marrying his mother. Upon the revelation of his wife's identity as his own mother, Oedipus blinded himself. *Oedipus at Colonus* tells the story of the end of the blinded king's life, when he was cast out of Thebes and left to find refuge in Colonus.

In *The Gospel at Colonus*, the clergy and choristers of a Pentecostal church dramatize this story just as if it were a parable found in

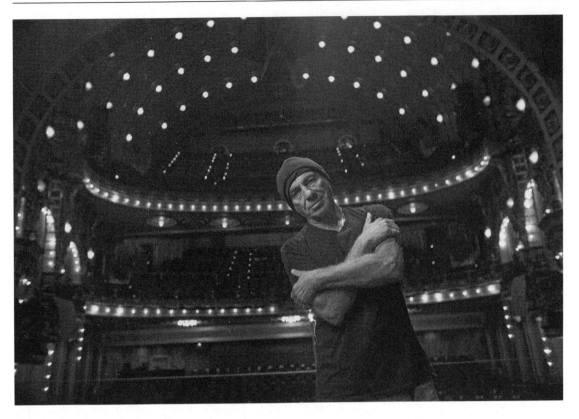

*Lee Breuer* (© *Boston Globe / Getty Images*)

the Bible. Small-scale versions of the play were performed in the years leading up to its debut as a full dramatic work on November 8, 1983, as part of the Next Wave Festival at the Brooklyn Academy of Music. Starring Morgan Freeman as Preacher Oedipus and blind gospel legend Clarence Fountain as Singer Oedipus, the production reached Broadway on March 11, 1988, at the Lunt-Fontanne Theatre. For its original Brooklyn production, *The Gospel at Colonus* won the 1984 Obie Award for Outstanding Musical.

## AUTHOR BIOGRAPHY

Asher Leopold Breuer was born on February 6, 1937, in Philadelphia, Pennsylvania, to an architect father and a designer mother. His youth was conventionally suburban, but his later life would prove a steady stream of mind-expanding multicultural experiences and creations. After his education at the University of California at Los Angeles, where he twice won the university's

best play award and earned a bachelor's degree in 1958, Breuer was both performing in and directing stage plays through the San Francisco Actors' Workshop by the mid-1960s. From 1965 until the end of the decade, he contributed to plays in Europe, in locales including Paris and Edinburgh. In the company of actress and director Ruth Maleczech, Breuer studied with the Berliner Ensemble, founded by Bertolt Brecht, and Jerzy Grotowski's Polish Theater Lab. Returning to North America in 1970, Breuer and Maleczech joined up with a couple more fellow avant-gardists intending to purchase a residence in the town of Mabou Mines, Nova Scotia. They bestowed the town's name on the theater company they cofounded that year (though, ironically, the residence would end up being in nearby Margaree Forks). With the company, Breuer variously filled the roles of actor, playwright, adapter, producer, and director.

Mabou Mines first produced a series of "animations," which—in addition to connoting the Latin *animus*, for "soul"—prioritized the presentation of moving and changing images accomplished through theatrical ingenuity, such as folding set pieces and actors entwining onstage to become different creatures. These productions included *Red Horse Animation* (1972), *B-Beaver Animation* (1974), and *Shaggy Dog Animation* (1978), which won the *Village Voice*'s Obie Award for the year's best play. Breuer and Maleczech married in 1978 and would have two children, named Clove Galilee and Lute Ramblin'.

Evoking Muslim culture with his 1982 performance poem *Hajj*, Breuer adapted Robert Fitzgerald's translation of the Sophocles play *Oedipus at Colonus* to write and direct *The Gospel at Colonus*, with music composed, arranged, and directed by Bob Telson. Officially debuting in 1983, the musical toured the United States and played on Broadway for several months in 1988. Through the late 1970s and early 1980s, Breuer served on the faculties of Yale Drama School, Harvard Extension School, New York University, and Stanford University and lectured at numerous other colleges. His later plays would draw on influences ranging from his Jewish heritage to Marxism to Zen Buddhism to Japanese Bunraku puppetry to African drumming to Hindu Kali worship and India's classic epic *The Mahabharata*. Breuer was awarded a MacArthur Foundation "genius grant" in 1997. Most recently, he lives in New York City and continues to serve as co-artistic director of Mabou Mines.

## PLOT SUMMARY

### Part I

*The Gospel at Colonus* opens in a Pentecostal church as the clergy and important members of the congregation make their entrances—they will be playing the various roles in the story to be told during the service. The preacher begins by declaring the service's source in the Book of Oedipus. He then starts telling Oedipus's story in the third person. Most audience members and readers will be aware that Oedipus, in the famous Greek legend, unknowingly murdered his father—although the preacher skips that part here—and married his mother, Jocasta, having children with her. In the preacher's telling, Jocasta, presumably having finally realized their incest many years later, committed suicide, and Oedipus, upon discovering the body and the particular brooches she wore, also realized the

# MEDIA ADAPTATIONS

- Recordings of the original cast singing the numbers from *The Gospel at Colonus* have been issued twice—by Warner Brothers on vinyl in 1984, after the Obie-winning Brooklyn performance, and by Nonesuch Records in 1988, after the show reached Broadway. The latter recording is available on CD.

- The first video presentation of *The Gospel at Colonus* aired on PBS on November 8, 1985, as part of the "Great Performances" series. This was filmed during the musical's performance at Philadelphia's Annenberg Center as part of the American Music Theater Festival on September 19, 1985. The recording is available on DVD and has been posted online on YouTube (https://www.youtube.com/watch?v=8ZyQP_zrD2U).

incest and promptly gouged his own eyes. The preacher makes reference to Oedipus's eventual death being recorded in the book of Exodus, and a quartet of lines attributed to Oedipus are quoted. These lines are found not in the biblical Exodus but in Sophocles's *Oedipus the King*, in a section sometimes labeled "Éxodos," at the end of Oedipus's last major speech in the play. The choir uses these words of wisdom as the basis of the invocation, the opening song, "Live Where You Can."

"Recapitulation from *Oedipus the King*," effectively the opening scene of the play within the play, shows the blinded Singer Oedipus advancing slowly, while the evangelist introduces him in his present state of affairs. She then descends a staircase to play the role of Antigone, his daughter, who is helping him find his way. With the preacher and Singer Oedipus now delivering some of Oedipus's lines in concert, one after the other, he and Antigone discuss his need to find refuge somewhere. They stop a man, described in the script only as a "friend," who reports in falsetto, a capella, that this is the blessed land of Colonus. Oedipus indicates that his death there has been ordained.

Oedipus urges Antigone to bring him forward, but the Choragos quintet and balladeer obstruct him, claiming, in the song "Stop Do Not Go On" that this is holy ground and Oedipus needs the gods' approval before proceeding. In the ensuing choral dialogue, the quintet members interrogate Oedipus, who, at his daughter's urging, admits his notorious identity.

At this point Ismene, another daughter of Oedipus, arrives, moved to tears at the reunion with her father. Ismene reports that there is trouble in Thebes between his sons: the younger, Eteocles, usurped the throne from the elder, Polyneices, who then joined forces with a neighboring army in Argos, intending to treasonously attack Thebes. The evangelist relates this backstory on Ismene's behalf, concluding by telling Oedipus that he must return, because Thebes needs him as protection against Polyneices. The evangelist then, as Antigone, converses with Oedipus. He is in disbelief that Eteocles and the Thebans would want him back, and Antigone points out that he is bound by his father's blood not to return to Thebes (as a consequence of his patricide). Oedipus declares that indeed the Thebans will never take possession of him but will be fated to keep fighting; if his sons are more concerned with being king of Thebes than with being dutiful toward their father, they will ultimately kill each other. Antigone suggests that the sons will feel the bitterness of his anger if and when they stand over his grave one day. For now, she indicates, he should ask forgiveness from those whose grounds they have "violated" in Colonus.

A prayer ritual, which the stage directions refer to as pagan in nature, is directed by evangelist Antigone and carried out by the preacher. It involves pouring water and honey on the earth and then covering it with olive (sprigs, as specified in Sophocles). At the end of the ritual, the preacher is "touched by the spirit" and now, for the time being, inhabits Oedipus in the first person.

Choragos leads a more detailed interrogation of Oedipus, confirming that his daughters Antigone and Ismene were conceived by his own mother with him, making them both his daughters and his sisters. This is scandalous enough, but Choragos also insists that Oedipus is guilty of patricide. Oedipus objects that he did not know his father Laius's identity at the time and was acting only in self-defense. Finally, Antigone

interrupts to beg that the interrogators show him mercy.

Singer Oedipus, a capella with his quintet, sings of being prophesied to die there in Colonus. He then preaches about his life, accompanied by the singing Balladeer, petitioning the goddesses for sanctuary.

Theseus, played by the pastor, arrives as the voice of authority in Colonus, declaring his acceptance of Oedipus's petition. He ushers Oedipus to the white piano at center stage. The Choragos quintet sings a welcome, and the Oedipus quintet joins in.

Creon, another blood relation of Oedipus's and the present king, arrives from Thebes, announcing that he intends to bring Oedipus back with him. Singer Oedipus objects that Creon mistreated him by exiling him before, but meanwhile Creon's two soldiers seize Antigone and Ismene and whisk them away. When Oedipus finishes his objections, Creon simply points out the absence of Oedipus's daughters and leaves. Oedipus, lacking Antigone's guidance, is left feeling utterly lost in the world.

As the section title here indicates, an ode is adapted from a set of lines spoken by the chorus in Sophocles's *Antigone*, lines sometimes called "The Ode on Man." Here the lines are delivered by the pastor, who then, in his role as Theseus, promises Oedipus that he will secure his daughters and return them to him. The Ismene quartet then sings an adaptation of the pastor's ode.

## Part II
The deacon playing Creon recalls the current circumstances for the audience, introducing Oedipus as he sings the lonely lament "Lift Me Up." After his quintet joins in, a testifier—Polyneices—steps up to plead for his father's blessing. With the balladeer singing under him, Polyneices admits to having failed to support his father but suggests that it is time for merciful forgiveness—since now he is in dire straits himself.

Theseus returns with Ismene and Antigone, who advances to her father's side. With Antigone and Oedipus receiving him politely, Polyneices complains of his brother's betrayal and reports that an oracle has said that only those blessed by Oedipus can come into the power of the throne. Polyneices proceeds to tout the valor of the captains serving under him, three of whom he introduces. Finally, with the captains singing under him, he asserts (somewhat brashly) that his position is just and that Oedipus should offer his blessing. Finally, Polyneices tells Oedipus that he will restore him to the throne.

Preacher Oedipus responds by accusing Polyneices of lying, of having betrayed Oedipus before, and of having traitorous intentions yet again. Oedipus prophesies that the two sons will kill each other in battle. At the end of his harangue, Polyneices and the captains collapse, dramatically representing their deaths in besieging Thebes.

The ensuing poem from *Antigone*, "Love Unconquerable," spoken by the evangelist, is taken from lines delivered by the chorus in the original play. Preacher Oedipus follows by delivering a meditation from the stage's pulpit. He suggests that at the end of a long and difficult life, salvation of the soul is the most important thing. At his words, through theatrical effects, lightning splits a prominent column on the stage and blackens the piano. This signals the time for Oedipus's death, and the pastor as Theseus ushers Singer Oedipus to the underworld. Oedipus blesses Theseus's Colonus as destined to long survive in practicing pacifism and leaving conflicts in the hands of God.

After the ode "Oh Sunlight," the blind Oedipus now miraculously leads Theseus to the place where he is to die, which is to remain secret from all his family. The Choragos quintet reprises the ode and then sings a sort of death lullaby, "Eternal Sleep." Singer Oedipus and his quintet ride the piano as it is lowered below the stage.

Antigone mourns her father, while the pastor eulogizes him and implores the women to trust in the divine benediction Oedipus has received rather than sorrowfully mourning him. With the singing of a doxology by the choir—a song of praise to God—raising Oedipus's name up to heaven, Oedipus and his quintet are raised back up to the stage, and everyone dances and celebrates.

A child of the choir approaches the preacher to ask if Oedipus's death was painless. The preacher replies by telling of Oedipus's final hours, when his daughters brought him fresh water for bathing and then cried as he prepared to leave them. The preacher relates that the voice of God was strong in urging Oedipus to go, it being his appointed time, and finally he left—and there is no accounting for how he died, but it was without suffering, making it a "wonderful" end to his life.

The Choragos quintet sings the closing hymn, "Let the Weeping Cease." The preacher delivers a benediction, echoing the hymn, and the service ends, with the cast all departing convivially while the gospel band plays on.

## CHARACTERS

### Evangelist Antigone
The evangelist—an additional reader, whether clergy or laity, for the church service—plays the second-largest part in narrating Oedipus's tale (behind the preacher). She steps into the drama when called for to play the part of Antigone. In the drama, Antigone stands as the most dutiful of Oedipus's children, serving as his eyes and helping him think things through during his exile from Thebes. She is honest and clearheaded and gives careful thought to matters of propriety.

### Balladeer
Offering occasional background singing and counterpoint lines, the balladeer is especially involved in helping Polyneices narrate his story.

### Captains
Polyneices vainly imagines that singing the praises of three of his captains—Tydeus, Capaneus, and Parthenopaeus—will sway Oedipus to offer the errant Polyneices his blessing. The captains appear courageous, but the plan fails.

### Child
A small child in the choir asks the preacher whether Oedipus felt pain during his death, allowing the preacher to deliver a sort of epilogue to the tale.

### Choragos Quintet
Representing the chorus from Sophocles's drama, Choragos (Greek for "chorus leader") and the quintet of which he is a part represent the concerns of the common people of Colonus. At first skeptical of Oedipus's integrity, the Choragos quintet ultimately welcomes him with open arms.

### Deacon Creon
A deacon—a clergy member ranking just below the pastor—plays the part of Creon. Although Breuer never makes clear Creon's relation to Oedipus, Sophocles identifies him as Oedipus's

brother-in-law (Jocasta's brother). Creon arrives in Colonus as the present king of Thebes, indicating that Oedipus's sons' fighting over "the crown" is more precisely a fight over being next in the line of succession. Creon makes an apparently forthright inquiry about the possibility of Oedipus returning to Thebes, but as Oedipus spurns him—a result Creon probably anticipated—his soldiers seize Oedipus's daughters, giving him leverage over Oedipus's actions. The reader gathers that Theseus's men manage to overtake Creon's men to allow Oedipus's daughters to return to Colonus.

### Eteocles
Not appearing in the play, Eteocles is the younger son of Oedipus who brings about the exile of the elder son, Polyneices, in order to make his own claim on the crown.

### Friend
A Friend gives Oedipus a hearty welcome to Colonus.

### Singer Ismene
A daughter of Oedipus, Ismene arrives early in the drama to report the conflict between Oedipus's sons. Thereafter, she plays a role subordinate to Antigone, singing but remaining mostly in the background during scenes of exposition. Played by a singer, Ismene is part of a quartet comprising two women and two men who sing and also act out parts of the drama through pantomime.

### Jocasta
Jocasta was Oedipus's mother and, after years apart, his wife. Years later, having borne at least four children with Oedipus, she realized his true identity and killed herself. She does not appear in the play but is mentioned in the backstory delivered by the preacher.

### Laius
Laius was Oedipus's father. In the son's telling, he killed his father only in self-defense, and he had no idea of the man's true identity.

### Preacher Oedipus
The preacher is visiting the church where *The Gospel at Colonus* is set, which allows him to better fill the role of Oedipus as beseeching stranger in Colonus. The preacher maintains some distance from his character in generally narrating Oedipus's lines indirectly, in the third person, often with Singer Oedipus meanwhile delivering them in the first person. However, the preacher also occasionally inhabits the role of Oedipus directly, in the manner of being inhabited by the Holy Spirit in a Pentecostal setting.

In terms of the drama within the church service, Oedipus starts out as a blind, lost, guilt-stricken wanderer. Gradually, he gains the sympathy of Theseus and the people of Colonus and, learning how the family members who wronged him are now fighting with each other, feels vindicated by their now begging him for assistance, which he steadfastly refuses to provide in any form. Feeling himself in the right at last, he is permitted to die an honorable death—and, not unlike the legendary fate of a young man from Nazareth, to rise from the grave to bring joy and salvation to those who would mourn him.

### Singer Oedipus
The singer who, alongside the preacher, also plays Oedipus does the majority of the acting and stage movement involved in the part. He is accompanied by a quintet, who like him are all blind and who collectively bring greater force to the persona of Oedipus.

### Testifier Polyneices
Stepping out of the audience as if a testifier at a Pentecostal service, Polyneices does his best to confess his sins, so to speak—that is, he admits them, but his remorse, if any, is all for show—in an attempt to get in his father's good graces. Preacher Oedipus calls him out as a liar and condemns him to die in the attack on Thebes; this is indeed depicted as his fate.

### Pastor Theseus
The resident pastor of the church in which the play takes place is well suited to the role of Theseus, the king and host who eventually welcomes Oedipus at Colonus. In the drama, claiming to have once been an exile himself, Theseus comes across as kindhearted, compassionate, and forgiving toward Oedipus and therefore deserving of the blessing that Oedipus gives to him and his kingdom.

# THEMES

## Religion

The unassuming audience member seeing *The Gospel at Colonus* for the first time likely has little idea what to expect from a reinterpretation of classic Greek drama in the form of a modern-day gospel service. However, one thing is made clear from the beginning: the sense of conviviality and general wellness with which the environment of a sincere church service is infused, through and through. There are "warm greetings" as the choir, band, and clergy members make their entrances, while the visiting singers "create a stir," leading up to the "hush" that falls over the congregation as the service is set to begin. Clearly everyone is happy to be there. They need not be instructed or directed, because they understand the ritual of the service and are willingly taking part in it, whether as participant or as spectator—that is, as participating spectator, since one of the ideas of the Pentecostal style of service is that not just choir and band members but everyone feels the joy of the gospel music and claps, sings, and/or dances.

Attending church is a therapeutic experience, especially when one has the chance to face up to one's own lesser actions and, through testifying or confession, whether aloud or merely in one's mind, to disown them—to move beyond one's sins and pledge to live a more ethical and fulfilling life. Regarding the power of the Pentecostal service, the words of the Reverend Earl F. Miller, who played Pastor Theseus in the original Broadway production, from the book's introductory matter can hardly be improved upon:

> Black preaching is body and soul. Black preaching like black religion is holistic. It engages the whole person. One of the clear things we can say is that the black religious experience is not just a meeting of the minds. It is an encounter with the living God. When we first started serving God, we didn't serve him with our words, we didn't serve him with our ideas, we danced him. We praised him with our whole being.

## Dysfunctional Families

As much as any man past or present, real or fictional, Oedipus is in serious need of redemption, because he was cursed to give rise to an exceedingly dysfunctional family. The fact of the incest between him and his mother is bad enough; the taboo against incest originates in the fact that combining genetic material derived too closely from the same source(s) greatly increases the risk of the perpetuation of detrimental genetic mutations. Oedipus can be glad that his children are apparently of sound mind and body, but things naturally took a turn for the worse in his and Jocasta's family when the wife killed herself and the self-blinded husband-son was left to take the blame.

People's actions often have great impact on the lives of those closest to them, which, in negative cases, can easily lead to lingering ill-will. Though he committed no conscious errors, Oedipus is naturally resented by the children left without a mother, which helps account for the sons' decision to exile and ignore the plight of their father. However, this decision has repercussions for the sons: having decided not to repair their family but to tear it apart completely, the brothers become enemies, and when they "need" their father again, he refuses them. Their rejection of him was too consequential, too hurtful, for him to simply forget about it, and the family's dysfunction is rendered permanent.

## Forgiveness

For all his misfortunes, Oedipus is the hero of *The Gospel at Colonus*, the one for whom the audience feels the most sympathy and roots most strongly—but one might argue that a share of the blame for the family's disintegration does fall with him at the last. After all, he himself expresses the notion that he is ultimately after revenge, a dark concept. When Creon comes (duplicitously) asking Oedipus to effectively forgive the family members who have wronged him and return to Thebes, Preacher Oedipus declares: "No! You'll not get reprieved! What you'll get is / All my vengeance active in that land forever!"

This implicit advocacy of revenge actually runs counter to the philosophy Oedipus propounds later in the play. In bestowing his blessing on Colonus, Oedipus suggests that a nation—or person—should remain pacific in responding to violence: "For every nation that lives peaceably, / Another will grow hard and push its arrogance, / Put off God and turn to madness. Fear not. / God attends to these things slowly; but he attends." Oedipus is fairly arguing the Christian point that judgment, and thus revenge, should be left to God. He himself has been judged and cast out of Thebes because of actions he committed that turned out to be "wrong" in ways he could not have known at the time, actions for which he has nevertheless shown

# TOPICS FOR FURTHER STUDY

- Read *Oedipus: Trapped by Destiny* (2016), a graphic-novel adaptation of *Oedipus the King* for young adults by French artist Yvan Pommaux, translated to English by Richard Kutner. Then write a paper in which you reflect on the similarities and differences between the processes of adaptation for Pommaux and for Breuer. Include discussion of the various ways in which the adaptations "reach" the reader or viewer, and try to draw a conclusion regarding which adaptation reaches the audience in the most meaningful way(s).

- Watch a video of a performance of *The Gospel at Colonus*, such as the production at the American Musical Theater Festival in Philadelphia in 1985, found on YouTube (https://www.youtube.com/watch?v=8ZyQP_zrD2U). Then write a paper in which you discuss the difference between reading the book version of the play and seeing a performance complete with all the music, both from a personal and from an objective standpoint. Include reference to at least one print and one online source regarding the physiological benefits of listening to music.

- After watching *The Gospel at Colonus* (see the previous topic), enlist as many musically inclined fellow classmates as you need to stage one of the numbers in your classroom, with the intent of re-creating the gospel atmosphere for your classmates to experience. As a prelude to your performance, instruct the rest of the class, your audience, as to how they can play the role of members of the congregation and perhaps sing along with a simple chorus part.

- Create a website designed as an homage to all the musical performers included in the original cast of *The Gospel at Colonus*, particularly Clarence Fountain and the Five Blind Boys of Alabama, J. J. Farley and the Soul Stirrers, the J. D. Steele Singers, and the Bob Telson Band. For each set of performers, offer a group biography (drawn from print and creditable online sources) and, if possible, at least one audio clip from a performance other than *The Gospel at Colonus*.

- Write a research paper or create a multimedia presentation on the history of Pentecostalism in America.

the utmost remorse. In effect, despite his inherent innocence, he has been persecuted, and such a person, above all others, deserves compassion and forgiveness.

Oedipus's sons, to the contrary, have played the role of judging and condemning their own father—and largely in the interest of better seizing whatever royal power they can. Even when they come to Oedipus seeking forgiveness, whether in person (as Polyneices does) or through an intermediary (as Eteocles effectively does, through Creon), they do so out of self-interest. In light of all these circumstances, it hardly seems that the sons deserve Oedipus's forgiveness. In fact, whether he forgives them is immaterial: what they want is action on his part, whether the bestowal of a blessing or accompaniment back toward Thebes, and yet certainly he owes them no positive action. In this sense, the vengeance he apparently seeks is not active violence but simply a withholding of potential salvation—a sort of passive vengeance. One might indeed argue that, as a father, in this case it is his duty to *not* offer forgiveness to his sons, because to offer it would be to fail to teach them a lesson about the consequences of their own failure to forgive.

## Love

Beyond the ethical complexities of forgiving and forgetting, the final message of both the service

*Breuer's play was adapted from the ancient Greek drama* Oedipus at Colonus *by Sophocles* (© K. Roy Zerloch / Shutterstock.com)

and the play is one of love. As the preacher relates, in telling the child about Oedipus's final hours, he said to his daughters, with regard to the extraordinary difficulties of their lives: "I know it was hard, my children, and yet one word / Frees us of all the weight and pain of life. / That word is love." He is referring not to the family love that bound them together through those difficult times, nor of romantic love (which, incidentally, was what brought about the troubles in the first place), but of God's love. In the gospel tradition, opening up the heart, mind, and body to the love of God, especially through song, is what frees the spirit from the burdens of life on earth. One need not be a deist, whether Christian, Muslim, or Jewish, to appreciate this message: feeling loved by God is quite equivalent to feeling embraced by Mother Earth, or getting in touch with the Buddha nature that pervades the universe, or being one with the Dao, to mention just a few traditions. As the preacher says just before the closing hymn, "The love of God will bring you peace." Oedipus gets the cathartic experience he needs from feeling that love and that peace, and the committed audience member or reader will be blessed with that same catharsis.

## STYLE

### Oratorio

The "Note on Production" in *The Gospel at Colonus* describes the play as an "oratorio." *Merriam-Webster's Collegiate Dictionary* defines *oratorio* as "a lengthy choral work usually of a religious nature consisting chiefly of recitatives, arias, and choruses without action or scenery." The nature of this particular work points to why Breuer has been considered a permanent member of American theater's avant-garde: because he tries new and interesting combinations of genre and form that carry a measure of risk in that they do not provide the conventional theatrical experience that more conservative theatergoers expect from a performance. The crux here is the lack of stage action. In a *Mother Jones* article, Charles C. Mann calls Sophocles's drama "powerfully written but almost devoid of dramatic action." Breuer told Mann,

> There was this great play, and *nobody* ever did it.... I had an intuition about it, and when I read it I realized I was right. It was much more like a rite, a ritual, than an ordinary play.

Many plays and musicals are heavily dependent on spoken or sung dialogue, but the actors and actresses will at least embody the physicality of their parts and make entrances and exits that enhance the sense of dramatic action. There is some dramatic action in Breuer's musical, but it is conducted only as acted out in pantomime by the clerics and singers who meanwhile frequently step out of their roles to play their part in the service. Preacher Oedipus is sometimes just the preacher, Evangelist Antigone is sometimes just the evangelist, and so forth. The play, then, really is much like the ritual of a gospel service, dependent less on the audience's immersion in the drama through the acting performances and more on their immersion in the music and the cathartic experience of the service.

## Greek Theater–Gospel Church

Breuer's combination of Greek theater with a Pentecostal church service is a unique and fascinating one. Given the blinded and beleaguered former king's trials and tribulations and his need for redemption, one might indeed ask, what better place could there be for him to go but to a gospel service? Of course, Breuer is not mixing his genres quite so thoroughly: Oedipus is not attending a gospel service, but rather the gospel service is telling through song the story of the final years of Oedipus's life. As described by the friend who introduces the place where Oedipus and Antigone find themselves, Colonus is a kingdom, not a church. However, the layering of one drama within another—the story of Oedipus being told within *The Gospel at Colonus*—has the effect of fusing the two settings in the audience member's mind, and, indeed, one cannot help but imagine Oedipus as gaining his redemption through the gospel tradition.

Breuer expressed, in speaking with Wendy Smith of the *New York Times*, what led him to think of Greek theater in terms of religious experience:

> The more I understood Greek theater, the more I began to feel—and this had something to do with being a child of the 60's—that the important element in it...was its spirituality. I lived in Greece for a year, and it was hard to walk around those theaters, with the altar in the center of the stage, and not know that they were basically churches.

In her essay "Dramaturgical Criticism: A Case Study of *The Gospel at Colonus*," Alicia Kae Koger confirms that theater was "Greek society's most public medium of religious ritual."

As Breuer told interviewer Gerald Rabkin, this was not the staid ritual of many churches; rather, "some scholars now feel that the tragedies were close to rock concerts, that there were responses from the audience like choral or choir responses in the church." Greek theatrical works are known for consistently featuring a chorus, which, functioning both without and within the drama at hand, enhances the musicality of the presentation and also helps accomplish a moral interrogation of the personae and their circumstances. This allows for a collective sense of resolution of both moral and emotional difficulties—a sense of *catharsis*. For Breuer, this sense is what lies at the heart of the connection between Greek theater and gospel. He told Smith, "What I found was that the Pentecostal, Afro-American church, which is part of the American language, gives you a living experience of catharsis in the world today." He then added, with regard to giving audiences a gospel-service version of Sophocles's drama,

> I wanted to show them: This is the cathartic experience, this is what Aristotle was talking about, this is what Greek tragedy is, this is what our entire Western dramatic culture is based on. You begin to understand catharsis by experiencing it.

## HISTORICAL CONTEXT

### Postmodernism

*The Gospel at Colonus* is considered a landmark piece of American theater. Coming at the crest of a spate of gospel musicals in the 1980s, Breuer's drama stood out for going beyond the appreciation of the musico-spiritual form itself to an attempt to make use of it to say something new. In addition, several of the play's qualities are characteristic of postmodernism, the literary style that was prevalent through the late twentieth century. Where the modernist credo of the early twentieth century, as proclaimed by poet Ezra Pound, was to "make it new," one of many possible credos for postmodernists has been to "re-make it new," or perhaps "re-new it"—to take a classic of literature or some other art form and repurpose it for the modern era. The most famous work to do as much is actually a modernist one, James Joyce's *Ulysses* (1922), which translates the events of Homer's *Odyssey* into a single day and night in the life of an ordinary man.

# COMPARE
# &
# CONTRAST

- **1980s:** In the wake of what is known as the golden age of gospel music, the two-decade period from 1945 to 1965, and after the mass popularity of the Northern California State Youth Choir's 1967 recording "Oh Happy Day," mainstream appreciation for gospel music has steadily climbed and persisted. Through the 1970s and 1980s, one or two gospel musicals appear in New York every year.

  **Today:** While gospel music remains popular in religious circles, more modern sounds, like rock 'n' roll and hip-hop, tend to have greater appeal among secular as well as pious youth. A landmark recording was *God's Property from Kirk Franklin's Nu Nation* (1997), featuring the hit single "Stomp"—with parts of George Clinton's "One Nation under a Groove" mixed in—which asserted urban culture's growing presence in the gospel tradition.

- **1980s:** The Church of God in Christ was formed at the turn of the twentieth century when a number of black preachers found that the spiritual experience of church felt complete only after direct connection with the divine, such as through speaking in tongues. Jesus's disciples experienced as much on the Jewish holiday of Pentecost, lending the new tradition the name of Pentecostalism. By the 1980s, the Church of God in Christ's membership has surpassed

  that of America's two major Presbyterian denominations combined.

  **Today:** As of 2012, the Church of God in Christ, a Pentecostal denomination of primarily African American membership, is the fifth-largest denomination in the United States, behind the Catholic, Southern Baptist, United Methodist, and Church of Jesus Christ of Latter-Day Saints (Mormon) churches.

- **1980s:** August Wilson has begun what will be called his American Century Cycle, or Pittsburgh Cycle, with one play devoted to African American history and culture in each decade of the twentieth century. Represented so far are the 1920s in *Ma Rainey's Black Bottom* (1984), the 1950s in *Fences* (1987), and the 1910s in *Joe Turner's Come and Gone* (1988), to be followed by the 1930s in *The Piano Lesson* (1990).

  **Today:** In the fall of 2013, at New York City's Greene Space in Lower Manhattan, nearly one hundred theater artists, including many who had worked on past productions of Wilson's works, convene to produce and record all ten plays in his American Century Cycle, which he completed with *Radio Golf*, representing the 1990s, in 2005. Nine of the ten plays are set in Pittsburgh, Wilson's birthplace. Wilson died at the age of sixty prior to *Radio Golf*'s Broadway premiere in 2007.

---

The classic-reinvention approach became more pronounced, varied, and fully explored in the postmodern era. Breuer has very much reinvented Sophocles's *Oedipus at Colonus*, giving it new relevance and energy by mixing in an entirely different genre, gospel music and ritual—and the mixing of genres is another postmodern trait. Third, the play breaks down the fourth wall, not just telling a story but telling the audience about the telling of a story, speaking directly to the audience. This brings the audience directly into the framework story—here, they are not just the audience in the theater but also the congregation in the church—enhancing the narrative experience.

One final postmodern trait evident on the surface of the work is the deliberate thwarting of audience expectations, for the purposes of reorienting one's perspective not only toward the

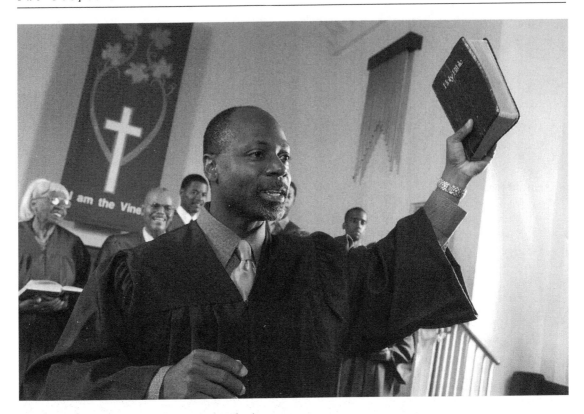

*The Pentecostal minister serves as the play's narrator* *(© sirtravelalot / Shutterstock.com)*

theater but toward the world as well. The people at the gospel service are not meant to act in a way that convinces the audience that they *are* the characters being portrayed—the evangelist frequently steps in and out of her role as Antigone, preempting belief in the illusion of her portrayal—even if this is what many people expect from Broadway. The unexpected nature of the universalized experience, that of a church service where belonging is determined not by belief in any particular religion but by belief merely in the fundamental importance of storytelling, is part of what makes it so powerful.

## Black American Theater

Breuer's musical holds an honored place in the history of black American theater—even though, one should recognize, Breuer himself is not African American, nor is Telson, the composer. Mimi Gisolfi D'Aponte, in her in-depth study "*The Gospel at Colonus* (and Other Black Morality Plays)," affirms that the musical is nonetheless a milestone in black theater's progression to "highly acclaimed dramatic art and

healthy Broadway box office," a progression keyed by Lorraine Hansberry's *Raisin in the Sun* (1959) and August Wilson's monumental cycle of plays representing African American history during each decade of the twentieth century. Although he was using a text written by a white man millennia ago, Breuer was most directly inspired by African American religion. He told Mann that with regard to American religion, only the Pentecostal tradition—that is, the African American gospel tradition—sought the same sort of holistic catharsis that was a goal of the Greek tradition. Going further back in history, Breuer pointed out that the entire experience of theater, of theatrical telling and retelling of a story, emerges from the African call-and-response tradition. As for what happened on the stage, Breuer relied heavily on the performance abilities of some legendary figures in theater and gospel, especially Freeman and Fountain, who for decades had been the famous leader of Clarence Fountain and the Five Blind Boys of Alabama.

Perhaps most to the point, Breuer allowed African American traditions themselves to govern the creative direction of the musical. He told Smith, with regard to the most formative period of the musical's evolution, in 1983 in Minneapolis, "My only direction . . . was, 'Do it like you do in church.' Every time I gave that direction it came out right." As a coda, the way that classic Western literature was used as a means of allowing people of all races and creeds to better access the gospel tradition—to better appreciate African American culture—was a substantial part of the drama's success. Composer Telson told Mann:

> It's wonderful that we've created something that black audiences could hear and feel right at home with . . . . But it's even more exciting for me to see middle-aged white people—people who would switch the channel if this music came on the radio—coming up to me after the show with tears of joy in their eyes. They've broken through something in themselves to be able to hear this music.

## CRITICAL OVERVIEW

*The Gospel at Colonus* earned rave reviews throughout its long life as a theatrical entity. D'Aponte tracks its evolution, which began with its conception at a workshop at New York's P.S. 122 in 1981; proceeded through an experimental/development tour in small theaters in Denver and Minneapolis as well as London, Edinburgh, Brussels, Paris, and Zurich; reached full production scale in Brooklyn in 1983, followed by extended tours across the United States; and ended with the Broadway run from March 11 to May 14, 1988. The run might have been longer, but as Breuer related in a *BOMB* interview with Michael Goldberg, he had once written a scathing letter to *New York Times* theater critic Frank Rich after the latter panned a 1981 Mabou Mines production of *A Prelude to Death in Venice*—the title alludes to a story by Nobel Prize winner Thomas Mann—as the work of "a bunch of drugged out hippies" who did not even deserve public funding. As evidence that Rich held a grudge, he gave the Broadway production of *Gospel* "the only bad review in over 800 reviews that the piece had received worldwide"— "an elitist, racist review," in Breuer's reasoned assessment. D'Aponte notes that the animosity between Breuer and Rich was well known in theater circles.

Alan Rich, of *Newsweek*, was among the first critics with national circulation to take stock of Breuer's creation in Brooklyn in 1983, as the opening lines of his review suggest: "An old-time Greek tragedy transformed into a new-time gospel musical? C'mon now; somebody's got to be kidding. Well, nobody is, and the living, dazzling, exhilarating proof is *The Gospel at Colonus*." The reviewer found that the show figuratively "sent up rockets," it was so powerful, as Breuer "has driven bright shafts of light into the murky textures of Sophocles." For Rich, the end of the play was marked by "a torrent of unbridled musical ecstasy," "peals of irresistible choral response," and "wave upon wave of thunderous joy." Mel Gussow reviewed the Brooklyn production for the *New York Times* and was similarly effusive. He called the genre mix "an unlikely but inspired marriage" and focused on how the "jubilant music . . . reaches toward ecstasy" in the multiple "soaring numbers." With the finale, Gussow wrote, "the stage threatens to lift off from its moorings, joining the show in an evangelical musical flight."

In the *Village Voice*, Michael Feingold found the 1983 production marked by conceptual "brilliance" that leads to "a wonderful, hypnotic, exhilarating evening." Regarding the execution of the concept, "the validation of Breuer's daring comes from the striking ease with which all of the elements of story and performance blend together." Assessing the 1988 Broadway production for *Newsweek*, Jack Kroll called it "one of the most marvelous shows of the decade, based on one of the most inspired ideas of any time." Kroll considers the music "superb," the cast "jam-packed" with vocal talent, and the show itself "a triumph of reconciliation, bringing together black and white, pagan and Christian, ancient and modern in a sunburst of joy that seems to touch the secret heart of civilization itself."

In D'Aponte's scholarly opinion, *The Gospel at Colonus* "offers a brilliant synthesis of an enduring classical plot wedded to the indigenous storytelling tradition, both narrative and musical, of its American Pentecostal church setting." The result, she affirms, is "gripping ritual drama" that leaves the audience "intimately enlightened." Perhaps the anecdotal assessments of the musical ring truest. D'Aponte cites Tom Disch of the *Nation*, who wrote of his theater-going experiences:

> I have seen *Gospel at Colonus* three times now . . . , and each time my heart has swelled, my throat has lumped and I've cried a steady flow of wedding-march tears, feeling foolish

and elevated and swept away. I'd happily go back and see it again tomorrow. I love it. I hope it runs forever.

## CRITICISM

### Michael Allen Holmes

*Holmes is a writer with existential interests. In the following essay, he reflects on the changes made by Breuer in adapting a dour ancient Greek tragedy to create the uplifting musical* The Gospel at Colonus.

Breuer is characteristically deferential in discussing the degree of credit he deserves as the auteur behind *The Gospel at Colonus*. With respect to the writing, he noted that Robert Fitzgerald's translation of Sophocles's *Oedipus at Colonus* was so poetic that he felt little need to make changes to the lines that he preserved for his adaptation. With respect to the theatrical tradition, he went well beyond modern-day African American productions to recognize the storytelling of African griots as essential to drama's foundation. Finally, with respect to the directing, he claimed to have done little more than simply ask the consummate gospel performers enlisted for his play to do everything just as they would in church. He practically positions himself as someone who simply happened to be in the right place at the right time, allowing the seed of the original conception of doing Greek theater gospel-style to first take root in his mind and then blossom entirely on its own. Reading through *Oedipus at Colonus*, however, makes clear that Breuer's selectivity and strategy in adapting Sophocles was essential to the success of the production.

One can see from the opening scene of *Oedipus at Colonus* how Breuer might have perceived the possibility of setting the drama in a modern-day church. Within the first ten lines of his opening monologue, Oedipus announces, "My sufferings have taught me to endure— / and how long these sufferings have lasted!" On this note, as Breuer told Smith, "The story of Oedipus is unmistakably one of salvation through suffering, than which there can be no more Christian theme." Oedipus soon turns to his daughter Antigone to ask if there might be any place in the vicinity to sit, perhaps "in the groves / belonging to the god?" Her response is that, judging from the laurel, olives, and vines as well as the nightingales

> IT HARDLY SEEMS THAT THE PLAY COULD END ON A POSITIVE NOTE UNDER THE CIRCUMSTANCES— UNLESS, THAT IS, A CHRISTIAN ELEMENT IS INTRODUCED."

singing, "this place is sacred." When she encourages him to "bend and sit" on a rock, it is very much as if she is ushering him to be seated on a pew inside a church, and the process of redemption is begun.

As the play proceeds, several types of alterations made by Breuer stand out. One of the first to be noticed is the occasional redistribution of lines between characters. For example, when Ismene comes upon the scene in Sophocles, she has a high degree of agency. She greets her father and reports on the unfortunate situation back in Thebes, all in her own words, peaking in a speech of some thirty lines. The dialogue goes on for some time as Ismene attempts to clarify who knew what when, such as regarding her brothers and pronouncements made by oracles. In *Gospel*, Ismene has far less agency. She does have her own quartet, with two men and one other woman to accompany her, lending weight to her stage presence, but after they sing "How Shall I See You through My Tears," establishing the emotional significance of the reunion, Ismene fades into the background. It is the evangelist, here, who steps forward to actually communicate the essentials of Ismene's tale. After she does so as her church persona, referring to Oedipus in the third person, she shifts—without any intervening dialogue from other characters—to become Antigone, addressing Oedipus in the second person, as "you." This self-accomplished shift fairly glosses over Ismene's presence in the scene.

The rationale behind this shifting of lines from Ismene to Antigone might be explained in several ways. First, having the evangelist be the narrator of Ismene's report allows the narrative to be summed up much more efficiently, the way a summary of a novel will be far shorter than the novel itself. Second, the use of the evangelist as narrator here represents a breaking of the fourth wall, as she speaks directly to

# WHAT DO I READ NEXT?

- *The Gospel at Colonus* was originally staged in briefer form as a companion piece to another genre-mixing effort of Breuer's, the doo-wop opera *Sister Suzie Cinema* (1980). This work and others can be found in the 1987 volume *Sister Suzie Cinema: The Performance Poetry of Lee Breuer, 1976–1986*.

- *Don't Bother Me, I Can't Cope: A Musical Entertainment* (1972), written by Micki Grant, is the book version of one of the first major plays to feature gospel music, in addition to soul, jazz, funk, and calypso. The musical was directed by Vinnette Carroll, the first African American director of a Broadway show.

- Perhaps the most famous example of African American theater produced by white writers is the opera *Porgy and Bess* (1935), with music composed by George Gershwin and libretto by Ira Gershwin and DuBose Heyward, based on Heyward's novel *Porgy* (1925). A film version of the opera was produced in 1959. With the hit song "Summertime," *Porgy and Bess*, depicting black street life in Charleston, South Carolina, is still produced frequently in regional theaters.

- Breuer acknowledges southern writer and anthropologist Zora Neale Hurston as the originator of his notion to channel ancient drama through contemporary African American culture. Her most famous novel is the novel *Their Eyes Were Watching God* (1937), about a locally disparaged woman's path to redemption.

- *The Gospel Goes to Broadway: Inspiration in Songs from Broadway Musicals* (2013), by Methodist pastor Dr. James R. McCormick, is an attempt to take lyrics and music written largely for the purpose of entertainment and root them back in scriptural lessons. Based on McCormick's own "Broadway Sundays" series of sermons, the twenty-six chapters draw from twenty-six different musicals.

- Breuer has declared himself greatly inspired by the renowned Czech writer Franz Kafka. One English edition of Kafka's writings is *Dearest Father: Stories and Other Writings* (1954), translated by Ernst Kaiser and Eithne Wilkins, which includes the section "Reflections on Sin, Suffering, Hope, and the True Way."

- The young-adult novel *Bull* (2017) by David Elliott is a modern retelling of the myth of Theseus and the minotaur in verse, echoing the style of Homer but using modern slang, speech patterns, and rhyming styles. The novel focuses on how the young outcast Asterion evolved to become the feared creature with the body of a man and the head of a bull.

---

the congregation/audience about what is taking place in the story. This enhances the postmodern style of the nested stories and audiences, involving the people watching the performance in a way that cannot happen if they are never addressed directly. Finally, and most practically, there is the fact that the woman who played Antigone, Isabell Monk, was one of only three professional actors used in the original staging of the show. The others were the incomparable Morgan Freeman as Preacher

Oedipus and Kevin Davis as Polyneices. Thus, it stands to reason that the professional actress would be given as many spoken lines as possible, relative to the gospel singers.

Part of Breuer's intent also seems to be to heighten the importance of the character of Antigone, as another shift of lines suggests. Just after the discussion with Ismene, Oedipus is both indignant and not quite sure what to do next. In *Gospel*, Antigone steps forward to suggest that before doing anything else, Oedipus needs to make amends for having fairly trespassed on sacred ground. In Sophocles, however, it is the chorus that makes this suggestion. In the context, having the chorus deliver this line seems to make more sense, as they are inhabitants of the area who can instruct newcomers on local custom. Yet leaving this suggestion to the chorus also gives weight to an otherwise generic persona; the audience never makes an emotional investment in the chorus the way it does in the stalwart Antigone, who has remained by her blinded father's side through thick and thin. Having Antigone instruct her own father as to this ritual makes her more of a repository of worldly knowledge, more of a guide for her beleaguered father, and thus a stronger character. It also increases the pathos of the father, who somewhat humbles himself in so obediently following the directions of his daughter, a young woman whom such an elder man, a father, would ordinarily consider subordinate to himself. For a modern era in which women generally have far more agency than they did in ancient Greece, it feels fitting that Antigone should be raised in both the audience's and Oedipus's esteem.

Also striking is the general elimination of lines and entire blocks of dialogue. For example, in Sophocles, Oedipus takes the opportunity, after Ismene arrives and reports on her brothers' doings, to articulate precisely how the young men had wronged their father in the wake of self-blinding and lingering shame over his misdeeds. Oedipus reiterates this same story when Creon arrives upon the scene—but Breuer has Oedipus explain his sons' misdeeds just once, in between those two scenes, when he is questioned for a second time by the Choragos. Such a revision is self-explanatory, but less clear is the reason for Breuer's compression of the scene involving the abduction of the daughters. In Sophocles, Creon and Oedipus exchange monologues, then engage in a prolonged dialogue, during which Creon reports having abducted *one* of Oedipus's two daughters, Ismene; Antigone temporarily remains, allowing for the most action-packed scene in the play to take place, with Oedipus declaring injustice, Creon asserting his right to the lives of Thebans, the chorus trying to intervene, and Antigone playing the damsel in distress. In *Gospel*, Creon simply announces that he has already abducted the two women, as the audience has witnessed, and he leaves. Breuer's making Antigone a stronger

character may be one reason for the minimization of this action, not prolonging the abduction and emphasizing Antigone's helplessness. Otherwise, it is somewhat curious that Breuer did not take advantage of the chance for a little more dramatic interplay between characters.

The explanation for the change seems to lie in the specific setting of *The Gospel at Colonus*—a church service. Breuer's intent is not simply to entertain the audience at as many turns as possible; rather, he is using a gospel service to present a depiction of Oedipus's life as a quasi-biblical parable. In this light, the sense of the trials endured by Oedipus are of the utmost importance, while the quibbling between Creon and the chorus and the action of the abduction are secondary. In fact, there is something almost unintentionally comical about the conflict between the blind, old Oedipus and his brother-in-law Creon, who once remarks, "I'll not hold back my anger. I will bring him away by force, / although I am alone and slow with age." To reinforce the point, he later quips, "Old as I am, I will try to act against you." When Theseus steps in to try to mediate the dispute, and Oedipus snaps at Creon for his "insult" and "taunts" over the "incest and calamity," the scene starts to feel like its own admixture of genres—like the pathetic bickering of *Grumpy Old Men* crossed with the dysfunctional family melodrama of television's *Geraldo*. Perhaps Breuer was wise to leave these exchanges out.

Arguably the most interesting changes made to Sophocles by Breuer come at the play's end. *Oedipus at Colonus* can hardly be seen to end on a high note. There is the reunion between Oedipus and his daughters and a measure of vengeance in his spurning Polyneices and sending him on his way. However, Polyneice's death is not abstractly portrayed in Sophocles as it is in *Gospel*, leaving the audience with no closure regarding the nefarious sons. Also, little solace is brought by Oedipus's death, with his daughters mourning severely and even losing their will to live. In fact, it hardly seems that the play could end on a positive note under the circumstances—unless, that is, a Christian element is introduced. Breuer was perhaps clued in to the opportunity to add this element by the speech given by the messenger reporting to the chorus how Oedipus met his end: "He was sent on his way / with no accompaniment of tears, no pain of sickness; / if any man ended miraculously, / this man did."

*The church choir plays the same role as the chorus in Greek theater* (© Joseph Sohm / Shutterstock.com)

The end met by the legendary Jesus of Nazareth may not have been painless, but it was certainly miraculous, and Breuer stressed this aspect of the tale.

To adequately revise Sophocles to a Christian context, Breuer needed to make a couple of important changes. The first concerns the idea of love. In Sophocles, the only solace Oedipus can offer his daughters is the fact of his fatherly affection for them. Regarding "the heavy task of tending" him through the end of his life, he states: "It was a cruel task, children, that I know, / but there's a single word that overthrows / all tasks of work. My love you had; no one / could love you more." Breuer, too, has Oedipus mention this, but in both works, there follows the unpleasant fact that his love will, with his death, be no more. In Sophocles, there is simply no other love to fill this void; the chorus implores the daughters to cease their mourning, but there is little emotional force behind the advice.

In *Gospel*, on the other hand, the preacher can fill the void by declaring, "Now let the weeping cease. / Let no one mourn again. / The love of God will bring you peace." Perhaps the more

important change concerns the direction in which Oedipus is headed. In Sophocles, he goes down to the underworld, where all shades of the deceased, good and bad alike, must go. But humans do not aspire to be burrowing creatures; they do not really want to go underground, whether in life or in death. To be "free as a bird," on the other hand, is a most human aspiration, and with the idea of Christian heaven, there is a different direction in which Oedipus must go: up. Having buried Oedipus, Breuer raises him back up to the stage, implying his rising gloriously higher. Thus, between God's love filling the void of the lost father's love, and Oedipus's final apotheosis—a Greek term meaning "*elevation* to divine status"—Breuer proved able to bring both Oedipus and many audience members to heights of ecstatic redemption that neither had ever known before.

**Source:** Michael Allen Holmes, Critical Essay on *The Gospel at Colonus*, in *Drama for Students*, Gale, Cengage Learning, 2018.

### Andrew White

*In the following review, White describes a particular production of the play as "brilliant."*

There's nothing kills a play's reputation like the label "Classic;" if you want to bury it even deeper, call it "Classical." We're allergic to the idea that the old stuff was actually worth watching, the dialogue worth listening to.

Sure, we'll go to see revivals of recent hits, the same way we get up and dance to the "golden oldies" which thrilled us in our misspent youth. But anything that smacks of timelessness and eternal truths? Meh.

And yet occasionally a theatrical genius will come along and, in a masterstroke, show us why some works endure. Lee Breuer, co-founder of the Mabou Mines company in New York, created a setting for Sophocles' great tragedy *Oedipus at Colonus* that became an instant hit; an instant, truly American hit. Not bad for a moldy, 2,400-year-old script.

Breuer's *The Gospel at Colonus* takes Sophocles' meditation on mortality, sin and redemption and brings it solidly into the American mainstream. Moving beyond the old concept of tragedy as emotional catharsis, Breuer shows how tragedy can actually fill us with joy and gratitude. He turns the theatre into an evangelical meeting house, the protagonist into a preacher; and for the chorus, the finely-tuned, passionate voices of praise that can fill the soul of a Sunday. It worked famously back in the 80's when first produced, and it works even more famously now.

*The Gospel at Colonus*, revived at WSC Avant Bard under the inspired direction of Jennifer I. Nelson, is one of the most joyous experiences in live theatre you are likely to see. This musical version of Greek Tragedy offers a meditation on the deeper meaning of one of antiquity's most notorious myths—of Oedipus, the king who infamously murdered his own father and married his mother.

In *The Gospel at Colonus* we find Oedipus, for years a wandering exile from his native city of Thebes, approaching his final resting place in Colonus, a village just north of Athens. His daughters, Antigone and Ismene, accompany him but because of his reputation, the local populace initially rejects him. As word of his arrival reaches the city, however, the mythical Athenian king Theseus comes out to greet him, welcomes him to his kingdom and vows to keep secret the precise location of Oedipus' passing. The city of Thebes, meanwhile, is in the midst of a civil war, with the struggle for succession fully engaged between Oedipus' two sons Eteocles and Polyneices. First Creon, his brother-in-law, and then Polyneices try to ensnare Oedipus in their plots for the throne; both are forcefully rejected. Oedipus moves on, stoically, to his final rest, with the turmoil of his life and Thebes firmly behind him.

One of Breuer's innovations was to have the role of Oedipus played by two actors, one for spoken dialogue and the other for the musical numbers. In WSC Avant Bard's production, the Preacher Oedipus is given a forceful turn by William T. Newman, Jr., while the Singer Oedipus is gloriously incarnated by DeMone, whose soaring voice fills the space at Theatre Two and leaves you breathless. Tiffany Bird and Ashley D. Buster offer touching turns as his daughters Antigone and Ismene, while the production's musical director e'Marcus Harper-Short has a subtle turn as Creon, Oedipus' scheming brother-in-law. There is a host of fine voices here, including Brandon Mack, Greg Watkins (who puts in a strong Polyneices) and topped off by Minister Becky Jays Jenkins and her Women's Ecumenical Choir.

The production is also graced by its setting; from the moment you enter the theatre you are embraced by Tim Jones's open space in spring, with birds chirping (courtesy Jason Schmitz's subtle sound design) and wisteria blossoms hung over the multi-level performance area. Danielle Preston has added contemporary and African motifs with her costume design, and choreographer Sandra Holloway manages the complex action of the play, creating some wonderful tableaux.

**Source:** Andrew White, "WSC Avant Bard's *The Gospel at Colonus* a Brilliant Revival," in *Broadway World*, March 10, 2017.

### Kevin J. Wetmore Jr.

*In the following excerpt, Wetmore discusses how Greek religion contrasts with Christianity.*

. . . Critics of *Gospel* argue that the philosophies and belief system behind Greek religion are incompatible with the philosophies and belief system of Pentecostal Christianity. Burdine, writing from the perspective of the theatricality of the black church, contends that the black church and Greek theatre are "too diametrically opposed" to allow *Gospel* to generate the meaning and experience for which its authors hope. Robert Brustein, writing as a theatre critic, in his original review of the Broadway production

> ALTHOUGH ONE CAN ARGUE THAT THE STRUCTURES WHICH SUPPORT THE INSTITUTIONS OF THE PENTECOSTAL CHURCH AND GREEK TRAGEDY ARE INCOMPATIBLE, THOSE STRUCTURES ARE RENDERED LESS IMPORTANT IF ONE ACKNOWLEDGES *GOSPEL* AS A POST-MODERN *BRICOLAGE* OF DELIVERANCE DRAMA AND PURE THEATRICALITY."

entitled "Transcultural Blends," complains, "I'm not convinced that the story of the blinded, feeble Oedipus...is entirely compatible with the rituals of Christian evangelism as practiced in the black church." He claims Breuer and Telson are "no[t] so much blending as banging" the two cultures together, ultimately doing a disservice to both. John Simon, writing in *New York*, even accuses Breuer and Telson of being "two white boys" who are "colonizing the gospel," appropriating African American culture and using it to frame European culture in order to enrich themselves. These critics raise three separate issues: the inaccuracy of representing Sophocles's play in the Gospel musical form, the incompatibility of Greek tragedy and Afro-Christianity and the appropriateness of two Euro-American males using African American religion in order to recreate Greek theatre. We shall deal with each of these issues separately.

In response to the criticism that the production does a disservice to Sophocles, Penelope Fitzgerald, wife of the translator Robert Fitzgerald, writes in the preface to the text of *Gospel* that, "*The Gospel at Colonus* uses the idea of reimagining in a striking and original way. The play is not meant to be Sophocles' *Oedipus*, but a whole new play derived from the original, different from it, and yet true to its original spirit." While Fitzgerald is essentially correct, that Breuer and Telson's play is not Sophocles', but a new work, just as Sophocles' was not the myth but a new work, her response raises as many questions as it does answers. What does it mean to be "true" to the original? Why should one be "true"? Can one even be "true"? Are there other allegiances and representations that

should be questioned here, such as the use of the Pentecostal church to represent ancient Greece?

Equally as problematic is Maryann McDonald's analysis of the play. She initially presents an almost "Black Athena" paradigm of the play, noting that, "It is possible that the African tradition from which Gospel music drew is even older than Greek tragedy." If this is the case, McDonald presents an interesting possibility—that Breuer and Telson are blending one ancient form with the modern version of another ancient form in order to create a unique fusion of European and African cultures, blending as equals, equally ancient, equally modern. McDonald, however, does not pursue this line, preferring instead to universalize and erase the difference between African America and Euro-America: "For the most part, black traditional music has become an American product," which is how two Euro-Americans, she argues, are "allowed" to use gospel music in Greek tragedy.

By calling black traditional music "an American product," McDonald focuses on the commodification of black culture while ignoring its origins. Cornell West can speak of "shared cultural space" when people of different ethnic backgrounds appreciate the same hip-hop music, or the work of an athlete, or a particular film, but this shared space does not in any way erase the origin of the form or suddenly transform it into national culture. For McDonald to say this is simply a way of avoiding the issue of "colonizing the gospel," and ignores the larger cultural issues that this piece of theatre engages, as shall be outlined below.

Alicia Kay [sic] Koger argues more forcibly and believably for a compatibility between the original and adaptation based on music, rhythm, and structure than on similarities between the church and the story of Oedipus's salvation. Koger claims that music plays "a role in the overall cathartic effect," and that this effect, present in the Greek original through the transformation of Oedipus, is achieved in *Gospel* through "layering." She argues that just as most songs in the musical begin "solo voice accompanied by one musical instrument" and build by adding others until, by song's end, all are blended together into a thunderous whole, the play itself also has a layered structure of cultures: "Greek, Christian, and contemporary African American," which are then layered together, not representative of any single one of them, but rather a blend of all, complete in and of itself only when mixed together. This musical metaphor of layered cultural structure offers a more suitable and interesting way of understanding how *Gospel* works as an Afro-Greek adaptation.

Mimi Gisolfi D'Aponte asserts that, "what takes place during *The Gospel at Colonus* is simultaneously, but in no hierarchical order, black church, participatory theatre, gospel concert, and Sophoclean drama. It is a combination which teaches, preaches, entertains and offers catharsis." Although one can argue that the structures which support the institutions of the Pentecostal church and Greek tragedy are incompatible, those structures are rendered less important if one acknowledges *Gospel* as a postmodern *bricolage* of deliverance drama and pure theatricality. The objections of critics who desire a one-to-one correspondence of Greek tragedy and black Christianity are countered by the argument that the elements that do not match are not what Breuer and Telson are highlighting. No one connected with the project has ever insisted that the theology of Greek tragedy is compatible with the theology of Christianity as practiced in the sanctified church. The name change from *Oedipus at Colonus* to *The Gospel at Colonus* suggests that the project is not merely an adaptation along the lines of a "Black Oedipus," but rather a new entity to be considered on its own terms, rather than whether or not it is truly representative of Greek tragedy or a Pentecostal church service.

There is a third cultural presence in the play that also supplements and links the first two. As Marianne McDonald indicates, church services don't have intermissions. They also usually don't have programs by Playbill, drinks for sale in the lobby, and different prices for different areas of seating. The conventions of modern theatre going, particularly those of the modern Broadway musical, are overlaid over the Pentecostal service and Greek tragedy. No audience member at the Lunt-Fontaine theatre, or any other theatre in which the piece has been presented, has believed that they were at an actual church service, although the familiar setting and conventions would cause some audience members to respond as if they were. Likewise, no audience member would believe they were watching historic Greek tragedy, with its mask and outdoor

theatre. Instead, the meeting point of these two cultures was the theatre itself, which has a different set of conventions and "rules" than these other two cultural forms.

Koger's and D'Aponte's analyses work best if one accepts that the shared sense of catharsis is what links these two plays, the original and its adaptation. In fact catharsis is the most popular critical response in the face of the issues listed above. Catharsis is arguably the solution to the critical problem of the incompatibility of belief systems. Aesthetic and intellectual distancing is the solution to the critical problem of inaccuracy of representation and even, possibly, to the "problem" of the ethnicity of the creators.

As noted above, Breuer argues that "communal catharsis" is the common ground between black church and Greek tragedy. In an interview with Gerald Rabkin, Breuer stated that he believed "that if you go one step further with cathartic theatre you might find pity and terror turning into joy and ecstasy." As noted above, Koger, D'Aponte and even Kramer acknowledge that it is the music of the production that makes it cathartic. As the famous Gospel singer Mahalia Jackson claims, "Gospel songs are songs of hope. When you sing them you are delivered of your burden." In other words, singing Gospel music is cathartic, at least for the singer. The effect, however, is also transferable to the congregation, in particular since the musical form is both individual and collectively expressed. The congregation joins the singer at certain parts of the song and are thus equally moved into catharsis. If tragedy is defined as a play that achieves catharsis for the audience, then *Gospel* is much more of a real tragedy (in the Aristotelian sense) than any other play considered in this study.

Interestingly, Morgan Freeman himself, in an interview with Glenda Gill, argues that catharsis is the common point between Greek tragedy and the black church. "That hollering and shouting we do must have been to [Breuer] what the Greek chorus was really about," Freeman states. "The Greeks were so emotional. You've just taken two traditions that were compatible and stirred them together." Freeman sees the two traditions as "compatible" based on their performance and on their effect—the celebration by black church or Greek chorus and the catharsis that either brings. Where European critics have seen only the incompatibility of theology and philosophy, Freeman sees the compatibility of effect and performance style.

Thomas M. Disch, in his review of the Broadway production for *The Nation*, wrote that he had seen the play three times, "and each time my heart has swelled, my throat has lumped, and I've cried a stead flow of wedding-march tears, feeling foolish and elevated and swept away." If that is not catharsis, what is?

The second method by which *Gospel* becomes an effective transculturation of Greek theatre is through distancing. As noted above, the intent behind *Gospel* was to challenge two potential audiences. Those familiar with Greek tragedy would have their preconceptions undercut by a "direct emotional experience," whereas those familiar with the form of Gospel musical would be distanced by the different subject matter, the "Book of Oedipus" instead of the Bible. For the former group, the cultural elite of the Northeast, "what began as an intellectual appreciation ended as an emotional experience," in other words, catharsis. Yet this very catharsis, this different experience of Greek tragedy, distances it, taking the familiar for this audience (the postmodern production of Greek tragedy) and radically transforming it. (Although, in fairness, as Coppenger argues, this approach is arguably class-specific and, what is more ethnic-specific.) However, the accusation of appropriation of African American culture is somewhat offset by those involved in the production, as will be argued below. For the latter, the conventions of church ritual are subsumed into the conventions of the Broadway musical and the subject matter of Christianity is exchanged for that of ancient Greece, also thereby presenting the familiar and unfamiliar simultaneously. It is the theatricality of the church that is used to rehistoricize the theatricality of Sophocles' text.

The African American church has its roots in Africa and in the slave experience in the New World. The figure of the preacher, "an icon among Afro-Americans and since," comes from West African priests, who were "spiritual leader, counselor, and politician" in the slave communities according to Walter C. Daniel. This communal role originated in Africa and continued in the New World, altering only slightly in the face of forced conversion to Christianity. The black preacher is a figure of religious, civic, and social power and importance who must be "a shrewd administrator and an engaging politician."

During the era of slavery, the preacher was not only a religious leader but a community leader and teacher. Even in the present day, many leaders in the African American community are also preachers or clergymen, such as the Reverend Jesse Jackson, Reverend Al Sharpton, and, of course, Dr. Martin Luther King.

In the early black church there was an emphasis on the Old Testament. Ulysses Duke Jenkins reports, "The plight of a people taken from their homeland became the text of their sermons and they could understand why Jeremiah asked, 'Is there no balm in Gilead?'" The focus of the amalgam of West African religious social structure and New World Christianity was the ideas of captivity and deliverance, presented in a highly performative style. Michael Weaver explains the two "modes" of preaching in the black church as "teaching" ("the dispassionate imparting of information") and "preaching" (the "physically enlivened and vocally arousing" performance of experience). Jon Michael Spenser, in his analysis of Gospel music, notes that the preaching of sermons is not simply the intoning of lines, but rather that there is musicality in black preaching. The preacher often delivers a "chanted sermon," accompanied by the organ, during which the congregation is expected to make responses via noises, phrases, clapping, etc., and which can rely upon such performance elements as melody, rhythm, repetition, call-and-response, polyphony, and improvisation. The preacher thus serves as a lead performer of sorts in a service that can combine individual and communal singing, narration through "testifying" and readings from the Bible, and interactive dialogue through call-and-response centered around a performance of teaching and preaching by the central authority figure. It is this highly theatrical religious service that Breuer and Telson used to develop their own Greco-religious service/performance....

**Source:** Kevin J. Wetmore Jr., "Ancient Plays in a New World: Multicultural Currents," in *Black Dionysus: Greek Tragedy and African American Theatre*, McFarland, 2003, pp. 106–110.

## SOURCES

"August Wilson's American Century Cycle," Greene Space website, http://www.thegreenespace.org/series/august-wilsons-american-century-cycle/ (accessed June 27, 2017).

Breuer, Lee, *The Gospel at Colonus*, with Bob Telson, Theatre Communications Group, 1989.

D'Aponte, Mimi Gisolfi, "*The Gospel at Colonus* (and Other Black Morality Plays)," in *Black American Literature Forum*, Vol. 25, No. 1, Spring 1991, pp. 101–11.

"Fast Facts about American Religion," Hartford Institute for Religion Research website, http://hirr.hartsem.edu/research/fastfacts/fast_facts.html (accessed June 27, 2017).

Feingold, Michael, "Gospel Truth," in *Village Voice*, November 22, 1983, p. 109.

Goldberg, Michael, "Lee Breuer," in *BOMB*, Summer 1996, http://bombmagazine.org/article/1981/lee-breuer (accessed June 25, 2017).

Gussow, Mel, "'Colonus' Mixes Songs with Sophocles," in *New York Times*, November 12, 1983, p. 12.

Hayes, John, "Church of God in Christ," in *New Georgia Encyclopedia*, December 4, 2013, http://www.georgiaencyclopedia.org/articles/arts-culture/church-god-christ (accessed June 27, 2017).

Koger, Alicia Kae, "Dramaturgical Criticism: A Case Study of *The Gospel at Colonus*," in *Theatre Topics*, March 1997, pp. 23–35.

Kroll, Jack, "An Oedipal Jamboree," in *Newsweek*, April 4, 1988, p. 75.

"Lee Breuer," MacArthur Foundation website, July 1, 1997, https://www.macfound.org/fellows/549/ (accessed June 25, 2017).

Mann, Charles C., "Doo-Wop Opera and Greek Gospel Tragedies," in *Mother Jones*, April 1987, pp. 28–31, 44–45.

Miller, Earl F., "Note on Performance," in *The Gospel at Colonus*, by Lee Breuer, Theatre Communications Group, 1989, pp. xiii–xiv.

Rabkin, Gerald, "Lee Breuer: On 'The Gospel at Colonus,'" in *Performing Arts Journal*, Vol. 8, No. 1, 1984, pp. 48–51.

Rich, Alan, "Oedipus Jones," in *Newsweek*, November 21, 1983, pp. 105, 107.

Smith, Iris L., "The 'Intercultural' Work of Lee Breuer," in *Theatre Topics*, March 1997, pp. 37–58.

Smith, Wendy, "Sophocles with a Chorus of Gospel," in *New York Times*, March 20, 1988.

Sophocles, *Sophocles I: Oedipus the King, Oedipus at Colonus, Antigone*, 2nd ed., translated by David Grene, edited by David Grene and Richmond Lattimore, University of Chicago Press, 1991.

"Timeline," Gospel Music History Archive, USC Digital Library, http://digitallibrary.usc.edu/cdm/timeline/collection/p15799coll9 (accessed June 27, 2017).

# FURTHER READING

Darden, Robert, *People Get Ready! A New History of Black Gospel Music*, Continuum, 2004.
   Darden provides one of the most comprehensive histories of the gospel tradition available, tracking gospel music back through African origins, the spirituals of the slavery era, the upheavals of the Civil War, and popularization during the twentieth century.

Foley, Helene P., *Reimagining Greek Tragedy on the American Stage*, University of California Press, 2012.
   Foley's scholarly volume looks at the various ways modern-day playwrights have tried to say new things with and about the Greek tragedies that have been gracing stages for thousands of years.

Jones, LeRoi, *Blues People: Negro Music in White America*, William Morrow, 1963.
   One of the most accomplished African American writers of the twentieth century, Jones is better known under the name he took in recognition of his African ancestry—and defiance of the names bestowed on Africans through slavery—Amiri Baraka. This volume is a seminal history on the influence of African American music on broader American culture.

Wilson, August, *Ma Rainey's Black Bottom: A Play in Two Acts*, New American Library, 1985.
   One of several of Wilson's American Century plays in which music plays a significant role, *Ma Rainey's Black Bottom* treats issues of race, religion, and art—and white producers' exploitation of black recording artists—in the 1920s.

———, *Seven Guitars*, Dutton, 1996.
   Another of Wilson's plays revolving around music, *Seven Guitars* treats the release of a blues singer from prison in the 1940s and his ensuing attempts to redeem himself.

# SUGGESTED SEARCH TERMS

Lee Breuer AND The Gospel at Colonus

Lee Breuer AND Mabou Mines

Lee Breuer AND avant-garde

The Gospel at Colonus AND Oedipus

Sophocles AND Oedipus at Colonus

Lee Breuer AND Sophocles

Pentecostalism AND gospel music

African culture AND call-and-response

black American theater

Broadway gospel musicals

# The Killer

## EUGÈNE IONESCO
## 1958

*The Killer* is one of Eugène Ionesco's most ambitious and successful plays. It is the first of four plays in which Bérenger is a major character, including *Rhinoceros* (1959), *Exit the King* (1962), and *A Stroll in the Air* (1963). These are sometimes known as the Bérenger plays. Ionesco wrote in French, and the French title is *Tueur sans gages*, which directly translates to "Killer without payment." A *tueur à gages* is the equivalent of a hit man in English, someone who kills for money. To kill for money is at least to have a reason, but to kill without payment, for no reward and perhaps no reason at all, is an even more frightening prospect.

The play is only Ionesco's second written with a traditional three-act structure, as his artistic project was to experiment not only with the subject of drama but with the form of the genre as well. Ionesco sought to bring high and low theater together and, as his obituary in the *New York Times* noted, Ionesco was "inspired by silent film clowns and vaudeville," elements he folded into to his plays in order to attack "the most serious subjects: blind conformity and totalitarianism, despair and death." For theatergoers used to an evening of light entertainment or even for those who expected the inspirational drama of tragedy, Ionesco's mixing of genres could prove a challenge.

*The Killers* explores this territory where drama and comedy overlap, in large part by

*Eugène Ionesco* (© *Science History Images | Alamy Stock Photo*)

overturning our expectations of what is a serious topic of drama. The murders take place offstage, and no one except the main character, Bérenger, seems particularly upset by them. The structure of the play is in many ways like a typical mystery: there is a murderer and a protagonist determined to identify that murderer. But Ionesco turns this classic quest for an external source of evil inside out, asking us to consider the ways in which we are all, as a society, complicit in violence.

## AUTHOR BIOGRAPHY

Ionesco was born in Slatina, Romania, on November 26, 1909, although he later claimed to have been born in 1912. He died in Paris on March 28, 1994. His father was Romanian, and his mother was French, and shortly after his birth they moved to Paris. French was his first language, and he did not learn Romanian until the family moved back there when he was

thirteen. Ionesco felt that France was always his true home. Martin Esslin, in his seminal book *The Theater of the Absurd*, quotes an interview Ionesco gave to the *Nouvelle Revue Français* in which he reflected on the effect on his work of the long-running classic Punch and Judy show in the Luxembourg Gardens. "It was the spectacle of the world itself, which . . . presented itself to me in an infinitely simplified and caricatured form, as if to underline its grotesque and brutal truth." In his early teens his parents divorced, and Ionesco had to move back to Romania. He went to high school and university there, and in 1936 he married Rodica Burileanu. In 1939 Ionesco returned to France to complete his PhD work in French literature, and he remained there for the rest of his life. His only child, a daughter, Marie-France, was born in 1944.

Ionesco's first play was *The Bald Soprano*, written in 1950 when he was struck by the banality of the dialogue in his English language textbook. After *The Bald Soprano*, Ionesco wrote a succession of plays very quickly (all originally in French). *The Lesson* was published in 1951; *Jack, or The Submission* and *The Chairs* in 1952; and *Victims of Duty* in 1953. *Amédée, or How to Get Rid of It* and *The New Tenant* were published in 1954. *The Killer*, published in 1958, is the first of the plays in which the character Bérenger appears, followed shortly by *Rhinoceros* in 1959 and *Exit the King* in 1962.

*Rhinoceros* was Ionesco's most famous play and has come to stand as a prime example of the theater of the absurd. Two of his plays, *The Bald Soprano* and *The Lesson*, have played continuously since 1955 at the Théâtre de la Huchette in Paris. In 1961 he was named an officer of the Ordre des Arts et des Lettres; in 1970 he was named a chevalier of the Légion d'Honneur. In 1970 he was elected a member of the Académie Française, and he was given the T. S. Eliot Award for Creative Writing from the Ingersoll Foundation in 1985.

## PLOT SUMMARY

### Act 1
The first act begins with lighting effects. The stage is lit like a gray winter day, with a little sound of wind or a leaf skittering across the stage. Suddenly, the light comes up to a bright white, accompanied by the vivid blue of the sky.

The stage remains silent with this blue and white light for at least a full minute before the actors appear. This light is, for Ionesco, the heart of the play, and Bérenger arrives onstage exclaiming about the beauty of the neighborhood. This is the radiant city, a neighborhood of the "mournful, dusty, dirty" expanse of districts in which Bérenger lives. In the radiant city, the weather is always beautiful, the streets are sunny, and the facades of the buildings are classical and yet not forbidding. Bérenger is amazed.

The Architect tells Bérenger that it is the rule in the radiant city that everything is lovely. The loveliness is "all calculated, all intentional. Nothing was to be left to chance." The climate is entirely artificial, the beautiful grass and flowers are watered from below, and every last detail has been designed to produce maximum pleasure. Unexpectedly, a telephone rings, and the Architect pulls a phone handset and cord out of his pocket. This play was written in 1958, several decades before portable telephones were invented, and so the idea that a person could have a telephone in his or her pocket would have been absurd.

Bérenger continues to rave about the convenience and beauty of the radiant city, especially in contrast to the area outside, which comprises "whole districts of people who aren't really unhappy, but worse, who are neither happy nor unhappy." Bérenger notes that while most people are unaware of this state, he was aware of it. He claims that this was "perhaps because I'm more intelligent, or just the opposite, *less* intelligent, not so wise, not so resigned, not so patient." He addresses the Architect: "Is that a fault or a virtue?" The Architect replies that he is incapable of judging, that "the logic department sees to that." Bérenger tells the Architect that he had once been filled with "a blazing fire" and "enormous energy," but it had dwindled away over the years. The whole time Bérenger has been speaking, the Architect has been on the telephone, and then he apologizes to Bérenger, saying he must go back to work. He leaves stage left, then returns a moment later with a small café table and a chair. He puts his briefcase on the table, takes the telephone from his pocket, and assures Bérenger that he can work and listen at the same time.

Bérenger carries on speaking, recounting a memory of "that dazzling radiance, that glowing feeling" that "gave fresh life to the force within me." The Architect continues having conversations on the phone, while encouraging Bérenger to keep speaking. Bérenger recounts a memory of being alone in a French country town and experiencing a moment of deep transcendental joy, a moment in which the light grew very brilliant, and all doubt and fear of death fell away. As he narrates this moment, the Architect is growing more and more agitated on the phone, trying to contact someone who turns out to be his female assistant, a woman who tells the Architect she is resigning her job. He refuses to accept her resignation, telling her she must come see him in person to resign. Meanwhile, Bérenger narrates the waning of his transcendent vision, the passing of which left him with "a kind of chaotic vacuum inside me." He was "overcome with the immense sadness you feel at a moment of tragic and intolerable separation." Bérenger tells the Architect that the light must be in him too, because "you have obviously recreated and materialized it. This radiant district must have sprung from you."

Bérenger calls into the wings on the right, "Mademoiselle, oh, Mademoiselle, will you marry me?" Just then, the Architect's secretary, Dany, enters. She negotiates with the Architect about leaving her job, and every time she says, "Yes, Monsieur," to the Architect, Bérenger takes it as an answer to his latest proposal. As Bérenger continues making romantic overtures to Dany, speculating on the happy life they will live in the lovely flats of the radiant city, she tells the Architect, "I hate the Civil Service, I detest your beautiful district, I can't stand any more, I can't bear it!" Dany leaves, followed momentarily by Bérenger, still proposing his love to her.

Bérenger tells the Architect that he wants to buy the white house that looks abandoned. As the Architect checks his watch, a stone falls between them. Then there is the sound of windows breaking. The Architect confesses to Bérenger that construction has ceased on the radiant city, and that its citizens want to leave but have nowhere to go. He takes Bérenger to the ornamental pool, where three bodies float, a boy, a man, and a woman. Every day, the Architect tells Bérenger, three people are found drowned in the pool. People are afraid to go out, leave their homes only in groups of ten or fifteen, but still, the murders continue. Gunshots are heard and Bérenger is frightened, but the Architect tells Bérenger that he is safe with him, because the killer does not attack civil servants.

The Architect walks Bérenger outside the radiant city to the tram depot. Once they are outside the gates of the radiant city, it is cold and rainy. The Architect and Bérenger step into a bistro for a drink. Bérenger is upset about the dead bodies, and the Architect, who is also both a doctor and the district Superintendent, tries to calm him. A homeless man comes in, but the Owner hustles him out. The Architect tells Bérenger that the Killer impersonates a beggar, then tries to sell his mark a few small items. The mark refuses, and the Killer follows the person to the edge of the ornamental pool, where the Killer offers to show the victim a photo of the Colonel. The prospect is tantalizing, and as the victim leans in for a better look, the Killer pushes the victim into the pool, to drown. Despite word being out, victims keep falling for the Killer's ruse. As they are speaking, a cry is heard, followed by the splash of a body falling into the water. The Owner rushes in, saying that it is Dany, the former assistant to the Architect. Bérenger runs off, in search of the Killer, while the Architect and the Owner finish Bérenger's sandwich and glass of wine.

## Act 2

Act 2 opens in Bérenger's room. It is a dark, low-ceilinged space, and as the curtain rises, Édouard is sitting in an armchair in the darkness. While during the first act, the stage was deliberately bare, in act 2 the stage is cluttered with furniture. The voice of the Concierge is heard offstage, singing a nonsense song, and a Man's voice is heard greeting her. There is a lot of noise from the apartment building and surroundings. A second man is heard in the hallway, speaking with the Concierge and asking for a Miss Columbine. The Concierge runs him off, claiming there are no foreigners in her building. Two old men are heard outside speaking about the weather, while the Clochard from act 1 comes onstage, speaking with them. The Grocer is heard shouting, as is the Schoolmaster, who is lecturing about Marie Antoinette. More conversations are heard from outside the apartment, sometimes speaking over one another. Eventually the Postman arrives with a telegram for Bérenger, but no matter how the Concierge bashes on his door, he is not home. She agrees to take the telegram, just as Bérenger returns home.

He is startled to find Édouard in his room. Édouard has keys, which is a surprise to Bérenger. Édouard is ill, coughing and feverish,

and the building is so cold that neither of them takes off his overcoat. Bérenger is shattered with grief over the death of Dany, who he refers to as his fiancée. Bérenger tries to explain to Édouard that it is the nature of evil that is upsetting him so much. Through his illness, Édouard keeps checking the big lock on his briefcase. He suggests to Bérenger that they go out, since it is probably warmer outside than in, and as they are leaving the room, Édouard's briefcase falls open, spilling its contents, including a stack of photographs.

Bérenger picks up the stack of photos, then realizes that these are photographs of the Colonel, like the ones the Killer has been using to lure his victims. Bérenger looks further into the briefcase, which disgorges objects like a sort of magic bag: Édouard has artificial flowers, pen holders, sweets, money boxes, children's watches. A proliferation of small objects covers the table as Bérenger keeps pulling objects out of the briefcase. Bérenger realizes that these are the same objects that the Killer has been using to lure his victims. Édouard denies that the items belong to him. Bérenger cries out that these are "the monster's things!" Édouard produces a little box from his pocket, which contains a notebook in which the Killer documents his murders. Bérenger is astonished at his friend, saying, "So many human lives you could have saved." He keeps asking Édouard how the objects got in his briefcase, but Édouard says that he does not know, that he cannot explain. He claims that the murderer sent them to him, to publish in a literary journal, but it was before the murders were committed.

Bérenger says they must go to the police, and he hurries Édouard, wanting to get there before the precinct closes. Édouard becomes flustered and puts the briefcase down as Bérenger pulls him out of the room. They bump into the Concierge as they leave and apologize, but she can be heard complaining as they go down the stairs.

## Act 3

Act 3 opens on an outdoor scene. The stage is set as a street with a raised walkway and railing at the back and, in the foreground, a small bench. As the curtain rises, the audience hears shouts of "Long live Mother Peep's geese!" from an unseen crowd.

Mother Peep is on the raised stage, and like the others present, she carries a green flag with a goose in the middle. She appears to be played by the same actress as the Concierge. Mother Peep is making a speech, urging her followers to "trust me with the chariot of state, drawn by my geese, so I can legislate." She can be heard speaking all through Bérenger and Édouard's conversation in the foreground. Bérenger enters, hurrying Édouard along, wanting to get him to the Superintendent/Architect before he goes home for the day and before the Killer has a chance to strike again.

Édouard insists on sitting down to rest, and Bérenger comments on the resemblance between Mother Peep and his Concierge. Édouard tells him he is seeing things, that she is "a politician, Mother Peep, a keeper of geese. A striking personality." Meanwhile Mother Peep is making campaign promises of a bombastic nature, promising to change everything and nothing. As the two men get up off the bench, Bérenger notices that Édouard no longer has his briefcase. They look all over the stage for it while Mother Peep continues to speak in contradictions and the crowd cheers for her. Édouard is increasingly mesmerized by Mother Peep and her speeches, while Bérenger becomes more and more agitated about the missing briefcase.

A drunk and disheveled man wearing a top hat appears, holding a briefcase. Bérenger tackles him while Édouard watches. The drunken man has been saying that he is "for the hero," and Édouard asks him what he means. As Bérenger discovers that the drunken man's briefcase contains no notes or trinkets, only bottles of wine, the drunken man says, "A hero fights his own age and creates a different one." As the crowd continues to cheer for Mother Peep, the drunken man shouts, "Down with Mother Peep!"

An Old Man enters from stage right, carrying a large briefcase just like the one Édouard has misplaced. Bérenger, Édouard, and the Man all surround the Old Man, trying to get the briefcase from him, and a slapstick routine ensues in which the Old Man's briefcase and the Man's briefcase get confused. All the while, Mother Peep is campaigning in the background, making promises that cannot be kept and finally leading the crowd in a goose-step march. The goose step is most famous for being the style in which Hitler's Nazi troops marched, stiff-legged and stiff-armed. The Man tells Mother Peep that science and art have done more for humanity than politics have, and she denounces him to the crowd. The Man climbs the steps to Mother Peep's stage, while Édouard pleads with him not to be a hero. Having sought it all the while, Bérenger at last discovers that there is nothing in the Old Man's briefcase just as Mother Peep raises a huge briefcase and hits the Man over the head with it. The Man and Mother Peep struggle, and she calls on her geese to "rally round." As the struggle grinds to a close, the stage directions specify that "MOTHER PEEP's *head reappears alone, for the last time: it is hideous.*" Mother Peep disappears into the crowd of her "geese."

As Mother Peep's head appears for the last time, the engine of a truck drowns out the crowd, and the three characters onstage continue talking and making gestures. An enormously tall Policeman appears. He should be so tall that perhaps he is on stilts, and the audience can see only the top half of the figure towering over the wall that forms the backdrop of the scene. With a long white stick, he is seen tapping the invisible people on the other side of the raised walkway. As the First Policeman is moving the crowd along, a huge military truck comes from the left and blocks the stage. Another military truck comes from the right, leaving just enough room for the First Policeman in between them. A young Soldier gets out of the truck holding a bunch of red flowers, which he uses as a fan. He sits on the edge of the wall, with his legs dangling, and fans himself.

Bérenger tells Édouard to return home for the briefcase while he hurries to the Superintendent's. Édouard says he will hurry, but he moves offstage very slowly, dodging the Second Policeman. The Old Man has been trying to find directions to the banks of the Danube, which is a river that runs through Germany, not Paris. Bérenger has told him to ask the Policeman, but both policemen are frantically trying to move the crowd on the far side of the stage out of the way. Bérenger is frantic to get by, but he cannot, and he is confused because the policemen seem to have the same voice. The Old Man continues to ask directions to the Danube, and the policemen become agitated and begin shouting and blowing their whistles. They frighten the Old Man, while Bérenger keeps trying to reason with them. The policemen begin arguing with the soldiers who are blocking the road.

Bérenger tries to convince the police that he is an honorable man on an important mission to the Prefecture (or police station), that he has vital information about the Killer. Finally, the trucks move back, and the policemen urge him on. Both police disappear, leaving Bérenger alone on a stage that has suddenly become bare and dark. Bérenger is very much alone, and the stage presents his walk as lonely and ominous. Bérenger sets off still agitated by the outrageous behavior of the policemen. He walks along, commenting on how much farther it is than he thought, how the street seems as though it will never end, while musing on the state of humankind and how much better everything will be once he catches the Killer. He calls for Édouard, but the echo indicates that Édouard will not be coming. He turns after calling for Édouard and comes face to face with the Killer.

The Killer is small, dressed in shabby clothes, with his toes peeping out of his broken shoes. He is standing on the wall at the rear, or on the bench, and he laughs derisively as he approaches Bérenger. The stage has gone even more bare, giving the impression that they are alone on a vast plain. Bérenger comments on how small the Killer is and says he will not hurt him, because he wants answers.

The Killer never speaks; he only answers Bérenger's monologue with a series of chuckles and shrugs. Bérenger confronts the Killer with a series of ideas. First he posits that the Killer hates happiness itself, but when he asks the Killer what his vision of happiness is, the Killer just shrugs. He asks him about specific victims, what animus he could possibly have had against them, but again he is met with only a shrug. Bérenger proposes that the Killer is taking pity on his victims, putting them out of their misery. The Killer shrugs. Bérenger tells himself not to lose his temper, that it is important that he understand why the Killer does what he does. The Killer merely chuckles. Bérenger makes the religious argument that Christ died for them all, including the Killer, that he is not beyond redemption. But the Killer only chuckles. He asks whether the Killer wants money or work and becomes increasingly frustrated as he cannot find a reason for the Killer to kill. As he argues, Bérenger finds himself growing increasingly angry, shouting at the Killer about how he is an imbecile, how Bérenger will now kill him. The Killer simply plays with his knife. Bérenger

points a gun at the Killer but stalls, crying out, "How weak my strength is against your cold determination, your ruthlessness!" As the Killer remains motionless, Bérenger drops to his knees in despair, and the Killer approaches, knife raised. The stage goes dark.

## CHARACTERS

### Architect

The Architect is the one who designed the radiant city and who shows Bérenger its features. He is a civil servant. Working in the French civil service is very different from being a government employee in America. In France, the civil service is a lifetime appointment, and applicants are admitted only after taking a very competitive series of exams. It is considered one of the most secure and prestigious professions in France, a security that is reflected in the play by the fact that even the Killer does not attack civil servants. The Architect is not only the designer of the radiant city, but he is also the district Superintendent and occasionally practices medicine. He is harried, doing business even as he shows Bérenger the features of the radiant city, not only via a telephone in his pocket (an absurd proposition at the time the play was written) but also via an enormous briefcase that dwarfs the small café table at which he works.

### Bérenger

Bérenger is the protagonist of *The Killer*. He is a very ordinary middle-aged man who is described by Martin Esslin in his seminal *The Theatre of the Absurd* as "a Chaplinesque little man, simple, awkward, but human." He is genuinely enraptured by the features of the radiant city and is just as genuinely upset when he discovers that there is a murderer ravaging its citizens. Although he falls in love with Dany at first sight, which seems improbable, he appears to be absolutely sincere about his feelings. After she is killed, Bérenger vows to find the Killer. He returns home to his dark and depressing apartment, only to find his friend Édouard waiting for him there. Édouard has all the accoutrements of the Killer in his own large briefcase, but Bérenger never suspects him and considers the contents of the case evidence. In his haste to get the evidence to the Architect/Superintendent to prevent future deaths, Bérenger enters a nightmare scenario of trying to navigate through a fascist rally, a military rally, and a traffic jam. When these obstacles are finally overcome, he finds himself in a vast wasteland, at the mercy of the Killer. Although he tries to persuade the Killer to cease, each of his arguments falls on deaf ears, and faced with the Killer's indifference to all his moral arguments, Bérenger loses faith in all of them, concluding, "There's nothing we can do. What can we do . . ."

### Clochard

The Clochard is a drunken beggar who first appears at the end of act 1, where the bistro Owner throws him out for drinking without paying. In act 2, he appears again, singing a nonsense song underneath the windows on the street, hoping people will throw him coins. The Concierge runs him off. The French clochard is a typical character. He is usually a homeless person who begs just enough to get food for the day and, in particular, to get wine. The drunken clochard is a cliché of French tourism, usually pictured sleeping under a bridge along the Seine.

### Concierge

The Concierge is the caretaker of Bérenger's building. She appears at the beginning of act 2, where she can be heard outside in the corridor, complaining about and keeping tabs on the residents of the building. She grumbles about people who have education and about how everything is getting harder, generally speaking in clichés. She shouts at the Clochard and runs him off. When the Postman arrives with a telegram for Bérenger, she pounds on his door, but he is not home, and Édouard does not answer. She is puzzled that Bérenger is not in, since she never saw him go out, but she reluctantly agrees to keep the telegram for him. Many French buildings have a concierge, who usually has an apartment on the ground floor near the building entrance. In French culture, the cliché of the concierge is that she (for it is usually an older, unmarried or widowed woman) is a busybody, always sticking her nose into the affairs of the residents.

### Dany

Dany is the Architect's secretary, which makes her a civil servant also. She is young and beautiful, with blonde hair, and wants to quit her job. The Architect refuses to take her resignation over the phone, insisting that she come to see him in person. He warns her about leaving the

civil service, both because it is such a secure, lifelong job and because remaining in the civil service protects her from the Killer. Bérenger falls in love with her and refers to her for the rest of the play as his fiancée. Just after quitting her civil service job, Dany becomes another of the Killer's victims, and her drowned body is found in the ornamental pond. Bérenger pledges to avenge her death by finding the Killer.

### Drunk in Top Hat and Tails
See *Man*

### Édouard

Édouard is Bérenger's friend. Bérenger is surprised to find Édouard sitting in a chair in his room when he returns home. Édouard is dressed in heavy, dark clothing, which might be mourning clothes, and is clearly ill. He coughs repeatedly and appears to have a fever. His right arm is slightly withered. He carries an enormous briefcase, which he holds close to himself the whole time that Bérenger tells him about the Killer. Bérenger's apartment is freezing cold, so the two men decide to go out for a walk and get some fresh air. As they are leaving, Édouard's briefcase falls open, revealing photographs of the Colonel, just like those the Killer uses to lure his victims. There are also small knickknacks of the sort that the Killer attempts to sell to his victims. As Bérenger pulls objects from the briefcase, it seems to be bottomless. Édouard denies any knowledge of how the objects got in the briefcase. When Bérenger finds visiting cards (a type of business card) with the Killer's name and address, as well as the Killer's address book and identity card and a box containing a notebook recording the dates and details of each death, Édouard claims, "I didn't know. I never know what I've got in my briefcase. I never look inside." When Bérenger persuades Édouard to go to the police with him, Édouard leaves the briefcase behind. He does not share Bérenger's urgency about the matter and dawdles at every opportunity. First he becomes mesmerized by Mother Peep; then, when they finally figure out that the briefcase must have been left behind, Édouard leaves to go fetch it with distinct indifference. Whether Édouard is the Killer or not is never made entirely clear.

### First Policeman and Second Policeman
The two policemen are each extraordinarily tall, perhaps played by actors on stilts. They first appear in order to move Mother Peep's mob

offstage just as the military trucks and the Soldier appear, blocking the street upstage. The policemen then become very agitated trying to control a traffic jam through the bottleneck, shouting indiscriminately at those left onstage as well as the imaginary people and vehicles blocking the road. Bérenger becomes increasingly agitated by their rudeness to the Old Man.

### Killer

The Killer turns out to be a short, slight person, perhaps a dwarf, with one eye that glitters in the stage lights. He appears toward the end of act 3, and throughout Bérenger's monologue he never speaks, simply chuckling once in a while. It is his silence that seems to drive Bérenger nearly to madness. Bérenger runs through all the arguments against murder that he can think of, but as the Killer remains unmoved, he undermines Bérenger's sense of surety about his own moral compass. In this way the Killer drives Bérenger to kneel before him, offering himself to the knife. While the Killer does not kill Bérenger in view of the audience, the implication is that he does so.

### Man

Designated simply as Man within the text, the Drunk in Top Hat and Tails is the chief voice who speaks up to challenge Mother Peep's demagoguery. Although he is very drunk, he is one of the only voices who speaks for reason, challenging Mother Peep and arguing for heroism. "A hero fights his own age and creates a different one," the Man notes. He confronts Mother Peep while forcing Édouard to drink wine. As he pours wine down Édouard's throat, he makes a speech about how progress comes not from politics, but from the arts and sciences. Mother Peep denounces him and sets her followers on him. The Man disappears into the mob, after which Mother Peep appears one more time to boast that her "geese have liquidated him."

### Mother Peep

Mother Peep is a demagogue, a politician who seeks support by appealing to the emotions and prejudices of a crowd, not by rational argument. She bears a striking resemblance to the Concierge and is played by the same actress. She is the keeper of the public geese. Because geese imprint at birth on a parental figure and follow that figure with great fidelity, they are considered a symbol of mindless or blind political allegiance. Mother Peep's name also harks back to nursery

rhymes, as it is a sort of mash-up of Mother Goose and Little Bo Peep. However, despite all the domestic connotations of her name, she is a satirical example of a fascist leader. Her speech is full of doublespeak, she encourages her followers to march in goose step, and, when challenged, she eggs them on until they "liquidate" the Drunk in Top Hat and Tails.

### Old Gentleman with the Little White Beard

See *Old Man*

### Old Man

Referred to in the text simply as the Old Man, the Old Gentleman with the Little White Beard appears with an umbrella and a large briefcase while Mother Peep is in the middle of her rally. Bérenger is desperate to see the contents of the Old Man's briefcase. The Old Man does not want to show them to Bérenger, and they struggle. The Old Man keeps asking for directions to the banks of the Danube. The Danube is a river in Germany, while the Seine is the river that runs through Paris. The Old Man claims to be a native Parisian, and yet he continues to ask directions to the Danube, not only of Bérenger but also of the two policemen. The policemen become impatient with the Old Man, and they frighten him. This enrages Bérenger, who insists that policemen are obligated to be polite to the public.

### Owner of the Bistro

The Owner of the Bistro greets the Architect/Superintendent and Bérenger warmly when they stop for a drink, but he is distracted by the Clochard, who is drunk and whom he throws out of his establishment. The Owner serves Bérenger and the Architect a glass of wine and a sandwich, but when he tells them it is Dany who has been killed, Bérenger runs off. The Architect tells the Owner to finish Bérenger's sandwich and glass of wine, and act 2 ends with the two men eating and drinking together.

### Soldier

The young Soldier arrives in one of the military trucks. He carries a bunch of red carnations, which he waves like a fan. He perches on the top of the wall at the back of the stage, his legs dangling over the ledge, in a posture that is not very military. He is entirely ineffectual in the face of the hostility exhibited by the two policemen, who eventually strip him of his flowers and slap him across the face before driving him back into his vehicle.

## Superintendent
See *Architect*

## Voices
There are a number of voices listed as parts, although Ionesco, in the opening stage directions, notes that these voices can be cut if time requires it. Further, he notes that "the director can choose those he likes," and their use "will all depend on the effectiveness of these voices and their absurd remarks." Ionesco further notes that the voices should be represented by "the greatest possible number of figures appearing in silhouette the other side of the window, as on a stage behind the stage."

# THEMES

## Existentialism
Existentialism is a set of literary and philosophical ideas that came to prominence in France in the years after World War II and which grew out of work by Albert Camus, Simone de Beauvoir, and Jean-Paul Sartre. The central idea is that the path to human freedom lies in freeing oneself from abstract universal ideas about what constitutes "the human condition." The thinkers who formulated existentialism were largely atheistic, but ethics were crucial to the project. They each stressed that it is the responsibility of the authentic human being acting with knowledge of one's existential dilemma to work for the collective good of one's fellow beings. Camus dramatized the plight of the existential hero in novels like *The Stranger* (1942) and *The Plague* (1947), where his protagonists are challenged to act with lucidity and take personal responsibility rather than fall back on the easy self-deception that Camus felt characterizes most human interactions. Simone de Beauvoir, in *The Ethics of Ambiguity* (1947) and *The Second Sex* (1949), attempted to frame an ethics of existentialism recognizing that radical human freedom entails a rejection of all socially constructed modes of being that are not authentic. Her work on the social construction of femininity in *The Second Sex* has made it a foundational text for modern feminist theory.

Jean-Paul Sartre's *Being and Nothingness* (1943) is perhaps the central philosophical text of the existential movement, attempting to reconcile the ontological conflict between existence, or being, and nothingness, which Sartre theorized as a type of freedom. In the wake of the atrocities of World War II, the existentialists were adamant that an authentic existence free from the constraints of society is worth pursuing because it allows one not only to take personal responsibility for one's own actions but also to act in a free manner for the good of society.

## Absurdity
It is Camus, in *The Myth of Sisyphus* (1942), who makes the distinction between the existential and the absurd. He links the absurdists to the Greek myth of Sisyphus, who was condemned by the gods to roll a big rock up a hill for eternity, a rock that would break loose just before the summit and roll back to the bottom, forcing him to begin again. For Camus this epitomized the absurdity of human life, as it is a project that can never be mastered and yet from which one cannot retire. For Camus, existential absurdity lies in what he sees as an inevitable gap between human reason and the effect of acting upon that reason. Esslin expounds on this notion in *The Theater of the Absurd*, where he explains, "'Absurd' originally means 'out of harmony,' in a musical context.... In common usage, 'absurd' may simply mean 'ridiculous,' but this is not the sense in which Camus uses the word." Esslin notes that Ionesco defines his own understanding of the term, in an essay on Kafka, as "that which is devoid of purpose.... Cut off from his religious, metaphysical, and transcendental roots, man is lost; all his actions become senseless, absurd, useless." For both Camus and Ionesco, the absurd is a state of metaphysical anguish.

This state of metaphysical anguish is not a subject for argument in the plays of Ionesco. Playwrights of this group were not interested in convincing an audience that the condition of human life is absurd, but rather they were interested in presenting and dramatizing the absurdity itself. Esslin notes, "It is this striving for an integration between the subject-matter and the form in which it is expressed that separates the Theatre of the Absurd from the Existentialist theatre."

# TOPICS FOR FURTHER STUDY

- In a radio interview broadcast on the BBC, as mentioned in a London *Telegraph* article, Terry Jones noted that the Monty Python troupe was influenced by the theater of the absurd: "'The absurdists were trying to do something that would shock, to stir their audience up to think in a different kind of way,' he says.... The Theatre of the Absurd valued incongruity above plot or character. It is not that much of a leap to an animated foot trampling on the screen or the fish-slapping dance." Research Monty Python sketches and, using YouTube, or another streaming service, choose one that seems particularly absurd to you. Watch it and try to classify three elements that make it absurd. Write up your definitions of those absurdities and then, with two or three classmates, write a new sketch using the same techniques. Perform it for your class.

- What is theater of the absurd? Research the avant-garde movement and prepare a presentation explaining general principles of this segment of theater history. Choose three playwrights who fit into this movement and summarize their work and why it is characteristic of the theater of the absurd. For each playwright, summarize one of their major works that fits into this rubric. Your presentation should include clips from theater productions, visual aids such as reproductions of theater posters, and quotes from directors and actors.

- Existential ideas like those that motivated Ionesco also motivated novelists of the era. Read Kurt Vonnegut's novel *Slaughterhouse-Five* (1969). World War II left many writers feeling that there is no purpose to life and that all action is futile. Compare the ways in which Vonnegut and Ionesco dramatize the futility of individual action in the face of the forces of evil. Write a paper comparing the two works and discuss how each addresses the question of the role of the individual in society.

- In *Under the Domim Tree* (1992), author Gila Almagor draws on her experiences as a girl to compose a portrait of an Israeli "youth village." In 1953, most of the teenagers living in Udim have lost one or both of their parents in the Holocaust, although many of them live with the hope that their lost parents are not dead and will come to find them. Where writers like Ionesco took from the experience of World War II that there is no meaning in life, these young people are busy trying to make sense of their own experiences and find the strength to move forward. In what ways do characters in this novel resemble those in *The Killer*, and in what ways are they different? Write a one-act play in which the characters in *Under the Domim Tree* find themselves confronted by the obstacles that frustrate Bérenger. Act it out for your classmates.

- *Waiting for Godot* (1953), by Samuel Beckett, is one of the key plays of the absurdist movement. Divide your class into groups and assign each group a separate section of the play. As a class, prepare to perform the whole play. Afterwards, each group should explain what they think their section of the play means and how it compares to *The Killer*.

---

In conversation with Claude Bonnefoy, Ionesco said,

The "absurd" is a very vague notion.... It is born of the conflict between my will and a universal will; it is also born of the conflict within me between me and myself, between my different wills, my contradictory impulses.

He continued, explaining that the central and eternal conflicts of life are inherently absurd, without logic, incapable of dialectical reconciliation:

*The protagonist, everyman Bérenger, appears in several of Ionesco's plays* *(© Ollyy | Shutterstock.com)*

*I have within me a movement both towards death and towards life. Eros and thanatos, love and hatred, love and destruction, it's a sufficiently violent antithesis isn't it, to give me a feeling of "absurdity."*

## Transcendence

The set directions for the opening of *The Killer* specify that the gray stage lighting should give way to "*a very bright, very white light; just this whiteness, and also the dense vivid blue of the sky,*" adding that "*the blue, the white, the silence and the empty stage should give a strange impression of peace. The audience must be given time to become aware of this.*" This moment of radiant light is key to the play, for it represents an experience of transcendence that happened to Ionesco as a teenager, the memory of which never left him. He described it in speaking with Bonnefoy,

I was about seventeen or eighteen. I was in a provincial town. It was in June, around

mid-day.... It seemed to me that the sky had become extremely dense, that the light was almost palpable, that the houses had a brightness I had never seen before, an unaccustomed brightness, free from the weight of custom.

This experience of joy lasted only for a few moments, but Ionesco described reliving it over and over, as a talisman in his memory. Ionesco told Bonnefoy explicitly that the city of light, the radiant city, of *The Killer* is based on this experience. He told Bonnefoy,

A lot of people have misunderstood *The Killer*. In the first act, Bérenger enters a radiant city. In a world that has been disfigured, he discovers a world transformed; he regains paradise after leaving the rainy town, after leaving the world of limbo.

Bonnefoy pressed him on this point, since the radiant city is terrorized by the Killer, who seemingly cannot be stopped. The paradise that Ionesco proposes is unsafe and broken. To this,

Ionesco replied, "Yes, it's the fall, it's original sin, . . . it's losing the faculty of wonderment." The dream of a world without pain, a world where sorrow and death are banished, is one of the oldest dreams of human existence, and some form of a transcendent world appears in the origin myth of nearly every religious tradition. Ionesco's play enacts the eternal story of the paradisical world infected by the force of unreasonable evil.

## STYLE

### Setting

Theater of the absurd often uses nonrealistic sets to foreground the artificial nature of the theater itself, as well as to underscore that authenticity comes not from verisimilitude and received ideas, but from one's own attempts to make sense of the nonsensical. Ionesco's *The Killer* opens on a bare stage and relies on specific visual effects to set the scene. The stage begins with dull gray lighting that implies a rainy day in fall or early spring, and then quite suddenly the lights change to "*a very bright, very white light; just this whiteness, and also the dense vivid blue of the sky.*" This lighting effect, in combination with the summery costume of the Architect and the small garden table with two chairs, constitutes the only indication that the radiant city is a place of eternal summer. Throughout act 1, the set remains bare as the Architect describes the features of the radiant city and as Bérenger exclaims over its beauty, its convenience, and how it is a place where every human comfort has been taken into account. The audience is forced to imagine the wonders of the radiant city, which are never presented to them in a realistic manner.

Act 2 opens on a more realistic set, the interior of Bérenger's apartment, with the stage directions specifying, "The decor of Act II is very much constructed, heavy, realistic and ugly; it contrasts strongly with the lack of decor and the simple lighting effects of Act I." Where the emptiness of act 1 invited the audience to construct a vision of paradise in their own minds, the realistic set of act 2 underscores the manner in which so-called realism can shut down the imagination and be an oppressive force, one that imposes preconceived ideas upon the imagination. The oppressive realism of the set decoration reinforces the difficulty Bérenger faces as he

attempts to interpret the meaning of the occurrences before him—Édouard's presence in his room, which he left locked, and the presence of the Killer's tools of the trade in Édouard's briefcase. Bérenger, being a person of good faith, does not suspect his friend, although the audience perhaps does.

If act 1 represents one pole of set design with its bare stage and act 2 represents the other with its oppressive realism, act 3 falls somewhere in between. The set represents one "*of the old streets of Paris, such as the Rue Jean de Beauvais.*" There is a wall at the back of the stage with a railing and a set of stone steps, and there is a bench in the foreground, but these elements are almost archetypal in their design. They could be any narrow street in an old city. As in the two other acts of the play, the set design in this act, with its mixture of realistic and symbolic elements, underscores the mixture of nightmarish and realistic actions.

### Dialogue

Dialogue in absurdist theater reflects a decay in the denotative function of language, expressing the authors' belief that the communicative function of speech has broken down. In conversation with Bonnefoy, Ionesco noted that one factor that distinguishes theater of the absurd from the ordinary theater of entertainment is that theater of the absurd takes as its central task "the problem of the human condition or of its ultimate purpose." The sort of theater that Ionesco is interested in is one that portrays "a very naked reality that is conveyed through the apparent dislocation of language." One sees this in action throughout *The Killer*. Although the first act begins with rather conventional dialogue of a transactional nature, as the Architect shows off the features of the radiant city and Bérenger admires them, it begins to dislocate, as Ionesco might say, when the Architect pulls the telephone from his pocket and starts carrying on two simultaneous conversations. While in modern days of cell phones this is a common occurrence, in the 1950s the prospect was at once absurd, inconceivable, and evidence of the breakdown of polite manners. While act 1 is notable for the sincere communication between the Architect and Bérenger while they are in the radiant city, that sincerity breaks down as soon as they leave it. In the bistro, the Architect becomes cynical and sarcastic, in contrast to his harried but sincere posture in the radiant city, while Bérenger, by contrast, remains constant in his sincerity, suffering real heartbreak when he learns that Dany has been murdered.

In act 2, the communicative function of the dialogue continues to fray. The act begins with several pages of cacophony as voices from the street mingle with the Concierge's gossip and complaints. Through it all, Édouard can be seen sitting motionless in the armchair, responding to none of the language that swirls around him. Once Bérenger arrives, the communicative function of conversation begins to slowly erode as he and Édouard talk over and past one another, escalating to the discovery of the Killer's accoutrements inside Édouard's briefcase. Édouard claims ignorance of them, including how they got there and what they are, and Bérenger never seems to suspect his friend of being the Killer.

In act 3, the breakdown of language continues. Mother Peep is a demagogue who speaks in empty slogans and contradictory clichés. Her language is useful only as a tool to whip her followers into a violent frenzy. The two policemen seem unable to direct anyone effectively, flailing around with their sticks, shouting at both Bérenger and the Old Man. And finally, Bérenger's inability to use language and reason to get through to the Killer, a character who does not speak at all, but merely chuckles, is the play's clearest indictment of the breakdown of language. Ionesco does not play this breakdown as comedy, although the play is very funny at times, but rather as a tragedy, one that ends in Bérenger's death at the hands of the Killer.

## HISTORICAL CONTEXT

### Intellectual Culture in Postwar France

France in the 1950s was a nation still reeling from war. World War II ended in 1945, having come a mere two decades after the devastating loss of life of World War I. World War II was one of the most deadly conflicts in human history, with high death tolls for civilians, combatants, and, of course, the six million Jews who were murdered in the camps. Those who survived the war were scarred not only by nearly a decade of terror and death but also by the experience of seeing neighbor turn on neighbor as Jews were rounded up and deported from those countries conquered by the Nazi regime. In France, the German defeat of the French forces in 1940 was experienced as a national humiliation, and the near triumph of fascism left intellectuals convinced that art must continue to engage with politics, even in the face of a world that seemed chaotic and meaningless.

The events of the first half of the twentieth century left writers like Ionesco convinced, as Martin Esslin outlines in his seminal book *The Theatre of the Absurd*, "that the certitudes and unshakable basic assumptions of former ages have been swept away, that they have been tested and found wanting, that they have been discredited as cheap and somewhat childish illusions." The destruction of these illusions, along with the decline of religious faith—which Esslin claims "was masked until the end of the Second World War by the substitute religions of faith in progress, nationalism, and various totalitarian fallacies"—left postwar writers like Ionesco with the sense that there was no certainty, and indeed no meaning at all. For Ionesco these experiences engendered a deep skepticism toward ideology, especially any ideology that became fashionable, because he had seen the way ideologies led seemingly reasonable people into conflict not just with their own neighbors at home but also across all of Europe.

Ionesco spent most of the 1930s in Romania, where he was a high-school and university student, and he has described the effect of watching the nation descend into fascism in an interview with Claude Bonnefoy:

> I had made a certain number of friends. And a lot of them—I'm talking about 1932, 1933, 1934, 1935—turned to Fascism. . . . There were a certain number of us who didn't want to accept the slogans and the ideologies that were thrust at us. It was very difficult to resist, . . . when you have newspapers, when you have a whole atmosphere, doctrines, a whole movement against you, it's really very hard to resist, hard not to let yourself be convinced.

This experience, as well as his postwar experience of watching his home country disappear behind the "Iron Curtain" with the establishment in 1948 of the People's Republic of Romania, a Stalinist state, all persuaded Ionesco to be, as he told Bonnefoy in the same interview, "suspicious of collective truths. I think an idea is true when it hasn't been put into words and that the moment it's put into words it becomes exaggerated."

# COMPARE
# &
# CONTRAST

- **1950s:** Samuel Beckett's *Waiting for Godot* is first performed on January 5, 1953, at the Théâtre de Babylone in Paris and has its English-language debut in London in 1955. Considered a foundational text of the absurdist theater, the play revolves around two characters named Estragon and Vladimir, who await in vain the arrival of someone named Godot. Despite its avant-garde credentials, the play speaks to audiences of all natures, as is demonstrated when the San Francisco Actor's Workshop presents it at San Quentin Prison in 1957.

  **Today:** While the play is still performed regularly, *Waiting for Godot* has settled so completely into popular culture that the phrase "Waiting for..." has been adapted in such diverse formats as the *Doonesbury* comic strip, *Sesame Street*, and the *Late Show with Stephen Colbert*. It has become shorthand for the comi-tragic hope that somehow our dreams will not be dashed, that the longed-for objects of our desires will be attained.

- **1950s:** Albert Camus is awarded the Nobel Prize for Literature in 1957. Camus, who was born in Algeria when it was a French colony, is one of the key writers developing the concept of the absurd in the mid-twentieth century. His philosophical treatise *The Myth of Sisyphus* questions whether life has meaning and, if it does not, asks whether the logical response is suicide. Although *The Myth of Sisyphus* was published in 1942, it is a key text for the playwrights of the theater of the absurd and has enormous impact during the 1950s.

  **Today:** Although existentialism, which was one of the biggest influences on the theater of the absurd, has largely been replaced by postmodernism as a philosophical mode, Camus remains a central figure to any reader or scholar interested in the intellectual history of the twentieth century. His work on the nature of freedom is as relevant as ever, and his novels *The Stranger* and *The Plague* remain cornerstones of the genre.

- **1950s:** Harold Pinter's play *The Birthday Party* premieres in London's West End in 1958. While it closes after only eight performances, it is enthusiastically reviewed and marks the beginning of his long career in the theater. While the English and French dramatic traditions are quite different, Pinter is often considered an heir to the absurdist tradition, especially in his early plays, which rely on misapprehension and seemingly inexplicable behavior by the characters. He strikes up a friendship with Samuel Beckett that lasts until Beckett's death.

  **Today:** Despite its initial failure, *The Birthday Party* has become one of Pinter's most-produced plays. His career as an actor, playwright, screenwriter, and director lasted for nearly fifty years. His career as a playwright spanned twenty-nine plays and spawned the adjective "Pinteresque" to describe his style, the hallmarks of which include the ways in which ordinary situations can become menacing, the slipperiness of memory, and the difficulty of truly communicating with another person.

---

The intellectual scene in Paris in the 1950s was a heady one. The city was known for its public intellectuals, people like Jean-Paul Sartre and Simone de Beauvoir, Albert Camus, Samuel Beckett, Jean Anouilh, and Jean Genet. The situation they were all attempting to address was, as Esslin describes, a "sense of the senselessness of life, of the inevitable devaluation of ideals, purity, and purpose."

Esslin points out that writers like Sartre, de Beauvoir, Camus, and Anouilh, who came to be known as the existentialists, approached this

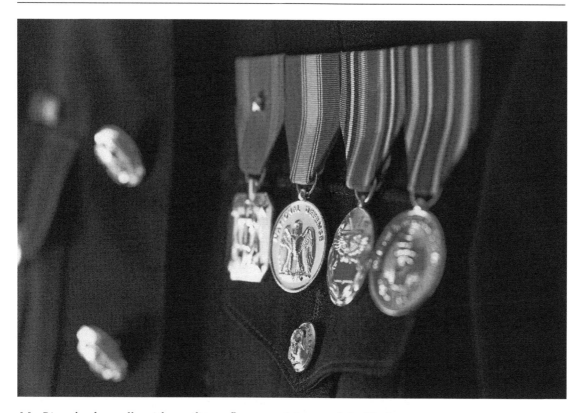

*Ma Piper leads a rally with a military flavor reminiscent of the Nazis (© JGGRMSON | Shutterstock.com)*

quandary by presenting "their sense of the irrationality of the human condition in the form of highly lucid and logically constructed reasoning." Those writers who came to be associated with the theater of the absurd, including Ionesco, Beckett, and Pinter, found that the only logical response to the illogic of existence was "the open abandonment of rational devices and discursive thought." In fiction, this time period saw the development of the *nouveau roman*, which challenged the traditional elements of the novel, much as the theater of the absurd challenged the traditional elements of the play. Some writers, like Samuel Beckett, worked in both genres, theater and fiction, and the undertakings in one often influenced the other. Writers experimented with such seemingly timeless elements of storytelling, whether on the page or on the stage, as chronology, narrative consciousness, and dialogue expressing the impossibility of communication.

The postwar period was crucial to the development of much modern philosophy, theater, and literature that followed, and the effects of the experimental work these writers did can be seen in modern movements like structuralism, poststructuralism, and postmodernism.

## CRITICAL OVERVIEW

Ionesco's play *The Killer* was first performed in Paris at the Théâtre Récamier in February 1959. While original reviews are difficult to find after all these years, Claude Bonnefoy includes quotations from the French press in his book *Conversations with Eugène Ionesco*. Robert Kemp of *Le Monde* felt that it is "a very cumbersome play, too cumbersome for the light-weight truths it bears. And for the spectator, however well-disposed, it is a crushing ordeal." But other critics were far more positive, even effusive. André Alter, writing in *Témoignage Chrétien*, found that "the world of the nightmare, which has never been suggested so convincingly, at last allows one to glimpse the possibility of an awakened world." In *Combat*, Marcelle Capron declared,

> *The Killer* seems to me the most important of Ionesco's plays ... because it deals with the most enormous subject there is, the one that contains all subjects: man in the presence of evil, fighting against evil—an evil which can take on any face, any form, even that of indifference, which is possibly the most demoralizing of all.

And Elsa Triolet, writing in *Les Lettres Françaises*, claimed that the play signaled the birth of an archetype: "What has just taken place at the Théâtre Récamier is the birth of a human type who should take his place in our language like a Panurge, a Don Quixote, a Pickwick, a Prudhomme."

Within a year the play had moved to New York, where it opened at the Seven Arts theater in 1960. It was reviewed in the *New York Times* by Brooks Atkinson, who praised Hiram Sherman for his portrayal of Bérenger, who "is not only a delight in this part of the play but also a droll representative of goodwill and credulity." Of the actor Louis Edmonds, who played the Architect, Atkinson said he "provides vivid contrast as the bloodlessly efficient civil servant who is capable of everything except serving human beings." Atkinson describes the first act as a "satire on the impotence of a technological civilization," while the second act "represents the muddle and squalor of life in an ordinary city," although he finds the final act "pretentious" and "prolix."

*The Killer* is the first of the series of plays in which Bérenger appears as a character, and it was the next play, *Rhinoceros*, that, as Mel Gussow notes in Ionesco's obituary in the *New York Times*, "proved to be his breakthrough play, enriched by Zero Mostel's virtuosic performance." As a result, *Rhinoceros* has tended to overshadow *The Killer*.

*The Killer* was not staged again in New York until 2014 at the Theatre for a New Audience. Directed by Darko Tresnjak, with a new English translation by Michael Feingold, the performance starred Michael Shannon as Bérenger, Robert Stanton as the Architect, and Kristine Nielsen as the Concierge/Mother Peeps. The performance received mixed reviews. Christopher Isherwood, writing in the *New York Times* said, "There are little-known plays by well-known writers that, when once viewed, strike you as being unjustly, even criminally neglected. Eugène Ionesco's 'The Killer' is not one of them." David Cote, at *Time Out New York*, was more enthusiastic, writing,

> Director Darko Tresnjak pulls out every stop for this bravura staging—amplified by Jane Shaw's dense sound design and buttressed by Michael Feingold's witty, musical translation. It's a dream cast (including Kristine Nielsen as a mouthy landlady), and you can feel their relish in wrestling with digging up the body.

Frank Scheck, in turn, writing for *Hollywood Reporter*, seems to agree with Isherwood:

> It's easy to see why the play has lapsed into relative obscurity. Despite its potent themes of the meaninglessness of life and the inevitability of death, it's a digressive, relentlessly talky affair that often feels like a slog during the course of its three-hour running time.

# CRITICISM

## *Charlotte M. Freeman*

*Freeman is a writer and editor who lives in Montana. In the following essay, she examines how absurdism differs from comedy in Ionesco's play* The Killer.

In common parlance the term *absurd* is understood to mean "comical," but this is not the way in which Ionesco and the other writers of the theater of the absurd used it. While in ordinary conversation one might use *absurd* as a synonym for *ridiculous* or to describe a comedic situation, Martin Esslin, in his seminal book *The Theatre of the Absurd*, published in 1961, notes that it refers to a form of theater that is essentially tragic. Esslin coined the term *theater of the absurd* and originally applied it to the work of Samuel Beckett, Arthur Adamov, Ionesco, Jean Genet, and Harold Pinter. He was careful to point out, however, that they "do not form part of any self-proclaimed or self-conscious school or movement." They were working separately when he saw what he felt to be considerable similarity in their work and set out to identify and document it. Esslin begins his discussion of absurdity as these writers practiced it by noting that the term comes from music theory, originally meaning "out of harmony" or "incongruous." He continues by explaining that he is using the term *absurd* in the way that Camus does in his groundbreaking philosophical work *The Myth of Sisyphus*. It is here that Camus describes a world in which reasoning no longer explains our situation, in which a man is

> deprived of memories of a lost homeland as much as he lacks the hope of a promised land to come. This divorce between man and his life...truly constitutes the feeling of Absurdity.

So while the theater of the absurd avails itself of many of the tools of comedy—mistaken identity, dialogue in which communication goes awry, even clowning and slapstick—it is in the service of a vision that is essentially tragic. In the wake of the horrors of World War II, writers like Ionesco felt that all the frameworks of meaning that human beings had previously used to guide their lives had been shown to be false. Religious faith had neither saved the six million from the death camps nor prevented ordinary German citizens from being persuaded to build and staff them and to denounce their Jewish neighbors. Philosophy and metaphysics had been shown to be useless against a rising tide of fascism that swept across Europe, and ethical arguments had not convinced any of the demagogues of the sort Ionesco satirizes in the form of Mother Peep from ceasing in their will to power. Esslin quotes Ionesco, writing in an essay on Kafka: "Absurd is that which is devoid of purpose.... Cut off from his religious, metaphysical, and transcendental roots, man is lost; all his actions become senseless, absurd, useless."

It is difficult to overstate the importance of the stage directions at the opening of act 1 to the artistic project of *The Killer*. Ionesco specifies that the stage should go quite suddenly from the gray light of an ordinary day in November or February to a "very bright, very white light; just this whiteness, and also the dense vivid blue of the sky." This lighting effect "should give a strange impression of peace. The audience must be given time to become aware of this." This radiant light was, for Ionesco the entire point of the play. When asked by Claude Bonnefoy in one of the interviews collected in *Conversations with Eugène Ionesco* if "you personally have ever been overwhelmed by a sense of light," Ionesco replied, "Yes. Once. And I've described it.... In *The Killer*. But nobody could understand what the radiant city mentioned in the play was. It's light, the city of light."

For Ionesco, light was a powerful symbol of transcendence, one that he carried all his life after an experience in his teenage years. As he told Bonnefoy, "It was in June, around mid-day. I was walking down one of the streets in this very quiet town. Suddenly it seemed to me...that I was in another world." He felt that the world had become brighter and more radiant, and as he told Bonnefoy, "It's very difficult to define it; perhaps the easiest thing to say is that I felt an enormous joy." The experience did not last long, but it stayed with Ionesco, and left him with a feeling that at any moment the ordinary things of the world could be illuminated with a transfiguring joy. He told Bonnefoy of another experience of the same type, when his daughter was a baby and they lived in a tiny apartment. They had strung her diapers (in those days there were only cloth diapers that needed to be washed) on a line across the apartment to dry. A friend had arrived and was moaning about how depressing life is, and Ionesco disagreed with him. He had an experience much like Bérenger in the radiant city, in which "everything is miraculous, everything is a glorious epiphany, the tiniest object looks resplendent." He tried to explain it to his friend and then later to Bonnefoy: "It had suddenly seemed to me that those nappies on the washing line had an unexpected beauty."

In light of these statements, it is important that we take Bérenger's joy in act 1 of *The Killer* as genuine. Esslin describes Bérenger as "a Chaplinesque little man, simple, awkward, but human." He is utterly sincere in his praise of the radiant city, and even in his instantaneous love for Mademoiselle Dany. In modern times it might be tempting to play Bérenger in an ironic way, as though his joy is somehow evidence that the radiant city is not as splendid as it seems, but this would be a mistake. As Ionesco explained to Bonnefoy, Bérenger "is amazed at his existence, at being in the world; and he finds this extraordinary and marvellous." Ionesco refers to this state as "the fundamental attitude," a phrase he uses to describe the state of oneness with all things that he experienced that day in the village in the south of France and at the sight of his daughter's nappies drying on the line. It is a state that can never be maintained for very long: "But later, this wondrous world falls apart, disintegrates. There's the problem of hatred, the problem of death, etc." The theater of the absurd uses comic devices—like the telephone in the Architect's pocket, and the demagogic excesses of Mother

# WHAT DO I READ NEXT?

- *Sarah's Key* (2006), by Tatiana de Rosnay—originally published in French as *Elle s'appelait Sarah*—dramatizes the sort of inhumane behavior during World War II that caused writers like Ionesco to lose faith that life has meaning. The novel follows two entwined plots. One is the story of Sara Starzynski, a young Jewish girl whose family is arrested by the Nazis in 1942 and held in the Vélodrome d'Hiver, the cycling stadium outside of Paris. As they were being arrested, Sarah locked her four-year-old brother in a cupboard to save him, thinking they'd be back in a few hours. The story of Sarah trying to get back to Paris to save her brother is intertwined with the story of modern American journalist Julia Jarmond, who has been assigned to write a story on the anniversary of the Vélodrome d'Hiver roundup, which has become a shameful moment in French history. The novel explores the manner in which the atrocities of World War II had repercussions down through subsequent generations.

- While Ionesco's plays are concerned with the effects of fascism and totalitarianism in Europe, these political scourges have affected nations around the world. Moying Li was only twelve years old when the Cultural Revolution swept across China. In *Snow Falling in Spring: Coming of Age in China during the Cultural Revolution* (2010), written for a young-adult audience, she tells the story of that traumatic time. Li takes refuge in books, but in a nation where all reading not specifically sanctioned by the party has been banned, even this activity puts her in danger.

- *Rhinoceros and Other Plays* (1994), translated by Derek Prouse, collects four Ionesco plays in a single volume, including his most famous play, *Rhinoceros*, in which the animal mysteriously appears in a small French village. Before long there are two rhinos and then three, as the citizens of the town are being transformed. This volume also contains the plays *The Leader, The Future Is in Eggs*, and *It Takes All Sorts to Make a World*.

- *Monty Python's Flying Circus: Complete and Annotated... All the Bits* (2012), by Luke Dempsey, compiles the scripts from every episode of the groundbreaking television show broadcast by the BBC from 1969 to 1974. Heavily influenced by the theater of the absurd, this troupe of actors who met at Cambridge University went on to create one of the most delightfully rude absurdist series ever broadcast on television. The collection contains annotations for the comedic references, photographs, and reminiscences by the actors, providing a good example of absurdism in action.

- Bertolt Brecht was one of the leaders of the avant-garde theater movement of the twentieth century. *Brecht on Theatre: The Development of an Aesthetic* (1964), edited and translated from the German by John Willett, collects his major essays written between 1918 and 1956. In these, Brecht discusses what he called "epic theatre" as well as his theory of how to induce alienation through directing, acting, and writing. The collection explores classic Brecht works such as *The Threepenny Opera, The Little Mahagonny, Mother Courage and Her Children, Mr Puntila and His Man Matti*, and *Life of Galileo*.

- Samuel Beckett was not only a key playwright of the absurdist school but a novelist as well. *Three Novels: Molloy, Malone Dies, The Unnamable* (1958) collects three of his fiction works in a single volume. Known collectively as "The Trilogy" these three are not only Beckett's greatest works of fiction but also keystone novels of the twentieth-century experimental tradition.

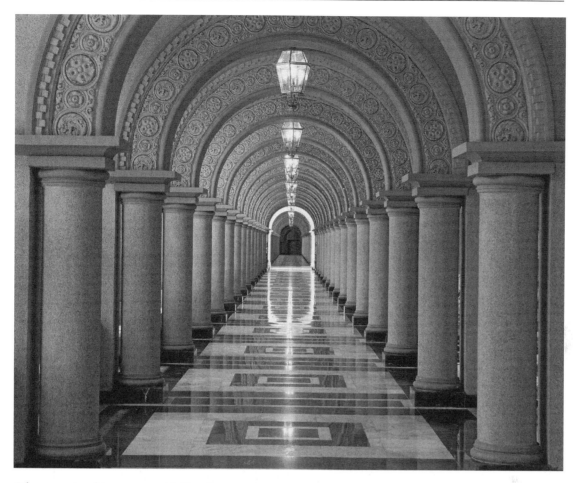

*Bérenger stumbles upon an idyllic city* (© Apples Eyes Studio / Shutterstock.com)

Peep's speeches, and the many incidents of mixing up the briefcases—in the service of serious theater that serves, as Ionesco explained to Bonnefoy, to "pose the problem of the human condition or of its ultimate purpose."

In this light, it is clear that one must also take the encroaching darkness of the final two acts as seriously as one takes the radiance of the first. Act 2 takes place in a claustrophobic apartment, one the stage directions note should be "*very much constructed, heavy, realistic and ugly; it contrasts strongly with the lack of decor and the simple lighting effects of Act I.*" Act 2 begins with a long period of cacophony as disembodied voices outside the apartment can be heard talking over and with the complaining Concierge. No one is saying anything of any importance, and no one is truly communicating with anyone else; it is all just noise. Finally Bérenger arrives, startled to find his sick friend already in his apartment, for he does not remember giving

him the key. They talk back and forth as Bérenger attempts to explain his experience in the radiant city, his sudden love for Dany, and his grief and horror at her murder. All the while, Édouard complains about the cold and his health and clutches an enormous briefcase to himself. He is not even as responsive to Bérenger as the Architect was in act 1, even as the latter was on the telephone.

Outside the radiant city, communication breaks down on many levels. Bérenger and Édouard cannot connect, and because of this they cannot act effectively. After Bérenger discovers the tools of the Killer's trade in Édouard's briefcase, he urges him to action, but Édouard is nearly impossible to rouse. He not only leaves the briefcase behind but, indeed, is nearly mesmerized by Mother Peep's speeches. Mother Peep, like all demagogues, relies not on reason but on emotion to move her charges or, as they are known in the play, her "geese." While she is a character with many comic attributes, from her nonsensical exhortations, to the fact that she urges her followers to use Hitler's "goose-step," to her monstrous appearance as she rises over the mob in her last appearance, she is also a terrifying figure. She whips her crowd into a frenzy, a frenzy that ends in the death of the Drunk in Top Hat and Tails, a character who stated, "I'm for the hero!" The nightmarish chaos of the first half of act 3 is as serious as the luminosity of the radiant city in act 1, for as Ionesco said to Bonnefoy,

> there's also a kind of absurdity that is unreason, contradiction, the expression of my being out of tune with the world, of my being profoundly out of tune with myself, of the world being out of tune with itself.

The play ends with a long monologue by Bérenger, as he attempts to reason with the Killer. Every argument he can come up with for why one should not kill one's fellow human beings is met with a shrug or a chuckle. The Killer refuses to engage, and this refusal sends Bérenger, our sincere man of belief, into yet another argument about why the Killer should cease. None of them work, and as Bérenger hears his own arguments fall on deaf ears, he ceases to believe them himself. Faced with the implacable face of the Absurd itself, Bérenger cannot go on. In conversation with Bonnefoy, Ionesco explained, "The absurd is also quite simply illogicality, unreason; so that history is not strictly speaking absurd, in the sense we've just established—it's nonsensical."

In a comic play, the characters would somehow celebrate this absurdity, but that Bérenger kneels at the end, offering himself as a sort of sacrifice to the force of death that has corrupted the paradise that is the radiant city, demonstrates the true seriousness of the theater of the absurd. Far from being a playwright of the nonsensical, as are groups like the Monty Python troupe, which claimed the absurdists as their inspiration, Ionesco in *The Killers* has written a heartbreaking play about the heroic task that is standing up in the face of life's ultimate meaninglessness. Bérenger dies at the play's end with the dignity of a true hero, while Ionesco's hopeful vision of a city of light lives on.

**Source:** Charlotte M. Freeman, Critical Essay on *The Killer*, in *Drama for Students*, Gale, Cengage Learning, 2018.

## Allan Lewis

*In the following excerpt, Lewis describes* The Killer *as "pessimistic" but "one of Ionesco's most effective dramas."*

### IV THE LAUGHTER OF EVIL—"WHAT GOOD ARE BULLETS AGAINST THE RESISTANCE OF AN INFINITELY STUBBORN WILL!"

... The play is Ionesco's most pessimistic statement, his most thorough rejection of existing norms, a grim portrayal of the prevalent anomie of the rule of reason, a confirmation of the death of God and the reign of chaos. The Killer may exist only in Bérenger's imagination, a projection of the subconscious in which the man of reason faces the animal part of his nature; the final helplessness may be a recognition of the absence of valid criteria. The Killer is not a paid assassin. The French title *Tueur sans gages* implies that his services are not for hire, that he has a metaphysical existence, unavoidable, ever-present, a force that established authorities are unable to eliminate. They may be partly responsible for his continuing presence. A simple, well-intentioned Bérenger makes the effort which turns out to be his own destruction. Ionesco repeats his preoccupation with death. In *Amédée* a corpse overwhelms the living, in *The Killer* a mysterious force kills, for there is no positive force to assert life.

The dramatic techniques work effectively with the content. Characters split, merge, and coalesce. The stage is extended to encompass any space. Language varies from the multiple, incoherent conversation of the street scenes and the repetition of nonsense to the well-organized, exhausting monologue of the final debate. *The Killer* is one of Ionesco's most effective dramas.

**Source:** Allan Lewis, "*Amédée* and *The Killer*," in *Ionesco*, Twayne Publishers, 1972, pp. 59–66.

## Leonard Cabell Pronko

*In the following excerpt, Pronko provides a broad analysis of* The Killer.

... Who is the Killer? Obviously it is not Edward. But then why does he carry a briefcase exactly like that of the Killer? And why does the Architect carry a briefcase? And the drunkard, the lost old man, and Mother Pipe? Because we are all killers. The Architect because he has become inhuman, coldly regulated, lost in his official functions; Mother Pipe because her ideology blinds her to men as individuals; Edward and the others, because of their resignation, their indifference and apathy.

In an article published in *Arts* when *The Killer* was first performed in Paris, Ionesco asks:

> Don't we have the vague feeling that beyond all ideologies we cannot help being at the same time murderer and murdered, . . . instrument and victim of death triumphant?
>
> And yet [he adds, leaving us some small hope in spite of the desperate ending of his play] we are here. It just may be that there is some reason, beyond our comprehension, for living. Everything is so absurd, that this too is possible.

Bérenger, I think, is Ionesco's most appealing character. Despite his pathetic naïveté, his almost ridiculous desire to match strength with incomprehensible evil, or rather precisely because of these qualities, we find Bérenger loveable and profoundly human. In him Ionesco has, except for one insignificant moment, forgotten his robots of the early works. Bérenger feels emotions he expresses, and his good will, however blind, is an indication of his commitment to man. Although he falls back upon the platitudes of our common heritage in his attempts to convince the Killer, he is no unthinking receptacle. In fact, his pain arises, like that of Beckett's characters, from an awareness of his situation. The men outside the radiant city, he tells the Architect, are drab and ugly, for they are neither happy nor unhappy, neither ugly nor beautiful, they feel no real nostalgia, and they suffer from life unaware that they are suffering. "But I was aware of the discomfort of living. Perhaps because I'm more intelligent, or on the contrary less intelligent, less wise, less resigned, less patient." Bérenger has had a glimpse of the happy city that man through strength of will might perhaps make his own. It reminds him of the paradise he once had lost. Unlike Vladimir and Estragon, he does not sit and wait for the arrival of an uncertain Godot to set things right. He decides to act for himself, but he encounters the same absurdity that lies behind the despair of Didi and Gogo and like theirs, his quest turns out to be fruitless . . . .

**Source:** Leonard Cabell Pronko, "Eugène Ionesco: From *The Bald Soprano* to *The Chairs—Victims of Duty, The New Occupant* and *Amédée—The Killer* and *Rhinoceros*," in *Avant-Garde: The Experimental Theater in France*, University of California Press, 1963, pp. 96–102.

## SOURCES

Atkinson, Brooks, Review of *The Killer*, Seven Arts, in *New York Times*, March 23, 1960.

Bonnefoy, Claude, *Conversations with Eugène Ionesco*, translated by Jan Dawson, Holt, Rinehart and Winston, 1971, pp. 22–23, 28–32, 120–21, 123, 125, 127, 177–79.

Cote, David, Review of *The Killer*, Theatre for a New Audience, in *Time Out New York*, June 2, 2014, https://www.timeout.com/newyork/theater/the-killer (accessed July 4, 2017).

Esslin, Martin, *The Theatre of the Absurd*, 3rd ed., Penguin Books, 1991, pp. 22–25, 133, 174, 178–79.

"France—Civil Service," in *Encyclopædia Britannica*, https://www.britannica.com/place/France/Civil-service (accessed June 23, 2017).

Gussow, Mel, "Eugene Ionesco Is Dead at 84: Stage's Master of Surrealism," in *New York Times*, March 29, 1994, http://www.nytimes.com/1994/03/29/obituaries/eugene-ionesco-is-dead-at-84-stage-s-master-of-surrealism.html (accessed June 23, 2017).

Ionesco, Eugène, *The Killer*, in *Three Plays: Exit the King, The Killer, and Macbett*, translated by Charles Marowitz and Donald Watson, Grove Press, 1973, pp. 5–109.

Isherwood, Christopher, "An Ideal Place, Except for All the Dead Bodies," in *New York Times*, June 1, 2014, https://www.nytimes.com/2014/06/02/theater/in-the-killer-ionescos-everyman-seeks-a-source-of-evil.html (accessed July 4, 2017).

McBride, William L., "Existentialism," in *The Cambridge Dictionary of Philosophy*, edited by Robert Audi, Cambridge University Press, 1995, pp. 255–56.

Scheck, Frank, Review of *The Killer*, Theatre for a New Audience, in *Hollywood Reporter*, June 2, 2014, http://www.hollywoodreporter.com/review/killer-theater-review-708522 (accessed July 4, 2017).

Wilson, Benji, "How Monty Python Was Formed," in *Telegraph* (London, England), August 4, 2010, http://www.telegraph.co.uk/culture/tvandradio/7927128/How-Monty-Python-was-formed.html (accessed June 26, 2017).

## FURTHER READING

Beckett, Samuel, *Collected Shorter Plays*, Faber and Faber, 1984.

> Beckett was one of the key figures of the absurdist movement. This volume collects twenty-five of his plays and "playlets," including *Krapp's Last Tape, Embers, Cascando, Play, Eh Joe, Not I*, and *Footfalls*. The book also brings together Beckett's mime dramas, all his radio and television plays, his screenplay for film, his adaptation of Robert Pinget's *The Old*

*Tune*, and the more recent *Catastrophe, What Where, Quad,* and *Night and Dreams.*

Bennett, Michael Y., *The Cambridge Introduction to Theatre and Literature of the Absurd,* Cambridge University Press, 2015.

This introduction sets the theater and literature of the absurd in its historical, intellectual, and cultural context. Bennett introduces the movement's key figures, including Beckett, Pinter, and Tom Stoppard, while tracing the history of the movement's origins, development, and how its influence continues to the present day.

Brecht, Bertolt, *Mother Courage and Her Children,* translated by John Willett, Methuen, 1980.

While Brecht was not considered an absurdist, his antiwar and antitotalitarian plays are widely considered some of the great dramatic creations of the modern stage. Set during the Hundred Years' War, this play follows Mother Courage, an itinerant trader, as she pulls her wagon of wares and her children through the blood and carnage of Europe's religious wars. In the enduring figure of Mother Courage, Brecht created one of the most extraordinary characters in literature.

Ionesco, Eugène, *The Bald Soprano and Other Plays,* translated by Donald M. Allen, Grove Press, 1982.

*The Bald Soprano* was Ionesco's first play, originally performed in 1950. He was inspired to write it by the banal dialogue of the English-language textbook he was studying, and it is a powerful exploration of the banality of language. The other three plays—*The Lesson; Jack, or The Submission;* and *The Chairs*—also demonstrate Ionesco's sense of the absurdity of ordinary life.

————, *Present Past, Past Present: A Personal Memoir,* translated by Helen R. Lane, Grove Press, 1971.

In this ruminative memoir, Ionesco muses on his past, especially his childhood, and through anecdote demonstrates how he came to feel so strongly that fad and cliché are forms of totalitarianism, which he spent his career trying to undermine.

————, *Three Plays: Amédée, The New Tenant, Victims of Duty,* translated by Donald Watson, Grove Press, 1958.

These three plays are, along with *The Killer,* considered some of the most important of Ionesco's career. In *Amédée* a couple have put up with a dead body in their bedroom for fifteen years, but now it is growing and crowding them out of the apartment. In *The New Tenant,* the characters are also being crowded out, but by furniture—furniture that speaks—while in *Victims of Duty,* Ionesco's characters must find a character known as "Mallot with a T."

## SUGGESTED SEARCH TERMS

Ionesco AND absurd

Ionesco AND existentialism

theater AND absurd

theater AND France AND postwar

The Killer AND Ionesco

Ionesco AND Jean-Paul Sartre

Ionesco AND Albert Camus

Ionesco AND Samuel Beckett

# *A Man for All Seasons*

**1966**

The 1966 film adaptation of Robert Bolt's 1960 play, *A Man for All Seasons*, is a masterpiece in character study. It is not a flashy production. It is rather a subtle story about Sir Thomas More, a quiet man with iron convictions. Strengthened by his devout faith, More withstands pressure from his king, his friends, and even his wife and daughter to swear to an oath that the courtiers surrounding him take lightly. Because he knows it is wrong, he refuses to swear, though it costs him his life. Themes of integrity and betrayal thread through this story of conscience.

Viewers may find it helpful to research the period before watching the film, for those who know nothing of Henry VIII's "great matter"—his six-year mission to have his marriage to his first wife annulled so that he might marry Anne Boleyn, which finally ended with the Church of England splitting away from the Catholic Church under the pope in Rome—may find themselves lost in the political intrigue of the Tudor court. Once one understands the situation, the film is a fascinating study of a tumultuous period in English history. *A Man for All Seasons* is the rare period film that sticks to the facts while developing the story in a literary frame.

## PLOT SUMMARY

The film opens with a fanfare playing over the image of statuary at a castle, likely Hampton Court Palace. Cardinal Wolsey finishes writing

*Robert Bolt* (© Trinity Mirror / Mirrorpix / Alamy Stock Photo)

a letter and gives it to his secretary, Thomas Cromwell, who then passes it on to a messenger. As the opening credits roll, the messenger travels along the Thames to the home of Sir Thomas More to deliver the letter. More's servant, Matthew, carries the letter inside. More; his wife, Alice; and his daughter, Margaret, or Meg, are entertaining guests, including Richard Rich and Thomas Howard, the Duke of Norfolk. More is summoned to the palace. He prepares to go immediately, though before he leaves, Norfolk warns him to be wary of Wolsey, who can be manipulative. As More walks to the boat, Rich catches up to ask whether More recommended him for a position at court, but More, in a hurry, puts him off.

When More arrives at the palace, Wolsey confronts him for being the sole voice of opposition in a council meeting, slyly teasing about More's "moral squint." More, however, considers the issue a "matter of conscience" and is not intimidated by Wolsey. A fanfare announces the return of King Henry VIII to the palace. Wolsey guesses that the king has been to visit his mistress, Lady Anne Boleyn, and asks More if he would support an effort to obtain permission from the pope for Henry to annul his marriage to Queen Catherine so that he can marry Anne. More refuses, and Wolsey declares them enemies.

When More leaves Wolsey, he is set upon by a crowd of people hoping to speak with him and hand him notes. An old couple offers some baked apples, hoping to sway More's judgment in their daughter's trial. A woman gives More a silver cup, saying that it is a gift "from some grateful poor folk, in Leicester." More gets a boatman to row him home. While they are moving along the river, More reads the inscription on the bottom of the cup and discovers that it is, in fact, a bribe; he throws the cup in the water, but the boatman fishes it out and gives it back to him.

When More arrives home, Rich is waiting to ask again about a position. More advises Rich to become a teacher instead of seeking a job at court. Rich is disgusted and says he will go instead to Master Cromwell. More gives the silver cup to Rich, who says he will sell it so he can afford a decent gown. More explains about the temptations he would face at court compared with the satisfaction of teaching and knowing that he is doing good work.

When More enters the house, Matthew informs him that Meg has a visitor: William Roper. He wishes to marry Meg, but More will not allow it because he considers Roper, who subscribes to the teachings of Protestant reformer Martin Luther, a heretic. After More sends Roper away, Meg asks about the conference with Wolsey, but More will not discuss it. More then talks with Alice, who expresses her hope that he might one day be Lord Chancellor, but More knows it is dangerous to even speculate about such a thing "while Wolsey lives."

Wolsey has fallen from favor because he was not able to secure the pope's permission for the king's divorce, and he is now on his deathbed. Norfolk rides through wintry weather to retrieve the gold chain that is the mark of Wolsey's office as Lord Chancellor. More is then made Lord Chancellor in a ceremony with a lot of pomp and circumstance.

King Henry comes on a visit More's house in Chelsea. It is meant to be a surprise, but More was forewarned that the king was on his way. Henry arrives by boat with a large retinue, greets Alice, and flirts a little with Meg. Once Henry has More alone, he insists that his marriage to Catherine cannot be valid because she was first married to his elder brother. Henry asserts that God is now punishing him for a sinful marriage and that is why Catherine has not borne him a son. The king wants More to agree with him

# FILM TECHNIQUE

- Although *A Man for All Seasons* was adapted from the original play, which the audience would obviously view from some distance, the film often uses close-ups, rather than wide shots, to allow the audience to study the actors' expressions.

- The interior movie scenes were all filmed on lavishly detailed sets in Shepperton Studios in Surrey, England, but many exterior scenes were filmed on location. For example, in the early scene in which More and Wolsey watch King Henry out the window, the actor did indeed dismount from his horse in a courtyard at Hampton Court Palace. Studley Priory in Oxfordshire, England, stood in for More's house in Chelsea, and the production's boats rowed down the picturesque Beaulieu River rather than the Thames, which has become too built up. The use of period-appropriate structures and outdoor settings adds to the film's realism.

- Throughout the movie, the filmmakers employ a few tricks to show the passage of time. Some are very simple, such as graying of More's hair to show his age and the stress of his ordeal. Some devices are a bit more involved. During a scene in Cromwell's office, we see wintry weather outside the window, which tells us that the matter of King Henry's divorce, which began in summer sunshine, is taking a long time. Similarly, when More looks out the window of the Tower of London near the end of the film, he first sees sun and green grass, then snow, and then summertime weather again. This illustrates how long he has been imprisoned. The change of seasons also reflects the title, for More is steadfast.

because he knows More to be an honest man—his approval means more than the approval of the courtiers, who will agree with anything the king says. Henry grows angry when More will

not go along with the idea of the divorce and returns to his boat without having any dinner, leaving his courtiers scrambling to catch up. As the royal party leaves, Cromwell sees Rich and beckons to him. Rich hesitates to go with Cromwell, and when he backs away, he slips in the mud. The crowd laughs, humiliating him.

More sits at the table with the abandoned feast that was laid out for the royal party. Lady Alice urges him to remain on King Henry's good side. Meg brings Roper into the room. He explains that his opinions on religion have changed. He no longer considers himself a Protestant, but he still strongly believes the church is in need of reform. Rich interrupts the conversation, and More introduces him to Roper. Rich tells More about Cromwell's questioning, pointing to the servant Matthew as one of Cromwell's informants. Once again, Rich asks More to give him a job, but More refuses, telling him directly that he is not strong enough to resist the temptation of corruption at court. After Rich leaves, Alice, Meg, and Roper all urge More to arrest him, believing him to be dangerous, but More insists on the importance of England's laws—and Rich has broken no laws.

Rich goes to see Cromwell, who has just been appointed Secretary to the Council. Cromwell explains that an administrator's duty is to "minimise the inconvenience of things," including the matter of the king's divorce. Rich says he would not disclose something said to him in friendship, but when Cromwell offers him a job, he tells all about the silver cup More gave him.

A nobleman reads a message from King Henry to a gathering of religious leaders led by Archbishop Cranmer. The king demands that he be named the "Supreme Head of the Church in England."

Surrounded by his family, More resigns from his post as Lord Chancellor. Norfolk comes to accept his resignation on behalf of the king, but neither he nor Lady Alice will help him remove the heavy gold chain symbolizing his office because they both feel the resignation is a mistake. Roper offers to help (More calls him "son," so it is to be assumed that he and Meg are now married), but More asks Meg to remove the chain. She complies.

More walks out to the riverbank with Norfolk and, after asking Norfolk to promise that their conversation will remain confidential, explains himself: he firmly believes that the pope is the head of the church and that the king is wrong to usurp that title in England.

More meets with his household staff, explaining that he must let some of them go because of his reduction in income now that he has resigned. Matthew steps forward to say that the servants all understand More's opinions and agree, but More firmly tells him not to speculate about or discuss such matters.

Lady Alice is angry that More has resigned, but More seems content to live a quiet life. He believes if he does not speak out against the king's course of action, he will be left alone, but Alice is afraid and wants him to explain. More refuses to speak frankly, wanting her to always be able to say honestly that he has not spoken to her on these issues.

Rich arrives at Cromwell's office to find him discussing the situation with Norfolk. Norfolk pushes Cromwell to leave More alone, as long as he is silent on the issue of the king's divorce, but Cromwell knows that More's reputation will be enough to convince the public that his silence indicates disapproval. Cromwell is determined to get a direct statement of More's loyalty to the king so that he will not be taken as a critic. Cromwell brings in the woman who gave More the silver cup, hoping to use the knowledge of the crime of accepting a bribe as leverage to force More to make a statement. Cromwell makes it clear that the king wants Norfolk to take an active interest in getting More in line, such as by urging More to attend the king's wedding to Anne Boleyn, which would imply his approval.

Church bells ring all over the countryside to celebrate the king's wedding. Henry seems happy, all smiles and singing with his bride, but when he mistakes a guest for More, his disappointment makes it clear that More's resistance to his will still rankles. More is summoned "to answer certain charges before Secretary Cromwell." Rich is present to act as secretary, and More pointedly compliments his gown (perhaps bought with the money he got for selling the silver cup and also monogrammed with King Henry's initial). Cromwell confronts More about his disapproving silence, using his contact with the "'Holy Maid' of Kent who was executed for prophesying against the King" to threaten him. More refuses to answer.

When More tries to find a boat to take him home, the boatmen snub him, likely already hearing rumors that he is out of favor with the king and his closest advisers. More turns to start walking and sees Norfolk, who urges More to give in to the king's wishes. When More refuses, they argue. Norfolk raises a hand to strike More. He ducks and falls to the ground. Their friendship is seemingly over.

Cromwell speaks to Parliament, explaining the necessity of rooting out anyone who does not support the king's marriage to Anne Boleyn. When More arrives home after the long walk from the palace, Meg is there to greet him. She explains about the new act of Parliament: everyone will have to take an oath to indicate they support the marriage. More hopes the wording will allow all of them to take the oath. However, the next scene shows More in the Tower of London—the oath was worded in such a way that he could not take it. He is kept in a damp cell with simple furniture and only a few books. He looks out the window as the seasons pass.

More is awakened in darkness and taken to Richmond Palace to be questioned by Cromwell, Norfolk, and Archbishop Cranmer. Rich is present as secretary. Norfolk declares this the "Seventh Commission" to look into the case, so the issue has clearly dragged on for a long time. More is willing to grant that Anne Boleyn is the queen and that any children she bears are the king's rightful heirs, but he remains silent on the matter of whether the king's marriage to Catherine of Aragon was unlawful. More, a lawyer, insists that his silence cannot be taken as treasonable.

After More is led away, Rich asks Cromwell about a new position: Attorney General of Wales. Cromwell is too distracted with More's case to give him an answer. Rich suggests putting More on the rack, but the king has forbidden torture.

Lady Alice, Meg, and Roper are allowed to visit More in the Tower, in his new cell, which is smaller, wetter, and altogether more grim than the first one. Meg has been pressured to persuade More to take the oath. Though she tries to reason with him, he is steadfast: he will not take the oath. More urges his family to flee the country, asking them to promise so he knows they will be safe. He makes a great show of enjoying the food that Alice has brought for him. She admits she does not understand why he is so stubborn in this matter and fears she will be angry once he is dead, but before the family are forced to leave, husband and wife reconcile.

More prays for his family before being taken into his trial, which is led by Cromwell. More denies that his silence in any way denied the king's position as head of the Church of England, but Cromwell counters that because all know More's opinions, they can safely assume he does not approve.

Cromwell calls Rich to testify. Rich claims that he heard More say he did not believe Parliament had the power to make the king the head of the church. More knows that this will be enough for Cromwell to justify his execution. Seeing the red dragon Rich wears on a chain, More asks about it and learns that Rich accepted the position of Attorney General there in exchange for his false testimony. The jury finds More guilty of high treason.

More goes to his death still professing himself "His Majesty's good servant" but believing his service to God is more important. Just before the executioner takes up his ax, More forgives him, asserting that he will go "to God" after he dies. A voice-over explains the fate of other major characters in the story before the final credits roll.

## CHARACTERS

### Lady Anne Boleyn
Anne Boleyn is played by Vanessa Redgrave. She appears only briefly in the film, on the day of her wedding to King Henry. She is happy and smiling, flirting and singing with the king.

### Archbishop Thomas Cranmer
Cranmer, played by Cyril Luckham, is adviser to King Henry. As Archbishop of Canterbury, Cranmer leads the court that declares Henry's marriage to Catherine of Aragon invalid and approves his marriage to Anne Boleyn. In the film, Cranmer is shown with the Duke of Norfolk and Thomas Cromwell, questioning More about his refusal to take the oath.

### Thomas Cromwell
At the start of the film, Thomas Cromwell (Leo McKern) is Cardinal Wolsey's secretary but clearly has ambitions for higher office. He later becomes secretary to the king's council of advisers. The film portrays Cromwell as jealous of More's position at court and as a schemer: when we first see him, he eavesdrops on More's conversation with Wolsey. Cromwell is staunchly Protestant, and as such he is firmly behind King Henry's divorcing Catholic Catherine of Aragon and marrying Lady Anne Boleyn.

### King Henry VIII
Rather than the bloated tyrant many think of when hearing the name King Henry VIII, Robert Shaw's Henry is still in the prime of his life. He is handsome and charming but already mercurial. His courtiers fear his temper, as is obvious in their behavior when Henry pays a surprise visit to More's home. Henry leaps out of the boat, only to land ankle-deep in mud, and all of his attendants freeze in horror until Henry bursts out laughing instead of becoming angry. Henry declares the Church of England as under his authority rather than that of the pope in Rome. However, he seems to be motivated more by self-interest than a genuine desire for religious reformation. Henry has no son to inherit his throne, and he has convinced himself that God is punishing him for marrying his elder brother's widow. Henry wants his first marriage to be declared invalid so that he might marry Anne Boleyn. In addition to hoping to secure an heir, Henry seems besotted with Lady Anne.

### Thomas Howard
*See* Norfolk

### Matthew
Matthew is one of More's servants. He does not want to be disloyal, but when More loses his position and must reduce his expenses, Matthew leaves to find a better-paying job, unwilling to accept a reduction in his wages.

### Lady Alice More
Lady Alice, played by Wendy Hiller, is More's wife. She is outspoken to the point of being unpleasant, but her frustration at the loss of social position as well as her fear for the safety of her family are understandable. Although she seems aware that More has greater love for their daughter than for herself, there is undeniable affection between husband and wife.

### Sir Thomas More
The character of Sir Thomas More is very closely based on the historical figure, with some of his dialogue even inspired by historical records and by his writings. From the very beginning, More is established as a kind man of principle. He is a loyal subject to his king, a hardworking public

servant, and a good husband and father, and he will not bend or compromise when he knows himself to be in the right.

When King Henry seeks to divorce his wife of more than twenty years so that he can marry Anne Boleyn, More does not speak out against the plan. He is even willing to accept any children from the king's second marriage as the rightful heirs to the throne, but he will not accept the king as the head of the church. A devoted Catholic, More believes that the first pope was designated by Christ himself and that therefore whoever holds that office is the only earthly authority over all matters spiritual. Because More refuses to swear the oath naming King Henry as the head of the Church of England, he is declared a traitor and executed. He dies bravely, pointing out that service to God is more important than service to his king.

## Norfolk
Nigel Davenport plays Thomas Howard, the Duke of Norfolk, who is one of King Henry's advisers. Although Norfolk considers himself More's friend, he urges More to swear the oath and save his life, not understanding that it is a matter of conscience. Norfolk is among the men who question More and who sit in judgment at his trial. Though he is saddened by More's stubborn refusal to give in, Norfolk will not risk his own position at court by defending him.

## Richard Rich
Rich (John Hurt) is a young man who asks for More's help in getting a position at court. More refuses, advising Rich to instead become a teacher. Disgusted, Rich goes to Cranmer and indeed rises to a high position. However, he clearly loses his integrity when he becomes entangled in court politics, because he lies on the stand at More's trial—likely at Cranmer's urging—claiming More asserted to him that Parliament did not have the power to make King Henry head of the Church of England.

## Lady Margaret "Meg" More Roper
Meg is the only one of More's four children to be portrayed in the film. In truth, More had three daughters and a son, all of whom were highly educated. It was rare for women to receive the same instruction as men, but More insisted on it for his daughters. Meg's unusual education is displayed in the film by her conversation in Latin with King Henry. Meg is close to her father and distraught by his refusal to save

himself by taking the oath. She is an affectionate person and seems happy in her marriage to William Roper. Susannah York fills the role of Meg.

## William Roper
Roper (Corin Redgrave) is a young man who lives near More's Chelsea house. He wants to marry Meg, but More at first refuses because he considers Roper a heretic for believing the teachings of Martin Luther. Later, when Roper comes back to what More considers the one true church, he and Meg are married. When More realizes that he cannot escape execution, he looks to Roper to protect Lady Alice and Meg by taking them out of the country.

## Cardinal Wolsey
Orson Welles plays Wolsey. At the start of the film's action, Wolsey is Lord Chancellor—King Henry's chief adviser—and he clearly resents More's opposition in council meetings. Wolsey later falls out of favor, largely because of his failure to negotiate the divorce the king so desperately wants. He is arrested but dies before he comes to trial.

## THEMES

### Integrity
The entire plot of *A Man for All Seasons* hinges on Sir Thomas More's integrity. More is established as a man of conscience when we first see him with Wolsey at the start of the movie. He defied Wolsey in a council meeting, even though he knew it would make the powerful Wolsey angry. Wolsey archly teases More for his "moral squint," but it makes More's character clear: he will not compromise on important matters, small or great, because he has great integrity. Because More is a man of his word and a man of honor, he believes the king is too. When first confronted by Cromwell, More refuses to believe that the king would lie, "because evidence is given on oath and he will not perjure himself."

More's integrity is also clear in his interactions with Richard Rich. More suspects that Rich is not strong enough to withstand the bribes and temptations at the royal court, and More's family urges him to take measures against Rich when he leaves the house angry that More will not give him a job. However, More does his best to protect Rich from himself, advising him to become a teacher instead of seeking a position at court. More also does nothing to stop Rich, such as

# READ.
# WATCH.
# WRITE.

- Watch the movie again to study the characterizations of the women. Lady Alice is outspoken, at times to the point of shrewishness; Lady Margaret is erudite and loving; and Anne Boleyn, though she is at the center of the political turmoil and by historical accounts an educated, intelligent woman, does not even speak, only appearing in the film to laugh, flirt, and sing while gazing at King Henry lovingly. Choose a few scenes from the movie and write them from the point of view of one of the female characters. With a group of classmates, perform your scenes for the rest of the class. Alternatively, film your scenes, post them online, and invite your classmates to view them.

- Imagine the story of Sir Thomas More as if it had taken place in a different period in history. How might his faith and conviction be different if he had lived two or three hundred years later? Or in modern day? Pick a historical period and write a summary of how you imagine *A Man for All Seasons* might play out in your chosen era. In addition, create sets and costumes for this period, either gathering pictures into a collage to represent your vision or sketching them yourself.

- Research period costumes appropriate to England in the early sixteenth century. Are the clothes and hats worn by various characters in the film accurate? Using examples from the film, create a multimedia presentation explaining how the fashions reflect the characters' social standing. Share your presentation with your class.

- Rewatch the movie, paying careful attention to the physical positions of characters in each scene. Often characters are placed behind desks to emphasize the authority of their offices, but More's presence seems to need no such props. Even when speaking to the king, he holds himself with dignity, and Henry himself, in his grand gilded outfit, carries his power with him even when walking under the trees. Write a paper comparing and contrasting the various characters, their confidence in their power and position, and the way they are staged in each scene.

---

arresting him, protesting that Rich has done nothing illegal. During More's trial, he seems disappointed rather than angered by Rich's perjury. More is likely aware that Cromwell would have found a way to get a condemnation no matter what, so Rich's false testimony is not truly the direct cause of More's execution, only a convenient way of speeding things up. When More confronts Rich, he seems genuinely saddened that Rich has sold his soul for a lucrative position.

## *Betrayal*

Another major theme in the film is on the opposite end of the spectrum from integrity: betrayal. At King Henry's court, most people seem to act only for their self-interest. Richard Rich's betrayal through perjury is discussed earlier. Indeed, Rich's treachery is straightforward, but there are other instances of betrayal that are far more difficult for More to bear, such as that of the Duke of Norfolk. When we first meet both More and Norfolk, they are in a large, laughing company in More's house in Chelsea. It is clear they enjoy each other's company and respect each other, and it is Norfolk who puts More forward as the next Lord Chancellor after Wolsey falls from favor and dies. However, time and time again, Norfolk urges More to take the oath, though he has a better understanding than most of why More resists. Norfolk sits on the panel that questions More and is present at his trial but does nothing to speak out for him, instead pressuring More to "give in."

Also painful to More is the betrayal by King Henry, for they were friends, after a fashion. The film suggests that the king might have let More

*Paul Scofield played the role of Sir Thomas More on both stage and screen* (© PA / AP Images)

live in quiet retirement. (This is not entirely historically accurate: Henry knew that More was a threat, and though in the film More professes to maintain his silence, in actuality More wrote several books that did not directly challenge the king's position as head of the Church of England but that made More's position clear.) However, Cromwell, in his jealousy of More's intellect, experience, and power, pushes the issue. Cromwell knows that he will never be able to buy More's cooperation and is determined to get rid of him. Both in the film and in truth, Henry allowed More to be tried and executed, though no one truly believed that More was anything but loyal to his king in matters of state. Historically, More's original sentence was to be hanged, drawn, and quartered, and the king granted him the mercy of a quicker death by beheading.

## STYLE

### Lighting

Throughout *A Man for All Seasons*, natural light is used as much as possible, which adds to the movie's realism. Indoors, at night, candles are

the only light source—for example, when More visits Wolsey in his office at the start of the film. When a scene occurs outdoors, the sun provides the light. King Henry's surprise visit to Sir Thomas's Chelsea house is cheerful, with bright sunshine. When we first see Henry VIII, he is at the top of the stairs by the river with the light of the sun behind him, almost blindingly bright. The beams of sunlight reflecting off his cloth-of-gold cape are like his royal glamour. In contrast to that scene's bright sun, there are cloudy skies over More's house when Norfolk comes to retrieve the chain of office, approximately halfway through the film. Again, the director uses natural light, but it is particularly well suited to the mood of the scene, because More is losing his position at court, falling from Henry's favor. Some outdoor scenes take place at night, such as when More falls out of favor and cannot get a boatman to take him home; he confronts Norfolk in the darkness near the palace. It is even darker and more difficult to see when More finally makes his way home and finds Meg outside waiting for him. The lack of light again reflect More's position at court: Henry has turned away, and the sun no longer shines on More.

### Soundtrack

The soundtrack of *A Man for All Seasons* is unusual in that it contains almost no music. The film opens with a fanfare of horns, as if announcing the king or some other noble personage. Then, during the opening and closing credits, music plays. Occasionally there is a song, as when King Henry and Anne Boleyn sing on their wedding day or when Henry's composition plays in the background at More's Chelsea home. However, this music is part of the action of the story. Through most of the film, the sounds are natural—only what one would hear if one were present in that place at that time. When the characters are outdoors, one hears birds chirping. When More or King Henry is traveling along the Thames, one hears the oars splashing in the water. Like the use of natural light and the historic settings, the lack of background music adds to the film's realism.

## CULTURAL CONTEXT

### Henry VIII's "Great Matter" and Reformation in England

When discussing his marriage to Catherine of Aragon, King Henry preferred to use the term *great matter* rather than *divorce*, for to use the

*Robert Shaw plays King Henry VIII, and Wendy Hiller plays Sir Thomas More's wife* (© Michael Ochs *Archives / Getty Images*)

latter would be to recognize that he had indeed been legally married. Instead, Henry wanted to claim that his marriage had never been valid because Catherine had first been married to Henry's elder brother, Arthur. Because Catherine was a princess of Spain, maintaining ties by marriage was desirable—the constant threat of war with France made an alliance with Spain particularly useful—so a dispensation was gained from the pope to allow Henry and Catherine to marry.

Catherine and Henry had only one living child: Princess Mary. Catherine had many miscarriages, stillborn babies, and infants who died very young. Based on an ambiguous passage in the Bible, Henry decided that being married to his brother's widow was a sin and that his lack of a male heir was God's punishment. He ordered his advisers to take up the matter once again with the pope so that his marriage to Catherine would be annulled, freeing him to marry a woman who could bear him a son. It must be said that Henry's desire for a new wife did not arise solely from guilt or fear that he had sinned in marrying Catherine. Henry had grown tired of his wife of twenty years and had fallen in love with Lady Anne Boleyn. Indeed, he was so besotted that some said she had bewitched him.

The pope refused Henry's first request for a dispensation. For six long years, Henry's counselors worked to obtain his divorce from Catherine until, in early 1533, Lady Anne realized that she was pregnant, which made matters more urgent. Henry, hoping for a son, pressured the Archbishop of Canterbury to grant him his divorce, against the pope's wishes, and Henry and Anne were married. Then, in 1534, by act of Parliament, Henry was made Supreme Head of the Church in England.

In addition to Henry's selfish desire to marry Anne Boleyn and the need—in that era when daughters were not considered proper future rulers—for a male heir, there was another factor that influenced the events surrounding Henry's "great matter." While many of Henry's advisers would have done anything their king asked, simply because they knew their position and wealth depended on staying in the king's favor, there were those with other motives for furthering Henry's cause: reformation of the church.

If Henry were made head of the Church in England, it could lead to reform in an institution that was seen as corrupt, with priests demanding payment to marry, baptize, and bury its parishioners. The Catholic Church was very rich. Later, Thomas Cromwell organized the dissolution of the monasteries, with all of the church's wealth going into the king's coffers—another helpful benefit to Henry of being Supreme Head of the Church of England, especially when he was spending so much to build defenses against possible attack by France.

There also were those who were genuinely devout and hoped to bring the common people closer to God. This faction hoped to have the Mass read in English rather than Latin and to have the Bible and prayer books also printed in English so that everyone might understand without the intervention of priests. After Henry was made head of the church, the Lord's Prayer began to be recited in English. Most prayers and services were still performed in Latin, but Henry's "great matter" was the start of a period of huge change in the Church of England that continued well after Henry's death. The politics of the country, including who was to take the throne after him, was closely tied to whether the people involved were Protestant or secretly loyal Catholics.

## CRITICAL OVERVIEW

Critical reception of *A Man for All Seasons* is overwhelmingly positive. It won countless awards, including several Golden Globes, several BAFTA awards, and Oscars for best picture, best actor in a leading role (Paul Scofield), best director (Fred Zinnemann), best adapted screenplay (Bolt), best cinematography (Ted Moore), and best costume design (Elizabeth Haffenden and Joan Bridge).

Film critics and serious academics alike are impressed by the film. As explained by Peter Marshall in his essay "Saints and Cinemas: *A Man for All Seasons*,"

> While most of Hollywood's forays into history are either ignored or disdainfully dismissed by experts in the field . . . Bolt's drama, and the film for which he wrote the screenplay, have for a generation and more been regularly referenced and critiqued in works of serious historical scholarship.

Moira Walsh, reviewing the film for *America* magazine, agrees that the movie is a great success, pointing out how "cinematic pacing, rhythm and verisimilitude are achieved in part by 'opening up' the film to just enough scenes of court pageantry and the sylvan loveliness of the Thames." Even more important than the spectacular settings, according to Walsh, "is the camera, artfully capturing the faces of superb actors speaking superb dialogue—dialogue that is the outward manifestation of electrifying confrontations and inner conflicts." The work of the director is also praised by *Variety*'s A. D. Murphy:

> Zinnemann's direction of his players seems uniformly excellent. In addition, he establishes mood and contrast in brief shots—placid, then turbulent waters, bustling minions—which are heightened further by versatile use of Technicolor, toned to the dramatic needs of the moment.

Murphy also singles out the "outstanding production design" of John Box and the camera work of Ted Moore, which "has caught all the nuances."

Bosley Crowther of the *New York Times* also mentions the "great pictorial conviction with the naturalistic style and the beautiful color photography of Ted Moore." However, Crowther asserts that the film's success is due in large part to the performance of Paul Scofield as Sir Thomas More. "Mr. Scofield is brilliant in his exercise of temperance and restraint, of disciplined wisdom and humor," Crowther writes. Then he continues: "In fact, it is this delineation of More's sterling strength and character, his intellectual vigor and remarkable emotional control, that endow this film with dynamism in even its most talky scenes." Crowther also singles out for particular praise the "truly diabolical malevolence" of Leo McKern's Thomas Cromwell and Robert Shaw's Henry VIII, who is "permittedly eccentric, like the sweep of a hurricane—now roaring with seeming refreshment, now ominously calm, now wild with wrath—as he shapes a frightening portrait of the headstrong, heretical King."

In discussing the cast, Murphy agrees that Scofield delivers an "excellent performance as More" and that "Robert Shaw is also excellent as the king, giving full exposition in limited footage to the character: volatile, educated, virile, arrogant, yet sensible." Murphy feels, however, that Leo McKern's work, though "restrained and chilling at first, unfortunately becomes too broad, almost that of a jolly rascal, effect being to flaw the dramatic impact at times." Murphy also highlights the performance of John Hurt as Richard Rich, "the ambitious young man whose loyalties and integrity are overcome by material desires"; Susannah York's "youthful air of knowing innocence" as Meg; and the "outstanding economy of expression" of Orson Welles as Wolsey.

# CRITICISM

## *Kristen Sarlin Greenberg*

*Greenberg is a freelance writer and editor with a background in literature and philosophy. In the following essay, she examines how Sir Thomas More's religious faith gives him strength in the 1966 film* A Man for All Seasons.

The 1966 film *A Man for All Seasons* portrays the dramatic end of the life of Sir Thomas More, a victim of political intrigue and the mercurial temperament of a king determined to have his way. More was a remarkable man. He held numerous public offices and was known as a man who worked tirelessly to improve the lot of the common man in England. A devoted scholar, he gave three daughters (only one of whom is portrayed in the movie) the same education as his son. His book *Utopia* (a word he himself coined) was translated all over Europe and earned him the reputation as one of the leading humanist thinkers of his day. More was sought out by King Henry VIII and his advisers for his brilliance, but in many ways he was not cut out to be a politician in this imperfect world, because he was not willing to bend when it came to matters of conscience.

The plot of *A Man for All Seasons* stays remarkably close to historical fact, though it glosses over some details. Throughout the film, we see the many challenges More faces in his endeavor to remain a man of integrity. Men in positions of great power in Henry's court try to

> MORE WAS SOUGHT OUT BY KING HENRY VIII AND HIS ADVISERS FOR HIS BRILLIANCE, BUT IN MANY WAYS HE WAS NOT CUT OUT TO BE A POLITICIAN IN THIS IMPERFECT WORLD, BECAUSE HE WAS NOT WILLING TO BEND WHEN IT CAME TO MATTERS OF CONSCIENCE."

manipulate and discredit More. Cardinal Wolsey even mocks him for his convictions, saying that without his "moral squint," he "could have made a statesman." More does not let Wolsey's disapproval fluster him. Instead, he calmly explains that "when statesmen forsake their own private conscience for the sake of their public duties they lead their country by a short route to chaos."

Thomas Cromwell, seeming almost jealous of More's success and power, sets up Richard Rich as his spy, desperate for any dirt on More. Cromwell sets out to prove that More took a bribe in the form of a silver cup; he learned about the cup only because once More realized it was indeed a bribe, he tried to get rid of it by giving it to Rich, who later told Cromwell. In spite of the machinations of men like Wolsey and Cromwell, More never stoops to their level. He trusts that if he himself acts morally, there is nothing he can be blamed or punished for, and therefore nothing truly bad will happen to him.

Lesser men than More, such as Richard Rich, lie to get ahead. During More's trial, he hears Rich's testimony—all lies—in horror and learns that Rich was compensated for his willingness to lie with a position as the Attorney General of Wales. Rather than become understandably angry at Rich's betrayal, More seems saddened that after all of the advice he offered about avoiding the temptations of the royal court, Rich gave in so easily to Cromwell's plans. "For Wales," More marvels. Then he continues: "Why Richard, it profits a man nothing to give his soul for the whole world. But for Wales." More himself gives up his very life to keep his soul without stain.

# WHAT DO I SEE NEXT?

- Like *A Man for All Seasons*, *Lady Jane* (Paramount Pictures, 1986, PG-13) is a drama based on a historical figure who falls victim to the political plotting of the Tudor royal court. Lady Jane Grey was Henry VIII's great-niece. After the death of Henry's only son, King Edward VI, she was hurriedly married off to the son of plotting palace adviser John Dudley and made queen in the hope of preventing Henry's eldest daughter, Mary—a staunch Catholic—from taking the throne and forcing Protestants into hiding. Jane was queen for only a matter of days before Mary took control, and Jane was later executed for treason.

- The title character of *Anne of the Thousand Days* (Universal Pictures, 1969, PG) is Anne Boleyn, who was married to Henry VIII for only a few years before being beheaded for treason, though her real crime was failing to give birth to a male heir.

- *Middle School: The Worst Years of My Life* (CBS Films, 2016, PG) was adapted from the young-adult novel of the same name. The movie tells the story of middle-school student Rafe, who decides to break each and every one of the rules in their tyrannous principal's Code of Conduct. Although the principal's misdeeds hardly compare to Henry VIII's wrath and whims and Rafe's pranks are a far cry from More's quiet dignity, both this film and *A Man for All Seasons* show a principled person going up against an unfair and arbitrary leader and his self-serving rules.

- Bolt wrote the screenplay based on Boris Pasternak's novel for *Dr. Zhivago* (MGM, 1965, PG-13), which stars Omar Sharif and Julie Christie.

- The protagonist in *The Mission* (Warner Brothers, 1986, PG), for which Bolt wrote the screenplay, is an eighteenth-century Jesuit priest who finds great strength in his faith, though it takes him to his death.

- Although the action in *The Lion in Winter* (Embassy Pictures, 1968, PG) takes place more than three hundred years before the reign of Henry VIII, the film portrays a similarly treacherous and plotting royal court of England. The three sons of King Henry II vie to inherit his throne, and his wife pushes him to make a choice. The cast features screen legends Peter O'Toole, Katharine Hepburn, and Anthony Hopkins.

---

The obstacles all come from men who set themselves in opposition to More because he will not do as they wish. However, even More's friends blithely urge him to abandon his principles. King Henry considers More a friend; in the scene of King Henry's surprise visit to More's house in Chelsea, he talks fondly to More, saying, "Thank God I have a friend for my chancellor." However, when he asks his thoughts on the matter of the divorce and it becomes clear that More does not approve, the king bursts out, "Then you haven't thought enough!" The king believes himself to be a good friend to More, but he is too accustomed to indulging his every whim and passion to consider any contradictory viewpoint.

Once he realizes that More will resist, the king hints at the rewards he would offer if only More will help him and approve his divorce: "If you could come with me, there's no man I'd sooner raise." In spite of this temptation, More still will not give in, much to Henry's frustration. "How is it that you cannot see?" Henry asks. "Everyone else does." He explains to More that he needs his support

> Because you're honest. And what is more to the purpose, you're known to be honest. Those like Norfolk follow me because I wear the crown.

Those like Cromwell follow because they're jackals with sharp teeth and I'm their tiger. A mass follows me because it follows anything that moves. And then there's you.

Henry knows that More is different—indeed that he is better than most men, which is why Henry so desperately wants his approval.

Perhaps even more difficult to resist is More's friend Thomas Howard, the Duke of Norfolk, who does not offer bribes or threats. Instead Norfolk begs, "Why can't you do as I did, and come with us, for fellowship?" He genuinely wants More to be safe. The explanation for More's amazing ability to resist all of this extraordinary pressure to give in lies in his response to Norfolk's plea. He asks the frustrated Norfolk, "And when we die, and you are sent to heaven for doing your conscience and I am sent to hell for not doing mine, will you come with me, for fellowship?" More is certain that to give in would be betraying himself and his God and therefore never wavers.

More is an intellectual—an intelligent, logical person—but it is his deep faith that gives him such great strength. He tells Norfolk, "Only God is love right through . . . and that's my self." His faith is the central part of his being. He lets it guide his behavior in everything and so is never tempted to back down, even in the face of a desperate appeal from his beloved daughter. In the Tower of London, Meg repeats back a lesson More himself taught her: "God more regards the thoughts of the heart than the words of the mouth." If this is true, she urges him, "say the words of the oath and in your heart think otherwise." However, More is not tempted to give in and swear to an oath that he knows to be wrong because he believes that "when a man takes an oath, he's holding his own self in his own hands like water. And if he opens his fingers then, he needn't hope to find himself again." He explains to Meg that an oath is "words we say to God," so he will not lie, even if no man on earth would ever discover the lie.

The last words More utters before going bravely to his death emphasize even more clearly his faith and the support it gives him. To the crowd that gathers for his execution, he humbly says, "I die His Majesty's good servant but God's first." He deeply believes that because he acted according to his conscience, he has nothing to fear, offering forgiveness to the executioner

*More was executed for not bending to the king's will* (© *John Springer Collection | Getty Images*)

and telling him, "Be not afraid of your office. You send me to God." More's quiet confidence when facing his death is in sharp contrast to Wolsey's desperate, gasping last words, which tie closely to More's own remark: Wolsey says, "If I had served God one half so well as I've served my king, God would not have left me here, to die in this place." Wolsey and those like him serve themselves, whereas More always thought of himself as working in service to God.

In 1886, the Catholic Church beatified More, and in 1935 Pope Pius XI canonized him—he is now a Catholic saint. What would More have thought of such an honor? He certainly does not seem the sort to seek praise or glory for doing what he saw as his duty to his own self and to God. However, perhaps it would be a comfort to him to know how many people around the world now understand his motives and admire his conviction, for as the fictional More said to his wife on their final meeting before his execution: "I'm sick with fear when I think of the worst they may do to me. But worse than that will be to go with you not understanding why I go." The film *A Man for All Seasons* illuminates his reasons and celebrates his integrity.

**Source:** Kristen Sarlin Greenberg, Critical Essay on *A Man for All Seasons*, in *Drama for Students*, Gale, Cengage Learning, 2018.

### Peter Marshall

*In the following excerpt, Marshall addresses the changes made from historical fact and analyzes the theme of religion.*

...In his *Preface* Bolt candidly conceded that he had 'appropriated a Christian Saint to my purposes'. These were to challenge the idea of the self as 'an equivocal commodity' in modern society, and to urge his contemporaries towards the realization of 'a sense of selfhood without resort to magic'. In an interview just before the first performance of the play in London, Bolt was still more explicit: More became a reluctant martyr because he had 'kept one small area of integrity within himself', and the powers-that-be could not rest until they had got at it. 'When he was attacked the Catholics thought he must be on their side. He was not. Both sides had the wrong end of the stick throughout.' In veering into historical assertion of this order, it was Bolt who had the wrong end of the stick. The one thing we *can* safely say about Thomas More is that he was on the side of the Catholics.

Ultimately, therefore, what a spectrum of commentators have objected to in *A Man for All Seasons* is that the writer fails imaginatively to enter and explore the contemporary mindset of its central protagonist. The portrayal is not so much inaccurate as inauthentic. Here we come up against an inescapable dilemma of representations of the past, particularly the distant past, in popular cultural media. It is relatively easy to get the small details right—the costumes, the buildings, even (with a little care) the outlines of events and something approximating to the speech patterns of the characters. But why should we expect modern audiences to be engaged or entertained by the predicament of individuals whose actions are based on attitudes and values almost entirely alien to those by which they live their own lives? To writers of creative fiction, even subtle and imaginative ones like Robert Bolt, the dilemma is unlikely, however, to present itself in quite the same terms. Frequently, the appeal of a historical setting is that it allows moral and political issues of the day to be explored in an oblique, but fresh and refocused way (something,

incidentally it has in common with science fiction). An ability to recognize the present-mindedness informing nearly all historical fiction is a useful skill for students and practitioners of history to possess. Yet it should not induce feelings of complacency on their part. For the dilemma of historical film—how to respect the autonomy of the past while rationalizing its representation in the present—is the dilemma of academic history also.

**Source:** Peter Marshall, "Saints and Cinemas: *A Man for All Seasons*," in *Tudors and Stuarts on Film: Historical Perspectives*, edited by Susan Doran and Thomas S. Freeman, Palgrave Macmillan, 2009, pp. 51–59.

## SOURCES

Crowther, Bosley, "A Sturdy Conscience, a Steadfast Heart: *A Man for All Seasons* Opens at Fine Arts," in *New York Times*, December 13, 1966, http://www.nytimes.com/movie/review?res=9B02EED8153CE43BBC4B52DFB467838D679EDE (accessed June 27, 2017).

"*A Man for All Seasons*," IMDb website, http://www.imdb.com/title/tt0060665/ (accessed June 26, 2017).

*A Man for All Seasons*, directed by Fred Zinnemann, Columbia Pictures, DVD, 2006.

*A Man for All Seasons* script, Drew's Script-o-Rama, http://www.script-o-rama.com/movie_scripts/m/man-for-all-seasons-script.html (accessed June 27, 2017).

Marshall, Peter, "Saints and Cinemas: *A Man for All Seasons*," in *Tudors and Stuarts on Film: Historical Perspectives*, edited by Susan Doran and Thomas S. Freeman, Palgrave Macmillan, 2009, p. 46.

Murphy, A. D., Review of *A Man for All Seasons*, in *Variety*, December 13, 1966, http://variety.com/1966/film/reviews/a-man-for-all-seasons-1200421180/ (accessed June 27, 2017).

"Sir Thomas More: Biography, Facts and Information," EnglishHistory.net, https://englishhistory.net/tudor/citizens/sir-thomas-more/ (accessed June 26, 2017).

Trueman, C. N., "Henry and Divorce," History Learning Site, http://www.historylearningsite.co.uk/tudor-england/henry-and-divorce/ (accessed June 27, 2017).

———, "The Reformation," History Learning Site, http://www.historylearningsite.co.uk/tudor-england/the-reformation/ (accessed June 26, 2017).

Walsh, Moira, Review of *A Man for All Seasons*, in *America*, May 13, 2013, https://www.americamagazine.org/issue/100/reviewing-man-all-seasons (accessed June 27, 2017).

## FURTHER READING

Fraser, Antonia, *The Wives of Henry VIII*, Knopf, 1992.

With meticulous research, Fraser presents King Henry's six wives as complex, intelligent women rendered powerless by the patriarchal political system in this highly readable history.

George, Margaret, *The Autobiography of Henry VIII: With Notes by His Fool, Will Somers*, St. Martin's Press, 1986.

George's novel imagines King Henry's story the way he himself might have told it, interspersed with occasional remarks from Will Somers, Henry's jester and friend.

MacCulloch, Diarmaid, *All Things Made New: The Reformation and Its Legacy*, Oxford University Press, 2016.

MacCulloch offers a detailed study of the way historians have looked at the Reformation in the past five centuries, exploring the religious, social, and political forces that shaped today's Christian world.

More, Thomas, *Utopia*, edited by Paul Turner, Penguin Classics, 2003.

This reprint of More's most famous book includes an introduction by editor Turner. More imagines an idyllic island without war, where property is shared and everyone receives an education.

Rinaldi, Ann, *The Redheaded Princess*, HarperCollins, 2008.

Rinaldi's young-adult novel tells the story of Elizabeth, Henry VIII's daughter with Anne Boleyn. Later, as queen, Elizabeth is confident and bold, but as a teenage girl her place in the world was uncertain: her mother executed by her capricious father and she herself not always welcomed at court.

Roper, William, *The Life of Sir Thomas More*, CreateSpace Independent Publishing Platform, 2014.

This is an affordable edition of the first biography of More, written by his son-in-law.

## SUGGESTED SEARCH TERMS

A Man for All Seasons AND film

A Man for All Seasons AND Robert Bolt

Sir Thomas More

Henry VIII AND great matter

Henry VIII AND Reformation

Thomas Howard, Duke of Norfolk

Anne Boleyn

Margaret More Roper

humanism AND Renaissance

# Night of January 16th

**AYN RAND**

**1934**

Ayn Rand's *Night of January 16th* (1933) was a successful Broadway play and has many attractive elements of a legal thriller: plot twists and suspense. Unfortunately, its gimmick of a jury drawn from audience members to decide the verdict of the trial that makes up the body of the play, and therefore the outcome of the final scene of the play, is not available to readers of the text. However, Rand considered far more important than any of the play's literary qualities its usefulness as a platform for projecting the ideals of her objectivist philosophy. Rand believed in a sort of hypercapitalism, in which leading entrepreneurs, whom she unashamedly thought to be on a higher level than most human beings, should be free to pursue their own interests with absolute selfishness and with everyone below acting in the same way but under their guidance, so that society as a whole would benefit as everyone fulfilled and enriched themselves. After writing successful novels in the 1940s and 1950s, Rand devoted herself to lecturing and writing solely to promote objectivism. She succeeded to the degree that many of her followers and readers obtained the highest government positions and worked to implement her ideas.

## AUTHOR BIOGRAPHY

Rand was born in St. Petersburg, Russia, on February 2, 1905. Her birth name was Alisa Zinov'yevna Rosenbaum, but throughout her

*Ayn Rand* (© *Library of Congress, Prints & Photographs Division, Reproduction number LC-USZ62-114904 (b&w film copy neg.)*)

adult life she used her pen name "Ayn Rand" (whose origin and meaning are obscure). Her family was Jewish but not particularly religious. Her father, Zinovy Zakharovich Rosenbaum, was a pharmacist; he owned a large building as a rental property, which contained his pharmacy and the family apartment. Rand attended a prestigious private school, the Stoiunina Gymnasium, where her best friend, Olga, was the sister of the later prominent novelist Vladimir Nabokov. After the Communist Revolution, Rand's family was dispossessed of its property, and during the Russian Civil War they fled to territory controlled by the White anti-Communist faction in the Crimea, making the thousand-mile trip on foot. They eventually ended up back in their home city in very reduced circumstances.

Because in the Soviet Union universities were free and open to women, Rand was able to take a degree in philosophy (though not without a hiatus caused by her expulsion for coming from a bourgeois background) and spent a year at graduate school in film studies. Rand took the opportunity in 1926 to travel to the United States, where she had relatives. She lived with her extended family in Chicago for several

months, perfecting her English, before they bought her a train ticket for Hollywood. They sent her with a letter of introduction from a relative who owned a movie theater to the prominent producer Louis B. Meyer. Rand took various jobs in Hollywood, working on the highly collaborative process of script production and acting as an extra (through which work she met Frank O'Connor, whom she married in 1929) and as a wardrobe mistress. Her main goal was to advance her own writing career.

The text that would become known as *Night of January 16th* (originally titled *Penthouse Legend*) was one of several screenplays and plays that Rand wrote in the 1920s and early 1930s, most of which would remain unfinished or unproduced. In order to promote the play, Rand offered it to be used for the senior play at Hollywood High School, but it was rejected. She turned down an offer by Al Woods to produce the play on Broadway; he naturally wanted to buy control of the text and eventually put on a successful production of the drama in a local theater in Los Angeles in 1934 (under the title *Woman on Trial*). Woods renewed his offer, giving Rand unusual, but not absolute control of the text. She accepted, and the play had a successful run on Broadway for several months in 1935–1936. Much of its appeal came from the play's gimmick of choosing a jury from the audience, whose verdict determined which of two possible endings were used in each performance. Rand, however, could not tolerate the normal changes in the text of any drama that are made during the actual production and spent years in legal wrangling with Woods over control of the text. *Night of January 16th* was made into a Hollywood film in 1941; Rand wrote a screenplay, but it was rejected. The production, critically and commercially unsuccessful, went ahead in a substantially different version.

With the profits from *Night of January 16th*, Rand was able to turn to writing novels and published *We the Living* (set during the Russian Revolution) in 1936 and the dystopian science-fiction novel *Anthem* in 1938. In 1943, Rand published *The Fountainhead*, which became a best seller. This novel reflects, in many respects, Rand's experience with *Night of January 16th*. It concerns the architect Howard Roark, who designs a building on the condition that it be built by its owner exactly as designed. When Roark returns from a vacation and finds significant alterations in his design, he blows up the building. He is acquitted in court, however, when his closing speech convinces the jury of the validity of his objectivist position. Rand returned to science fiction in her final novel, *Atlas Shrugged* (1957), in which a group of objectivist supermen blow up not a building but all of human civilization, after control of society is wrested from them by collectivist moochers.

Throughout the 1950s and 1960s, Rand devoted herself to building up an objectivist movement, lecturing and writing essays for various objectivist pamphlets and newsletters. Rand gathered around herself a group of young followers who included future Federal Reserve chairman Alan Greenspan. The group took the self-mocking name the "Collective." One of its most important members was the psychologist Nathaniel Branden, and the organization founded to spread objectivism was originally called the Nathaniel Branden Institute. Rand not only began an affair with Branden but also held a meeting with her lover; her husband, Frank; and Branden's wife, explaining to them that the affair was perfectly rational and necessary and that Frank had to absent himself from their apartment on Tuesday afternoons and Thursday evenings when Rand and Branden would meet. This event is generally seen as the cause of Frank's alcoholism. If anyone in the Collective disagreed with Rand, she would convene a meeting of the group and, for all intents and purposes, hold a trial and force the other members to vote the offender out. This happened to Branden himself when Rand discovered he was having an affair with another woman. Leonard Peikoff (Greenspan's cousin) took over leadership of the objectivist movement.

Rand regained full control of the text of *Night of January 16th* and in 1968 published a final, definitive edition. This was produced off-Broadway under the title *Penthouse Legend*, but it did not meet with commercial success. Rand was a lifelong smoker and was diagnosed with lung cancer in 1974; one of her lungs had to be surgically removed. She quit smoking, and members of the Collective urged her to speak out about the dangers of smoking. Rand refused, insisting that her condition was only a coincidence and that the statistical correlation between smoking and lung cancer had been manufactured by collectivist forces within the government to attack the entrepreneurs who ran the tobacco industry. Rand died of pneumonia at her home in New York on March 6, 1982. Peikoff inherited her estate, which

came to about one million dollars, an unusually small sum after so successful a literary career. Rand had never invested any money, unwilling to pay taxes to the government on her profits.

## PLOT SUMMARY

The texts of dramas are inherently unstable compared with other genres, since directors often feel free to make any changes they consider necessary for their production. The history of the text of *Night of January 16th* is especially troubled: although it was composed in 1933 by Rand, ownership of it was split with her producer, Al Woods. Rand envisioned the play as an ideological statement, while Woods was interested in adapting it to the needs of a commercial audience. Productions he oversaw (as well as versions published under his control) were often very different from Rand's text. After a long legal dispute, Rand resecured sole ownership of the text and edited and published a new and revised version in 1968 that she considered definitive. This is the text followed here. Rand's preferred title for the work was *Penthouse Legend*. (Woods declined to use the title on the ground that it would be commonly understood in a salacious manner and damage the work's reputation; the play was staged in the 1970s, unsuccessfully, under that title off-Broadway.) Rand finally republished the play under *Night of January 16th*. By then, the work was well known by that title, but it is often referred to in objectivist literature as *Penthouse Legend*.

### Note to Producer
In a brief notice intended for the production staff of the play rather than the audience, Rand explains the gimmick of the play, that the verdict of the trial conducted during the play can go either way and will be decided by a jury selected from the audience.

### Act One
The curtain opens on a courtroom, with the lawyers and court officials but not the judge in place and the audience in the same position as the audience in a real courtroom. The judge, William Heath, enters and orders the bailiff to empanel the jury. He does so, calling audience members by name. (Presumably the audience members willing to participate registered beforehand and were

## MEDIA ADAPTATIONS

- Rand's play was filmed as *The Night of January 16th* in 1941, directed by William Clemens, produced by Sol C. Siegel and starring Robert Preston and Ellen Drew. It was released by Paramount.

- In 1989, a Hindi language adaptation of *Night of January 16th, Gawaahi*, was filmed by Anant Balani, produced by Rajiv Mehra and Adityaraj Kapoor. It starred Zeenat Aman and Ashtosh Gowariker. This adaptation was a musical with lyrics by Sardar Anjum and music by Uttam-Jagdish.

- A television adaptation of *Night of January 16th* was broadcast in New York on July 12, 1952, on WOR-TV's *Broadway Television Theatre*, starring Neil Hamilton and Virginia Gilmore.

- Another adaptation appeared on May 10, 1956, on CBS's *Lux Video Theatre*, starring Phyllis Thaxter.

- *Night of January 16th* became the *ITV Play of the Week* in Britain on January 12, 1960, starring Maxine Audley and Cec Linder.

- A radio production of *Night of January 16th* appeared on the BBC on August 4, 1962.

picked at random before the performance began; however, in the Broadway run, celebrities were often invited to the play and served on the jury alongside audience members.)

Flint, the prosecutor, begins his opening argument. He describes how, on the night of January 16, the body of Bjorn Faulkner, the Swedish financier, had fallen fifty stories from his penthouse apartment onto Broadway. This was at first thought to be a suicide motivated by Faulkner's financial ruin. Though his business turns out to have been mostly based on fraud, at one time it was among the largest in the world to the extent that its gold-mining concerns made it important in maintaining the world economy, which was then based on the gold standard. Flint

suggests, however, that Faulkner was attempting to save his financial empire through a new deal with another millionaire, John Graham Whitfield, and, in fact, had married his daughter, Nancy Lee. This has caused him to break with this mistress, Karen Andre, whom he fired as his secretary. Flint accuses her of murdering Faulkner in revenge for her romantic loss.

The first witness is Dr. Thomas Kirkland, the coroner who examined Faulkner's body. He tells Flint that because of the cold, there is no way to precisely establish Faulkner's time of death. Moreover, the body was too badly damaged to rule out death sometime before the fall. Kirkland is followed by John Joseph Hutchins, the night watchman in Faulkner's building. He testifies that Faulkner and Andre had lived in the penthouse of the building, but after his marriage Faulkner moved out. The only time he saw him come back was on January 16, when Faulkner, Andre, and two men Hutchins didn't know (one of whom was noticeably drunk) came in through the lobby and went up to the penthouse. After a short time, the drunken man left, driving away and followed by another car. Ten minutes later, the other guest left too, and then Faulkner's body hit the pavement. When he went out to see what had happened, Andre soon came down and crouched weeping over the body.

The next witness is Homer Van Fleet, a private detective that Faulkner's wife had hired to follow her husband. He tells essentially the same story as Hutchins, but he had been on the roof of a nearby building looking down on the penthouse and testifies that Andre had shoved Faulkner's unconscious or already dead body over the railing of the penthouse. Under cross-examination by Stevens, Van Fleet admits that he had been drinking prior to witnessing the scene on the rooftop. Stevens also insinuates that the detective had been paid to perjure himself by Faulkner's widow.

The next witness is Elmer Sweeney, the police inspector who investigated Faulkner's death. He relates how at the crime scene Van Fleet gave him the same information he had testified to, in front of Andre, which caused her to laugh hysterically. Andre said then that she had struggled with Faulkner to keep him from jumping and explained that the two men who were with them were associates of Faulkner's she did not know and gave them what turn out to be false names. Magda Svenson, an old retainer of the Faulkner family who was the housekeeper in the penthouse, is the next to testify. It is clear she loathes Andre as a corrupting influence on Faulkner, whose nursemaid she had been when he was a child. She begins to describe Andre's and Faulkner's love life in very salacious detail, causing Stevens to call for a mistrial since the testimony is irrelevant and might prejudice the jury. Andre blurts out that it might prejudice them in her favor, but the motion is in any case overruled. On the day of Faulkner's wedding, Svenson saw Andre entertain another man in the penthouse, namely, the sober man who came with Andre and Faulkner on January 16.

Svenson's testimony is interrupted when Faulkner's widow, Nancy Lee, comes into the courtroom. She has been thought to be grieving in seclusion in California but has now come forward to testify. She paints a highly romanticized picture of her courtship with Faulkner that runs counter to everything we otherwise know of his objectivist ideals. When asked whether Faulkner had loved her, she replies rather that she owned him. The act ends in an outburst by Andre shouting that it is perfectly obvious which of the two women Faulkner had loved and one can hardly deny this.

## Act Two

The second act begins with the testimony of John Graham Whitfield, Faulkner's father-in-law. He verifies that he had loaned Faulkner twenty-five million dollars (probably close to a billion in today's money) not only for the sake of his daughter but also to avoid the economic chaos that would follow the collapse Faulkner's business concerns were facing.

James Chandler, a police handwriting expert, next testifies that he believes Faulkner's suicide note was in his own handwriting. Siegurd Jungquist, Faulkner's bookkeeper and replacement for Andre as his secretary, testifies next. When asked if he was aware of Faulkner's financial irregularities, he seems shocked, since in his view a great man like Faulkner could do no wrong. Stevens receives an anonymous message that Andre should not testify until the unknown sender arrives in the courtroom, but Andre insists on testifying immediately.

Like Faulkner's widow, she describes their whole relationship at length. When she first started to work for him, she was subjected to severe sexual harassment by Faulkner, including

an offer of prostitution and a threat of rape, but that was what she wanted, to be dominated by a man even stronger than she herself. She describes Faulkner's fraud in more detail. She acted fully as his partner and had no moral qualm, since she considered that the drive to gain greater power and wealth justified everything. Their scheme started to come apart when Whitfield would not extend a loan of ten million dollars. Whitfield used this leverage to blackmail Faulkner into marrying his daughter. In the end, however, Whitfield refused to give him an agreed-upon additional twenty-five million loan, so Faulkner and Andre simply took it by forging Whitfield's signature. She was obviously leading up to an account of how Faulkner had killed himself rather than face jail and bankruptcy when Whitfield exposed this, but before she can finish, the gangster "Guts" Regan rushes into the courtroom and says that Faulkner is dead. Andre faints.

## Act Three

Recomposed, Andre continues her testimony. Far from killing himself, Faulkner made an elaborate plan to fake his suicide and take Whitfield's money and flee to Argentina with Andre. They were assisted by Regan. He agreed because he, too, loved Andre and was the man Svenson had seen kissing her. He procured the body of a gangster who had died in a shoot-out with other criminals, and that was the body dumped over the penthouse ledge. The dead body, carried by Regan and Faulkner, had been the supposedly drunken man seen by the night watchman. But now, Faulkner was actually dead. In cross-examination, Flint still pursues his original theory of the crime, suggesting that Andre had murdered Faulkner and plotted to run off with Regan and the stolen money. Her motive is now that Faulkner had been reformed by his wife, come to his senses, and rejected Andre. Still, Andre insists that Faulkner could never have been turned into the altruistic monster his widow had described.

Regan testifies next. After they left the apartment, he and Faulkner were to drive separately to a small airfield in what is now the middle of Brooklyn and fly directly out of the country. As arranged, Faulkner got there first. When Regan arrived, he found that his car was there but Faulkner was not. Moreover, the plane was gone, and Regan could tell from tire tracks that it had taken off, but Faulkner didn't know how to fly. There was also another empty car there. Regan waited to see whose it was, and the owner walked up to it about dawn. Regan threatened to report to his contacts with the newspapers whatever the man had been up to and received a check for five thousand dollars for his silence. However, this was only a ruse so he could find out the man's identity. It was Whitfield. He couldn't threaten him into saying anything about Faulkner, so he let him go.

Regan eventually found his plane in an abandoned airfield in New Jersey, burned up and with a charred body inside he judged to be Faulkner's. Through his questioning, Flint slightly alters his theory of the crime, suggesting that Andre and Regan together murdered Faulkner. In cross-examination, Stevens rather suggests that Whitfield was the man who drove after Faulkner (identified as the drunken man in earlier testimony) and that he had killed Faulkner. Trying to divert suspicion, Whitfield points out that even if he had wanted to do such a thing, he could not have known of the plot about the fake suicide and decide to take action just then. This causes Jungquist, the bookkeeper, to return to the stand to testify that he, in fact, had told Whitfield about the transfer of the stolen money to a bank in Argentina on the afternoon of January 16, proving Whitfield has just perjured himself.

After the attorney's summations, the bailiff leads the jury offstage, where they actually deliberate and deliver a verdict. This time is filled onstage by a remarkably cinematic device, with all of the witnesses coming back onto a darkened stage to stand one by one in a spotlight and recite key lines from their earlier testimony.

### Not Guilty Ending
Andre thanks the jury on behalf of Faulkner.

### Guilty Ending
Expecting to be executed for murder, Andre thanks the jury for sparing her from having to commit suicide. She clearly has no interest in living without Faulkner.

## CHARACTERS

### Karen Andre
Andre represents the ideal type of Rand's super-entrepreneur, someone whose competence sets her far above the norms and calls of ordinary society. Laws and morality do not apply to her, and the satisfaction of her selfish desires takes precedence over, for example, the needs of the poor during the depth of the Depression. She is subservient only to her lover, Faulkner, who possessed the same qualities to an even greater degree. This isolation and removal from human norms are what Rand is getting at in her description of Andre in the stage directions: "One's first impression of her is that to handle her would require the services of an animal trainer, not an attorney." She is not wild in appearance, but rather unusually calm, yet "one feels the tense vitality, the primitive fire, the untamed strength in the defiant immobility of her slender body."

At one point in the play, Andre's housekeeper, Svenson, testifies about her mistress's sex life with Faulkner (which clearly shows that, despite her claims of piety and virtue, she was actively spying on them). The fact that they were not married violated most social norms that would have been shared by an American jury in the 1930s. Nevertheless, even in the midst of her trial for murder, when Andre hears Svenson's testimony, she cannot help but fall into a reverie, recalling her past joys. She is so convinced of her own true virtue (as opposed to the collectivist virtue of mass society that she considers to be a form of oppression) that she imagines the jury will be prejudiced in her favor by Svenson's testimony. This is all the more incredible because Svenson described as part of their practices a specially made nightgown wrought from a mesh of fine platinum wire, which even in Depression era money must have cost tens of thousands of dollars to produce during a time when millions of men could not find jobs to feed their families and those who could were happy to work for ten dollars a week. But Andre—which is to say Rand—cannot imagine that such indulgence in the midst of such want might be viewed negatively, since Andre was merely exercising her true superior nature. While Rand says in the introduction of the play that the question of guilt or innocence is finely balanced, an objective reading of the play leaves little doubt of Andre's guilt (not of murder but certainly of numerous other crimes), and, as Rand admits, what the jury is choosing between is Andre's morality of selfishness and indulgence and a collective sense of justice.

### James Chandler
James Chandler is the handwriting expert who authenticates Faulkner's suicide note.

## Court Attendants

Verisimilitude requires various staff members in a fictional courtroom, including bailiffs, guards, the court reporter, and others. While they must be present onstage, they are in either nonspeaking roles or speak no more than is required to ask the jury to enter or leave the courtroom.

## Nancy Lee Faulkner (née Whitfield)

Faulkner's widow is presented in stereotypical terms as a superficial socialite, as when Homer Van Fleet, the private detective she hired to shadow her husband, is asked how she reacted when told her husband was continuing to see Andre regularly. He answers that "Mrs. Faulkner is a lady and, as such, she has no reactions." When she enters the courtroom, the stage directions describe her as "twenty-two, blonde, delicate, perfect as a costly porcelain statuette." The contrast of her artificial beauty with the untamed natural beauty of Andre is purposeful. The most revealing thing about Nancy Lee, from the point of view of objectivism, also comes from Van Fleet, who says, "Mr. Faulkner was the most devoted of husbands and he loved his wife dearly." This is tellingly accompanied by one of the play's few stage directions: "He declaims in a slightly unnatural manner." Rand needs the audience to read a great deal into this odd phrase and its odd pronunciation.

Rand's super-entrepreneurs are based on Friedrich Nietzsche's ideal or superior man. Part of the excellence of the superior man in Nietzsche's thought is that he accepts reality as it is and his place in that reality, his fate, in other words. Inferior men, whom the superior man must control and use, however, construct a false version of reality, comforting to their own weakness and helplessness. Since it is clear that Faulkner had no romantic interest in his wife and was never in love with anyone except Andre, the line parroted by Van Fleet must have been something that he heard Nancy Lee say all the time, something she repeated as a mantra. It is the opposite of the truth, but it was vital to her identity, so she spoke it as if it were the truth and as if repetition could make it true like speaking a spell. For Rand, there could hardly have been a clearer characterization of Faulkner's widow than what she called a collectivist creep.

One can compare this, however, to Rand's relationship with her husband, Frank. When asked about him by audience members at her lectures, she claimed that Frank was essentially the same person as Howard Roark, the entrepreneurial superman main character of her novel *The Fountainhead*. In fact, he was perfectly content to run his small business out of their farm in California, selling flowers to nurseries. Yet Rand claimed that she hated the farm, and his desire to leave it was the reason they moved to New York, although this seems rather to have been motivated by her desire to be nearer to her lover, Nathaniel Branden. Rand also spent considerable effort in later life denying that Frank developed Alzheimer's disease and tried various techniques to train him to not lose his memory. In *Night of January 16th*, when asked under oath whether her husband had loved her, Faulkner's widow pointed replies, "Bjorn Faulkner was mine." Although Rand may have imagined herself as Karen Andre, this line seems more truly reflective of the author's life.

## Homer Van Fleet

Van Fleet is the private detective Faulkner's widow hired to follow her husband or to protect him, as she later testifies.

## District Attorney Flint

Flint, the prosecutor, is presented as a stereotypical representation of respectability. At the same time, he has to represent for Rand the collective mass of society that stands in opposition to her superhuman entrepreneurial heroes. Through this equation, Rand sets up her own position as countercultural, something that mainstream society inherently rejects. Since he is a prosecutor in New York City, one would have to consider that Flint ought to be the kind of talented and successful man that Rand admires. However, Rand's follower Mimi Reisel Gladstein, in the character sketches in *The New Ayn Rand Companion*, classifies him as part of the "secondary unworthy or villainous characters" precisely because he represents the interest of society against the right of Rand's heroes to dominate it. At the same time, in his opening statement to the jury, Flint is responsible for describing Faulkner in Randian hero-worshipping terms. Rand considered that her works demonstrated her philosophy, and the fact that such a black-and-white division of characters is possible shows how simplified her characterization was in service of that aim.

## Judge Heath

Though Heath literally looks over the entire play from the bench, his part does not allow much scope for character development. He does little more than sustain or overrule objections.

## John Hutchins

Hutchins is the night watchman in Faulkner's building.

## Siegurd Jungquist

Jungquist had been Faulkner's longtime book-keeper and succeeded Andre as his secretary. He displays, from the objectivist viewpoint, the proper respect and difference of an ordinary man to so great an entrepreneur.

## Dr. Thomas Kirkland

Kirkland is the coroner who examined Faulkner's body.

## Lawrence "Guts" Regan

Regan is the gangster who assisted Falkner in faking his suicide. He rather melodramatically claims that he acted as he did out of his love for Andre, even while realizing that it was impossible.

## Defense Attorney Stevens

While Stevens is no less respectable and no less gray in hair and clothing than the district attorney, he has the air of "a man of the world." Because he defends Andre, Stevens is a loyal servant of Rand's superhuman heroes if not one himself.

## Magda Svenson

Svenson was Faulkner's housekeeper; she had begun working for his family in Sweden thirty-eight years earlier. Rand goes out of her way to describe her as unpleasant, giving her one of the longest descriptions in her stage directions: She "waddles toward the witness stand. She is fat, middle-aged, with tight, drawn lips, suspicious eyes, an air of offended righteousness. Her clothes are plain, old-fashioned, meticulously neat." Swenson hates Andre because she views her as having corrupted Faulkner, whom she thought of almost as her son. In other words, Svenson symbolizes everything in collective culture that stands opposed to Rand's superhuman entrepreneurs. Rand also makes her fanatically religious. When Swenson is sworn in to testify in court, "she takes the Bible, raises it slowly to her lips, kisses it solemnly, and hands it back, taking the whole ceremony with a profound religious seriousness." Rand considered religion to be as grotesque and false as she does Svenson's person and character, but associating religious display with this obviously unpleasant character is as far as Rand dared to go in criticizing religion in a popular play in the 1930s. In contrast, Andre's blasé declaration of atheism when offered the Bible to swear on would probably seem prejudicial to the audience.

## Elmer Sweeney

Sweeney is the police officer who oversaw the crime scene at Faulkner's suicide. The stage directions imply that he is rather childish. Rand is utilizing here the stereotype, common in 1930s films, of the Irish cop, bumbling and incompetent. His fond memories of seeing Andre's collection of nightgowns and his wish that he had seen Andre's dress, torn supposedly in the struggle with Faulkner, fall off are pure comic relief.

## John Graham Whitfield

Whitfield, like his daughter, symbolizes the tyranny of collectivist society that oppresses her entrepreneurial supermen. He wished to acquire and control Faulkner for his daughter. His further testimony that he was also concerned about saving the small investors that would be wiped out if Faulkner's business empire collapsed has to be considered in the light of objectivism. While, to the typical audience member, this may seem like a virtuous covering over his self-interested actions, to objectivism this kind of altruism is the height of vice. We can thus believe that Rand intended him to be understood sincerely and that this sentiment painted him as a villain. Similarly, his statement concerning Faulkner's character, "We were as different as two human beings could be: I believe in one's duty above all; Bjorn Faulkner believed in nothing but his own pleasure," to objectivist ears shows Whitfield as corrupt and Faulkner as a hero.

## THEMES

### Sex Roles

Karen Andre recounts on the witness stand how she became Bjorn Faulkner's lover:

> He said he'd give me a thousand kroner if I would go into the inner office and take my skirt off. I said I wouldn't. He said if I didn't, he'd take me. I said, try it.

# TOPICS FOR FURTHER STUDY

- *The White Tiger*, by the Indian novelist Aravind Adiga, won the Booker Prize in 2008. It is the autobiography of an Indian man who rises from the lowest level of Indian society to run a successful taxi company, at the cost of abandoning his family and committing murder to advance his career. The main theme of the novel is that Indian society is a metaphorical rooster coop that holds everyone in the place to which they have been allotted, even the rich. The hero, forced to maintain his company though bribery of corrupt officials, has only moved to a different part of the coop. The book not only obviously incorporates many of Rand's favorite themes but also comes to conclusions different from hers. Write a paper analyzing the book from an objectivist viewpoint.

- Largely ignored by the academic community, objectivism has become a creature of new media, and, for instance, most contemporary objectivist fiction takes the form of self-published e-books. By the same token, perhaps the single most important critical writing on Rand has been undertaken by Adam Lee. He published an extensive section-by-section review of *Atlas Shrugged* in the form of a series of posts on his blog *Daylight Atheism* (http://www.patheos.com/blogs/daylightatheism/series/atlas-shrugged/) with a precis at Salon.com (http://www.salon.com/2014/04/29/10_insane_things_i_learned_about_the_world_reading_ayn_rands_atlas_shrugged_partner/). It should be noted that although Rand was a strident atheist, the contemporary atheist community is remarkably hostile to her, since the movement is for the most part politically progressive. Create your own blog with a series of posts devoted to the critical interpretation of *Night of January 16th*.

- *Theodore Boone: Kid Lawyer* (2010) is the first of a series of young-adult courtroom dramas by John Grisham. Write a paper comparing this novel to *Night of January 16th* in terms of how they both use their courtroom settings to create drama and suspense.

- *Night of January 16th* is filled with legal incongruities, from the admission of hearsay evidence to the order of the attorney's closing statements. Write a paper analyzing the play from the point of view of legal procedure.

---

It seems clear that Andre consented to the encounter, but it might not have looked that way to an outside observer. Rather than force or coercion being used in the encounter, it seems that the participants fetishized a sort of role playing of inequality in their sex roles, that both participants want the man to be domineering and aggressive. These are characteristics that belong to Rand's type of the objectivist hero in his business dealings and all other aspects of his life. Rand is careful to have Andre say that this was the first time she ever had sex, suggesting that she had never before met such an overwhelmingly heroic figure as Faulkner. Moreover, every romantic relationship in all of Rand's later novels is presented in exactly the same terms.

While Andre and Rand's other female characters represent her heroic type as much as her male characters, there is nevertheless a hierarchy of heroism, and the objectivist naturally looks toward the more perfect business hero as someone to follow and even submit to. The basic fantasy that Rand incorporates into her dramatic narrative is the mainstay of romance novels and must have wide appeal to female taste. This general theme of Rand's has attracted the attention of feminist scholars. The title of Susan Brownmiller's "Ayn Rand: A Traitor to Her Own Sex" suggests the general tenor of the response, but Robert Sheaffer, in his "Rereading Rand on Gender in the Light of Paglia," gives a more sensitive reading, suggesting that Rand is simply reverting

*The medical examiner cannot determine whether Faulkner fell to his death or was thrown out of the penthouse, or even whether he was alive when he fell* *(© Jacqueline Klose / Shutterstock.com)*

to the normal circumstances of traditional patri-archal sexuality.

## Crime

Rand and her objectivist philosophy have a curi-ous relationship with crime. She considered to be right, just, and moral the very things that society condemns, such as selfishness and ruthless self-interest, and the very things that society upholds, such as altruism, to be vice and crime. When, in *Night of January 16th*, the prosecutor Flint reminds Andre of the various laws she has broken, she responds, "Laws made *by* whom, Mr. Flint? And *for* whom?" She genuinely can-not understand that the law applies to people like her and Faulkner.

Although Rand was too committed to nineteenth-century liberalism to move far in the direction of anarchist libertarianism, her characters inevitably find that their objectivist ideals move them outside the law. The injustice of the law turns her heroes into outlaws. In the 1968 intro-duction to the play, she writes, "For the purpose of dramatizing the conflict of independence versus conformity, a criminal—a social outcast—can be

an eloquent symbol." Howard Roark, in *The Foun-tainhead*, dynamites a building he designed but did not own to prevent his ideals from being compro-mised, while in *Atlas Shrugged* Francisco d'Anco-nia blows up the facilities at several copper mines that were owned by shareholders in his company when he turns his back on the society he thinks of as moochers. Also in *Atlas Shrugged*, the Taggart family fortune was begun by the heroine Dagny's grandfather, who murdered a state legislator who was about to help pass legislation regulating his business.

In *Night of January 16th*, Rand considered the gangster "Guts" Regan as one of her entre-preneurial supermen thwarted by the conven-tions of collectivist society and forced to run a protection racket. Faulkner's business empire, too, was based on fraud, as was the case with his real-life model Ivar Kreuger. Faulkner's shady past is interestingly problematized in the play through the testimony of his widow:

> I told him that it was our duty to save his enterprises, our duty to the world he had wronged, not to ourselves. I made him realize his past mistakes and he was ready to atone for

them. We were entering a new life together, a life of unselfish devotion to the service and welfare of others.

An objectivist would immediately realize that Faulkner could never have been persuaded of any such thing. What she espouses is precisely the opposite of objectivism, which holds selfishness and self-interest to be the only ideals.

What the jury has to decide is whether the objectivist morality that would hold Faulkner blameless is correct, whether his heroism washes away all guilt, or whether the laws and morality of the society he set himself against are correct. Stevens says as much to the jury, when he tells them that Faulkner "had put himself beyond all present standards; whether it was below or above them, is a question for each of us to decide personally." Although Rand clearly believed that a not guilty verdict represented an endorsement of objectivism, this is not necessarily the case. In the fictive world of the play, that is to say in Rand's imagination, it seems quite clear that Andre did not kill Faulkner and the members of the jury could vote that way without endorsing her personal ideology or approving the innumerable crimes of which she clearly is guilty but which are not before the jury in this case.

# STYLE

## *Drama*

Just as objectivism as a whole is deeply indebted to nineteenth-century liberalism, Rand's aesthetic theory looks back to Aristotle, whom she considered virtually the founder of Western civilization. Aristotle's *Poetics* is an expression of his aesthetic theory, based on criticism of the preceding century of Greek drama (the works of Aeschylus, Sophocles, and Euripides and many dramatists whose texts are now lost). Aristotle considered that a good play preserves what he calls the dramatic unities: the play should take place in a single location represented onstage and in real time, no longer than the performance of the play itself lasts. In terms of film, one would say that a play ought to be a single shot, as if it was a real event captured in documentary footage.

Rand does a good job of following these rules in *Night of January 16th*. The entire drama takes place inside the courtroom, with the trial collapsed into a single morning, during a time no

longer than the performance. Only the verdict and brief ending are meant to take place a short time later, following the deliberation of the jury. (The stage direction indicates the second act takes place on the following day, but this is for verisimilitude within the American justice system and is probably not noticed by most audience members.)

In other respects, however, Rand misunderstands Aristotle or, perhaps one might say, reads her own ideas into the philosopher. For her, the Aristotelian aesthetic requires that the story of the play concerns a heroic character building up his own soul, his own consciousness through his own efforts, which is undoubtedly and avowedly the main theme of all Rand's works. For Aristotle, however, the term *tragedy* passes from the name of a genre to its modern meaning of an event of great sadness, in that the dramas he studied invariably concerned the destruction of a great man by forces outside his control, more particularly if they emanated from the divine world or, as moderns would say, from within the hidden depths of the great man's own character. *Night of January 16th*, however, comes closer to Aristotle's original idea than any of Rand's other works. Faulkner is destroyed by the bargain he makes with Whitfield but which he cannot keep because it is contrary to his character.

## *Melodrama*

The term *melodrama* originally applied to any stage play with a musical score designed to heighten the emotional intensity of the accompanied scenes. It evolved in critical usage through the nineteenth century to mean a work that sought an exaggerated emotional intensity through sensationalistic events as a substitute for involving the audience in the emotional lives of the characters. Rand comments on the technique within the text of the play when the private detective who had been following Faulkner on the night of the fake suicide describes "Miss Andre sobbing over it [i.e., the body], fit to move a first-night audience." Rand means that her performance was melodramatic acting so intense that it would have affected even experienced theatergoers. *Night of January 16th* has substantial elements of melodrama.

Rand, in her introduction to the 1968 edition of the play, criticized Woods, her producer, for being able to see the potential only for melodrama in the play but at the same time admitted that such a view was not entirely invalid: "Melodrama was the only element of my play that [Woods] understood." She does not deny that there is a melodramatic element in the play. Her conflicts with Woods arose over his attempt to intensify the play's melodrama. She continued:

> He introduced, in small touches, a junk heap of worn, irrelevant melodramatic devices that clashed with the style, did not advance the action and served only to confuse the audience—such as . . . a flashy gun moll, etc.

Melodramatic elements in the play as Rand wrote it include the exaggerated description of Andre that Flint, the prosecutor, gives to the jury in his opening statement, describing her as Faulkner's "notorious mistress" and accusing her of murder in an overwrought metaphor, making her "the hands that helped to raise Bjorn Faulkner high over the world; the hands that threw him down, from a great height, to crash into a pavement cold as this woman's heart." Rand becomes so carried away in her rhetoric that what crashes from a great height is the syntax of the sentence.

## HISTORICAL CONTEXT

### Ivar Kreuger

The figure of Bjorn Faulkner, the overshadowing presence of *Night of January 16th*, who has, in fact, died before the action of the play starts, was based on a real person, Ivar Kreuger, the Swedish match king. In her introduction to *Night of January 16th*, Rand describes Kreuger as "a mysterious figure, a 'lone wolf,' celebrated as a man of genius, of unswerving determination and spectacular audacity." By the early 1920s, Kreuger had become one of the most powerful and most famous businessmen in the world, though he does not quite fit the mold of Rand's idealized tycoon. Kreuger had been born in Sweden, on March 2, 1880. He was not, like the heroes of Rand's novels, the creator of a new architectural style or a new industrial process but rather founded his fortune by buying the Swedish and German patent rights to a new steel-and-concrete construction technique developed by American engineers. He became a prominent building contractor, for example, constructing the stadium for the 1912 Olympic

Games in Stockholm. In 1917, Kreuger spun off the building company to his partner, the engineer Paul Toll, and converted his own considerable profits, together with his father's match factory, into a financial holding company and rapidly expanded, taking over company after company.

At one point, Kreuger owned half of the world's iron ore deposits. However, his greatest success was with matches. Beginning with acquiring other match manufacturers in Scandinavia, Kreuger quickly gained an effective monopoly on matches worldwide. While matches may seem like a trivial item, they were indispensable at the time, before gas or liquid fuel lighters were common. They were used not only for smoking but also for lighting stoves and similar tasks, so people had to buy them. Once Kreuger had a monopoly, he was free to price gouge at almost any level he wished. He was able to get around antitrust laws in many countries by giving loans to the local governments.

As successful as Krueger's efforts were, he expanded much too quickly, and he had to resort to crime to keep his enterprises expanding. Pioneering the same techniques that would later be used in the Enron Ponzi scheme (and which are recalled in some detail in *Night of January 16th* as Faulkner's methods), Kreuger would secure loans based on profits that were manufactured through false bookkeeping. He would then pay out the money in high dividends to attract investors, whose money was paid back to them and used to lure other investors, to keep inflating the whole scheme. Krueger may well have believed that his enterprise (which at one point had a theoretical value of one hundred billion dollars in modern money, more than a quarter of which existed only on paper) would eventually grow into solvency. When it became clear that it would not, Kreuger killed himself in his Paris apartment on March 12, 1932. In the 1960s, Kreuger's brother, Torsten, began writing a series of books arguing that his brother had been murdered, spawning a minor conspiracy theory, though, of course, Rand could have had no insight into this. Today, Krueger's enterprises have several successor companies, including Swedish Match, which dominates the cigar and chewing tobacco market in the United States.

*Karen Andre is on trial for Faulkner's murder, but at first she thinks his death is fake* *(© Everett Collection / Shutterstock.com)*

## CRITICAL OVERVIEW

Rand scholarship is in a somewhat unusual position. Her philosophy of objectivism was decidedly political and is deeply implicated in contemporary American politics. Alan Greenspan, chairman of the Federal Reserve Bank from 1987 to 2006, was one of Rand's chief disciples, while Paul Ryan, the Speaker of the House, makes *Atlas Shrugged* required reading for his staff. In addition, Rand has a dedicated following working to promote, rather than criticize and evaluate, her ideas. Her work has generally been ignored by academics to a degree remarkable for an author of her cultural importance; they tend to view objectivism as rather old-fashioned nineteenth-century philosophy. According to her entry in the *Stanford Encyclopedia of Philosophy*, academics also find that "her polemical style, often contemptuous tone, and the dogmatism and cult-like behavior of many of her fans also suggest that her

work is not worth taking seriously." As a result, most writing about Rand's thought is undertaken by either fervent objectivists or authors who feel that her political writing is dangerous to society. So any work about Rand must be carefully evaluated in terms of the prejudices of the author.

The main source for the history of *Night of January 16th* and its various productions is Rand's own introduction to the 1968 edition, supplemented, for instance, by Barbara Branden's biography, *The Passion of Ayn Rand*, which points out the importance of the income derived from the play in Rand's personal life, allowing her to write full time. Mimi Reisel Gladstein, in *The New Ayn Rand Companion*, gives extensive coverage of *Night of January 16th*. Aside from detailed character sketches, Gladstein observes that "*Night of January 16th* is significant for dramatic ingenuity and thematic content." The themes that were the very

# COMPARE & CONTRAST

- **1930s:** The year 1933 was the worst of the Great Depression in terms of unemployment, with a quarter of all American workers unemployed. This crisis followed a stock market crash in 1929 whose effects the government could do very little to alleviate, since the United States and most other Western countries had a gold-standard currency.

  **Today:** In terms of unemployment, the United States is now fully recovered from the 2008 stock market crash, after which the Federal Reserve created demand by expanding the fiat currency, limiting unemployment compared with the 1930s both in the percentage of unemployed and the duration of depressed employment levels.

- **1930s:** In *Night of January 16th*, Faulkner plans to flee the country in a private plane flown from an isolated rural airstrip in Brooklyn, New York.

**Today:** Urban sprawl has completely covered Brooklyn, and no plane could hope to get in the air near New York without being detected by the local air traffic control.

- **1930s:** Sexual harassment is illegal, but prosecutions are rare (and civil cases unheard of) as much because of the usual disparity in social rank between the criminal and the victim as a pervasive legal culture that imagined that such crimes were uncommon and also deeply queried the woman's role as a temptress.

  **Today:** Sexual harassment in the workplace is much more widely recognized as a serious problem, prosecutions are more common, and a wide variety of governmental bodies exist to deal with the problem. Large institutions make an effort to police themselves and prevent harassment, but many of the same barriers of class and gender discrimination persist.

---

source of the play's existence were also the cause of Rand's difficulties with Woods, the play's producer, since he felt its political and social content would be of little interest to the theatergoing public. Gladstein also surveys journalistic reviews of the play's theatrical productions, which reflect Woods's point of view. They are generally mediocre, reacting to the gimmick of the play in creating a jury drawn from the audience, and take no notice of its philosophical message. She concludes this section with the comment:

> Both sympathetic and hostile reviewers recognize Rand's dramatic power and passionate intensity. The sympathetic reviewers find that these qualities sweep them along; their interest never flags.... Negative reviewers scorn Rand's intensity as overwrought and her drama as melodramatic.

In *The Ayn Rand Cult*, Jeff Walker suggests that one factor that drew Rand to the real-life character of Ivar Kreuger as the basis for the character of Bjorn Faulkner in *Night of January 16th* was his connection with the tobacco industry, since Rand was fascinated with tobacco and it was one of the few indulgences she allowed herself.

## CRITICISM

### Bradley A. Skeen
*Skeen is a classicist. In the following essay, he explores the influence of the philosopher Friedrich Nietzsche on Rand's philosophy of objectivism as it is expressed in* Night of January 16th.

Rand was perfectly candid that *Night of January 16th* and all of her fiction was merely a platform for the symbolic or metaphorical exposition of her philosophy of objectivism. In a speech given in 1963 (reprinted in *The Ayn Rand Reader*), Rand clarified the form that this

IN OTHER WORDS, THE ACTIONS OF RAND'S
CHARACTERS WILL ALWAYS ILLUSTRATE
OBJECTIVISM."

takes: "The motive and purpose of my writing is *the projection of an ideal man*" (italics in original). Rand elaborates on this further in the introduction to the final edition of *Night of January 16th*, where she clearly and rationally describes the play in terms of her objectivist aesthetic theory as "a sense of life play . . . a preconceptual equivalent of metaphysics, an emotional, subconsciously integrated appraisal of *man's relationship to existence*." "Its events," she continues, "are not to be taken *literally*; they dramatize certain fundamental psychological characteristics, deliberately isolated and emphasized in order to convey a single abstraction: the characters' attitude toward life." In other words, the actions of Rand's characters will always illustrate objectivism. In order to understand *Night of January 16th*, therefore, it is necessary to understand objectivism, so it will be useful to inquire more closely into the character and origin of Rand's philosophy.

The early years of the Communist regime is an era known as the silver age in the history of Russian philosophy, and Rand was educated in this period, when Nietzsche was the dominant figure; she is known to have read extensively in the works of that philosopher. Nevertheless, Rand cannot be simply reduced to a strict Nietzschean. Even so, there are many Nietzschean ideas embedded in objectivism, especially its early forms, as demonstrated in *Night of January 16th* and *Anthem*—for example, the idea that the true and only worthwhile motivation for action is joy. Later in life, Rand wanted to downplay her debt to Nietzsche, stressing instead her originality, and rewrote *Anthem* accordingly. Thus, an objective understanding of the influence of Nietzsche on *Night of January 16th* can be had only by comparing some of Nietzsche's ideas with Rand's in the play.

A central idea of Nietzsche's philosophy—certainly the one most important in his reception by Rand—is expressed in the well-known but little-understood idea of the *will to power*. Nietzsche

uses power in its two senses, as the ability to accomplish something and as the ability to control others. The exercise of the will to power begins with a self-directed agent's attempting to reach some goal for his own purposes, proceeds with that agent's directing subordinate processes or other agents to achieve it, and is always subordinated toward the goal to be achieved. The exercise of power and the achievement of any worthwhile goal can come about only in the face of some resistance that must be overcome, coming either from other agents with contrary goals or from the difficulty of the process itself. The achievement of successfully overcoming resistance to reach the goal is what Nietzsche referred to as joy, which is ultimately the goal of all action. To explain through a trivial example, climbing two miles up a mountain gives one a greater sense of accomplishment than walking along sidewalks for two miles. Note that a climber is said to *conquer* a mountain. The will to power is a dialectical process through which creativity is released by overcoming obstacles, with each success becoming the basis for new achievement. In Nietzsche's view, two friends are paradoxically also competitors engaged in a conflict that builds up their friendship through the will to power.

Nietzsche developed, or rather explained, his ethical system by imagining a rather fanciful situation in the past, in much the same kind of thought experiment that Karl Marx and Sigmund Freud used to illustrate their ideas. Nietzsche imagined an ancient Greek hero who possessed all the qualities that would be defined as good, in contrast to his slave, who possessed all the qualities that could be defined as bad. The slave is physically incapable of using violence to gain his freedom, as his master presumably would in the same situation. Thus he reacts by striking at his heroic master intellectually, characterizing him as an oppressor, and twisting all of his virtues into vices. This clearly is not meant to be taken as a literal discussion of historical masters and slaves but rather is meant to suggest that the master and slave roles as he defines them are necessary to the will to power. In a notebook, posthumously published as *The Will to Power*, Nietzsche says that "a great man [i.e. the master] . . . wants no 'sympathetic' heart, but servants, tools; on his intercourse with men he is always intent on *making* something out of them." So the creativity necessary to reach the goal also elevates and transforms the subordinates who are used for that purpose.

# WHAT DO I READ NEXT?

- Some of Rand's private writings have been edited and published by David Harriman as *Journals of Ayn Rand* (1997). These documents are highly relevant both to Rand's biography and to the development of objectivism. Harriman is an objectivist (and the introduction to the book is written by Peikoff), so the selection of texts may have been made to promote that philosophy. For instance, Rand worked to distance herself from the influence of Nietzsche's philosophy, and Chris Sciabarra, in his *Ayn Rand: The Russian Radical*, suggests that a full publication of her journals from the early 1930s would help to clarify the issue of her philosophical originality or dependence.

- *Atlas Shrugged* (1957) is Rand's magnum opus, in terms of both its literary achievement and the developed form of objectivism presented in the novel.

- *Ayn Rand at 100* (2006) is an anthology of essays on Rand published by the Liberty Institute, the main objectivist organization in India, and edited by Tibor R. Machan. The essays either are by Indian authors or concern the relevance of objectivism for Indian society.

- Other than Rand herself, objectivism has not produced any important literary authors writing purely on that theme as Rand did, although a small number of dedicated objectivists self-publish their work, which may be in line with the libertarian streak of objectivism and seems to be preferred in many cases to more traditional publishing. However, the popular fantasy author Terry Goodkind is an avowed objectivist and often incorporates Rand's ideas into his novels. His book *The First Confessor* (2012) is often mentioned on objectivist discussion boards and concerns a society where magical powers seem to stand in for the supercapitalist qualities of Rand's heroes.

- Rand called *Calumet "K"* (1901), by Henry Kitchell Webster and Samuel Merwin, her favorite novel, and it was certainly one that had a great impact on her writing. Rand also wrote the introduction to a reprint edition. The story concerns the struggles of an independent businessman to construct a grain elevator on the outskirts of Chicago.

---

Remember, too, that the process is dialectical: like two friends working together, the master and slave exchange roles at each step of the forward or upward progress toward the object of the will to power. The superman (a word Nietzsche used only rarely for the master type) is a role, and each individual plays it in some situations when he is acting with the will to power. In other situations an individual will be the slave type or directed agent, helping fulfill the vision of someone else. He expresses this again in *The Will to Power* when he says, "There is a divine love that despises and loves, and reshapes and elevates the beloved." Nietzsche was by no means naïve enough to believe that there are real people who are all good or all bad and still less that everyone is one or the other.

The outlines of Rand's indebtedness to Nietzsche are already becoming apparent. Her superhuman entrepreneurs, Faulkner and Andre in *Night of January 16th*, are akin to Nietzsche's master. If anything, however, Rand's work is indebted to a more popularized form of his philosophy. For example, Rand's defense of selfishness, which one could call just as easily a critique of altruism, is derived from Nietzsche. The criticism takes the call for altruism and turns it around, questioning the motives of anyone who makes it, suggesting that it is really made out of interest by people who have little to give and would gain much from the redistribution of wealth. Further, this line of thought sees calls for altruism as an attempt to manipulate those in a position to give by playing on their own guilt.

---

This is Nietzsche's wily slave twisting the role of the master. However, Rand's popularity is largely based on the permission she gives her readers to actually be selfish without guilt. She loses the distinction between selfishness being a false accusation and selfishness being defensible as a virtue.

Rand makes another mistake about, or transformation of, Nietzsche's philosophy through simplification. In the Nazi misreading of Nietzsche, the superman and the subhuman are mistaken as inherent human characteristics, as if there is something superior about the Aryan race that makes them better and fitted to command the inferior Jewish race. Rand was by no means a Nazi, but she makes the same type of error in her analysis of Nietzsche. For Rand, there is no dialectical process in which the master and slave roles are exchanged; rather, a small elite is gifted with talents that make them inherently superior and fit to excel if not rule. The rest of humankind is of an inferior grade and as a collective takes on Nietzsche's slave role of slyly criticizing and secretly working against the master (Whitfield and his daughter in the play). Rand presents this idea in no uncertain terms in *Night of January 16th*. Even Flint, the tool of the collective, recognizes that Faulkner occupied the "throne of the world's financial dictator." He bestrode the globe, "with kingdoms and nations in the palm of one hand—and a whip in the other." Andre says of Faulkner's marriage, "We had always faced our business as a war. We both looked at this as our hardest campaign," meaning that they considered they were at war with and trying to conquer and enslave all of humankind (at least in some metaphorical sense). By the same token, Faulkner in his suicide note says,

> I found only two enjoyable things on this earth whose every door was open to me: My whip over the world and Karen Andre. To those who can use it, the advice is worth what it has cost mankind.

Faulkner's death would be a loss to humankind because only he was fit to lead it. The inferior collective, on the other hand, wants only to tear down and destroy their natural masters—even though this would cut their own throats, since they would be leaderless and doomed (the theme of *Atlas Shrugged*). Flint makes this relationship clear in his closing statement when he urges the jury, "Let your verdict tell us that none shall raise his head too high in defiance of our common standards!" Andre is the same type of superior human being, if a little

less so, than Faulkner. This explains the strange nature of their romantic relationship (an element repeated identically in Rand's novels): she searches out the one man strong enough to be her master, and he finds joy in dominating her. Even here, however, one dominates the other with no give-and-take.

The difference between real divisions that Rand believed existed between real people, as opposed to the theoretical Nietzschen dialectal process with which she began, cannot be stressed enough. In the "Note to Producer" in *Night of January 16th*, Rand says, "The decision will have to be based upon the jurors' own values and characters . . . [because] its underlying conflict is the basic conflict of two different types of humanity." Besides concretizing Nietzsche's superman in the form of real men, she also imagined a different relationship between them and their underlings. Jeff Walker, in *The Ayn Rand Cult*, quotes from Rand's journals a note about the character of Howard Roark in *The Fountainhead* (but the same applies to all of her ideal heroes). She says that he was "born without the ability to consider others. . . . Indifference and an infinite contempt is all he feels for the world and for other men who are not like him." The love of the master for the slave and the goal of the superior building up the inferior are gone. Rand clearly held the same views herself about all-too-real people.

Thanks to her prominence as an ideologue, Rand was invited to Cape Canaveral to witness the launching of the Apollo 11 mission in 1969. Writing about the experience (in an essay reprinted in *The Ayn Rand Reader*), she redoubled her certainty that nothing could be achieved by what she called collectivism. (For many years she insisted *Sputnik* had been a hoax, since she could not accept that collectivist Soviet science could have made such a breakthrough.) She claimed,

> The fact that man is the only species capable of transmitting knowledge and thus capable of progress, the fact that man can achieve a division of labor, and the fact that large numbers of men are required for a large-scale undertaking, do not mean what some creeps are suggesting: that achievement has become collective.

She closed the essay by arguing that

> those who suggest that we substitute a war on poverty for the space program should ask themselves whether the premises and values that form the character of an astronaut would be satisfied by a lifetime of carrying bedpans and teaching the alphabet to the mentally retarded.

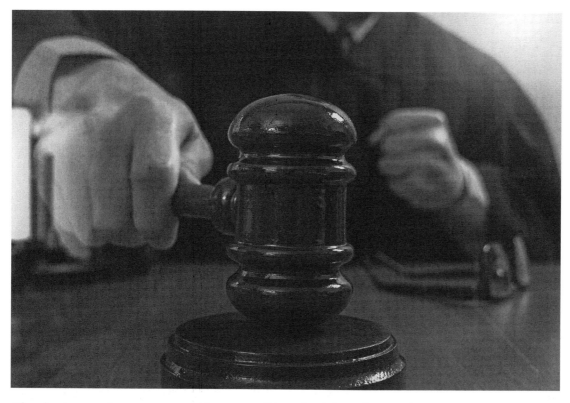

*The play has a unique structure, with two possible endings depending on the jury's verdict* (© everything possible / Shutterstock.com)

Besides what today would be a shocking insensitivity to the intellectually handicapped, it seems hard to deny that what she has in mind here is really the collective, which, if not subhuman, is at least *sub* her entrepreneurial supermen. Jeff Walker, in *The Ayn Rand Cult*, observes that "scarcely a Rand novel, play, or short story is complete without a gratuitously snide reference to some variation on the 'Vocational School for Subnormal Children.'" This is the contempt that Faulkner and Rand's other super entrepreneurs feel for those beneath them.

**Source:** Bradley A. Skeen, Critical Essay on *Night of January 16th*, in *Drama for Students*, Gale, Cengage Learning, 2018.

## Ayn Rand

*In the following excerpt, Mayhew gathers some of Rand's interview answers that illuminate her ideas about literature.*

### ...AYN RAND'S FICTION

In "The Goal of My Writing" (in The Romantic Manifesto), AR writes: "As far as literary schools are concerned, I would call myself a Romantic Realist."

*What do you mean in calling yourself a Romantic Realist? Which of the writers that you like are also Romantic Realists?*

My school of writing *is* romantic realism: "romantic" in that I present man as he ought to be; "realistic" in that I place men here and now on this earth, in terms applicable to every rational reader who shares these values and wants to apply them to himself. It's realistic in that it's possible to man and applies to this earth; it's romantic in that it projects man and values as they ought to be, not as statistical averages.

The writer I consider my closest ancestor literarily is Victor Hugo. He is a romantic writer who presented values as they apply to human life. He's one of the few who attempted—"attempted" hell, I apologize—who *wrote* a great novel in contemporary terms, *Les Misérables*. Offhand I can't think of another romantic novel presented in realistic terms, His other novels take place in earlier periods, but *Les Misérables* is a novel of Hugo's own time and society.

"

O. Henry is a romantic writer with a strong sense of values translated into concrete action in the modern period, in almost journalistic terms. Yet he never presents a "realistic" study of the characters he creates; he presents essences. He presents wealthy men, working girls, and con men tremendously idealized or stylized. They are not statistical copies of the people he saw. They are creations out of his own abstraction of what human beings could be and ought to be. The overall moral message of O. Henry is: "Isn't life interesting?" That's the benevolent universe element in him. He presents not what people do statistically but what people could make of life if they were imaginative. [FW 58]

*Why do you consider yourself a Romantic Realist?*

I consider myself a romanticist, and believe my values are relevant to and possible on Earth. I deal with realistic issues in a romantic way. "Realism" and "naturalism" were once considered interchangeable, though I use "naturalism" for novels that are plotless and based on a deterministic metaphysics. So if I called myself a romantic naturalist, that would be a contradiction. But "realism" means "based on reality," and doesn't imply naturalism or determinism.

Joseph Conrad also called himself a Romantic Realist. I don't like him, but I think he is correct in so labeling himself. He treats his novels realistically, but not naturalistically. So even though my values are quite different from his, I agree with that designation. He expressed his values and, in that sense, he was a romantic— only his settings and characters are much more realistic than I'd ever select. But he was not a naturalist. [NEW 69]

*In your fiction-writing course, you say that* We the Living *has your best plot. Could you explain why this is so?*

Yes, because it's a simple story. A plot is a purposeful sequence of logically connected events. *We the Living* has a narrower theme, and therefore has almost a classic progression of one event leading to another—with a definite subplot, the story of Kira's cousin Irina—and it's one event depending on the other. The events are interconnected almost as tightly as the plot of a good detective story.

*Anthem* has no plot at all. *The Fountainhead* and *Atlas Shrugged* have plots, but on so grand a scale, and with so many involvements, that they are not as perfect one-line plots as in *We the Living*. *We the Living* has the best single-line plot, and it's the easiest on which to learn what a plot is. So it's better to start with a novel like *We the Living*—even to read it, let alone write it—before coming to *Atlas Shrugged*. [PO11 76]

*Throughout her life, AR maintained what she called the "Benevolent Universe Premise"—the conviction that we live in a world in which man can succeed and achieve his values, and where evil is ultimately impotent.*

*If the universe is benevolent, why does Kira die at the end of* We the Living, *just as she's about to escape?*

This is concrete-bound. [In "Let Us Alone" (in *Capitalism: The Unknown Ideal*), AR describes the concrete-bound mentality as the "inability to grasp principles, to distinguish the essential from the nonessential."] I did not sit there and decide arbitrarily to let Kira die. A novel isn't written that way. If you want to know about anything in a novel, ask what its theme is. The theme of *We the Living* is the individual against the state. I present the evil of dictatorship, and what it does to its best individuals. If I let Kira escape, I leave the reader with the conclusion that statism is bad, but there's hope because you can always escape. But that isn't the theme of *We the Living*. In Russia, a citizen cannot count on leaving or escaping. Someone who does escape is an exception, because no borders can be totally closed. People do escape, but we'll never know the number of people who died trying. To let Kira escape would have been pointless. Given the theme of *We the Living*, she had to die. [PO8 76]

*Was Howard Roark, in* The Fountainhead, *based on Frank Lloyd Wright?*

Absolutely not. Some of his *architectural* ideas were, as was the pattern of his career.

I admire Wright as an architect; but as a person—as a character—Roark's philosophy is almost the opposite of Wright's. [FHF 74]

*Why did you choose architecture as the central profession in* The Fountainhead?

The theme. I wanted to show individualism and collectivism in psychology: Roark versus Toohey as the two extremes. I had to show how this works in a creative profession. I chose architecture because it combines science and art. It involves a great deal of engineering and esthetics.

After choosing architecture, I did a lot of research on it, in order to originate dialogue that would sound true to the profession. It's funny that I still receive fan mail inviting me to speak on architecture. People assume I love the subject, but I don't. I like architecture as an art. But after *The Fountainhead*, it had no special meaning to me—less so than music or painting. I'm glad if I convinced people that I like it, but what I actually did was translate into architecture what I felt about writing. My research material for the psychology of Roark was *myself*, and how I feel about my profession. [NFW 69]

*In* The Fountainhead, *why did Dominique act as she did against Roark? Particularly, why did she marry Peter Keating?*

I explain that in *The Fountainhead*, through Dominique's own words, but I'll elaborate. Dominique's error is one from which many good people suffer, only not in so extreme a form. She was devoted to values, was an individualist, had a clear view of what she considered ideal, only she didn't think the ideal was possible. Her error is *the malevolent universe premise*: the belief that the good has no chance on earth, that it is doomed to lose and that evil is metaphysically powerful.

Many people make that mistake, and the reason is that they form their conclusions by statistical impressions. As a person grows up, he looks around and certainly sees more evil than virtue. So he is disappointed more often than pleased; he's often hurt and sees a lot of injustice. And with each generation, given the present culture, it gets worse and worse. By emotional overgeneralization from these first impressions, a great many people whose basic premises are good decide to become (in effect) philosophical subjectivists. They conclude that their values can never be shared by others or communicated to others, and therefore that they can never win in reality.

That was Dominique's mistake. She acted against Roark because she was convinced that he should retire and never open himself up to be hurt by the world—that he shouldn't attempt to fight the world, because he was too good to win. Observe that her actions against Roark were in fact superficial: she did not create any major damage to him, and she never would. But her actions implied a great compliment to him: her understanding and valuing of him as a great man and a great creative talent. It was the misguided application of her estimate of the world that caused her to do what she did.

Why did she marry Peter Keating? Because he was the least worthy of her. It was her symbol of rebellion, in this way: She never made the mistake of thinking that since the world is evil, she must make terms with evil and try to be happy on those terms, as Keating and Wynand tried. She was too good for that. She would not seek happiness in a world she considered evil. So she married a man she could not love or respect, as a symbol of her defiance and desire *not* to seek anything in a world as low as she thought it was. Well, she learned better. By the end of the book, she discovered why she had been wrong, and why Roark was right. Before that, Roark did not attempt to stop her. He was right to conclude that she must correct her error herself.

If you translate this abstraction into less extreme forms, I'd say that most men share Dominique's error in some form or another. You may not try to stop the career of the person you love; but any time you have a good idea or an important value, you will tend to repress it. You'll tend to feel "This is good and I know it, but nobody else will understand me; nobody else will share it. Why be hurt?" Any time you experience an emotion of that kind, you are acting on Dominique's error, and you'd better correct it. [FF 61]

*AR wrote the screenplay for the film version of* The Fountainhead *(Warner Bros., 1949).*

*The climax in your novel* The Fountainhead *seems to contradict the climax of the movie version. Did you have any control over the film?*

If you were any kind of dramatist—if you understood literature and the difference between a novel and a screenplay—you'd take your hat off to me for what I accomplished in that movie. [FHF 70]

In *Introduction to Objectivist Epistemology*, AR describes an experiment that established that crows could deal with only three units at a time.

She points out that man, too, can deal with only a limited number of units. This fact about human cognition is sometimes referred to in Objectivist literature as "the crow epistemology."

*How does the principle of the crow epistemology apply to the presentation of ideas in your novels?*

By the time I come to an abstract speech, I've given you all the concretes required for you to draw a conclusion—and then I draw the conclusion. I present the concretes at a certain pace so that you don't have to take in the whole theme all at once. This is why *Atlas Shrugged* is so long: I give you certain concretes in action before I explicitly and at length mention the abstraction they're based on. [OC 80]

*In* The Art of Fiction, *AR makes the following suggestion: "do not use slang in straight narrative."*

*At the end of Part 2 of* Atlas Shrugged, *Dagny "rents" a plane, writing "a check for fifteen thousand dollars . . . as deposit against the return of the Sanders plane—and . . . another check, for two hundred bucks, for his (the airport attendant's) own, personal courtesy." Given your views on slang, why did you use "bucks" instead of "dollars"?*

Look at the context. It's not fully narrative. It's written as a paraphrase of what they [Dagny Taggart and Owen Kellogg] told him. It's paraphrasing the kind of dialogue that went on between them and how they assured him that they're on a special mission from mysterious authorities, and he thinks of Washington, and so forth. When I use "bucks," it was precisely to give coloring to a condensed synopsis of an actual conversation, and this is the terms in which *he* would think of it. And what was achieved is a stress on the lack of dignity of the man and the whole procedure. He gives to total strangers a $15,000 airplane for a two-hundred-buck bribe. That's why I used the word, and that doesn't contradict what I said about slang. [FW 58]

*In* The Art of Fiction, *AR says: "It is proper to laugh at evil . . . or at the negligible. But to laugh at the good is vicious."*

*You've said that one should never laugh at the good—for example, at heroes—but there's a scene in* Atlas Shrugged *that's funny, though the humor seems to be directed at Dagny. She is in the valley, and after coming across an automobile manufacturer who runs a grocery store, a judge who runs a dairy farm, a writer who works as a fishwife, and so on, she meets a man who "looked like a truck driver," and she asks: "What were you outside? A*

NORMALLY CULTS REACH OUT AND ASSERTIVELY RECRUIT. THE RAND CULT WAS FORTUNATE: THERE WAS NO NEED FOR HARD MISSIONARY WORK."

*professor of comparative philology, I suppose?" The man replies: "No ma'am . . . , I was a truck driver." Could you explain this joke?*

It's Dagny, for a moment, who is contradictory, so the joke is on her She has made a mistake in judgment. She concludes that since everybody in the valley is something more than what he's doing at the moment, and since this man looks like a truck driver and is doing unskilled labor, he's undoubtedly a professor. Therefore, it's her judgment that one is laughing at. But it's not malicious humor, because it's not an important error of judgment. That's good-natured humor. Dagny is having an unusually good time in her bewilderment, so if she makes a mistake of that kind, it underscores the benevolent preposterousness of the whole situation. That's why one can afford to laugh at it.

The same is true of Noel Coward's "Mad Dogs and Englishmen." In effect he's saying: "How irrational the Englishmen are! When everybody else collapses, they still go out in the sun dressed formally." Is that an insult to the English? No, he's laughing at the natives snoozing there, *not* at the English. [FW 58] . . .

**Source:** Ayn Rand, "Esthetics, Art, and Artists," in *Ayn Rand Answers: The Best of Her Q & A*, edited by Robert Mayhew, New American Library, 2005, pp. 188–94.

### Jeff Walker

*In the following excerpt, Walker discusses the cult of personality that developed around Rand.*

Nearly always, new converts to Objectivism are *young*. In the 1960s, the core of the Objectivist rank-and-file consisted of college kids, many of them converted or first attracted when in high school. Even Rand's inner circle, the Collective, mostly comprised "thirsty" young people drinking up her ideas, ideas so potently spiked with her charisma as to be absolutely convincing. "She could convince you to walk into a firing squad," declares Erika Holzer.

Ron Merrill opens his book on Rand's ideas with: "I was fifteen—a common age for converts to the ideas of Ayn Rand." Barbara Branden read *The Fountainhead* at age 15. Eric Nolte was 16. Libertarian philosopher and former Objectivist Eric Mack first read Rand as a high school junior. Roy Childs felt obliged to remark upon his "late" start, not reading Rand until his last year of high school because he wasn't normally a reader of fiction. Sympathetic critic Robert Hunt suggests that *Atlas Shrugged* "demands the fervent elitism of late adolescence in order to be read with conviction. A taste for Rand must be acquired early or not at all." A former Objectivist recalls that when he was a teen, in the spring of 1966, the assistant pastor at the Lutheran Church he attended gave him his copy of *Atlas Shrugged*, much the way that eventual neo-Objectivist leader David Kelley discovered Ayn Rand. Says Kelley, "By the time I went to college,... I knew these were my basic values."

Normally cults reach out and assertively recruit. The Rand cult was fortunate: there was no need for hard missionary work. At the back of every copy of *Atlas Shrugged*, one paperback page-turn after the inspiring conclusion, the young reader scarcely having had a moment to catch his or her breath, found "A MESSAGE FROM THE AUTHOR," virtually an invitation to join the Objectivist movement. It was a highly unusual pitch for the 1960s, if not for later decades. These back-of-the book invitations help to explain the growth and resilience of the Rand cult, then and now. The sales of Rand's novels are so high, year after year, that a tiny percentage of readers responding to these invitations supplies the official Objectivist organization with a steady flow of new recruits.

The youthful students of Objectivism who were recruited in such surprising numbers in the 1960s typically came equipped with a basic education but little or no prior knowledge of the subjects that Objectivism pronounced upon, subjects like philosophy, history, economics, and literature. Typically, recruits learned the Objectivist line on all these subject areas, and *then*, perhaps, began to learn a little about them. The students' first exposure to these subjects was through a Randian lens.

Pierpont describes Rand's readership as the largely abandoned class of thinking nonintellectuals. Joan Kennedy Taylor concurs: "Many thought that Rand had invented laissez-faire capitalism.... dentists, engineers, and so on loved this vision of a technologically advancing logical world, but this was the first they had dealt with ideas in any grand sense." Taylor, having grown up with people in the arts and having gone to a liberal arts college, was not quite as overwhelmed by Rand's ideas as most of her fellow students of Objectivism, for whom these were the only ideas in the world.

Many former cultists say that early college classes destabilized their worldview and bewildered them, preparing them for the certainty offered by the cult. Rand criticized professors for disorienting students, while in effect capitalizing upon the disorientation. Kay Nolte Smith recalls that a friend took her in 1957 to an NYU lecture by Rand who said that everyone has a philosophy of life, the only choice being whether one is going to know it consciously or not. For Smith this was "a blinding epiphany. I thought 'my God, she's right'—everybody's actions are governed by some kind of thoughts," so it's incumbent on us to know consciously what those are. "And the idea that one could be consistent in one's thoughts, I found wonderfully attractive."

*Atlas Shrugged* was most people's entry to the cult. The part that casual readers skip is the part Objectivists-to-be dwell upon: Galt's 35,000-word speech, which Jane Hamblin called the longest burst of sustained histrionics since Wagner's *Ring of the Nibelungs*. Rosalie Nichols recalls that reading *Atlas Shrugged* a second time snapped the last ties holding her to her pre-Objectivist friends. "I had always been lonely, and it had been getting worse with every shattered relationship. Now I felt totally isolated. But then I reasoned: I exist. Ayn Rand exists. There must be others. I have to find them." For Nichols, Rand's philosophy "made it easier to understand people and harder to get along with them,... easier to identify the influences in our culture and harder to live in it,... stimulated my desire to study and made it almost impossible to read a textbook,... fueled my ambitions and convinced me how difficult it would be to achieve them in this society.... I became more and more particular and less and less satisfied."

### THE SPELL OF AYN RAND

*Newsweek* remarked about Rand in 1961 that no she-messiah since Aimee McPherson could so hypnotize an audience. Of the Rand-based figure in her novel, *Elegy For a Soprano*, Kay Nolte Smith writes that, "people responded less to her ideas than to the strength with which they were held." There can be something peculiarly magnetic about someone who seems completely unconflicted. Those lacking self-confidence tend to look to such a person for certainty In Mary Gaitskill's Objectivism-satirizing novel *Two Girls, Fat and Thin*, the Randian-in-the-making character, recalling her first attendance at a lecture by the great Granite (Rand), rhapsodises, "I imagined myself in a psychic swoon, lush flowers of surrender popping out about my head as I was upheld by the mighty current of Granite's intellectual embrace."

Rand was impressive on an interpersonal level, according to followers. Even John Kobler, an unsympathetic 1960s journalist, could not avoid mentioning her "huge blazing hazel eyes" that fronted a "personality as compelling as a sledgehammer." "We were young and she was not," recalled Kay Nolte Smith. "I thought she was a genius. One of the things that was dazzling to me was her superb command of the language. She could just talk magnificently on any subject without any hemming or hawing or note consulting, and then she could marshal an argument on practically any subject, that—at least at that time in my life, given my age and knowledge and experience—I was simply unable to refute, had I cared to. And if you think to yourself, I have to be able to go by rational arguments, and you're unable to refute them, then you're really in a bind, which is where we all were." Rand spent virtually all of her productive time after the publication of *Atlas Shrugged* in 1957 consolidating and communicating what she believed to be rational arguments *for* her ideas and *against* opposing ideas. She became good enough at it to dazzle already-starstruck university students.

To former student of Objectivism Ron Merrill, it seemed that Rand *radiated* intelligence. "You could almost physically feel it . . . you would ask her a question and she would look at you with those incredible eyes and you could just see—almost like a fire burning behind them— the power of her intelligence . . . she was never at a loss . . . ask her a question and instantly out came an answer that you could never have thought of on your own." She could improvise on the spot, with a perfect answer, even regarding something she hadn't previously thought about, "in perfect sentences, with all the grammatical elements in the right place." Merrill could well understand how people "would give

up anything to be so close to a person of such stellar intellect." It doesn't come across when you see her from a distance or on tape, Merin insisted. "You had to get up close, talk to her, her attention focused on you," like a magnifying glass in the sun. Merrill is correct that neither razor-sharp intelligence nor unusual articulateness is evident on extant video and audio tapes of Rand.

Former associates cite Rand's unshakeable arrogance and self-assurance, emulated by the follower, who, secretly not so self-assured, relied heavily upon Rand. She came to embody Reason. The highest value became earning her approval, the gravest sin—incurring her displeasure. Kramer and Alstad suggest that a guru can become a disciple's personal living god, igniting even greater emotion than an ethereal one. An early 1970s open letter to Ayn Rand proudly confessed its author a Randian cultist. "I worship you . . . . I owe you my life . . . . I think you are the greatest thinker and writer who ever lived . . . ." Published albeit obscure novelist Shane Dennison recalls that, as imagined from afar in the 1960s, Rand and Branden "were *gods*, man, they'd said it all."

Rajneesh's sannyasins came to view their Master as a powerful, unquestioned, and unquestionable authority Likewise Kay Nolte Smith recalls the "commonly held and voiced view that Ayn was *never* wrong . . . about anything having to do with any aspect of thought or of dealing with human beings." Leonard Peikoff, today's Pope-like leader of orthodox Objectivism, tells us that Rand "discovered true ideas on a virtually unprecedented scale" and that a moral person would greet this "with admiration, awe, *even love* . . . . If you . . . accept Objectivism, you live by it," and you revere Ayn Rand for defining it. To her most devoted followers, Rand is very much an 'Eastern' guru, that is, perfect enlightenment in the flesh. In the West, the only perfection is heavenly. In the East, the guru's enlightenment is all-encompassing, applying everywhere in the past, present, and future. Peikoff echoes that sense of finality with respect to Rand . . . .

**Source:** Jeff Walker, "The Cult While the Guru Lived," in *The Ayn Rand Cult*, Open Court, 1999, pp. 11–15.

### T. H. McCulloh

*In the following review, McCulloh characterizes Rand's play as a product of its time.*

Ayn Rand's courtroom drama *The Night of January 16th* is one of the more dated theater pieces that still pops up every once in a while. It was written in an era when authenticity was not top priority and when simplism ran rampant in dramatic structure.

Not only does Rand allow her defendant, Karen Andre, to jump up and insist on questioning a witness—the judge and her attorney allow it—but the playwright's familiarity with actual legal procedure seems sketchy.

She also has a penchant for creating characters who are stereotypical icons for the opposing forces in her monolithic drama. And then there's the sociopolitical agenda at the core of all Rand's writing—that power, whether political or economic, is sure to corrupt. Considering today's headlines, that still sees to be true, but Rand's coloring-book minimization hits you over the head with it.

The only thing a theater company can do is play her *January 16th* absolutely straight, with a B-movie flavor, as a period piece. That's exactly what director Marc LeBlanc does with his staging at Westminster Community Theatre. Sandi Newcomb's authentic period costumes set the time, and the acting echoes the high coloring of the genre.

Even those actors who seem to go a little overboard bring back memories of second features at Saturday matinees. Jennifer Boudreau's janitor's wife, with her trashy Southern accent, Tony Grande's smart-aleck private eye, Joel Ray Ibanez's wonderfully amused New York cop, Kip Hogan's religious housekeeper, Laurie LeBlanc's outrageous gun moll, Mark J. Mallo's gangster in love with Andre, and Aaron Abrams' well-defined jailbird bookkeeper—are all in that mode, with the erzatz dialects of the period right on the button.

Balancing them are pretty realistic and effective performances by the main players in Rand's tale of the world's greatest financial swindler, his mistress Andre, their plan to desert a crashing empire with $10 million, and the complicated phony murder they concoct to get away with it.

Lisa Harvey's Andre is as cocksure and savvy as she can be, her attorney is played with wonderful sincerity by Warren Draper, and the prosecuting attorney is given a good angry, flustered edge by Edward J. Stenecik. Jasmine Trepte is the perfect icy Rand foil as the financier's duped society wife, and Warren Y. Harker is properly stuffy as her evil banker father. The whole cast fits right into the mold.

The play's gimmick has the audience as the jury, which ultimately decides Andre's guilt or innocence, and Rand provides alternative endings for either decision—this long before the more recent *Mystery of Edwin Drood* used the same gimmick.

If you can't find the excellent 1941 film version of *January 16th* on video, this production will give you a good idea of how they used to do this type of thing.

**Source:** T. H. McCulloh, "Rand's *Night of January 16th* Has a Good Day in Court," in *Los Angeles Times*, January 25, 1995.

## SOURCES

Aristotle, "Poetics," in *The Complete Works of Aristotle*, Bollingen Series 71, edited by Jonathan Barnes, Princeton University Press, 1984, Vol. 2, pp. 2316–40.

Badhwar, Neera K., and Roderick T. Long, "Ayn Rand," in *The Stanford Encyclopedia of Philosophy*, edited by Edward N. Zalta, Fall 2016, https://plato.stanford.edu/archives/fall2016/entries/ayn-rand/ (accessed June 5, 2017).

Binswanger, Harry, ed., *The Ayn Rand Lexicon: Objectivism from A to Z*, New American Library, 1986, p. 188.

Branden, Barbara, *The Passion of Ayn Rand*, Doubleday, 1986, pp. 110–18.

Brownmiller, Susan, "Ayn Rand: A Traitor to Her Own Sex," in *Feminist Interpretations of Ayn Rand*, edited by Mimi Reisel Gladstein and Chris Matthew Sciabarra, Pennsylvania State University Press, 1999, pp. 63–65.

Bulrazik, Mary, *Sexual Harassment at the Workplace: Historical Notes*, http://bcrw.barnard.edu/archive/work force/Sexual_Harassment_at_the_Workplace.pdf (accessed June 24, 2017).

Gladstein, Mimi Reisel, *The New Ayn Rand Companion: Revised and Expanded Edition*, Greenwood, 1999, pp. 10, 37–38, 51–52, 56, 61–62, 65, 117.

Heller, Anne C., *Ayn Rand and the World She Made*, Doubleday, 2009, pp. 77, 92–93.

Hull, Gary, and Leonard Peikoff, eds., *The Ayn Rand Reader*, Plume, 1999, pp. 135–39, 451.

Hunt, Lester H., "Thus Spake Howard Roark: Nietzschean Ideas in *The Fountainhead*," in *Philosophy and Literature*, Vol. 30, No. 1, April 2006, pp. 79–101.

McConnell, Scott, *100 Voices: An Oral History of Ayn Rand*, New America Library, 2010, pp. 8–9, 16–17, 33.

Nelson, William E., "Criminality and Sexual Morality in New York, 1920–1980," in *Yale Journal of Law & the Humanities*, Vol. 5, No. 2, 2013, pp. 265–341.

Nietzsche, Friedrich, *The Will to Power*, translated by Walter Kaufmann and R. J. Hollingdale, Vintage, 1968, pp. 505–506.

Partnoy, Frank, *The Match King: Ivar Kreuger, The Financial Genius behind a Century of Wall Street Scandals*, Public Affairs, 2009, pp. 193–200.

Rand, Ayn, *The Ayn Rand Reader*, edited by Gary Hull and Leonard Peikoff, Plume, 1999, pp. 124–39, 451–60.

———, *Night of January 16th: A Play*, World, 1968.

Sciabarra, Chris Matthew, *Ayn Rand: The Russian Radical*, Pennsylvania State University Press, 1995, pp. 100–106.

Sheaffer, Robert, "Rereading Rand on Gender in the Light of Paglia," in *Feminist Interpretations of Ayn Rand*, edited by Mimi Reisel Gladstein and Chris Matthew Sciabarra, Pennsylvania State University Press, 1999, pp. 299–317.

Walker, Jeff, *The Ayn Rand Cult*, Open Court, 1999, pp. 244–77.

## FURTHER READING

Cunningham, Darryl, *The Age of Selfishness: Ayn Rand, Morality, and the Financial Crisis*, Abrams Books, 2015.
    Writing in the form of a graphic novel, Cunningham presents a critical biography of Rand and shows how her ideas infiltrated into the government through her personal followers like Alan Greenspan and disciples of her writing like Paul Ryan, who shaped policies that contributed to and worsened the 2008 financial crisis.

Podritske, Marlene, and Peter Schwartz, eds., *Objectively Speaking: Ayn Rand Interviewed*, Lexington, 2009.
    This volume collects transcripts of several of the countless interviews Rand gave during her life, ranging from local newspapers in California in the early 1930s as her writing began to gain recognition to the height of her popularity at college campuses and on television during the 1960s.

Rand, Ayn, *The Fountainhead*, Bobbs Merrill, 1943.
    *The Fountainhead* is equal in popularity and importance among Rand's works to *Atlas Shrugged*. Like all her work, it is an exposition of objectivist philosophy.

———, *Letters of Ayn Rand*, edited by Michael S. Berliner, Dutton, 1995.
    This volume is a valuable collection of Rand's letters, but it represents less than half of her correspondence that exists in manuscript and was chosen to highlight her exchanges with the famous and notable; in many cases the volume contains a series of letters back forth between Rand and her correspondent. The manuscripts remain under the control of Rand's chosen ideological successor, Leonard Peikoff, who also wrote the introduction to this volume.

## SUGGESTED SEARCH TERMS

Ayn Rand

Night of January 16th

Penthouse Legend

objectivism

Great Depression

Ivar Kreuger

Al Woods

courtroom drama

# Seven Guitars

## AUGUST WILSON
## 1995

*Seven Guitars*, first performed in 1995, is a play by August Wilson, one of America's foremost playwrights. The play opens and closes with a small gathering after the funeral of its central protagonist, Floyd "Schoolboy" Barton, a blues guitarist on the cusp of professional success, and concerns the events leading up to his death. His doomed struggle to succeed as a musician, and to win back the love of a woman he abandoned, is interwoven with the lives of this woman and several other friends and acquaintances, which play out in the backyard of a modest boarding-house in Pittsburgh.

The play is the fourth part of Wilson's Pittsburgh Cycle, also called his American Century Cycle, a group of ten plays which explore African American life in a Pittsburgh neighborhood. Each play is devoted to a particular decade of the twentieth century, with *Seven Guitars* set in the 1940s. It features the street-corner speaking style of the Hill District neighborhood where Wilson grew up, a distinctive hallmark of all of his plays, and explores issues of race, relationships, and fate. It won the 1996 New York Drama Critics' Circle Award for Best Play, and it was nominated that year for both the Pulitzer and the Tony for best dramatic production.

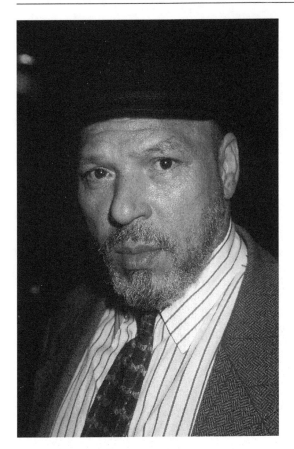

*August Wilson* (© *ZUMA Press, Inc. / Alamy Stock Photo*)

## AUTHOR BIOGRAPHY

Wilson was born on April 27, 1945, in the Hill District of Pittsburgh, Pennsylvania. He was named Frederick August Kittel Jr. after his father, a white German immigrant and infrequent presence in the household. His mother, Daisy Wilson, an African American, encouraged all of her children to read at an early age. August received his first library card at the age of five and read voraciously, and his zeal for words was evident early on, as for example in a love poem he composed in the sixth grade, cited in the *New Yorker*: "I would I could mend my festering heart / Harpooned by Cupid's flaming dart ..."

As a freshman at Central Catholic High School, Wilson remarked in his 2001 interview with the *New Yorker*, "There was a note on my desk every single day. It said, 'Go home nigger.'" After attending several more schools, Wilson, now fifteen, dropped out and immersed himself in the life and culture of the Hill District's street

corners; his observations would later inform much of his writing.

At eighteen he officially assumed the name August Wilson and dedicated himself to the writer's life, working odd jobs while composing poetry. At twenty-three, influenced by the black nationalist movement, he helped found the Black Horizon Theater in Pittsburgh. His first play, *Recycle*, was performed in 1973. Five years later, having immersed himself in drama and the work of African American playwrights in particular, he moved to Saint Paul, Minnesota, where he joined the Penumbra Theatre Company.

One of Wilson's plays from this period, *Jitney*, a later version of which would become the eighth play in his Pittsburgh Cycle, was produced in Pittsburgh in 1982. In this same year the National Playwrights Conference invited him to develop a play there. This would become *Ma Rainey's Black Bottom*, the third play in his cycle, and in 1985 it won the New York Drama Critics' Circle Award for Best American Play.

Success and widespread recognition came not long after. In 1987 Wilson's play *Fences* won the Pulitzer Prize for Drama, the Tony Award for Best Play, and other awards, and he was named Artist of the Year by the *Chicago Tribune*. He won critical acclaim over the following several decades, especially for his skill in capturing the natural cadences of speech in black communities and for showcasing these communities themselves and the issues experienced by the people.

Paramount Pictures purchased the film rights to *Fences* in 1987, and in 1990 Wilson generated some controversy by insisting on a black director. This was not, he insisted, separatism; in a speech at Princeton University in 1996, he argued,

> The American theatre ... is the theatre that we have chosen to work in. And we embrace the values of that theatre but reserve the right to amend, to explore, and to add our African consciousness and our African aesthetic to the art we produce.

Wilson continued writing without cease throughout his life and was decorated with two Pulitzers, two Tonys, and numerous other awards. In 1995 he wrote *Seven Guitars*, and in 2005 he completed the Pittsburgh Cycle with its tenth play, *Radio Golf*, which premiered at the Yale Repertory Theater on April 22. Two months later, Wilson was diagnosed with liver cancer. He died on October 2, 2005, in Seattle, Washington.

# PLOT SUMMARY

## *Act 1*

### SCENE 1

*Seven Guitars* opens in the backyard of a boardinghouse in the Hill District of Pittsburgh, Pennsylvania. Five mourners have gathered here after the funeral of their friend Floyd "Schoolboy" Barton. They are Canewell and Red Carter, Floyd's friends and occasional bandmates who recorded with him in Chicago; Vera, Floyd's former lover; Louise, owner of the boardinghouse; and Hedley, a seemingly mentally unbalanced boarder and peddler who keeps chickens in the yard.

They sit and discuss the funeral. Vera says that she witnessed six angels coming out of the sky, and the rest debate the identity of these figures, some arguing that they were working for the funeral home, others that they were otherworldly or at least strangely inappropriate in their behavior. The discussion turns briefly to the possibility of foreknowledge of one's own death. Vera goes inside. A brief back-and-forth about alcohol is interrupted by Floyd's voice from inside the house singing his hit single, "That's All Right."

### SCENE 2

The play flashes back to several days before Floyd's death. Floyd and Vera are in the backyard dancing to the same song playing on the radio. He tries to kiss her, but she rebuffs him. He insists that his life is empty without her; she reminds him testily that he left her for another woman. Floyd tells Vera that his musical career is about to begin in earnest, with a recording contract offered by the same company that produced "That's All Right." He only has to retrieve his guitar from the pawn shop, for which he may have to pawn his .38 handgun in return. She assures him that she still has the gun. He will have to travel to Chicago to record but has bitter memories of his last trip there, which ended in a ninety-day jail sentence for vagrancy. He urges her to travel there with him, but she refuses. The two reminisce about their first encounter, but Vera reveals how traumatized she was when he left her for someone else.

Louise appears, and it is obvious that she and Floyd have little regard for one another. She complains about her niece, who is coming from Alabama to stay with her after one man killed another in a lover's dispute over her.

### SCENE 3

The following morning, Hedley begins constructing a chicken-killing station. Louise appears and badgers Hedley for cigarettes; when he asks for payment, she reminds him that he is two days behind on his rent. She also insists that he should go see a doctor, since he has been spitting up blood, but he prefers to visit a local folk healer.

Canewell shows up with a goldenseal plant for Vera. The three banter about Floyd and Vera, religion, and chickens, until Canewell undertakes to rouse Floyd, who has indeed, against Louise's wishes, spent the night with Vera. Hedley returns to his basement.

Floyd encourages Canewell to return to Chicago with him to cut another record, but Canewell was also arrested there and is uninterested in going back.

Hedley emerges from his basement, and Floyd greets him with a line from Jelly Roll Morton's song "I Thought I Heard Buddy Bolden Say," a tune Hedley frequently sings as a kind of prayer or meditation about money. This encourages Hedley to indulge in a rambling fantasy, part biblical and part political, in which he will be given money, power, and land. This is evidently a recurring fantasy of his; Canewell describes Hedley's much more detailed version of the same fantasy from two nights earlier.

After a back-and-forth about religion, the curative powers of goldenseal, and relationships, Floyd determines to retrieve money he is owed for his labor in the Chicago workhouse during his jail time, so that he can buy back his guitar.

### SCENE 4

Several hours later, Vera and Louise are preparing food in the yard. They talk about Louise's niece, then about Floyd. Louise compares him to her ex-husband, who abandoned her. Floyd and Canewell appear, Floyd much agitated because his reimbursement for labor in the workhouse was denied.

Red Carter appears, and Floyd tries to persuade him to record with him in Chicago, but Red is uncertain. The four discuss card games and how to cook greens. The women leave, and the conversation turns to cigar brands, comic verse, the similarities between watermelons and women, and the difficulties in managing multiple love affairs. Joe Louis will be fighting Billy Conn this evening, and everyone plans to listen to the match on the radio.

Hedley begins quoting the Bible, and the men debate religion, power, time, and women's cooking abilities. The conversation turns more serious when Floyd and Red discuss their economic disempowerment, their fighting skills, and their talents as musicians. None of them trust the music industry in the slightest, having been taken advantage of by unscrupulous producers, and they vow not to allow themselves to be shortchanged again. The conversation ends with a mournful recollection of their dead loved ones and acquaintances.

### SCENE 5

The six friends are gathered around a radio listening to the boxing match. When Joe Louis triumphs, they rejoice. Red Carter and Vera begin to dance, but Floyd, jealous, interrupts them. He and Red threaten one another, but before it can become violent, Louise's niece Ruby, an attractive young woman, appears with a suitcase. The men are intrigued, but she dodges their attentions and enters the house. The party takes up a game of cards, and Canewell, with a rooster crowing nearby, gives a brief lecture to the group about roosters, using the topic to discourse about slavery and emancipation. Hedley leaves abruptly. Ruby reappears and joins them at the card table. Then Hedley enters the yard, carrying the rooster. He makes a strange speech, part prophecy and part sermon, and kills the rooster, then leaves. Everyone is stunned.

## Act 2

### SCENE 1

Hedley is making egg-salad sandwiches in the yard. Ruby appears, and the two of them make small talk while Hedley openly ogles her. Hedley admits to having killed a man for refusing to call him by his first name, King. He propositions her, but she turns him down, and he retires to the basement. Floyd appears and chats with Ruby. Hedley returns, Ruby leaves, and Floyd complains to Hedley about his failure to redeem his guitar from the pawn shop. Floyd plays along with Hedley's favorite fantasy about money and power. Hedley warns that Floyd is marked for greatness and that this puts him in mortal danger from the world of white men.

### SCENE 2

Louise and Vera discuss Ruby, then Floyd's plans, and Vera confesses that she is curious about Chicago. Louise advises her against following him there. Ruby enters the yard, and the three of them discuss the jealousy of men; Ruby reveals that she is pregnant by one of the lovers she fled.

Floyd and Canewell arrive in high spirits: Floyd's manager is going to give him an advance, a gig has been set up at a local dance hall for Mother's Day, and they have a date with the Chicago recording studio. Hedley appears in a dark mood, denouncing racial injustice faced by his father. After he leaves, Louise explains that Hedley has tuberculosis but believes that his summons by the board of health to a TB sanitarium is a white plot designed to disempower him.

### SCENE 3

Floyd and Canewell discuss Floyd's newest difficulties: his manager has missed an appointment to give him the promised advance, so he cannot retrieve his guitar, without which he cannot play the Mother's Day dance. Floyd's fantasies about success in Chicago grow ever more grandiose.

Red Carter appears and notifies the others that Floyd's manager has been arrested for selling fraudulent insurance policies. The news devastates Floyd. He recalls his mother's extreme poverty, vows that he will not live that way, and leaves swearing to make it to Chicago.

### SCENE 4

Vera, Louise, and Ruby listen as Red Carter laments the ways in which laws have made it increasingly difficult to eke out a living. Then they all express concern about Floyd, who has been missing since the night before.

Hedley enters the yard singing and carrying something wrapped in his apron. He recounts his relationship with his father, who once kicked him in the mouth and berated him as a failure; Hedley apologized to his father at his deathbed without realizing that the man was already dead. But his father appeared to him in his dreams, promising him wealth, and today, while making arrangements to provide sandwiches at a wedding, the father of the bride gave him a machete, which Hedley proudly unveils from the apron. He says he is ready now for the white man to attempt to take him to the sanitarium.

## SCENE 5

Hedley is in the yard by himself, holding the machete and engaging in a Bible-inflected monologue about black empowerment. Ruby appears, and Hedley proclaims his otherworldly mightiness to her. She takes the machete from him, whereupon he forces himself on her, kissing her. She realizes his desperation and surrenders to him.

## SCENE 6

Floyd is burying something in the garden. He has a guitar case and a dress box with him and brandishes both proudly to Vera when she appears. The guitar is brand-new, and so is the dress; he bought it for Vera to wear to his gig that evening. In addition, he has two bus tickets for Chicago. She asks him whence the money came with which to buy all this, but he refuses to tell her. Instead, he proclaims his commitment to her. She shows him a bus ticket she purchased herself, from Chicago to Pittsburgh, good for one year, and vows to keep it with her but hopes she will never have to use it. They embrace.

## SCENE 7

Louise muses to herself about the events of the last few days. When Vera appears, dressed for the Mother's Day show, they talk about Ruby, who has gone to church with Hedley. Ruby appears without Hedley, who is apparently visiting a friend to buy moonshine. Ruby says she intends to tell Hedley that her baby is his.

Canewell appears and tells them that a loan office has been robbed; one of the robbers was shot, but two others fled with the money. Louise and Ruby leave to prepare for the dance, and Vera tells Canewell that she and Floyd are going to get married. Canewell congratulates her but also tells her of his own deep love for her, which she has refused in the past but which is as strong as ever.

Red Carter enters the yard, and finally Floyd comes out of the house in a new suit and carrying his new electric guitar. Canewell has his harmonica with him, and Red Carter's drums are ready at the dance hall.

## SCENE 8

Floyd, Vera, Louise, and Canewell have returned from the show, which was a huge success. Canewell notices that the goldenseal plant he purchased for Vera has been uprooted; Floyd tells her that they will take care of it, and the women go inside. While Floyd is distracted watching the women leave, Canewell digs around the goldenseal and unearths a handkerchief wrapped around $1,200. Floyd warns him that the money is his, and the two men argue until Floyd pulls out his .38 and admits that he was one of the men who robbed the loan office. Canewell surrenders the money to him.

Canewell leaves. Floyd is alone in the yard when Hedley appears and sees Floyd standing there with the money. He begins laughing and crying simultaneously and addresses Floyd as Buddy, the musician in his favorite song who promises money and power. He tells Floyd to give him the money; Floyd warns him to go to bed, and after a brief tussle, Hedley goes into the basement.

While Floyd is burying the money, Hedley reappears with his machete. Floyd turns just in time to have his throat cut.

## SCENE 9

The play picks up where the opening scene left off, just after Floyd's funeral, with his song "That's All Right" playing from inside the house. Red Carter, Louise, Canewell, and Hedley are listening to it. Hedley appears drowsy. The others discuss the police investigation of Floyd's murder.

Ruby emerges from the house to put a blanket on Hedley, and Red Carter takes her out for a beer. Vera describes her vision of angels carrying Floyd into the sky. Canewell sings the first line of "I Thought I Heard Buddy Bolden Say." Hedley asks him what Buddy said; Canewell recites the next line, "Wake up and give me the money," but Hedley corrects him: Buddy, in his version of the song, gives the money freely. He then holds up a handful of the money he took from Floyd, lets it fall to the ground, and begins to sing the song himself.

## CHARACTERS

### *Floyd "Schoolboy" Barton*

The tragic central character of *Seven Guitars*, Floyd is a musician who, after some setbacks, appears to be at the edge of professional success: one of his songs has become a hit on the radio, and he has been invited by the Chicago studio that produced it to return for another recording.

But his road to success is threatened by a lack of money. After his recording stint, he was arrested (unjustly, he maintains) for vagrancy and sent to a Chicago jail for ninety days. He has returned home to the Hill District of Pittsburgh, and his guitar is in a pawn shop; all he has left of value is his .38 handgun and an older guitar, and without the pawned guitar he cannot record. Throughout the play, his efforts to retrieve the guitar are stymied by his economic and social position. His manager is impossible to find, and when at last Floyd manages to secure the promise of an advance, the deal falls through; the money he is owed from his labor at a Chicago workhouse is unobtainable because he lacks the proper paperwork; the guitar has been in the pawn shop too long and can no longer be redeemed. Desperate, he participates in a robbery, and while the spoils enable him to buy a new guitar and a ticket to Chicago, they also result in his murder when a mentally unbalanced acquaintance sees him with the money.

The pathos of his desperate actions and violent end is maintained and simultaneously balanced by his relationship with an ex-lover, Vera. Although he abandoned her once for another woman, he has realized his error and ardently pursues her throughout the play. His feelings are genuine: this is made clear in the stage directions, and Vera finally responds to his attention. But his love for her only increases his desperation, since he feels that he can deserve her only if he succeeds professionally. His mental agony is tied in part to his memories of his own mother's poverty; just before he resolves to attempt the robbery, he recalls that she did without and died without anything of value.

Floyd's character displays a wide emotional range: pride, grief, love, anger, solicitude, and regret equally define him. But his quick temper is on display as well, first in a fit of jealousy after his friend and bandmate Red Carter dances with Vera and later when his other friend and bandmate, Canewell, discovers the money Floyd has buried and he threatens Canewell with his gun. He dreams big and refuses to resign himself to failure, and these qualities, in conjunction with his rashness, spell his doom.

### Canewell

Canewell is a harmonica player and close friend of Floyd's who recorded with him in Chicago and was also arrested, in his case for playing his harmonica on the street. He is uninterested in returning to Chicago now and has a deep mistrust of the music industry in general, but their

friendship is deep enough that he accompanies Floyd on each of his various endeavors to secure the money necessary for success. The only adventure they do not share is Floyd's robbery of the loan office, which Floyd never mentions until Canewell discovers the money himself. This scene, the penultimate one of the play, marks the one moment of real tension between the men, with Floyd pulling his .38 on Canewell.

Yet there is one other potential source of tension between the two men, and it is a testimony to the depth of their friendship that it never threatens their bond: this is Vera, whom both men love. Canewell's affection for her is obvious early on, as he has already purchased her a record player and brings her a goldenseal plant as a gift. (She uses this record player to play Floyd's song "That's All Right" after the funeral, and the assembled friends fall silent listening to it; one can only guess at Canewell's state of mind as it plays.) He refers openly to his love for Vera when she informs him that she and Floyd have decided to marry, and he has evidently professed this love once before, without success. His decency compels him to congratulate her despite his disappointment and to remark on Floyd's great fortune in winning her affections.

### Red Carter

Red, a drummer, is Floyd's close friend and erstwhile bandmate, like Canewell. But his friendship with Floyd is not quite as close; he is much less interested in going to Chicago and does not accompany Floyd on any of his wild-goose chases after money. When Red dances with Vera, Floyd is roused to violent jealousy, which Canewell's gifts to Vera never cause despite Canewell's actual love for her. He is a sharp dresser and boasts of his experiences with women, describing, for example, his comical efforts to juggle relationships with seven women at once. This braggadocio may lie at the heart of his lesser intimacy with Floyd, since Floyd, too, hungers for all the signifiers of success, purchasing a beautiful new suit for himself after the robbery at the loan office. The two men also both carry guns for self-defense (Floyd a Smith & Wesson .38, Red a snub-nosed .32), while Canewell carries a more old-fashioned knife.

Red's place in the play is more as a comic foil than anything else, but his longest speech is about the increasing difficulties in simply getting by. He has surrendered his pistol to buy his drums back from the pawn shop and feels helpless without it, given the growing violence in the streets.

## Hedley

Hedley, a boarder at Louise's house who keeps chickens in the backyard, peddles various goods (such as cigarettes and candy bars) around town. This, plus income from catering funerals and weddings with modest fare like chicken and egg-salad sandwiches, enables him to pay for a space in the house's basement.

He is the play's most enigmatic character. Apparently somewhat mentally deranged, Hedley is prone to disjointed speeches full of biblical imagery about wealth and power. At times, these rambling monologues include prophecy-like visions and vague threats. While other characters occasionally mention the world of white men and its effects on their lives, they do so for the most part as an afterthought; the indignities they suffer because of racial injustice are so commonplace, one senses, as to be scarcely worth mentioning, except for a few isolated occasions. But Hedley is constantly attuned to racial injustice and views the power of white people as an existential threat, to all blacks but particularly to himself. The others gently mock his fixation but respect his choice to live and think as he pleases; they never treat him as a lunatic, interacting with him instead as a natural and intimate element of their lives, discussing religion with him and bantering affectionately with him. In fact, his ostensibly crazy speeches are, in some ways, more accurate descriptions of the challenges they themselves mention only in passing.

Yet Hedley lives in a mental world far different from theirs. His delusions of power infuse much of his decision making. Far from harmless, these delusions empower him to take control of his world in ways the others are simply unable to embrace. This is made clear at the end of act 1, when he kills a rooster after a speech about the iconic place the rooster occupies in their lives, when he recounts murdering a man who refused to call him by his first name, King, and later when he forces himself on Ruby in a violent spasm of lust. Its clearest manifestation, of course, is when he cuts Floyd's throat. He exists in the play to bring into the open all of the hidden forces that alternately imperil and motivate the other characters.

## Louise

The strong-willed owner of the boardinghouse in whose backyard the play takes place, Louise is the most sensible of the seven. She dispenses down-to-earth advice to both Vera and Ruby, her pregnant niece, about relationships and sums up the unpredictable events of the play in a comic monologue just before the Mother's Day show as, essentially, much ado about nothing. She is a protective, matronly presence, resentful of Floyd for the instability and emotional pain he has introduced into Vera's life, and impatient with her niece's inexperience and flightiness. But for all her no-nonsense approach to life, she has a softer side: she demonstrates a willingness to forgive Floyd to some degree, for example, when she encourages him to play cards with her, and she is close to Hedley, aware of the little traumas of his life in ways the others are not (as when she reveals to them that he is upset over his Board of Health summons to a sanitarium for tuberculosis).

Louise's approach to life's difficulties is clearest when she describes to Vera her own abandonment by her husband. This, she claims, was the best thing that ever happened to her. On the other hand, she reveals that she still has the razor and pistol he left upstairs, as if as keepsakes, so she is evidently not as hardheaded as she pretends.

## Ruby

Ruby is the most thinly drawn character in the play. This is partly accounted for by the fact that she is also the youngest, but her role is chiefly as an attractive young woman, and some critics have taken Wilson to task for the way he portrays such women. She is the only character absent from the post-funeral gathering in her aunt's backyard that frames the play, and one presumes that Wilson would have found it difficult to give her anything meaningful to say.

One scene that defies expectation, and perhaps belief, is when Hedley forces himself upon Ruby, and she readily surrenders to his advances; the stage direction says that she "*gives herself to him out of recognition of his great need*," and later she seems to have decided to form a relationship with him. But she has witnessed his ranting, has seen and been shocked by his inexplicable killing of an inoffensive rooster, and has been receptive enough to the more balanced male characters' attentions, so her own character seems less than fully coherent.

Nevertheless, Ruby, like the others, has a distinctive voice all her own, and her self-absorption and naivete provide the play with some of its funnier moments, as when she complains that she will develop muscles in her legs if she has to walk too much along the steep streets of Pittsburgh's Hill District.

## Vera

Vera and Floyd together occupy the emotional center of *Seven Guitars*: they invest one another with special power, mutually destructive on the one hand and redemptive on the other. The play's second scene establishes this, as Floyd struggles to express his longing for her, while Vera remains tender but resolutely at arm's length.

Like the other characters, Vera is haunted by the past: Floyd abandoned her for another woman, and the pain is recent enough that it prompts some of the play's most overtly poetic lines from her. But in her case the past is now inverted, with Floyd increasingly desperate to win back her love and driven to a jealous fit when she dances with Red Carter. Wilson plays this out as a classic tragedy, with their reconciliation and hopes for the future dashed by Floyd's big dreams and rashness. At no point does she lose herself in her refound love for him; indeed, she shows him the return ticket she has bought in case their relationship does not survive Chicago. But after his death, her grief is powerful enough that she sees angels carrying Floyd aloft.

## THEMES

### African American Culture

*Seven Guitars* is in some ways a tribute to the African American experience. Its characters are individuals, yet they re-create a sense of history greater than the merely personal. The Hill District was Pittsburgh's Harlem in the 1940s, but in the ensuing years the area was redeveloped, and with its lost identity came a long decline. At the time the play is set, the neighborhood is a music center, and the lives of its male characters, at least, are all intertwined with the blues. Wilson, using notes and observations made as a young man in this area, expertly captures the diction of Pittsburgh's black community as well; in a play especially, purely speech- and action-driven, voice is of the utmost importance, and Wilson's voices impressed critics. Finally, he exposes the lives and struggles of black characters within the context of a black community for predominantly white theatergoing audiences. The play lacks even a single white character, nor does it wear social critique on its shoulder. Indeed, white audience members may be struck more by the largely matter-of-fact attitude toward racial injustice and the sense that such injustices are commonplace, worth mentioning only briefly, than they would be by an overt political sensibility. Nevertheless, Wilson makes it plain that injustice plays an enormous role in his characters' lives.

### Love

Love-bound motivations propel much of the play's central plot arc. Floyd is desperate to win back Vera's love, and his sense that she will be drawn to him by the prospect of fame and fortune drives him to commit the robbery that leads to his life's end. Other characters speak of love as well, notably Louise, for whom the best approach to disappointment in love is to proclaim herself better off without it. Her character is more resolute than Vera's, who finds herself unable to fully resist Floyd's blandishments despite her reserved demeanor. Canewell is the second character defined at least in part by disappointment in love, as well as by loving perseverance: he has professed himself to Vera before, and while he accepts her denial and wishes her the best, he continues to hold a torch for her. But romantic love is not the only variety that impels these characters forward. In Hedley's case especially, familial love, and the pain it can engender, is a motivating force: the audience learns of his brutal treatment at the hands of his father, who kicked him in the mouth for being a failure. He may have always been mentally unbalanced, but his response to abuse is to retreat further still into fantasy: his delusions of power are endlessly tied together with memories of his father and his yearning for a father's acceptance. Love, in Wilson's telling, can be a dangerous force.

### Desperation

Floyd exemplifies the theme of desperation. Driven to ever further extremes by his limited circumstances on the one hand and the prospect of success on the other, his desperation finally becomes the ultimate tragic force. Along the way, it brings a series of disruptions to his life. When he sees Red Carter dancing with Vera, for example, he senses that his relationship with

# TOPICS FOR FURTHER STUDY

- Wilson's ideas about race and the American stage invited plenty of controversy during his lifetime, particularly when he advocated for a black director for *Fences* and when he criticized the notion of "color-blind" casting, for example, using an all-black cast for the Arthur Miller play *Death of a Salesman.* This led to a public debate with Robert Brustein, the artistic director of Boston's American Repertory Theater, in 1997. Research the arguments presented by these two men. Then write a paper in which you place their debate in historical context. Spike Lee, for example, has made the similar argument that films about African American life require African American directors. How often are black characters created, written, or directed by white, not black, artists? Do these treatments in various media affect widespread perceptions of race?

- Write a one-act play that uses the local speaking style of the area you grew up in. The authenticity of Wilson's dialogues are frequently praised by critics: they are characterized by the faithful reprise of the grammar, rhythm, and inflection of the language of Pittsburgh's Hill District, with rare embellishment. Speaking styles can be difficult to capture; exaggeration is one notable pitfall, cliché another, so take care to avoid these. Give each of your characters a distinctive voice. The primary action of *Seven Guitars* is motivated by economic distress, but the play is as much about spiritual pain, strength, and disempowerment; use your play to explore the effects of inner turmoil on outer events.

- Create a PowerPoint presentation about the ways in which Pittsburgh has changed over the twentieth century. The Pittsburgh Cycle focuses on one neighborhood in that city, so broaden your presentation to cover the entire city (architecture, industries, population, politics) to put Wilson's work in context. The website Historic Pittsburgh, hosted by the University of Pittsburgh's University Library System at http://digital .library.pitt.edu/images/pittsburgh/, is a good resource for images, and there is a wealth of books about city history available in libraries.

- *Monster*, a young-adult novel by Walter Dean Myers, is narrated by Steve Harmon, a sixteen-year-old African American awaiting trial in prison after having participated in a robbery that resulted in murder. Harmon, an aspiring filmmaker, alternately presents his experiences in diary form and as a screenplay (a format similar to that of *Seven Guitars*). Both *Monster* and *Seven Guitars* have elements of a classical tragedy, in which a protagonist's own actions bring him ever closer to doom; Myers's novel, however, is in part Harmon's analysis of tragedy after the fact. Write an essay in which you analyze these works as tragedies. Do Myers and Wilson handle tragic elements differently? How much of a role in these stories do they assign to cultural and social context?

---

her—the real foundation of his hopes for the future—is threatened, and in his anxiety he almost causes a violent physical confrontation with his close friend. Later, when Canewell, with whom he is closest, discovers and claims the robbery money, Floyd aims his gun at him. His desperation, then, is sundering his most important connections to others. And just when he believes that he has finally safeguarded his future as a musician with a loving partner, Hedley appears to claim the profits of his most desperate act; the past does not merely haunt Floyd but kills him too. Hedley, too, is desperate, dreaming obsessively of power and glory, and

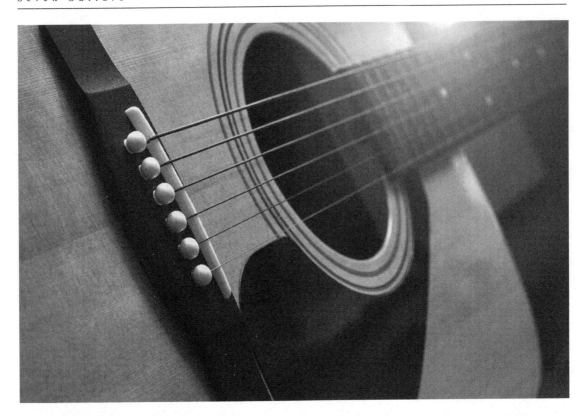

*Floyd was an up-and-coming jazz musician* (© *l0vE l0vE | Shutterstock.com*)

their twin desperations bring them together in a final act of violence.

### Destiny

As in a classic tragedy, the past holds special power over the lives of these characters, shaping their futures in ways beyond their control. Floyd believes that he is meant for greatness, and Hedley agrees, warning him that, marked as a hero, Floyd is in danger of his life. But Floyd's past and his nature doom his dreams and govern his final days. He once turned his back on the love of his life; when he makes it his quest to win her back and atone for his past, he finds that the path to his imagined destiny is blocked at every turn by his own actions. His hot temper wins him an extended sentence in a Chicago jail; he has lost the paperwork that would have secured payment for his labor at the workhouse; he has allowed too much time to elapse to redeem his guitar. Even when matters are beyond his control, however, they work against him—his manager is a crook, for example, and gets arrested before he can advance Floyd the money for his guitar and a ticket to Chicago. His social position as an African American man plays a crucial

role, steadily limiting his options until only the starkest choices around success and failure remain. In the end, most fatefully, his response to life is never to surrender but to fight to the last, and his willingness to use violence ultimately resolves his destiny.

## STYLE

### Diction

Diction is, simply, the selection and arrangement of words in speech and writing. In a play, diction is of the utmost importance to character development. Where a novel, for example, can employ many kinds of figurative language and symbolism to illustrate character, and a film can use the same figurative language in its camera work, a play has only dialogue and limited stage directions to give individuality to its personae. Wilson pays special attention to diction in his plays, adapting and refining it in different ways for each character. It is noteworthy for its fealty to the actual diction of the Hill District streets where *Seven Guitars* is set. Wilson employs colloquial diction, or language used in everyday speech, and slang, or newly coined words and other terms not accepted in formal usage, to give his characters a sense of authenticity. He also pays careful attention to cadence, the natural rhythm of language caused by the alternation of accented and unaccented syllables, especially in the peculiar diction used by Hedley. The play's title makes clear the primacy of diction to Wilson: the seven guitars are his seven characters, each an instrument giving voice to a specific vocal music.

### Structure

The form taken by a piece of literature is its structure. In *Seven Guitars*, the structure is not chronologically linear. Instead, it begins and ends with a brief gathering after Floyd's funeral. The gathering bookends the main action of the play, which takes place beforehand. This structure has the effect of rendering the play an elegy, or lament for the dead; the audience knows that Floyd will die, and this knowledge makes even more acute the theme of destiny.

Interestingly, the few specific hints as to a date in the play are contradictory. The boxing match between Joe Louis and Billy Conn is the only reference to a specific year in *Seven Guitars*. The actual match took place on June 19, 1946; later, however, Canewell announces that their date with the recording studio is for June 10, while Floyd says that they have a gig arranged at a local dance hall for Mother's Day, which was on May 12 in 1946. This free-floating temporality is not at odds with the simple framing device; the Pittsburgh Cycle is about eras, not days.

Regardless, the structure of the frame story is an ancient one. Wilson, a devoted student of the stage, was well aware of its classical roots and felt free to utilize classical elements to tell a modern story.

## HISTORICAL CONTEXT

The year 1995 was a time of contradiction in America, politically and culturally. A *New York Times* headline from October 1994 summed this up as the "Paradox of '94: Gloomy Voters in Good Times." The country was in an economic boom, with job growth, low inflation, increased productivity, and a healthy stock market, but the general mood and outlook of the citizenry were grim: some 70 percent of the public was gloomy about the future. This was due in part to the use of the gross domestic product (GDP) as the primary gauge of America's economic health. The GDP is a measure of the amount of wealth changing hands and ignores disparities along class lines. Generally, people were working longer and for less money, and the gulf between a diminishing middle class and the richest citizens was growing. Crime, too, was on the rise.

This was evident among the country's African Americans. Since the early 1970s, the unemployment rate among blacks had been 2 to 2.5 times higher than that among whites. In some ways opportunities were improving for black America: contrary to the national trend, certain statistics showed a growing black middle class, and more African Americans were college graduates than at any other time in American history. But these trends were extremely gradual, and by some measures the black middle class had contracted along with its white counterpart.

Politically, while blacks remained dramatically underrepresented on Capitol Hill, there was progress. In the year in which *Seven Guitars* was first performed, Jesse L. Jackson Jr., son of the renowned civil rights activist, won election to the House of Representatives; Ron Kirk was elected mayor of Dallas, the first African American to hold that office; and Lonnie Bristow was the American Medical Association's first African American president. On October 16, over eight hundred thousand black Americans gathered in Washington for the Million Man March, to demonstrate the population's vigor, optimism, and importance to America. But other developments pointed to a long struggle still under way. Seven months before, Mississippi finally ratified the Thirteenth Amendment—the last state to officially approve the abolition of slavery. And the Million Man March had been organized partly as a response to the election of the 104th US Congress, in which Republicans controlled both the Senate and the House. Many black leaders objected to the Republican Party's Contract with America, in which, among other things, criminal penalties and prison funding were increased, while social welfare programs and public school budgets were cut.

Culturally, as ever, the country was of two minds about race. The 1995 event that best demonstrated this state was the O. J. Simpson murder

# COMPARE
# &
# CONTRAST

- **1940s:** The electric guitar, long experimented with by designers and musicians, is on the cusp of widespread popularity. A solid-body electric guitar is built in 1940 by Les Paul using an acoustic arch top, a $4'' \times 4''$ wood post, and homemade pickups. Other designs follow rapidly, and the device gains in popularity especially among country and jazz musicians; country-and-western star Merle Travis and blues musicians T-Bone Walker and Muddy Waters are early enthusiasts.

  **1995:** Innovations in electronic music are proceeding at a breakneck pace with the use of computers. Propellerhead's music-loop editing software ReCycle, for example, can alter the tempo of a music sample without changing its pitch, so that DJs can splice tracks together more easily, and is widely available. So is the Korg Prophecy, an affordable synthesizer featuring "physical modeling," that is, the accurate electronic reproduction of acoustic sound, such as from brass and reeds.

  **Today:** Innovations in computers have made musical production via electronic means available to virtually anyone. A digital audio workstation, or DAW, is software that acts as a complete recording studio, enabling users to record, edit, and produce audio files of many types. Such software handles information on the order of the terabyte, or a million million bytes.

- **1940s:** President Franklin D. Roosevelt signs Executive Order 8802 on June 25, 1941, prohibiting racial discrimination in the defense industry. The head of the Brotherhood of Sleeping Car Porters, A. Philip Randolph, previously urged the president to end such discrimination, only to be rebuffed; only when Randolph threatens a massive march on Washington to protest such discrimination does Roosevelt acquiesce to his demands.

  **1995:** Following the 1994 Contract with America platform adopted by the Republican Party, which promises (among other things) to increase prison construction and law enforcement funding while cutting social welfare programs, the Million Man March is held on October 16 in Washington, DC. This mass gathering of African Americans, estimated at eight hundred thousand participants, is held to raise awareness of minority issues.

  **Today:** The Congressional Black Caucus (CBC), an organization of the African American members of the US Congress, meets with newly elected President Donald Trump to discuss the economic and social obstacles faced by African Americans and possible solutions. In June, the CBC declines an invitation to a second meeting, citing what it describes as actions taken by the Trump administration to the detriment of the African American community.

- **1940s:** The Great Migration, a massive movement of African American populations from the South to the North begun around 1910, increases rapidly due to several industrial trends, including the invention of the mechanical cotton picker and a demand for labor in northeastern factories. By 1950, African Americans constitute over 12 percent of Pittsburgh's population, up from 5.3 percent in 1910. Most blacks, however, still live in the South as laborers and sharecroppers.

  **1995:** Economic opportunity and political changes are once again causing African American migration, this time from the North to the South. Atlanta, a popular destination in the 1990s, sees its black population increase by around 160,000. Houston, Miami, Dallas–Fort Worth, Norfolk, Orlando, and Washington, DC, also experience rapid growth in their black populations.

  **Today:** The southward movement of black families is ongoing, with black populations in southern cities growing annually at a rapid pace. Many African Americans involved in this migration are college educated and see in the South a new land of opportunity, more affordable than cities in the North and West and with family connections ready to be re-established.

*Before his death, Floyd had been recently released from jail* (© Gts / Shutterstock.com)

trial, which transfixed the nation; 71 percent of blacks polled believed that he was innocent, while 72 percent of whites thought him guilty. In other ways, black culture was making steady inroads into mainstream America. Hip-hop was the country's best-selling musical genre. Movies like *Dead Presidents*, *Higher Learning*, *Clockers*, and *Bad Boys* put the issues facing black America front and center, while television shows like *Fresh Prince of Bel Air*, *Martin*, and *The Wayans Bros.*, if not perfectly representative of African American life at large, nevertheless presented black lives to national audiences.

## CRITICAL OVERVIEW

*Seven Guitars* has received near-universal praise. Vincent Canby, in a review for the *New York Times* in 1996, called it a "big, invigorating . . . play whose epic proportions and abundant spirit remind us of what the American theater once was." Character definition, he wrote, is "Mr. Wilson's singular gift as a writer." But he saw Hedley as overinvested with "heavy significance" and suggested that the second act "seems slightly out of balance. . . . The play's ending is . . . less stunning than muffled."

The writing itself won special praise from across the board, as when Jeremy Gerard, reviewing the play for *Variety*, called it "haunting" and "rich with exceptionally vivid characters" whose "voices and songs are the confident creations of a writer at the very top of his form." Ben Brantley, writing for the *New York Times* in 2006, ten years after the play's first performance, praises "the life force that courses through every word Wilson wrote." He compares it to "a song whose dominant strands blare, tickle, lilt and, above all, exhilarate."

## CRITICISM

### William Rosencrans

*Rosencrans is a writer and copy editor. In the following essay, he examines Wilson's* Seven Guitars *as a balancing act between the phenomenon of the white gaze and cultural expectations for black theater as a political tool.*

Wilson, as recorded in *Conversations with August Wilson*, has said that the function of black theater is the same as that of white theater: "to create art that responds to or illuminates the human condition." Nevertheless, particular challenges are faced by black playwrights and other black artists. The desire to create an art form that is specifically

> IN THE END, THIS ANGER IS TURNED NOT
> AGAINST ANY WHITE FIGURE BUT AGAINST A FELLOW
> AFRICAN AMERICAN. THE VIOLENCE IS DIRECTED AT
> A SUBSTITUTE TARGET; WHITE AUDIENCES, HOWEVER,
> HAVING BEEN PRIMED BY HEDLEY'S FURIOUS
> ORATIONS ABOUT RACIAL INJUSTICE, CANNOT HELP
> BUT REMEMBER THE ORIGINAL TARGET WHEN
> FLOYD'S WINDPIPE IS SEVERED."

African American—one that is truly reflective of African American experience, in addition to the general human condition—has engendered long-running debates about the nature of art as a social construct and has created a veritable obstacle course of philosophical, cultural, and racial pitfalls. Wilson began writing long after the obstacles had first been acknowledged, but they were (and are) still formidable for black artists; *Seven Guitars* is representative of the way Wilson runs that course.

The source of these difficulties is racial context. An art form created, for example, in an Africa never exposed to white culture, designed solely for black eyes, would be free to explore the human condition without reference to race, while still being uniquely African. But all art in America is produced and presented in the context of an art world overseen by white critics, producers, and the like, a world where whites are economically and culturally dominant.

The black artist is inescapably subject to what critics have long referred to as the "white gaze." The scholar W. E. B. Du Bois first articulated the quandary of constant exposure to this gaze in 1903:

> It is a peculiar sensation, this double-consciousness, this sense of always looking at one's self through the eyes of others, of measuring one's soul by the tape of a world that looks on in amused contempt and pity. One ever feels his twoness,—an American, a Negro; two souls, two thoughts, two unreconciled strivings; two warring ideals in one dark body, whose dogged strength alone keeps it from being torn asunder.

Five decades later, Frantz Fanon referred to the same sensation:

> I am being dissected under white eyes, the only real eyes. I am *fixed*. Having adjusted their microtomes, they objectively cut away slices of my reality.... I cannot go to a film [with a black character] without seeing myself. I wait for me.... The people in the theater are watching me, examining me, waiting for me.

The issue is that the white gaze (as well as any other) inevitably brings with it a particular point of view, with particular assumptions. Philosophers like Edmund Husserl have explored the nature of the first-person point of view and the ways in which it governs our perceptions of reality; with regard to race is one of those ways. This conflict between the perceiver and the perceived has not changed since the days of Du Bois and Fanon, and the dynamic remains for theater as for any other form. The Broadway League, the trade association for the Broadway theater industry, reports that 77 percent of Broadway theatergoers in 2015–2016 were white. Given that the work of African American artists who make it beyond community theater and onto the national stage will inevitably be viewed by white audiences, many questions must be asked. How can black experience be accurately communicated to white audiences? Must social injustice be addressed, or is this too reductive of black experience? Is it even necessary to acknowledge the presence of white audiences, or can the white gaze be ignored?

Some of the roots of this debate were explored in the 1920s during a long-running debate between Du Bois and another African American scholar, Alain Locke. Du Bois, revolted by the musical comedies that showcased parodies of African American life, advocated a distinctly political theater of black experience: protest theater. Locke argued for a theater presenting African American life as experienced in a day-to-day sense. No one in theater captured the pain of existing, white-penned presentations of black characters better than Bert Williams, an actor who wrote in 1921:

> I shuffle onto the stage, not as myself, but as a lazy, slow-going negro.... The real Bert Williams is crouched deep down inside the coon who sings and tells stories.... I'd like a piece that would give me the opportunity to express the whole of the negro's character.... If I could interpret in the theatre [an] underlying tragedy of the race, I feel that we would be better known and better understood. Perhaps the time will come when that dream will come true.

# WHAT DO I READ NEXT?

- The coming-of-age novel *Show and Prove* (2015), by Sofia Quintero, is set in the Bronx in the summer of 1983. It follows Smiles and Nike, two young men, friends whose lives take unexpected turns in the context of Reagonomics, hip-hop, urban woes, and racial tension. Issues surrounding both lower- and middle-class black youth are explored.

- *A Raisin in the Sun*, a play written by Lorraine Hansberry that first debuted in 1959, was the first written by a black woman to be performed on Broadway. Its almost exclusive depiction of one African American family's interrelationships, revolutionary for white-majority audiences, was nominated for four Tonys and was named the year's best play by the New York Drama Critics' Circle.

- Wilson is best known for *Fences* (1985), a Pulitzer-winning play and the sixth in the Pittsburgh Cycle: in the 1950s, a former baseball-playing father struggles to support his wife and son, while they receive, and must learn to cope with, the brunt of his resentment. The play was made into a movie in 2016, directed by Denzel Washington.

- *Rust Belt Boy: Stories of an American Childhood* (2016), a memoir written by Paul Hertneky, has been praised for its authenticity

much as Wilson's work has. The grandchild of immigrants, Hertneky covers the transformation of Pittsburgh from a center of industry to a failing city during his boyhood; it is an elegy to the metropolis, to which he learns to say good-bye.

- *Bless Me, Ultima*, written by Rudolfo Anaya in 1972, depicts life in the 1940s from a Latino point of view. This novel, set in rural New Mexico, recounts the youth of Antonio and his connection with a folk healer who moves into his house; his coming of age is related against a backdrop of mysticism. It is the best-selling Chicano novel of all time.

- *Black Boy* (1945), by Richard Wright, is a memoir about the author's youth in the South and young adulthood in Chicago, his fight for dignity, his observant eye and imagination, and his political outrage at the injustices he and other African Americans endure. This is an abiding classic of African American literature.

- *Praying for Freckles: Growing Up Maronite in Pittsburgh's Hill District* (2016), by Gene Kail, is the story of his childhood as a Lebanese American in Pittsburgh's Hill District. The book chronicles the sense of being a cultural outsider and the process of assimilation.

---

Du Bois's and Locke's two approaches have informed the work of black playwrights ever since the 1920s, with the majority of plays striking a balance between them. Wilson perfected this balance. Critic Samuel A. Hay summarizes Wilson's balancing act well:

> His decadent stories about often clowning people were the kind of plot DuBois had feared would feed traditional prejudices.... They are, instead, the "open and free" characters of Locke expressing DuBois's frustrated hopes. Wilson's themes, like those of DuBois, espouse positions on racism, politics, and economics.

Yet Wilson attempts to prick African American consciences—not white ones.

Wilson himself put his method quite simply in a 1987 interview recorded in *In Their Own Words*: "All of my plays are political but I try not to make them didactic or polemical."

What, exactly, are some of the techniques he uses to manage the obstacle course? Wilson had the advantage of writing for a post–civil rights era audience, in a country whose schoolbooks included many of the darker chapters of African American history, so he was at greater liberty to

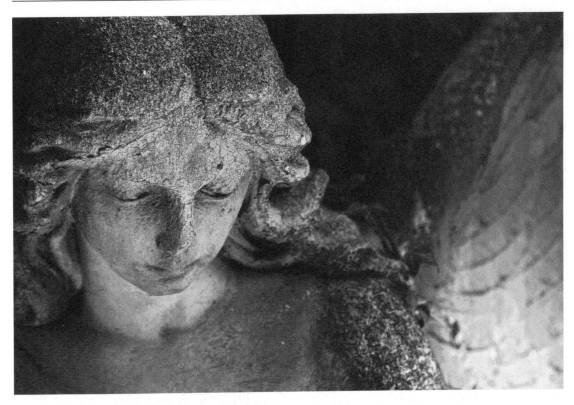

*Some of the characters see angels in the cemetery at Floyd's funeral* (© Zwiebackesser / Shutterstock.com)

focus on black lives in and of themselves than his forebear. *Seven Guitars* features an all-black cast. The only white presence is the voice of the radio announcer who narrates Joe Louis's victory over Billy Conn. Immediately, then, the pressure is off for Wilson to write lines for characters as they consciously interact under a white gaze; they are free to be themselves, however the artist conceives their identities, unmediated by an overt white context. Their desires, pleasures, angers, hopes, and regrets are expressed without an interracial filter; their only filters are those innate to the human condition referred to earlier—the desires to impress, to love, to succeed, and so on.

This is the crux of Wilson's approach. His aim is always to demonstrate that black life is a totality, a cultural whole expressive of everything necessary to its self-fulfillment, without the need for mediation from other cultures. He has stated,

> Black life is large enough; there is no idea that it cannot contain that is not already a part of it— so that you have a whole—complete. This is not a "sub-culture"! You have a whole complete world view—a whole complete cultural philosophy, religion, mythology, history . . .

The strictly African American interactions in *Seven Guitars* enable Wilson to present the effects of racial injustice more subtly. This is a key to the success of his plays as political works. Indeed they are not, by any stretch of the imagination, polemical; instead, mention of racial injustice comes almost as an afterthought. These characters have a shared background in this context, and so a white audience is invited into this background. Where an unjust arrest might inflame deep outrage in a white character, for example, Canewell has not even seen fit to mention it to his friends. "What you went to jail for?" asks Louise. "You ain't told us all that. You just say you didn't like [Chicago]." Canewell briefly summarizes his arrest, ending simply with, "I ain't going back up there." "I don't blame you," responds Louise, who then immediately changes the subject: "Where's Vera, Floyd?" And with that the matter is dropped. White audiences may be struck by how much a part of the fabric of black life such events involving white condescension and oppression are: so commonplace as to be scarcely worth mentioning.

These sidelong mentions of disparity are unobtrusive, but they are nevertheless frequent.

Floyd, desperate for his manager's promised advance, without which his dreams for the future will crumble, says, "If I knew where he lived I'd go over to his house." "They don't like that," cautions Canewell. "They don't like you coming over to their house." The interaction lasts only a few seconds but suggests a lifetime constricted by racial mores.

Another of Wilson's methods for balancing the personal against the political is illustrated in the character of Hedley. Hedley's off-kilter ramblings are clearly the result of mental instability, but they are the play's most overt references to racial oppression. By putting angry political denunciations in the mouth of a mentally ill man, Wilson accomplishes many things. Most important, while white (and black) audiences will not fail to register them as genuine outrage, the other characters generally ignore or dismiss them. "He talking all this plot-against-the-black-man stuff," Louise scoffs. "You know how he is." "Everything is a plot against the black man to Hedley," agrees Canewell.

Wilson also frames these obsessions of Hedley's as manifestations of religious mania, which has the effect of removing them from the earthly plane, where they might take effect, to the spiritual one, as if they were safely behind a preacher's pulpit. The fervor of Hedley's pronouncements, the biblical imagery, and the prophecies of empowerment and violence coalesce as overt and perfectly righteous expressions of anger, which could be expected to discomfit white audience members—were they delivered by a man in his right mind. In the end, this anger is turned not against any white figure but against a fellow African American. The violence is directed at a substitute target; white audiences, however, having been primed by Hedley's furious orations about racial injustice, cannot help but remember the original target when Floyd's windpipe is severed.

Wilson's work, then, expertly navigates a historically treacherous racial terrain. It is in many ways the fulfillment of the dream of Langston Hughes, who in his 1926 essay "The Negro Artist and the Racial Mountain" wrote:

> We younger Negro artists who create now intend to express our individual dark-skinned selves without fear or shame. If white people are pleased we are glad. If they are not, it doesn't matter.... If colored people are pleased we are glad. If they are not, their displeasure doesn't matter either. We build our temples for tomorrow, strong as we know how, and we stand on top of the mountain, free within ourselves.

> WHEN READERS EXAMINE WILSON'S INCLUSION OF ESSENTIAL AFRICAN AMERICAN HISTORY IN *SEVEN GUITARS*, THEY GAIN PERSPECTIVE OF THE PLAY'S CONFLICTS BY CONSIDERING HOW AND IN WHAT WAY CERTAIN HISTORICAL EVENTS TRANSCENDED DECADES."

**Source:** William Rosencrans, Critical Essay on *Seven Guitars*, in *Drama for Students*, Gale, Cengage Learning 2018.

### Ellen Bonds

*In the following excerpt, Bonds examines the importance of history in* Seven Guitars.

In the prefatory "Note" to *Seven Guitars*, August Wilson avers that he pursued his "interest in history" by imbuing his plays with an "overall historical feel" and foregrounding his characters' "personal histories" as he fit them into the "historical context in which they live." Throughout his cycle, Wilson's interest in history centers on African American history: slavery and its aftermath from the Middle Passage to the Great Migration. And while he sets each of his plays within an historical context of a particular decade, he relies on the culture of that time more so than political events to provide historicity. In *Seven Guitars* Wilson does not recount World War II history; rather, he focuses on the characters' post-World War II struggles to overcome broken promises, social, civil, and economic injustices, and continued conflict on both an internal and communal level—to progress beyond the war and its aftermath.

Still, an understanding of the political history as well as the cultural contexts of the World War II period (late 1930s-late 1940s) helps inform our reading of *Seven Guitars*. If, as Harry J. Elam contends in his *The Past as Present in the Drama of August Wilson*, history can both "shackle" and "empower" African Americans, readers should investigate how Wilson situates his characters within World War II history, in particular African American involvement in the war effort as well as the cultural history represented (in part) by Joe Louis. By considering these essential contexts, readers understand that *Seven Guitars* fulfills Wilson's often-stated purpose: to illustrate the "most important issues confronting black Americans for that decade" (qtd. in Shannon *Dramatic Vision* 3). At issue in 1940s America is the usurpation of racial progress that preceded and exceeded the World War II era and that produced rising frustrations as the consequence of false promises made by white political leaders (including, in particular, Franklin Delano Roosevelt).

Understanding Wilson's incorporation of history in his plays can be challenging because of his use of "deliberate anachronisms" or "multifarious temporalities." In his "Introduction" to *August Wilson: Completing the Twentieth-Century Cycle*, Alan Nadel explains the reciprocal relationship between drama and history as Wilson represents it. Wilson's use of "multifarious temporalities" produces "multifarious perspectives [that] give the specific conflicts of the play their historic dynamics [as] these dynamics give the play's conflicts their historical specificity" (3). Sandra Shannon maintains that Wilson's manipulation of time takes audiences on a "non-linear journey" where the boundaries between "uppercase" events in History and the equally important but often disregarded personal experiences of history are blurred. It is a place where the historical past meets the present. But in *Seven Guitars*, the present environment reflects a determination to move on and forget the past including the war.

A single reference to World War II appears in Scene 4 of *Seven Guitars* where Floyd says, "That's why we won the war.... They got the atomic bomb and everything" (44). Here, Wilson's use of two competing pronouns—"we" and "they"—indicates the uncertain inclusion of African Americans in the national victory. Without Floyd's comment, only the cultural references to Joe Louis and certain blues songs (e.g., "That's All Right") provide clues to the time in which the play is set. Even then, readers must consider not only the post-war year, 1948 or even the decade of the 1940s, but a time that exceeds and transcends categorization along conventional thinking of historical chronology.

Readers can determine the historical time period that informs the play by employing William James' "saddle-back" technique (looking to both the past and the future from the vantage point of the present). Doing so helps reveal the "overall historical feel" of this era, one of racial

oppression and African Americans' resistance to oppression, a degree of progress in terms of racial equality, but America's resistance to said progress. *Seven Guitars*, set in 1948, occupies a mid-point in the twentieth century and the midpoint in Wilson's cycle. Looking to the past, readers can note both political and cultural events that helped create the post-war environment in which the characters live. For example, riffing on the number seven from the play's title (as Tony Kushner suggests in his Foreword to *Seven Guitars*), readers can recall that seven years in the past, 1941, the United States entered World War II and Joe Louis fought Billy Conn for the first time. The World War II political history for African Americans involved the fight to overcome continuing oppression on the home front as much as the battle against the enemy overseas. The cultural history, Louis's victory over Conn, provided hope that progress in terms of racial equality could be achieved. The characters in *Seven Guitars* continue to resist injustice as they hope for a better future. Readers can consider how the fight for racial justice during World War II continued seven years into the future, 1955 (the year many consider as the start of the Civil Rights movement). Significantly, scholars have credited African Americans' fight for racial justice during World War II with serving as an origin for the Civil Rights movement of the 1950s.

Even though *Seven Guitars* begins and ends in 1948, the origins of the story's conflict and the consequences of its violent resolution exceed a single year, indeed a single decade. Wilson, no doubt, recognized that the distinction between start dates and origins is important because history cannot be restricted to rigid time lines. In his "Beginning Again, Again," Alan Nadel differentiates between origins and starts, examining the ways that Wilson "[reconfigured] the before/after relationship that informed his history" (15). Since *Seven Guitars* functions as a flashback, its starting point could be Floyd's death or his pre-death. For the history that informs the play, the starting point could be even more ambiguous since the causes of World War II originated decades before 1939, even before the start of the 20th century. Moreover, in *Seven Guitars* Wilson illustrates how the effects [of] racism that existed before and during World War II remained after 1945 (the end date of the war), indeed into the following decades.

In addition to realizing that historical origins and influences transcend decades, readers can benefit from recognizing how the overlap between and among Wilson's plays reinforces the significance of the way that Wilson structured his cycle. Once again, applying James' saddle-back perspective to 1948, ten years earlier takes us to the year after *The Piano Lesson* ends. Ten years into the future takes us to the year after *Fences* begins. As Harry Elam suggests in "*Radio Golf* in the Age of Obama," readers should consider these temporal possibilities since Wilson was interested "in the gaps and fissures in history" into which African Americans' experience (their lower case history) "have too often fallen" (195). Wilson situates his plays to fill in the gaps not only retrieving but more importantly revitalizing African American experience. In *Seven Guitars*, for example, Wilson includes essential history from the past of slavery to the present of continued discrimination and segregation, from the past of the pre–World War II period to the present post-war period which may be hard to distinguish as a new and different time.

When readers examine Wilson's inclusion of essential African American history in *Seven Guitars*, they gain perspective of the play's conflicts by considering how and in what way certain historical events transcended decades. For example, Wilson's reference to the Great Migration helps express his reservations about this key event: c.f., Red Carter's comment, "There ain't nothing but niggers from Mississippi in Chicago. The Sixty- One highway . . . run straight north . . . [and more importantly] wore many a man out" (I: 5, 59). But significantly, for the purpose of understanding Wilson's choice of the year in which he set the play, readers need to know that the pre–World War II geographical shift in African American population continued to increase during and especially after the Second World War. "Seventy-seven percent of the African American population [were living] in the South in 1940 [but] nearly 50 percent" were living in the North by 1960 ("Postwar Prosperity"). During this second-wave emigration, blacks continued to encounter "overcrowding, discrimination, and violence" in Northern cities ("Postwar"). In her reading of *Seven Guitars*, Sandra Shannon contends that Floyd "Schoolboy" Barton's plight is an affirmation that the "transplant of [the Great Migration] did not take" ("A Transplant"). The characters in *Seven Guitars* as part of a second-wave Great Migration demonstrate that not only did the Great Migration "not take" in 1948 but also for many African American migrants, it did not live up to the widespread myth of the North's being the Promised Land.

To help illustrate the pervasive oppression African Americans experienced during the World War II period, Wilson dramatizes the quest to achieve racial progress through the metaphor of moving—not only from the South to the North, from Pittsburgh to Chicago, but also past the overwhelming presence of death that existed at the end of the war. From the opening scene where they return from Floyd's funeral to Hedley's resistance to admitting the severity of his tuberculosis to Canewell's reaction to the news that George Butler died—"Every time I look up, somebody's dying . . ."—their attempts not to dwell on death and to move on represent the pervasive post–World War II attitude in America. However, the ability to forget the past and progress to a better future is compromised by their position in American society—a position that has changed little despite African Americans' significant contribution to the war effort.

Although Wilson foregrounds his characters' personal histories in *Seven Guitars*, he noted the significance of World War II political history in his comments about the play's setting. For example, Wilson cited African American's participation in the war effort as the determiner of his choice of year in which to set the play. In an interview with the *Seattle Times*, Wilson maintained that he considered both a pre-war and post-war setting for *Seven Guitars* and chose 1948 because post-war African Americans were full of hope and "I wanted to touch on that period of hopefulness" (I-Chin Tu). But John Lahr, in his *New Yorker* piece "Black and Blues: *Seven Guitars* a New Chapter in August Wilson's Ten-Play Cycle," reads the play's characters as "poised between their greatest hope and their greatest heartbreak," quoting Wilson, "'We had just gone off and demonstrated our allegiance and willingness to fight and die for the country. . . . We actually believed that things would be different, and that we would be accorded first-class citizenship. We came back after the war, and that was not true'" (99–100).

Certainly, before World War II, America's political history in terms of race relations made it difficult to believe that "things" could ever be different for African Americans. The history of the United States' treatment of African Americans before World War II affects the world in which *Seven Guitars'* characters live after the war. Here, readers can note the "before/after" relationship that Nadel cites as essential for informing Wilson's plays. For example, in the years leading up to World War II, African Americans continued to fight racist perceptions and discrimination on the home front. This pervasive discrimination emanated from the top. In one notable event, President Roosevelt refused to support an anti-lynching bill in 1935, a bill that had been sorely needed for decades. However, since the Dyer Bill's defeat by Senate filibuster in 1922, no anti-lynching legislation had been introduced to Congress. Walter White initiated a new proposal—the Costigan-Wagner Bill—but as in 1922 it was defeated. Essentially, Roosevelt capitulated to the southern seniority in Congress to ensure their cooperation on future legislation (Goodwin 163). Some New Deal programs did expand to become more inclusive by 1939, but any progress in racial justice was incremental and met with pragmatic concessions and outright resistance. Overall, the country-wide racism that existed during the Great Depression persisted as the United States geared up for the war.

A study of the history of African Americans' determination to participate in the war effort before and during World War II helps inform the motivation of *Seven Guitars'* characters who remain both determined to strive for a better life and frustrated by continued racial discrimination in post–World War II America. This injustice existed in 1940 as patriotic fervor and calls for national unity were increasing (Goodwin 165). However, once again African Americans were excluded from participating in supporting their country, both in the defense industry and the military. Plants across the country issued statements that blatantly rejected black workers. For example, Vultee Air in California dictated, "'It is not the policy of this company to employ other than of the Caucasian race'" (qtd. in Goodwin 247). A Catch-22 existed that prohibited blacks from being hired to work unless they were union members; however, the union accepted white members only. Still, African American leaders resisted. For example, throughout early 1941, A. Philip Randolph and Milton Webster planned a march on Washington to "[win] Democracy for the Negro [by] Winning the War for Democracy." Wilson may have been alluding to the history of Randolph and Webster's advocacy and the general "willingness

> THERE IS NO IDEA THAT CANNOT BE CONTAINED BY BLACK LIFE. WE HAVE THE ENTIRE WORLD HERE."

[of African Americans] to fight and die for their country" in his comments to Lahr in the *New Yorker* piece. Previously, Wilson had commented on his characters' motivations in his "Sailing the Streams of Black Culture." In this 2000 *New York Times* essay, Wilson wrote that the characters in his plays act heroically because they "still place their faith in America's willingness to live up to the meaning of her creed so not to make a mockery of her ideals" despite America's history of racial injustice. . . .

**Source:** Ellen Bonds, "World War II History/history: Essential Contexts in *Seven Guitars*," in *August Wilson's Pittsburgh Cycle: Critical Perspectives on the Plays*, edited by Sandra G. Shannon, McFarland, 2016, pp. 60–65.

### Carol Rosen and August Wilson
*In the following excerpt, Wilson talks about his plays, including* Seven Guitars.

*. . . Theater Week:* Seven Guitars *is set in 1948. Is this play the only missing piece in the cycle as you conceived it?*

*AW:* Well, *Seven Guitars* is one of the missing pieces . . . .

Okay, let's back up a minute. 1911 is *Joe Turner*. 1927 is *Ma Rainey's Black Bottom*. 1936 is *The Piano Lesson*. 1948 is *Seven Guitars*. 1957 is *Fences* and 1969 is *Two Trains Running*. And I have a seventies play, *Jitney*, included as part of my cycle.

*TW: If you continue to track history by dramatizing decades, will you next depict contemporary life, the period of your own adulthood?*

*AW:* The sixties was actually my adulthood. I came into manhood in the early sixties. *Two Trains Running* was that period of time. In 1969, I was twenty-four years old.

So what's left is the eighties and nineties when you deal with my adulthood as a middle-aged man as opposed to as a young man.

*Seven Guitars* is the forties and it fills in that gap there. Then I have the two ends to work on.

So next I'm working on the eighties and then I'll do the early 1900s, the first decade of the twentieth century, and be done with that part of it. I'll never stop working, but I'll be done with that part.

*TW: You said once that* Fences *began for you with an image of a middle-aged man holding a baby. Do you always start with an image?*

*AW*: Sometimes it's with an idea. Sometimes it's with a line of dialogue. Sometimes it's just a burning passion to say something, even if you don't know what it is you want to say. [Laughs]

This play started with an image of seven men with guitars on stage. Someone named Floyd—it was Bannister at the time—but someone named Floyd Barton had been killed, and these men were in a lineup and they were responding to this unheard and unseen voice, this disembodied voice. "No, sir," "Well, I know Floyd for however many years," etc.

I thought by doing that, I would go on to do two things. I wanted to expose—sort of look behind—the songs, to the interior psyche of the individuals who create the songs so you see how the blues are created and where in essence they come from.

I was interested in showing the relationship between those men and white society, and between those men and black society, where from one viewpoint, they're seen as drunkards and vagrants and things of that sort, and then from the other, they're seen as carriers of the tradition, a very valuable and integral part of the community and the culture.

So I began to work at putting these scenes together. This all happened in my mind, of course, but one of the guys came to me and said, "What the hell she doin' here? Tell her to get the hell out of here. You say this an all-man play."

I looked over and there was this woman sitting on the stage. "Tell her to get the hell...." I said, "No, I'll take care of it, man." So I went over, and I said, "Excuse me, what are you doing here?" She said, "I want my own space." I said, "You want your own scene?" She said, "No, I want my own space."

I didn't know what she meant by that. So I said, "I don't know how I'm going to deal with this." I closed my tablet and I walked away. A couple of months later, I sat down one day and I opened my tablet. I said, "Okay, you've got your own space." There was a knock at the door and a woman answered the door. There was a man standing there with a radio and a chicken and he had come courting. That turned out to be Vera. And the man ended up being Floyd. It was various other men at different times.

And then I let Vera in and then these other two women walked in behind her. [Laughs] So I ended up with four men and three women.

*TW: So now the play has seven characters, but only one guitar. Why do numbers crop up so often in the dialogue, even in the title? Does the number seven have special significance?*

*AW*: I don't have the men with seven guitars on stage anymore.

At one point, as I was writing the play, there was something called "The Numbers Section." In everything in that particular section, I tried to deal with numbers, various dates and any way that you could get a number—how long the records were, two minutes, thirty-seven seconds, whatever—I dealt with numbers.

I didn't consciously do that. Of course, there's seven birds over there, and seven is a mystical number and involved a lot in superstition and things of that sort, and it's a winning number on the dice, things of that sort. Hedley says, "Inside each man is seven generations," but he says, "The seventh son of the seventh son is a big man, but I am not the seventh son. I'm just a poor black man who has grown up without knowing the joys of a woman."

*TW: Do you think of the seven characters as guitars themselves?*

*AW*: Absolutely. Yes, that's why there are seven characters. As it turned out, they are the seven guitars. They each have their individual voices and their individual characters. And if they're the guitars, then I guess I'm the orchestra. I'm not sure. [Laughs]

*TW: Could you be the guy in the pawn shop?!*

*AW*: That I'm *not*. I am not the guy in the pawn shop! However you want to cut it.

*TW: This production of* Seven Guitars *has traveled across America. How has the play taken shape in the course of its journey?*

*AW*: We had a much longer journey with *Piano Lesson*. This has been relatively short. We started it last January at the Goodman Theater and we went from there. In September, we mounted the show at the Huntington Theatre in Boston. And then we went to ACT in San

Francisco and then down to the Ahmanson and then to New York. That's a much shorter journey than most of my plays have taken.

I don't think it's changed its shape, but I think it's changed considerably since Chicago. I rewrote and added scenes, for instance. That was a big change. I didn't add any characters, but I tried to define them better and I added a couple of scenes that I thought would help to do that. And I continued working on it since then.

*TW: I've heard that the first scene of the play was originally part of the final scene.*

*AW*: No, no. It functions as a bookend; it functions as a flashback. We begin the play the day of the burial of Floyd Barton as the characters have come back from the cemetery And then we flash back—I hate that word, but we do, we flash back—to Floyd's life. Then at the end of the play, we come back to them in the yard after they've come back from the funeral.

*TW: Why don't the characters identify the killer? Are they protecting him?*

*AW*: He's not being protected. No one knows he's done it, first of all. Canewell suspects it. He says, "What did he give you?" and having seen Floyd in the yard with the money, he has it sort of figured out, but they don't know that he did it. *He* [the killer] doesn't know he did it.

*TW: The audience suspects he is going to do it, the minute he shows up with a machete.*

*AW*: I did not know he was going to do it the minute he showed up with a machete. Maybe the audience does.

It took me a long while to figure out who was going to do it. [Laughs] I started out knowing that Floyd Barton was murdered and I had no idea.

*TW: Your choice of the killer makes the death of Floyd all the more wrenching. As in* Fences *and* The Piano Lesson, *you create a no-win situation, evoking a sense of loss and bewilderment because no resolution is possible. If the police killed him it would all be so cut and dried.*

*AW*: It's tragic. It wouldn't be tragic if the police killed him. Hedley—yes, it's very interesting that their paths cross. Of course, Floyd has to assume the responsibility for his own death, his own murder. Had he not been standing in the yard with the money, then Hedley never could have assumed that he was Buddy Bolden, etc. Had he not robbed the place, then had the

money, he wouldn't have been standing there. So whatever events conspired to have him standing in that yard at that precise time, he has to himself bear the responsibility for that.

It was difficult to kill him that way. . . . Once I knew that someone was going to kill Floyd Barton, I toyed with the idea of having it be someone outside the play. But that didn't work And once it was going to be someone inside the play, I liked my characters and I didn't want to make any of them murderers. [Laughs] So I came up with a way to have that happen without Hedley being the murderer per se.

You see, if Buddy Bolden is bringing some money from Hedley's father, he represents his father's forgiveness. Also, Hedley is going to use the money to buy a plantation, not to get rich, but so the white man doesn't tell him what to do anymore, to become independent, land being the basis of independence.

In a way, the play says that anyone who is standing in the way of a black man's independence needs to be dealt with. So it's very necessary that Hedley decides that Floyd, as Buddy Bolden, is the messenger, the courier who would like to keep the money, who will not give him his money so he can buy his plantation. It means it's a betrayal of Hedley's father.

Of course, the tragedy is he's not Buddy Bolden, that he is Floyd Barton. It's a mistake. It's an honorable mistake, but it is a mistake.

*TW: Would you consider Floyd to be your first tragic hero?*

*AW*: No, not the first hero. Boy Willie [in *The Piano Lesson*] is very heroic. Troy [in *Fences*] is a very heroic man. Sterling [in *Two Trains Running*] is very heroic; Levee [in *Ma Rainey's Black Bottom*—even though he kills, for all his misguided transferred aggression and misguided heroics—he still has that warrior spirit.

*TW: These other characters you mention are compromised heroes, but Floyd has a strong sense of his own place in the world, of his special value to the community as an artist. He is going somewhere.*

*AW*: Yes, yes. His death is a most unfortunate occurrence. One of the things that is interesting is Floyd goes out and gets the instrument of his hero, Muddy Waters, and Hedley goes out and gets the machete, which is the instrument of his hero, Toussaint L'Ouverture.

They both feel compelled to get these things. And Hedley is warning Floyd. He loves him; it's like his son and he would do nothing to harm this man. He's rooting for him and looking out for him, telling him, "Watch your back; they're after you." The last thing he would do would be to harm Floyd. And they don't know, but it's just fated that their paths were just crossing.

*TW: Somewhat like Gabriel in* Fences, *Hedley is a loose-cannon character who inhabits a realm other than that of your more realistic characters. His actions take on a symbolic valence. He does not behave according to laws of logic, but he functions as an instrument of death.*

*AW:* They have their own interior logic. For instance, Hedley refuses to go to the sanitarium. Now, if my father died from lack of proper medical care, then all of the sudden you want to give me—"I don't know, it's a trap."

See, so it's also where he's been, the truth that he has accumulated in his life. It's no different than when I get a letter from AT&T saying they want me to join a Reach Out America plan, that they can save me some money on my long-distance calls. I look at that with great suspicion and go, "Wait a minute, this is not right. You guys rarely try to save anybody any money. You know you're out to maximize your profits. What do you mean, you're going to save me some money?"

It's the same thing. "Come on, we want you to go into the sanitarium?" And you go, "I don't know, it's a trap." Every encounter he's had with white society has been a trap of some sort. So why wouldn't he assume that? So the logic is not the common logic, but he has his own interior life and his own interior logic that is rooted in *this* world. He doesn't go around saying he's a prophet or a Messiah or anything. He talks about Marcus Garvey, he talks about how he wants to be the father of the Messiah.

*TW: In the script there was a moment when the characters all take turns speculating about what each one would do if he or she were God.*

*AW:* That's no longer in.

There was a bunch of stuff—I took a lot of stuff out. Otherwise, it would be a four-and-a-half-hour play. I had to try to find those moments that best served the material. This [section] was an addendum to the story, to the actual events of the play. Particularly with my plays, it's sometimes necessary, because it illuminates the characters and illuminates their logic and their thoughts and the world that they live in. You have to make choices. Sometimes it's difficult.

*TW: That passage shows how cynical the characters are about the possibility of being saved by some outside force.*

*AW:* Oh, you're never saved by any outside force. It all comes from within you.

*TW: Some of your stage directions, particularly at climactic moments, seem very difficult to realize in performance. In* Fences, *for example, Gabriel is described as letting out an "atavistic cry" and dancing with such abandon that he "opens the gates of Heaven." In the movie industry, such a description is termed "hyping the script"— when the writer eloquently calls upon the actors and the director to deliver the impossible.*

*AW:* It's a great theatrical moment. Make of it what you want. It's a challenge to the actors. I think people take that moment and do something really stunning with it. Other people don't rise to the occasion or the challenge.

What do you do? I almost wrote a moment like that for Hedley in *Seven Guitars*. He had realized that this is Floyd.

*TW:* Fences *was going to be adapted for the screen. It has not yet been turned into a film, has it?*

*AW:* So far, no.

*TW: Are you still expecting it to become a film?*

*AW:* I am, yes.

*TW: What is holding up the project?*

*AW:* The problem was: a black director. They have since agreed to hire a black director. We may do that; we may make the film with John Singleton. You know Hollywood.

*TW: Do you consider your plays autobiographical?*

*AW:* They are not autobiographical. All the characters are entirely invented. They're not based on anyone that I know or anyone I know about. None of the events of the play is based on my life or anyone's life that I know. These are just things I make up. In the sense that all of the characters all come out of me, they are probably all me, the different aspects of my personality. But it's not my life, and it's not anyone who I know.

*TW: Are there things in your life that you would not write about?*

*AW:* No, I can't think of anything. But there's nothing in my life I *would* write about. I don't have any secrets, but I don't think it's that important . . . . You make art out of your life and you have one life and you have small art. I'm not interested in that.

I'm interested in something larger than that. I have a four-hundred-year autobiography, if you will. Since 1619, the early seventeenth century, my ancestors have been here in this country and I claim all of that. I can write about that experience and any part of it.

*TW: Would you consider yourself a political playwright?*

AW: Absolutely. All art is politics. I'm one of those warrior spirits. The battle since the first African set foot on the continent of North America has been a battle for the affirmation of the value and worth of one's being in the face of this society that says you're worthless, etc. In that sense, everyone's history has its own political dictates, and so I attempt to follow them.

I think that as blacks, we need to alter the relationship that we have to the society. In the sixties, the catchword was Black Power. And equally important, perhaps more so, we need to alter the shared expectation that we have of each other as blacks. My art hopefully contributes to that.

*TW: You are describing the potential effect of your plays on both white and black audiences. Do you write for any particular audience?*

*AW:* No. I write for an audience of one, which is the self. I write basically and selfishly for myself as the artist. [It's] the same as Picasso when he painted a picture, and he put red here and he put blue there. He's not painting for anyone; he's doing the expression to this thing that beats in here [he thumps on his chest], and whatever artistic tenets that he may follow, whatever he's trying to accomplish in his art, that's what you do.

I do place black Americans at the center of the universe, in the world. As Africans prior to coming over here, they existed, and they were the center. Everything revolved around them in their world view. Over here, all of that has been taken and stripped away. So I say, "Let's look at it. The world is right here in this back yard." There is no idea that cannot be contained by black life. We have the entire world here.

*TW: Your plays show the heroic side of characters whose lives have been devalued by the dominant white society.*

*AW:* Absolutely. You get a different perspective. The people always knew they had a

> INSTEAD OF USING CHRISTIANITY'S MORAL FOUNDATIONS TO UPHOLD THE DIGNITY OF BLACK AMERICA, HE REVELS IN SLAUGHTER, DAMNING TO ENDLESS TORMENT ANYONE WHO GETS IN HIS WAY."

value. They had fallen into a political circumstance in which they were enslaved, but they always knew that there was a value to them, even if their captors and their enslavers did not see that or recognize that. The people always knew and they continued to pray to their gods.

Someone else looking over here would look at them and say, "They're very strange people. They don't have no language, they don't have no custom, they run around half-naked, this, that, the other." But it all depends on where you're standing. If I'm standing over here, I can understand how you could see that. But the people knew themselves . . . .

**Source:** Carol Rosen and August Wilson, "August Wilson: Bard of the Blues," in *Conversations with August Wilson*, edited by Jackson R. Bryer and Mary C. Hartig, University Press of Mississippi, 2006, pp. 190–97.

## Peter Wolfe
*In the following excerpt, Wolfe provides a character analysis of Hedley.*

### THE WINGS OF ETHIOPIA

. . . The psychological, spiritual, and political energies infusing *Seven Guitars* all converge in Hedley in a context of Shakespearean anxiety about nature robbed of its order. Hedley's suspicion that he serves this disorder has heightened his anxiety. Instead of using Christianity's moral foundations to uphold the dignity of black America, he revels in slaughter, damning to endless torment anyone who gets in his way. A major component of his mind-set is the belief that the soil soaked with the blood of his forebears will enrich his soul. It's inevitable that he hates whites because *their* blood and *their* collective memories both bar them from his messianic fantasy.

Neither clown nor demon, this troubled, complex man drips death. He first appears right after the funeral of his murder victim, which he attended, and two scenes later he's making the chicken sandwiches he hopes to sell to the guests at another funeral service (7G, 18). The same death that helps his business has marked him. What keeps him in death's domain is his pentecostal fury. This would-be figure of wrath and destruction calls himself a hurricane, a lion, and a warrior (88–89). His creed is one of blood and thunder: "'Ethiopia shall stretch forth her wings and every abomination shall be brought low'" (19), he raves, paraphrasing Psalms 68:31. This scourge (whom Shafer calls "a mystic" [1998, 37]) sees himself as larger than life, comparing himself to Toussaint L'Ouverture, Marcus Garvey, and Joe Louis. His heroic self-image declares itself in the opening words of the song he chants to begin act 2, scene 5: "Ain't no grave... can hold my body down" (7G, 88). To ratify his exalted self-concept, he traces a circle in the yard with his steps as soon as he finishes his song, repeating the circular pattern he made with the blood he squeezed from the neck of the rooster he killed in act 1, scene 5. (The lack of authorial squeamishness Trudier Harris noted in Bynum's sacrificial pigeons in *Joe Turner* intensifies with the rooster in *Seven Guitars*, the slaying of which isn't merely described but, rather, portrayed.)

As has been seen, the eternity symbolized by these circles excludes white people. It's therefore bogus. Defining conflict racially, he warns the others, "The white man got a big plan" (7G, 69). This plan, if it exists, can't be any uglier than his. Just as his black father nearly kicked him to death, he, Hedley, had already killed one black man before the play's continuous action, and he kills another during it. If anything, he does the white man's dirty work of annihilating black people. The born ruler's persona he affects while singing and making sandwiches in the scene immediately before the one where he kills the rooster is fatuous. This renegade who refuses to be treated by white doctors and tries to sneak out of paying his rent is strictly small-time.

His legacy of wrongdoing extends most clearly from his father. Besides being mad, Hedley Sr. named his son King, after Charles "Buddy" Bolden (1877–1931), founder of New Orleans's first jazz band and also the first king in a line of New Orleans cornetists that included Joseph "King" Oliver and Louis Armstrong. Madness darkened Bolden's last years, which suggests that Hedley Sr. might have disclosed in himself a prophetic streak when he named his son. Bolden, "a riveting performer of personal charisma and crowd-pleasing musical power," had to be institutionalized after going "spectacularly insane" during a street parade (Carr, Fairweather, and Priestley, 66). The insanity that caused this flare-up worsened. After drunkenly attacking both his mother and his mother-in-law, Bolden spent his last 24 years in a mental home (Carr, Fairweather, and Priestley, 66).

Hedley regrets having been named after this mad jazz king. The honorific name has pumped him up with so many delusions of grandeur that, when a fellow black refused to call him King, Hedley murdered the man. His grandiose self-image still clings to him, but in an altered form: though he'll still compare himself to Moses and Jesus, he's ready to settle for becoming the father of the Messiah; his monumental impact on posterity will occur through his son. The allure created by this impact consumes him. Though impelled by apocalyptic visions, he takes the initiative rather than waiting for the divine will to express itself. His lust roused by his messianic gabble, he has sex with Ruby. The next scene starts with Floyd alone on stage burying the money the theft of which will soon cost him his life. Death has become the offspring of Hedley's rut with Ruby. And logic decrees that more death will follow, an idea supported by the play's color symbolism. Besides expressing itself in the blood shed by Hedley's two victims, red, the color of martyrdom, asserts its might in the roses engraved on Floyd's mother's headstone, in the papier-mâché floral decorations Louise makes for Mother's Day, and in the flaming red dress Ruby (whose name denotes red) wears to the big dance.

Hedley traduced nature by f—ing Ruby, a woman 35 years his junior, just as his fantasy of starting a plantation in Pittsburgh (7G, 24) traduces reason. Not only does Pittsburgh lack the climate, the available land, and the workforce to support a plantation; any farm Hedley installed there, against all odds, with its crops of tobacco and oats, would turn him into a facsimile southern white landlord. He would thus be one with his sworn foe. But as he did in *Trains* with the sale of Memphis's building to the city, Wilson again invites the possibility that the black man can beat the odds, even when he seems to have no chance. Granted, Hedley's turbulence and extravagance have raised the odds against him.

But this excessiveness hasn't killed hope. Most of Wilson's plays end on a note of guarded acceptance, the pulse of life continuing to throb in a painful, frightening, yet beautiful world. Sometimes the throbbing will seem like a descent of grace or a divine intercession, ironically those very mercies that Hedley, who could profit a great deal from them, has banished from his militant theology.

The closing scenes of the three plays separating *Fences* from *Guitars* include the muted promise of renewal through sexual love. In *Guitars* the promise, though present, is even more muted. The prospect of fathering the Messiah seems to have humanized Hedley. He agrees to go to the sanitarium for treatment, and he also attends church—as does Ruby, for the first time in 20 years. Another ray of hope glances from the child she's carrying. Plays like *Fences*, *Joe Turner*, and *Piano Lesson* featured children in scenes near final blackout to signal hope. Perhaps Ruby's unborn child augurs the same brightness and cheer. When it's born, Hedley will be too euphoric to count the months since he first lay with her. But the future holds dangers, too. How will Hedley react if she has a girl? And even if a boy is born to her, the ordeal he faces as Hedley's son could thwart his healthy growth. Violent fathers inscribe violence into their sons. Also, as Hedley's burdensome first name shows, his father had the same wild hopes for him that he has for *his* unborn son. And Hedley became a murderer.

His murdering days may not be over. He and Floyd have the following exchange in act 1, scene 3:

> FLOYD: "I thought I heard Buddy Bolden say . . ."
> HEDLEY: What he say?
> FLOYD: He said, "Wake up and give me the money."
> HEDLEY: Naw. Naw. He say, "Come here. Here go the money."
> FLOYD: Well . . . what he give you?
> HEDLEY: He give me ashes.
> FLOYD: Tell him to give you the money. (7G, 23–24)

Their exchange recurs with variations three more times (7G, 39, 70, 103–104). The last of them begins with Wilson saying of a drunken Hedley, "*He has waited many years for this moment*" (103). Hedley has stumbled into the yard at the very moment when Floyd is burying the remainder of his stolen cash. In his stupor Hedley mistakes Floyd for Buddy Bolden (Lahr, 101). Hedley's father had told him years before that one day Buddy would bring him the money

to buy his plantation. When Floyd refuses to give Hedley the loot, he's killed. Hedley still has it in his pocket the day after Floyd's funeral. In the play's dying moments, he and Canewell do their own version of the litany Hedley had performed four times with Floyd. Canewell's taking Floyd's part in the litany implies that he'll become Hedley's next victim, an outcome darker and more wrenching than that of the last scene of *Ma Rainey*, which depicted the slaughter of one musician by another. The final exchange between Canewell and Hedley and the latter's response to it reveal that Canewell's life may be hanging by a thread:

> CANEWELL (singing): "I thought I heard Buddy Bolden say . . ."
> HEDLEY: What he say?
> CANEWELL: He say, "Wake up and give me the money."
> HEDLEY: Naw. Naw. He say, "Come here, here go the money."
> CANEWELL: What he give you?
> HEDLEY: He give me this.
> (HEDLEY *holds a hand handful of crumpled bills. They slip from his fingers and fall to the ground like ashes.*) (7G, 106–107)

Hedley won't profit materially from his murder of Floyd because he knows that money won't buy what he needs. He craves power. If he had the chance, he'd kill the great black heroes of the past because he wants to take their place. He even says of the just-slain rooster to the six characters assembled in the yard at the end of act 1, scene 5 (the only time in the play that the whole cast appears on stage together), "This rooster too good for your black asses" (7G, 64). The mythical grandeur building from the sexual symbolism of the rooster has dwarfed him. Hedley has always hated the masculine power he pretends to admire because it reminds him of his puniness. This childless man resents the rooster for the same reason. His stand in both cases is that of the loser. Knowing he can never attain the eminence of paragons like Joe Louis or Marcus Garvey, Hedley would kill them if he could. Only by destroying them can he wipe out the reproach they threaten him with.

One of these paragons is Canewell, Floyd's harmonica player and the script's griot, or raisonneur. Canewell's name suggests his and the other characters' rural southern origins, and it's Canewell who brings Vera the medicinal goldenseal plant Floyd will later uproot while hiding the money he stole. It's through Canewell, too, that Wilson rehearses some of the play's most disturbing ideas. For instance, Canewell faults Jesus for raising Lazarus from the dead. Life's laws, Canewell believes, are intrinsic. Besides violating this self-sustaining order, Jesus exposed the resurrected Lazarus to more of the pain he had put behind him by dying (7G, 25–26). Voicing an attitude conveyed by Floyd's hit song, Canewell will also claim that love that's not appreciated or returned still has value. Sufficient unto itself love need pay no dividends. Perhaps he means that life is so bitter that any outgoing of the heart will redeem it. It's difficult to say because his role is much more rhetorical than it is dramatic. Wilson put him in the play to talk. Perhaps talk is all he's good for besides playing the harmonica. At the play's outset, a more opportunistic, alert character grabs a piece of pie Canewell had singled out for himself....

**Source:** Peter Wolfe, "All Right with Whom?," in *August Wilson*, Twayne Publishers, 1999, pp. 139–43.

## SOURCES

Brantley, Ben, "Weaving Blues of Trying Times and Lost Dreams," in *New York Times*, August 25, 2006, http://www.nytimes.com/2006/08/25/theater/reviews/25guit.html (accessed June 16, 2017).

———, "The World That Created August Wilson," in *New York Times*, February 5, 1995, http://www.nytimes.com/1995/02/05/theater/theater-the-world-that-created-august-wilson.html?pagewanted=all (accessed June 10, 2017).

Canby, Vincent, "Unrepentant, Defiant Blues for 7 Voices," in *New York Times*, March 29 1996, http://www.nytimes.com/1996/03/29/theater/theater-review-unrepentant-defiant-blues-for-7-voices.html (accessed June 16, 2017).

Cobb, Clifford, Ted Halstead, and Jonathan Rowe, "If the GDP Is Up, Why Is America Down?," in *Atlantic*, October 1995, https://www.theatlantic.com/past/docs/politics/ecbig/gdp.htm (accessed June 16, 2017).

Du Bois, W. E. B., "Of Our Spiritual Strivings," in *The Souls of Black Folk*, Penguin, 1996, p. 5.

Fanon, Franz, "The Fact of Blackness," in *Black Skin, White Masks*, Grove Press, 1967, pp. 116, 140.

Gerard, Jeremy, Review of *Seven Guitars*, in *Variety*, March 28, 1996, http://variety.com/1996/legit/reviews/seven-guitars-3-1200445186/ (accessed June 10, 2017).

Hay, Samuel A., *African American Theatre: An Historical and Critical Analysis*, Cambridge University Press, 1994, pp. 2–5, 71–72.

Hughes, Langston, "The Negro Artist and the Racial Mountain," in *Modern American Poetry*, University of Illinois website, http://www.english.illinois.edu/Maps/poets/g_l/hughes/mountain.htm (accessed June 10, 2017); originally published in *Nation*, 1926.

Isherwood, Christopher, "August Wilson, Theater's Poet of Black America, Is Dead at 60," in *New York Times*, October 3, 2005, http://www.nytimes.com/2005/10/03/theater/newsandfeatures/august-wilson-theaters-poet-of-black-america-is-dead-at-60.html (accessed June 16, 2017).

Krasner, David, *Resistance, Parody and Double Consciousness in African American Theatre, 1895–1910*, St. Martin's Press, 1997, p. 10.

Lahr, John, "Been Here and Gone: How August Wilson Brought a Century of Black American Culture to the Stage," in *New Yorker*, April 16, 2001, http://www.newyorker.com/magazine/2001/04/16/been-here-and-gone (accessed June 10, 2017).

Moore, Opal, "Learning to Live: When the Bird Breaks Free from the Cage," in *Maya Angelou's "I Know Why the Caged Bird Sings,"* edited by Harold Bloom, Chelsea House Publishers, 1998, p. 180.

Morales, Michael, "Ghosts on the Piano: August Wilson and the Representation of Black History," in *May All Your Fences Have Gates: Essays on the Drama of August Wilson*, edited by Alan Nadel, University of Iowa Press, 1994, pp. 105–15.

Rawson, Christopher, "The Next Page: An Ambitious Renovation of August Wilson's Boyhood Home Will Be Good for Pittsburgh and the Arts," in *Pittsburgh Post-Gazette*, April 24, 2016, http://www.post-gazette.com/opinion/Op-Ed/2016/04/24/The-Next-Page-An-ambitious-renovation-of-August-Wilson-s-boyhood-home-will-be-good-for-Pittsburgh-and-the-arts-writes-Christopher-Rawson/stories/201604240020 (accessed June 16, 2017).

Savran, David, *In Their Own Words: Contemporary American Playwrights*, Theatre Communications Group, 1988, p. 304.

Shafer, Yvonne, *August Wilson: A Research and Production Sourcebook*, Greenwood Press, 1998, pp. 42–43, 103–108.

Shannon, Sandra G., and Dana A. Williams, "A Conversation with August Wilson," in *Conversations with August Wilson*, edited by Jackson R. Bryer and Mary C. Hartig, University Press of Mississippi, 2006, pp. 247, 249; originally published in *August Wilson and Black Aesthetics*, edited by Dana A. Williams and Sandra G. Shannon, Palgrave Macmillan, 2004, pp. 187–95.

Sinclair, Abiola, "Black Aesthetic: A Conversation with Playwright August Wilson," in *Conversations with August Wilson*, edited by Jackson R. Bryer and Mary C. Hartig, University Press of Mississippi, 2006, pp. 94, 97–98; originally published in *New York Amsterdam News*, May 19, 1990.

Wilkerson, Margaret B., "Critics, Standards and Black Theatre," in *The Theatre of Black Americans: A Collection of Critical Essays*, edited by Errol Hill, Applause Theatre Book Publishers, 1987, pp. 319–26.

Wilson, August, "August Wilson's 1990 *Spin* Essay on *Fences*: 'I Don't Want to Hire Nobody Just 'Cause They're Black,'" in *Spin*, February 22, 2017, http://www.spin.com/featured/august-wilson-fences-paramount-pictures-race-essay-october-1990/ (accessed June 10, 2017).

————, "Feed Your Mind, the Rest Will Follow," in *Pittsburgh Post-Gazette*, March 28, 1999, http://old .post-gazette.com/magazine/feedmind.asp (accessed June 10, 2017).

————, *The Ground on Which I Stand*, Theater Communications Group, 2000, p. 41.

————, *Seven Guitars*, Plume, 1997.

## FURTHER READING

Dicker/sun, Glenda, *African American Theater: A Cultural Companion*, Polity Press, 2008.

This study of the history of African American drama and the ways it has been affected by social realities brings together the personal and the scholarly. It includes creative exercises to help illustrate the social and artistic trends it explores.

Elkins, Marilyn, ed., *August Wilson: A Casebook*, Garland, 2000.

This introduction to Wilson's work consists of twelve essays, especially exploring his metaphorical use of the black body; his collaboration with Lloyd Richards, notable African Canadian scholar and director of Yale's theater school; and influences on his work. The book includes an interview with Wilson.

Hays, Samuel P., ed., *City at the Point: Essays on the Social History of Pittsburgh*, University of Pittsburgh Press, 1991.

Essays by thirteen historians illuminate a variety of areas of Pittsburgh history, providing perspective on the city itself and on the general process of urbanization. The book will be of interest to social historians and curious lay readers alike.

Nadel, Alan, ed., *May All Your Fences Have Gates: Essays on the Drama of August Wilson*, University of Iowa Press, 1994.

This collection of essays is a critical examination of Wilson's work, delving into five plays and in the process exploring gender relations, music and cultural identity, the relationship of African ritual to African American drama, and other topics by a number of scholars.

Wilkerson, Isabel, *The Warmth of Other Suns: The Epic Story of America's Great Migration*, Random House, 2010.

Wilkerson offers six hundred pages of information and anecdote in this thorough account of the Great Migration of American blacks from the South to the North in the twentieth century. She creates a nuanced chronicle of the migration's benefits and disadvantages and describes a wide variety of individual experiences.

## SUGGESTED SEARCH TERMS

August Wilson

August Wilson AND Seven Guitars

Pittsburgh Cycle

Pittsburgh AND Hill District

African American theater

African American theater AND social critique

critical racial theory

white gaze

# *Tribes*

**NINA RAINE**

**2010**

*Tribes* is an award-winning play composed by noted British playwright Nina Raine for the English Stage Company. It was first performed in October 2010 at London's Royal Court Theatre and has since become a stage favorite across the English-speaking world. An intimate, emotionally nuanced play, *Tribes* engages with the dynamics of the modern family and the profound social alienation experienced by the deaf. It is at once a compelling drama and a romance, examining a wide array of mental, emotional, and physical handicaps through the lens of a loving, albeit discordant, family. The play poses essential questions about the impact of communication upon character and about the value of expression, in all its myriad forms, in healing estrangement and nurturing human connection. *Tribes* offers an unflinching, ultimately optimistic commentary on the social stigmas that divide people, and on the common humanity, too often overlooked, that brings people together.

## AUTHOR BIOGRAPHY

The daughter of celebrated poet and Oxford University don Craig Raine and noted Oxford lecturer Ann Pasternak Slater, grandniece to novelist Boris Pasternak, Raine was born in Oxford, England, in 1975. She grew to adulthood in the company of three brothers, one of

*Nina Raine* *(© Ferdaus Shamim / Getty Images)*

them also a budding playwright, and early on demonstrated the creative talents and inclinations that would later propel her to theatrical fame. In 1998, Raine graduated with top marks from Christ Church College of Oxford University with a degree in literature. Almost immediately, the young graduate began to pursue her growing passion for theater and the dramatic arts, lending her creativity to a wealth of directors and playwrights in their own creative endeavors. Even in secondary roles as assisting writer or producer, Raine was recognized for her creative talents and sensitivity to human rights issues.

The playwright's first independent success, her performance *Rabbit*, premiered to positive reviews in Britain's Red Lion Theatre in 2006 and soon made the jump across the Atlantic to be performed in New York and on other American stages. This achievement was followed by a second play, *Tiger Country*, and shortly thereafter, in 2010, by her biggest critical success to date, *Tribes*, which won the Drama Desk Award for Outstanding Play, the Offie Award for Best Play, and the New York Drama Critics' Circle

Award for Best Foreign Play. It has since become an international phenomenon.

Despite her growing recognition in dramatic circles, Raine remains steadfastly private in aspects of her personal life and divulges details sparingly, largely through the context of intimate interviews. She continues to create and direct plays that, while rich in the poignancy and complexity of everyday life, leave her own largely to the imagination.

## PLOT SUMMARY

### Act One

#### SCENE ONE

The curtain for *Tribes* opens on an erudite, middle-class family preparing to sit down to a carefully prepared dinner. Present are middle-aged Christopher and Beth and their three children, all in their twenties, Daniel, Ruth, and Billy. The conversation is intelligent but abrasive, much of it lost to the household's youngest son, Billy, who is deaf and picks up only intermittent snatches of conversation through the use of hearing aids. The father of the household, spurred on by clever commentary provided by his eldest, Daniel, is deriding his wife for the inadequacy of the food at the table and his daughter for her infatuation with a considerably older suitor. Through conversation, it is revealed that Billy is a recent graduate of university and has returned home for temporary lodging while he pursues the next step in his life. Daniel interrupts the dinner by answering a phone call that leaves him visibly shaken and leads Billy to fear for the happiness of his brother.

#### SCENE TWO

Billy is in attendance at a party, waiting outside the door of the bathroom for the present occupant to emerge. A young woman named Sylvia exits the bathroom and apologizes to Billy, through the use of sign, for having kept him waiting while she made a private call to her boyfriend. Billy tells Sylvia that although he is deaf he relies solely upon lip-reading and the assistance of his hearing aids to engage in conversations. The two new acquaintances fall to talking, and the conversation reveals that Sylvia is the daughter of two deaf parents and that her own hearing is beginning to fail. Somewhat

# MEDIA ADAPTATIONS

- A promotional video from opening night of the Barrow Street Theatre production, Off-Broadway in New York City, was made available online by the play's creative team, at https://www.youtube.com/watch?v=hpo Lgc98haQ. Other videos concerning or sampling scenes from *Tribes* can also be found on YouTube.

unexpectedly Billy kisses Sylvia, and the two part in sweet anticipation of future meetings.

### SCENE THREE

Daniel is in the kitchen, complaining in his usual comical manner while his mother tends to his wounded foot. After it is dressed, Daniel turns his attentions to Ruth, and the two begin a vicious argument over their stymied aspirations, both having returned to live at home for wont of opportunity after pursuing higher education. Billy, up to this point distant and aloof, attempts to play peacemaker between his two squabbling siblings. Despite Billy's best efforts at healing the household, Christopher makes matters worse by intruding and verbally belittling the entire family. To change the tide of conversation, Billy begins to tell those assembled about his growing relationship with Sylvia. His speech is cut short by the failing batteries of his hearing aid.

### SCENE FOUR

Billy returns home late after a planned meeting with Sylvia to find a sleepless Daniel smoking a cigarette at the kitchen table. Daniel confesses that auditory hallucinations are preventing him from rest but remains tight-lipped about the finer details of his experiences. Perhaps to redirect attention from himself, Daniel inquires after Sylvia and attempts to furnish his younger brother with unasked-for romantic advice.

### SCENE FIVE

Ruth and Daniel are engaging in their characteristic abusive banter in the kitchen while

assisting with dinner preparation. They express mutual dread over the visit of Billy and Sylvia to the household. Upstairs, the siblings can hear the noise of their father berating their mother for the use of clichés in her writing and the growing distress of Beth as her novelistic ambitions are belittled. Ruth reveals to Daniel that Billy is learning sign language under the mentorship of his girlfriend, a revelation that upsets him greatly. He expresses his fear that Billy will become stigmatized through closer association with the established deaf community and will be cut off from his rightful opportunities in life. Ruth suggests that Daniel's motives underlying his views are selfish and possessive.

Billy and Sylvia arrive in the midst of this general tumult and are initially greeted with a tense, awkward silence. After somewhat stilted introductions, the assembled party sit down to their first joint meal. Almost immediately, the conversation turns to the deaf community, which Sylvia openly admits is hierarchical and incestuous. Somewhat rudely, Beth disrupts the growing rapport and openness at the table to answer a call from a religiously observant relative, Zach, which excites the unseemly derision of Christopher and Daniel. This signals an unpleasant turn in the tone of the scene, and the family openly questions Sylvia's teaching of sign language to Billy. Christopher makes the argument that sign is restrictive in its eloquence and expressiveness, further implying that the deaf are consequently limited in their moral character and understanding of empathy. Sylvia becomes tearful and explains her hurt in terms of her own loving, deaf family. Uncharacteristically, Christopher apologizes to the girlfriend of his youngest son. Sylvia sits down at the family piano and plays classical music from memory, a symbolic act that stuns even the most vicious of tongues into temporary silence.

## Act Two

### SCENE SIX

Sylvia spends the night with Billy at his family's house. While she is upstairs preparing for bed, Billy and Daniel engage in a cold, clipped conversation regarding the future of his budding relationship. Billy reveals to his older brother that Sylvia makes him feel complete, heard, and understood in a way that he has been denied for many years. He accuses Daniel, somewhat justly, of speaking from a place of jealousy caused by the shift in Billy's affections.

Sylvia enters, and Billy excuses himself, claiming the need for sleep and relief from the abusive banter of the family. Sylvia sits down and joins Daniel in a late-night cigarette, charming him with her candid and clever gift for conversation. Daniel breaks away from the dialogue and listens intently to something Sylvia cannot hear. Daniel then takes Sylvia in his arms and kisses her, an affront neither rebuffed nor embraced, and begs her not to take his younger brother away from the house.

**SCENE SEVEN**

Ruth and her mother speak to each other in hushed tones while Christopher is listening to his language-learning tapes through a soundproof headset. They talk of the worsening of Daniel's imagined voices and the recurrence of his crippling stutter, a tendency he has not manifested since early childhood. The topic of Billy's new job, lip-reading security tapes for police investigations, and the recognition of his talents by a local newspaper arise. Ruth expresses jealousy of her younger brother's success and begins to cry over her own lack of fulfillment and deep-seated loneliness. Beth attempts to comfort her daughter as best she is able.

Christopher breaks from his auditory lesson and calls repeatedly to Daniel to come downstairs. Daniel finally emerges, looking somewhat dazed, and claims he can no longer distinguish the voices within from the voices without. His father scoffs at this confession and cites his son's growing reliance upon marijuana as the source of his hallucinations.

Billy and Sylvia enter the scene in grave, ominous silence. Sensing the emergence of a confrontation, the family inquires about the reason for their visit to the house and for their uncharacteristic silence. Billy remains mute except to sign to Sylvia, who, with some reluctance, translates his meaning into words. Through the medium of his girlfriend, the youngest son of the household informs his family that he will no longer converse with them unless they undertake a study of sign. He expresses his resentment at being molded to their expectations for so long and his newfound resolve to cut off all contact unless his demands are met. He makes known that he feels no love for the oppressive insanity of the household and feels closer kinship with Sylvia's family. Ruth and Beth react with immediate apology for their treatment of Billy, while the father of the household, in keeping with his character, becomes enraged and washes his hands of the situation in self-righteous indignation. Daniel's veneer of anger quickly turns to pleading as he entreats Billy, through a pitiable and crippling stutter, to reconsider his ultimatum and remain in the family fold. Unmoved, Billy forcefully removes his hearing aids and leaves with Sylvia.

**SCENE EIGHT**

Sylvia approaches Billy in their common living room while he is hard at work reviewing security tapes. After some prompting, she declares that she will no longer be attending meetings for the deaf, which she finds increasingly hierarchical, alienating, and even emotionally confining. Billy is surprised and dismayed by this admission on the part of his girlfriend and attempts, to no avail, to dissuade her from the resolution. Sylvia concedes that her decision stems partially from panic, as her condition progresses and she loses her perception of tone, but holds firm to her belief that she must preserve the nuance and expression afforded her by language through other means than sign language.

When Sylvia urges her boyfriend to return and make peace with his family, Billy becomes irate and confesses that he has been guessing at lip-reading, and in some cases fabricating dialogue, in his work in order to fund a life for the two of them. He also admits that he enjoys the ambiguity of his work, even when it carries dire, perhaps unjust consequences for those who incur blame, and that it allows him to feel powerful despite his disability. Sylvia is horrified by this confession and parts ways with Billy.

**SCENE NINE**

After a long separation from the household, Sylvia approaches a resentful Daniel and Ruth to discuss Billy, who is currently under investigation for manipulation of evidence. She demands of Daniel the reason for his unwanted advances, which he explains as a desperate, ill-advised ploy to keep his brother under the same roof. Daniel's condition is greatly worsened, and between his stutter and the imaginary voices intruding on the conversation, he is nearly unable to communicate. In an act of empathy, Sylvia offers to try to help ease the auditory hallucinations, but Daniel, ashamed and despairing, refuses all assistance.

## SCENE TEN

Billy approaches Daniel in reconciliation as a condition imposed by Sylvia for their renewed relationship as boyfriend and girlfriend. He is hesitant but sincere in his actions and weathers the broken barrage of Daniel's anger with grace. Both brothers exchange secrets of their private lives and transgressions and mutually forgive one another. Other members of the family join the reunion. In a failed attempt to express his emotions through language, Daniel instead forms the sign for "love" and is mirrored by Billy. The two young men embrace, and the play concludes.

## CHARACTERS

### Beth

The most marginalized character in the play, Beth struggles under the burden of her husband's verbal abuse and feels powerless to ease the suffering of her children. Beth harbors the dream of achieving recognition as a novelist, an endeavor scorned by those closest to her, and seeks to express herself on paper in a way denied her in her own life. She performs all the daily duties of the household without the reward of recognition or support.

### Billy

The youngest child of the household and the central character of the play, Billy emerges as enigmatic and self-assured despite his lifelong handicap of deafness. In contrast to the other members of his family, the young man remains largely aloof to the cruel and belittling gossip that dominates the household and pursues his own goals. Under the tutelage of his newfound love, Sylvia, Billy takes up the study of sign language in preference to his hearing aids, a practice resented by those closest to him for its imagined stigma and snobbery.

### Christopher

Christopher is a brash, vain man of advancing years and the head of the household around which the play revolves. An academic turned writer, Christopher uses his erudition and imagined authority to wound and belittle the other members of his family. He is largely unsympathetic to the physical and emotional ailments of his children and mocks his wife's creative ambitions. Shielded by his tremendous ego, Christopher is not a man to compromise or adjust to the viewpoints of others. When not deriding them, Christopher isolates himself from his family and their most intimate concerns by practicing foreign languages through the use of a soundproof headset.

### Daniel

The oldest child of the household, mired in a perpetual crisis of identity, Daniel is the most erratic and emotionally unstable of his siblings. He has recently returned from his higher studies and resents once again living at home under the auspices of his abusive father and doting but ineffectual mother. Daniel's brilliant wit and gift for imitation disguise his deep depression and his torment by auditory hallucinations, which afflict him with growing frequency and prevent him from sleeping. To cope with his demons, Daniel turns to periodic drug use and the attention afforded him by one-sided, unhealthy relationships. He is the most affected by his younger brother's departure from the household, a separation that greatly worsens his underlying conditions.

### Hayley

Finding representation only through her implied presence on the other end of telephone conversations, Hayley is the unhealthy fixation of Daniel's love life.

### Rebecca

The faceless wife of Zach, Rebecca is cruelly mocked by Christopher and Daniel solely on the basis of her appearance.

### Ruth

Ruth is the middle child of the family and the close, if occasionally contentious, confidant of Daniel. An aspiring opera singer, Ruth struggles not so much with her abrasive home life as with her deep-seated loneliness and feelings of inferiority in relation to her more successful peers. Her personal romantic choices, in particular her penchant for older suitors, is a source of constant derision from her father. She is a firm, if generally unheard, advocate for Billy's happiness.

### Sylvia

A young woman raised by two deaf parents and a deaf sibling, Sylvia is becoming newly reconciled to her genetic predisposition and the gradual loss of her own hearing. Although she weathers this difficult transition with grace and humor, Sylvia is secretly paralyzed by the implications of the loss of verbal communication on her engagement with the world around her. Although she begins the play with an implied boyfriend, Sylvia becomes deeply romantically involved with Billy and eventually joins her life with his. Despite her affection, Sylvia remains her own woman throughout the play and refuses to be discouraged or corrupted by the abuses of either Billy or his family.

## Zach

A distant family member on Beth's side, Zach is a source of disdain and amusement for Christopher and his eldest son on the basis of his religious scruples and adherence to a brand of Orthodox Judaism long since abandoned by Beth and Christopher's more secular household.

## THEMES

### Communication

*Tribes* explores the theme of communication in a stunning diversity of forms and emotional nuances. Raine juxtaposes the literal deafness of Billy with the more abstract, but no less profound, failure of the household to listen to or properly communicate with one another. While the play affirms the incredible wealth of expression afforded by spoken language, it questions the extent to which verbal communication is taken for granted and even abused by its practitioners. Through the interactions of her unique characters, Raine demonstrates the interconnectivity of verbal expression with the equally visceral language of sign, posing a possible solution to limitation to any one single form of communication.

Through her dissection of the myth of simple communication, the playwright questions the ability of mere artistry of language to represent truth and relay empathy. The flood of erudite, witty, and often cutting conversation that dominates the better part of the performance proves itself to be largely empty of import compared to wordless expressions of love, physical embraces, and the deeply felt passion of piano music. Because they are comparatively infrequent and often obscured by the relentless banter of Billy's household, concrete actions, as opposed to words, frequently emerge in Raine's play as the most effective vehicle for communication and expression. *Tribes* concludes with this understanding when Daniel, struck dumb by a crippling

speech impediment and the imagined voices in his head, resorts to the unaffected, silent language of the heart to welcome his younger brother home. Despite the absence of words, his message is understood clearly by all.

### Family

The small cast of characters in *Tribes*, coupled with the domestic settings, marks the play as an intimate family drama. The majority of its dialogue takes place at the dinner table, a hallowed meeting place of households across the world. In keeping with her dramatic complexity and insight, Raine balances the value associated with family and other modes of human connection with its inevitable, and sometimes substantial, complications. Christopher and Beth endure an openly abusive marriage, while Daniel and Ruth resent the stifling environment of the household and the discouraging influence of their parents on their dearly held dreams. The faceless Zach and his wife, Rebecca, are subject to cruel ridicule by members of their family, and every outsider to the household is subjected to intense and abusive scrutiny. Billy, his individuality crushed under a childhood of impossible expectations, openly rebels against what he views as the madness of his own home and forsakes his own family for Sylvia's. Nor are the romantic pairings in the play represented as idyllic or free from strife. Daniel is tortured by his one-sided adoration of Hayley, Ruth struggles in her relationship with an older, attached man, and Billy, through his misplaced anger towards those closest to him, allows the woman he most loves to grow distant.

Yet, despite Raine's raw representation of the confinement and trauma too often associated with family, each of her characters yearns for a loving community, a tribe, to call one's own. For each character, this is a struggle marked by intense introspection and painful bouts of rejection. The established deaf community to which Billy feels such a strong connection excludes Sylvia on the basis of her partial hearing loss. Meanwhile, Billy and his siblings experience alienation from their own family and seek in vain to form meaningful romantic attachments. Ultimately, however, the otherwise disparate and deeply flawed personalities that compose Raine's cast of characters are forced to examine their own egos and discriminatory tendencies and find fulfillment in one another. Family, Raine suggests at the closing of the play,

# TOPICS FOR FURTHER STUDY

- In keeping with the play's exploration of alternate forms of communication and the inadequacy of verbal speech to convey all emotions with appropriate depth, use print or online library resources to translate an uplifting compliment for one of your classmates into sign language. Perform your message to its intended party in front of your class and draft a short written reflection detailing the difficulties and triumphs involved in your translation.

- As the title of Raine's play suggests, individuals instinctively associate and align themselves with others as a basis for community. Using poster board, create a family/community tree of those you feel the closest kinship to, including a brief explanatory description next to each entry. If you feel comfortable, present your creation to the class.

- Contrary to their expectations, the members of Billy's family are awed by the expressive beauty of the sign language Sylvia performs at their dinner table. Using online resources, research the available wealth of sign-language poetry, and select a presentation that has special resonance with aspects of your own experience. In your notebook, create a bullet-point list of adjectives you associate with the performance and craft these adjectives into a description of what separates, or elevates, your chosen enactment from a mere verbal recitation.

- Much of *Tribes* revolves around the family dinner table, a meeting place that provides no end of entertaining banter, cutting criticism, and poignant insight. Organize yourselves into groups and, utilizing your joint creativity, draft a single scene of your own play revolving around a cast of imaginary characters assembled for their nightly meal. Assign roles among your group members, and act out the scene in front of the audience of the larger classroom.

- Watch Rachel Kolb's insightful and haunting video on the imperfect art of lip-reading and its expressive counterpart, sign language, found on Vimeo at https://vimeo.com/148127830. Armed with this new perspective, compose a dramatic monologue for Raine's character Billy, articulating his complex feelings regarding the world of sound in which he is immersed and his perceived place within it as a member of the deaf community. Attempt, to the best of your ability, to craft your piece in harmony with what you know to be Billy's own perspective and temperament from reading the play.

- Many of the characters in *Tribes*, in particular Sylvia and Beth, attempt to cultivate their powers of empathy through various means related to language and intimate human interaction. This emphasis on perspective and relation to other experiences is pivotal not only for this particular performance but also in Raine's famously immersive approach to writing all of her plays. In conscious imitation of Raine's creative methods, spend a few hours engaged in an activity foreign to your usual lifestyle. Afterward, compose a representative scrapbook of your experience to be shared with your classmates, broadening their perspective and exposure to the world around them.

- Alienation and the difficulty of maintaining human connection in the face of differences, real and perceived, figure largely in *Tribes*. To further explore this theme across literature, undertake a reading of the classic young-adult novel *Cheshire Moon* (1996), by Nancy Butts. Take notes on the obstacles faced by its main character, Miranda, as she struggles to forge new and meaningful relationships in her own life and understand the import of her recurring dream. Translate your notes into a wordless, visual representation of Miranda's dream isle through an artistic medium of your choice to share with and explain to your classmates.

*Much of the play's action takes place around the family dining table* (© *Pandora Studio | Shutterstock.com*)

is less a ready-made social construct than a personal and evolving commitment.

### Stigma

The intensely self-conscious family at the heart of Raine's play underscores the societal tendency to favor trappings of hierarchy, value, and perceived status over emotional integrity. As such, her eclectic cast of characters variously struggle under the burden of stigma and traumatizing, often-forced adaptation to unrealistic social expectations. Billy is instructed from birth to eschew all the connotations of his disability, while his two siblings, Daniel and Ruth, are afforded the best education and training available, only to be criticized for their perceived shortcomings and inadequacy. All the children of the household, along with their mother, feel overshadowed by the self-styled success and erudition of Christopher. Likewise, Sylvia is diminished by what she views as the strict hierarchy of the established deaf community and goes to great lengths to prove herself in their eyes.

The characters in *Tribes* value empty distinctions of status above all other considerations, a weakness that contributes to their ongoing misery and the gradual dissolution of their personal lives. By taking a stand against the tyranny of his own household toward the end of the play, Billy is rejecting not only the expectations of individual family members but also the larger societal standards that govern almost every aspect of their lives. This singular act of courage forces the other characters of the drama, most especially Daniel, to prioritize concrete emotional needs over the facade of carefully guarded appearances. Implicit to the youngest son's rejection of stigma, however, is also a consuming anger that works for, rather than against, the pride and overdeveloped egotism that accentuate the household divisions. Sylvia's moderating effect upon her boyfriend's understandable but misplaced anger, alongside the humbling of characters like Daniel through emotional honesty, ultimately wins the day to elevate considerations of love over the trappings of societal acceptability. Each character is forced to acknowledge one's own true motivations and character flaws before extending that same acceptance to each other.

# STYLE

## Conflict

The drama of Raine's play is held in tension almost entirely by conflict and the friction of distinct, combative personalities. The playwright utilizes conflict to great effect to expose the inherent weaknesses of the family unit and to suggest the dire consequences of their continued lack of communication. The overarching conflict of *Tribes*, namely, the inability of Billy's family to acknowledge the nature of his disability and dislodge their preconceived notions of social stigma, is augmented by smaller but no less compelling dramas throughout the play. Even characters afforded no actual stage appearances, like Daniel's girlfriend Hayley and the much-derided Zach and Rebecca, serve to accentuate the poisoned environment that characterizes the household and restrains the people therein from realization of deeper emotional truths.

## Drama

As opposed to the ancient connotations of tragedy, with sweeping epics inciting fear and pity in the audience, modern drama typically constitutes a more intimate and subtle expression of infinitely complex human interactions. The relative dearth of characters, the events of great magnitude, and even the confinement of the setting to mundane home environments all mark *Tribes* as a deeply social and psychological drama that elevates the experience of the individual over that of the larger tide of humanity. The intimacy of the play, however, does not diminish the tremendous implications of its drama. Rather, Raine examines essential human truths and damaging social compulsions through the far more manageable and widely relatable lens of family and the love that binds, and sometimes suffocates, its individual members.

## Foil

Particularly in its dramatic foundation of biological family and connections formed through intense affection, the play relies upon the stylistic device of the foil, distinct characters evolved through comparison with one another, to highlight the many personalities and motivations populating the household. Most striking among these pairings is Billy and his older brother, Daniel. Both struggle, through markedly different methods, to find a measure of peace and fulfillment despite their difficulties of communication. Through this comparison, Billy emerges as courageous and self-assured, while Daniel reveals himself to be evasive, fragile, and weak-willed. Raine upends the purely oppositional dynamic of the literary device, however, when she brings the two brothers together at the end of the play. In the final scene, the differences between Billy and Daniel become the vehicle for reconciliation and newfound compassion and humility that strengthen the characters of both men and inspire their shared family.

## Motif

In a clever fusion of the literary device of the *motif*, a persistent theme or fixture marking a dramatic composition, and its musical counterpart establishing an aural impression, Raine punctuates her performance with iconic musical movements and onstage representations of the instruments that produce them. The family collection of heirloom instruments, most notably the piano Sylvia plays to stun the family into silence, are joined by Ruth's operatic outbursts and Daniel's persistent barrage of brilliant, if often offensive, vocal imitations. *Tribes* is a play awash in sound and its physical and aural representations, a motif made all the more evocative by the inability, and in some cases the unwillingness, of the characters to listen.

# HISTORICAL CONTEXT

## Deafness in European History

The history of societal treatment of deaf individuals and the gradual evolution of alternate forms of communication is an ancient and complex one. Its trajectory is most fully recorded through the context of European history, which informs the play's depiction of deafness in a modern British household. In the classical age of the Greeks and the Romans, scarce attempts were made to understand or embrace the disability, and it was largely dismissed as an overwhelming obstacle to higher education and full societal inclusion. The theological shapers of fledgling Christianity demonstrated an increased if conflicted interest in the deaf, simultaneously demonizing it in afflicted individuals and elevating silence as a sacred charge among many of the religion's most prominent orders.

Although there are records of communication by sign existing as early as the Dark Ages,

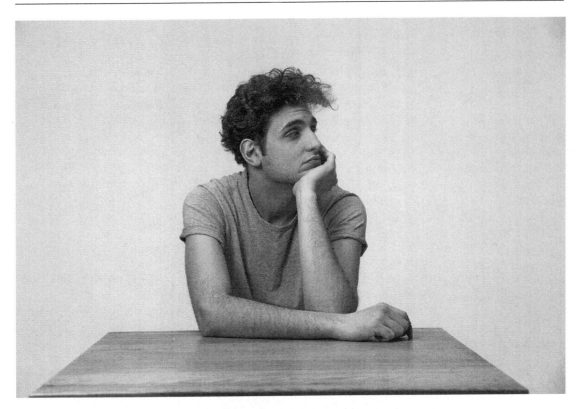

*Billy's deafness isolates him somewhat from the rest of the family* (© *Dean Drobot | Shutterstock.com*)

existing systems were isolated and not yet codified, and the first attempts at a system of standardization did not emerge until the 1500s in Italy. This singular project was taken up and expanded upon with increasing vigor for the following two centuries by the other countries of central and southern Europe, culminating in the first establishment of an official school for the deaf by an American pupil of continental sign language in 1817.

From that time until the present day, the advancement of education of the deaf and their intrinsic human rights have increased steadily and diversified into a complex and formidable field of study. Legislation regarding the deaf community and others with forms of sensory impairment continue to be a source of great deliberation in the present day. At the time of the writing of Raine's *Tribes*, British prime minister David Cameron was widely accused of betraying his own background, as both a son and a father to individuals afflicted with profound disability, and shifting legal and monetary priorities away from consideration for these valuable and most vulnerable members of society.

## CRITICAL OVERVIEW

Raine's intimate and moving stage drama is well regarded from myriad international and cultural perspectives. Despite its complex subject matter and setting within a hypercritical, disconnected, largely unsympathetic household, reviewers note the play's accessibility, and relevance, to a broad public audience. Of deep and lasting import, the play bears the trappings of erudition without distancing itself from the swell of everyday life. In her 2015 review of a performance for the *Denver Post*, Joanne Ostrow writes, "Raine's plot holds surprises on the way to a satisfying ending in a truly transporting play...that's psychologically minded but not overly intellectual."

Ostrow's *New York Times* counterpart Ben Brantley echoes this praise and also draws attention to the playwright's skill in balancing distinct and interrelated themes, with seeming ease, throughout an intimate drama with sweeping implications. Even more impressive, the reviewer asserts, is the play's masterful inclusion of pointed musical and auditory elements that, given the prevailing theme of deafness, allow the audience to feel personally immersed in its pathos and unique conditions of silence. In part because of the incredible strength of the first act, however, with the supersensitivity of a person who is hard of hearing instilled in the audience through the staging, Brantley takes issue with what he views as the diminished subtlety and overly explicit nature of the play's second half. The reviewer explains the source of this weakness by writing,

> Though this heightened sensibility is sustained throughout, the second act is a bit of a letdown. That's when the Plot, with a capital P, takes over, and self-conscious Important Moments occur. People start explaining, with labored specificity, aspects of themselves that we have already inferred. It's a bit as if Ms. Raine suddenly felt obliged to translate for the hard of understanding.

Maddy Costa, a reviewer for the London *Guardian*, is fascinated less by the stylistic aspects of the performance than by its inherent psychological weight and by the creative process and unique experience that went into its making. Costa intersperses her review with biographical segments and interviews taken from Raines and her colleagues and family to pose compelling questions regarding the play's inspiration. Above all, Costa praises what she views as Raine's greatest and most singular strength, her "great ear for anger." She further lauds the playwright for transmuting that most divisive of human tendencies, the drive toward strife, into a vehicle for more uplifting sentiments. She writes of *Tribes*, "As in *Rabbit*, the characters are scathing and antagonistic—although here, arguing is shown as proof of love."

Interestingly, subtle but poignant inclusions of cultural and religious significance are also noted by reviewers of the play, not least of all by critics within the Jewish community. In her article "Comedy-Drama 'Tribes' Communicates Dysfunction of British-Jewish Family," Naomi Pfefferman of the *Jewish Journal* notes the direct reference within the play to the family's more religiously observant cousins, Zach and Rebecca, and connects this suggested complexity to Raine's relationship with her own Jewish heritage. Through discussion with the playwright herself, Pfefferman roots the title of the play, and its obsessive occupation with inclusion and exclusion, in the cultural confusion inherent to growing up Jewish in a British household and to balancing a modern, secular lifestyle with ancient, deeply felt traditions.

> IRONICALLY, IT IS THIS VERY DIFFERENCE, A NEBULOUS CONCEPT AT THE HEART OF RAINE'S LATER PLAY, THAT WORKS AGAINST ITSELF TO CREATE AN IMPRESSION OF UNIVERSAL HUMANITY."

## CRITICISM

### Jeffrey Eugene Palmer

*Palmer is a scholar, freelance writer, and teacher of high-school English. In the following essay, he examines the hypocrisy of stereotypes in Raine's* Tribes *and in the works of her Victorian predecessors.*

While at first glance it may seem illogical to examine a modern British household through the lens of distant cultural predecessors, the unnamed family of Raine's *Tribes* demonstrates the same unyielding adherence to social hierarchy, refinement, and love of knowledge, balanced against inherent prejudice, which so characterized the Victorians of the late nineteenth century. The family's singular, arguably inconsiderate stance toward their youngest son, Billy, and his lifelong condition of deafness is a testament to this parallel and helps to underscore the inherent bias that increasingly defines the family over the course of the play. This bias shapes not only Billy's circumstances but also the lives of his two older siblings, Daniel and Ruth, and even the servile stance of their mother, Beth, within an outwardly erudite family mired in the restrictive prejudices of a bygone age.

In her scholarly article "'I Listened with My Eyes': Writing Speech and Reading Deafness in the Fiction of Charles Dickens and Wilkie Collins," Jennifer Esmail explores in great detail the early stigmatization of members of society afflicted with auditory impairment and the clear distinction Victorians drew between deaf individuals who either remained mute or attempted forms of verbal communication and those who resorted to methods of sign. In her description of so-called "Oralists" and disciples of theirs who advanced verbal forms of communication for the hearing impaired, Esmail quotes a two-hundred-year-old outlook on the

# WHAT DO I READ NEXT?

- A 2001 novel by young-adult writer Jean Ferris, *Of Sound Mind* masterfully explores the complex interrelationships between a primarily deaf household and its few hearing members.

- Rising British novelist Howard Jacobson wrote *The Finkler Question* in 2010, a well-crafted examination of friendship and enduring anti-Semitism in modern British society.

- Originally written for the stage in 1949, Arthur Miller's celebrated play *Death of a Salesman* is an archetypal family drama that suggests the empty, damaging nature of bluster and the ability of one man to poison an entire household.

- A 1957 novel in Russian by novelist Boris Pasternak, great-uncle to Raine, *Doctor Zhivago* is a sweeping epic of life and love during the traumatic Russian Revolution and remains a well-loved classic of literature to this day.

- Written for the stage by Raine's younger brother, Moses Raine, in 2014, *Donkey Heart* combines the familial fixation of *Tribes* with elements of the Russian heritage common to the sibling playwrights.

- A celebrated work of great pathos and complexity, Philip Roth's 1997 novel *American Pastoral* provides a riveting glimpse into the damaging influence of societal expectations on an otherwise idyllic family.

- Oliver Sacks released his intriguing work *Seeing Voices: A Journey into the World of the Deaf* in 1989 as a seminal study of the unique engagement of deaf individuals with spoken and perceived language.

- *Hearing Voices: A Common Human Experience* is a 1998 study by John Watkins that aims to elucidate the phenomenon of auditory hallucinations and dispel the most damaging stigmas surrounding it.

- Nina Raine's *Rabbit* (2006) propelled her to theatrical recognition and anticipated the success of her future productions. *Rabbit* explores the gritty reality of romantic relations, unrequited affections, and seething rivalries.

- *The Glass Menagerie*, the 1945 play that propelled playwright Tennessee Williams to fame, details a life of self-imposed isolation in a broken household.

---

limitations of sign language—from an 1827 Harriet Martineau novel—that bears striking resemblance to the outlook expressed by the highly educated father presiding over Raine's modern British household.

> Like the Oralists who disputed the linguistic sophistication of signed languages, Martineau mistakenly accused signers of being "incapable of any high degree of intellectual and moral cultivation, by being cut off from all adequate knowledge of the meaning of language, and from the full reception of most abstract ideas."

Not only are these accusations voiced as boldly, and with even less sensitivity, by the verbose and abusive Christopher, but moreover the anxieties they generate in other characters, like Sylvia, cannot be underestimated. In keeping with the claims of her accusers, both historical and contemporary, the young woman comes to perceive her plight of impending deafness as an attack on two sides of her character. She claims a growing alienation both from the signing deaf community she once so fully embraced, and by extension Billy, and from the members of her own hearing-impaired family on the basis of their inexplicable emotional differences. Sylvia expresses to her boyfriend that she dreads not only the growing flatness of her voice but also the perceived separation from conversational abstractions, in particular the irony upon which she had in the past so heavily relied. Thus she shifts from support of the beautiful sign language she so deftly practices to an aversion to that alternate form of language. Most of all, however, Sylvia fears that, in keeping with the views espoused by armchair critics like

Christopher and Victorian thinkers of an earlier age, if she transitions to signing, she will lose her emotional depth and the ability to fully empathize with others.

The roots of this modern-day tragedy of perception fueled by age-old prejudice are explored in great detail by Esmail through the writings of Charles Dickens and Wilkie Collins and their famously deaf heroines in "Doctor Marigold" and *Hide and Seek*, respectively. She undertakes the admirable project of highlighting the efforts of both authors to combat misconceptions regarding disability in their own age, but she also brings attention to the inadequacy, and even at times unintentional adherence to damaging implications, of their methods:

> While Collins and Dickens were sympathetic to deaf people's insistence on the sufficiency and suitability of signed languages despite Oralists' claims, both writers have difficulty overcoming the cultural prejudice that constructed signed languages as more embodied, and therefore more iconic, concrete, and primitive than spoken languages.

Inherent to this aforementioned difficulty, the scholar explains, is the reliance of both men on their characteristic blend of flippant social humor, idealization of perceived defect, and innocently intended, albeit ultimately damaging, conflation of hearing loss with physical degeneration through their profusion of comical, elderly characters. The shortcoming of this approach is twofold in nature. First, it reinforces the divide between those steeped in a world of sound and those deaf to it. Second, and perhaps more important, their writing combats sweeping social prejudice without managing to adequately explore or depict the underlying condition of deafness and its full impact upon distinct individuals.

This conflict between the bigger picture and its finer details exists to the same extent in Raine's play but with a fuller knowledge of the inadequacy of this tension to do justice to the full complexity of the human condition. A more thorough examination of this flawed dynamic in Victorian fiction, as well as its evolution through the medium of twenty-first-century theater, would serve to complement rather than detract from the fine scholarship of Esmail in dissolving damaging social constructs that persist in the modern day. Intrinsic to this project is an understanding of the continued fascination of both with elements of the grotesque, pointed distortions of human traits that underscore the inherent absurdity, ugliness, and multifaceted nature of the reality we too often take for granted. Esmail posits this fascination as one of the defining hallmarks of the nineteenth-century novel, describing it as "a genre that famously makes use of physical difference to develop narrative, affect, realism, or sensation." Ironically, it is this very difference, a nebulous concept at the heart of Raine's later play, that works against itself to create an impression of universal humanity.

In the case of *Tribes*, with the intimate cast of characters in sharp contrast to the deluge of protagonists, villains, and arbitrary caricatures that populate most Victorian novels, the family unit, literally and figuratively, takes center stage. Raine makes use of this far smaller, if no less exclusionary, community to represent a more manageable and viscerally piercing microcosm of societal hypocrisy. Christopher, the unsavory head of the household as an oppressive arbiter of acceptability who attempts to bully and demean his family into conforming to unrealistic expectations of normalcy, becomes himself an emblem of absurdity. Further, his stubborn, self-imposed blindness to reality and his excessive use of verbal bluster suggest a grotesque element to the empty rhetoric that so often underlies social conformity. This caricature of shallow, misappropriated verbosity finds its parallel in numerous Dickensian characters, not least of all in Mr. Turveydrop of the author's self-professed opus, *Bleak House*, who takes pride in patrician inactivity and relies upon his overtaxed children to tend to his every need. Turveydrop, like his modern counterpart Christopher, values appearances, what he terms "deportment," over all matters of substance or consideration for others. He addresses his son, Prince, in language simultaneously condescending, inflated, and ludicrous:

> "My son," said Mr. Turveydrop, "for those little points in which you are deficient—points of Deportment which are born with a man—which may be improved by cultivation, but can never be originated—you may still rely on me.... If you have ever contemplated your father's poor position with a feeling of pride, you may rest assured that he will do nothing to tarnish it. For yourself, Prince, whose character is different (we cannot be alike, nor is it advisable that we should), work, be industrious, earn money, and extend the connexion as much as possible."

What emerges in Victorian social critiques as a largely humorous and harmless trope, however, bears grotesque fruit in the context of Raine's modern depiction of the relationship between a father and his son. The lifelong verbal abuse inflicted by Christopher on Daniel emerges in the young man's auditory hallucinations—the psychological embodiment of empty language—which mock him to the point of physical exhaustion and despair and begin to obscure his powers of auditory comprehension. In a horrifying and gruesome inversion of Billy's own congenital condition, his older brother suffers not from the absence of words but rather from their profusion. He is figuratively deafened by them.

Flippantly, both in a characteristically Victorian context and with brutal realism in Raine's modern production, spoken language emerges as a vehicle for both personal stagnation and the abuse of others. By contrast, although tight-lipped characters of both genres are of variously good and evil dispositions, their common reliance upon concrete action over empty proclamations belies a graceful, competent nature. This trait of taciturn resolve is best embodied in *Tribes* by Billy, with his hard-won distinction of being the only member of his household to achieve a measure of independence, and Sylvia, with her determination to grapple with her demons in the realm of action and on her own terms. Both reject the dictates of society for their own, admittedly markedly different, brands of moral justification.

This striking inversion, in Raine's play, of tropes of normalcy and the linguistic burdens imposed by society contains revelations that can be neither silenced nor fully dismissed by the audience. Like her Victorian forerunners, the playwright acknowledges the innate hypocrisy of these expectations, but she takes greater care to emphasize the shortcomings of verbal expression through example and through contrast. She transmutes the ironclad distinction between characters of word and of action upheld by novelists like Dickens—which tends towards a heavy-handed didacticism, more pitying than enlightening—into more subtle, innate, and empathetic indicators of a universal human condition. *Tribes* confronts a truth that most examples of Victorian drama stopped short of addressing directly, namely, that there are many ways to be listened to, but only one to be heard. Without an understanding and acceptance of our differences, and a clear will to give meaning to careless and indefinite words, language in all its manifestations is as futile and as fleeting as wind.

*Sylvia's hearing loss does not prevent her from playing the piano* (© Netfalls Remy Musser / Shutterstock.com)

**Source:** Jeffrey Eugene Palmer, Critical Essay on *Tribes*, in *Drama for Students*, Gale, Cengage Learning, 2018.

### Charles McNulty

*In the following review, McNulty admits the play is "a tad overwritten" but still "emotionally stirring."*

In the intellectually raucous British household of Nina Raine's *Tribes* family members don't so much talk as assault each other with monologues.

The dinner table cacophony consists of scraps of debate, ironic jabs, aesthetic proclamations, academic gobbledygook, politically incorrect polemics and insults both sophisticated and juvenile.

With everyone boisterously holding forth as though the fate of the Western world rested upon their tongue, it's no surprise that listening is a negligible activity—an elective course no one has bothered to sign up for.

This smart and sensitive (if slightly over-padded) play, which centers on a young deaf man in the throes of love struggling to claim an independent identity within his quarreling clan, divides the world into two categories—those who cannot hear because of physical impairment and those who cannot hear because they can't shut up long enough to take in someone else's reality.

Critically esteemed off-Broadway, *Tribes* arrives at the Mark Taper Forum with its New York production, directed by David Cromer, largely intact. It takes a little time to adjust to the clamor, especially when Christopher (Jeff Still), the family patriarch and public intellectual who writes "argumentative" books, is haranguing his nearest and dearest at full blast.

The opening scene, in which dinner discussion proceeds like a contact sport, is the opposite of ingratiating. I found myself wincing at the hubbub, wishing there were a mute button I could press. The commotion may be unduly exaggerated by Cromer and his cast, but the point is as much thematic as theatrical in a play that is a study in contrasts of communication styles.

Raine ranges over a vast territory here. She's interested in deafness as both a disability and an alternative way of experiencing the world. But she's also preoccupied with the limitations of language, exposing the gaps in what even the most highly accomplished speakers are able to impart.

The play is focused more on the psychological than the philosophical aspect of this, but the linguistic line is pursued to its outer limits, where questions of truth and sanity are briefly engaged.

If *Tribes* seems a tad overwritten, it's no doubt because Raine has compiled a doctoral dissertation's worth of ideas on her subject. But at the center of the work is an emotionally stirring hush, an eloquent stillness that is an oasis from the punishing din.

This is the space occupied by Billy (Russell Harvard, in a wonderfully anchoring performance), the youngest of the siblings, who has been deaf since birth and who has long given up trying to keep pace with the bantering gymnastics.

A stranger to sign language when the play begins, Billy undergoes a change of consciousness after meeting Sylvia (a superb Susan Pourfar), who is losing her hearing because of an inherited condition.

Raised by deaf parents, Sylvia is in many ways more at home in the deaf community than Billy, though she's terrified of the silence that's rapidly engulfing her. Their quickly developing romance sets in motion changes that prompt Billy to challenge his family's status quo.

Although treated straightaway like a member of this confrontational family, Sylvia is perceived as a threat by Billy's father, who is proud that Billy has been raised almost exclusively within the hearing world, and Billy's brother, Daniel (Will Brill), whose psychiatric problems are ignited by his fear that Billy will abandon him.

Beth (Lee Roy Rogers), Billy's mother, a late-blooming writer with a bohemian flair, tries to defuse the tension of this overcrowded household, as does Ruth (Gayle Rankin), Billy's sister, a performer whose venture into opera provokes a tangential disquisition on the nonverbal possibilities of artistic expression

But the hostilities are brought to a head when Billy announces through Sylvia that he won't have anything more to do with his family until they can speak to him in sign language, which he has finally acquired. He's tired of accommodating himself to them and wants to be treated as an adult son, not the family mascot.

The production, revolving mostly around the dinner table of this *Guardian*-reading, book-crammed household (compactly arranged by scenic designer Scott Pask), employs supertitles and projections (the work of Jeff Sugg) to create a sense of what it's like to live in the interstices of conversation. Daniel Kluger's sound design contributes to this effect, which is a welcome departure from the play's otherwise traditional brand of domestic realism.

This family is clearly an extreme case, but I wondered whether *Tribes* would have been more persuasive if Cromer had toned down the rackety belligerence. Does Still's Christopher have to be so insufferable? His type exists no doubt in academic and journalistic circles (please don't ask me to name names), but couldn't he have been dappled with a little charisma?

The connection Raine insinuates between Daniel's faltering mental health and the family's dysfunctional mode of communication seems overly literary. Poor Brill is subjected to thematic overload, having to play a character who not only develops a colossal stammer but also starts hearing voices. The strain leaves him hunched and haggard.

The second act gets tangled in plot strands that could easily be trimmed. What rescues

**IN FRONT OF AN AUDIENCE, IT WAS VERY
POWERFUL."**

"Tribes" is the honest poignancy of Pourfar, who beautifully balances Sylvia's strength and insecurity, and the captivating interior glow of Harvard, who conveys everything he needs to about Billy through his physical bearing.

With actors this emotionally connected, words are secondary. More to the point of Raine's play, hearing is shown to depend more on an open heart than fully functioning ears.

**Source:** Charles McNulty, "*Tribes* Will Be Heard—and Felt," in *Los Angeles Times*, March 11, 2013.

### Nina Raine

*In the following essay, Raine describes working with Nobel Prize–winning playwright Harold Pinter.*

I was 23 and working in London at The River Cafe. I was a cashier: my friend Katherine Tozer, a talented young actress, manned the phones. In an act of typical generosity, our boss, Ruthie Rogers, suggested we make our London debut putting on a play in her house, a Richard Rogers-designed epic space. She would do bruschettas, and invite her friends. We jumped at the offer, and I chose Harold Pinter's two-hander, *Ashes to Ashes*.

I wrote to Pinter, asking permission, and got a call. Pinter wanted to meet. I stood, extremely nervous and one hour early, in Campden Hill Square. When I finally buzzed the door, I was so adrenalised all I remember of Pinter's study was a blur of brown—it could have been velvet or leather—and a round curved mirror on the wall, the type that shows you if there's a car coming fast round a corner. I sat on a sofa opposite Pinter and we discussed the play. He was charming. To my surprise, he was easy to talk to. Pinter asked for only two things: that he attend a final rehearsal; and that he invite a small list of his friends to the event.

We hadn't yet cast the other part. My father, Craig Raine, had seen a brilliant actor called Elliot Levey perform in a student production in Oxford. I offered him the part unseen.

Three weeks of testing rehearsals followed.

Anxiety in the cast was high. Elliot was a brilliant actor, but nervous. He was older than me and had no idea if I could direct. People were keen to see us perform a Pinter play in the Rogers' house in a way that they would never have in a more conventional venue. Kathy's agent insisted we invite the great and the good, including Peter Hall and Richard Eyre, and everyone, to our terror, said yes.

There were arguments about pauses. Elliot distrusted them. We chiselled over every breath. Did Kathy really have to take a pause if, for instance, there were dot-dot-dots in the text? I said yes. Elliot said no. I rang Pinter for support. 'Yes,' Pinter said, patiently. If there were dot-dot-dots, it was a good idea to mark them with a slight pause. Triumphantly, I went back to Elliot with this news. Elliot said Pinter was wrong.

But somehow, the play began to take shape.

One day, near the end of rehearsals, rather like whipping cream, simply through sheer repetition, the play stiffened and found its tone and shape. The actors field it—the mixture of play, speed, ease and unease needed to make the piece sing. Not through any skill of mine, but simply, as Pinter has said, through 'saying the f***ing lines.' It was time for Pinter's rehearsal.

We sat miserably, waiting in the Rogers' great atrium. Strict instructions had been given to the Rogers' extended family and staff to guard against any interruption or noise.

Periodically, we looked out of the window for Pinter. Finally we saw him approaching, in a beige mac, tinted glasses and black trousers.

He sat on a chair in the huge, high-ceilinged reception room. We began the play. I've never seen two actors more nervous. No one was thinking about the play. All any of us could think of was the man watching it. Then, suddenly, I heard the sounds of washing up, a room away. I couldn't interrupt the performance. Suddenly Harold spoke.

'I'm sorry, but this is just impossible.' We looked at him. Did he mean the acting? He gestured towards the noise. 'What is that? Can you tell them to stop?' I bolted through to the scullery and found Ruthie's Brazilian cleaning lady, Rosa, busy at the sink. I told her to leave it. I terrified her. We began again. The actors were transformed. I think we all felt that it couldn't be that bad: Pinter hadn't told us to stop altogether.

Then Pinter gave his notes. They were detailed, clear, and basic. He liked it, but he wanted certain words to be more audible.

On the night itself, neither actor was as nervous as that afternoon. No one could be more intimidating than Pinter's audience of one.

In front of an audience, it was very powerful.

Afterwards, Pinter made a speech referring to me as 'the cat's whiskers' and, after a few drinks, told Matthew Evans, then chairman of Faber and Faber, to f*** off because he hadn't yet read his new play.

The next day I got a parcel with a letter of thanks. It was *Celebration*, Pinter's new play. Set in a high-end restaurant, the action cuts between two tables: a bickering couple, Suki and Russell, and the wedding anniversary of two couples—two sisters who have married two brothers. The characters are boozed up, violent, vulgar and funny. They are attended to by a smooth maitre d', his sexy maitresse d', and a waiter who continually interrupts the tables to recite long lists of literary celebrities his grandfather knew. Pinter said this was based on his own experience of working as a waiter. He overheard a conversation on a table about TS Eliot, which he dared to interrupt. He was sacked the same day.

Pinter, in his note to me, said he was going to direct the play and had an idea about us. Did we want to meet him for lunch and discuss? Kathy and I, broke as ever, decided we must treat Pinter to the River Cafe (staff got a discount). We sat outside, Pinter's glasses black in the sunshine. The play was set in a restaurant. Plates would need to be cleared, drinks brought on. Would we like non-speaking roles as waitresses? Sitting there in the River Cafe, the irony was not lost on us. I was thrilled but terrified. I'd never worked as a waitress, only a cashier, because my hands shook and I was intimidated by clearing plates in front of River Cafe customers. How much worse, balancing plates in front of an audience at the Almeida? Plus, I got stage fright. I decided I would take beta-blockers. Kathy had the opposite reaction. She was a bit disappointed that this was the extent of our challenge. For the next month I learned how to carry a pile of plates on my wrist. And I got a prescription for beta-blockers.

Susie Wooldridge and Lindsay Duncan were playing the sisters in *Celebration*: Andy de la Tour and Keith Allen were playing the brothers. Lia Williams and Steven Pacey were playing the bickering couple on the other table. On the first day of rehearsals only one actor hadn't turned up: Keith Allen. We sat and waited for Keith. I felt a strange reversal taking place. From everyone's tremendous respect and fear of Pinter at the start of the morning, there began to grow a definite feeling of the greatest living playwright being cheeked. 10.30, 10.45, 11.00 ticked by...finally Keith turned up. We read through both plays.

Harold's charisma and presence were palpable. I watched every minute of rehearsals and was never once bored. Afterwards, as an assistant director watching other directors at work, I realised how rare this is. Not only was Harold charismatic, he was funny. Usually when he was at his most irritable. One coffee break, he started to complain about Tony Blair. He had written a letter a week or so before to the PM complaining about government funding of a Turkish dam that would deprive Kurds of their homes. 'Well, I got a letter today from 10 Downing Street, you know? It began, "Dear Harold", and ended "Yours ever, Tony!" I've never met the man!' Sometimes, one could see how these episodes fed directly into Harold's work. There is an exchange in *Celebration*, between the maitresse d' and her guests, where she talks about men she has known who were 'very interested in sex.' Harold told us this came from a conversation he had had with Lady Richardson, a close friend of Vivien Leigh. What was Vivien like, Harold had asked her. 'Oh, very interested in sex', said Lady Richardson. 'And that was it!' said Harold. 'I wanted to say...could you be...a bit...more specific!' And he gave a rare blush. Harold's openness was very winning. On the subject of children, who are also touched on in *Celebration*, Harold said, 'I was an incredibly morbid, morose child. My parents never had another after they saw how I turned out.' Then, as an afterthought, he added brightly, 'I cheered up later, though.'

...I thought the cast vaguely unfriendly. I realise now it was stress and nerves. Despite Pinter's charm, everyone was frozen by the fear of displeasing him. Keith, out of all the actors, seemed to be the least ruffled by Pinter's way of working. Often, he arrived hungover, and snored softly in the corner as others ran their scenes. Once he came in with a strange blood-stained scratch down his cheek. We asked what had happened. 'Someone said Beckett was better than Pinter. So I started on them.' And as everyone 'lurched around in the mud', as Pinter put it to the deputy stage manager, trying to remember their lines, with questioning looks on their faces, Keith would cock up his lines 40 times in a row without an atom of embarrassment. There was one line in particular he found seemingly impossible to remember in *The Room*—"So you're the wife of the bloke you mentioned then." In the end, Harold said, 'The day you get that line right, Keith, I'll give you a chocolate pudding.' Rehearsing the opening of *Celebration*, Keith repeatedly lit a fresh fag before the waiter's first line which opens the play. In the end Harold asked what on earth he was doing.

'A subtle joke—you know, the food arrives and I have to put it out.' 'Bit early in the day to be subtle, isn't it?' said Harold.

'Yeah,' said Keith, 'but I wanted a laugh before the first line of the play.' By the time we hit the theatre, Pinter had endorsed the fag, even telling the waiter to give a pause after Keith lit his cigarette in the darkness before coming on— 'I want the audience to be frightened of that glowing cigarette.' We waitresses also got our moment of love.

Kathy and I were on right at the start of *Celebration*—the play opens with the anniversary table being served their food. It was our job to come on with the plates behind the waiter, Danny. Then, after the action had switched to the other table, we appeared again, to clear the plates. The first time we did it, Harold praised us, saying 'it went like f*** ing clockwork.' Then, when we hadn't been on for a while, but were waiting at the back for our moment, he turned round and said, 'I miss you. What can we do about it?' There had been no explosions and although the actors might have been sitting on a lot of repressed tension and fear, generally the feeling was harmonious. Harold had been extremely affectionate to Kathy and me, and I had even had the joy of being able to contribute materially to rehearsals. Lindsay said a line in one of the last runs and something extraordinary happened. Harold said to Lindsay, 'I don't know what it is that you did, but it worked, so do it again if you can.' I had noticed the same moment, and thought that Lindsay had sounded suddenly younger, almost childlike. After rehearsals I went up to Harold and told him.

'You're absolutely right,' he said, and passed the note on to Lindsay.

I was very pleased, but this was probably a contributing factor to the fatal error I then made with Harold, on the last lap. We had all been invited to drinks, to meet the other company rehearsing at the Gainsborough Studios. Chatting away with Harold and a couple of others, I remarked how accurate a note Harold had given was. 'Thank you,' he said. But, I foolishly added, the actor in question still wasn't doing it. At that point, Ralph Fiennes, who was in one of the other plays, walked past and left the party, without, I think, having introduced himself to Harold. And Harold's mood suddenly flipped. Smiling coldly, he turned to me and said, 'Darling—you must never give me notes.' Everyone in the circle went quiet. 'Oh dear,' he said. 'I seem to have cast a froideur.'

I felt completely unable to mend the awkwardness and was bitterly embarrassed by my presumption. I don't think Harold knew what to do either, and so he ignored not only me, but Kathy too, all through tech, dress and previews. As a result, I couldn't enjoy the excitement of hearing, seeing, and being in the show for the first time. I felt I had ruined something and I didn't know how to put it right.

On press night, after a very good show, we all gathered for prosecco in the Green Room. Harold said 'Where are my girls?' and kissed Lindsay and Lia. Then he kissed Kathy, and said, 'Where's Nina?', and then kissed me. At the end of the night I thanked him for everything—it had been fascinating so far and I was sure it would continue so. 'Everything?' he said. 'Everything', I said, and he smiled and kissed me again on the cheek.

**Source:** Nina Raine, "The King and I," in *London Evening Standard*, June 19, 2009.

# SOURCES

"ASL Timeline," ASL Poetry, http://deafjam.org/time-line.html (accessed June 20, 2017).

Atkinson, Rebecca, "How David Cameron Has Betrayed People with Disabilities," in *Guardian* (London, England), April 15, 2015, https://www.theguardian.com/commentisfree/2015/apr/15/david-cameron-betrayed-disabled-coalition-retrogression (accessed June 20, 2017).

Brantley, Ben, "World of Silence and Not Listening," in *New York Times*, March 5, 2012, http://www.nytimes.com/2012/03/05/theater/reviews/tribes-by-nina-raines-at-the-barrow-street-theater.html (accessed June 20, 2017).

Costa, Maddy, "Nina Raine: A Great Ear for Anger," in *Guardian* (London, England), October 11, 2010, https://www.theguardian.com/stage/2010/oct/11/nina-raine-tribes-tiger-country (accessed June 20, 2017).

Dickens, Charles, *Bleak House*, W. W. Norton, 1979, p. 294.

Esmail, Jennifer, "'I Listened with My Eyes': Writing Speech and Reading Deafness in the Fiction of Charles Dickens and Wilkie Collins," in *ELH*, Vol. 78, No. 4, Winter 2011, pp. 991–1020.

Moore, John, "'Tribes' and the Tyranny of Language and Listening," Denver Center for the Performing Arts website, September 30, 2015, https://www.denvercenter.org/blog-posts/news-center/2015/09/30/tribes-and-the-tyranny-of-language-and-listening (accessed June 20, 2017).

Morris, Steven Leigh, "Nina Raine's Play *Tribes* Depicts a Family That Talks a Lot but Doesn't Listen," in *LA Weekly*, March 14, 2013, http://www.laweekly.com/arts/nina-raines-play-tribes-depicts-a-family-that-talks-a-lot-but-doesnt-listen-2613331 (accessed June 20, 2017).

"Nina Raine," Vermont Stage, http://www.vermontstage.org/nina-raine-bio.html (accessed June 20, 2017).

Ostrow, Joanne, "'Tribes' Review: Nina Raine's Moving Play Resonates in Denver," in *Denver Post*, October 20, 2015, http://www.denverpost.com/2015/10/20/tribes-review-nina-raines-moving-play-resonates-in-denver/ (accessed June 20, 2017).

Pfefferman, Naomi, "Comedy-Drama 'Tribes' Communicates Dysfunction of British-Jewish Family," in *Jewish Journal*, March 13, 2013, http://jewishjournal.com/mobile_20111212/113936/ (accessed June 20, 2017).

Raine, Nina, *Tribes*, Dramatists Play Service, 2013.

Rees, Jasper, "Nina Raine: 'I Started Getting a God Complex,'" in *Telegraph* (London, England), January 3, 2011, http://www.telegraph.co.uk/culture/theatre/8236794/Nina-Raine-I-started-getting-a-God-complex.html (accessed June 20, 2017).

———, "Theartsdesk Q&A: Playwright Nina Raine," The Arts Desk, December 6, 2014, http://www.theartsdesk.com/theatre/theartsdesk-qa-playwright-nina-raine (accessed June 20, 2017).

## FURTHER READING

Innes, C. D., *Modern British Drama: The Twentieth Century*, Cambridge University Press, 2002.
> This volume is a formidable examination of a golden age of theatrical expression.

Lane, Harlan, *When the Mind Hears: A History of the Deaf*, Vintage Books, 1989.
> Lane wrote this text in 1989 as a comprehensive and poignant examination of the complex disability at the heart of Raine's play.

Raine, Craig, *My Grandmother's Glass Eye: A Look at Poetry*, Atlantic Books, 2016.
> A work of recent criticism by Raine's father, this volume provides readers with a compelling glimpse into the style and sentiments of a man widely believed to be the basis for the playwright's character of the relentlessly critical Christopher.

Sulloway, Frank J., *Born to Rebel: Birth Order, Family Dynamics, and Creative Lives*, Vintage Books, 1996.
> A compelling, well-researched examination of evolving family dynamics in a modern age, this book provides valuable insight into the inner workings of the household portrayed in *Tribes*.

Vasishta, Madan, *Deaf in Delhi: A Memoir*, Gallaudet University Press, 2006.
> Vasishta lost his hearing at a young age after suffering a long illness but, through continued perseverance and optimism, found fulfillment in a famously intolerant society for the deaf.

## SUGGESTED SEARCH TERMS

Nina Raine

Nina Raine AND Tribes

Moses Raine AND playwright

Craig Raine AND poet

Boris Pasternak

deaf identity AND Nina Raine

family conflict AND Nina Raine

deafness AND communication

# Une Tempête

## AIMÉ CÉSAIRE

## 1969

*Une tempête* (*A Tempest*) is a play by Martinique poet, dramatist, and politician Aimé Césaire. An adaptation of William Shakespeare's play *The Tempest* from a postcolonial perspective, *A Tempest* was first performed and published in 1969. Its full title was *Une tempête: D'apres "La tempête" de Shakespeare, adaptation pour un théâtrenègre*. An English version of the play, translated by Emile Snyder and Sanford Upson, was published in New York in 1975 by the Third World Press. Another translation, on which this entry is based, was made by Richard Miller and published in 1986. It is subtitled *Adaptation of Shakespeare's The Tempest for a Black Theater*. The play had its American premiere at the Ubu Repertory Theater in New York City on October 9, 1991. The play is important because it is a representative work of early postcolonial drama, a type of literature in which writers from colonies and former colonies present the colonial experience from the point of view of the indigenous people who have suffered under foreign domination.

## AUTHOR BIOGRAPHY

Césaire was born on June 25, 1913, in Basse-Pointe, Martinique. He had his initial education in Martinique and then went to Paris in 1932, where he entered the Lycée Louis-le-Grand,

*Aimé Césaire* *(© Lipnitzki / Getty Images)*

where he studied philosophy. In 1934, he published an article in *L'etudiant noir*, a journal he cofounded, which used the word *negritude* for the first time. Césaire was to emerge as one of the three leaders of the Negritude cultural and literary movement that sought to advance black consciousness. The following year he was accepted into the prestigious École normale supérieure. In 1937, he married Suzanne Roussy, a writer. Two years later, in 1939, he published the long autobiographical poem *Cahier d'un retour au pays natal* (*Notebook of a Return to the Native Land*), which protests against the conditions endured by black people in Martinique. This was also the year that World War II began, and Césaire and his wife returned to Martinique, where they taught in the public schools. In 1941, he was one of the cofounders of the review *Tropiques*, which contained criticism of the wartime Vichy government in France and established Césaire as a political figure. In 1945 he became mayor of Fort-de-France and was elected deputy of the Communist Party to the National Assembly in Paris; he was instrumental in arranging for Martinique and Guadeloupe to become overseas departments of France in 1946.

Between 1944 and 1960, Césaire published four books of poetry: *Les armes miraculeuses* (1944; Miraculous Weapons), *Soleil cou coupé* (1948; Beheaded Sun) *Corps perdu* (1949; Lost Body); and *Ferrement* (1960; Shackles). He also published nonfiction, including the influential

essay *Discourse sur le colonialisme* (*Discourse on Colonialism*, 1957) in 1950. In 1956, Césaire took part in the First International Congress of Black Writers in Paris, and he also left the Communist Party.

In addition to his poetry and nonfiction, Césaire was a dramatist. In 1956, he wrote the tragedy *Et les chiens se taisaient* (And the Dogs Were Silent), followed by *La tragédie du roi Christophe* (1963; *The Tragedy of King Christophe*, 1969); *Une saison au Congo* (1966; *A Season in the Congo*, 1968), and *Une tempête* (*A Tempest*, 1975), an adaptation of Shakespeare's play, *The Tempest*. In 1983, *Aimé Césaire: The Collected Poetry*, translated by Clayton Eshleman and Annette Smith, was published by the University of California Press. Césaire remained mayor of Fort-de-France until his retirement in 2001. He had occupied the position for over fifty years. He died of heart failure on April 17, 2008, at the age of ninety-four, in Fort-de-France.

## PLOT SUMMARY

### Prologue
The actors enter, and each selects a mask. As they do so, the master of ceremonies makes brief comments about the characters, giving clues as to the character of some of them and the roles they will play. The master of ceremonies himself picks two actors to portray the wind and the captain of the ship.

### Act 1, Scene 1
On the ship, as the storm rages, Gonzalo, Antonio, and Sebastian try to discuss the situation with the boatswain, who is doing his best to supervise the efforts of the crew to keep the ship afloat. The boatswain tells them they would be better off below deck, in their cabins. Gonzalo speaks to him in a disparaging way. There is thunder and lightning, and the ship sinks.

### Act 1, Scene 2
On the island, Prospero explains to his daughter, Miranda, how they came to be on the island. Prospero used to be the duke of Milan, but his position was usurped by his brother, Antonio, aided by Alonso, the king of Naples. They denounced him to the Inquisition. A flashback follows in which Prospero is denounced as a heretic by a friar, representing the Inquisition.

# MEDIA ADAPTATIONS

- A version of the play is available on YouTube, at https://www.youtube.com/watch?v=RzY OnRde1pw, directed by Kamaluddin Nilu and performed by students in the Department of Theatre Arts of the University of Hyderabad, India, on March 13, 2014. The run time is two hours, six minutes.

Prospero then tells Miranda that no trial ever took place; instead, Prospero ended up marooned on the island. Gonzalo supplied him with food, clothing, and books to make his exile tolerable. Now his enemies have come to the deserted island, seeking to claim it as their own, but Prospero, with the help of Ariel, has been able to create the storm that has wrecked the ship.

Ariel enters, unhappy at what he has been made to do. He wants his freedom and says that Prospero has told him thousands of times that he would be freed. Prospero says he will free Ariel only when he is ready to do so.

Prospero summons Caliban. They exchange insults. Prospero expects gratitude for what he has taught Caliban, but Caliban denies that Prospero taught him anything. Instead, it was the other way round. Caliban taught Prospero about everything on the island, such as the trees and the fruits, but Prospero made him live in a dirty cave. Prospero accuses him of having tried to rape Miranda, but Caliban denies it. Prospero orders him back to work, bringing wood and water, threatening to whip him if he refuses. Caliban announces that he no longer wishes to be known as Caliban, which was the name Prospero gave him. He tells Prospero to call him X, since Prospero stole his identity from him.

Caliban exits, and Ariel enters as a sea nymph. Prospero tells Ariel that Caliban is the enemy, not the people on the shipwreck. He tells Ariel they are not to be harmed. He will forgive them if they repent and ask forgiveness. After all, they are men of his race and rank. He tells Ariel

that he wants Alonso's son, Ferdinand, to marry Prospero's daughter.

Ferdinand enters and sees Miranda. Ferdinand explains that he is a victim of the shipwreck and that his father is dead. Miranda offers him her support. Prospero enters and tells Miranda she is being too hospitable to Ferdinand, whom he accuses of being a traitor and a spy. He says he will make Ferdinand his house servant. Ferdinand accepts his fate willingly because he has fallen in love with Miranda.

## Act 2, Scene 1

Caliban sings in his cave. Ariel enters, and they have a discussion about how best to end their suffering and oppression. Ariel warns Caliban that Prospero is out for revenge against him and that Caliban will lose because Prospero is stronger. For his part, Caliban scorns Ariel for obeying Prospero; Caliban says that Prospero's promise to free Ariel means nothing. Ariel says that, unlike Caliban, he does not advocate violence. Instead, he hopes he can make Prospero himself change and end the injustice he currently oversees. Ariel believes that Prospero can be made to acquire a conscience. Caliban dismisses the idea as nonsense. Prospero will never collaborate with them to make the world better. All he understands is power and domination. Caliban promises violent rebellion.

## Act 2, Scene 2

Gonzalo, Sebastian, Alonso, and Antonio discuss their situation and the island on which they find themselves. Gonzalo thinks the island is rich with natural resources that they could exploit. His idea is to colonize the island, although he does not wish to oppress the native population. Music is heard, and Prospero and Ariel enter, both invisible. Other figures enter, carrying a table with food laid out on it. They invite the castaways to eat. Then they disappear. The castaways, astonished, get ready to eat, but then elves come and take the table away. Shortly after, the elves return with the food. Spooked, Alonso says he will not eat the food. This upsets the still invisible Prospero, who takes it as an insult. He wants to exert his power over them by making them eat. The castaways then eat, and Alonso thinks sadly of his son, Ferdinand, whom he believes to have drowned. Then they all sleep.

## Act 2, Scene 3

Antonio and Sebastian come upon the sleeping men. Antonio wants to kill Alonso, the king, while Sebastian, Alonso's brother, decides to murder Gonzalo. They draw their swords, but before they can act, Ariel intervenes and wakens the sleepers and tells them what was about to happen. He also tells Alonso that Prospero sent him and that Prospero rules the island. However, Prospero will forgive them their sins against him if they repent. Ariel tells Antonio and Sebastian that they will also be forgiven, if they, too, repent. They agree to do so, although Gonzalo reproaches them for what he sees as their insincerity. Ariel, on behalf of Prospero, invites them all to the celebrations for the engagement of Ferdinand and Miranda. Alonso is overjoyed that his son is alive and praises God.

## Act 3, Scene 1

Ferdinand is working very hard with a hoe all day, and he appears not to be used to such exertions. Miranda wants to help him. Ferdinand asks her what her name is, but Prospero has forbidden her to say. Caliban whispers it to him, though, and Ferdinand pretends he is christening her with a name he has chosen. Miranda thinks she has been subject to a trick of some kind. Prospero enters and tells Ferdinand he has done enough work for one day and can stop. He orders Caliban to finish the work, much to Caliban's resentment and disgust. Caliban says that he will get his revenge one day.

## Act 3, Scene 2

Trinculo enters, singing in the rain. He thinks he is the only survivor of the wreck. He sees Caliban sheltering under a wheelbarrow and crawls under the cover. He thinks he may be able to take Caliban prisoner, take him back to Europe, and exhibit him in a carnival.

Stephano enters, singing and drinking from a wine bottle. He sees Caliban's head sticking out from under the cover and, like Trinculo, thinks there is money to be made from him in a carnival. He gives Caliban a drink from the wine bottle. Then he sees Trinculo's head under the other side of the cover and, because he is drunk, thinks he has stumbled upon a two-headed monster. After a moment or so, he realizes it is Trinculo. They discuss Caliban, calling him an Indian and thinking him a savage. Stephano says he wants to civilize him and offers him more wine. Caliban drinks. Stephano and Trinculo plan to exploit

him. Stephano, thinking that he and Trinculo are the only survivors, proclaims himself king of the island. Caliban finds his voice and hails him as the king but tells him to be wary of Prospero. If Stephano wants to rule the island, he will have to defeat Prospero. Stephano replies that it will be easy for him to get rid of Prospero. He puts Trinculo in charge of Caliban and says their forces will march on the enemy at dawn the following day.

## Act 3, Scene 3

In his cave, Prospero summons gods and goddesses as part of the celebrations for Ferdinand and Miranda. Juno, Ceres, and Iris appear, as do some nymphs, who dance. But then another god, the black devil-god Eshu, enters. Miranda thinks he looks more like a devil than a god, and Eshu says he is a god to his friends but a devil to his enemies. Prospero thinks that Ariel must have made a mistake in summoning him. Eshu says that he was not invited but came anyway. Prospero tells him to go, and Eshu does so, but not before he has sung a bawdy song that offends the other gods.

After all the gods exit, Prospero is worried. He knows Caliban is plotting against him, and he plans to punish him for his rebellion.

## Act 3, Scene 4

At night, the spirits of the tropical forest can be heard. As dawn comes, Caliban goes off to fight Prospero, singing his battle song. Stephano and Trinculo enter, and the three join forces, although the two castaways have contempt for Caliban and call him a savage. They see some bright clothing hanging from a rope (which Prospero deliberately placed there earlier to distract Caliban), and Stephano and Trinculo get into a fight about who should have the clothes. Caliban, contemptuous of them and with his weapon drawn, advances on Prospero, who has just appeared. Prospero challenges Caliban to kill him, and Caliban hesitates, saying he is not a murderer. Prospero summons Ariel, and Stephano, Trinculo, and Caliban are taken prisoner.

## Act 3, Scene 5

In Prospero's cave, Ferdinand and Miranda are playing chess. Ferdinand cheats, but Miranda forgives him. The nobles enter, and Alonso is thrilled at the wedding of the two young people, as is Gonzalo. Prospero enters and tells them that their ship is safe, as are their crew. Prospero says he will return with them to Europe. He turns to Ariel and tells him he will be free that day.

Stephano, Trinculo, and Caliban enter. Stephano and Trinculo are not well received, and they make their excuses. Prospero tells them go and sleep off the effects of the wine they have drunk. As for Caliban, Prospero refers to him as devilish, which leads Gonzalo to try to exorcise Caliban, who merely laughs at the notion. Prospero asks Caliban what he has to say in his own defense. Caliban replies that he will not defend himself. He says that his regret is that he has failed to win his freedom. Prospero adopts a conciliatory tone and says there should be peace between them. Caliban replies that he is interested only in being free. He speaks about what he has suffered at Prospero's hands and says that eventually he will win and Prospero's world will come crashing down. Prospero rejects this, saying that he will go on getting stronger. Caliban remains defiant, and he and Prospero end up saying that they hate each other. Prospero then informs the nobles that he has decided to stay on the island and continue his work on what he thinks of as creating civilization and harmony, which he believes he alone is able to do.

After everyone other than Prospero and Caliban exit, Prospero says he has tried to save Caliban from himself but that Caliban has only ever answered with anger and hostility. From now on, Prospero says, he will answer Caliban's violence with violence of his own.

Some time passes. Prospero enters, looking old and tired. He grumbles about how the island seems now to be overrun with opossums. Firing in all directions, he vows to protect civilization. Then he says that the climate on the island has changed. It is cold now. He wonders what Caliban is up to and shouts out to him. A snatch of Caliban's song is heard. He is singing of freedom.

# CHARACTERS

### Alonso

Alonso is the king of Naples and father of Ferdinand. Before the events depicted in the play take place, he colluded with Antonio to help Antonio seize Prospero's lands. Shipwrecked on the island, Alonso at first believes that Ferdinand has perished, and he is grief-stricken over his loss as well as distressed by the fact that he has likely also lost his throne and his country.

He is overjoyed when he discovers Ferdinand is alive, and he also blesses the marriage between his son and Miranda. He expresses genuine remorse for his wrong actions in the past.

### Antonio

Antonio is the duke of Milan and Prospero's younger brother. He conspired with Alonso, the king of Naples, to seize Prospero's dukedom. The storm delivers him into Prospero's hands. Antonio, who has a conceited and exaggerated notion of his own importance, is about to kill the sleeping Alonso and thereby make himself king of Naples, when Ariel intervenes and stops him. Ariel tells him that Prospero will forgive him, on condition that he abandon his plans. Antonio, thinking that he has been overcome by magic, agrees to Prospero's request.

### Ariel

Ariel is a mulatto who has been enslaved by Prospero. Prospero uses Ariel to put his magic into action. Ariel, for example, creates the storm that leads Prospero's enemies to the island. He also creates the illusory banquet. Many times Prospero has promised to free Ariel, and, unlike Caliban, Ariel believes that it is possible to appeal to Prospero's conscience and get him to acknowledge that he is guilty of injustice. Then he will change, and they will be free. At the end of the play Prospero finally tells Ariel he will be free that very day.

### Boatswain

The boatswain tries to save the sinking ship in the first scene of the play.

### Caliban

Caliban is a black man who has been enslaved by Prospero. Caliban was one of the original inhabitants of the island. He does not accept his enslavement and plots to fight back against Prospero's ill treatment of him. He has a vision of attaining his own freedom by violent rebellion, and by the end of the play he is still carrying on the fight.

### Captain

The captain gives instructions to the boatswain during the storm in the first scene.

## Ceres

Ceres is one of the gods summoned by Prospero to celebrate the betrothal of Ferdinand and Miranda. She complains that Eshu's song is obscene.

## Eshu

Eshu is described as a "black devil-god." As the gods and goddesses summoned by Prospero dance in celebration of the betrothal of Ferdinand and Miranda, he enters uninvited and shocks the other gods with his earthy, bawdy talk and songs.

## Ferdinand

Ferdinand is the son of Alonso. The nobles put him to work cultivating the land on the island, and he finds it hard work. It is also arranged for him to marry Miranda. At the end of the play, Ferdinand and Miranda, now married, are ready to return to Europe, and Prospero wants them to preside over a combined kingdom of Milan and Naples.

## Gonzalo

Gonzalo is a worthy old counselor to Alonso the king. He is dignified, if somewhat long-winded and preachy in his speech. Sebastian and Antonio find him exasperating, but Alonso appreciates him.

## Iris

Iris is one of the gods summoned by Prospero to celebrate the betrothal of Ferdinand and Miranda. She is shocked by Eshu's antics.

## Juno

Juno is one of the gods summoned by Prospero to celebrate the betrothal of Ferdinand and Miranda. She gets upset by the presence of Eshu and leaves.

## Master of Ceremonies

The master of ceremonies appears just once, in the prologue. He instructs the actors to put on the masks that represent the characters they are playing.

## Miranda

Miranda is Prospero's young daughter. She was born in Milan and was little more than a baby when Prospero took her with him into exile. Her only memories are of life on the island, where she is happy. She becomes betrothed to Ferdinand, and they marry. Miranda has a forgiving nature,

although she might also be thought to be naïve, given her youth.

## Prospero

Prospero is the former duke of Milan who now rules the island. Prospero lost his dukedom when his brother, Antonio, as well as Alonso, conspired against him. He was sent into exile and found himself on the island. He was able to take his books with him, so he continued to have access to esoteric knowledge, which allows him to summon Ariel at will. Prospero made himself master of the island by enslaving not only Ariel but also Caliban, who was the original inhabitant. Prospero thinks that he taught Caliban language and tried to civilize him, but Caliban holds a decidedly different view. Prospero finally forgives his enemies and at first says he will go back to Europe with them, but then he changes his mind, deciding to remain on the island with Caliban.

## Sebastian

Sebastian is Alonso's brother and an associate of Antonio's. When he and Antonio come upon Alonso and Gonzalo sleeping, Antonio tries to get Sebastian to kill Alonso and therefore inherit the throne of Naples. Sebastian refuses because he cannot kill his own brother. However, he is willing to let Antonio commit the murder while he, Sebastian, kills Gonzalo. Their murderous plot is foiled by Ariel's intervention.

## Stephano

Stephano is a drunken sailor who wanders around the island with Trinculo. He proclaims himself king of the island and, with Trinculo and Caliban, tries to overthrow Prospero. But the quarrelsome Stephano and Trinculo get into a fight with each other and are then captured by Prospero. Prospero calls them scoundrels and sends them away to sleep off the wine they have imbibed. He does not prevent them, however, from returning to the ship and sailing for Europe with the others.

## Trinculo

Like Stephano, Trinculo is a disreputable drunken sailor, but Stephano is the stronger personality; he dominates Trinculo and orders him around. Trinculo and Stephano join forces with Caliban in an attempt to overthrow Prospero, but they are soon captured.

# THEMES

## Colonialism

In drawing out some of the implications present in Shakespeare's play, *The Tempest*, on which *A Tempest* is based, the dramatist makes the issue of colonialism and how to combat it front and center. Prospero is the representative of an imperialistic European culture that has colonized this unnamed tropical island. Prospero has enslaved Caliban, who represents the indigenous people of the island, and forces him to work hard supplying Prospero's needs.

In the dialogue between them in act 1, scene 2, the issues are laid out clearly. Prospero and Caliban have diametrically opposed views regarding the situation. Referring to Caliban as a "savage," Prospero claims that he taught Caliban to speak and educated and trained him, trying to civilize him. In other words, he justifies himself, as advocates for colonialism often did, by claiming to be a benefactor rather than an oppressor. But Caliban refutes the argument forcefully, first by speaking a word in his own language, showing that he had language before Prospero ever came along. Caliban also says that Prospero did not really educate him either, merely forcing him to do all the manual labor that Prospero was too lazy to do. Prospero kept his real learning to himself. Caliban thus presents the argument that the colonizing powers limited the education of the native population because they did not want them to gain any knowledge that would enable them to challenge the established colonial order. Caliban also explains that his mother, Sycorax, was a kind of earth goddess, and he regards the earth itself as alive, which is why he respects it and lives in harmony with it. Prospero, on the other hand, adopts the predominant Western belief that the earth is essentially just inert matter and can be exploited and polluted in any way the ruling class wishes in order to create material abundance for the few. As a result of this greed, the indigenous population is forced to live in impoverished ghettos, as Caliban complains.

It is also clear that Prospero's rule is maintained by brutality and violence. When Caliban says he has done enough work, Prospero threatens him with a whipping if he does not continue. The play therefore offers the view that all colonial regimes are founded on violence and oppression. Despite this, Prospero persists till the end in believing that actually he has tried to save Caliban from himself rather than steal from him everything he has, including his identity.

# TOPICS FOR FURTHER STUDY

- Choose a scene from *A Tempest* and act it out with classmates.

- Does Césaire present Prospero in an entirely negative light, or does he show positive qualities as well? Write an essay in which you discuss Césaire's characterization of Prospero.

- Describe colonialism and how it worked. What was the political and economic system that colonizing powers put in place in their colonies? What were the main beliefs of the colonizers that allowed them to do this? Create a time line that outlines the major events in European colonialism from the sixteenth to the twentieth century. Give a class presentation in which you describe the colonial system, with specific examples.

- Go to glogster.com and create a glog that could be used to advertise a performance of *A Tempest*.

- Read the prose retelling of Shakespeare's *The Tempest*, in *Shakespeare's Stories for Young Readers*, by E. Nesbet, or *Stories from Shakespeare*, by Geraldine McCaughrean. Then write your own retelling of Césaire's *A Tempest*, not exceeding 2,500 words.

Prospero continues to believe that Caliban is simply ungrateful, rejecting all that Prospero has offered and responding only with continual anger and hostility. When Prospero finally declares at the end of the play that he will fight Caliban's violence with violence of his own, it is not only a striking exception to his forgiveness of the nobles who wronged him, it is also simply an extension of the violence he has practiced all along, which he has refused even to acknowledge.

The different strategies that might be employed in opposing colonialism are also laid out early in the play, in the debate between Caliban and Ariel in act 2, scene 1. Ariel takes a different approach from Caliban's. He advocates appealing to the moral conscience of the

*Like Shakespeare's play, Césaire's* Une Tempête *takes place on a remote island (© Rene Holtslag / Shutterstock.com)*

colonizer Prospero and tells Caliban that he does not believe in violence. Instead, Prospero must be made to see the injustice of the system over which he presides. When he does so, he will voluntarily end it and join with the formerly oppressed people to create a better society. Caliban, however, scoffs at this. "Prospero is an old scoundrel who has no conscience," he says. Caliban intends to go on planning to fight Prospero, even though Ariel warns him that Prospero is stronger than he is. Caliban sees no other way of approaching the situation; he would rather die than submit to Prospero's tyranny.

### Forgiveness

Somewhat overshadowed by the colonialism theme, and certainly receiving less prominence than in Shakespeare's play, forgiveness is nonetheless present. Prospero has every right to feel anger and the desire for revenge against Antonio, Alonso, and Sebastian, given how his dukedom was stolen from him. However, he offers Alonso forgiveness because he sees that the king is showing genuine repentance for his misdeeds. He also forgives Antonio and Sebastian on the condition that they renounce their plans to kill Alonso and Gonzalo, since such plans are doomed to failure. Antonio and Sebastian agree to the conditions, but scarcely from the goodness of their hearts. They realize they have been outwitted.

Prospero's reasons for offering forgiveness should also be noted, since they intersect with the colonialist theme. He can forgive the malefactors because they are of his own rank and race, as he says explicitly in act 1, scene 2. Not so Caliban, which is why Prospero declares that it is Caliban who is the enemy, not the castaways, even though it was the latter group that wronged him. This reveals that even when generosity and forgiveness seem to prevail, the underlying injustices based on race and power continue to exert their hold.

## STYLE

### Imagery

The imagery of the play helps to create a vivid impression of the tropical island, which may be in the Caribbean or somewhere off the coast of Africa. There is frequent reference to the flora and fauna that exist there. Miranda, who has lived on the island almost all her life, seems to love it, especially the birds, and she offers to show Ferdinand all the fruits and flowers that flourish there. Of the castaways, it is Gonzalo who is most appreciative of what he sees as he and the other nobles explore the island. He calls it "a magnificent country! Bread hangs from the trees and the apricots are bigger than a woman's full breast" (act 2, scene 2). Ariel, in his guise as a sea nymph, sings of it as almost an island paradise: "Sandy seashore, deep blue sky, / surf is rising, sea birds fly / here the lover finds delight" (act 1, scene 2).

It is Caliban, though, who adds a sharper definition to this imagery. He is aware of the power of the god Shango on the island. Anyone who offends Shango will suffer for it. (Shango is the name of a god in some Caribbean and African cultures.) In other words, in Caliban's view one must live in harmony with the laws that govern the island, and everything will be fine; otherwise, expect to reap the consequences. Caliban evokes the birds of the island, hailing the "black pecking creature of the savannas" (act 3, scene 2); his imagery has a violent tinge as well as racial implications as he sings, "The white blossoms of the miconia / Mingle with the violet blood of ripe berries / And blood stains your plumage, / traveller!" (act 3, scene 2). Caliban considers himself to be a friend and advocate of all life on the island, even such things as "snakes, scorpions, porcupines!" (act 3, scene 4). He claims, after all, to be challenging Prospero on behalf of everything that lives there, he says, and he regards Prospero as the "Anti-Nature."

## Allegory

The play takes *The Tempest*, Shakespeare's romance set on a magical island, and while retaining much of that play's action turns it into an allegory of Western colonialism. An allegory is a literary work that, in addition to the literal level of meaning, contains a second set of ideas that adds another level of meaning to the work. In this case, different characters represent aspects of the colonial experience. Prospero represents the European colonizers from several nations who from the sixteenth through to the mid-twentieth century colonized large areas of Africa, Asia, and the Americas. Caliban represents the indigenous population of these areas, who were dominated by the colonizing powers who exploited the natural resources of the colonized nations and kept the indigenous people in a state of subservience. Ariel represents the mulatto (mixed race) population of the colonized areas.

## HISTORICAL CONTEXT

### Postcolonial Literature

Postcolonial literature emerged as a result of the process of decolonization that gathered force after World War II and continued into the 1950s and 1960s. The European colonizing powers, which included France, the United Kingdom, Portugal, and Belgium, relinquished control of many of their colonies in Asia, Africa, and the Caribbean during this period.

Césaire was a leading voice in the anticolonial movement that developed after World War II. In the 1930s, he had been one of the three founders of the Negritude movement, which sought to promote pride in black identity. In 1950, his *Discourse sur le colonialisme* (*Discourse on Colonialism*) was one of many critiques of colonialism that appeared. Robin D. G. Kelley, in "Poetry and the Political Imagination: Aimé Césaire, Negritude & the Applications of Surrealism," observes that according to Césaire,

> colonialism works to "decivilize" the colonizer: Torture, violence, race hatred, and immorality constitute a dead weight on the so-called civilized, pulling the master class deeper and deeper into the abyss of barbarism. The instruments of colonial power rely on barbaric, brutal violence and intimidation, and the end result is the degradation of Europe itself.

Also, according to Kelly's summary of Césaire, the "colonial ideology" of "racial and cultural hierarchy . . . is as essential to colonial rule as the police and the use of forced labor."

Another anticolonial work was Frantz Fanon's *Black Skin, White Masks* (1952). Like Césaire, Fanon was from Martinique and at one point was taught by Césaire. Yet another such work was Tunisian writer Albert Memmi's *The Colonizer and the Colonized*, which appeared in 1957.

As the tide turned against colonialism and more and more colonies gained their independence, postcolonial literature began to flourish. This filled a gap in literature, since for the first time a body of work sprang up, much of it written in the languages of the colonizing powers, that presented an alternative point of view to that of the colonizer. Colonized people began to tell their own stories of what it was like to be under the rule of a foreign power, and such works challenged the prevailing colonial view of indigenous cultures as backward and their people inferior. One of the most famous of early postcolonial works is *Things Fall Apart*, a novel written in English by Nigerian author Chinua Achebe in 1958. Set in the nineteenth century, it deals with life in Nigeria both before and during the period of colonial rule. (Nigeria would gain independence from Britain two years later, in 1960.) *Wide Sargasso Sea* (1966), by Jean Rhys, is another early postcolonial novel. Rhys

*The ship of the King of Naples is caught in a storm and wrecked on Prospero's island* (© Susanitah /
*Shutterstock.com*)

lived most of her life in England but was born in
Dominica, an island in the Caribbean, and her
novel, set in the nineteenth century, is about a
Creole woman who endures an unhappy
arranged marriage to an Englishman.

Postcolonial drama also came into existence
during these decades, in an attempt to come to
terms with the colonial experience through theater.
Césaire, Nigerian Wole Soyinka, and West Indian
Derek Walcott were early postcolonial dramatists.

## CRITICAL OVERVIEW

In October 1991, D. J. R. Bruckner reviewed the
American premiere of *A Tempest*, produced at
the Ubu Theater in New York City, in the *New
York Times*. He describes it as "a bright political

comedy"; the production is a "sprightly and song-
filled enchantment." Bruckner writes that "the
luminous intelligence of Mr. Cesaire's meditation
on the absurdities of colonialism shines through
the antics of the bewildered characters." He also
notes that "good humor is the key to the play's
meaning.... Mr. Cesaire is a gentle mocker of
self-delusion." Bruckner's conclusion is that "the
playwright seems to be saying, freedom depends
on grasping the truth about our common humanity more than on holding political power."

Janis L. Pallister, in *Aimé Césaire*, describes
the play as "a lucid and complex dramatization of
many political postulations." She goes on to
remark: "The various characters reflect many
social strata so that the play is also the dramatization of prevailing socioeconomic conditions."
Pallister also notes that "Prospero's position of

# COMPARE
# &
# CONTRAST

- **1960s:** During this decade a large number of French and British colonies in Africa and the Caribbean gain their independence. In 1960, France grants independence to African nations that include Benin, Upper Volta, Cameroon, Chad, Republic of the Congo, Ivory Coast, Togo, and Madagascar. Algeria gains independence from France in 1962. The United Kingdom grants independence to the Caribbean nations of Jamaica and Trinidad and Tobago in 1962 and to Barbados and Guyana in 1966.

  **Today:** France no longer has colonies, but there remain eleven territories overseas that France administers. These territories send representatives to the French parliament, and their populations are citizens of France. These territories include Martinique and Guadeloupe in the Caribbean, French Polynesia in the South Pacific, and French Guyana on the North Atlantic coast in South America.

- **1960s:** As former colonies become independent, postcolonial literature, in which writers assess the impact of colonialism and develop a new national literature, flourishes. In 1960, Nigerian playwright Wole Soyinka writes *A Dance of the Forests*, a complex play about Africa's past and the path it must tread in the future. The play is published in 1963.

  **Today:** Sir Derek Walcott, a leading postcolonial writer from Saint Lucia, remains an active writer into the 2010s. His play *Pantomime* (1978) explores relations between colonizing and colonized people. The play is one of his most popular works and is frequently revived in the twenty-first century. Productions are staged by the Pegasus Players in Chicago in 2006; there is a production at the University of Essex in England in 2012, as well as productions in the Caribbean, such as at the Little Carib Theatre in Trinidad and Tobago in 2013 and at the Palladium, Sandals Grande, Saint Lucia, in 2014.

- **1960s:** There is a movement in Martinique for independence, but economic recession, including high unemployment, works against any push for independence. Also, France responds to the movement by giving the island more autonomy.

  **Today:** In 2010 voters in Martinique reject proposals for greater autonomy. The independence movement still exists, however, in the form of the Martinican Independence Movement, a political party that holds one seat in the French National Assembly. Martinique remains part of France and as such is a member of the European Union.

---

colonial-style domination" is "tenuous" because of the multitude of threats he faces. Caliban turns to violence because he is "desperate for reform," but his rebellion does not succeed "in part because he has formed dangerous and unfruitful alliances with Trinculo and Stephano, two drunken wastrels. He slowly comes to realize that he must fight his battles alone."

Mary Gallagher, in her essay, "Aimé Césaire and Francophone Postcolonial Thought," in *Postcolonial Thought in the French-Speaking World*, notes how Césaire replaced the definite article in the title of Shakespeare's *The Tempest* with an indefinite article, which

> makes of Césaire's play a hyponymic variant. The work could thus be regarded as explicitly writing back, and the tenor of this relation between classic and variant, between a text of empire and a text of the post-colony could be seen as fundamentally postcolonial.

Gallagher also observes that the "play's thesis underlines the imprisonment of all of the characters, including the master, within rigid hierarchical positions."

# CRITICISM

## *Bryan Aubrey*

*Aubrey holds a PhD in English. In the following essay, he examines how in* A Tempest *Césaire reshaped the traditional interpretations of Shakespeare's* The Tempest.

It is not difficult to see how Shakespeare's play *The Tempest* might be adapted and represented from an anticolonial viewpoint. Shakespeare certainly provided the raw materials for such an interpretation, although, writing at a time when Western colonialism had barely begun—the play was likely written in the early 1610s—he had other ideas and themes in mind. One prominent theme is nature versus art. Humanity in its precivilized state of nature, as represented by Caliban, is contrasted with art, as represented by Prospero, and understood as the ability to gain mastery not only over the lower aspects of human nature but also over the created world. Prospero is thus presented as the wise man, the magus. Another theme is education, or learning. Miranda, Prospero's daughter, is capable of it, but Caliban is not. Also, the natural nobility of Miranda and Ferdinand is contrasted with the bestiality of Caliban. Freedom is a theme, too. Antonio and Sebastian seek it through political power, illegally gained. Caliban, when he joins with them, thinks he can gain freedom by changing his master, while this in fact merely alters the conditions of his slavery.

The theme of destiny is also evident. The hand of Providence is at work; it was Providence that first brought Prospero and Miranda to the island, and it is providential destiny that brings his enemies to the same island. Both Gonzalo and Ferdinand refer to the workings of Providence, and this theme is naturally linked to the fundamental religious concerns of sin, redemption, and the workings of grace. It is also linked to the themes of forgiveness and reconciliation, which are common to all Shakespeare's late plays, known as romances. (In addition to *The Tempest*, these are *Pericles, Cymbeline,* and *The Winter's Tale*). The island itself is in the Shakespearean tradition of unlocalized zones of transformation (like the Forest of Arden in *As You Like It*), where normal social roles break down in the face of an expansion of experience and consciousness. The island is different to different people; how they see it reflects the sort of people they are, and this is linked to Shakespeare's

> CÉSAIRE DOWNPLAYED MANY OF THE THEMES THAT EARLIER INTERPRETERS HAD SEEN AND INSTEAD CRAFTED A PLAY THAT SHARPLY IDENTIFIES CALIBAN AND ARIEL AS EXAMPLES OF DISPOSSESSED INDIGENOUS PEOPLES, VICTIMS OF THE BRUTAL POLICIES AND PRACTICES OF THE COLONIZERS."

long-lasting concern with appearance and reality. For example, it transpires that the storm that wrecks the ship is not real, but an illusion created by Prospero, and this is also true of the banquet and the masque—they are symbolic visions created by Prospero to confront the castaways with the truth about their own selves. Prospero is therefore likened to a playwright, creating the action of a play according to his own designs.

Critical interpretations of *The Tempest* in the first two-thirds or so of the twentieth century elaborated for the most part on these standard themes. For example, John Middleton Murry, in his 1936 study, *Shakespeare*, writes:

> The Island is a realm where God is Good, where true Reason rules; it is what would be if Humanity—the best in man—controlled the life of man. And Prospero is a man in whom the best in man has won the victory.... The Island is a realm ...controlled by a man who has become himself, and has the desire, the will and the power to make other men themselves.

Murry continues:

> Poised between Caliban, the creature of the baser elements—earth and water—and Ariel, the creature of the finer—fire and air—is the work of Prospero's alchemy: the loving humanity of Ferdinand and Miranda.

The possibility that Caliban might be seen as representing oppressed indigenous peoples, trodden down by the colonizing powers, did not usually present itself during this period. Instead, Caliban was often seen more in a universal, psychological light as the darker, uncivilized elements in every man's nature, elements that if overcome would be for the betterment of all. One would not wish to denigrate the work of Murry, who was a brilliant and perceptive critic, much renowned in his day, but it is fair to say that in the 1930s, while

# WHAT
# DO I READ
# NEXT?

- *Aimé Césaire: The Collected Poetry*, translated, with introduction and notes by Clayton Eshleman and Annette Smith (1984), is the definitive edition in English of Césaire's poetry. It also includes Césaire's *Notebook of a Return to the Native Land*. This edition contains an introduction and notes as well the original texts in French.

- *The Tragedy of King Christophe* (1963, revised 1970) is a play by Césaire set in Haiti in the early nineteenth century. It follows the rise of the historical figure of Henri Christophe, a slave who became a general in the army of Toussaint Louverture and then declared himself king in 1811. Christophe ruled northern Haiti until 1820, and the play traces his evolution from liberator to tyrant. The play is available in a 2015 edition published by Northwestern University Press, in a translation by Paul Breslin and Rachel Ney.

- *Postcolonial Plays: An Anthology*, edited by Helen Gilbert (2001), is a collection of contemporary postcolonial plays from diverse countries and regions, including Canada, the Caribbean, South and West Africa, Southeast Asia, India, New Zealand and Australia. The introduction describes major themes of the plays, which include race and class, slavery, political corruption, and nationalism.

- Poet and playwright Sir Derek Walcott, from the Caribbean island of Saint Lucia, won the Nobel Prize in Literature in 1992. *Dreams on Monkey Mountain and Other Plays* (1970) is a collection of four of his plays. In the title play, a drunken man, sent to jail to get sober, has a vision in which he becomes a healer and a leader. The play was awarded the 1971 Obie Award for Distinguished Foreign Play when it was produced in New York.

- Nigerian playwright Wole Soyinka was awarded the Nobel Prize in Literature in 1986. His tragedy *The Strong Breed* (1964) is based on a ritual tradition of the Yoruba people in which one man atones for the sins of the community by going into exile. In this case, the man concerned also loses his life. The play can be found in the first volume of Soyinka's *Collected Plays* (1973).

- *Short Plays for Young Actors* (1996), edited by Craig Slaight and Jack Sharrar, is a collection of plays for actors from the age of fourteen to twenty-two. The plays, which range from the serious to the comic, are mostly new works, although some classic plays are also included. There is a substantial introduction about the basics of acting.

- *From Columbus to Castro: The History of the Caribbean, 1492–1969* (1984), by Eric Williams, is a history of the people of the Caribbean islands such as Jamaica, Haiti, Barbados, Trinidad, and Martinique. The book covers slavery and its abolition, the vital importance of sugar, and the various systems of colonialism set up by the Western powers, including Spain, France, and Great Britain.

---

the British Empire remained mostly intact, the rights of colonized peoples was not a topic exactly in the forefront of most people's minds, including those of literary critics.

That began to change in the 1960s, when the pace of decolonization in Africa, the Caribbean, and Latin America increased and a new, postcolonial literature began to spring up. A new awareness began to dawn in the West of the injustices inflicted by the colonial powers during the many decades in which they had ruled countries far from their own shores, largely to their own advantage. Such an awareness also began to seep into criticism of Shakespeare's play.

Postcolonial criticism of *The Tempest* has been examined by Jyotsna Singh in her essay in *Shakespeare: An Oxford Guide*. She notes that by the 1980s, it was common for literary scholars to be less willing to accept the traditional view of Prospero as a godlike figure and to be more sympathetic to the plight of Caliban and the arguments Caliban presents in the play—that the island is his and that he initially welcomed Prospero but was betrayed and enslaved by him. Singh writes,

> Unlike generations of earlier readers, post-colonial critics view Prospero's and Miranda's relations with Caliban as an allegory of European colonialism—one that reveals Shakespeare's own ambivalence toward Prospero's power. Europeans' colonising activities among non-European natives they encountered in the Americas, Africa, and the Caribbean were based on the premise of the "civilising mission." This mission assumed that the natives lacked any culture or formal language until the Europeans brought them the "gifts" of Western language and culture. If the natives resisted European paternal rule, then they were labelled as "savages," beyond redemption.

More than a decade earlier, Césaire had made his own contribution to the re-visioning of *The Tempest*, in the form not of a critical essay but of a creative work in its own right. For *A Tempest*, Césaire took the basic plot and all the characters from Shakespeare's play, although in a mischievous touch he added Eshu, the dark god who plays havoc with the neoclassical divinities summoned to celebrate the betrothal of Ferdinand and Miranda. Césaire downplayed many of the themes that earlier interpreters had seen and instead crafted a play that sharply identifies Caliban and Ariel as examples of dispossessed indigenous peoples, victims of the brutal policies and practices of the colonizers.

To advance his new perspective on an old play, Césaire changed a number of aspects of the dynamic between Caliban and Prospero. In Shakespeare's play, Caliban does not dispute the truth of Prospero's statement that he, Prospero, taught Caliban language, which fits with the notion that before Prospero arrived, Caliban was a "savage," little better than an animal. (Indeed, Miranda, in act 1, scene 2 of *The Tempest*, refers explicitly to Caliban as a "savage.") In Césaire's *A Tempest*, however, Caliban does not let such a statement by Prospero go unchallenged. When Prospero, who refers to Caliban as a "savage...a dumb animal" (act 1, scene 2)

claims that he taught him how to speak, Caliban denies it: "You didn't teach me a thing! Except to jabber in your own language." To make the point explicit, just a few lines earlier in the same scene, Césaire's Caliban utters a word, "Uhuru," in his own language, and Prospero even acknowledges that Caliban is speaking in his "native language" again. The implication is clear: if Caliban had a language before the colonizer Prospero arrived, he also had a culture—a culture that, it is revealed, included respect for the earth, as Caliban explains when he tells Prospero about his mother, Sycorax, a kind of earth goddess. Prospero did not understand or respect this indigenous culture and was instrumental in suppressing it. (Incidentally, *Uhuru* is a Swahili word that means "freedom.")

Césaire also changes how the conflict between Caliban and Prospero plays out. In Shakespeare's play, Caliban softens in the final scene. He refers subserviently to Prospero as his "master" (act 5, scene 1, line 262). After Prospero has indicated that he might pardon him for joining Stephano and Trinculo's plot to kill him, Caliban says, "I'll be wise hereafter / And seek for grace" (act 5, scene 1, lines 294–95), a conciliatory but submissive gesture that the Caliban in *A Tempest* would never even dream of making. Unlike in Shakespeare, there will be no forgiveness between the two; instead, they declare their hatred for each other. Césaire's Caliban pledges continual violent opposition to Prospero, a commitment that makes sense in the light of Césaire's alteration of the ending of the play. In Shakespeare's play, Prospero returns with the other nobles to reclaim his dukedom in Italy, presumably leaving Caliban to reclaim the island. But in *A Tempest*, Prospero changes his mind about leaving, convincing himself he has a duty to stay on the island. As a result, he and Caliban are left alone together to battle it out. Césaire's point seems to be that the colonizer will never leave voluntarily, as in Shakespeare's play; he must be forced out by violent opposition. The ending of *A Tempest* suggests ongoing racial conflict between colonizing whites and colonized black people, and it is clear also that the latter are gaining the upper hand as Prospero grows old and weary.

There is also the matter of Ariel and the changes Césaire rings on that character. In Shakespeare, Ariel is not human but a spirit whose element is the air; it is Ariel who creates

*Miranda and Ferdinand fall in love, but Prospero enslaves Ferdinand* (© *maradon 333 / Shutterstock.com*)

the storm that wrecks the ship and also creates and dissolves the illusory banquet that is set before the nobles. In *A Tempest*, however, Ariel is described as a mulatto slave. This enables Césaire to acknowledge the complexity of colonization, in which white settlers often had sexual relations with the indigenous people, thus producing offspring of mixed race. Making Ariel a mulatto slave who still, it seems, is able to perform all the magical tricks that Shakespeare's airy spirit is capable of is somewhat problematic, of course, but Césaire, whose goal was to develop his political themes, was unlikely to have been bothered by such niceties. Césaire also accepts the ending of Shakespeare's play, in which Ariel is finally granted his freedom, but unlike in Shakespeare, he gives Ariel a cryptic speech in which he hints that he will use his freedom to help others gain theirs, a statement that fills Prospero with a feeling of unease.

Another reason it is important for *A Tempest* that Ariel, like Caliban, be a human slave is that those two characters can then have their debate (in act 2, scene 1) about how best to oppose Prospero. It has been remarked (by a scholar

named Michael Benamou, cited by Janis L. Pallister in *Aimé Césaire*) that the different positions of Ariel and Caliban with regard to that issue resemble the positions taken by Martin Luther King Jr. and Malcolm X during the American civil rights movement of the 1960s, which might well have been in the back of Césaire's mind as he wrote *A Tempest* toward the end of that decade. As Ariel does in the play, King favored nonviolence and an appeal to the moral conscience of white people. In contrast, Malcolm X believed that violence could be justified if it was necessary to achieve civil rights for black people. Interestingly, in *A Tempest*, Caliban tells Prospero that he no longer wishes to be known as Caliban, which is a name Prospero gave him. Instead, he wants to be known as X, "like a man without a name. Or, to be more precise, a man whose name has been stolen." Similarly, Malcolm X was born Malcolm Little, but he rejected that last name as being imposed by a slave owner long in the past and chose X instead, to signify his lost name.

Thus did Césaire tweak Shakespeare's approximately 350-year-old play from an anticolonial point of view to create a new work that

> **IN ESSENCE, CÉSAIRE AFRICANIZES AND NEGRIFIES SHAKESPEARE'S PLAY, TO DEAL WITH THE ETERNAL THEME OF HIS POLITICAL THEATER: AFRICA'S PAST AND PRESENT, AND THE DILEMMA OF THE ENCOUNTER WITH THE EUROPEAN MASTER."**

offered food for thought for a radically different age; the play was a clarion call for the rights of the dispossessed and disempowered peoples across the colonized world. Nearly fifty years later, during a time of continuing global racial and economic inequality, *A Tempest* retains its startling and disturbing relevance.

**Source:** Bryan Aubrey, Critical Essay on *Une Tempête*, in *Drama for Students*, Gale, Cengage Learning, 2018.

### Femi Ojo-Ade

*In the following excerpt, Ojo-Ade examines how Césaire adapts Shakespeare's play to relate to the African diaspora.*

. . . It is not surprising that Prospero's island (deliberate assignment of ownership) is often identified as Bermuda, commonly recognized in Shakespeare's times, as Haiti and/or Cuba. Why not other places, such as Hawaii or Australia or New Zealand? No need to respond. So, Césaire joins the ongoing interpretation, by accepting Caliban's identity as black, but not as an ugly black, and the island as black, but not in the absolute, geographical sense. He eschews the *civilized* proposition of Gonzalo's Utopia, and focuses on the more relevant matters of Slavery and Colonialism and Racism. While Shakespeare does not bother to populate his island even as he and his audience would imagine it to be in the Caribbean (another play on words would suggest the relationship between Caliban and Caribbean), Césaire calls attention to a fact too often forgotten, that the original owners of the islands were Indians (or Caribs), whom the invaders from Europe worked mightily hard to eliminate. Césaire's stroke of genius is in making the two bumbling drunkards, Stephano and Trinculo, identify Caliban as Indian.

In essence, Césaire Africanizes and negrifies Shakespeare's play, to deal with the eternal theme of his political theater: Africa's past and present, and the dilemma of the encounter with the European master. By modifying the qualifier of the English play's title from the definite to the indefinite, from the absolute to the particular, Césaire again subtly calls attention to the singularity of the African experience. Regarding the island, we have already mentioned that the insularity and solitariness go beyond geography to connote psychology in the context of colonialism and slavery. Thus, he uses his artistic magic, so to speak, to include the United States (e.g., Caliban's reference to dogs hounding the slave, p. 88) and to combine slavery and colonialism into a macrocosm of continuous dehumanization and exploitation, thus inextricably linking Africa to the Diaspora.

Part of the process of particularity is the new character construct of Ariel as a mulatto. Shakespeare's choice of name has been debated: Is it an allusion to "aerial," to imply invisibility, or does it have to do with the biblical character (Isaiah, chapter 29) known as "Lion of the Lord?" The latter attribute suggests that Ariel is superior to Caliban and closer to Prospero, lord of the island. And while Shakespeare's Ariel has had a change of gender over the years (first, male; then female from about 1930 until recent times, when it again became male), Césaire's has always been male. In African diasporic history, the mulatto presence has been an integral part of the conundrum, with the constants of white at the top and black at the bottom of the hierarchy.

Let us point out other important differences between Shakespeare and Césaire. After being given alcohol by the drunk Stephano, Caliban accepts him as a god and as his new master and urges the inebriate to avenge him by torturing Prospero and becoming lord of the island. In the end, Caliban learns that Stephano is no god, and that Prospero is invincible. He agrees to obey the latter again and is pardoned for his bad behavior. On the contrary, Césaire's Caliban considers Stephano and Trinculo as partners in the plot and never stops rebelling against Prospero as slave master. In addition, Prospero's and Miranda's contention that Caliban tried to rape her is denied by Césaire's character.

Now, Césaire's play, representing an in-depth study of the encounter between Europe and Africa, establishes African cosmology from the very beginning. Besides what he calls "two supplementary precisions" (Ariel as mulatto and Caliban as black slave), he offers, first, an "addition" of Eshu, "black god-devil," and then the instruction: "The actors enter one after the other and each chooses a mask at his convenience." Before act 1 comes the *meneur de jeu*, a sort of director recalling other theatrical creations of Césaire's, such as the Presenter-Commentator (*Christophe*) and the "Bonimenteur" (*Saison*). The difference here is that this is a psychodrama, and the mask is a symbol of identity and personality, indeed, the essence of the human being. Precisely in Yoruba mythology, there is the legend of the choice of one's head: Ajala is in charge of giving out heads to all human beings coming to earth. One may make a good or bad choice; at times, people refuse a particular head or decide to have it remolded according to their taste. Since Ajala is also known to be a drunk, he sometimes makes mistakes. All this proves the fact of destiny, the possibility to change one's fate and the constancy of struggle in life. Césaire's *meneur* resembles Ajala as he dispenses the masks. It is interesting that he himself chooses the Tempest, "enough to break everything," in order to maintain control and to be certain of the adequacy of the setting. Prospero, remarkably, too, chooses his own mask, which underscores the singular will to power of the civilized tyrant and tormentor. Indeed, Prospero behaves like the unforgiving God: When Ariel asks him to bear with Caliban, who has been revealed to be trying to attack him, Prospero vehemently rejects the notion. "By this insubordination, it's the whole world order he is questioning. Divinity [indulgent] may laugh at it! Me, I have a sense of my responsibilities!" (71). A reminder it is, of M'Siri's pompous assertion in *Saison*, with Katanga expressing the commitment to liquidating Lumumba as a sort of Christian duty. Factoring in the man's magic, one would think of Prospero as a Supreme Being; a paradox it would be, since he is complaining of his dukedom having been usurped by his brother. Furthermore, he becomes a double usurper by taking over the island from Caliban and Ariel.

Regarding Eshu, his presence in the play is a clear statement on the impact of African religion in the Diaspora. In that religion, human destiny is not determined in the absolute by a harsh, unforgiving God of vengeance. There are mobility and movement, will and possibilities for change. In the universe, Eshu, trickster and tempter and tester, is stationed at the crossroads where good and evil meet and can be confused. Forever the prankster, he teases and taunts, underscoring existential flexibility and myriad dangers and challenges facing humans. He can lure one into sin. Therefore, in order to be safe, one appeases him with a sacrifice, thus seeking his favor and assistance. As stated above, the freedom to choose masks implies human will. As the Yoruba say, *Owo eni l'aa fii tunwa eni se* (We can ameliorate our character through our own volition). It is possible to influence fate by insisting, by resisting, by acting with conviction and integrity. One remembers the Sanza Player's statement in *Saison* (act 3, scene 8) urging consideration for Mokutu, that he, like all humans, can change. Unfortunately, the leopard does not change its spots. We shall further explore African religious presence in the psychodrama. As for Christianity, it is linked with the *mission civilisatrice* of slavery and colonialism.

Césaire defines European civilization in terms of capitalist mercantilism. Witness the actions of the two bungling drunks, Trinculo and Stephano. Lost on the island, Trinculo comes upon Caliban lying under a wheelbarrow. Immediately, his racist and materialist mind goes to work:

> Wow! an Indian! Dead or alive? With these non-French races, one never knows…Peuh! In any case, that's all right by me! Dead, I shall find shelter under his rags; I'll make a coat out of it, a cover, a parapet. Alive, I'll make him a prisoner and take him back to Europe and, there, my word, my fortune is made! I'll sell him to a non-resident. No! I'll display him myself in the fairs! My goodness, what a chance! Let's settle down in the warmth and let the storm roar! (58)

Here is the classic predator, the vulture swooping on its prey. It is the businessman counting his booty with no concern for the victim. And one is reminded of the famous colonial fairs in Paris and Brussels and elsewhere, with Africans in cages like exotic animals. And one recalls that, in certain cases, the victims of Europe's exploitation and exhibitionism and sick entertainment never returned home, remaining in the winter wilderness where, destitute, they died of cold and were buried in unmarked, mass graves. Naturally, Trinculo is not too inebriated to affirm his racial superiority or to calculate his potential fortune.

His compatriot and brother in the bottle, Stephano, soon arrives on the scene. Deeper into the bottle, he is tongue-twisted and, seeing Caliban, calls him *Zindien* instead of *Indien*. Still, he is not too far gone into the land of Bordeaux *rouge* or *blanc* to be unable to count the yield of his unexpected booty:

> My word! but it's true, a *Zindian*! Great! No doubt that I am lucky. Imagine, a *Zindian* like that, but that's money! Displayed in a fair! Between the bearded woman and the breeder of fleas, a *Zindian*! An authentic *Zindian* from the Caribbean! Cash, I tell you, or I am the last of the madmen!

> (*Touching Caliban*) But he is very cold! I don't know the *Zindian's* blood temperature, but that one seems very cold to me! Provided he does not die! (59)

The farce gets worse when Stephano makes Caliban drink some alcohol, to warm him up, only to discover a second head, that of Trinculo, which he believes to be Caliban's own! Thus, his capitalist imagination runs wilder than before: "Fantastic! A simple *Zindian*, that's already something, but one with two heads, a Siamese *Zindian*, a *Zindian* with two mouths and eight feet, extraordinary! My fortune is made!" When the two potential traders of *Zindian* exoticism find out about each other's survival of the storm, their common selfishness and shared sense of exploitation—the core of capitalism—reveal the element of conflict often overlooked in civilization. And it all goes back to the mission: After dishonoring their vaunted religion by explaining their safety to the magnanimity of the Drunkard God, they agree to use him. Stephano intones: "He doesn't appear stupid, if one judges by the slope of his throat! I shall endeavor to civilize him…Oh, not too much! But enough for us to be able to *profit from it*" (60, emphasis mine).

Succinctly stated, the civilizing mission is not meant to ameliorate the condition, to humanize or edify Europe's victims, but to establish and maximize their usefulness in the enterprise of exploitation. Stephano's expert estimation of Caliban's character by examining his throat, falls in line with the great scientific accomplishments, from measuring the mass of black brain, the length and brea[d]th of the head, and other body parts, to determine intelligence, an exercise that always led to the conclusion that blacks were/are less intelligent and less endowed than whites in matters going beyond instinctive action . . . .

**Source:** Femi Ojo-Ade, "*Une Tempête*: The Dilemma of the African Diaspora," in *Aimé Césaire's African Theater: Of Poets, Prophets, and Politicians*, Africa World Press, 2010, pp. 252–56.

> **"AIMÉ CÉSAIRE'S MULTI-LEVEL EXPLOITATION OF THE POSSIBILITIES OF THE PLAY-IN-PLAY DEVICE THUS GIVES MASTERFUL EXPRESSION IN THIS TEXT TO HIS POLITICAL MILITANTISM AND IDEOLOGICAL CONCERNS"**

### Maurice Blackman
*In the following excerpt, Blackman analyzes the play-within-a-play device.*

#### … THE PLAY WITHIN THE PLAY

As will already be apparent from this rapid presentation of Césaire's adaptation of *The Tempest*, the doubling device of play-within-play dramaturgy can be seen to function on a number of levels of both the text and the performance of *Une Tempête*. I want to try now to enumerate and comment on these multiple framing or doubling devices before moving on to a more thorough interpretation of them.

Starting from the basic fact of *Une Tempête* being an adaptation—or better, an intercultural appropriation—of a prestigious Shakespearean original, we need to bear in mind that, on the performance level, what we see onstage is constantly framed for us by the representational strategies chosen by Césaire: the play is performed as a psychodrama or elaborate role-play by a group of black actors who don masks to perform both white and black characters, masters and slaves. This performance aspect is foregrounded in the text by the prologue, in which Césaire has the 'Meneur de jeu' call for volunteers or select players for each role. This outer framing device (reminiscent of Genet's use of a similar device in *The Blacks*) has the effect of turning the inner play from an allegory into a symbolic drama embodying the performance styles of traditional African theatre: this performance style is carried through Césaire's text as he introduces elements of black idiolect and of African music and dance, all of which are designed to bring out the Negro values embedded in Césaire's rewriting—the mythical recreation of the world through music and dance; the expression of essential realities through images which often have a sexual or animistic basis outside European cultural norms. Shakespeare's *Tempest*, of course, contains a few well-known songs, but Césaire develops and extends the role of music in his adaptation. He keeps elements of Shakespeare's original songs for Ariel and some of the other characters, but in particular he introduces some songs for Caliban (who has none in Shakespeare): Caliban sings his gods each time he feels threatened by Prospero, and his songs are a kind of survival tactic—indeed, the last word of the play is the chorus of Caliban's song of freedom.

Césaire's appropriation is thus a political act, both in its content—he 'Africanises' Shakespeare's iconic play and brings out a latent political message—and in its performance: the psychodrama will stage a series of dramatic scenes with the aim of liberating the audience (whether black or white) from its complexes through a consciousness-raising exercise.

On the level of the text itself, *The Tempest* is one of the best-known examples of Shakespeare's playful exploitation of the metaphor of theatrical illusion, with its complex interplay of theatre within theatre. At the first degree, the play presents a spectacle in which Prospero is one of the characters; at the second degree, the play presents spectacles of which Prospero is both the director and one of the performers; and at the third degree, the play contains a masque performed by the gods and arranged by Prospero in honour of Miranda and Ferdinand. The whole complex system delights in creating the theatrical illusion and simultaneously reminding the spectator that he or she is watching the performance of a piece of theatre.

Césaire wholeheartedly embraces the Shakespearean game of theatrical illusion in his rewriting, and as we have seen, foregrounds it in a particularly political way in his added prologue. His Prospero, too, is a kind of magus or alchemist, crossed with a theatrical director whose magical powers can impose illusions on the other characters in the play and create spectacles which dazzle both us and the characters. *Une Tempête* recapitulates all of the levels of the play within the play that are already present in *The Tempest*—initial dramatic spectacle of the tempest itself, called up by Prospero; the trial imposed on Ferdinand before he can win the hand of Miranda; the magical illusions and distractions imposed on the other characters; the celebratory masque (whose

decorum is interrupted by the priapic Eshu in Césaire's version)—and even adds a flashback scene to the exposition in Act I in which we see a priest of the Holy Office summoning Prospero before the Inquisition. Césaire's concluding scene is also overtly theatrical, with the passing of time symbolised by the partial lowering and raising of the curtain, and with Prospero visibly aging before our eyes.

But the most striking element of the play within the play, as we have noted above, is the representational strategy of the psychodrama and the masked black actors: these are a constant reminder to the spectator of the theatrical illusion created in *Une Tempête*, presented as the performance of a performance.

## INTERPRETATIONS

Césaire's adaptation and extension of the play-within-the-play devices of the original thus have a primary political function: he refocuses the play's action on Caliban's relations with Prospero, adds some African and Caribbean cultural references to the text, and most importantly, repositions the play in a new outer frame which foregrounds a specifically African style of performance. This deliberate 'Africanisation' or 'negrification' of an iconic text from the dominant culture is a political gesture in itself, which can be read as a post-colonial act of self-liberation through the reconquering of black history, in a sort of parallel to Caliban's effort to reconquer his island from the European usurper.

The outer framing device also represents an act of self-liberation on a personal level, both through the retelling of the story from the black point of view, and from the raised consciousness brought about by the analysis of the colonial relationship expressed in the text. On the one hand, Césaire reveals the 'Prospero complex'—that is, the dilemma of the white coloniser who has to exert his power and exploit the black, but who at the same time resents the fact that he is ultimately dependent on the black in order to continue to be the dominant power. As Prospero says in the final scene (III.5):

> Well I hate you too! For you are the one through whom, for the first time, I have come to doubt myself [...] And now, Caliban, it is me against you! What I have to say to you will be brief: ten times, a hundred times, I have tried to save you, first of all from yourself But you have always responded with rage and venom, like the opossum which hoists itself up on the

rigging of its own tail in order to bite the better the hand that is dragging it out of the darkness of its ignorance! Well, my boy, I will do violence to my normally indulgent nature, and henceforth to your violence I will respond with violence! (pp. 90–91)

On the other hand, Césaire shows Caliban throwing off the colonised black mentality which finally accepts the mythical image of itself imposed by white authority: he refuses Prospero's mystification and imposition of a cultural pattern which makes the black an historically inferior being. The point is made in Caliban's final tirade:

> You must understand me, Prospero: for years I have bowed my head, for years I have accepted, accepted everything: your insults, your ingratitude, and worse, more degrading than all the rest, your condescension. But now it's finished! Finished, you hear! Naturally, for the time being, you are still the stronger one. But I don't give a damn for your strength, nor for your dogs, for that matter, nor for your police, nor your other inventions! And you know why I don't give a damn? Do you want to know? It's because I know that I will have you. Impaled! And on a stake that you yourself have sharpened! Impaled on yourself! Prospero, you are a great illusionist: you know all about lies. And you have lied to me so much, lied about the world, lied to me about myself, that you have ended up imposing on me an image of myself: an underdeveloped man, as you say, an incapable man, that's how you have obliged me to see myself, and it is an image that I hate! And it is false! But now I know all about you, you cancer, and I know myself as well! (pp. 90–91)

On another level, the 'negrification' of Shakespeare's *Tempest* can be seen as a direct expression of an important theme in Césaire's doctrine of negritude—the theme of liberation through cultural expression. Césaire believes that a reaffirmation and adaptation of Negro culture to the modern world, and the abandonment of a servile imitation of dominant white culture, are necessary conditions for the full rehabilitation and liberation of the Negro. His intercultural appropriation of an iconic text about the colonisation of the Caribbean thus represents an act of black cultural rehabilitation that frames the central theme of self-liberation.

In turn, Césaire's appropriation of Shakespeare's text has fascinating parallels with the theme of language as power expressed in the central relationship in his play. Prospero's power comes ultimately from his superior knowledge, his secret books, his control over language. He is the one who named Caliban, and, as he reminds Caliban in Act I scene 2, who taught him to speak and who educated him out of his animal-like state. Caliban's first utterance in the play is 'Uhuru!' the Swahili word for 'freedom', just as his final utterance at the end of the play is the word 'freedom' itself, and his first act of defiance is his verbal assault on Prospero when he greets him in Act I scene 2:

> Good day. But a good day filled as much as possible with wasps, toads, pustules and shit. May today hasten by ten years the day when the birds of the sky and the beasts of the earth gorge themselves on your rotting flesh! (p. 24)

This is the beginning of Caliban's self-liberation, as he rejects the prison of language and the name imposed on him by Prospero and gives himself the possibility of expressing himself in his own terms. Although he initially opposes Ariel's politics of patience in Act II scene 1—

> What I want is (*He shouts*) 'Freedom now!' (p. 36)

—Caliban finally renounces violence in his confrontation with Prospero and instead affirms through song his cultural independence and self-liberation (III.5: p. 89). On the other hand, Prospero's power over language gradually deserts him in his final speech: the stylised process of aging in the final moments of the play is mirrored in his regressive speech patterns, as he passes from declamatory blank verse to nonstandard idiomatic speech, and finally to an almost childish babble (III.5: pp. 91–92)

Aimé Césaire's multi-level exploitation of the possibilities of the play-in-play device thus gives masterful expression in this text to his political militantism and ideological concerns. The very act of appropriating and 'negrifying' Shakespeare's text and refashioning it into a psychodrama of self-liberation from the false consciousness of the colonial mentality and its associated complexes provides an outer frame, in both formal and thematic terms, to the drama that unfolds within it, and represents a highly original use of the device of the play within the play which has both cultural and political ramifications.

**Source:** Maurice Blackman, "Intercultural Framing in Aimé Césaire's *Une Tempête*," in *The Play within the Play: The Performance of Meta-Theatre and Self-Reflection*, edited by Gerhard Fischer and Bernhard Greiner, Rodopi, 2007, pp. 302–306.

### Lucy Rix

*In the following excerpt, Rix considers the play in the context of politics.*

#### THE LATER STAGE: TURNING TO THEATRE

... After completing a model assimilationist education, mainly in Paris, Césaire returned to Martinique in 1939. After the war, he was invited to run on the Communist party ticket in the municipal elections and was elected mayor in 1945. The following year he successfully oversaw Martinique's transition from a colony to a department of France. This was something that he had long struggled for, and which he believed to be a positive change. However, it was to be the first disappointment in a long and often disillusioning political career. It actually resulted in the loss of the limited, but real influence that local people could bring to bear on colonial governors and officials. The whole decision-making process was transferred to Paris, and the colonial governors, who were often residents of Martinique, were replaced by prefects who were less sensitive to local needs. From 1958 to 1964, the sugar industry, which had produced almost all of Martinique's exports, went into serious decline and unemployment rose to 25 per cent. The riots of 1959 in Fort-de-France were directed 'not against the local white Creoles, but against metropolitans ... the metropolitan had, in scarcely more than a decade, become a popular scapegoat for the disruptions and disappointments of departmentalization.' Césaire formed the Parti Progressiste Martiniquais in 1958: its aim was not independence, but autonomy. The colonial legacy of social, economic and psychological destruction has left Martinique significantly dependent on France for financial support (in the 1970s, France was supplying half Martinique's revenue). Although nominally it has been abandoned, colonialism remains both overtly and insidiously in place, as Susan Frutkin notes: 'French assistance has been along social rather than developmental lines, and, while a higher standard of living has accompanied the infusion of public funds, in reality it reflects an inflated state of welfare living rather than any improvement in the island's productive capabilities.'

This was the political climate in which *Une tempête* was written, Césaire having turned to theatre for a more accessible cultural channel through which to communicate his views:

> Blacks from now on must make their history. And the history of the blacks will truly be what they will make of it ... a black writer cannot enclose himself in an ivory tower. There are things to be understood ... it is necessary to speak clearly, speak concisely, to get the message across—and it seems to me that the theatre can lend itself to that.

Although Césaire here stresses the importance of transmitting 'the message', the particular form of theatre to which he turned was actually one of great flexibility. It seems that what may be interpreted as a desire to find a more transparent medium resulted in the discovery of a highly diverse and shifting site of performance. Jean-Michel Serreau, who collaborated with Césaire on all three of his plays (Césaire has said that Serreau's death contributed to his decision not to continue writing drama), sought 'an open or exploded scenic space, overtly constructed rather than self-enclosed, an environment for registering rhythmic movement rather than capturing a static scene'. In making explicit the process of construction and impermanence, this theatre could be mobile and provisional: it could adapt itself to an individual environment rather than the audience adapting themselves to the institutional stasis of traditional theatre. The message, then, becomes an integral part of the dramatic process, as Césaire highlights in the opening masking scene of *Une tempête*. In this scene, what was originally intended to be an entirely black cast dons masks in order to designate the race of each character. Césaire suggests that the allocation of masks (and therefore race) is an arbitrary process by showing each actor to be choosing his or her mask:

> Come gentlemen, help yourselves. To each his character and to each character his mask. You, Prospero? Why not? His is an unfathomable will to power. You, Caliban? Well, well, that's revealing. You, Ariel! I have no objections. And what about Stephano? And Trinculo? No takers? Ah, just in time! It takes all sorts to make a world.

One of Césaire's pointed changes to Shakespeare's cast list was to specify Caliban as a black slave and Ariel as a mulatto slave. Prospero's race and nationality are left unspecified and, although the obvious assumption is that the actor will don a white mask, Césaire avoids any assumption that 'white' is a neutral or normative race—because every actor wears a mask, the white race is displayed as equally constructed and performed. As Robert Eric, Livingston comments: 'The effect of the maskplay is to de-essentialize the construction of race, to set up a tension between the racial script and its performance'. From the outset, therefore, Césaire undermines his own racial stereotyping of a black Caliban as the violent rebellious slave (the 'Malcolm X' figure) and Ariel as the 'whitened', Christian 'Uncle Tom' mulatto, who hopes to assert change through non-violent means (the Martin Luther King figure). The overlaying of a specifically American colonial situation (which Césaire himself posited and which is evident in the echoes of the US black leaders' speeches in the speeches of Caliban and Ariel) adds to the play the contemporary politics of the Black Power movement. This compression of colonial history (remembering that the first performance of the play was set in pioneer America) produces a reinforcing of the simultaneous commentary offered by the play on both the historical condition of slavery and its effect on contemporary Martinique. Universal themes of power and colonialism are shown to be locked in constant combat with specifics of time and locality. As Homi Bhabha points out in this essay's second epigraph, the disruption of the traditional Western teleological conception history offers one way of levering open the holes and voids of the colonial story.

Re-tracing 'black history' on the stage reveals what Glissant has observed to be a vertiginous process: 'For history is not only absence for us, it is vertigo. The time that was never ours we must now possess. We do not see it stretch into our past and calmly take us into tomorrow, but it explodes in us as a compact mass, pushing through a dimension of emptiness where we must with difficulty and pain put it all back together.' Césaire's choice of dramatic form destabilizes authorial control and rejects the concept of uncontaminated reading. As Helen Gilbert and Joanne Tompkins note, 'most postcolonial criticism overlooks drama, perhaps because of its apparently impure form: playscripts are only a part of theatre experience, and performance is therefore difficult to document.'

Despite Césaire's achievement of both beginning to develop a specific space for 'black' culture and, at the same time, highlighting the constructed nature of racial identity, there remain apparent racial cliches in the play that are less straightforward to explain or justify. For example, Western culture is characterized as the height of Enlightenment rationalism (epitomized by the measured dance and mannered speeches of the prudish Olympian goddesses) and 'black culture' is portrayed in an equally hackneyed manner, as a vibrant glorification of chaos and untamed nature, personified by Eshu (the Yoruba god of boundaries between worlds) . . .

. . . This opposition feels uncomfortable because it seems to perpetuate stereotyping that was, and continues to be, employed by colonialists. However, read within the context of a play that Césaire specified as having the 'ambience of a psychodrama', to simplify his treatment as stereotyping or essentialism would be reductive. In fact, by placing such blatant stereotypes on the stage, Césaire reveals and displays internalized and entrenched racial images, and thereby provokes discussion.

Additionally, the manner in which Césaire juggles and undermines rôles and characters ensures that an atmosphere of impermanence and humour is maintained. From the very start of the play, Prospero's role as theatre director is usurped by the mysterious 'Messeur de jeu' who supervises the random distribution of actors' parts and who also generates the tempest itself. Thus, despite Prospero's later rantings about conducting the score of the island, during the first scene we see him relegated to an anonymous actor. Not only are racial rôles displayed as being constructed through masking, but the play is also frequently interrupted by characters usurping the rôles of others: Césaire himself takes Shakespeare's place; Eshu intrudes into the Western pantheon; Ferdinand plays at being a slave and Stephano and Trinculo at being kings and generals. Rôles and subjects are exploded and temporary, they can be taken or handed out; despite Césaire's desire to write the black subject into existence, the play's self-conscious treatment of performance tends repeatedly to shake off the potential solidification of racial essence.

*Une tempête* is also an urgent play of protest, written at a time when Césaire could see the possibility of autonomy for Martinique (let alone independence) slipping further and further out of reach. Although *négritude* and its association with a return to African roots has been heavily criticized for its reductionism, Césaire needed to maintain the momentum of a waning struggle. He was well aware that *négritude*'s creation of Africa was a textual process: 'Of course my knowledge of Africa was bookish; I and my whole generation were dependent on what whites wrote about it' The very textuality of Africa enables its appropriation to an anticolonialist cause. As Benita Parry observes:

> As I read them [Césaire and Fanon], both affirmed the invention of an insurgent, unified black self, acknowledged the revolutionary energies released by valorizing the cultures denigrated by colonialism and, rather than construing the colonialist relationship in terms of negotiations with the structures of imperialism, privileged coercion over hegemony to project it as a struggle between implacably placed forces, an irony made all too obvious in enunciations inflected, indeed made possible, by these very negotiations....

**Source:** Lucy Rix, "Maintaining the State of Emergence/y: Aimé Césaire's *Une Tempête*," in *The Tempest and Its Travels*, edited by Peter Hulme and William H. Sherman, Reaktion Books, 2000, pp. 241–45.

## SOURCES

Bruckner, D. J. R., "Theater in Review," in *New York Times*, October 16, 1991, http://www.nytimes.com/1991/10/16/theater/theater-in-review-112191.html?mcubz=2 (accessed June 10, 2017).

Césaire, Aimé, *A Tempest*, translated by Richard Miller, TCG Translations, 2002.

Cornevin, Robert, "Martinique," in *Encyclopædia Britannica*, https://www.britannica.com/place/Martinique (accessed June 10, 2017).

Gallagher, Mary, "Aimé Césaire and Francophone Postcolonial Thought," in *Postcolonial Thought in the French-Speaking World*, edited by Charles Forsdick and David Murphy, Liverpool University Press, 2009, p. 35.

Kelley, Robin D. G., "Poetry and the Political Imagination: Aimé Césaire, Negritude & the Applications of Surrealism," in *A Tempest*, by Aimé Césaire, TCG Translations, 2002, p. xi.

Murry, John Middleton, *Shakespeare*, Jonathan Cape, 1936, reprint, 1954, pp. 395–96, 402.

Pallister, Janis L., *Aimé Césaire*, Twayne Publishers, 1991, pp. 89, 96.

Shakespeare, William, *The Tempest*, Methuen, 1980, pp. 32, 129, 131.

Singh, Jyotsna, "Post-colonial Criticism," in *Shakespeare: An Oxford Guide*, edited by Stanley Wells and Lena

Cowan Orlin, Oxford University Press, 2003, https://www.bl.uk/shakespeare/articles/post-colonial-reading-of-the-tempest (accessed June 21, 2017).

## FURTHER READING

Arnold, James A., *Modernism and Negritude: The Poetry and Poetics of Aimé Césaire*, Harvard University Press, 1981.

> This study focuses on Césaire's poetry but has commentary on the drama as well, including *A Tempest*.

Loomba, Ania, *Colonialism/Postcolonialism*, 3rd ed., Routledge, 2015.

> Loomba examines all aspects of colonial and postcolonial studies, including history and significant features, anticolonial thought, recent developments and how feminist and postcolonial thought intersect. The third edition includes a new introduction and sections on such contemporary issues as globalization and environmental crises.

Ojo-Ade, Femi, *Aimé Cesaire's African Theatre: Of Poets, Prophets and Politicians*, Africa World Press, 2010.

> This is a critical reading of Césaire's work in drama that assesses his historical importance from both colonial and postcolonial perspectives. It also includes all Césaire's plays in English translation and an interview with Césaire.

Young, Robert J. C., *Postcolonialism: A Very Short Introduction*, Oxford University Press, 2003.

> In this survey, Young discusses the history and significance of postcolonialism, with specific historical examples. He also examines the fiction of postcolonial writers such as Gabriel García Márquez and Salman Rushdie, and postcolonial theorists such as Edward Said, Frantz Fanon, and Gayatri Spivak.

## SUGGESTED SEARCH TERMS

Aimé Césaire

Césaire AND A Tempest

Césaire AND A Tempest AND allegory

Césaire AND A Tempest AND Shakespeare

postcolonial literature

anticolonial literature

Caribbean drama

Negritude AND Césaire

Césaire AND Martinique

# A View from the Bridge

**ARTHUR MILLER**

**1955**

*A View from the Bridge*, by famed American playwright Arthur Miller, is a psychological family tragedy set in the largely Italian neighborhood of Red Hook, Brooklyn. The play is retrospectively narrated by a lawyer, Alfieri, who makes clear from his opening monologue that the episode in question came to an unfortunate end. It revolves around a longshoreman—a laborer who loads and unloads docked ships—named Eddie, who must cope with two challenging transitions in his life: his beloved niece's reaching maturity and starting to make her own way in the world, and his wife's welcoming two Sicilian cousins to stay with them in a time of need. Despite having several interactions with Eddie, Alfieri can do little more than stand by as the dramatic tale unfolds.

As Miller related in other settings, the foundation for the play was a story told to him by a real-life lawyer in the Brooklyn waterfront area named Vinnie Longhi, about a man who found himself in precisely the situation described for Eddie. Initially shying away from the story, which he heard in 1947 and which seemed already too complete, Miller at last returned to it with the first one-act production of *A View from the Bridge*, which debuted at New York's Coronet Theater on September 29, 1955. Not entirely satisfied, Miller revised and extended the play, in part by changing monologues originally written in free verse or blank verse into prose, for a two-act production staged at London's Comedy

*Arthur Miller* ( © *Library of Congress, Prints & Photographs Division, Reproduction number LC-USZ62-109630 (b&w film copy neg.)* )

Theatre beginning October 11, 1956. The original version is the one found in *A View from the Bridge: Two One-Act Plays* (1955). The two-act version, which is discussed here, is found in Miller's *Eight Plays* (1981) and other omnibus editions, such as *The Penguin Arthur Miller: Collected Plays* (2015).

## AUTHOR BIOGRAPHY

Arthur Asher Miller was born on October 17, 1915, in Manhattan, New York City, to a well-off Jewish couple who lived in then-prosperous Harlem. His father owned a coat-manufacturing business. The young Arthur was not inclined toward intellectual pursuits, preferring almost anything that involved physical activity. He enjoyed playing baseball and football, ice skating, and swimming, and by his teen years he was dabbling in carpentry—gaining enough skill to build a back porch for his family's home. The family moved to the relatively rural Midwood area of Brooklyn in 1929, as the coat business first slackened, then collapsed entirely with the stock-market crash that year. Common labor

soon became a mainstay of Miller's young-adult life; over the next few years he would hold jobs ranging from bakery delivery boy, dishwasher, and waiter to warehouse clerk, truck driver, and factory hand. After he graduated from high school, he took a position as a clerk, during which time he first found himself engrossed in literature—starting, of all places, with *The Brothers Karamazov*, Fyodor Dostoevsky's greatest masterpiece. Miller suddenly felt that he was born to be a writer.

Successfully arguing that his poor high school grades did not reflect his capacities, Miller enrolled at the University of Michigan as a journalism student in 1934. He once joked that he chose journalism because he heard that that department gave out prizes—and indeed he proceeded to start winning prizes, not for journalism but for plays that he wrote. He won the university's Avery Hopwood Award for best play of the year twice, and another honor earned him a substantial cash prize and brought his work to the stage in Detroit. Graduating in 1938 and returning to New York, he worked with the Depression-era Federal Theatre Project and married his college sweetheart, Mary Grace Slattery, with whom he would have two children. He began writing and selling radio plays as well as film scripts—and thereby realizing how beholden scriptwriters were to the advertisers and executives of the stations and companies that produced them. During World War II, though he was unable to serve in the military due to an old injury, Miller toured army camps and wrote both a fictional movie and a nonfiction book based on the experience. His first Broadway play, *The Man Who Had All the Luck*, was produced in 1944; its run lasted less than a week.

Miller's level of success rose over the course of the following decade. He won the New York Drama Critics' Circle Award for *All My Sons* (1947) and that same award as well as the Pulitzer Prize for Drama for his renowned *Death of a Salesman* (1949). His works were steadily adapted for radio, television, and film, sometimes by himself, and his presence in Hollywood allowed him to meet the woman who, after he divorced his first wife, became his second, film star Marilyn Monroe. *A View from the Bridge* (1955) represented the height of his success—not because his talents waned after that, but because he became a target of the House Un-American Activities Committee (HUAC) and Senator

Joseph McCarthy's dogged hunt for Communist sympathizers. Miller had indeed supported far-left political causes, some of which involved the Communist Party, but only until 1950, and he declared before HUAC in 1956 that he would no longer support a Communist cause. What became a bigger problem was his morally upstanding refusal to name names of others who had participated in the same activities he had. He was ultimately convicted of contempt of Congress in 1957 and fined, though the following year an appeal reversed the conviction. Miller wrote very little during this period, and though his career was far from over, his greatest works were behind him.

In the last several decades of his life, Miller published additional plays as well as journals, short stories, and essays. His later plays were produced in such esteemed sites as the Lincoln Center Repertory Theater, but not on Broadway. In his personal life, he divorced Monroe and in 1962 married photographer Ingeborg Morath, with whom he would have two more children. He held a number of highly esteemed positions—including president of PEN and delegate to Democratic National Conventions—and eventually lived mainly in his country home in Roxbury, Connecticut. He died there of congestive heart failure at the age of eighty-nine on February 10, 2005.

## PLOT SUMMARY

### Act One

*A View from the Bridge* opens on a set with multiple stage areas: in the center is the living/dining room area of Eddie and Beatrice's apartment, to the front and sides are the street outside the apartment building, to the right is a desk representing Mr. Alfieri's law office, and there is also a telephone booth. Mr. Alfieri enters, passes two men on the street, and stations himself inside his office at his desk. He speaks directly to the audience—he is both character and narrator—about the seedy nature of the Red Hook docks area of Brooklyn and his quirky interest in working there. He suggests that the fascinating case the audience will soon witness led to a bloody end.

Having entered on the street, Eddie chats briefly with his friends Louis and Mike and then heads into the apartment. His niece, Catherine, is buoyant about a new skirt and plans to

# MEDIA ADAPTATIONS

- Renzo Rossellini composed an Italian opera based on Miller's play, *Uno sguardo dal ponte*, with the libretto adapted by Gerardo Guerrieri. The opera premiered on March 11, 1961, in Rome, and the first US performance came in Philadelphia on October 17, 1967.

- A 1962 film bearing the French title *Vu du pont* was directed by Sidney Lumet and produced by Transcontinental Films, with an adapted screenplay by Norman Rosten and a running time of 110 minutes. The film was released in the United States with Miller's original title.

- A New Zealand production of Miller's play directed by Ivo van Hove on July 5, 2015, was released as *National Theatre Live: A View from the Bridge*.

go out. Eddie judgmentally expresses his concerns about the attention she has been attracting from men on the street, almost bringing her to tears. Changing the subject, he announces that Beatrice's cousins have arrived, which sends Beatrice into a panic, because she has not fully prepared the apartment, having expected them the following week. Eddie expresses his concern that the cousins' staying with them will lead to his sleeping on the floor, so Beatrice coddles him.

Catherine excitedly reports having gotten a stenographer's job at a local plumbing company, but Eddie objects—though he softens at mention of the pay of fifty dollars per week. Still, he had wanted her to get a classier job, to help her move up in the world. Eddie finally agrees to let her take the job, but he specifies that she should not trust any of the men there. Regarding the cousins, when Catherine asks Eddie what to do if someone asks about them, he insists that everyone must say absolutely nothing; apparently they are undocumented immigrants. When Catherine steps out to get Eddie a cigar, he and Beatrice show signs of relational stress, both imagining that the other has been angry.

When the lights go down on the scene, Alfieri appears now at the front of the stage, affirming that Eddie was a good man. The cousins had come at ten o'clock.

A friend named Tony escorts Marco and Rodolpho to the apartment door and leaves them there. They knock, Eddie lets them in, and they all make introductions. Marco thanks Beatrice and Eddie for letting him and his brother live with them for the time being. He wants to send as much money as possible home to his malnourished wife and three children in Sicily. Eddie starts to show a dislike of Rodolpho, who is boisterous with laughter and questions, while Catherine shows particular interest in him. Rodolpho dreams of being a motorcycle messenger working grand hotels in Italy. He is also a singer, and he demonstrates his talent with the jazz song "Paper Doll." Eddie politely suggests that being quieter would be prudent. When Eddie notices that Catherine is wearing high heels, he tells her to change; when she comes back, she offers Rodolpho sugar for his coffee.

The scene ends, and Alfieri ponders the fact that Eddie, though he could not have anticipated it, turned out to have a destiny. Weeks passed, and he was troubled.

As Beatrice approaches the house, Eddie, standing in the doorway, mentions that it is after eight, and she suggests that the movie at the Paramount ran long. In response to his questions, she reveals that Catherine is indeed thinking about marriage. In turn, Eddie questions Rodolpho's behaving like "a weird," occasionally bursting out in song and making everyone laugh too much. Beatrice expresses her own concern about when she is going to "be a wife again"— that is, when they will renew intimate physical relations. He evades the line of questioning and reaffirms his doubts about Rodolpho's character.

Beatrice goes inside, and Louis and Mike pass by. Mike's comments seem to confirm the strange impression Eddie has gotten of Rodolpho. As the two longshoremen leave, Catherine and Rodolpho return. Though Eddie expresses not wanting Catherine to go outside of Brooklyn, Rodolpho starts trying to persuade Eddie to let them go to Broadway. Soon Rodolpho goes for a walk, leaving Eddie to chat alone with Catherine. He eventually declares that Rodolpho is using her to get a passport, and she enters the house sobbing indignantly. Beatrice chews Eddie out, and he goes for a walk. Beatrice

counsels Catherine to take her life into her own hands and marry Rodolpho.

The lighting shifts, and Eddie arrives at Alfieri's office. After Alfieri narrates his impressions upon Eddie's entrance, he turns and picks up the conversation at the point where Eddie has just finished explaining the situation with his niece. Alfieri does not understand whether Eddie has any question actually concerning the law. Eddie reiterates his uncomfortable feelings about Rodolpho, but Alfieri advises him to let the situation alone, because he has no legal recourse—presuming that he does not want to threaten their presence in America by calling immigration officials. Eddie acknowledges that he does not. Alfieri suggests that Eddie loves Catherine too much, that a man raising a niece to maturity might get mixed up about his feelings for her. Eddie sidesteps the implicit accusation by returning to the question of Rodolpho's character. Eddie departs, and Alfieri narrates how he was left feeling very alarmed, though there were yet no concrete misdeeds to point to.

Eddie, Beatrice, Catherine, Marco, and Rodolpho are finishing dinner. The Italians regale the Americans with stories of the old world. As they speak of how "free" things are with regard to men and women in America, Eddie indicates that Rodolpho has in fact been feeling too free with Catherine and gets riled up about the situation. When he calms down and sits on his rocker, Catherine provocatively puts "Paper Doll" on the phonograph and asks Rodolpho to dance. As Eddie gets tense again, it comes out that Rodolpho is also an excellent cook, and Eddie flares up once more. He suggests that what the men should really all do is go to a boxing match, and he prods Rodolpho into taking an impromptu lesson. They jab lightly at first, but Eddie escalates the intensity until getting a square blow to Rodolpho's face. Rodolpho shakes it off and resumes dancing with Catherine. Marco challenges Eddie to pick a chair up by the bottom of one leg, but Eddie cannot; Marco can, lifting the chair threateningly over Eddie's head and smiling. The curtain drops.

### Act Two

Alfieri, at his desk, narrates that on December 23, a case of whisky slipped out of its net on the docks. Beatrice was shopping, Marco was working, and Rodolpho, who was not hired that day, was left home with Catherine.

Rodolpho mentions the money he has saved up, and Catherine asks whether he would want to take her back to Italy. He balks, wondering why he would leave a rich country to bring a wife to a poor country while having no job or prospects. When she asks whether he would still marry her if they had to go back, he replies that he would not marry her only to bring her to Italy, because he wants to live in America with her—and is insulted that she would suggest he just wants the necessary papers to stay in the country. They talk about Eddie, then Beatrice, and finally Rodolpho coaxes Catherine into joining him in the bedroom.

Eddie appears on the street, drunk. He goes in the house, and Catherine emerges from the bedroom straightening her dress. When Rodolpho soon also emerges, Eddie tells him to leave immediately, without Catherine. She objects, but he seizes her and kisses her on the lips; when Rodolpho tries to intervene, Eddie grabs him, holds him for a moment, and kisses him too. Believing he has proven something, he reasserts his order for Rodolpho to leave, alone, then stumbles out.

Alfieri reports that he next saw Eddie on December 27, when their exchange left Alfieri feeling strangely powerless. Eddie enters the office, and the conversation picks up with Alfieri asking about Rodolpho's refusing to leave. After Eddie sticks to his talking points about his responsibility toward Catherine and Rodolpho's insufficiently masculine nature, Alfieri begs him one last time to leave them alone; to do otherwise will only alienate him from everyone around him. Eddie leaves, stubborn, and Alfieri follows, calling to him hopelessly.

Eddie appears at the phone booth. He calls the Immigration Bureau and reports, anonymously, the pair of undocumented men staying on the ground floor of 441 Saxon Street in Brooklyn. After hanging up, he passes Louis and Mike on the street. Eddie enters his house, where Beatrice is packing up Christmas decorations. She has already helped her cousins move to Mrs. Dondero's apartment upstairs. When Eddie starts up about restraining Catherine's activities, Beatrice loses her temper. Puffing his chest, Eddie vaguely demands respect, finally saying that he is tired of the questions about what he does or does not want to do in the bedroom. Eddie tries to blame her for having changed and demands that she take him at his

word no matter what. As for Catherine, Beatrice points out that if he had not sheltered her so much, she might not have fallen in love with the first decent and interesting man who happened along. He tries to suggest that he will let her go out in the evenings now, but she points out that it is too late. She tries to persuade him to go to their niece's wedding next week. When Catherine comes down, Beatrice gets her and Eddie to reconcile for the moment. Catherine gets permission to bring more pillowcases upstairs for the two other boarders also there, but Eddie suddenly objects to putting all the submarines—a term for those arriving below-decks as undocumented immigrants—together.

Two immigration officers knock, and Eddie instructs Catherine to run up the fire escape and lead Marco and Rodolpho out. She is confused and upset, but the officers start hollering, and she rushes out. The officers enter, sweep around the apartment, then split up to head upstairs via both the inside and outside stairways. Soon after, the officers, the four Italians, and Catherine come down the stairs, with Catherine pleading desperately for Rodolpho's freedom. When he gets a chance, Marco breaks free in order to spit in Eddie's face. Enraged, Eddie starts yelling, but when they get outside, Marco publicly accuses Eddie of killing his children (by ruining Marco's chances of continuing to send money home to them). All the neighbors, including Mr. Lipari, Louis, and Mike, walk away, ignoring Eddie's pleas for sympathy. Still enraged, Eddie says he will kill Marco.

The lights rise on a prison reception room (perhaps, depending on the performance, the same desk used to represent Alfieri's office). Alfieri insists that Marco agree not to commit any crimes before he bails him out. Rodolpho insists too, even though Marco's deportation is certain, so that Marco can work in the meantime. Rodolpho and Catherine will solve things for him by marrying.

In the apartment, Eddie is in his rocker, and Beatrice appears in fine clothes. She says she is going out, but Eddie reiterates his decision that if she goes, she can never come back. Catherine appears and says they need to get going because the priest will not wait; when Beatrice says Catherine should go without her, Catherine berates Eddie for his selfishness. Rodolpho arrives, ominously indicating that Marco is coming—as soon as he finishes praying. Catherine and Beatrice start begging Eddie to leave, and Rodolpho offers a humble apology for any wrongdoing, but Eddie remains indignant and unyielding over Marco's insults. Marco arrives outside and vindictively calls to Eddie, who steps outside. Eddie demands a public apology from Marco, then promptly attacks him, but Marco fends him off with a blow to the neck and calls Eddie an animal. Eddie takes out a knife, and Louis tries to intercede, but Eddie raises the knife threateningly. Marco still will not apologize, so Eddie rushes him, but Marco manages to deflect and redirect his arm so that Eddie stabs himself, falling to the ground. Eddie dies in Beatrice's arms.

Alfieri steps out of the crowd to deliver an epilogue about respecting Eddie, to an extent, for living out his feelings to the fullest—though "it is better to settle for half"—and about his mourning Eddie with a sense of alarm.

# CHARACTERS

## Mr. Alfieri

The lawyer who narrates the drama is in his fifties and somehow feels an important connection with Brooklyn's Red Hook area. His wife and friends think he should prefer something classier, but he realizes that laborers like Eddie are the sorts who do not just "settle for half" when it comes to engaging with life, and he appreciates that. Still, he laments that he felt powerless to alter the course of Eddie's life—and death—despite his repeated efforts to persuade Eddie to just let go of Catherine. Alfieri even quite forthrightly suggests that there is something unwholesome about Eddie's affection for Catherine—that he loves her more than an uncle should love a niece—but it seems Eddie is too wrapped up in that love to let the admonition sink in. For Alfieri to have pressed the point further might have risked an explosion of violence then and there, especially given how Eddie reacts *furiously* when Alfieri insinuates that deep down Eddie wants to marry Catherine himself. After all, Alfieri is only a lawyer, not a psychotherapist.

## Tony Bereli

Tony is the friend—and apparent Mafia connection—who ushers Marco and Rodolpho to Eddie and Beatrice's doorstep and also coordinates their work situation.

## Beatrice Carbone

Eddie's spouse is, as was common in that era, largely constrained to the role of housewife; that is, Eddie does his best to constrain her to that role. But she clearly has her own opinions and understands the complicated family situation far better than Eddie realizes, leading her to urge Catherine to take advantage of Rodolpho's wholehearted affections and get out of the house while she can. Beatrice is surely partly hoping that Catherine's departure will encourage Eddie to refocus his romantic energy toward his wife, as he most certainly ought to. For all his difficulties and challenges, Beatrice greatly mourns her husband's death.

## Eddie Carbone

Eddie and his complicated psychology are at the center of the play. Here he is, having helped raise his niece in place of her deceased parents, and all he wants, or so he thinks, is what is best for her. As affectionate parents or surrogate parents are liable to do, however, he believes that what is best for her is sheltering her and shielding her from all the possibilities in the world. Now comes along a charming young gentleman whom she falls for, and Eddie cannot stand the idea of her running off with him—because Rodolpho's situation as an immigrant seems too desperate, and Rodolpho himself seems, in Eddie's bigoted opinion, insufficiently manly. Eddie takes this as evidence that Rodolpho "ain't right"—that is, that he is homosexual—and cannot be serious about his affection for Catherine. Unfortunately, Eddie gets too bottled up in his own ill-informed perspective, his indignity over the situation gradually turns to rage, and when his rage gets redirected toward himself, he dies.

## Catherine "Katie"

Catherine is usually called "Katie" by her aunt and uncle, Beatrice and Eddie, who have raised her since an unspecified age. Katie has reached a level of maturity that means she is ready to go out into the world and not only meet people but also explore her own identity through relationships with them. The only problem is that her uncle has grown too attached to her and does not want to let her engage in that exploration. Beatrice does not exactly blame Katie for her uncle's attachment, but she does point out that sitting on the tub to chat with Eddie while he shaves in his underwear, for example, as well as walking around the house in her slip, makes the wrong impression, or sends the wrong message, or no longer seems appropriate—or all of the above. As a young girl, of course, Katie could be close with her uncle in an entirely innocent way, and, as she aged, she maintained this innocence about the relationship. But Katie realizes that Beatrice is right about her needing to get out of the house when the drunken Eddie seizes and kisses her on the lips, in what amounts to an act of sexual assault. As Katie later implicitly but caustically informs him, with this heinous act he lost any right to reprimand anybody else about their actions, and at this point she is finally indeed more than happy to get out of the house. Nevertheless, like Beatrice, she mourns Eddie's death.

## Charley

The character identified in the script as the First Immigration Officer is named Charley. The two officers are quite efficient at getting their job done, covering the escape routes in the apartment building so that the men they are seeking are effectively trapped inside.

## Dominick

The Second Immigration Officer is named Dominick.

## Mrs. Dondero

Not appearing in the play, Mrs. Dondero is the older woman upstairs with extra space to rent out to Marco and Rodolpho as well as the two newcomers.

## Mr. and Mrs. Lipari

Mr. Lipari is the neighborhood butcher, and a nephew of his is one of the newly arrived men rounded up by the immigration officers. When Eddie pleads with him not to believe Marco's accusation, Mr. Lipari and his wife simply turn away. This does not exactly bear out Eddie's earlier heated suggestion that the Lipari family is bad-tempered.

## Louis

A fellow longshoreman of Eddie's, Louis always hangs out with Mike. They like to go bowling.

## Marco

An Italian mason and general handyman, Marco, alongside his younger brother, Rodolpho, goes to work as a common docks laborer upon his arrival in the United States. His wife and three children back in Sicily are essentially starving, and at least one seems to have tuberculosis, so he has come to the United States to try to earn and send home as much money as possible. Referred to only as the "syndicate" in the play, the Mafia are the ones who have arranged the brothers' illegal immigration and daily work. Marco is immensely strong but also described in the stage directions as "*tender*" and "*quiet-voiced*." He is friendly with his cousin Beatrice and her husband, but when he and Rodolpho are rounded up by immigration officers, Marco quickly realizes that Eddie—who had made clear his hostility toward Rodolpho—was responsible. It is not clear whether Marco is intent on taking his revenge to the level of murder: he ultimately engages in a fight with Eddie without bearing any weapons and turns Eddie's knife back on himself only in what seems like legitimate self-defense.

## Mike

A friend of Louis and Eddie's, Mike enjoys bowling. When he recalls all the funny things Rodolpho has said and done, he can hardly stop laughing.

## Nancy

Catherine's mother, Nancy, was Beatrice's sister. Eddie suggests that he is the one who specifically promised to the dying Nancy that he would be responsible for her daughter, Katie. It would seem more likely that Nancy would have expected such a promise from her sister, Beatrice—but it is possible that Nancy was enough under the sway of patriarchal American culture to consider Beatrice's husband the one in the position of ultimate authority in the relationship. Or perhaps Eddie simply assumed that authority for himself and made a promise that the dying Nancy did not need or even want from him in particular.

## Rodolpho

Marco's brother, Rodolpho, is, quite simply, the most pleasant person in the play. He is always quick with smiles, laughs, buoyant comments, and a positive attitude. Liable to burst into song among the presumably stoical, practical longshoremen at the docks, he delights even them. Eddie fears that this delight is actually derogatory—that everyone is laughing *at* Rodolpho for acting so differently from them. He especially fears that this difference is a sign of homosexuality. But when Eddie speaks with Louis and Mike, it is not at all clear that Mike's delight carries any derogatory sense. In Mike's words, when Rodolpho's around, "everybody's happy." It is, in fact, comically ironic that Eddie should think that there is something wrong with someone because he makes everyone around him happy. Although Eddie refuses to believe it, by the play's end it seems clear that Rodolpho truly loves Catherine and wants to spend his life with her.

### Two "Submarines"

As they are called in the dramatis personae (the list of characters at the beginning of the script), the Two "Submarines," or undocumented immigrants, who take refuge in Mrs. Dondero's apartment include a nephew of Mr. Lipari's.

## THEMES

### Patriarchy

From early in the opening scene, it is apparent that the Carbone household is under the influence of ideas of patriarchy—that the man who earns the money considers himself the one in charge and expects his word to amount to law. Eddie's dominating words and actions make this perfectly clear, but it is also apparent in the attitudes of Catherine and Beatrice. Whether or not they believe that men should hold all positions of authority and women should defer to them, they have little choice but to function in both a society and a family organized as such. Catherine evidently possesses an extraordinary intelligence, one allowing her to graduate from high school at the age of sixteen and be on the verge of graduating at the top of her class in stenographer's school at the age of seventeen. And yet if she performs so well intellectually, the modern reader wonders, why is she only going to stenographer's school?

One reason is that in the 1950s, when the play is understood to be set, many colleges did not yet admit women, especially into programs for white-collar professions. On top of this, perhaps stenographer's school is all Eddie could afford—or all he cared to decide that he could afford. Thus, the highly intelligent Catherine is delighted at the prospect of getting a stenographer's job at a plumbing company, while Beatrice is delighted at the prospect that "some day she could be a secretary." Only in a painfully patriarchal society must intelligent women be content to aim so low in their professional lives.

# TOPICS FOR FURTHER STUDY

- Do some investigation into the psychological theories of Sigmund Freud, and then write a paper examining the inner workings of Eddie's mind from a Freudian perspective. If possible, find a way to explain Alfieri's notion that people usually "settle for half" in Freudian terms.

- The title of Miller's play *A View from the Bridge* bears little relation to the action, with the only prominent mention of a bridge coming in Alfieri's reference to the Brooklyn Bridge in his opening monologue. Write a paper in which you reflect on the connotations and possible meanings of the title, researching and elaborating on the symbolic, philosophical, and existential significance of bridges as appropriate.

- Read the young-adult novel *Mafia Girl* (2015), by Deborah Blumenthal, which follows the very interesting Manhattan life of Mia, who is the daughter of a notorious Mafia boss—and who develops affection for a police officer. Then write an essay in which you compare and contrast the situations of Mia and Catherine with respect to developing romantic sentiments that run counter to their fathers' (or, in Catherine's case, father figure's) interests. Conclude by offering your opinion about which young woman's situation is more difficult and why.

- Write one more scene to attach to the end of *A View from the Bridge* to depict where the surviving characters' lives will take them next. You may need to do a little research about 1950s America for clues and guidance. You can pick up right where the play leaves off, with Beatrice and Catherine embracing the dying Eddie in the street, or start with a fresh scene. Once the scene is written, recruit a few classmates to act out and film it, and share it with the class. Post the video online and allow your classmates to comment.

## Father-Child Relationships

In the context of the family, there might be such a thing as a benevolent patriarchy, with a husband and father who cares about everyone and, though recognized as the family's ultimate authority, believes in equality of influence between himself and his wife. Eddie is no such husband—and ultimately no father at all to the niece he has raised like a daughter. It is bad enough that he belittles the seventeen-year-old young woman as "kid" when he is in the process of judging her for the clothes she favors. It is worse that he embarrasses her in front of company by not only insisting that she change her shoes but, indeed, effectively insisting that she do so without his needing to make the demand explicit, placing her in the position of mutely deferential servant. And it is both terrible and terrifying that he thinks—while drunk—that his position gives him any right to seize his grown niece and force a kiss from her. It seems that the sense of patriarchy is rooted so deeply in his mind that he literally believes that whatever he thinks or wants to do is "right." It goes to show how easily patriarchy can evolve into outright tyranny.

An interesting thing about drama, as well as fiction, is that the author may only be attempting to truthfully portray a single, unique situation involving a particular group of people, but presenting an audience with that portrayal can make certain generalized statements whether the author intended it or not. Specifically here, Eddie is a man who is not related to Catherine by blood—she is his wife's sister's daughter. Miller, then, might be seen as suggesting that such a situation is in part problematic because the incest taboo is a step removed—the essential blood relation is lacking. Indeed, in an interview with Ronald Hayman, Miller reported that versions of the story he heard from Longhi seemed to be well known in Italian American circles, as if it were a folktale, with "the orphan girl or the niece who is not quite a blood relation living in the house" being a fixed element. In the play, Miller hints at the seriousness of such a problem in having Eddie simply kiss Catherine, but this speaks to situations where the abuse is far more serious. The play functions as a warning, then, about situations where a controlling and possessive man ends up having an intimate relationship with a young woman who is not his own daughter. People's looking out for each other—as Beatrice looks out for Catherine—is an important means of preventing sexual abuse and assault.

## Immigrant Life

In what begins in an entirely different type of story from that of Eddie and Catherine's relationship, Beatrice's cousins arrive in Brooklyn as immigrants from Italy. Miller says much about how difficult—as well as promising—life can be for such immigrants, whether they are documented or not. Marco's situation at home is as desperate as a situation can be: there is not enough work to be done back in Sicily, and so he cannot make enough money to adequately feed his family. It may be risky to slip into a country without proper documentation and try to make a living there, but with a little help getting overseas passage and work once arrived, it can be done. The upside of the risk is made clear when Marco starts to make enough money to ensure that his wife and children are getting both food and medicine. The downside includes the cramped living quarters and the humble occupations that immigrants end up in—occupations that need no training and likely pay a low wage, since employers can take advantage of the fact that undocumented immigrants have no legal recourse for demanding higher wages. Some people reflexively feel that undocumented immigrants, having broken the rules of entry, have literally no right to exist in the country where they find themselves, meaning if they are found, they should be deported. In taking a humanistic view of immigration, Miller's play makes a profound statement in favor of the acceptance of undocumented immigrants.

## Justice

Although the events never reach the courtroom, Miller's play ends up hinging on concepts of justice. Alfieri makes a point, in his opening monologue, of mentioning, "Justice is very important here." He also subtly makes the more controversial point that the law alone cannot be expected to ensure justice in the world. He says, "Oh, there were many here who were justly shot by unjust men," suggesting that even though the men enacting the punishment were themselves neither official nor unofficial upholders of the law, the punishment inflicted—such as on gangsters like "Frankie Yale"—was, in itself, just. In other words, sometimes, as the lawyer Alfieri suggests, regardless of what the law says, it may be fair for people to take justice into their own hands.

This is what Marco does, or means to do, in his antagonism toward Eddie. Marco declares his conviction that among honorable men, and

*Eddie works as a longshoreman* (© *T-Design | Shutterstock.com*)

in particular according to Sicilian codes of family honor, Eddie would not be left alive after his betrayal of his wife's two cousins. Marco realizes that being sent back to Italy will ensure that he will once again be unable to provide for his family, quite possibly leading to their premature deaths. The presence of the other two submarines in the building makes Eddie's betrayal worse, since two additional men against whom Eddie has no right to hold a grudge will likely also not be able to provide for themselves and their families. Marco's sense of honor, his sense of justice, prods him not only to spit in Eddie's face and make a public accusation with regard to the unjust betrayal but also to summon him to a showdown. Even then, obstinately holding his ground, Eddie gives himself an unfair advantage with the knife. The audience may, indeed should, mourn Eddie's lost life, but many may feel that, for putting so many immigrants at risk for no other reason than his own petty and bigoted resentments, Eddie deserves to die. Importantly, though, this sentence was carried out not by Marco—who declined to try to commit cold-blooded murder, which would have remained a morally questionable act—but, in effect, by fate.

## STYLE

### Foreshadowing

In telling the tragic story of Eddie's demise retrospectively, as a memory recalled at a later time, Alfieri gives almost nothing away—except for the fact that the end is a tragic one. At the end of his opening monologue, he vaguely reveals that there was some complaint that left him feeling powerless, unable to do anything but watch "it run its bloody course." With such an introduction to the drama, most audience members will be looking, whether intentionally or not, for the seeds of the problem and how it might lead to a violent end, which may or may not involve someone's death. This foreshadowing, ensuring that the audience's senses are primed from the beginning, allows Miller to be subtle with the action as it proceeds.

The dramatic action is fairly subdued through the early scenes—people are interacting, and they do not always agree, but it is hard to see how anyone involved could be moved to violence. An audience member might even lament that there is not enough action in these early scenes, but the prospect that some violence will indeed occur helps sustain interest. The characters gradually reveal antagonisms that are liable to deepen over time, and Alfieri also steps in several more times to help advance the narrative—and drop further foreshadowing hints about what will take place. At one point he mentions that Eddie in particular has "a destiny" to fulfill, which leaves Eddie with potentially either a subjective or an objective role to fill—he might be either the inflicter or the victim of violence (and turns out to be both). Later Alfieri narrates, after a visit from Eddie, that he "could have finished the whole story that afternoon." By now the audience or reader realizes that Eddie is going to do something of great consequence, but tension remains about what that something will be.

### Stage Directions

Dramatists almost invariably use stage directions to indicate the physical actions taking place on the stage, including gestures and facial expressions. Some of Miller's directions here are intriguing because, rather than simply indicating outward action, he describes the innermost feelings and mind-sets of the characters. For example, when Eddie is finally relenting with regard to Catherine's desire to get a job, he is said to deliver one of his lines *"with a sense of her childhood, her babyhood, and the years."* The line itself is only "All right, go to work," but the specificity of the direction speaks to the deeper emotional sense underlying the otherwise nondescript line. Similarly, when the Carbones are asking Beatrice's cousins about their home back in Italy, Rodolpho delivers a line not just while smiling, but while *"smiling at the smallness of his town."* This detailed description might seem unnecessary, because the line that follows makes the sense fairly clear: "In our town there are no piers, only the beach, and little fishing boats." But Miller's specificity indicates that he has a most complete image of the dramatic action in his mind, and the smile he describes is indeed a very specific kind of smile—not just a proud smile, as one might otherwise imagine—and for the reader, at least, recognizing the fullness of Miller's vision can evoke confidence in his dramatic talents and in this play in particular.

### Theatrical Fluidity

As is often done with a large enough stage, Miller's play calls for it to be divided up into several different scenes, so that dramatic action can take place in several different locales without any need for curtain use or prop rearrangement. As convenient as this is, it also calls for a slightly higher level of dramatic talent on the part of the actors, especially, in this case, Alfieri. On several occasions, he must turn from narrating the play while facing the audience to engaging with another character visiting his office. This must be done in a way that allows the audience to understand the distinction between the modes of his speech, perhaps with some assistance from lighting, and also retains their suspension of disbelief with regard to the "reality" of what is taking place.

## HISTORICAL CONTEXT

### To Red Hook, from Sicily

The Brooklyn neighborhood of Red Hook—located on the western coast of the borough, adjacent to Governors Island and opposite the Statue of Liberty—was a thriving seaport through the early twentieth century. The area was first named Roode Hoek by the Dutch for the hooklike shape of the peninsula protruding into Upper New York Bay and for the redness of the soil found there. Settled as a village in the seventeenth century, it became an especially important port in the mid-nineteenth century with the opening of the Atlantic Basin, an artificial harbor, in 1847. On the south side of the hook, the similar Erie Basin opened in 1864, with Red Hook becoming the end point of shipping going up and down the Erie Canal.

Meanwhile through the end of the nineteenth century, the essentially feudal society that persisted in southern Italy meant that life was extremely difficult for peasants, and by the turn of the twentieth century they were seeking passage to America in droves. The southern mountain region of Basilicata, for one, lost some 40 percent of its population to emigration between 1906 and 1915. Life was especially difficult for many in Sicily, where the influence of the Mafia had been growing since the early nineteenth century. With secretive, community-based hierarchies of individuals gaining widespread control of businesses and governmental positions—such as by hiring or appointing only people associated with their organization—profits from the daily economy as well as influxes of governmental investment in infrastructure

# COMPARE
# &
# CONTRAST

- **1950s:** With over twenty thousand residents, many of whom work the docks and about half whom live in public housing, Red Hook is cut off from the rest of Brooklyn by a highway and is known as a tough area—sometimes called a slum—where Italian American gangsters thrive.

  **Today:** Having seen its docks eclipsed by larger-scale waterfront operations elsewhere, Red Hook, now home to just over ten thousand residents, has recently seen a modest resurgence with the relocation of middle-class artists, technology firms, and creative companies to the area. One of the key harbors was bought out and taken over by an Ikea furniture superstore.

- **1950s:** As of 1950, more than 1.4 million individuals who were born in Italy are residing in the United States. The figure has been slowly dropping since the mid-1930s, when more restrictive immigration policies were put in place. Special allowance is made for immigration from Italy, which is still suffering from defeat in World War II, from 1952 to 1962, and through those decades, there are more foreign-born Americans from Italy than from any other nation.

  **Today:** Although immigration policies opened back up in 1965, the years of peak

migration from Italy had already passed. The number of foreign-born Italian Americans reached a low of 580,000 in 1990, climbing back up to just over 600,000 in 2000. As of the year 2000, New York State is home to over 2.7 million Italian Americans.

- **1950s:** In an era inhibited by suburban religious values as well as Cold War fears, many homosexual people remain closeted. But milestones in the 1950s, including the publication of a book about homosexuals as a national minority, the formation of gay support organizations, and the extensive sexuality research conducted by Dr. Alfred Kinsey and his associates, pave the way for wider understanding and appreciation of homosexuality and sexual difference.

  **Today:** Laws forbidding homosexual activity have been struck down across America, the Supreme Court legalized gay marriage nationwide in 2015, pride parades are common in urban centers and elsewhere, many high-profile celebrities have publicly revealed their sexual preferences, and with the additional support of social media, more people than ever are empowered to be forthright about and happy with their sexual orientation no matter what it is.

were siphoned through Mafia members' self-serving hands, leaving that much less for the common people. Mafia job preferment and the slow ruination of the economy meant that work grew scarce for those without connections, leaving the unemployment rate consistently hovering around 30 percent, a devastating proportion.

The occasional involvement of Mafia-linked figures in crimes in America, including violent crimes, contributed to stereotypes regarding the character of Italians generally. American officials eager to find a basis for discrimination

were able to rely on the theories of the racist northern Italian doctor Cesare Lombroso, who concluded through measurements of body parts, including heads (a practice called phrenology, which has long since been dismissed as a pseudoscience), that southern Italians were inherently inclined toward criminality. Thus did the US Immigration Commission's 1911 Dillingham report, cited by Helene Stapinski in the *New York Times*, conclude, "Certain kinds of criminality are inherent in the Italian race. In the popular mind, crimes of personal violence, robbery, blackmail and extortion are peculiar to the

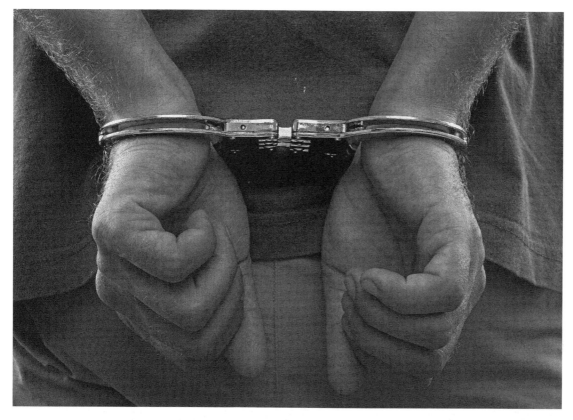

*Eddie calls immigration to report Rodolpho and Marco, and the two young men are arrested* (© Jinga /
*Shutterstock.com*)

people of Italy." The commission had been further encouraged to stem Italian immigration by
Italian politicians who realized that their nation
was bleeding manpower at an incredible rate,
thanks to conditions that left the common people
"suffering" and "starving," in Stapinski's words.

All this ultimately led to the Immigration
Act of 1924—referred to by Eddie in Miller's
play as "the Immigration Law"—which cut immigration from Italy by some 90 percent. Naturally,
this meant that emigration from Italy, which
remained necessary for many under the intolerable conditions there, was put more in the control
of organized crime, increasing the Mafia's influence in America. Not until after World War II,
when Italian Americans served in the military in
disproportionately high numbers, did the Italian
character—outside of organized crime, that is—
gain favor and respect in the popular American
imagination.

For all its success as a port, Red Hook
became dominated by the sorts of Italian Americans who found themselves atop the hierarchy
of organized crime and thus gained a reputation
as an especially tough part of the city. As Alfieri
reports in the beginning of *A View from the
Bridge*, Al Capone and Frankie Yale were just
two of the best-known mobsters who graced (so
to speak) the streets of the district. In light of the
abundance of low-income dockworkers and
their families, the area became home to one of
the first federal housing projects in 1938, the Red
Hook Houses. By 1950, some twenty-one thousand residents were compressed into Red Hook;
for comparison's sake, the population was down
to eleven thousand in the early twenty-first
century. Also by 1950, however, the area was
becoming increasingly isolated, by virtue of the
construction of the Gowanus Expressway in
1946 and the Brooklyn Battery Tunnel in 1950,
both of which cut Red Hook off from mainland
Brooklyn. Moreover, shipping practices shifted
to the use of large metal containers that required
more dock space and fewer dockhands, and
ports developing in New Jersey began to thrive.
The culture of Italian American longshoremen
in Red Hook had seen its peak.

## CRITICAL OVERVIEW

Although Miller is now regarded as one of the greatest playwrights in American history, critics in his era were not always favorable toward him, whether due to his politics, his personal life, their own expectations, or, on occasion, the actual quality of the play in question. Coming a half decade after Miller's 1949 masterpiece *Death of a Salesman*, *A View from the Bridge* found a critical community primed to judge his work with the highest of standards. In the *New York Daily News*, John Chapman called the play a "modern classic," observing, "What happens in it simply has to happen, and this is the inevitability of true tragedy." Chapman declared:

> This is an intensely absorbing drama, sure of itself every step of the way. It makes no false moves, wastes no time and has the beauty that comes from directness and simplicity.... Miller has come a long way in our theatre, and he will go much farther, for his mind is a mind that won't stay still.

Walcot Gibbs, in the *New Yorker*, was generally appreciative, admiring the "broken rhythms and mindless repetitions" that lend a "grotesque eloquence" to the characters' working-class speech. The reviewer adds that Miller's "command of the idiom is nearly perfect and his treatment of the dramatic incident is beyond criticism." Leonard Moss, writing in 1980 in *Arthur Miller*, would show similar admiration for the subtlety of the dialogue in *A View from the Bridge*. He observes that the scene introducing Marco and Rodolpho "splendidly illustrates Miller's ability to encompass strong anxiety in commonplace talk." In the same vein, once the false love triangle develops, "the inception of the sex-rivalry is conveyed entirely through Eddie's ominous silences and through the connotations of his sullen dialogue."

Gibbs's one major complaint, echoed by Moss, was that Alfieri makes for an unnecessary and somewhat unwelcome narrator, as if Miller felt a need to dress up his humble play in fancier clothes to make it more acceptable to elitist audiences. Gibbs notes of Alfieri, "It was my feeling that he served merely to bring a superfluous and rather pretentious air of classroom erudition to an otherwise admirably forthright play." He affirmed that the excellent play needed no such "genteel embroidery." Moss suggests that, even though Alfieri effectively serves the classical function of the Greek chorus, he is found "constantly interrupting the cumulation of tension," and overall his "contribution... seems seriously limited."

The expanded two-act version of *A View from the Bridge* debuted in London in 1956, and Samantha Ellis, in a 2003 retrospective for the London *Guardian*—after pointing out that Marilyn Monroe stole the show on opening night in a scarlet satin gown—quotes several reviewers' opinions of the production. As quoted by Ellis, Milton Shulman of the *Evening Standard* found the play "so bulging with dramatic muscles that it is constantly on the verge of bursting its seams." *Sunday Times* reviewer Harold Hobson, Ellis writes, who had seen the New York production and considered it a "masterpiece," was slightly less pleased with the London version, writing: "It has been decorated. Things which brooded in the dark recesses of undefined feeling have been brought into the light." The playwright's communication with the audience, he felt, amounted to "special pleading; though the special pleading is very good."

Like Gibbs, a London *Times* reviewer (also quoted by Ellis) found that Alfieri's narration contributed to the result's being "a good picture in a pretentious frame." In the reviewer's opinion, the play represented "the miscarriage of an intention to elevate these ordinary men and women to the rank of heroes and heroines of high tragedy." Far more positively, Ellis reports that Kenneth Tynan, writing in the *Observer*, found the London production "uncannily good" and the play itself "just short of being a masterpiece." Ellis also notes that Cecil Wilson, writing in the *Daily Mail*, considered the play "savage, searing and spellbinding," a work that "though no shocker, will shake you to the core." James J. Martine, in an introduction to the 1979 collection *Critical Essays on Arthur Miller*, sums up the playwright's importance in stating, "Miller is one of the most important dramatists of this century."

## CRITICISM

### Michael Allen Holmes

*Holmes is a writer with existential interests. In the following essay, he examines the importance in* A View from the Bridge *of Rodolpho's upending gender roles of 1950s America.*

# WHAT DO I READ NEXT?

- Like this play, Miller's Pulitzer- and Tony-winning masterpiece, *Death of a Salesman* (1949), also deals with the end of an era for a certain breed of conventional, patriarchal husband and father. The play's runaway success immortalized the tragic character of Willy Loman, a salesman in his early sixties who finds himself flummoxed by reality.

- The seedier side of Brooklyn was immortalized in Hubert Selby Jr.'s perceptive novel *Last Exit to Brooklyn* (1964), which zeroes in on Red Hook dockworkers, union corruption, and underworld violence.

- American novelist William Styron made his debut with *Lie Down in Darkness* (1951), a book revolving around a relationship between a father and a daughter in which the former harbors too much love for the latter, with ultimately tragic consequences.

- Miller and director Elia Kazan were once friends and associates—until Kazan chose to name names when he was brought before the House Un-American Activities Committee in 1952, four years before Miller. The two had been collaborating on a screenplay for an anti-union-corruption film set in Red Hook, called "The Hook," but it never got made. Kazan, however, went on to direct the similarly set but anti-Communist film *On the Waterfront* (1954), which brought Marlon Brando to fame. The screenplay was written by Budd Schulberg, who went on to publish both *On the Waterfront: A Screenplay* (1981) and *On the Waterfront: A Play* (2001), the latter coauthored with Stan Silverman.

- Miller has said that one drama in particular made an especially profound impression on him during his university days: Norwegian playwright Henrik Ibsen's *A Doll's House* (1879). The play is distinctly feminist in an era before feminism was even a word, promoting freedom of action for a married woman in oppressive patriarchal circumstances.

- An American teenager who gets involved with an Italian who may or may not be trouble is also a feature of Kristin Rae's young-adult romance *Wish You Were Italian* (2014), in which Pippa's parents send her to Florence, Italy, to attend art school, but Pippa is more interested in having nonacademic cross-cultural experiences.

- *Images of Red Hook, Brooklyn* (2012), by Thomas Rupolo, provides some 120 photographs of the neighborhood, ranging from the distant past to the present, along with a brief history, informative captions, and commentary from residents and laborers who have known the area best.

- Enoch Brater's *Arthur Miller: A Playwright's Life and Works* (2005) is among the most recent treatments of the important events in Miller's life as well as the cultural relevance of his writings.

---

In considerations of Miller's social drama *A View from the Bridge*, Eddie is invariably given the lion's share of attention. He is undeniably the central character, even if not the most ethical, with the play's conflict created by his unbalanced responses to the family circumstances in which he finds himself. His psychology is ripe for examination from a Freudian perspective, given how thoroughly he has sublimated his romantic difficulties and confusions, and even in a more casual framework, there is much to be said about him. In view of all this, perhaps not enough is said about the man who serves as Eddie's foil and the instigator of his wayward opinions and emotions, Rodolpho. Miller was known to inhabit a far-left perspective with regard to governmental politics, but his portrayal of Rodolpho merits fuller recognition as advancing liberal ideas in gender politics as well.

"

AS FOR HIS RELATIONSHIP WITH KATIE, IN

PERHAPS THE MOST IMPORTANT PART OF HIS

DEFIANCE OF THE GENDER ROLES OF THE DAY,

RODOLPHO HIMSELF POINTS OUT A CRUCIAL

ASPECT OF THAT RELATIONSHIP—AN ASPECT

LACKING FROM EDDIE'S RELATION TO HIS NIECE."

The fifties are widely recognized as the pinnacle of inhibition and repression in America. Earlier in the century, the Roaring Twenties were full of liberal behavior, while the thirties saw everyone so preoccupied with the Great Depression that moral concerns received less attention. In the forties, World War II swept America back into an era of prosperity—and as more and more people aspired to the middle and upper-middle classes, more and more did their very best to conform to what they perceived as class expectations. And nowhere were expectations made clearer, it can be argued, than on television. The medium had swept the nation at midcentury, meaning great numbers of people were being exposed to a commercialized popular culture that highlighted and rigidified behavioral norms already in place. Advertisers wanted only the cleanest-cut families populating sitcoms, families where everyone fit "just right," so to speak, specifically with a manly breadwinning father, a happily subjugated mother, and clever but never-*too*-troublesome children. With only a handful of channels available in the beginning, practically everyone was watching the same things and absorbing the same cultural messages, whether implicit or explicit.

An *Artifice* essay delves into the problems created by the strict gender roles seen on television nationwide—including problems of violence. Situation comedies like *Leave It to Beaver* and *Father Knows Best* (the title of which, honestly, says it all) may not have centered on episodes of violence or even depicted them at all, but the rigidity of the gender roles could indirectly lead to violence. The *Artifice* writer begins her argument by working up to the point where she can observe, "For boys in the 1950s, 'being a man'

and never doing anything that anyone could consider feminine was a lesson taught to them by their fathers and by the popular culture of the time." With situation comedies, a cultural mainstay from their inception, invariably centered in the home, fathers like Ward Cleaver had very limited repertoires of behavior, generally leaving for work in the morning, coming home at night, and solving problems for their children with neat dispensations of wisdom. Women, invariably, were the ones doing household chores like laundry, washing dishes, cooking, cleaning, and catering to the needs of the other family members. The *Artifice* writer thus points out, "It is the absence of the men in the home in these television shows that reinforces that boys and men simply do not belong there." The writer proceeds to cite a 2012 study finding that the stricter a man's conceptions of gender roles are, the more likely he is to act out in violence. The *Artifice* writer can at this point affirm, "Trying to over-fulfill one's manliness because of the fear of not being manly enough often times leads to violence."

Here, then, we have Eddie's situation expressed perfectly. He meets his end, at the play's end, largely because he cannot bear Marco's threats to his masculinity. Once Marco has insulted him by spitting in his face and publicly accusing him, Eddie feels that he has a right to do anything to get back what he refers to as "my name," which sounds much like code for his masculinity. For Eddie to back down and apologize would be, from his perspective, a humiliation, indeed an emasculation. His frustration over Marco's matching—and more ethically grounded—refusal to back down is what brings out Eddie's knife and brings about his death.

As far as homosexuality was concerned, the fifties were a time of slow but increasingly inevitable change. Homosexuality had been an acknowledged, if not publicly discussed, facet of American culture for decades, especially in urban centers. National attention was drawn to the issue, however, when Senator McCarthy roused people to the indignant fear that homosexuals were disproportionately likely to be either Communist sympathizers (as Communists did, after all, believe in equality among all peoples) or vulnerable to Soviet blackmail. Alongside the Red Scare, focused on Communism itself, this became known as the Lavender Scare. It was in response to these affronts that organizations offering community and support to gay and lesbian individuals, calling themselves *homophile*, first started forming. The Mattachine Society was founded by several gay men who indeed had Marxist backgrounds and perspectives, although, as the Cold War thickened, they saw fit to disavow radical Marxism. Additional organizations included the West Coast's One, Inc., founded in 1952, and the lesbian network Daughters of Bilitis, founded in 1955. The topic of homosexuality was also directly broached in literature, with Donald Webster Cory publishing *The Homosexual in America: A Subjective Approach* in 1951, affirming that homosexuals represented not a biological aberration but a legitimate minority population.

It was in this broader cultural context that *A View from the Bridge* was first presented to New York audiences in 1955. And in light of that context, the significance of the depiction of Rodolpho becomes all the clearer. While his sexuality is beside the point when he and Marco first appear, his conviviality and positive attitude are indisputable. One might think that, after stowing secretly away on a ship, facing a new situation in a new country, he would be guarded and wary, like the "*suspicious*" Marco. Yet Rodolpho's first three spoken sentences, about the relative richness of Eddie and Beatrice's building, all end in exclamation points. And even before he first speaks in the Carbone family's presence, specifically to Catherine, he is "*ready to laugh*" over her astonishment at his light complexion. After asking Eddie about Tony's honesty—which makes Eddie laugh—Rodolpho either smiles or laughs, according to the stage directions, seven times in the course of his next seven comments. Eddie may be accustomed to a certain stoic, unemotional masculinity on the part of his fellow longshoremen—there does not seem to be much room for humor in his exchanges with Louis and Mike—a far cry from Rodolpho's forthright, engaging personality.

Rodolpho might be seen as asserting his masculinity in a sense when he declares that his dream is to earn enough money to purchase a motorcycle, a source of transportation generally considered risky and thus manly; very few women were riding motorcycles in the 1950s. Yet what Rodolpho wants to do with this motorcycle is fill a subordinate role in society, that of messenger. And he does not necessarily seem to believe in the manliness of the motorcycle itself; he avows that "the machine is necessary," but he

does not seem to be enamored of the machine the way a conventionally manly man would be. To the contrary, he is acutely aware that the motorcycle has value not so much in and of itself but largely as a signifier, one that makes loud noises and suggests to potential clients that he holds a legitimate place in society. Tellingly, in the middle of his speech about the importance of the machine, Rodolpho "*helps Beatrice set out the coffee things*," signaling his indifference to conventional masculinity.

Rodolpho's recognition of the significance of appearances is something that arouses Eddie's suspicion in other respects, such as regarding his "wacky" hair. In commenting, "I just hope that's his regular hair, that's all I hope," Eddie indicates how upset he would be if it turned out Rodolpho dyed, styled, or even permed his hair. Yet if one is interested in singing, acting, and Broadway, as Rodolpho is, appearances are a necessary concern—and onstage, even the men wear makeup. Male tenors are also an important part of many harmonic and choral arrangements, regardless of Eddie's aversion to a man who can sing in a high voice.

Gender roles are further broken down by Rodolpho's ensuing actions. Eddie is inclined to interpret Rodolpho's failure to ask his permission to simply take Katie to a movie as a sign of disrespect. It might be an omission for Rodolpho not to make any formal display of seeking such permission in the extreme case of marriage, perhaps, but for going to see a movie, Rodolpho's neglect of this "duty" might be seen not just as permissible but as a distinctly feminist move. Katie does not belong to her uncle, however he might wish her to, but to herself, and thus why should Rodolpho need consult anyone besides Katie about her public behavior? It is as if he recognizes that she ought to be able to do what she wants and see whom she wants—and that requesting a male guardian's permission to accompany his young female relation somewhere is an act of deferral to patriarchy—and deferring to something like patriarchy only strengthens it.

In turn, Rodolpho may be good at cooking, another conventionally feminine task in the eyes of 1950s America, but the circumstance in which his skill comes in handy attests to the gender neutrality the task ought to have. On a fishing boat, much like on a larger military vessel or whaler—all of which then represented "manly"

*When Marco confronts Eddie about the arrest, Eddie pulls a knife and is fatally stabbed in the scuffle*
*(© CoolR / Shutterstock.com)*

occupations, involving difficult physical activity for the attainment of food, wealth, or power—women are unlikely to be present, and so the task of cooking necessarily falls to a man. As an excellent cook, then, Rodolpho both defies the conventional American gender role and is proof of how illogical that gender role is. As for his relationship with Katie, in perhaps the most important part of his defiance of the gender roles of the day, Rodolpho himself points out a crucial aspect of that relationship—an aspect lacking from Eddie's relation to his niece. Rodolpho affirms, "I have respect for her, Eddie." In other words, he does not and has no intent to subordinate Katie; he wants to be her partner, on equal footing, through and through.

There is, it should be admitted, in the staging of Miller's play, room for Rodolpho to be played as overtly homosexual and for the romance to be played up as possibly indeed what Eddie fears it is—a front for Rodolpho as he seeks permanent residence in the United States. After all, the slickest of con men would say everything that Rodolpho says for as long as necessary—until

after the curtain drops, preventing the audience from witnessing his ultimate betrayal. But such a staging of the play would validate all of Eddie's bigoted fears and accusations and put the audience or reader in the awkward position of having to admit that the sexually assaultive, knife-wielding Eddie was right. No director could stage the play this way and claim to be following the spirit of Miller's original intent. Of course, the fact that Rodolpho is *not* homosexual, after all, might be seen to compromise the relevance of his status as someone who does not conform to accepted gender roles. The audience can accept Rodolpho, ultimately, specifically because he *is* heterosexual, if that is how they want or need to accept him—as if his behaviors might be excused only by the validation of his attraction to women. But in the end, Rodolpho's precise sexual identity is beside the point. He is a person who naturally acts the way he is inspired to act, even in the face of derision and prejudice, and the ability to do this is just as important for straight people as it is for gay people. The breaking down of gender roles not just by homosexual,

> *A VIEW FROM THE BRIDGE* IS A TRAGEDY
> OF THE COMMON MAN, AS DEFINED BY MILLER, IN
> WHICH THE HERO, REGARDLESS OF HIS STATION IN
> LIFE, IS TOTALLY COMPELLED 'TO EVALUATE
> HIMSELF JUSTLY.'"

bisexual, and transsexual people but by people whose sexualities cover the entire spectrum from gay to straight is what will ultimately allow the American public not just to acknowledge but, indeed, to accept and welcome people no matter what their sexuality might be.

**Source:** Michael Allen Holmes, Critical Essay on *A View from the Bridge*, in *Drama for Students*, Gale, Cengage Learning, 2018.

## Alice Griffin

*In the following excerpt, Griffin characterizes the play as a tragedy.*

The story of *A View from the Bridge* was told to Arthur Miller by a friend who worked among longshoremen in Red Hook, home of the real-life Eddie Carbone. Miller originally conceived the play in one act in the classical mode: "a hard, telegraphic, unadorned drama" that moved to its catastrophe in a "clear, clean line." Not unlike heroes of Greek tragedy, Carbone is gripped by an overwhelming passion which leads him to a fatal decision: he betrays the social code by which he lives and for which he dies in an attempt to regain his good "name." Lawyer Alfieri is a chorus character who introduces, participates in, and interprets the action, which moves inevitably to a conclusion feared yet anticipated by the audience. As Miller notes, "It must be suspenseful because one knew too well how it would come out, so that the basic feeling would be the desire to stop this man and tell him what he was really doing to his life."

Miller hoped the play would produce the wonderment evoked by Greek tragedies at "the awesomeness of a passion which, despite its contradicting the self-interest of the individual it inhabits, despite every kind of warning, despite even its destruction of the moral beliefs of the individual, proceeds to magnify its power over

him until it destroys him." Like some classical heroes and heroines, longshoreman Eddie is gripped by an incestuous sexual passion, here for the niece to whom he has been a father. Unknown and unacknowledged by him, his desire for seventeen-year-old Catherine intensifies when two of his wife's relatives arrive in the country illegally from Sicily. Catherine, who has led a sheltered life, is attracted to and soon falls in love with the younger of the two men, Rodolpho.

When they announce their decision to marry, Eddie' s uncontrollable rage and jealousy lead him to break the code of his Sicilian society regarding illegal immigrants. Informing on them to the Immigration Service is a betrayal, punishable by lifelong ostracism, by one's friends, neighbors, and family. As officers lead the brothers away before onlooking neighbors, Marco, the older, points accusingly at Eddie as the informer. In a final fight with Marco, Eddie draws a knife, insisting, "I want my name." The knife is turned against him, and he dies, asking "Why?" The inexorability of events suggested the style to Miller, the "myth-like march of the tale" calling for an unadorned, straightforward fashion, "a fine, high, always visible arc of forces moving in full view to a single explosion."

Miller states that the play was "not designed primarily to draw tears or laughter from an audience" but, rather, to evoke their "astonishment at the way in which, and the reasons for which, a man will endanger and risk and lose his very life." Whether by "distancing" the action to allow audience to think as well as feel or by directing actors in a realistic rather than a heightened style, the production was judged "cold" by the reviewers when it opened on Broadway in 1955.

Two years later, when director Peter Brook scheduled the London premiere of *A View from the Bridge*, Miller expanded the work to two acts. It is this revised version that is analyzed here, with references to the earlier one-act play as indicated. As Miller explains in the introduction to the revised version, published in 1960, Brook's production helped achieve the play's aims: the set, which "soared to the roof with fire escapes [and] passageways, suggested apartments, so that one sensed that Eddie was living out his horror in the midst of a certain normality, and that invisibly...he was getting ready to invoke upon himself the wrath of his tribe."

The classically trained British actors, accustomed to playing Shakespeare, easily handled the larger-than-life style the play requires, and the "pay scales of the London theater made it possible to do what I could not do in New York—hire a crowd," reports Miller. When the neighborhood was represented by twenty actors instead of four (Broadway's affordable maximum), the larger group, like a Greek chorus, enhanced the audience's understanding of the main character, says Miller: "the mind of Eddie Carbone is not comprehensible apart from its relation to his neighborhood, his fellow workers, his social situation. His self-esteem depends upon their estimate of him, and his value is created largely by his fidelity to the code of his culture." In the revised version, "once Eddie had been placed squarely in his social context, among his people, the mythlike feeling of the story emerged of itself, and he could be made more human and less a figure, a force," notes Miller.

The chorus character of lawyer Alfieri opens and closes the play. In the two-act version he speaks prose instead of verse, although it is rhythmic, poetic prose. At the beginning Alfieri's cadence also strikes the note of inevitability: "Every few years there is still a case, and as the parties tell me what the trouble is, the flat air in my office suddenly washes in with the green scent of the sea, the dust in this air is blown away and the thought comes that in some Caesar's year . . . another lawyer, quite differently dressed, heard the same complaint and sat there as powerless as I, and watched it run its bloody course. . . . This one's name was Eddie Carbone."

In expanding the play, Miller developed the character of Eddie's wife, Bea, so that she becomes a sympathetic, wronged woman as well as a chorus character less exalted than Alfieri. If he is the voice of society and human nature, she is the voice of the individual neighbors. Another change is the expansion of Catherine's role. The passive recipient of others' attention in the earlier version, she is now active in her own right, a teenager in the flush of first love, anxious to begin a job in the outside world. In the first scene, demurring at the prospect of her working, Eddie finds fault with the neighborhood and the company: "Near the Navy Yard plenty can happen. . . . And a plumbin' company! That's one step over the water front. They're practically longshoremen." Bea asks: "You gonna keep her in the house all her life?"

At their first meeting with the brothers whom they will harbor, Catherine and Bea are enthusiastic, but Eddie is suspicious, and when blond Rodolpho becomes the center of attention by singing "Paper Doll," Eddie warns him to be quiet: "You don't want to be picked up, do ya?" Helpless in the face of Catherine's obvious attraction to Rodolpho, Eddie tries to undermine him by casting doubt upon his manhood. He complains to Bea in the next scene that the younger man sings at work and is "like a weird." "And with that wacky hair; he's like a chorus girl or sump'm." Eddie consults Alfieri to complain that "the guy ain't right" and to inquire whether there is a law against "a guy which he ain't right can go to work and marry a girl and—?" Eddie's obsession with Catherine increases with the growing threat of Rodolpho, while Bea attempts to avoid an eruption she senses is imminent. In the second scene in act 1 she asks Eddie, "When am I gonna be a wife again?"

An added scene in act 1 develops the characters of both women. Beatrice cautions her niece: "I told you fifty times already, you can't act the way you act. You still walk around in front of him in your slip." She reminds Catherine that she is now a grown woman: "You're a woman, that's all, and you got a nice boy, and now the time came when you said good-by. All right?" Catherine is "strangely moved at the prospect." In the parallel scene that follows, Eddie is warned by Alfieri, who is as direct as he can be: "We all love somebody, the wife, the kids—every man's got somebody that he loves, heh? But sometimes. . . . there's too much," he cautions, "too much love for the daughter, there is too much love for the niece."

When Alfieri says, "Let her go," Eddie's response leaves no doubt that the obsession is sexual: "I take the blankets off my bed for him, and he takes and puts his dirty filthy hands on her like a goddam thief!" Alfieri replies: "She wants to get married, Eddie. She can't marry you, can she?" Eddie "furiously" charges, "I don't know what the hell you're talkin' about!" Warnings have no effect on Eddie's mounting anger and desperation.

Act 1 concludes on a note of high emotion, as Eddie's oral threats turn physical. Catherine insists on dancing with Rodolpho, whom Eddie, sitting and twisting his newspaper, begins to insult, impugning his manhood. Then his manner changes to cordial. He invites the brothers to a boxing bout, offers to teach Rodolpho, and exchanges a few light blows. Eddie moves in, "feints with his left hand and lands with his right. It mildly staggers Rodolpho." As he and Catherine resume their dancing, Marco challenges Eddie to lift a chair from the bottom of one of its legs, Eddie tries and fails, and Marco "slowly raises the chair higher and higher.... like a weapon over Eddie's head—and he transforms what might appear like a glare of warning into a smile of triumph."

The next scene will reach a climax even more intense. Alone in the house with Rodolpho for the first time, Catherine asks if they might live in Italy after they are married: "I'm afraid of Eddie here." Catherine's expanded role reveals her as an active, sympathetic young person in place of the passive object of Bea's and Eddie's wrangling in the first version. She is torn between love for Rodolpho and loyalty to Eddie. Rodolpho urges the weeping girl to make the break and leads her into the bedroom.

As they emerge, Eddie enters, drunk. Eddie orders him out; Catherine says she will go too. Eddie forbids it. "He reaches out suddenly, draws her to him, and as she strives to free herself he kisses her on the mouth." Rodolpho frees her and spins Eddie around. "Rodolpho flies at him in attack. Eddie pins his arms, laughing, and suddenly kisses him." Eddie threatens: "Watch your step, submarine," and warns, "Just get outa here and don't lay another hand on her unless you wanna go out feet first."

Eddie's kissing Catherine confirms his incestuous passion; it is an unguarded act he would never have committed unless both drunk and driven beyond reason by what he perceives to have occurred between her and Rodolpho. It shocks the audience, but even more shocking is his kissing Rodolpho. It culminates Eddie's hints and accusations about Rodolpho's manhood, Eddie's major line of attack. (He also has assured Catherine that the marriage is only to legalize Rodolpho's immigrant status and eligibility for citizenship.)

Have the critics been uncomfortable with this play and especially with this scene? After the initial reviews of both the shorter and longer versions of *A View from the Bridge*, there has been little serious analysis, except for Miller's own comments. Benjamin Nelson feels that there is a "possibility" of "latent homosexuality" in Eddie, because of "his obsession with Rodolpho's 'queerness,' which he attempts to substantiate by humiliating the boy with a savage kiss [that] obviously reveals more about Eddie than

about Rodolpho." But this interpretation is unconvincing in the context of Eddie's intensifying sexual obsession with his niece, even to the extent of betraying his community and destroying his own good name.

In a crazed belief that his suspicions have been confirmed by kissing Rodolpho, Eddie pays a last visit to Alfieri, who is dubious: "You didn't prove anything about him. It sounds like he just wasn't strong enough to break your grip." The lawyer warns him that "the law is nature. The law is only a word for what has a right to happen.... Let her go." As Eddie leaves, Alfieri suspects that, to destroy Rodolpho, Eddie will even destroy himself.

Alfieri voices the apprehension and fears of the audience about the catastrophe that is to ensue. Eddie phones the Immigration Bureau and informs on Rodolpho and Marco. "The betrayal achieves its true proportions as it flies in the face of the mores administered by Eddie's conscience—which is also the conscience of his friends, co-workers, and neighbors," notes Miller.

Like Oedipus, Eddie will be thrust from the community for an act that harms it. He also resembles John Proctor in his determination to preserve his good name at any cost, even death. A climactic scene closes the play. Having spit in Eddie's face and denounced him in front of the neighbors, Marco returns. He and Eddie both seek the final encounter. Eddie rejects Rodolpho's apology and insists that he wants his "name," which Marco took from him. Beatrice attempts to bar Eddie's way and cries out the truth: "You want somethin' else, Eddie, and you can never have her!"

To the surrounding neighbors, Eddie attempts to justify himself as one wronged by strangers he sheltered: "to come out of the water and grab a girl for a passport?... Wipin' the neighborhood with my name like a dirty rag! I want my name, Marco." He attacks Marco, who strikes him; Eddie goes down, then springs a knife and lunges with it, but Marco turns the blade back to him and presses it as Eddie falls to his knees. He dies in Beatrice's arms, and Alfieri steps from the crowd to speak the final words:

> Most of the time now we settle for half and I like it better. But the truth is holy, and even as I know how wrong he was, and his death useless, I tremble, for I confess that something perversely pure calls to me from his memory—not purely good, but himself purely, for he

> EDDIE CARBONE IS A TRAGIC FIGURE, MILLER CLEARLY FEELS, BECAUSE IN THE INTRANSIGENCE OF HIS ACTIONS THERE IS AN IMPLICIT FIDELITY TO THE SELF, AN INTEGRITY TO ONE'S OWN BELIEFS NO MATTER HOW PERVERSE THEY MAY BE. "

allowed himself to be wholly known and for that I think I will love him more than all my sensible clients. And yet, it is better to settle for half, it must be! And so I mourn him—I admit it—with a certain . . . alarm.

*A View from the Bridge* is a tragedy of the common man, as defined by Miller, in which the hero, regardless of his station in life, is totally compelled "to evaluate himself justly." Eddie, like Willy Loman, is unwilling "to remain passive in the face of what he conceives to be a challenge to his dignity, his image of his rightful status." Miller notes that "the commonest of men may take on . . . [tragic] stature to the extent of his willingness to throw all he has into the contest, the battle to secure his rightful place in his world." His plight evokes fear in the audience, "fear of being displaced, the disaster inherent in being torn away from our chosen image of what and who we are in this world." . . .

**Source:** Alice Griffin, "*A View from the Bridge*," in *Understanding Arthur Miller*, University of South Carolina Press, 1996, pp. 81–81.

## Arthur D. Epstein
*In the following excerpt, Epstein offers a character study of Eddie.*

. . . Critics have completely overlooked, evidently viewing it as purely representational, Rodolpho's singing of "Paper Doll," except to indicate that Martin Ritt, the stage director of the New York production, caught the satire of Italian singers who consciously imitate the singing style of American crooners. However, what is much more crucial is that, like many of the songs in Shakespeare's plays, the lyrics of "Paper Doll" in *A View from the Bridge* illuminate the dilemma of the tragic hero . . . .

. . . The dominant theme of the lyric is that the singer is going to buy a paper doll that other fellows cannot steal; in other words, an object of

love which will obviate the possibility of rivalry and theft. The relevance to Eddie Carbone is striking. Throughout the play (which incidentally is interwoven with imagery of thievery) Eddie repeatedly accuses Rodolpho of having stolen Catherine from him or alludes to it. Catherine is Eddie's paper doll. Rodolpho is the flirty, flirty guy, and the interesting fact that the singer intends to "buy" a paper doll parallels exactly Eddie's attitude that he has a basic right to control Catherine's actions because of the enormous personal sacrifices he has made in order to raise her:

> I worked like a dog twenty years so a punk could have her, so that's what I done. I mean, in the worst times, in the worst, when there wasn't a ship comin' in the harbor, I didn't stand around lookin' for relief—I hustled. When there was empty piers in Brooklyn I went to Hoboken, Staten Island, the West Side, Jersey, all over—because I made a promise. I took out of my own mouth to give to her. I took out of my wife's mouth. I walked hungry plenty days in this city!

Eddie's hostility toward Rodolpho is revealed in his thinly veiled suggestion of his suspicion of Rodolpho's homosexuality, first mentioned to Beatrice. Never concrete in his accusation, the closest Eddie comes to specific identification is to label Rodolpho a "weird." "Queer," the more common pejorative for a homosexual, could easily have been used by Miller, but the selection of the word "weird" subtilizes Eddie's suggestion and is more appropriate to the texture of shadowy innuendo in which he is working. Rodolpho, we and Beatrice are informed, is now known by Eddie's longshoreman pals as "Paper Doll . . . Canary." He does "a regular free show"; and it is unnecessary, I think, to belabor the sexual overtones of this phrase. His hair is "wacky . . . he's like a chorus girl or sump'm," Eddie tells us. In this dialogue Eddie is the accuser, making sly, damaging suggestions, while Beatrice attempts to defend Rodolpho against such innuendoes and to dismiss their relevance. Set in striking juxtaposition to this scene is the following with Eddie and his friends, Louis and Mike. A surface glance reveals its comic relief. But there is something more. Actually what Miller has done (again reminiscent of Shakespeare's use of comic scenes) is to illuminate the earlier scene by reversing Eddie's role. In his meeting with Louis and Mike, it is Eddie who is placed in the uncomfortable position of defending Rodolpho against the same innuendoes now being leveled at him by Mike and Louis. This has gone completely unnoted by critics. Notice the striking similarity between Beatrice's and Eddie's language in trying to explain Rodolpho's odd behavior on the waterfront piers:

> Beatrice [to Eddie]: Well, he's a kid; he don't know how to behave himself yet.
> Eddie [to Louis and Mike]: Yeah, I know. But he's a kid yet, y'know? He—he's just a kid that's all.

An echo of Beatrice's words. An ironic reversal of roles. Furthermore it is Mike, in the comic scene, who assumes Eddie's role of the insinuator in the previous scene. Not only does this scene help to illuminate through comedy and juxtaposition the earlier scene and help to establish the discomfort of Eddie's dilemma, but it lends credence to Eddie's suspicion that Rodolpho is a homosexual by buttressing through representation the reactions of Eddie's pals to Rodolpho, reactions which Eddie had just described to Beatrice in the previous scene. It seems to me to be one of the major deficiencies of the criticism of A View from the Bridge that no recognition has been made of Miller's abundantly clear attempt to make *some* case for Eddie's behavior. Eddie's reaction to Rodolpho is not as isolated, as bizarre and monstrous, as the critics suggest. On the contrary, we have seen (and I shall later point out additional textual evidence) that other characters in the play, namely, Eddie's longshoreman pals—whose background is similar to Eddie's and whose views are not distorted by incestuous desire for Catherine—also read Rodolpho as a "weird." Eddie Carbone, as Arthur Miller has carefully created him, is not isolated in his reactions to Rodolpho.

Eddie's meetings with his confidant, Alfieri, provides a closer look into Eddie's private world. The suggestion that Rodolpho is a homosexual, which he never makes concretely to Beatrice, is more directly stated to Alfieri (although the word "homosexual" is never used). The jibs of Eddie's peers are revealed as he attempts to construct a case against Rodolpho to convince Alfieri that the young submarine is a homosexual. What emerges as a central issue in this scene is that under the written law Eddie Carbone has no recourse *even* if his accusation is true.

Eddie's accusation reveals a mind tortured by the fear that he is about to lose Catherine, and his distress is compounded by his suspicion that Rodolpho is a homosexual. Yet this suspicion, ironically, provides Eddie with a seemingly innocent motive for opposing the marriage of Catherine and Rodolpho. Eddie's accusation of inversion is the foundation upon which he attempts to structure a case against Rodolpho. His efforts to enlist the assistance of Alfieri on his behalf are based upon convincing Alfieri of Rodolpho's homosexuality—of convincing Alfieri that Rodolpho "ain't right." The zeal with which he takes up his hostility to Rodolpho externalizes the intensity of his own passion for Catherine, and obviates any necessity for self-examination which might expose this underlying passion—an exposure Eddie is unable to face. Witness, for example, Eddie's horror when Beatrice confronts him at the end of the play with an open declaration of his subconscious feelings for his niece:

> *Eddie, crying out in agony*: That's what you think of me—that I would have such a thought? *His fists clench his head as though it will burst.*

And, similarly, during his first interview with Alfieri, Eddie reacts furiously to Alfieri's suggestion that he may want Catherine for himself: "What're you talkin' about, marry me! I don't know what the hell you're talkin' about!"

Alfieri, with sagacity and insight, realizes that the real problem involved is Eddie's excessive love for Catherine:

> You know, sometimes God mixes up the people. We all love somebody, the wife, the kids—every man's got somebody that he loves, heh? But sometimes . . . there's too much, and it goes where it mustn't.

Alfieri suggests that this excess of love (and Alfieri never challenges Eddie's genuine protective love for Catherine) may begin to overflow in unnatural directions. Law, Alfieri explains to Eddie, is merely a codification of what is natural and has a right to happen. Eddie's frustration in learning that the law is uninterested in his case against Rodolpho breaks through in an impassioned speech which echoes the theme of "Paper Doll":

> And now I gotta sit in my own house and look at a son-of-a-bitch punk like that—which he came out of nowhere! I give him my house to sleep! I take the blankets off my bed for him, and he takes and puts his dirty filthy hands on her *like a goddam thief*!

Let us listen again to those all-important lyrics: "I'm gonna buy a paper doll that I can call my own. / A doll that other fellows cannot steal." And now Eddie crying to Alfieri: "He's stealing from me!" The robbery motif, the imagery of thievery in Eddie's anguished speech and in the lyrics of "Paper Doll" is clearly not accidental.

Symbolically, Alfieri (Reason) is contrasted with Eddie (Passion); Eddie is a man governed by his passions, and in *A View from the Bridge* Miller is showing us the deficiencies of an impulsive man who operates without the moderation imposed by reason. Yet, one of the elemental ironies of the play is that Alfieri, a symbol of rational thought, a man of legal training, ordered procedure, wisdom, and basic native intelligence, is also powerless to stop the onrushing tide and sweep of the horrible events in this play. Alfieri realizes the direction in which Eddie is heading, but is puzzled by his own inability to halt him. His only gesture is to consult, in an admission of personal helplessness, "a certain old lady in the neighborhood, a very wise old woman" (a practice common among many clannish societies), and is told to "Pray for him." The written law, man's own law, is inadequate here, Miller seems to be saying. Eddie Carbone's fate is in the hands of the Gods. How much like Greek tragedy!

Earlier I mentioned that there is additional evidence to support Eddie's view that Rodolpho is a homosexual, evidence which suggests that not only Eddie thinks Rodolpho is a homosexual. Eddie, recall, visits Alfieri after the famous scene in which he seizes Rodolpho and, in front of Catherine, kisses him. Alfieri, who tries to dissuade Eddie from informing and senses that he is now so inclined, shouts to Eddie after an interview: "You won't have a friend in the world, Eddie! Even those who understand will turn against you, *even the ones who feel the same* will despise you!"

Despite the fact that he recognizes the thoughtlessness of Eddie's action, Alfieri is nevertheless unmistakably aware that others, namely Eddie's fellow longshoremen, also suspect that Rodolpho is a homosexual. Moreover, the scene with Eddie and his friends, Louis and Mike, is instructive here in pointing up that others besides Eddie share his suspicions about Rodolpho. The diction and the tenor of the dialogue clearly suggest that the longshoremen, of whom Louis and Mike are representative, respond to Rodolpho as does Eddie. In the conversation outside Eddie's house, for instance, Louis and Mike, after expressing amazement at Marco's masculine strength, confirm Eddie

in his suspicions. Immediately following their words about Marco, we have this glaring contrast:

> *Mike, grinning*: That blond one, though—
> *Eddie looks at him*. He's got a sense of humor.
> *Louis snickers*.

Miller is careful to note that Mike's words about the "blond one" are framed with a grin, and that Louis then snickers, a direction that significantly reveals that something is being withheld in this conversation. The character of what Mike has to say to Eddie reinforced by Louis' response, does not indicate an appreciation of Rodolpho's humor per se; on the contrary, Mike's words refer to the young submarine's odd behavior on the waterfront. Continuing, Mike relates to Eddie in a fit of hysterical laughter: "You take one look at him—everybody's happy." One day while working with Rodolpho at the Moore MacCormack Line, the other longshoremen "was all hysterical." Miller's stage directions following these words should not be neglected: "*Louis and he* [Mike] *explode in laughter*." Furthermore, it is worth noting that Eddie, Miller tells us, is "*Troubled*" by this conversation. In essence, the significance of this scene is to solidify Eddie's private suspicions of Rodolpho's weird behavior by displaying a public representation and confirmation of these suspicions through the personae of Louis and Mike.

The working environment of which Eddie is a part, specifically, longshoremen, consists of a group of men who depend for their livelihood upon their physical power. Loading and unloading cargo is grueling, physical, masculine labor. I emphasize what is obvious because I wish to make strikingly clear that longshoremen would quite naturally associate physical labor with masculinity. Rodolpho, on the other hand, can sew, sing (in a very high voice, perhaps somewhat effeminate?) and cook—all aptitudes which in the minds of longshoremen, or for that matter any working group which relies upon sheer masculine physical power, are associated with feminity. Plainly Rodolpho is not a homosexual because he sings in a high voice and can cook and sew. But because of their background and work it is understandable that Eddie and his peers regard Rodolpho as they do. And this is why Alfieri, who appreciates the psychology of his Red Hook clients, can say "*even the ones who feel the same will despise you*." It is fallacious to suggest that Eddie Carbone is isolated in his response to Rodolpho. What does finally isolate Eddie from his community is not his innuendoes or even his attempt to degrade Rodolpho in front of Catherine. Rather, it is his overt act of betrayal, of informing the immigration authorities that Rodolpho and Marco are submarines. By this one decisive act, Eddie commits the unforgivable sin of informing, with the inevitable consequence of isolation from his social context.

For betrayal, Marco's spitting in Eddie's face is a symbolic murder which foreshadows his act of murder at the conclusion of the play. The spitting, coupled with a public accusation ("That one! He killed my children! That one stole the food from my children"), underscores the imagery of theft. According to Eddie, Rodolpho has stolen Catherine; Marco has stolen Eddie's "good name." Balancing Eddie's victimization, Marco feels that Eddie has stolen a chance for the life of his children. We might also note that although Eddie's betrayal was not designed to net the two submarine nephews of the butcher, Lipari, both the neighborhood and Lipari condemn and punish Eddie just as severely as if Eddie's act had been originally perpetrated against Lipari and his family. In other words, it is inconsequential against *whom* Eddie informs; the act of informing is what is unforgivable and unforgettable in the Red Hook mind.

Marco is a symbol of primitive justice. Like Eddie, he will not settle for half. The symbolic murder of spitting in Eddie's face does not satisfy his appetite for revenge. As he says to a fearful Alfieri: "In my country he would be dead now. He would not live this long." Marco is a product of the Old World. "Not quite civilized, not quite American," he insists upon a primitive form of justice. Ironically, Marco is as dissatisfied with the law as Eddie. Both want from the law what the law has not been designed to provide—indiscriminate punishment; in a word, retributive justice. An interesting parallel is evident: Eddie seeks recourse to the law to prevent Catherine from marrying someone who "ain't right." When recourse to the law fails, he informs. Marco too wants Eddie punished for degrading his brother, robbing his children, mocking his work. Learning there is no law for that, he reneges on his word to Alfieri and ultimately kills Eddie. Marco's code of law is primitive, punitive justice. As he takes Marco's hand (the same hand that held the chair as a threatening weapon) Alfieri counsels him: "This is not God, Marco. You hear? Only God makes

justice." Interestingly enough, both Eddie and Marco receive warnings from Alfieri; both men reject his advice.

Alfieri, the romantic, makes the clearest statement of authorial opinion we have in *A View from the Bridge*. He recognizes the waste of Eddie's death and the violation of a code of honor. But Alfieri, in his Epilogue following Eddie's death, assigns a dignity to Eddie's action which would otherwise be ambiguous:

> I confess that something perversely pure calls to me from his memory—not purely good, but himself purely, for he allowed himself to be wholly known and for that I think I will love him more than all my sensible clients.

Eddie Carbone is a tragic figure, Miller clearly feels, because in the intransigence of his actions there is an implicit fidelity to the self, an integrity to one's own beliefs no matter how perverse they may be. However wrong he may have been, and Alfieri is not unmindful of Eddie's tragic deed, Eddie nonetheless pursues what he regards as a proper course of action. Reason was absent in his behavior, but the irony is that Alfieri, a product of the compromising attitude of the Italian-American community of Red Hook ("we settle for half"), still loves a man who did not settle for half. Alfieri, the romantic, admires the purity of Eddie's emotions, not the rightness or wrongness of them. Of Alfieri's rewritten Epilogue in the revised version of *A View from the Bridge* Miller has this to say, which I think suggests how desperately he wanted to make clear that Eddie is a tragic figure:

> In revising the play it became possible to accept for myself the implication I had sought to make clear in the original version, which was that however one might dislike this man, who does all sorts of frightful things, he possesses or exemplifies the wondrous and humane fact that he too can be driven to what in the last analysis is a sacrifice of himself for his conception, however misguided, of right, dignity, and justice.

Although Miller considers Eddie a tragic figure, he nonetheless apparently has never had any clearly defined outline of the emotions toward Eddie which he wanted to elicit from his audience. A comparison of his own statements reveals this uncertainty. In the introduction of his *Collected Plays*, Miller suggests that the changes he made in revising the original version had this result: "It was finally possible to mourn this man." On the other hand, three years later, in a new introduction to the paperback reprint of the play, Miller had this to say: "Eddie is still not a man to weep over." Miller's confusion, I think, is the result of his preoccupation with the moral element in *A View from the Bridge* rather than eliciting specific emotions. The dilemma of a man—Eddie—betraying the code of his social milieu is of paramount consequence to Miller, and is what engages his creative energy. His failure to clarify what emotions the audience will feel reveals itself even in the statement about Eddie that he makes Alfieri deliver in the Epilogue to the play. Alfieri, like Miller, has ambivalent feelings toward Eddie: "And yet, it is better to settle for half, it must be! And so I mourn him—I admit it—with a certain . . . alarm."

Despite Miller's recognition of Eddie's moral flaw, he (and I think this is typical of Miller's vision of life) cannot ignore the essential humanity of his characters. His faith in the dignity of man is what leaves him unable to dismiss completely the humanly fallible Eddie Carbone from the race of humanity. Perhaps Linda's words in *Death of a Salesman* can illuminate for us what Miller really thinks of Eddie Carbone:

> I don't say he's a great man. Willy Loman [Eddie Carbone?) never made a lot of money. His name was never in the paper. He's not the finest character that ever lived. But he's a human being, and a terrible thing is happening to him. So attention must be paid. He's not to be allowed to fall into his grave like an old dog. Attention, attention must be finally paid to such a person.

**Source:** Arthur D. Epstein, "A Look at *A View from the Bridge*," in *Critical Essays on Arthur Miller*, edited by James J. Martine, G. K. Hall, 1979, pp. 110–16.

## SOURCES

"Arthur Miller, Legendary American Playwright, Is Dead," in *New York Times*, February 11, 2005, http://www.nytimes.com/2005/02/11/theater/arthur-miller-legendary-american-playwright-is-dead.html (accessed July 1, 2017).

Carson, Neil, *Arthur Miller*, Grove Press, 1982, pp. 1–13.

Cavaioli, Frank J., "Patterns of Italian Immigration to the United States," in *Catholic Social Science Review*, Vol. 13, 2008, pp. 213–29, https://www.pdcnet.org/collection/fshow?id=cssr_2008_0013_0213_0229&file_type=pdf (accessed July 4, 2017).

Chapman, John, Review of *A View from the Bridge*, in *File on Miller*, compiled by C. W. E. Bigsby, Methuen, 1988, p. 37; originally published in *New York Daily News*, September 30, 1955.

Ellis, Samantha, "*A View from the Bridge*, October 1956," in *Guardian* (London, England), July 16, 2003, https://www.theguardian.com/stage/2003/jul/16/theatre.samanthaellis (accessed July 1, 2017).

Gibbs, Walcot, Review of *A View from the Bridge*, in *File on Miller*, compiled by C. W. E. Bigsby, Methuen, 1988, pp. 37–38; originally published in *New Yorker*, October 8, 1955.

Hayman, Ronald, "Interview," in *Conversations with Arthur Miller*, edited by Matthew C. Roudané, University Press of Mississippi, 1987, p. 192; originally published in *Arthur Miller*, Heinemann, 1970.

"LGBT History Month: The 1950s and the Roots of LGBT Politics," Human Rights Campaign website, October 10, 2014, http://www.hrc.org/blog/lgbt-history-month-the-1950s-and-the-roots-of-lgbt-politics (accessed July 3, 2017).

"The Mafia," Best of Sicily, http://www.bestofsicily.com/mafia.htm (accessed July 2, 2017).

Martine, James J., *Critical Essays on Arthur Miller*, G. K. Hall, 1979, p. xxii.

"Masculinity, Gender Roles, and T.V. Shows from the 1950s," in *Artifice*, October 18, 2014, https://the-artifice.com/masculinity-gender-roles-tv-1950s/ (accessed July 3, 2017).

Miller, Arthur, *A View from the Bridge*, in *Arthur Miller: Eight Plays*, Nelson Doubleday, 1981, pp. 393–470.

Morris, Bonnie J., "History of Lesbian, Gay & Bisexual Social Movements," http://www.apa.org/pi/lgbt/resources/history.aspx (accessed July 3, 2017).

Moss, Leonard, *Arthur Miller*, rev. ed., Twayne Publishers, 1980, pp. 1–10, 44–49.

"The 1950s–1960s," in *Italian Tribune*, August 24, 2016, http://www.italiantribune.com/the-1950s-1960s/ (accessed July 2, 2017).

"Red Hook," South Brooklyn Network, http://www.southbrooklyn.com/neighborhood/red-hook (accessed July 2, 2017).

"Red Hook History," Waterfront Barge Museum website, http://waterfrontmuseum.org/red-hook-history (accessed July 2, 2017).

"Red Hook Justice," PBS website, http://www.pbs.org/independentlens/redhookjustice/redhook.html (accessed July 2, 2017).

Stapinski, Helene, "When America Barred Italians," in *New York Times*, June 2, 2017, https://www.nytimes.com/2017/06/02/opinion/illegal-immigration-italian-americans.html (accessed July 2, 2017).

"*A View from the Bridge*," in *File on Miller*, compiled by C. W. E. Bigsby, Methuen, 1988, pp. 36–39.

Wertheim, Albert, "*A View from the Bridge*," in *The Cambridge Companion to Arthur Miller*, 2nd ed., edited by Christopher Bigsby, Cambridge University Press, 2010, pp. 104–17.

# FURTHER READING

Gilbert, James, *Men in the Middle: Searching for Masculinity in the 1950s*, University of Chicago Press, 2005.
Gilbert delves into the roles that mass media played in both promoting male conformity and introducing people to differences in ways that laid the groundwork for the social revolution of the 1960s. Among the celebrated men focused on are playwright Tennessee Williams and sex researcher Alfred Kinsey.

Mello, William J., *New York Longshoremen: Class and Power on the Docks*, University Press of Florida, 2010.
Interactions between waterfront companies, union leaders, and governmental officials—especially as influenced by organized crime—made for big news at times in the twentieth century. Mello's history explores the public and private currents that determined the course of labor-related events in the city.

Miller, Arthur, *Timebends: A Life*, Grove Press, 1987.
The most definitive—and acclaimed—treatment of Miller's life is his own, written toward the end of his active writing career and reflecting not only on the events that mattered most to him but also on the broader trajectory of the American twentieth century.

Morreale, Ben, and Robert Carola, *Italian Americans: The Immigrant Experience*, Beaux Arts Editions, 2013.
In a history book full of black-and-white photographs that bring it to life, Morreale and Carola describe the course of Italians' history as a minority population contributing to the honor, success, and fascination of America.

# SUGGESTED SEARCH TERMS

Arthur Miller AND A View from the Bridge

A View from the Bridge AND New York OR London

Red Hook AND Brooklyn

Red Hook AND waterfront

New York longshoremen

Italian American AND culture OR history

Sicilian Mafia AND Brooklyn

Arthur Miller AND Communism OR HUAC

Arthur Miller AND Marilyn Monroe

# Who's Afraid of Virginia Woolf?

**1966**

*Who's Afraid of Virginia Woolf?* is the screenwriter Ernest Lehman's 1966 adaptation of the Tony Award–winning drama by Edward Albee that debuted in 1962. Controversy surrounded the play when it was named the winner of the 1963 Pulitzer Prize in drama but the prize was not awarded owing to the play's subject matter and coarse language. Albee's play reflects the growing tensions of the Cold War and disillusionment with the American dream as the characters cruelly exploit each other. The film launched the film-directing career of the theater veteran Mike Nichols. Nichols and Lehman left much of the original dialogue intact. *Who's Afraid of Virginia Woolf?* violated the antiquated movie censorship rules of the Hays Code. Its approval for release helped to end the Hays Code and bring about the current rating system. The film removed some of the more offensive language and takes some scenes outside of George and Martha's house, which is the only setting of the play.

The stars of the film, Elizabeth Taylor and Richard Burton, married at the time, skillfully performed the roles of a dysfunctional middle-aged couple and generated a great deal of interest. *Who's Afraid of Virginia Woolf?* became one of the highest-grossing films of 1966 and earned Academy Awards for best actress, best actress in a supporting role, best art direction, best cinematography, and best costume design.

*Edward Albee (© Library of Congress, Prints & Photographs Division, Reproduction number LC-USZ62-116771 (b&w film copy neg.))*

## PLOT SUMMARY

This black-and-white film begins with a shot of the moon and pans across a college campus, establishing the setting. Sad but calm music plays as Martha and George, a middle-aged couple, leave a party. They are walking home in and out of the shadows as the credits role. He hushes her because it is after 2:00 a.m., but they are amiable on their walk.

The darkness dramatically shifts as the couple turns on the bright light in their disheveled house. Martha is drunk, and George looks tired. As they enter, Martha says, "What a dump," a line made famous by a character Bette Davis played in the movie *Beyond the Forest*. Martha asks George which film the line is from as he cleans up after her, and they walk into the kitchen. George does not know, but Martha, while eating chicken, continues to ask him and to berate his ignorance. He complains about being tired, and she criticizes him for not doing anything. She demands a drink and informs him that they have company coming because her "daddy," the head of the college, has told her to "be nice" to them.

Annoyed, George follows Martha upstairs to the bedroom, where they argue, and she hides things in a halfhearted attempt to clean. He lies on the bed, and she sings "who's afraid of Virginia Woolf?" to the tune of "Here We Go Around the Mulberry Bush" while bouncing on him. They continue to insult each other and laugh as the shots shift between close-ups and medium shots. George rejects her advances, and they go downstairs. The verbal sparring continues, and she clumsily hides debris. She orders him to answer the door, and he warns her not to talk about "the kid." She yells an insult at the same moment the door opens.

The younger couple, Nick and Honey, are obviously uncomfortable entering the tense atmosphere. George and Martha insist that they stay, and George makes drinks. The polite Honey and Nick listen to George and Martha fling insults at each other with each compliment about the house and college. Cutaway shots show their unease. When Honey praises Martha's father, Martha takes the time to insult George for wasting the opportunity that being married to the president's daughter provides. Honey quickly jumps up from the sofa and asks for directions to the bathroom. Martha shows her the way.

George and Nick are alone, and George irritates Nick by attempting to spar verbally. The blond Nick is a biologist, and George is a history professor. Between making comments about the two women, George hypothesizes that science will destroy cultures. Nick reveals that he and Honey do not have children. Honey comes downstairs and mentions George and Martha's son. The expression on George's face changes with a close-up, and he looks upstairs in a rage as if accepting a challenge. He tells Nick and Honey to stay.

Martha enters in a tight outfit and insults George's work when he comments on it. She openly flirts with Nick while berating George. The camera cuts away, focusing on the different speakers and occasionally gives insight to the responses of the characters listening. Martha tells a story about beating George at boxing, and he leaves the room. In low-key lighting, he walks in and out of shadow to get a rifle, building tension for the viewer. George returns to the living room and aims the rifle at Martha. Honey screams, and there is a close-up reaction shot of

# FILM TECHNIQUE

- A low-angle shot is filmed from below the subject. In *Who's Afraid of Virginia Woolf?* the low-angle shot emphasizes the character with the upper hand. For example, Martha and Nick are filmed at a low angle when they dance and humiliate George.

- High-angle shots are filmed from above and can be used to make people or objects appear smaller or less powerful. Martha is filmed in a high-angle shot after George ends the illusion that they have a son.

- A close-up reveals the detail of the character by focusing on a single subject. For example, Martha's monologue in the kitchen is a close-up that allows the audience to see the emotional revelation of her love for George and sadness over their lives together.

- Extreme close-ups do not show the entire face of the characters. An extreme close-up of Martha yelling at George, for example, shows both her emotional response and the strong shift in action.

- Medium-wide shots are also called American shots, according to *Elements of Cinematography: Camera*, posted at the University of Texas at Dallas website. The shots show the upper bodies of the characters, cutting out the legs. These shots, such as that of Martha and George in the kitchen when they arrive home, provide a good view of the characters' facial expressions without using a full close-up.

- A reaction shot shows a character's reaction to the preceding shot, according to *Film Glossary*, posted at the Rice University website. A reaction shot is used in the film when Honey tells George that Martha has mentioned his son's birthday. George displays shock and anger, which motivates the final scene.

- An establishing shot is an extremely long shot at the beginning of a scene that gives the viewer the context of the ensuing closer shots, according to *Film Glossary*. An establishing shot is used to show the college campus as Martha and George leave a party.

---

Martha's face before George fires an umbrella. Everyone laughs, and Martha kisses George.

Honey asks about their son, and Martha attempts to change the subject, saying that she is sorry that she has mentioned him. George keeps talking, and they argue about the color of the son's eyes. Martha begins insulting George again for losing the opportunity to become president and compares him to Nick. George breaks a bottle in anger during her tirade. He finally grabs Honey and starts dancing while singing "Who's Afraid of Virginia Woolf?" The spinning makes Honey feel sick, and she runs out of the living room.

Martha makes coffee while George walks to the swing outside the house. Nick watches him in a long shot and joins him with a bottle of liquor. Nick says that his wife is always sick. The shot is of their backs and takes place in low-key lighting.

The shot moves to one of George and Nick from the front. Nick reveals that he has married Honey because she was pregnant, but it was a hysterical pregnancy. They laugh about it. George tells the story of a friend who accidentally killed both of his parents. He says that the man is in a mental hospital from the shock.

George makes a comment about Martha not having pregnancies and begins to present a revelation of his own when Martha walks out and interrupts, standing in the darkness in the background. Nick also admits that money motivated his relationship with Honey. Her father was an evangelist who made a fortune and left it to Honey. George says that Martha's stepmother was wealthy and died soon after marrying Martha's father. The men joke about fathers-in-law.

George warns Nick that he sees him as a threat, and Nick tells George his plan to take over the university. He makes a comment about having an affair with Martha. They argue when George tries to give Nick advice about the college and insults his character as they return to the house. Nick calls Honey and gets their coats. Martha becomes very upset when Nick says they are leaving. George gets the car to take their guests home.

The scene moves to the interior of the car. George and Martha are in the front and Nick and Honey in the back. George and Martha insult each other's parenting, each one accusing the other of harming their son. Honey is extremely drunk and tries to calm the situation. Finally, she talks about dancing. She asks whether they can stop at a roadhouse she sees. Martha agrees with her and insists that George stop the car. He gives in, and there is a shot of his foot on the pedal.

An overhead shot shows that Honey is dancing alone without music. The effect is jolting. George puts classical music on the jukebox to annoy the others in the roadhouse as he and Martha discuss who will dance with whom. Honey is angry when Nick tries to make her stop dancing and tells him to leave her alone. Martha changes the music, and Nick and Martha dance together closely in low-angle shots while George and Honey watch in the background. Martha continues to belittle George, which Nick enjoys. Martha decides to tell a story about George's novel. She explains that her father refused to allow publication of the book, which is about a boy who kills his parents. George unplugs the jukebox and yells at her to stop. She reveals that the story is George's autobiography. Enraged, George attacks Martha, calling her Satan, and Nick pulls him away. The bartender comes from the back to investigate and announce the bar is closing. George tells the bartender that they are playing a game. He persuades the bartender to give them a final round before they leave so they can play another game.

George plays Get the Guests. He also asks them whether the story of his first novel is true and admits that he wishes Martha had not said anything about it. He goes on to describe the plot of his second novel. At first, Honey wants to listen to the story, but she becomes upset when she realizes that it is the story of Nick's marrying her because of a hysterical pregnancy and her father's money. She asks George to stop and then runs out. Nick is angry that George has caused trouble for him. He threatens George as

he follows Honey, insisting they walk home. Martha is furious, but George says the game has been an amusement for her benefit.

In the parking lot, tempers flare again, and Martha attacks George. A handheld camera catches the motion of the fight. He threatens to have her committed, and the two declare war in a close-up that resembles a couple about to kiss. Martha drives away, leaving George in the parking lot. George watches her pick up Nick and Honey at the side of the road.

George walks home and finds Honey alone in the backseat of the car. The chain is on the house door, and he accidentally rings the doorbell as he breaks in. On the stairs, he finds the clothes Martha has been wearing. In a low-angle shot, George begins laughing as he walks to the steps, where he starts crying. Honey, extremely drunk, gets out of the car and asks him about the bells she has heard, meaning the doorbell. From the front yard, George sees the silhouette of Nick and Martha upstairs. He quietly whispers a promise to get even with Martha and asks Honey if she knows what is happening. She says that she does not want to know. Honey begins rambling about not wanting a baby and being afraid of childbirth. George confronts her aggressively, guessing that without Nick's knowledge she has prevented herself from becoming pregnant. Honey continues asking about the bells, and George has an idea. He tells Honey that the sound is a messenger delivering the news of his son's death. He practices delivering the news to Martha.

There is a shot of the moon with Martha's voice in the background. The camera pans to outside the house, where Martha is looking for the rest of the party and screaming for George. She has a clinking glass in her hand. Nick comes outside and tells her that she and everyone else have lost their senses. He has just left Honey on the floor of the bathroom, whispering that she is hiding. They are sitting on the porch, and Martha tells Nick that he is not better than anyone else, implying that he has been impotent with her.

In the kitchen, Martha looks out the back door and admits that George is the only one who has ever made her happy. The monologue uses a close-up of her face. She punishes him for loving her and expects a terrible end to their relationship. The doorbell rings, and Martha orders Nick to answer it, calling him her houseboy. She mocks his attempt to seduce her to benefit his career and tells him that he must be of use in some way.

Nick answers the door, and there is a close-up of some white snapdragons. George is behind, saying something in Spanish that translates to "flowers for the dead." He mocks Nick with Martha, first referring to him as his son and then calling him the houseboy. Nicks says that he can never determine when George is telling the truth, and both George and Martha explain that the truth does not matter. Martha protects Nick's feelings by allowing George to believe that he has slept with her. George demands that they play a final game and tells Nick to bring Honey back to the living room. Alone, George puts his arm around Martha, and she asks him to stop the games. He slaps her hand away from him and insists that she be angry for their last battle.

The group is together, Honey is very drunk and hops into the room. George begins the game by talking about his and Martha's son. George insults Martha's parenting before she tells the story of the birth and childhood of the son she wanted. The camera cuts away between Martha and George, who reminds her of details. Honey is moved by the story and proclaims her desire for a baby.

Martha then begins to insult George's parenting and explain how she tried to protect their son from his influence. Meanwhile, George is reading Latin. The text is the Mass of the dead. When Martha finishes, George tells her that he has news. Honey tries to stop him, but George describes their son's death. Martha is angry and devastated. She tells George that he cannot make these decisions and blames George for killing their son. Nick holds her back from attacking George. She demands evidence of their son's death, and George says that he has eaten the telegram with the announcement.

In a close frame, Nick has a realization and says that he understands what is happening. Their son is not real. George tells Martha that he has decided to kill their son because she has broken their rule and told Honey about him.

George announces that the party is over as the sun rises in the background. A devastated Martha admits that she and George could not have children, and George escorts Nick and Honey out, interrupting Nick from making his final comment. George turns out the lights and tells Martha that it is time for bed. He sits down

next to her and puts his hand on her shoulder. He strokes her hair, telling her that it was time, and she tries to accept the change in their lives. George sings "Who's Afraid of Virginia Woolf?" and Martha admits that she is. The camera zooms in for a close-up on the clasped hands before the exit music plays without any credits.

# CHARACTERS

### Bartender
The roadhouse bartender is a small role. He checks on the commotion between George and Martha and tells the groups that the bar is closing.

### Bartender's Wife
The wife of the bartender noiselessly gives the group their last round of drinks.

### George
George is a middle-aged associate professor in the history department who is married to Martha, the daughter of the university president. Although he is highly intelligent, George has little ambition. He resents his father-in-law's influence on Martha and her expectations for his career. George may have accidentally killed his parents and written about it in a novel, but he never admits the story is true.

George appears to be dominated by Martha, but he is an equal partner in their games. He finds Nick to be a threat to his career and relationship. George is deeply devoted to Martha despite their tumultuous marriage. Still, he deals the final blow in their war by killing their imaginary son and removing the illusion from their lives.

Richard Burton played George on screen and earned an Academy Award nomination for best actor. He was married to Elizabeth Taylor as the film was entering production and encouraged her to take on the role of Martha.

### Honey
The wife of Nick, Honey is young and naïve. Although she seems a doting wife, she reveals her fear of pregnancy and childbirth, and she secretly hides her family planning from Nick. She is easily shocked and sickened by stress. Honey may have been pregnant when she married, but Nick believes it was a hysterical pregnancy. She is also the daughter of a corrupt evangelist who gathered a fortune from the

faithful. Her interactions with Nick indicate an unhappiness in their relationship that she attempts to avoid by staying ignorant of his transgressions.

Sandy Dennis played Honey and won an Academy Award for best supporting actress.

## *Martha*

Martha is the daughter of the president of Carthage University. She is in her fifties and married to George, who is younger than she is. Martha always compares her husband to her father and publicly berates him for his failure to move up in the college and follow her plan for their lives. Martha drinks too much and reveals her greatest secret to Honey, causing George to remove the lie from their lives.

Although Martha attempts to sleep with Nick, she reveals that George makes her happy. She punishes George because of her own self-hatred and disappointment in herself. Martha's desire for a child that she could never have is what leads to the creation of an imaginary son with her husband. When her son is gone, she fears living with George in reality.

Elizabeth Taylor gained weight and wore makeup to age her for the role of Martha. She was only in her thirties at the time, but her convincing portrayal of an unhappy woman in her fifties won an Academy Award for best actress.

## *Nick*

Nick is blond, thirty, physically fit, and highly intelligent, having achieved a master's degree by the age of nineteen. He is a biologist with a plan for moving up in the college. His ambition attracts Martha, and he has the idea to sleep with her and other faculty wives as a way to improve his career.

Nick's marriage to Honey is one of convenience. She was supposedly pregnant when they married, and he was attracted to her family money. Nick shows little regard for his wife's happiness. He flirts in front of her and leaves her passed out in the car when he attempts to sleep with Martha. Nick finds himself frustrated as he becomes entangled in the games of George and Martha. He finally realizes the truth about Martha's secret game. He attempts to address George before leaving, but George does not allow him to speak.

George Segal was nominated for an Academy Award for best supporting actor for his portrayal of Nick.

## THEMES

### *Success*

The theme of success runs throughout *Who's Afraid of Virginia Woolf?* Martha is deeply unsatisfied with George's unsuccessful academic career. She tells the story of their early relationship, when she and her father both considered George a worthy successor to his father-in-law. She had great plans for them, and she is humiliated and frustrated to be married to an associate professor rather than the head of the history department. Nick is the antithesis of George. He has plans to move up at Carthage University, which initially attracts Martha. She uses Nick as a tool to punish George for his lack of ambition.

When Nick and George speak alone, the audience understands that Nick's ambition drives all of his actions. His marriage to Honey is based on his desire for her family money and the obligation of a possible pregnancy. He admits his plan to take over the roles of older professors and sleep his way to the top. He jokingly tells George that he should start with Martha because of her connection to the president. When Nick does make his move, however, Martha is not deceived. She confronts him with the truth of his actions, pointing out that ambition, not passion, is his motivation. The price he pays for her help in his success is pretending to be her houseboy.

George does not fit the traditional definition of success. He is not wealthy or powerful. He has married for love and has not tried to exploit his relationship with the university president's daughter. Martha and Nick humiliate him, but George manages to gain the upper hand in his sparring with both Nick and Martha. George is flawed but is repulsed by Nick's selfish need to destroy others for his career. He also fears what Nick and a society ruled by science and ambition would mean for culture and diversity.

### *Illusion (Philosophy)*

In an interview with the *Paris Review*, Albee admits that the play is about the fear of lost illusion: "And of course, who's afraid of Virginia Woolf means who's afraid of the big *bad* wolf... who's afraid of living life without false illusions." The movie maintains this theme. Different stories are told throughout the film, but their truth is uncertain. For example, George tells Nick a story about a young man who accidentally kills

# READ.
# WATCH.
# WRITE.

- The film *Who's Afraid of Virginia Woolf?* deviates from the play by moving the characters outside and to a roadhouse. What purpose did these changes serve? Use an application such as easel.ly to create a list of ideas about how these changes affect the story compared with the staging of the play. Present your findings and explain why you do or do not agree with the writer's and director's choices.

- Pay close attention to Martha in the film. Write a report on her based on her behavior, language, dress, and mannerisms. How do the other characters react to her? What could explain her behavior and the need to live apart from reality?

- Martha and Honey are both miserable women. How does the film address femininity and women's roles? In a small group, discuss these characters and whether they represent any tropes or stereotypes. Create a web page to share your discoveries. Provide links to any examples of stereotypes or tropes that you feel are relevant.

- Divide into pairs. Prepare and perform an interview with Nick or Honey that takes place after their encounter with George and Martha and upload it using an application such as Edpuzzle. How would the character feel after that night? What, if anything, changed for the character? What would the interviewer ask, and what would the character say?

- Watch the 1941 movie *Citizen Kane*, considered a masterpiece that is still studied by directors. The movie follows the life of Kane, an ambitious man who ruins those around him. Compare the themes between the two films and the techniques used to tell the two stories. What similarities and differences are there? Break into small groups and create a blog. Ask each student to write one entry about their observations for the blog.

- Watch the 1968 film *A Lion in Winter*, which is the story of the English King Henry II and his wife, Eleanor of Aquitaine, and their destructive marriage. Break into pairs and create a list of similarities and differences between the stories; display them using a Venn diagram. Regroup and share your observations with the rest of the class.

---

his parents. Martha later reveals that the story is about George, but neither one has a history of being truthful, making every anecdote questionable. A frustrated Nick finally admits that he cannot determine when George is lying. Both George and Martha tell him that he should not know the difference.

In the end, both couples see past their own illusions about themselves and their relationships. Honey and Nick are not a happily married young couple. Rather, they deceive each other and keep secrets. George removes the central illusion of the play when he tells the story of his and Martha's son's death, which mirrors the death he describes to Nick. He ends the story of their son, forcing Martha to live in reality with him. George refuses to resurrect the illusion for Martha. When he sings, "Who's Afraid of Virginia Woolf?" to her, she admits that she is. She is afraid of living a life without illusion.

### American Dream

At first glance, Nick is the all-American ideal working hard to achieve the American dream. He is a blond athlete who is also intelligent. His work in science reflects the growing interest in scientific discoveries of the 1960s. Nick plans to be successful in his work and reach the pinnacles he desires. The young character, however, deviates from the traditional American dream of

*Mike Nichols* (© *Tinseltown | Shutterstock.com*)

finding success through hard work by showing a lack of integrity. He chooses to use selfish and underhanded tactics to move forward.

Nick finds financial security by marrying Honey and shows little consideration for her feelings. He tells George the story of her hysterical pregnancy within hours of meeting him. When George reveals knowledge of Honey's secret, Nick is angry about how this revelation will affect him. It is possible that Nick will achieve what he sets out to accomplish as he tries to manipulate people to advance him. The question remains, however, what is the cost of the American dream?

As the young wife of a man who has a bright future, Honey also seems to be living the dream of many American women. The only thing to complete the image is motherhood. Honey, however, has no desire to have children. She keeps her fears and actions to prevent pregnancy secret. It is unlikely that Nick, who cares about appearances, would support her decision. Honey, who is obviously not happily married, rejects the last step of

the American dream for women. She seems to change her mind toward the end, but it is possible that she is only momentarily moved by Martha's story because of her drunken state.

## STYLE

### Black and White
*Who's Afraid of Virginia Woolf?* is shot in monochrome, or black and white, which uses an emulsion that changes colors into various shades of gray. In the 1960s, most black-and-white movies were art films or movies with small budgets. Nichols's choice of black and white was deliberate. J. W. Whitehead explains in *Mike Nichols and the Cinema of Transformation* that Nichols's "interpretation of Albee's play [was] an artifice aware of its artificiality, not a work of kitchen-sink realism." Whitehead quotes Nichols as saying, "The whole idea of movie as metaphor changed with color.... In *Virginia Woolf*, the whole thing is an *idea* of reality." The black-and-white medium was the best way to illustrate the themes of truth and illusion that the play presents.

### Sound
The score of *Who's Afraid of Virginia Woolf?* helps to establish the mood of the film. In the moonlight, for example, the music is calm and melancholy. It contrasts the coming action of the movie while giving expression to the personal feelings of the characters. The action that follows is in stark contrast to the music, making the shift even more jarring.

### Low-Key Lighting
The light and shadow in *Who's Afraid of Virginia Woolf?* help develop emotion within different scenes. The low-key lighting in the film allows characters to move from the shadow. For example, low-key lighting is used to develop suspense and a sense of foreboding when George goes to get his gun from the closet. The low-key lighting also creates a somber tone when George is alone on the swing at night.

### Mise-en-scène
The mise-en-scène, which includes the set, lighting, and costumes, provides greater insight into the characters and develops the tone. The chaos

of Martha and George's house reflects the chaos of their relationship.

### Cinema Verité

Cinema verité implemented a handheld camera and was originally used in filming documentaries. Stephen J. Bottoms explains in *Albee: "Who's Afraid of Virginia Woolf?"* that this technique combined with a real-life location "provided Nichols with an appropriate means of bringing the cinema audience into George and Martha's intimate delusionary world." The effect of using a handheld camera allows the film to reflect the drunken confusion that the characters experience.

## CULTURAL CONTEXT

### Women in the 1960s

The second wave of feminism began in the 1960s. Betty Friedan's book *The Feminine Mystique* (1963) explored the dissatisfaction women felt in being placed in the sole role of wife and mother and encouraged them to look for their personal fulfillment. During the 1960s, women faced many limitations. The birth control pill, for example, was not approved by the US Food and Drug Administration until 1960, and it was available to married women only, according to Katie McLaughlin in "5 Things Women Couldn't Do in the 1960s." Women also could not obtain credit cards in their own names or serve on juries. They were also prevented from attending Ivy League universities and taking on professional roles.

The 1960s, however, was also a time of change for women. Sex discrimination in the workplace was included in Title VII of the 1964 Civil Rights Act. The National Organization for Women formed in 1966 to, according to its statement of purpose, to "take action to bring women into full participation in the mainstream of American society...exercising all the privileges and responsibilities thereof in truly equal partnership with men" and further

> to initiate or support action...to break through the silken curtain of prejudice and discrimination against women in government, industry, the professions, the churches, the political parties, the judiciary, the labor unions, in education, science, medicine, law, religion and every other field of importance in American society.

Many people, however, saw the women's movement as a danger to traditional American values and a threat to society.

Martha's frustrations reflect the limitations placed on women in the 1960s. In almost every way, she is the antithesis of the socially acceptable woman. Martha does not keep a tidy home or cater to her husband's needs. She is strong and aggressive and desires authority. She is an ambitious woman who, unfortunately, can realize her ambitions only through her husband. As a woman, Martha would not likely have had the opportunity to become a professor, and she definitely would not be able to follow in her father's footsteps and take on a role of authority. George's lack of ambition frustrates her because she has no option to make her own way. Honey's desire to take control of her reproduction also reflects the limitations and viewpoints of the time.

### The Cold War and the 1960s

The Cold War started shortly after World War II. The rise of communism in the Soviet Union and Eastern Europe was seen as a threat to Western democracy. In 1947, President Harry Truman introduced the Truman Doctrine in a speech. This doctrine promised to support other nations in the fight against communism. Although the Soviet Union and the United States were allies in World War II, the relationship between the two countries was tense for decades as each side tried to gain the upper hand in weapons and technology. In 1960, Cuba became an ally of the Soviet Union, and the threat of war came closer to American shores. In 1962, ballistic missiles and nuclear warheads arrived in Cuba. President John F. Kennedy demanded their removal and created an American naval blockade to prevent the Soviet Union from supplying more weapons. Finally, the Soviet Union agreed to remove the missiles in exchange for a US promise not to invade Cuba. The United States also removed missiles from Turkey.

The play *Who's Afraid of Virginia Woolf?* opened the same year as the Cuban missile crisis and reflected the anxiety of the Cold War. As an entry in the *Encyclopedia of War and American Society* explains, "Americans confronted the prospect of imminent nuclear war as one might expect: some were fatalistic, others lived in denial, but nearly all felt a most palpable fear and many panicked."

*Elizabeth Taylor, George Segal, Richard Burton, and Sandy Dennis* (© *Keystone | Getty Images*)

*Who's Afraid of Virginia Woolf?* reflects the stress of the Cold War. Military terminology and war references abound in the film. Albee admitted that George and Martha were named after George and Martha Washington. The tension between George and Martha and George and Nick escalates over the course of the film. Eventually, the skirmishes lead to a declaration of war. George unleashes his version of the nuclear bomb by killing his and Martha's nonexistent son.

### Changing Art and Culture in the 1960s

The 1960s saw a change in what Americans found socially acceptable. Through much of the decade, films were subject to the Motion Picture Production Code, also called the Hays Code, created in 1930 and named after Will Hays, who served as president of the Motion Picture Producers and Distributors of America (MPPDA) at the time. The MPPDA eventually became the Motion Picture Association of America (MPAA). The code was initially not well enforced but soon became the standard as a seal of approval was needed for films to appear in most theaters. Bob Mondello, in "Remembering Hollywood's Hays Code, 40 Years On," points out the restrictions: "The mocking of religion and the depiction of illegal drug use were prohibited, as were interracial romance, revenge plots and the showing of a crime method clearly enough that it might be imitated." Sexual topics, pregnancy, abortion, and coarse language were also addressed in the Hays Code.

*Who's Afraid of Virginia Woolf?* created a conflict with the Hays Code before shooting even started. Harry M. Benshoff, citing the work of Leonard J. Leff and Jerold Simmons, writes in *American Cinema of the 1960s*: "For over two years the film's producers tried in various ways to rewrite the script, but eventually it was filmed with most of its raunchy and/or blasphemous dialogue intact." The code seal had been initially denied but was granted after an appeal. Warner Bros. released the movie with the stipulation that no one younger than eighteen be allowed to view it without a parent. The release of *Who's Afraid of Virginia Woolf?* and other films the same year brought about the end of the Hays Code. The MPAA rating system was implemented in 1968, allowing viewers to decide for themselves what they found offensive.

## CRITICAL OVERVIEW

Nichols's vision of Albee's play was considered shocking at the time of its release because of the language and honest discussion of matters that were not typically addressed in films. Although twenty-first-century audiences might find it tame, there was concern at the time over how the public and critics would react.

*Who's Afraid of Virginia Woolf?*, however, was both a commercial and critical success. The *Variety* review, for example, proclaims that the "direction by Mike Nichols in his feature debut, and four topflight performances score an artistic bullseye." Some critics, however, found the choice to move part of the action out of George and Martha's house a poor decision. Stanley Kauffmann's review for the *New York Times* states, "He has also placed one scene in a roadhouse, which is a patently forced move for visual variety." Still, Kauffmann praises the overall effect of the movie, calling it "one of the most scathingly honest American films ever made."

Even critics who were less than enthusiastic about the subject matter of the play brought to the screen were thrilled with the acting and directing. In a review in the *New York Daily News*, Kate Cameron calls the greatest element of the film "the magnificent manner in which Elizabeth Taylor, Richard Burton, George Segal and Sandy Dennis take hold to their respective roles and deliver them to the audience in an uncompromising manner."

## CRITICISM

### April Paris

*Paris is a freelance writer with a degree in classical literature and a background in academic writing. In the following essay, she argues that Martha*

> THEY ARE TWO BROKEN AND FLAWED PEOPLE. THEIR PERSONAL FEELINGS OF GUILT AND SELF-LOATHING LEAD THEM TO A DYSFUNCTIONAL AND DESTRUCTIVE MARRIAGE THAT RELIES ON GAMES AND ILLUSION TO SURVIVE. THEIR LOVE BECOMES TWISTED, AND THEIR ONLY HOPE OF SALVATION IS THROUGH FACING THEIR REALITY."

*and George love each other and that their dysfunction stems from their personal unhappiness and need to live in illusion.*

At its heart, *Who's Afraid of Virginia Woolf?* is a movie about love and marriage. George and Martha may have a vicious relationship, but they are genuinely devoted to each other. They are two broken and flawed people. Their personal feelings of guilt and self-loathing lead them to a dysfunctional and destructive marriage that relies on games and illusion to survive. Their love becomes twisted, and their only hope of salvation is through facing their reality.

J. W. Whitehead points out in *Mike Nichols and the Cinema of Transformation* that Nichols used the opening scene in which George and Martha walk home together to establish their connection: "It is crucial that, through all that follows, much of it vile, vindictive, and injurious, we return to an understanding of this essential companionship." For all their flaws, George and Martha are strongly motivated by love for each other.

In the beginning, the games that George and Martha play are almost a form of romance. For example, George shoots at Martha with a prop gun, startling her. Rather than being frightened or angry, Martha briefly praises the ingenuity of the game. George does not enjoy her constant humiliation, but he has learned how to play her game. As he tells Nick, "Martha and I are having... nothing. Martha and I are merely exercising... that's all, we're merely walking what's left of our wits. Don't pay any attention to it." Martha, in her turn, praises George's ability to keep up with the game as fast as she changes the rules. The games provide a distraction for their discontent and allows them to flee or engage their personal demons.

# WHAT DO I SEE NEXT?

- Released by MGM in 1967, *The Graduate* was Nichols's second film and earned him an Academy Award. The movie is rated PG and tells the story of a college graduate who has an affair with an older woman and of the fallout that ensues.

- *Schindler's List* (Universal Amblin Entertainment) opened in 1994. The director, Stephen Spielberg, used black-and-white technique to film this R-rated movie about the Holocaust.

- Twentieth Century Fox released *Gone Girl* in 2014. This R-rated thriller directed by David Fincher addresses the theme of truth and reality as a married couple engages in a psychological war against each other.

- Albee's play *A Delicate Balance* was adapted into a PG-rated film directed by Tony Richardson and produced by American Film Theater in 1973. Like *Virginia Woolf*, the film addresses the theme of illusion in a dysfunctional family.

- *Cleopatra* was the first film starring Elizabeth Taylor and Richard Burton. MGM's historical drama, released in 1963 and rated G, was directed by Joseph L. Mankiewicz with uncredited direction by Rouben Mamoulian and Darryl F. Zanuck. The two leads showed great chemistry and soon became a couple who would go on to star in eleven movies together.

- Nichols's *Silkwood* was released by MGM in 1983. Based on a true story, the R-rated film shows the versatility of Nichols as a director. The movie stars Meryl Streep, who plays a whistleblower at a nuclear power plant.

- The *Bridge to Terabithia* is based on the children's book by the same name. Released in 2007 and rated PG, the main characters create a fantasy world to hide from reality.

- Based on Yan Martel's novel of the same name, *Life of Pi* was released in 2012 and rated PG. Pi Patel recalls the incredible story of surviving a shipwreck and his view of the world and reality.

---

The couple efficiently exploits the weaknesses that they know to win their games. Although the audience hears some of their past, George and Martha's insistence that one cannot know the difference between truth and illusion makes the full story difficult to pin down. George tells Nick the story of a young man who kills his parents and spends the rest of his life in a mental hospital. Martha later reveals that the story is about George and that his including it in his novel has killed his future at the college. George's rage at Martha and his insistence that the game is over gives the impression that there is truth to the tale. Still, he does not admit it. "True or false? I mean, true or false that there ever was such a thing. Anyway, she told you about it, my first novel, my memory book which I'd sort of preferred she hadn't."

Regardless of which details are true, George is apparently overcome by a sense of guilt and self-loathing. Stanley Kauffmann explains in his review for the *New York Times* that Burton is a "specialist in sensitive self-disgust" and is "convincing as a man with a great lake of nausea in him, on which he sails with regret and compulsive amusement." This regret allows him to accept Martha's cruelty but not embrace her love. He rejects each act of love or tenderness that she shows as the games escalate. He is better equipped to handle a barb than he is a kiss.

Martha initially appears to be a shrew with no love for her husband. She takes every opportunity to emasculate him. For example, she tells a story about beating him in boxing. She also compares him to Nick and her father, bemoaning being trapped in his failure. The truth,

Story-in-Pictures    "WHO'S AFRAID OF VIRGINIA WOOLF?"    Photo 2

Martha, a sloppy, matronly and fading voluptuary, hides her tumultuous frustrations and feminine vulnerability behind a loud-mouthed vulgarity. Her father is president of the college and she berates George for his lowly professional status.
© 1966 BY WARNER BROS. PICTURES INC.    COUNTRY OF ORIGIN U.S.A.

*Elizabeth Taylor won an Oscar for her performance* (© *Michael Ochs Archives / Getty Images*)

however, is that Martha hates herself more than she does anyone else. In a monologue delivered as she looks out the back door, she reveals that George is the only man who could ever make her happy. Her self-hatred, however, keeps her from being happy, and she punishes George for the sin of loving her.

On the night on which the film takes place, the games escalate as the illusions fall away. George's illusion is in the past as he rewrites the story of his parents' deaths, making it a work of fiction rather than fact. C. W. E. Bigsby explains in *Journal of American Studies*, "George, the historian, looks to the past both as protection from present reality and a welcome relief from an enervating conformism." Martha's decision to tell their guests about the novel eliminates illusionary escape. Her decision to mention both the novel

and their son incites George's anger and brings them to a declaration of war. Martha ups the stakes by choosing to shift from aggressive flirting with Nick to an attempted affair. When George finds her clothes on the stairs, his heartbreak is palpable. Still, he chooses to continue their game and strike the final blow, forcing Martha into reality with him. Martha's great illusion is one that she shares with her husband: their son.

Martha and George's consoling mythology both unites and divides them. According to Bigsby, "far from facilitating human contact, illusions rather alienate individuals from one another and serve to emphasize their separation." Over the course of the action, the son moves from being a comfort to both characters to being a weapon that they wield. Each one hurls insults at the other's parenting ability to shock the guests. This shift in illusion comes with Martha's great mistake of revealing the son to Honey and making him public.

George talks Martha into sharing the story of their son with the guests as part of the final game. She gives an emotional account of his birth and childhood, causing George to declare her a true mother. Her story is then met with his announcement of their son's death. Martha is enraged at George for making the decision to kill their son, which initially confuses Nick and Honey. Still clinging to her illusion, she demands that George show her evidence of the message informing them of their child's death. Nick finally understands that George and Martha never had a son. He has existed as a game to distract from their childless marriage. By informing Martha of the son's death, George ends the game and strips away her illusions.

Left alone, George and Martha are at a crossroads. She is afraid of Virginia Woolf, that is, of living a life confronted with reality. George promises that it will be better and refuses to bring the illusion back into their lives. As they hold hands at the end, there is the possibility for their love to survive. As Bigsby writes, quoting Henrik Ibsen's play *The Wild Duck*, "the ending, although not definitive, does hold out hope for 'a real companionship, founded on truth and purged of all falsehood'." Whatever choice they make, it will be grounded in reality.

**Source:** April Paris, Critical Essay on "Who's Afraid of Virginia Woolf?," in *Drama for Students*, Gale, Cengage Learning, 2018.

### *Matthew C. Roudané*

*In the following excerpt, Roudané provides a character study of Nick.*

... Nick is a caricature. The newly appointed assistant professor of biology seems to represent an innocent midwesterner. The theatergoer initially sympathizes with the young man: he appears too polite to refuse Martha's invitation to the after-party party at her home, too aware of departmental politics to offend those in lofty places (George and Martha, after all, are fixtures at the college), and too obedient to extract himself and Honey from what instantly escalates into a socially awkward endurance test. Most in the audience have some sympathetic correspondence with a person who tells George, "I just don't see why you feel you have to subject *other* people" to

THROUGH NICK, ALBEE REINVENTS IN DRAMATIC TERMS WHAT TOCQUEVILLE OBSERVED IN HISTORICAL TERMS A CENTURY BEFORE: THAT PRIVATE SELF-INTEREST, UNCHECKED BY MORAL CONSCIENCE, INEVITABLY LEADS TO SELF-COLLAPSE."

ridicule (91). Albee stresses the social uneasiness of Nick and Honey, particularly at the moment of their entrance, and the audience feels for the naive, well-meaning couple that is ambushed and unwittingly trapped in the emotional cross fire.

Nick is no match for his guests. From the moment he makes his awkward appearance, George tests the intelligent, youthful scientist one moment, derides him the next, ever shifting any comfortable field of social reference so that Nick can never be sure if he is interpreting signals accurately. Near the beginning of the action, for instance, Nick recognizes that his host will involve him in social game-playing and will verbally spar with the younger amateur boxer:

All right...what do you want me to say? Do you want me to say it's funny, so you can contradict me and say it's sad? or do you want me to say it's sad so you can turn around and say no, it's funny. You can play that damn little game any way you want to, you know! (33)

In spite of Nick's protest and impulse to leave—the remarks that he prefers never to "become involved" in the "affairs" of business associates (34)—George refuses to let him escape. George delights in keeping Nick off-balance, ever beguiling, cajoling him into lowering his public guard and surprising the thirty-year-old when, in a gesture of "*comforting a child*," he declares that becoming involved in business associates' affairs is the norm at the college: "Musical beds is the faculty sport around here" (34). Lured, no doubt, by continual drink, George goads Nick, who takes his clues from George and goes along with the games while simultaneously playing into George's hand, because he is never sure of the exact rules. Although he is clearly the object of manipulation, Nick only gives George more reason to attack when confessing that his professional ambition marginalizes human concerns. This is a Nick who will, on a professional level, (plot to) take over courses from his older colleagues in the biology department, will "start some special groups" for himself, and above all will "plow a few pertinent wives..." (112). Of course, Nick in one sense merely plays along with his adversary; he is a reluctant participant in drunken banter—it is his supposedly innocuous way of enduring a very long business obligation. But Albee's theatrical strategy depends on (or encourages) the collapse of traditional truth and illusion distinctions, as seen when Nick raises the ante in the game, suggesting that he will seduce Martha. "Well now, I'd just better get her off in a corner and mount her like a goddamn dog, eh?" (114). The exchange turns more threatening after George entices, then implicates, his rival:

> *George*: Why, you'd certainly better
>
> *Nick*: (*Looks at George a minute, his expression a little sick*) You know, I almost think, you're serious.
>
> *George*: (*Toasting him*) No, baby...*you* almost think you're serious, and it scares the hell out of you. (114)

Nick's eagerness to rise in the profession through sexual proclivity soon deflates itself for, when put to the test, he fails in one of the games, "Hump the Hostess." Martha's flirtation with Nick is simply her way of escalating her war with her husband. Nick is reduced to an impotent boy. Martha chides him, George humiliates him. "Look! I know the game! You don't make it in the sack, you're a houseboy" (202).

The audience's impressions of Nick as innocent midwesterner changes to Nick as opportunistic scientist. In many ways, he stands as the latest version of the Albeean American Dream figure. In *The American Dream*, The Young Man defines an absurdist type, an exaggerated spineless caricature who is the target of Albee's satire. The Young Man, like Nick, is "almost insultingly good looking in a typical American way. Good profile, straight nose, honest eyes, wonderful smile" (*AD*, 107). More importantly, behind the attractive facade, Albee implies, lies a defleshed functional type, a vain incarnation of a sterile culture, one who readily admits that he, as consummate conformist, will "do almost anything for money" (*AD*, 109). As another kind of conformist, "a pragmatic extension of the big dream" (145), Nick also will do almost anything to rise in professional rank, including sabotaging

anyone blocking his efforts to succeed. The Young Man of the earlier play appears drained of all substance and individuality, one of the few figures in the Albee canon who can be regarded as a truly absurdist character. Nick, on the other hand, becomes more than a blatantly dislocated stock American Dream figure; worse, he has evolved into a more sophisticated, intelligent, elaborately detailed, indeed, a more sinister extension of The Young Man. Significantly enough, only Nick lacks, not just a past family history and personal biography, but some traumatic event that has forever altered his being. (The only details Albee provides are that Nick and Honey's families have been lifelong acquaintances, he earned a master's at nineteen, and he was a good boxer.) Denied a past, Nick squares his synthetic hopes on a future that will be solely determined by distilled scientific truths forged from an amoral and sterile present. Within Albee's scenario, Nick lacks the moral gravity of George, and such moral inadequacy, for George, must not go unchallenged this particular evening.

Nick represents what Henry Hackamore in Sam Shepard's *Seduced* symbolizes—the "nightmare of the nation." For Albee as for George, Nick stands for a new generation of scientists who subordinate human ideals to a pragmatic view of life. Such an attitude certainly permeates Nick's personal life, as evident when he reveals that family pressure and social decorum, not love, motivated him to marry Honey. "I wouldn't say there was any...particular *passion* between us, even at the beginning...of our marriage, I mean" (105). Like Peter's Marriage in *The Zoo Story* or Tobias's in *A Delicate Balance*, Nick's marital relationship seems physically as well as spiritually inert. His stance toward Honey devalues any heroic romantic ideals; replacing passion and love are biology and finances. Nick admits that Honey's father, a corrupt evangelical, left his daughter financially secure, which undoubtedly attracted Nick to her even more. Nick and Honey are Albee's clearest symbols of public and private sterility, and complement his larger thematic concern in the play. *Who's Afraid of Virginia Woolf?* is Albee's grand lament for a loss of love, a loss of humane values, a loss of the self and the other. Nick's directing force in life centers on professional and monetary, not familial, satisfaction; and Honey, by not resisting, only ratifies their American Dream pursuits. Nick will be successful, Albee implies, because of the young scientist's a priori belief in the myth of the American Dream and a society that prizes the pragmatism of these "wave-of-the future boys" (107). His innocence long ago corrupted, as ideals gave way to expedient compromises, Nick places his faith and love in an entrepreneurial America and has become almost machinelike: he possesses "steely-blue" eyes, a "solid gold groin" (111). Nick represents a new and disturbing kind of professoriate of which George wants no part and against which he rebels. "I will fight you, young man . . . one hand on my scrotum, to be sure . . . but with my free hand I will battle you to the death" (68). Appalled by everything Nick stands for, George admits that he feels threatened on a private level (Nick may seduce his wife) and on a public level (he may undermine the Jeffersonian principles so dear to George).

Feelings of threat and subversion partially account for George's deliberate melding of boundaries separating truth and illusion. Indeed, George shifts alliances with Nick constantly. He creates the impression, in Nick's mind at least, that there exists some kind of male bonding between them and that, as faculty of a small liberal arts college, they somehow share certain educational principles—hence their ostensible collegiality and drunken banter about their wives and how they came into some inheritance. In fact, quite the opposite is the case, as George, while suddenly shifting some unstated alliance with Nick, admits:

> You realize, of course, that I've been drawing you out on this stuff, not because I'm interested in your terrible lifehood, but only because you represent a direct and pertinent threat to my lifehood, and I want to get the goods on you. (111)

Such potential threats, Albee suggests, emerge from much more than the possibility of Nick seducing Martha. Albee's real interest lies with charting broader social mythologies. The lessons of history, and how they have been conveniently ignored, lie at the heart of Albee's masterwork. Nick, the potential shaper of future history, faces George, the torchbearer for past history. George takes it upon himself, as a Thoreauvian surveyor of human history, to assume a liberal humanistic stance toward the outer world.

Nick, a seemingly indeterminate figure, plays an integral role in the playwright's ideographic presentation: his single-minded, scientific vision of experience, and all the dehumanizing cultural connotations which Albee would like the audience to ascribe to Nick, elevate him to the status of a decadent, even evil, major character. Nick acts as a foil to George and all the ideals on which George bases his life. Nick and George create a marvelous dialectic within the play, dramatizing as they do Albee's exploration of the connections between the individual's sense of public responsibility and his or her definition of private liberties. This is essentially a Tocquevillian dialectic that, on the one hand, recognizes the individual's right to pursue vigorously professional and entrepreneurial interests. Nick fills this role within the paradigm. On the other hand, this Tocquevillian dialectic also posits that in an ideal world, such private interests should, but do not, exist in equipoise with a purposeful sense of civic and moral duty. George, of course, represents this part of the paradigm. Albee's dialectic and its underlying tensions produce in Nick and George divided alliances and contribute to the play's multivalency and ambivalent intensity.

Albee seems drawn toward certain civic issues with which Alexis de Tocqueville grappled in *Democracy*, his seminal examination of American culture and thought. The heart of Tocqueville's beliefs, explains historian Arthur Schlesinger, centers on the ambiguous (and probably irreconcilable) interconnections of public ideals and private interests: "The great distinction, in short, between the classical republics and modern democracy lay in the commercial motive. . . . The problem was to make private interest the moral equivalent of public virtue. This could be achieved through the disciplinary influence exerted by society on its members—an influence embodied in the mores and in law and institutions. *Self-interest rightly understood:* this Tocqueville saw as the key to the balance between virtue and interest in commercial values." The delicate moral balance between the public and the private which so engaged Tocqueville exerts an equally strong influence on Albee's aesthetics in general, and his conceptualization of George and Nick in particular. In Albee's scheme, George is the standard-bearer of noble public virtue, Nick of smug self-serving enterprise and self-aggrandizement.

In *The Sandbox* and *The American Dream*, Albee anticipated all that Nick symbolizes through an investigation of the same ideological and mythic terrain forming the crucible from which rises the American Dream myth. Such a cultural milieu invites an ironic treatment of experience and, in *Who's Afraid of Virginia Woolf?*, Nick and Honey become the primary agents producing, and absorbing, such ironic satire. Echoing his prefatory remarks to *The American Dream*, Albee alludes to the historiography of *Who's Afraid of Virginia Woolf?* by naming George and Martha as he did. In 1965 Albee remarks that "there was some notion in my mind, while I was working on the play . . . which is the reason actually that I named the couple George and Martha—after General and Mrs. Washington. There might be an allegory to be drawn, and have the fantasy child the revolutionary principle of this country that we haven't lived up to yet." Later Albee again makes the analogy: "Indeed," Albee said in 1966, "I did name the two lead characters of *Virginia Woolf* George and Martha because there is contained in the play . . . an attempt to examine the success or failure of American revolutionary principles" (*CEA*, 58). And two decades after the debut of the play, he remarked that *Who's Afraid of Virginia Woolf?* was "the result of my examination of the 50s, as much as anything. Many of us suspected that even though we were terribly enthusiastic about the Thousand Days of Kennedy before terribly long it would be business as usual and things could slide back to the way they were. And, indeed, quickly enough they did" (*CEA*, 162). Through Nick, Albee objectifies not merely a post-Eisenhower belief in science as truth (a notion made more urgent when Albee conceded that he named Nick after Nikita Khruschev), but a lament for a decline of values in Western civilization. Through Nick, Albee reinvents in dramatic terms what Tocqueville observed in historical terms a century before: that private self-interest, unchecked by moral conscience, inevitably leads to self-collapse. In summing up Tocqueville's theories, Schlesinger writes: "Self-interest wrongly understood tilts the balance away from republican virtue and from public purpose. The individual withdraws from the public sphere, becomes isolated, weak, docile, powerless. Individualism in the Tocquevillian sense leads to apathy, apathy to despotism, despotism to stagnation, stagnation to extinction. The light dwindles by degrees and expires of itself." Albee places Nick in just such a dismal pattern. In *Who's Afraid of Virginia Woolf?*, informed social or public responsibility threatens to turn into anomie. Only through the paradoxical nature of George and Martha's cleansing influence will Nick and Honey be able to break out of this destabilizing pattern. For Albee, as for Tocqueville before him, self-interest rightly understood is "the key to the balance between virtue and interest in commercial democracies." Within Albee's presentation, George understands this vital distinction. Nick does not . . . .

**Source:** Matthew C. Roudané, "The Characters," in *Who's Afraid of Virginia Woolf?: Necessary Fictions, Terrifying Realities*, Twayne Publishers, 1990, pp. 75–81.

# SOURCES

Beasley, Heather A., "Women's Rights," in *America in Revolt during the 1960s and 1970s*, edited by Rodney P. Carlisle and J. Geoffrey Golson, p. 159.

Benshoff, Harry M., "1966 Movies and Camp," in *American Cinema of the 1960s: Themes and Variations*, edited by Barry Keith Grant, Rutgers University Press, 2008, p. 164.

Bigsby, C. W. E., "*Who's Afraid of Virginia Woolf?* Edward Albee's Morality Play," in *Journal of American Studies*, Vol. 1. No. 2, October 1967, pp. 257–68.

"Black-and-White Film," in *The Columbia Film Language Glossary*, https://filmglossary.ccnmtl.columbia.edu/term/black-and-white-film (accessed July 3, 2017).

Bottoms, Stephen J., *Albee: "Who's Afraid of Virginia Woolf?"*, Cambridge University Press, 2000, pp. 51, 52.

Cameron, Kate, "*Who's Afraid of Virginia Woolf?* Is Magnificent: 1966 Review," in *New York Daily News*, June 24, 1966, http://www.nydailynews.com/entertainment/movies/review-mike-nicholas-afraid-virginia-woolf-article-1.2019400 (accessed July 3, 2017).

"Cuban Missile Crisis," in *Encyclopedia of War and American Society*, Vol. 1, edited by Peter Karsten, Sage Publications, 2005, p. 201.

Dietrich, Alicia, "Making Movies: *Who's Afraid of Virginia Woolf?*" in *Cultural Compass*, http://blog.hrc.utexas.edu/2010/07/15/making-movies-whos-afraid-of-virginia-woolf (accessed July 3, 2017).

"Establishing Shot," in *Film Glossary*, Rice University website, http://www.owlnet.rice.edu/~engl377/film.html (accessed July 3, 2017).

Flanagan, William, "The Art of Theater No. 4: Edward Albee," in *Paris Review*, No. 39, Fall 1966, https://www.theparisreview.org/interviews/4350/edward-albee-the-art-of-theater-no-4-edward-albee (accessed July 3, 2017).

Friedan, Betty, "Statement of Purpose: The National Organization for Women's 1966 Statement of Purpose," NOW website, October 29, 1966, http://now.org/about/history/statement-of-purpose (accessed August 3, 2017).

Katz, Ephriam, "Low Key," in *The Film Encyclopedia*, 6th ed., HarperCollins, 2008, p. 885.

Kauffmann, Stanley, "Screen: Funless Games at George and Martha's: Albee's *Virginia Woolf* Becomes a Film," in *New York Times*, June 24, 1966, http://www.nytimes.com/movie/review?res = 9E04E3DA1731E43BBC4C51DFB066838D679EDE (accessed July 3, 2017).

Leff, Leonard J., and Jerold Simmons, "*Who's Afraid of Virginia Woolf?*" in *The Dame in the Kimono: Hollywood, Censorship, and the Production Code*, University of Kentucky Press, 2001, pp. 241–66.

McLaughlin, Katie, "5 Things Women Couldn't Do in the 1960s," CNN website, August 25, 2014, http://www.cnn.com/2014/08/07/living/sixties-women-5-things/index.html (accessed July 3, 2017).

"Medium Wide Shot" in *Elements of Cinematography: Camera*, UT Dallas website, https://www.utdallas.edu/atec/midori/Handouts/camera.htm#ecu (accessed July 3, 2017).

Mondello, Bob, "Remembering Hollywood's Hays Code, 40 Years On," in *All Things Considered*, NPR website, August 8, 2008, http://www.npr.org/templates/story/story.php?storyId = 93301189 (accessed July 3, 2017).

"Reaction Shot," in *Film Glossary*, Rice University website, http://www.owlnet.rice.edu/~engl377/film.html (accessed July 3, 2017).

Review of *Who's Afraid of Virginia Woolf?* in *Variety*, December 31, 1965, http://variety.com/1965/film/reviews/who-s-afraid-of-virginia-woolf-3-1200420919/ (accessed July 3, 2017).

Whitehead, J. W., *Mike Nichols and the Cinema of Transformation*, McFarland, 2014, pp. 26, 28.

"*Who's Afraid of Virginia Woolf?*: THR's 1966 Review," in *Hollywood Reporter*, November 20, 2014, http://www.hollywoodreporter.com/news/whos-afraid-virginia-woolf-read-750750 (accessed July 3, 2017).

# FURTHER READING

Beaver, Frank, *Dictionary of Film Terms: The Aesthetic Companion to Film Art*, 5th ed., Peter Lang, 2015.
> This dictionary is a useful source for film terms. It includes an artist index.

Bottoms, Stephen, ed., *The Cambridge Companion to Edward Albee*, Cambridge University Press, 2005.
> This collection of essays examines Albee's work, including *Who's Afraid of Virginia Woolf*, and the themes and styles he used. The essays provide greater insight into the film because so few changes were made between play and film.

Callan, Jim, *America in the 1960s*, Fact on File, 2005.
> This young-adult history text provides a brief overview of the decade. It is a valuable starting point for better understanding of American society during the writing and filming of the movie.

Schuth, Wayne, *Mike Nichols*, Twayne Publishers, 1978.
> This text examines the director's early life and career. It is an excellent source that includes *Who's Afraid of Virginia Woolf?* and notes on filmography.

# SUGGESTED SEARCH TERMS

Who's Afraid of Virginia Woolf?

Who's Afraid of Virginia Woolf? AND Mike Nichols

Who's Afraid of Virginia Woolf? AND film technique

Who's Afraid of Virginia Woolf? AND Edward Albee

America AND 1960s AND social change

Who's Afraid of Virginia Woolf? AND criticism

Who's Afraid of Virginia Woolf? AND film

America AND Cold War

# Witness for the Prosecution

## AGATHA CHRISTIE

## 1953

*Witness for the Prosecution* is one of the most famous and most frequently performed plays of the twentieth century. It was written by Agatha Christie, whose many novels made her the best-selling author of modern times, second in sales only to William Shakespeare and the Bible.

Like many of Christie's works, the play presents a murder mystery being played out among the upper class of Great Britain. The story revolves around the trial of Leonard Vole, a charming young man accused of murdering Miss Emily French, a single, wealthy woman considerably older than he. Vole claims that he and Miss French were nothing more than friends; his wife testifies that he was home when the murder took place; evidence implies that the killing was done by robbers. Soon, however, the robbery story falls apart, and the wife, on the witness stand, testifies that she lied to the investigators. Then new evidence shows that she might be lying when she says she was lying. Vole's defense team, led by the quirky intellectual Sir Wilfrid Robarts, has trouble keeping up with the twists in the story, as they and the audience try to discern truth from illusion.

Christie originally wrote *Witness for the Prosecution* as a short story called "Traitor Hands," which was published in 1925. After the success of her play *The Mousetrap*, which started in London's West End in 1952 and is still running, she quickly adapted "Traitor Hands" to

*Agatha Christie* (© *Chronicle* / *Alamy Stock Photo*)

*Witness for the Prosecution*, which opened in London in 1953 and then at Henry Miller's Theater in New York in December of 1954. It had an impressive run of 645 performances and won the New York Drama Critics' Circle Award for Best Foreign Play and Tony Awards for its lead actors. The text of *Witness for the Prosecution* is available in *The Mousetrap and Other Plays*, published by Dodd, Meade in 1978. That book is still available, currently published by NAL/Dutton, and the play is also available by itself in paperback form from Samuel French.

## AUTHOR BIOGRAPHY

Christie was born Agatha Mary Clarissa Miller on September 15, 1890, in Devon, England. She was homeschooled, mostly by her American-born father until his death when she was eleven. She and her mother were very close. In 1914, at age twenty-four, she married Colonel Archibald

Christie, a pilot with England's Royal Flying Corps. During World War I she served as nurse in a local hospital. Her first published novel, 1920's *The Mysterious Affair at Styles*, introduced the character of Hercule Poirot, a Belgian detective who would appear in thirty-three of her novels and fifty of her short stories.

Christie suffered a mental calamity in 1926: her mother died that year, and she found out that her husband was involved with another woman. She disappeared for eleven days, sparking a nationwide police manhunt and creating a mystery about her whereabouts that has not been solved to this day. She finally showed up at a hotel registered in the name of her husband's lover. After divorcing Archibald Christie in 1928, she remarried in 1930 to Max Mallowan, an archaeology professor.

Her writing career went on to chalk up unimaginable commercial successes. Over the course of her career, Christie published nearly seventy murder mysteries. In 1955, the Mystery Writers of America made her the first-ever recipient of the Grand Master Award, the organization's highest honor. She is one of the best-selling authors in all of history, with two billion books sold. she is arguably outsold only by William Shakespeare, who had a four-hundred-year head start, and the Bible. She also made a lasting influence in the theater: her play *The Mousetrap* became the longest-running play in London in 1957, five years after it opened, and in 2012 celebrated its 25,000th performance and is still running. Christie died of natural causes on January 12, 1976.

## PLOT SUMMARY

### Act One

The first act takes place in the chambers of a lawyer, Sir Wilfrid Robarts, Q.C., in London, late one afternoon. Sir Wilfrid's typist, Greta, enters to get a piece of paper; then Carter, Sir Wilfrid's chief clerk, comes in. The phone rings, and Carter answers it. He explains that Sir Wilfred is out and that he is expecting Mr. Mayhew, another lawyer, to arrive soon. Carter and Greta talk about the importance of accuracy and of court cases they have both heard of where simple mistakes have caused terrible results.

Carter tells Greta to make tea because Mr. Mayhew will arrive soon. He mentions Mayhew's client, Leonard Vole, and Greta is

# MEDIA ADAPTATIONS

- The first adaptation of Christie's short story, already renamed "Witness for the Prosecution" before the play was even written, was for British Broadcasting Company television, in 1949. Mary Kerridge played Leonard's presumed wife Romaine Heilger (referred to as "Romaine Vole" earlier in the play). Dale Rogers played Leonard Vole, and Derek Elphinstone played Sir Wilfrid Robarts. This adaptation was written by Sidney Budd and directed by John Glyn-Jones.

- The play was adapted for American television in 1953, while it was playing in London. The CBS broadcast starred Tom Drake as Leonard, Andrea King as Romaine and Mrs. Mogson, the alias Romaine uses to sell Sir Wilfrid the letters that incriminate Romaine, and Edward G. Robinson as Sir Wilfrid. Anne Howard Bailey wrote the adaptation, which was directed by Richard Goode.

- The most famous adaptation is the 1957 film of *Witness for the Prosecution*, a major release for MGM studios. It starred Tyrone Power as Leonard and Marlene Dietrich as Christine (the name given to the character of Romaine Vole in this production) with Charles Laughton as Sir Wilfrid. Billy Wilder and Harry Kurnitz wrote the screenplay, which was adapted by Lawrence B. Marcus, and Wilder directed. This version is available on DVD and Blu Ray from Kino Lorber films.

- A 1982 version of *Witness for the Prosecution* for Hallmark Hall of Fame Television starred Beau Bridges as Leonard, Diana Rigg as Christine, and Ralph Richardson as Sir Wilfrid. John Gay wrote the adaptation, and Alan Gibson directed. This version is available as an Amazon exclusive as a two-film disc, along with the film *Avanti!*, from TGG Direct.

- A 2016 adaptation for BBC One, called *Agatha Christie's Witness for the Prosecution*, ran as a two-part, two-hour miniseries. It stars Billy Howle as Leonard, Andrea Riseborough as Romaine, David Haig as Sir Wilfrid (called Sir Charles Carter in this production), Kim Cattrall as Emily French, and Toby Jones as John Mayhew. Julian Jarrold directed. It was produced by Mammoth Screen, Agatha Christie Productions, and the BBC, in association with Acorn Media Enterprises, Acorn TV and A + E Studios.

excited: she has read about the Vole case in the newspaper. All she knows about Vole's legal situation is that Vole has been asked by the police to give a statement.

Mayhew arrives with Leonard. Carter is nervously excited. He leaves to get Sir Wilfrid, who has been in court. It is clear that Greta is charmed by handsome Leonard Vole, and she rushes out to get some tea for him.

Mayhew and Leonard, left alone, discuss the severity of the case in which Leonard is involved. He may be charged with murder. Responding to Mayhew's questions, Leonard admits that he has had a checkered past, losing a series of dead-end jobs. He met his wife when he was in Germany, in the army.

Sir Wilfrid enters and makes small talk with Mayhew. Mayhew has Leonard explain why he thinks he is in legal jeopardy. Leonard explains his relationship with Miss Emily French, who has been murdered. He met her by chance one day, about six weeks earlier, helping her when she dropped her packages while crossing a busy street, and then he ran into her at the theater a few days later. They formed a relationship. He would go a few times each week to her house, where she lived with Janet MacKenzie, who was her housekeeper, and eight cats. Miss French probably knew that he had a wife, he says, though he never talked about her, allowing Miss French to hold romantic notions about him. He hoped to persuade her to invest in an invention he had made. He was helping her with her finances. He explains to Sir Wilfrid and Mr. Mayhew that he is aware how this might make him look like a scheming gold digger. Sir Wilfrid explains that he should just tell the truth, that it could actually even benefit his case if it looked as though he was indeed trying to swindle Miss French, as it would eliminate any motive for killing her.

On the night of the murder, Leonard went to Miss French's home because, he says, he had found a new invention that he thought would interest her—a different kind of cat brush. He knew Janet MacKenzie would be off for the night. He says that he arrived at quarter to eight, had some coffee with Miss French, and played cards with her. The police have said that MacKenzie came home early and heard someone talking to Miss French after nine, but Leonard says that it must have been someone else, that he had gone by then. Nobody saw him walk home, but his wife, Romaine, will testify that he was home by nine-thirty, the time that evidence shows the murder to have taken place.

As he explains his movements that evening, Sir Wilfrid reads in the newspaper that Miss French's will left her entire estate to Leonard, who is shocked to hear this. Soon Detective Inspector Hearne arrives with a police officer to arrest Leonard, who finds it hard to believe that he is a suspect.

When Leonard leaves with the police, Sir Wilfrid and Mayhew discuss his case. Sir Wilfrid cannot decide if Leonard is extremely naïve for not understanding the legal danger he is in or is extremely clever. They worry that a jury will not believe the testimony of his wife, a foreigner, and the wife is the only evidence he has to offer in his defense. Still, Sir Wilfrid agrees to help Mayhew with the case.

Romaine Vole arrives, saying that Mayhew's office said her husband would be there. They explain that he has been arrested. As they explain the story Leonard told them, Romaine seems surprised that her husband described her as being devoted. She characterizes his faith in her as foolish. She also does not believe that Miss

French viewed Leonard as a son or nephew, which was the impression Leonard gave the lawyers. She agrees to their line of defense, but reluctantly: when they ask if it is true that Leonard was home at nine-thirty, the time of the murder, she makes it clear that she is saying that is true only because Leonard said so. She states clearly that she will support his story if doing so will acquit him, though she does not believe the jury will believe her.

Sir Wilfrid explains that a wife cannot be compelled to testify against her husband, and Romaine reveals shocking information: she was already married when they met in Berlin, so she is not legally his wife. When pressed for the truth, she again unconvincingly repeats the story that will help Leonard's case: that he came home at nine-thirty and did not leave again. She even confirms that this should give him his alibi.

When she leaves, the lawyers are dismayed. She has said that she will testify on Leonard's behalf, and Leonard himself seems to be completely convinced that she will be loyal, but her cold attitude reveals a lack of enthusiasm, or even resentment, toward him.

## Act Two

The second act takes place in the Central Criminal Court, commonly referred to as the "Old Bailey," in London. It is a morning six weeks after the events of the first act. Court is already in session, and jurors are being sworn in at the murder trial of Leonard Vole. Leonard enters a "not guilty" plea, and the judge, Mr. Justice Wainwright, reminds the jurors to forget all of the news they have read about the trial and to focus on what they hear in the courtroom.

Mr. Myers lays out the prosecution's case. Leonard Vole and Emily French were friends. On the evening of October 14, she was killed. Janet MacKenzie, the housekeeper, was out for the evening, but she returned to the house around 9:25 to pick up a knitting pattern that she wanted to take over to a friend's house and heard a voice in the next room with Miss French, identifying the voice as Leonard's. She did not think much of it and left. When she came home again around eleven o'clock, Janet MacKenzie found Miss French dead. Inspector Hearne, the investigating policeman, takes the stand and gives the coroner's time of death and observations about the window in the murder room, which he believes was broken from the inside.

The only fingerprints in the room were those of Emily French, Janet MacKenzie, and Leonard Vole. Although the room looked as if a robbery might have taken place, Miss French was wearing expensive jewelry.

On cross-examination by Sir Wilfrid, acting as Leonard's attorney, the inspector discusses a kitchen knife found at Leonard and Romaine Vole's apartment. This brings up the subject of blood stains on Leonard Vole's shirtsleeve: he says that he had cut himself slicing a ham with this knife earlier in the night, and his wife has supported that claim in her statement to the police. Mr. Myers asks if the cuts could have been intentionally inflicted, and Sir Wilfrid accuses him of leading the witness. The blood on Leonard's coat is later revealed to be Miss French's type but is also Leonard's type, so either of them could be the source. Dr. Wyatt, the police surgeon, says that it appears Miss French was struck from behind by a left-handed person. Leonard is left-handed.

Janet MacKenzie takes the stand to talk about the night of the murder. Mr. Myers's examination of the witness goes from finding the body to Miss French's relationship with Leonard in general. She testifies that Miss French did not know that Leonard was married and that she had taken to reading novels about older women who have romantic relations with younger men.

Sir Wilfrid gets Janet MacKenzie to admit that she did not like Leonard. She also admits that she would have been the heir in Miss French's will but that Miss French changed it to leave her money to Leonard. Although she says that she heard Leonard's voice, Sir Wilfrid gets her to admit that she might have just heard a radio program, demonstrating to the court how weak her hearing is.

A forensic scientist from New Scotland Yard testifies to the blood that was found on Leonard's coat sleeve even after it was cleaned and that it was Miss French's type. Sir Wilfrid points out that Leonard is the same blood type, so the blood could be his.

The climactic moment of the second act is the testimony of Leonard's "wife," Romaine, who is called as a witness for the prosecution, not a witness for the defense. Everyone is surprised to hear her called to the stand as "Romaine Heilger." She explains that she never divorced her first husband in Berlin, Otto Gerthe Heilger, whom she married in 1946, so she was

never legally married to Leonard. He is therefore not shielded by laws that prohibit spouses from being compelled to testify against each other.

Romaine testifies that on the night of the murder, Leonard actually arrived home after ten, and not, as she had said earlier, at 9:30. It would therefore have been possible for him to commit the murder in the time established by the coroner and still make it home. She says that, upon arriving home, he told her, "I have killed her." He then instructed her to say he had been home much earlier. She also says that he arrived home with blood on the sleeve of his jacket and asked her to wash it out for him. The story about cutting himself while slicing ham was one that Leonard made up later, when the police lab found the blood on the jacket. When asked, Romaine says that she is changing her testimony because she feels she cannot help hide a murder and because she never loved Leonard and married him only to get out of Germany.

When Sir Wilfrid calls Leonard Vole to testify, he talks about his friendship with Miss French. He was not leading her on romantically, he says; he thought of her as an aunt. His testimony reviews the things he has asserted all along: that he spontaneously went to Miss French's house the night Janet MacKenzie was off because he wanted to show her a new invention, that he went home before nine-thirty, that he cut his wrist carving a ham, and that Romaine washed his coat the next morning. He did not know that he was to be the beneficiary of Miss French's will. The testimony that Romaine gave against him, he says unequivocally, is untrue. On cross-examination, Mr. Myers focuses on Leonard's low-paying job, which he quit recently, and the fact that he helped Miss French with her taxes and therefore knew her approximate net worth. Mr. Myers points out that he had been talking to travel agents about how much a cruise would cost at the time of the murder, which implies that he knew he was coming into an inheritance, but Leonard explains it as mere curiosity. He does not know why Romaine changed her testimony, and as the curtain falls he is still declaring his innocence.

### Act Three, Scene One

The first scene of the third act takes place in the evening of the same day as the events in the previous act took place, in the chambers of Sir Wilfrid—the same setting as the first act. Sir

Wilfrid and Mayhew are discussing how badly the day in court went for the defense. They cannot understand why Romaine changed her testimony: even if she was not legally married to Leonard, she still should have been indebted to him for getting her out of postwar Germany. After Sir Wilfrid's housekeeper, Greta, expresses her confidence in Leonard, based on her impression of him, the two lawyers talk about what a charming man he is and how having a woman on the jury would help get him freed.

Sir Wilfrid explains that the detail of Leonard's making travel plans is not strong evidence: for fun, his own wife plans itineraries to exotic places she knows she will never visit. Mayhew says his wife looks at houses that she has no intention to buy.

Sir Wilfrid's clerk, Carter, comes in with an unnamed woman. She speaks with a Cockney accent, and her hair and makeup hide much of her face. She offers to sell them letters written by Romaine. They bargain her price down from a hundred pounds to twenty pounds. She says that Romaine stole a man away from her, and when confronted that man slashed her face with a razor. She stole these letters from his apartment. While Mayhew and Sir Wilfrid discuss the importance of the letters, the woman slips away. They determine that she does not want to risk being assaulted by her ex-boyfriend again if he found out she had helped them question Romaine.

### Act Three, Scene Two

The second scene of this act takes place in the courtroom at the Old Bailey, the same setting as the second act, on the following morning. Sir Wilfrid introduces into evidence the letters, which a handwriting analyst has confirmed were written by Romaine. After some discussion about whether it is legal to introduce new evidence so late in the trial, the judge allows it. Romaine is called to return to the stand.

When asked about "Max," the man to whom the letters are addressed, Romaine is rattled. The particular letter Sir Wilfrid asks about is from October 17. In it, she tells this "Max" that the death of Miss French could be used to free her from her marriage to Leonard, so that she and Max can be together. The letter outlines how she plans to frame Leonard for the murder. The actual details that she relates are the facts that support Leonard's alibi: the facts that she has refuted on the witness stand. The jury leaves and

then comes back with a "not guilty" verdict. Romaine is arrested for perjury.

While they are waiting in the courtroom for the crowd of spectators outside to disperse, Romaine talks to Leonard, with his lawyers standing close. Sir Wilfrid talks about what a wicked woman she has been, and she laughs. It was her testimony that freed Leonard, she brags. She talks in her Cockney voice, and Mayhew and Sir Wilfrid realize that the woman who brought the letters to them was Romaine, in disguise.

She went through all of this because she knew that Leonard actually *was* guilty of murdering Emily French. Sir Wilfrid asks if she isn't afraid of being involved with a murderer, but she says that the love between her and Leonard is real.

A girl enters the courtroom and runs up to Leonard. She explains that she is his girlfriend and that now they can be together and leave on a cruise. As Leonard gloats about being freed and inheriting Miss French's fortune, Romaine, in a jealous fit, picks up the knife from the evidence table that he allegedly cut his hand with and stabs him dead. She looks up to the judge's seat and announces, as if formally entering a plea, that she is guilty.

## CHARACTERS

### Carter

Carter is the chief clerk in Sir Wilfrid Robarts's law office. Early in the first act, while he and Greta, Sir Wilfrid's typist, are preparing for their boss to return from court, they set the stage for how serious and formal Sir Wilfrid can be. They also discuss the impending arrival of Leonard Vole, giving audiences background to the case that is to be the play's focus.

### Mr. Clegg

Clegg is an assistant in the forensics laboratory at New Scotland Yard, the central investigative authority in London. He is the person who investigated Leonard Vole's coat, finding that it still had blood on it, even after being washed. The blood type he found is type O, which was Miss French's type, but it also turns out to be Leonard's type.

## Emily French

Miss French does not appear as a character in this play, but the action all centers on her death. She was an unmarried elderly woman who entered into a relationship with Leonard Vole when they met on the street. For weeks, he would go to her house for visits, playing cards with her and chatting about the news. She relied on him for financial advice. She had her will changed, leaving most of her estate to Leonard. Most of the evidence implicates Leonard in her death: he admits to having been at her house on the night of the murder, a night that he knew her housekeeper, Janet MacKenzie, would be out, and he has blood on his jacket sleeve that is her blood type. Still, he has an alibi.

Much of the drama centers on Leonard's motive, which would depend on whether Miss French viewed Leonard in a maternal way, like a son or nephew, or if she had romantic interests toward him. The prosecution tries to show that Leonard manipulated the emotions of this older woman who was vulnerable to romance. This is the position taken by Janet MacKenzie. Leonard, however, proposes that they were just friends.

## Girl

At the end of the trial, when Leonard Vole has been acquitted, an unnamed girl jumps into his arms. She claims to be his girlfriend, which he quickly confirms. He states that he plans to run away with this girl before Romaine, the woman who is going to go to jail for committing perjury for him, kills him.

## Greta

Greta is formally Sir Wilfrid Robarts's typist, but in keeping with the standards of the time, she is also responsible for domestic chores around the office, such as making and bringing tea. Christie uses Greta's fawning attitude toward Leonard Vole to inform audiences of the charming hold he has over women.

## Inspector Hearne

Inspector Hearne is the police detective who arrests Leonard Vole at Sir Wilfrid Robarts's office. He is later called to the stand as the prosecution's first witness, to explain the crime scene and the discovery of the blood-stained jacket.

## Romaine Heilger

*See* Romaine Vole

## John Mayhew

Mayhew is the solicitor who is handling Leonard Vole's case before the play begins. In the British legal system, a solicitor is a trained lawyer who is authorized to handle specific legal requirements, while not being licensed to argue before a court. He brings the case to Sir Wilfrid Robarts, a certified barrister, when it becomes clear that Leonard is likely to be arrested and forced to stand trial.

Sir Wilfrid and Mayhew work this case together, bouncing ideas off each other. As their social status implies, Sir Wilfrid is more astute than Mayhew, who does not come up with any particular insights himself.

## Janet MacKenzie

MacKenzie was the housekeeper for the late Miss French. She was named Miss French's heir in a previous version of her will, before it was changed to make Leonard Vole the heir. She disliked Leonard even before finding out about the will, however. The play does not make it clear if she dislikes him simply because he has interrupted her personal relationship with Miss French or if she truly does see that he is the kind of conniving criminal that he turns out to be in the end. Her cold, awkward manner makes it difficult for anyone else on stage to give much credence to her suspicions.

## Mr. Myers, Q.C.

Myers is the head of the prosecution team. He is clever and has done his research, several times surprising the defense led by Sir Wilfrid Robarts. He is also tripped up a few times by Sir Wilfrid, who wins objections from the judge when Myers tries to phrase things in ways that misrepresent what the witnesses have said. The competition between Myers and Sir Wilfrid is somewhat personal. Early in the play, Mayhew points out that Sir Wilfrid takes particular pleasure from beating Myers in court.

## Sir Wilfrid Robarts, Q.C.

Sir Wilfrid is the play's central character. The audience approaches the central mystery of Miss French's death through his eyes, being tricked by Leonard and Romaine Vole when Sir Wilfrid is tricked and figuring out more and more parts of the puzzle as Sir Wilfrid figures them out.

Sir Wilfrid is presented as a well-respected man with keen intelligence, able to listen to the situation laid out for him and interpret the truth at the center of it. At the same time, he is a representative of his client: he does not judge, for instance, whether it is a good thing that Leonard might have been leading Miss French on romantically or not, but only whether that impression might or might not help Leonard's case.

He is quite sexist in his views. He is suspicious of Romaine and advises his friend Mayhew that one should never trust a woman; later, at the start of the third act, he characterizes women as "ungrateful beasts." He is married, though, and uses his wife's habit of planning trips that she will never take to help himself understand how Leonard's arrangements for a cruise might just be idle speculation. Sir Wilfrid is more comfortable among men and clueless about women, which blinds him to the devotion that drives Romaine to perjure herself on Leonard's behalf and the complex ruse she goes through to make her perjury believable.

## Leonard Vole

Leonard is the defendant being prosecuted in *Witness for the Prosecution*. He is a charming man whom the one woman in his lawyer's office, Greta, swoons over, proclaiming that he must be innocent because he seems so nice. Since much of his defense is built on his relationship with the rich Miss French and his wife, Romaine, audiences rightfully wonder throughout the play whether he is being honest or has been using his likability to bend women and the trained lawyers as well to do his bidding.

The details of Leonard's background make him seem likely to be a petty swindler. He has not been able to hold a job because of his temper. His story about bumping into Miss French by coincidence after their first meeting is the kind of thing that a person stalking her would say. His insistence that he just hoped to get her backing for his invention but that he was not trying to trick her into signing over money to him would be rejected if it were not told with such earnestness.

He has a handy explanation for every piece of evidence that arises to make him look guilty. When his jacket sleeve is brought up because it has blood on it, Leonard says he cut himself earlier in the day, while slicing a ham. When Miss French's will leaving him a fortune is brought up, he says that he had no idea she had done that.

In the end, it turns out that Leonard is, in fact, a murderer after all: everything about his story that seemed shaky actually was shaky. He is even worse than he seemed: he has used his wife, Romaine, setting her up for a jail sentence for perjury while planning all the time to run off with a young girl. He used Miss French for her money, and he used Romaine to cover up his killing, abusing their love for him.

## Romaine Vole

Romaine is the "witness for the prosecution" referenced in the title. That description is ironic: she begins the play as a witness for the defense, intended to supply the alibi that will prove that Leonard Vole did not kill Emily French. She initially tells investigators that Leonard arrived home around nine-thirty, the time when the murder was taking place across town. She also said that the blood on Leonard's jacket came from a cut when he was carving a ham for dinner. On the witness stand, she reverses what she said: he came in after ten, she testifies, and said that he had just murdered Miss French. He gave her the jacket and told her to wash the blood out; when that did not work, he cut himself with a knife to support the ham-carving story. The defense team is aghast. They object that a wife cannot testify against her husband this way, but the prosecution shows that Romaine never divorced her husband, Otto Heilger, in her native Germany, so her marriage to Leonard is void. "Heilger" is Romaine Vole's real name. Although she has been living for years as Leonard Vole's wife, she is not technically his wife.

Because she is a German and has already told two versions of the story, jurors are inclined to be confused about what to believe. Their confusion is cleared up by evidence provided by a mysterious Cockney woman, who sells to the defense team letters Romaine wrote. The letters show that Romaine planned to run off with a lover, Max, and therefore gave incriminating information to get Leonard put in jail. The jury believes that her incriminating testimony was false and that therefore the alibi she originally gave must be true.

In the last scene, she reveals that the mysterious Cockney woman was actually Romaine herself. She used the disguise to make the evidence proving that she, Romaine, was a liar look more credible. She is willing to go to jail for perjury in order to save Leonard's life because she really does love him. When she finds out that he is running off with another woman, though, she stabs him to death.

### Mr. Justice Wainwright
Wainwright is the judge in the case.

### Dr. Wyatt
Wyatt is a police surgeon. He conducts the autopsy on Emily French, testifying that the killer was probably left-handed, as Leonard Vole is, but also that the fatal blow could equally have been struck by a woman or a man.

## THEMES

### Deception
One way that *Witness for the Prosecution* is able to mislead its audience is by the deceptive nature of Leonard Vole. Leonard Vole asserts that he is innocent when talking to Sir Wilfrid and Mr. Mayhew. It is only when the trial is over and he knows that he cannot be tried again for Emily French's murder that he tells his lawyers the truth.

Vole's wife, Romaine, deceives the lawyers as well. She wants to help secure Vole's release, but she does so by tricking everyone, including his very lawyers, into thinking that she hates him, so that the jury will feel sympathy for Leonard. She helps hide the actual truth—that he came home that night, confessed to the murder, and asked her to help him cover up the evidence. Romaine knows the fantasy that he wants to convince people of, and she works to make the deceptive version more real.

Christie builds to a climax by having Leonard and Romaine drop their deceptions in the last act. Romaine is proud to have lied on Leonard's behalf, even though doing so means that she will likely go to jail for perjury. Leonard admits that he actually did kill Emily French and that he has been misleading his lawyers all along in order to mislead the jury more convincingly. But then he admits to an even greater deception: he is not in love with Romaine and finds her sacrifice to be very convenient. It keeps him out of jail, but it also ensures that she will be put in jail, taking her out of the way so he can run off with another woman.

### Credibility
Most witnesses who take the stand at a trial try to convince juries of their credibility. This

expectation is one of the key factors in helping Romaine pull off a convincing deception and helping Christie mislead her audience. Romaine does not want to support her credibility and, in fact, wants to undermine it. She wants the jury to believe the opposite of what she says.

To damage her own credibility, Romaine makes the jury as well as the defense team believe that she is an immoral, conniving woman. She reverses her initial statement when she is on the witness stand, which she is allowed to do when evidence proves that, owing to an earlier marriage, she and Leonard Vole are not actually married.

At this point, the new story that she tells is more credible than the original version she gave. If the jury believed that she was providing Leonard with an alibi only because she was his loving wife, then she would have no reason to turn against him, but she says that she is turning against him because she is compelled to tell the truth. Then new evidence comes to light that she is in love with another man, which gives her a self-centered reason to lie about Leonard's innocence. This ruins the credibility of her anti-Leonard testimony.

The jurors do not find out what audiences find out in the end: the evidence that damaged Romaine's credibility was planted by Romaine herself, in disguise. She destroyed her credibility so that the jury would do just what she hoped they would and, rejecting her, find Leonard to be the one telling the truth.

### Identity
One way that Christie keeps this story alive is by changing the identity of one of the main characters several times. At first, Romaine Vole is a devoted wife who believes that she must support the story her husband tells about the night of Emily French's murder. When the trial begins, though, she is not considered Leonard's wife but is instead known as Romaine Heilger, a woman who used Leonard to escape the poverty and chaos of postwar Berlin. At this point, both personalities could cancel out each other's testimony, if not for the sudden appearance of the unidentified Cockney woman who claims to have been the ex-girlfriend of Romaine's lover and co-conspirator. The lawyers believe this woman, not realizing that she is Romaine in disguise, and use the evidence she gives them to secure Leonard's freedom.

# TOPICS FOR FURTHER STUDY

- John Grisham became one of the best-selling novelists of all time between the end of the twentieth century and the beginning of the twenty-first century by writing thriller novels set in the American legal system. In his Theodore Boone series he writes for a young-adult audience. The books feature a young man (Boone) who acts as an amateur attorney. Read one of the Boone books (*Theodore Boone: Kid Lawyer, Theodore Boone: The Abduction, Theodore Boone: The Accused, Theodore Boone: The Activist, Theodore Boone: The Fugitive*, or *Theodore Boone: The Scandal*). Using what you learned from this contemporary YA book, create a blog post and point out at least five ways that you think the trial of Leonard Vole would not take place in modern-day America. Allow your classmates to comment on your post.

- Leonard Vole says that he left Miss French's house and walked home but that nobody can corroborate his alibi until he arrived home to his wife. Chart three ways that a pedestrian in London would be tracked during his walk if it had happened today; then show three different ways his presence would probably have been noted in the 1950s.

- Christie has written this play from the point of view of the members of the prosecution and their interactions with the defendant and the witnesses. The jury deliberations are not presented. Have your class play the role of the jury. Assign some students to represent the merits of Leonard Vole's case and some to support the evidence of Romaine's conflicting testimony. Be sure to look up which evidence is admissible and which is not.

- Who do you think is the real protagonist of this story: Sir Wilfrid Robarts or Leonard Vole? Make a list of characteristic elements you think define the protagonist of a drama and show how details about each character's depiction in the play apply to the items on your list, to support one solid conclusion to the question.

- Having Romaine bring evidence to the defense team while dressed in disguise and using a phony voice seems like a stunt on the part of Christie. Could it work? Research cases where people have actually had run-ins with the law while wearing physical disguises and draw comparisons to this story. Write a brief essay on whether physical disguises are at all credible in real life.

When Romaine tells them of her plan in the end, she is the loving wife she was in the first act, but more clever and cunning than the lawyers ever could have guessed. She is, once again, a different person than any they thought they knew.

## Female-Male Relations

In using his personal magnetism and allure to get women to support him, Leonard Vole is adapting the role traditionally played in films by women. In the first act, audiences can see the effect that he has on women even before he has appeared for the first time onstage, in the way Greta, at Sir Wilfrid's office, discusses how nice he seems, even though she knows of him only from pictures in the newspapers. When she is in the same room with Leonard, Greta is eager to serve him, and she later dismisses any doubts about his innocence because she is so thoroughly smitten.

Over the course of Leonard's testimony, it becomes apparent that Miss Emily French felt the same way about him. Even though he pretends not to have noticed, there is plenty of evidence that she was so charmed by him that she read up on how a relationship like theirs, between a younger man and an older woman, might work, and she ended up changing her will to benefit this stranger whom she had known for only a few weeks. Her housekeeper, Janet

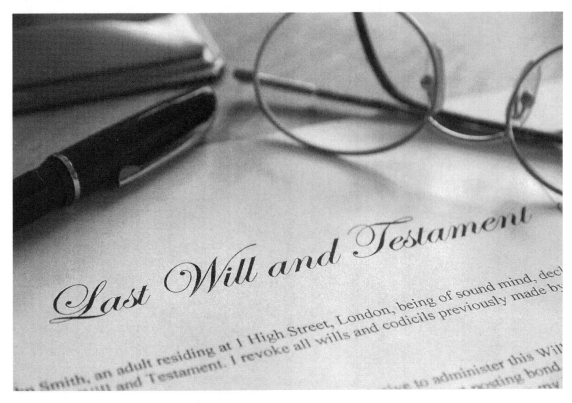

*Leonard Vole is a prime suspect for Emily French's murder because he was heir to her wealth*
*(© SteveWoods / Shutterstock.com)*

MacKenzie, is immune to Leonard's charms, identifying him as clearly being a manipulator and a killer, but no one believes Janet exactly because she is so harsh toward a charming man. The common view seems to be that being cold and asexual has made Janet jealous of Leonard.

In the end, like a traditional femme fatale, Leonard uses his sexual wiles to get Romaine to destroy her life on his behalf. He has cast a love spell over her that is so strong that she is willing to go to prison if it means that Leonard will go free. The only thing that can turn her against him is jealousy, which is activated with the late appearance of the young, pretty girlfriend whom he might love more than Romaine.

## STYLE

### Courtroom Drama

Christie is said to have been hesitant to adapt her short story about a woman who lied in court to the stage because she felt uncertain of being able to write a courtroom drama. A courtroom drama is a specific subcategory of the detective story. A detective story focuses on a protagonist's discovery of the facts of a mystery, then coming to a personal understanding of what they mean, and then perhaps explaining how the events occurred. Audiences follow along with the detective through the narrative or, as in the case of Dr. Watson in the Sherlock Holmes stories, through a surrogate who watches as the detective figures out the crime. In a courtroom drama, the facts of the case are presented both to the jury and to the audience. There is drama in the way that the characters have to follow within the structure of legal traditions: one side or the other may be prohibited from introducing certain evidence, for instance, or a statement may be stricken from the record, or what seems a logical conclusion may be overruled.

The courtroom drama is a staple of television and movies today. At the time *Witness for the Prosecution* was first performed, Erle Stanley Gardner had already published about forty novels starring his signature character, Perry Mason, who was adapted to television in the late 1950s with a television series that is still run on stations across the land.

## Happy Ending

Originally, this play ended with Leonard Vole's admitting that he had actually murdered Emily French. That ending would have left audiences leaving the theater with a bad feeling for several reasons. The most obvious one would be that it supports the opposite of the commonly accepted adage that crime does not pay. Going back to Aristotle, there has been a sense that art has a moral responsibility to show the consequences of criminal activity. Murderers are generally punished in art—not because artists have a moral obligation but to make the story satisfying. Society has no interest in promoting antisocial behavior, so a play that shows a criminal's getting away with his crimes would naturally make law-abiding citizens uncomfortable.

Another, more aesthetic reason this ending would be unpopular is that it makes fools of the protagonists. Audiences form bonds with characters they follow throughout a story. In this case, the protagonists are Sir Wilfrid Robarts and his cohorts, Carter and Mayhew. To show in the end that they have been foolishly serving a guilty man makes a mockery of them and, by extension, of the members of the audience who identified with them. Audiences do not mind being tricked cleverly, but being lied to by the murderer is not particularly clever.

The play is a success because Christie added the unnamed girlfriend at the end. Instead of being so smart that he fooled the judge, the jury, the prosecution, and the defense lawyers, Leonard proves dumb enough to be driven by plain, basic lust for a younger woman. The play retains the clever twist that Leonard and Romaine have beaten the legal system, but it also is able to have them punished when Romaine plunges a knife into him—the very knife that was in court to defend the phony story about Leonard's cutting himself while slicing a ham. By adding just a few lines, Christie is able to show justice served and to switch Romaine from a pathetic dupe to a master of her own fate, allowing audiences to leave the theater feeling satisfied.

## HISTORICAL CONTEXT

### Mystery Fiction

Christie is celebrated for having sold more books than anyone except William Shakespeare, but her literary reputation is limited because she wrote "genre fiction." In Christie's case, the particular genre is mystery fiction, a popular format that really existed for only about a century before *Witness for the Prosecution* was first performed. In the mystery story, a crime that seems unsolvable is often carefully and methodically examined, clue by clue, by someone dedicated to unraveling the mystery, until the truth is revealed.

One of the first examples of the mystery story, according to crime fiction historians, is *Things as They Are; or, The Adventures of Caleb Williams*, a 1794 novel by William Godwin (the father of *Frankenstein* author Mary Wollstonecraft Shelley). In this book, the protagonist, Williams, uses investigative techniques like those used in today's mystery novels to determine just how his employer killed a neighbor and framed another man for the murder.

Edgar Allan Poe, who is today often remembered for his stories and poems depicting the macabre and supernatural, is generally considered one of the people to solidify the methods of the mystery story. In his 1841 short story "The Murders in the Rue Morgue," Poe introduced the first detective in fiction, C. Auguste Dupin. Though he is not formally a detective—the word *detective* was not even in use at the time—Dupin solves crimes in that story and in two subsequent stories: "The Mystery of Marie Rogêt" in 1842 and "The Purloined Letter" in 1845. In writing about the solution of crimes, Poe sought to use engaging circumstances to examine the mysteries of the criminal mind.

Another early mystery writer was Charles Dickens. Although history has remembered Dickens for his literary masterpieces about social injustice, such as *Oliver Twist, A Tale of Two Cities*, and *David Copperfield*, he was a well-known popular writer of genre fiction in his time. Among his works that dealt with solving crimes were the 1841 novel *Barnaby Rudge: A Tale of the Riots of '80* and *Three Detective Anecdotes*, published in the early 1850s, which focused on new developments in crime solving used by the police of that day. The novel that Dickens was writing at the time of his death in 1870, *The Mystery of Edwin Drood*, shows his

# COMPARE & CONTRAST

- **1953:** Forensic science can determine the blood type of a sample, even if someone has tried to wash it away, but it cannot differentiate one person's blood from another person's if they are in the same blood group.

  **Today:** DNA markers, which have more than a 99 percent likelihood of accuracy, have been used in criminal cases since 1987. Today, criminals can be convicted on the evidence of a single hair or a drop of blood, while cases of wrongful conviction that are decades old are often reversed owing to DNA evidence.

- **1953:** In addition to being a typist, a woman like Greta can be ordered to make and serve tea in the office of Sir Wilfrid Robarts because she is a woman.

  **Today:** The stereotype of assigning domestic chores to a female professional because of her gender is well known and has been the subject of many gender-discrimination lawsuits.

- **1953:** To determine Emily French's idea of a romance between herself and Leonard Vole, the prosecution in Vole's case introduces the titles and subjects of the books that she ordered from the library concerning relationships between older women and younger men.

  **Today:** A more thorough and comprehensive look at French's interests could be gained by going through her online browsing history, which is why such information is routinely examined in criminal investigations.

- **1953:** A man like Leonard Vole who has invented something like a new kind of windshield wiper might look for a person with a lot of available money to invest, such as Emily French, for the financial backing he needs to develop it.

  **Today:** A person who has invented a new product would get backing from Kickstarter, Indiegogo, or several other websites organized to put investors in touch with inventors.

---

continued interest in mystery and detective writing. Biographers have also noted that Dickens was writing *Drood* to compete with his friend and sometime collaborator Wilkie Collins, whose 1859 novel *The Woman in White* is often identified as the groundbreaking first English detective story.

Collins and Dickens paved the way to one of the most famous detectives in fiction, Sherlock Holmes. Holmes first appeared in 1887 in the novel *A Study in Scarlet* and continued to appear until shortly before the death of his author, Sir Arthur Conan Doyle, in 1930. Popular culture's fascination with Holmes's method of using precise examination of specific, small details to draw broader conclusions about events is evident in the way that after a hundred years, new movies and television shows imagining further adventures by this character are constantly appearing.

In the twentieth century, British and American mysteries followed separate paths. "Dime novels" that were made to appeal to people of low income seeking thrills gave rise to the hard-boiled detective in America, as exemplified by the works of Dashiell Hammett, author of *The Maltese Falcon* and *The Thin Man*, and later by Raymond Chandler, whose Philip Marlowe character came to exemplify the lone-wolf private detective over the course of eight books from the 1930s to the 1950s. At the same time, British writers were producing what were often referred to as "drawing room mysteries" and sometimes as "locked room mysteries." Set in upper-class genteel locations, such as a country estate or a posh resort, these stories focused on the work of a quiet, insightful, unlikely detective, such as Christie's Miss Marple, an aged spinster. Dorothy L. Sayers, G. K. Chesterton (creator of

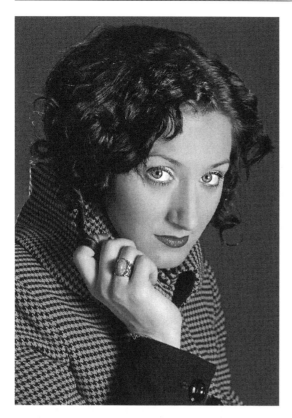

*Romaine testifies on behalf of the prosecution while plotting to undermine her own words with fabricated evidence (© Vlasov Volodymyr | Shutterstock.com)*

the crime-solving priest Father Brown), and, later, Dick Francis (whose mysteries were set in the world of international equestrian circles) are examples of the British drawing room writers, as well as, of course, Christie herself.

## CRITICAL OVERVIEW

*The Mousetrap*, Christie's immediate predecessor to *Witness for the Prosecution*, turned out to be her biggest stage hit and the longest-running play in theater history. It began in 1952 and has run for over twenty-five thousand performances in London; it is expected to pass thirty thousand in 2026. Still, it was *Witness for the Prosecution*, with a London run of 488 shows and a New York run of 646, that Christie herself pegged as her best, most satisfying play. When it opened on Broadway in December of 1953, the New York drama critics were generous with their praise. According to Charles Osborne, author of *The*

*Life and Crimes of Agatha Christie*, the critics were "unanimous in finding it one of the most exciting and best acted plays seen in New York for years." It won the New York Drama Critics' Circle Award for Best Foreign Play of the 1954–1955 season.

In the twenty-first century, *Witness for the Prosecution* is still frequently performed in local theaters around the world. Most people know it from film and television adaptation, particularly the 1957 film, which was nominated for nine Academy Awards. As with many long-running stories, the play has evolved over the decades: for instance, the 2016 television miniseries by writer/producer Sarah Phelps focuses on John Mayhew not Sir Wilfrid Robarts, with a star turn by Toby Jones in that role, and fleshes out Romaine's life as a theater showgirl during World War I. Maureen Ryan of *Variety* found this version very engaging, saying: "If I call 'Witness' a very high-level, meaty 'Law & Order' episode executed with period flair, I mean that as a serious compliment," she wrote, before noting that the show captures the "ambiguity and thoughtfulness" that most people fail to appreciate in Agatha Christie's best works.

## CRITICISM

### David Kelly

*Kelly is an author and a teacher of creative writing. In the following essay, he examines whether the abrupt appearance of Leonard's girlfriend in* Witness for the Prosecution*'s final moments works as more than just a popular move and whether it is artistically legitimate.*

Christie's 1953 stage drama *Witness for the Prosecution* has long been held up as an example of the kind of intellectual puzzle that keeps audiences guessing until the very last moment, never quite sure until the final curtain of who did what and why. During its first run, posters in movie theater lobbies teased mystery fans by begging them to keep quiet about the surprise ending, implying that their friends who were made aware of the play's final twist would be robbed of a delightfully sublime experience, cheated of the joy of being able to say, "I *knew* it all along!" or "I guess I should have seen that coming."

Well, here is the final twist in the mystery of who killed Miss Emily French and staged the murder scene to look like a burglary gone

> BOTH THE WOMAN AND THE GIRL COULD BE INTERPRETED AS PSYCHOLOGICAL MANIFESTATIONS, WRAITHS WITH LITTLE SUBSTANCE IN THE HEAVY, FORMAL, LAW-BOUND WORLD OF THE PLAY."

awry: a bear did it. That is not true, of course. But in some respects it seems as likely as the surprises Christie springs in the last few minutes of the show.

Throughout the story, audiences see charming young inventor/unemployed car mechanic Leonard Vole charged with the murder, being the most likely suspect. He is, after all, something of a drifter, unable to hold a job for more than a few months by his own admission. In the few weeks that he knew Miss French, he got her (though he denies that it was his idea) to change her will, leaving her significant fortune to him. Evidence puts him in the house on the night of the murder. The only alibi to show that he was not in that area at the very time Miss French was killed and to explain the blood on Leonard's coat sleeve is the testimony of his wife, Romaine—the "witness" of the play's title.

The story's first, greatest twist is when Romaine flips her story. She goes from defending Leonard to condemning him, declaring her original testimony to have been coerced and false. This is followed by a series of aftershocks. She is found to have a previous marriage and therefore to not be Leonard's wife after all. Then a mysterious woman with a scarred face and a Cockney accent sells letters to the defense lawyers that show Romaine scheming with her secret lover to lie in court and have Leonard sent away for the murder so that they can be together. When the letters are submitted into evidence and the jury realizes that Romaine has been setting Leonard up, they reach a "not guilty" verdict.

After the trial, a series of surprise revelations pop up at breakneck pace. Leonard admits to his lawyers that he really did kill Miss French after all. Romaine admits that she was the mysterious Cockney woman, disguising herself with fake scars to make the lawyers she sold the letters to believe her evidence was real. It appears that Romaine intentionally perjured herself while testifying against Leonard, so she is facing a prison sentence. She accepts her fate as the price that must be paid to help Leonard, even though, she admits now, she knew all along that he was guilty. And then, seemingly from nowhere, a girl walks up claiming to be Leonard's true girlfriend, which means that Leonard took advantage of prison-bound Romaine to save his own neck. Leonard admits this. Romaine, it turns out, is going to prison because Leonard is a cad. So Romaine grabs a knife and stabs him to death.

The surprise twist that audiences were supposed to keep quiet and not reveal is the final one, the existence of the girl. Throughout the play Leonard has charmed ladies, such as the typist in his lawyer's office and, of course, Miss French, but being charming does not necessarily mean that he was actually cheating on his wife. It is no great shock that an oily character like Leonard Vole would end up taking advantage of a woman, even if it is his wife, who has just saved him from execution, but to have a new character show up on the last page of the script and speak eight sentences of dialogue that reverse all that audiences know about what came before seems terribly close to cheating. The point of a mystery story is that the audience members can match wits against the author, not that the author can come up with surprises by making up new, unexpected turns of events. If "unexpected" were the only standard we held for engaging mysteries, then what would *not* be acceptable? An anvil falling from the sky? The revelation of an evil twin? A bear?

The girl who appears at the end of the play seems to be an example of wish fulfillment on the part of Christie. She is said to have fought for this ending, over the objections of pretty much everyone else involved in the original production. She did not want the play to end with Leonard's confessing to murder and then walking free, but she also had much invested in the central concept that Americans call "double jeopardy"—that the law could not prosecute him a second time after an "innocent" verdict has been rendered. At the end of the play Romaine has just perjured herself to hide Leonard's guilt, so she, of course, would not be the device to punish him for being guilty. The girl's appearance lets Romaine end the play regaining her dignity, and the guilty murderer dies. Ignoring all artistic fairness, this ending serves the concept of popular entertainment well.

# WHAT DO I READ NEXT?

- Christie was an interesting person as well as an engaging writer. She told the story of her life in the 1977 book *An Autobiography*. The book is rich with detail, but it conspicuously skips her disappearance for eleven days in 1926, which has been the subject of speculation for fans throughout the decades. Her autobiography is still published in print and as an e-book by William Morrow Paperbacks.

- *Witness for the Prosecution* was a short story before Christie adapted it for the stage. It was originally published in 1925 as "Traitor Hands" in *Flynn's Weekly* magazine and was renamed for inclusion in Christie's collection *The Hound of Death* in 1933 under the name "The Witness for the Prosecution." It is included in *The Witness for the Prosecution and Other Short Stories*, published in 2012 by William Morrow.

- Christie's mystery writing has always been compared to that of her contemporary, Dorothy L. Sayers. One of Sayers's most popular novels is *Gaudy Night*, featuring the recurring characters Lord Peter Wimsey and Harriet Vane in a setting that resembles the London of Christie's play. (Local theater productions have adapted Sayers's book for the stage.) *Gaudy Night* was first published in 1935 and is currently in print from Harper Perennial.

- Young adults who like Christie's writing style may be attracted to Carola Dunn's Daisy Dalrymple mystery series, about a young woman from an aristocratic family who solves crimes in England in the 1920s. The list of Dalrymple novels is long, but the one most like *Witness for the Prosecution* might be *Fall of a Philanderer*, a 2011 story that follows Daisy and her husband, Alec, as they solve the murder of a philandering playboy while on vacation.

- Walter Dean Myers's 2004 novel *Monster* tells the story of a sixteen-year-old African American teenager on trial for a murder that occurred during a robbery in which he was involved. The book is written as a screenplay in the mind of the protagonist, making it resemble the courtroom drama of *Witness for the Prosecution*. It was showered with awards, including the Michael L. Printz Award and an ALA Best Book. Likewise, it was named a Coretta Scott King Honor selection and a National Book Award finalist. It is available from Amistad Publishers.

- The year that *Witness for the Prosecution* opened on Broadway, another much-lauded murder mystery, *The Bad Seed* (1954), also opened. This story revolves around a child who may have killed the boy who won a penmanship medal she felt she deserved, and her mother's investigation of the horrible prospect that she may have raised a youthful murderer. Based on a novel by William March, *The Bad Seed* was adapted for the stage by Maxwell Anderson, one of the great playwrights of mid-century Broadway. Anderson's oft-produced play is available from Dramatist's Play Service; March's novel is in print, published by Harper Perennial.

---

To be artistically fair, the appearance of the girl would have to be unexpected but at the same time would also have to have been already foreshadowed in earlier events onstage. Fortunately, there is some symbolic legitimacy for this character: she is a mirror image of the character Romaine made up to conveniently pass along bogus information, the woman with the Cockney accent. The Cockney woman's story is very psychologically revealing about the woman who made her up, Romaine. She says that she has been dropped by her boyfriend for a woman whom she calls a "trollop," "a wicked one," and "a Jezebel." She says that Leonard has

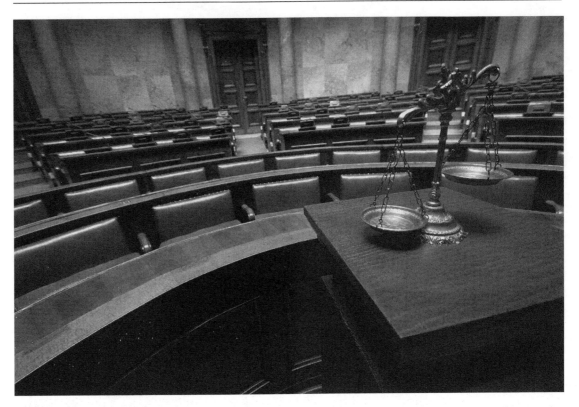

*Christie wrote different endings for the play, and none of them feature a traditional form of justice for the murderer* *(© corgarashu | Shutterstock.com)*

"been took in by her (Romaine) all right." She knows that Romaine, her rival, is better looking than she is because her boyfriend has ruined her looks, cutting her face, like the criminal that he is, though she still loves him nonetheless.

Perhaps Romaine has subconsciously known all along what Leonard's game is and where she herself fits into the love triangle, and so she has dreamed up a character who is to her criminal boyfriend what Romaine is to Leonard: a devoted but used-up ex-lover. In a sense, Romaine is anticipating the arrival of Leonard's girlfriend. Her Cockney woman projects Romaine as the beautiful young home wrecker, the exact opposite view of the girl who says in the last scene, "You're years older than him, and you just got hold of him—and you've done your best to hang him. But that's all over now." In addition to being younger—that is, unscarred—the surprise girlfriend is also more refined than Romaine, as is made clear in her opening lines: "Len, darling you're free. Isn't it wonderful?" she chirrups, as if meeting him on the badminton court and not in the court of law. She is young and vibrant and

sophisticated. She is naïve, too, in that she takes the testimony against Leonard at face value and thinks Romaine has been a threat, not Leonard's accomplice. She is to Romaine what Romaine was to her imaginary Cockney woman character: an unfeeling snob who has wedged herself into true love for her own shallow amusement.

There is even more symmetry in the way the script presents these two characters. Christie tags the dialogue of the nameless Cockney character with "Woman," while the nameless girlfriend is identified in the script as "Girl." And if the girl seems to show up out of nowhere in the last scene, her appearance is no more or less sudden than the disappearance of the woman from her one scene, as the excited lawyers are looking over the evidence she has brought them. Both the woman and the girl could be interpreted as psychological manifestations, wraiths with little substance in the heavy, formal, law-bound world of the play. One is the manifestation of the mind of a character, however, while the other serves the author as a handy device to fulfill the plot's requirement that the killer be exposed and brought to justice.

Because of Christie's reputation for being a popular writer but not necessarily a literary one, it seems unlikely that she would justify a popular twist by saying that it is symbolic. She probably wouldn't feel the need to justify herself in any way. Still, the sudden appearance of the girl does work symbolically. It fulfills audiences' simple, basic need to see Leonard, the "bad guy," punished, but satisfying what audiences want to see does not make a move right. However, when the character of the girl is held up against the character of the woman, interesting and magical things occur. Either character alone is closer to being a hack writing device than *Witness for the Prosecution* earns, but when you put these two characters together, they make art.

**Source:** David Kelly, Critical Essay on *Witness for the Prosecution*, in *Drama for Students*, Gale, Cengage Learning, 2018.

### Deb Miller

*In the following review, Miller describes the play as "thoroughly engrossing."*

A grand presentation of Agatha Christie's popular whodunit of 1953, *Witness for the Prosecution*, closes out Bristol Riverside Theatre's 30th anniversary season with a bang. Directed by Susan D. Atkinson, the play (later adapted for the 1957 hit film starring Charles Laughton, Marlene Dietrich, and Tyrone Power) not only offers a thoroughly engrossing courtroom drama/murder mystery filled with the all-time best-selling author's signature twists, turns, and surprise ending, but also presents a savvy look at pre-feminist mid-century attitudes towards women.

Accused in 1950s London of murdering a wealthy spinster who befriended him, the unemployed American Leonard Vole proclaims his innocence to investigators, attorneys, and the court, but his German-born wife Romaine is the only one who can provide him with a solid alibi. When she takes the stand against him and swears that he confessed his guilt to her, the lawyers, judge, and jury must consider all of the testimony and evidence, along with the characters' disparate personalities and ulterior motives, to determine what really happened and who is telling the truth—the ingenuous and amiable man or the cold and calculating woman.

Alternating between scenes in the defense counsel chambers and The Old Bailey Central Criminal Court, the intriguing production is performed by a top-notch cast that delivers both the increasingly tense drama and the intermittent counterpoints of humor. Keith Baker is a standout as Queen's Counsel Sir Wilfrid Robarts, committed to the case, commanding in court, and convinced of his client's innocence, until growing suspicions make him reevaluate his confidence in the accused. Carl Wallnau as Vole's solicitor Mr. Mayhew gives Baker fine support, as they discuss the points of the confounding crime, sneak cigars and liquor when they should be drinking tea, and consider the credibility of the suspect and the witnesses against him, with misogynist comments like "Never trust a woman" and "Mrs. Vole is an evil woman"—which elicited nervous laughter from the opening-night audience.

Matt Leisy is fully affable and believable as Leonard Vole, as he offers his voluntary statements, describes his genial relationship with the victim, and reacts with heartfelt dismay to the incriminating testimony. Eleanor Handley as Mrs. Vole is, by contrast, harsh, unsympathetic, and "cool as a cucumber" in her unexpected betrayal of her husband. Sharon Alexander turns in a powerful performance as Janet MacKenzie, the victim's housemaid, who gives an impassioned account of her distaste for Vole and her unshakeable belief in his guilt. Leonard C. Haas as Mr. Myers, the prosecuting Q.C., provides some bits of comic relief with his exaggerated throat-clearing and less-than-brilliant objections and arguments, as does Kyra Leeds as Robarts' ditzy secretary Greta, and James Luse as the incompetent forensic expert Mr. Clegg.

Along with the professional cast, a large ensemble of community players fills out the roles of jurors, barristers, and court staff and adds to the production's look of realism, and dialect coaching by Rebecca Simon contributes to the actors' array of authentic-sounding European accents. Jason Simms' imposing set design evokes the hallowed English aged-wood interiors and efficiently switches from chambers to courtroom, while costumes by Gina Andreoli include vintage-style clothing and traditional wigs and silks.

**Source:** Deb Miller, "Review of *Witness for the Prosecution* at Bristol Riverside Theatre," in *DC Metro Theater Arts*, May 12, 2017.

## SOURCES

"Agatha Christie," in *Biography*, April 27, 2017, https://www.biography.com/people/agatha-christie-9247405 (accessed June 16, 2017).

Christie, Agatha, *Witness for the Prosecution*, in *The Moustrap and Other Plays*, Dodd, Meade, 1978.

"Christie's Life," Agatha Christie website, http://www.agathachristie.com/about-christie#christies-life (accessed June 16, 2017).

"History of the Mystery," MysteryNet.com, 2016, http://www.mysterynet.com/timeline/history-of-mystery/ (accessed June 17, 2017).

Mason, Emma, "The Mysterious Disappearance of Agatha Christie," in *HistoryExtra*, October 22, 2014, http://www.historyextra.com/feature/weird-and-wonderful/mysterious-disappearance-agatha-christie (accessed June 16, 2017).

Masters, Kristen, "A Brief History of the Mystery Novel," in *Books Tell You Why*, September 13, 2014, https://blog.bookstellyouwhy.com/a-brief-history-of-the-mystery-novel (accessed June 17, 2017).

Osborne, Charles, *The Life and Crimes of Agatha Christie*, Holt, Rinehart and Winston, 1982, p. 175.

Ryan, Maureen. "TV Review: 'Witness for the Prosecution' on Acorn TV," *Variety*, January 30, 2017. http://variety.com/2017/tv/reviews/witness-for-the-prosecution-acorn-tv-agatha-christie-1201973484/ (accessed June 30, 2017).

"Timeline of Life of Conan Doyle," Conan Doyle Info website, 2017, http://www.conandoyleinfo.com/life-conan-doyle/timeline/ (accessed June 17, 2017).

## FURTHER READING

Barnard, Robert, "Counsel for the Defense," in *Agatha Christie: Modern Critical Views*, edited by Harold Bloom, Chelsea House Publishers, 2002, 83–99.
> Despite its title, Barnard's article is not focused on Christie's work with courtroom dramas but is instead an extended explanation and appreciation of the style that has made her an international celebrity. Her talent as a crime writer in general is the driving force behind this work.

Gill, Gillian, *Agatha Christie: The Woman and Her Mysteries*, Free Press, 1990.
> Gill takes a feminist approach to both the author and her characters, which gives her room for interpreting *Witness for the Prosecution* and other works and weaving an engaging story out of Christie's view of the world.

Green, Julius, *Curtain Up: Agatha Christie: A Life in the Theatre*, HarperCollins Publishers, 2015.
> Having produced several Christie plays for the stage, Green is considered a bit of a Christie expert. This book covers her development as a playwright chronologically, from the 1930s through the end of her life, showing how her understanding of stagecraft matured.

O'Donnell, Bernard, *The Old Bailey and Its Trials*, Burke, 1952.
> At the time when this book was published and when *Witness for the Prosecution* was first performed, the Central Court of Justice of London had been in operation for nearly four hundred years (in a "new" building since 1907). A sense of this historical weight and the tradition behind it (like the barristers' wigs) helps readers feel the gravity of the decisions weighed within the play.

Trewin, J. C., "A Midas Gift for the Theater," in *Agatha Christie: First Lady of Crime*, edited by H.R.F. Keating, Holt, Rinehart and Winston, 1977, 131–54.
> Trewin's style is grand and theatrical itself, but he does cover the range of Christie's experience in writing for the theater. This essay is illustrated with many photos of actors in the middle of first-run performances of Christie plays.

## SUGGESTED SEARCH TERMS

Christie AND Witness for the Prosecution

Witness for the Prosecution AND Mousetrap

Witness for the Prosecution AND courtroom drama

Witness for the Prosecution AND adaptations

Agatha Christie AND dramatic twist

Agatha Christie AND London stage

Witness for the Prosecution AND postwar Germany

Agatha Christie AND feminism

Agatha Award for cozy mystery

# Glossary of Literary Terms

## A

**Abstract:** Used as a noun, the term refers to a short summary or outline of a longer work. As an adjective applied to writing or literary works, abstract refers to words or phrases that name things not knowable through the five senses. Examples of abstracts include the *Cliffs Notes* summaries of major literary works. Examples of abstract terms or concepts include "idea," "guilt" "honesty," and "loyalty."

**Absurd, Theater of the:** See *Theater of the Absurd*

**Absurdism:** See *Theater of the Absurd*

**Act:** A major section of a play. Acts are divided into varying numbers of shorter scenes. From ancient times to the nineteenth century plays were generally constructed of five acts, but modern works typically consist of one, two, or three acts. Examples of five-act plays include the works of Sophocles and Shakespeare, while the plays of Arthur Miller commonly have a three-act structure.

**Acto:** A one-act Chicano theater piece developed out of collective improvisation. *Actos* were performed by members of Luis Valdez's Teatro Campesino in California during the mid-1960s.

**Aestheticism:** A literary and artistic movement of the nineteenth century. Followers of the movement believed that art should not be mixed with social, political, or moral teaching. The statement "art for art's sake" is a good summary of aestheticism. The movement had its roots in France, but it gained widespread importance in England in the last half of the nineteenth century, where it helped change the Victorian practice of including moral lessons in literature. Oscar Wilde is one of the best-known "aesthetes" of the late nineteenth century.

**Age of Johnson:** The period in English literature between 1750 and 1798, named after the most prominent literary figure of the age, Samuel Johnson. Works written during this time are noted for their emphasis on "sensibility," or emotional quality. These works formed a transition between the rational works of the Age of Reason, or Neoclassical period, and the emphasis on individual feelings and responses of the Romantic period. Significant writers during the Age of Johnson included the novelists Ann Radcliffe and Henry Mackenzie, dramatists Richard Sheridan and Oliver Goldsmith, and poets William Collins and Thomas Gray. Also known as Age of Sensibility

**Age of Reason:** See *Neoclassicism*

**Age of Sensibility:** See *Age of Johnson*

**Alexandrine Meter:** See *Meter*

**Allegory:** A narrative technique in which characters representing things or abstract ideas are used to convey a message or teach a lesson. Allegory is typically used to teach moral, ethical, or religious lessons but is sometimes used for satiric or political purposes. Examples of allegorical works include Edmund Spenser's *The Faerie Queene* and John Bunyan's *The Pilgrim's Progress.*

**Allusion:** A reference to a familiar literary or historical person or event, used to make an idea more easily understood. For example, describing someone as a "Romeo" makes an allusion to William Shakespeare's famous young lover in *Romeo and Juliet.*

**Amerind Literature:** The writing and oral traditions of Native Americans. Native American literature was originally passed on by word of mouth, so it consisted largely of stories and events that were easily memorized. Amerind prose is often rhythmic like poetry because it was recited to the beat of a ceremonial drum. Examples of Amerind literature include the autobiographical *Black Elk Speaks,* the works of N. Scott Momaday, James Welch, and Craig Lee Strete, and the poetry of Luci Tapahonso.

**Analogy:** A comparison of two things made to explain something unfamiliar through its similarities to something familiar, or to prove one point based on the acceptedness of another. Similes and metaphors are types of analogies. Analogies often take the form of an extended simile, as in William Blake's aphorism: "As the caterpillar chooses the fairest leaves to lay her eggs on, so the priest lays his curse on the fairest joys."

**Angry Young Men:** A group of British writers of the 1950s whose work expressed bitterness and disillusionment with society. Common to their work is an anti-hero who rebels against a corrupt social order and strives for personal integrity. The term has been used to describe Kingsley Amis, John Osborne, Colin Wilson, John Wain, and others.

**Antagonist:** The major character in a narrative or drama who works against the hero or protagonist. An example of an evil antagonist is Richard Lovelace in Samuel Richardson's *Clarissa,* while a virtuous antagonist is Macduff in William Shakespeare's *Macbeth.*

**Anthropomorphism:** The presentation of animals or objects in human shape or with human characteristics. The term is derived from the Greek word for "human form." The fables of Aesop, the animated films of Walt Disney,

and Richard Adams's *Watership Down* feature anthropomorphic characters.

**Anti-hero:** A central character in a work of literature who lacks traditional heroic qualities such as courage, physical prowess, and fortitude. Anti-heros typically distrust conventional values and are unable to commit themselves to any ideals. They generally feel helpless in a world over which they have no control. Anti-heroes usually accept, and often celebrate, their positions as social outcasts. A well-known anti-hero is Yossarian in Joseph Heller's novel *Catch-22.*

**Antimasque:** See *Masque*

**Antithesis:** The antithesis of something is its direct opposite. In literature, the use of antithesis as a figure of speech results in two statements that show a contrast through the balancing of two opposite ideas. Technically, it is the second portion of the statement that is defined as the "antithesis"; the first portion is the "thesis." An example of antithesis is found in the following portion of Abraham Lincoln's "Gettysburg Address"; notice the opposition between the verbs "remember" and "forget" and the phrases "what we say" and "what they did": "The world will little note nor long remember what we say here, but it can never forget what they did here."

**Apocrypha:** Writings tentatively attributed to an author but not proven or universally accepted to be their works. The term was originally applied to certain books of the Bible that were not considered inspired and so were not included in the "sacred canon." Geoffrey Chaucer, William Shakespeare, Thomas Kyd, Thomas Middleton, and John Marston all have apocrypha. Apocryphal books of the Bible include the Old Testament's Book of Enoch and New Testament's Gospel of Peter.

**Apollonian and Dionysian:** The two impulses believed to guide authors of dramatic tragedy. The Apollonian impulse is named after Apollo, the Greek god of light and beauty and the symbol of intellectual order. The Dionysian impulse is named after Dionysus, the Greek god of wine and the symbol of the unrestrained forces of nature. The Apollonian impulse is to create a rational, harmonious world, while the Dionysian is to express the irrational forces of personality. Friedrich Nietzche uses these terms in *The Birth of Tragedy* to designate contrasting elements in Greek tragedy.

**Apostrophe:** A statement, question, or request addressed to an inanimate object or concept or to a nonexistent or absent person. Requests for inspiration from the muses in poetry are examples of apostrophe, as is Marc Antony's address to Caesar's corpse in William Shakespeare's *Julius Caesar*: "O, pardon me, thou bleeding piece of earth, That I am meek and gentle with these butchers! . . . Woe to the hand that shed this costly blood! . . . "

**Archetype:** The word archetype is commonly used to describe an original pattern or model from which all other things of the same kind are made. This term was introduced to literary criticism from the psychology of Carl Jung. It expresses Jung's theory that behind every person's "unconscious," or repressed memories of the past, lies the "collective unconscious" of the human race: memories of the countless typical experiences of our ancestors. These memories are said to prompt illogical associations that trigger powerful emotions in the reader. Often, the emotional process is primitive, even primordial. Archetypes are the literary images that grow out of the "collective unconscious." They appear in literature as incidents and plots that repeat basic patterns of life. They may also appear as stereotyped characters. Examples of literary archetypes include themes such as birth and death and characters such as the Earth Mother.

**Argument:** The argument of a work is the author's subject matter or principal idea. Examples of defined "argument" portions of works include John Milton's *Arguments* to each of the books of *Paradise Lost* and the "Argument" to Robert Herrick's *Hesperides*.

**Aristotelian Criticism:** Specifically, the method of evaluating and analyzing tragedy formulated by the Greek philosopher Aristotle in his *Poetics*. More generally, the term indicates any form of criticism that follows Aristotle's views. Aristotelian criticism focuses on the form and logical structure of a work, apart from its historical or social context, in contrast to "Platonic Criticism," which stresses the usefulness of art. Adherents of New Criticism including John Crowe Ransom and Cleanth Brooks utilize and value the basic ideas of Aristotelian criticism for textual analysis.

**Art for Art's Sake:** See *Aestheticism*

**Aside:** A comment made by a stage performer that is intended to be heard by the audience but supposedly not by other characters. Eugene O'Neill's *Strange Interlude* is an extended use of the aside in modern theater.

**Audience:** The people for whom a piece of literature is written. Authors usually write with a certain audience in mind, for example, children, members of a religious or ethnic group, or colleagues in a professional field. The term "audience" also applies to the people who gather to see or hear any performance, including plays, poetry readings, speeches, and concerts. Jane Austen's parody of the gothic novel, *Northanger Abbey,* was originally intended for (and also pokes fun at) an audience of young and avid female gothic novel readers.

**Avant-garde:** A French term meaning "vanguard." It is used in literary criticism to describe new writing that rejects traditional approaches to literature in favor of innovations in style or content. Twentieth-century examples of the literary *avant-garde* include the Black Mountain School of poets, the Bloomsbury Group, and the Beat Movement.

# *B*

**Ballad:** A short poem that tells a simple story and has a repeated refrain. Ballads were originally intended to be sung. Early ballads, known as folk ballads, were passed down through generations, so their authors are often unknown. Later ballads composed by known authors are called literary ballads. An example of an anonymous folk ballad is "Edward," which dates from the Middle Ages. Samuel Taylor Coleridge's "The Rime of the Ancient Mariner" and John Keats's "La Belle Dame sans Merci" are examples of literary ballads.

**Baroque:** A term used in literary criticism to describe literature that is complex or ornate in style or diction. Baroque works typically express tension, anxiety, and violent emotion. The term "Baroque Age" designates a period in Western European literature beginning in the late sixteenth century and ending about one hundred years later. Works of this period often mirror the qualities of works more generally associated with the label "baroque" and sometimes feature elaborate conceits. Examples of Baroque works include John Lyly's *Euphues: The Anatomy of Wit,* Luis de Gongora's *Soledads,* and William Shakespeare's *As You Like It.*

**Baroque Age:** See *Baroque*

**Baroque Period:** See *Baroque*

**Beat Generation:** See *Beat Movement*

**Beat Movement:** A period featuring a group of American poets and novelists of the 1950s and 1960s—including Jack Kerouac, Allen Ginsberg, Gregory Corso, William S. Burroughs, and Lawrence Ferlinghetti—who rejected established social and literary values. Using such techniques as stream of consciousness writing and jazz-influenced free verse and focusing on unusual or abnormal states of mind—generated by religious ecstasy or the use of drugs—the Beat writers aimed to create works that were unconventional in both form and subject matter. Kerouac's *On the Road* is perhaps the best-known example of a Beat Generation novel, and Ginsberg's *Howl* is a famous collection of Beat poetry.

**Black Aesthetic Movement:** A period of artistic and literary development among African Americans in the 1960s and early 1970s. This was the first major African-American artistic movement since the Harlem Renaissance and was closely paralleled by the civil rights and black power movements. The black aesthetic writers attempted to produce works of art that would be meaningful to the black masses. Key figures in black aesthetics included one of its founders, poet and playwright Amiri Baraka, formerly known as LeRoi Jones; poet and essayist Haki R. Madhubuti, formerly Don L. Lee; poet and playwright Sonia Sanchez; and dramatist Ed Bullins. Works representative of the Black Aesthetic Movement include Amiri Baraka's play *Dutchman,* a 1964 Obie award-winner; *Black Fire: An Anthology of Afro-American Writing,* edited by Baraka and playwright Larry Neal and published in 1968; and Sonia Sanchez's poetry collection *We a BaddDDD People,* published in 1970. Also known as Black Arts Movement.

**Black Arts Movement:** See *Black Aesthetic Movement*

**Black Comedy:** See *Black Humor*

**Black Humor:** Writing that places grotesque elements side by side with humorous ones in an attempt to shock the reader, forcing him or her to laugh at the horrifying reality of a disordered world. Joseph Heller's novel *Catch-22* is considered a superb example of the use of black humor. Other well-known authors who use black humor include Kurt Vonnegut, Edward Albee, Eugene Ionesco, and Harold Pinter. Also known as Black Comedy.

**Blank Verse:** Loosely, any unrhymed poetry, but more generally, unrhymed iambic pentameter verse (composed of lines of five two-syllable feet with the first syllable accented, the second unaccented). Blank verse has been used by poets since the Renaissance for its flexibility and its graceful, dignified tone. John Milton's *Paradise Lost* is in blank verse, as are most of William Shakespeare's plays.

**Bloomsbury Group:** A group of English writers, artists, and intellectuals who held informal artistic and philosophical discussions in Bloomsbury, a district of London, from around 1907 to the early 1930s. The Bloomsbury Group held no uniform philosophical beliefs but did commonly express an aversion to moral prudery and a desire for greater social tolerance. At various times the circle included Virginia Woolf, E. M. Forster, Clive Bell, Lytton Strachey, and John Maynard Keynes.

**Bon Mot:** A French term meaning "good word." A *bon mot* is a witty remark or clever observation. Charles Lamb and Oscar Wilde are celebrated for their witty *bon mots.* Two examples by Oscar Wilde stand out: (1) "All women become their mothers. That is their tragedy. No man does. That's his." (2) "A man cannot be too careful in the choice of his enemies."

**Breath Verse:** See *Projective Verse*

**Burlesque:** Any literary work that uses exaggeration to make its subject appear ridiculous, either by treating a trivial subject with profound seriousness or by treating a dignified subject frivolously. The word "burlesque" may also be used as an adjective, as in "burlesque show," to mean "striptease act." Examples of literary burlesque include the comedies of Aristophanes, Miguel de

Cervantes's *Don Quixote*, Samuel Butler's poem "Hudibras," and John Gay's play *The Beggar's Opera*.

# C

**Cadence:** The natural rhythm of language caused by the alternation of accented and unaccented syllables. Much modern poetry—notably free verse—deliberately manipulates cadence to create complex rhythmic effects. James Macpherson's "Ossian poems" are richly cadenced, as is the poetry of the Symbolists, Walt Whitman, and Amy Lowell.

**Caesura:** A pause in a line of poetry, usually occurring near the middle. It typically corresponds to a break in the natural rhythm or sense of the line but is sometimes shifted to create special meanings or rhythmic effects. The opening line of Edgar Allan Poe's "The Raven" contains a caesura following "dreary": "Once upon a midnight dreary, while I pondered weak and weary...."

**Canzone:** A short Italian or Provencal lyric poem, commonly about love and often set to music. The *canzone* has no set form but typically contains five or six stanzas made up of seven to twenty lines of eleven syllables each. A shorter, five- to ten-line "envoy," or concluding stanza, completes the poem. Masters of the *canzone* form include Petrarch, Dante Alighieri, Torquato Tasso, and Guido Cavalcanti.

**Carpe Diem:** A Latin term meaning "seize the day." This is a traditional theme of poetry, especially lyrics. A *carpe diem* poem advises the reader or the person it addresses to live for today and enjoy the pleasures of the moment. Two celebrated *carpe diem* poems are Andrew Marvell's "To His Coy Mistress" and Robert Herrick's poem beginning "Gather ye rosebuds while ye may...."

**Catharsis:** The release or purging of unwanted emotions—specifically fear and pity—brought about by exposure to art. The term was first used by the Greek philosopher Aristotle in his *Poetics* to refer to the desired effect of tragedy on spectators. A famous example of catharsis is realized in Sophocles's *Oedipus Rex,* when Oedipus discovers that his wife, Jacosta, is his own mother and that the stranger he killed on the road was his own father.

**Celtic Renaissance:** A period of Irish literary and cultural history at the end of the nineteenth century. Followers of the movement aimed to create a romantic vision of Celtic myth and legend. The most significant works of the Celtic Renaissance typically present a dreamy, unreal world, usually in reaction against the reality of contemporary problems. William Butler Yeats's *The Wanderings of Oisin* is among the most significant works of the Celtic Renaissance. Also known as Celtic Twilight.

**Celtic Twilight:** See *Celtic Renaissance*

**Character:** Broadly speaking, a person in a literary work. The actions of characters are what constitute the plot of a story, novel, or poem. There are numerous types of characters, ranging from simple, stereotypical figures to intricate, multifaceted ones. In the techniques of anthropomorphism and personification, animals—and even places or things—can assume aspects of character. "Characterization" is the process by which an author creates vivid, believable characters in a work of art. This may be done in a variety of ways, including (1) direct description of the character by the narrator; (2) the direct presentation of the speech, thoughts, or actions of the character; and (3) the responses of other characters to the character. The term "character" also refers to a form originated by the ancient Greek writer Theophrastus that later became popular in the seventeenth and eighteenth centuries. It is a short essay or sketch of a person who prominently displays a specific attribute or quality, such as miserliness or ambition. Notable characters in literature include Oedipus Rex, Don Quixote de la Mancha, Macbeth, Candide, Hester Prynne, Ebenezer Scrooge, Huckleberry Finn, Jay Gatsby, Scarlett O'Hara, James Bond, and Kunta Kinte.

**Characterization:** See *Character*

**Chorus:** In ancient Greek drama, a group of actors who commented on and interpreted the unfolding action on the stage. Initially the chorus was a major component of the presentation, but over time it became less significant, with its numbers reduced and its role eventually limited to commentary between acts. By the sixteenth century the chorus—if employed at all—was typically a single person who provided a prologue and an epilogue and occasionally appeared between acts to introduce or underscore an important event. The chorus in William Shakespeare's *Henry V* functions in this way. Modern dramas rarely feature a chorus, but T. S. Eliot's *Murder in the Cathedral* and Arthur Miller's *A View from the Bridge* are notable exceptions. The Stage Manager in Thornton Wilder's *Our Town* performs a role similar to that of the chorus.

**Chronicle:** A record of events presented in chronological order. Although the scope and level of detail provided varies greatly among the chronicles surviving from ancient times, some, such as the *Anglo-Saxon Chronicle,* feature vivid descriptions and a lively recounting of events. During the Elizabethan Age, many dramas—appropriately called "chronicle plays"—were based on material from chronicles. Many of William Shakespeare's dramas of English history as well as Christopher Marlowe's *Edward II* are based in part on Raphael Holinshead's *Chronicles of England, Scotland, and Ireland.*

**Classical:** In its strictest definition in literary criticism, classicism refers to works of ancient Greek or Roman literature. The term may also be used to describe a literary work of recognized importance (a "classic") from any time period or literature that exhibits the traits of classicism. Classical authors from ancient Greek and Roman times include Juvenal and Homer. Examples of later works and authors now described as classical include French literature of the seventeenth century, Western novels of the nineteenth century, and American fiction of the mid-nineteenth century such as that written by James Fenimore Cooper and Mark Twain.

**Classicism:** A term used in literary criticism to describe critical doctrines that have their roots in ancient Greek and Roman literature, philosophy, and art. Works associated with classicism typically exhibit restraint on the part of the author, unity of design and purpose, clarity, simplicity, logical organization, and respect for tradition. Examples of literary classicism include Cicero's prose, the dramas of Pierre Corneille and Jean Racine, the poetry of John Dryden and

Alexander Pope, and the writings of J. W. von Goethe, G. E. Lessing, and T. S. Eliot.

**Climax:** The turning point in a narrative, the moment when the conflict is at its most intense. Typically, the structure of stories, novels, and plays is one of rising action, in which tension builds to the climax, followed by falling action, in which tension lessens as the story moves to its conclusion. The climax in James Fenimore Cooper's *The Last of the Mohicans* occurs when Magua and his captive Cora are pursued to the edge of a cliff by Uncas. Magua kills Uncas but is subsequently killed by Hawkeye.

**Colloquialism:** A word, phrase, or form of pronunciation that is acceptable in casual conversation but not in formal, written communication. It is considered more acceptable than slang. An example of colloquialism can be found in Rudyard Kipling's *Barrack-room Ballads:* When 'Omer smote 'is bloomin' lyre He'd 'eard men sing by land and sea; An' what he thought 'e might require 'E went an' took—the same as me!

**Comedy:** One of two major types of drama, the other being tragedy. Its aim is to amuse, and it typically ends happily. Comedy assumes many forms, such as farce and burlesque, and uses a variety of techniques, from parody to satire. In a restricted sense the term comedy refers only to dramatic presentations, but in general usage it is commonly applied to non-dramatic works as well. Examples of comedies range from the plays of Aristophanes, Terrence, and Plautus, Dante Alighieri's *The Divine Comedy,* Francois Rabelais's *Pantagruel* and *Gargantua,* and some of Geoffrey Chaucer's tales and William Shakespeare's plays to Noel Coward's play *Private Lives* and James Thurber's short story "The Secret Life of Walter Mitty."

**Comedy of Manners:** A play about the manners and conventions of an aristocratic, highly sophisticated society. The characters are usually types rather than individualized personalities, and plot is less important than atmosphere. Such plays were an important aspect of late seventeenth-century English comedy. The comedy of manners was revived in the eighteenth century by Oliver Goldsmith and Richard Brinsley Sheridan, enjoyed a second revival in the late nineteenth century, and has endured into the twentieth century. Examples of comedies of manners include William Congreve's *The Way of the World* in the late seventeenth century, Oliver Goldsmith's *She Stoops to Conquer* and Richard Brinsley Sheridan's *The School for Scandal* in the eighteenth century, Oscar Wilde's *The Importance of Being Earnest* in the nineteenth century, and W. Somerset Maugham's *The Circle* in the twentieth century.

**Comic Relief:** The use of humor to lighten the mood of a serious or tragic story, especially in plays. The technique is very common in Elizabethan works, and can be an integral part of the plot or simply a brief event designed to break the tension of the scene. The Gravediggers' scene in William Shakespeare's *Hamlet* is a frequently cited example of comic relief.

**Commedia dell'arte:** An Italian term meaning "the comedy of guilds" or "the comedy of professional actors." This form of dramatic comedy was popular in Italy during the sixteenth century. Actors were assigned stock roles (such as Pulcinella, the stupid servant, or Pantalone, the old merchant) and given a basic plot to follow, but all dialogue was improvised. The roles were rigidly typed and the plots were formulaic, usually revolving around young lovers who thwarted their elders and attained wealth and happiness. A rigid convention of the *commedia dell'arte* is the periodic intrusion of Harlequin, who interrupts the play with low buffoonery. Peppino de Filippo's *Metamorphoses of a Wandering Minstrel* gave modern audiences an idea of what *commedia dell'arte* may have been like. Various scenarios for *commedia dell'arte* were compiled in Petraccone's *La commedia dell'arte, storia, technica, scenari,* published in 1927.

**Complaint:** A lyric poem, popular in the Renaissance, in which the speaker expresses sorrow about his or her condition. Typically, the speaker's sadness is caused by an unresponsive lover, but some complaints cite other sources of unhappiness, such as poverty or fate. A commonly cited example is "A Complaint by Night of the Lover Not Beloved" by Henry Howard, Earl of Surrey. Thomas Sackville's "Complaint of Henry, Duke of Buckingham" traces the duke's unhappiness to his ruthless ambition.

**Conceit:** A clever and fanciful metaphor, usually expressed through elaborate and extended comparison, that presents a striking parallel between two seemingly dissimilar things—for example, elaborately comparing a beautiful woman to an object like a garden or the sun. The conceit was a popular device throughout the Elizabethan Age and Baroque Age and was the principal technique of the seventeenth-century English metaphysical poets. This usage of the word conceit is unrelated to the best-known definition of conceit as an arrogant attitude or behavior. The conceit figures prominently in the works of John Donne, Emily Dickinson, and T. S. Eliot.

**Concrete:** Concrete is the opposite of abstract, and refers to a thing that actually exists or a description that allows the reader to experience an object or concept with the senses. Henry David Thoreau's *Walden* contains much concrete description of nature and wildlife.

**Concrete Poetry:** Poetry in which visual elements play a large part in the poetic effect. Punctuation marks, letters, or words are arranged on a page to form a visual design: a cross, for example, or a bumblebee. Max Bill and Eugene Gomringer were among the early practitioners of concrete poetry; Haroldo de Campos and Augusto de Campos are among contemporary authors of concrete poetry.

**Confessional Poetry:** A form of poetry in which the poet reveals very personal, intimate, sometimes shocking information about himself or herself. Anne Sexton, Sylvia Plath, Robert Lowell, and John Berryman wrote poetry in the confessional vein.

**Conflict:** The conflict in a work of fiction is the issue to be resolved in the story. It usually occurs between two characters, the protagonist and the antagonist, or between the protagonist and society or the protagonist and himself or herself. Conflict in Theodore Dreiser's novel *Sister Carrie* comes as a result of urban society, while Jack London's short story "To Build a Fire" concerns the protagonist's battle against the cold and himself.

**Connotation:** The impression that a word gives beyond its defined meaning. Connotations may be universally understood or may be significant only to a certain group. Both "horse" and "steed" denote the same animal, but "steed" has a different connotation, deriving from the chivalrous or romantic narratives in which the word was once often used.

**Consonance:** Consonance occurs in poetry when words appearing at the ends of two or more verses have similar final consonant sounds but have final vowel sounds that differ, as with "stuff" and "off." Consonance is found in "The curfew tolls the knells of parting day" from Thomas Grey's "An Elegy Written in a Country Church Yard." Also known as Half Rhyme or Slant Rhyme.

**Convention:** Any widely accepted literary device, style, or form. A soliloquy, in which a character reveals to the audience his or her private thoughts, is an example of a dramatic convention.

**Corrido:** A Mexican ballad. Examples of *corridos* include "Muerte del afamado Bilito," "La voz de mi conciencia," "Lucio Perez," "La juida," and "Los presos."

**Couplet:** Two lines of poetry with the same rhyme and meter, often expressing a complete and self-contained thought. The following couplet is from Alexander Pope's "Elegy to the Memory of an Unfortunate Lady": 'Tis Use alone that sanctifies Expense, And Splendour borrows all her rays from Sense.

**Criticism:** The systematic study and evaluation of literary works, usually based on a specific method or set of principles. An important part of literary studies since ancient times, the practice of criticism has given rise to numerous theories, methods, and "schools," sometimes producing conflicting, even contradictory, interpretations of literature in general as well as of individual works. Even such basic issues as what constitutes a poem or a novel have been the subject of much criticism over the centuries. Seminal texts of literary criticism include Plato's *Republic,* Aristotle's *Poetics,* Sir Philip Sidney's *The Defence of Poesie,* John Dryden's *Of Dramatic Poesie,* and William Wordsworth's "Preface" to the second edition of his *Lyrical Ballads.* Contemporary schools of criticism include deconstruction, feminist, psychoanalytic, poststructuralist, new historicist, postcolonialist, and reader-response.

# D

**Dactyl:** See *Foot*

**Dadaism:** A protest movement in art and literature founded by Tristan Tzara in 1916. Followers of the movement expressed their outrage at the destruction brought about by World War I by revolting against numerous forms of social convention. The Dadaists presented works marked by calculated madness and flamboyant nonsense. They stressed total freedom of expression, commonly through primitive displays of emotion and illogical, often senseless, poetry. The movement ended shortly after the war, when it was replaced by surrealism. Proponents of Dadaism include Andre Breton, Louis Aragon, Philippe Soupault, and Paul Eluard.

**Decadent:** See *Decadents*

**Decadents:** The followers of a nineteenth-century literary movement that had its beginnings in French aestheticism. Decadent literature displays a fascination with perverse and morbid states; a search for novelty and sensation—the "new thrill"; a preoccupation with mysticism; and a belief in the senselessness of human existence. The movement is closely associated with the doctrine Art for Art's Sake. The term "decadence" is sometimes used to denote a decline in the quality of art or literature following a period of greatness. Major French decadents are Charles Baudelaire and Arthur Rimbaud. English decadents include Oscar Wilde, Ernest Dowson, and Frank Harris.

**Deconstruction:** A method of literary criticism developed by Jacques Derrida and characterized by multiple conflicting interpretations of a given work. Deconstructionists consider the impact of the language of a work and suggest that the true meaning of the work is not necessarily the meaning that the author intended. Jacques Derrida's *De la grammatologie* is the seminal text on deconstructive strategies; among American practitioners of this method of criticism are Paul de Man and J. Hillis Miller.

**Deduction:** The process of reaching a conclusion through reasoning from general premises to a specific premise. An example of deduction is present in the following syllogism: Premise: All mammals are animals. Premise: All whales are mammals. Conclusion: Therefore, all whales are animals.

**Denotation:** The definition of a word, apart from the impressions or feelings it creates in the reader. The word "apartheid" denotes a political and economic policy of segregation by race, but its connotations—oppression, slavery, inequality—are numerous.

**Denouement:** A French word meaning "the unknotting." In literary criticism, it denotes the resolution of conflict in fiction or drama. The *denouement* follows the climax and provides an outcome to the primary plot situation as well as an explanation of secondary plot complications. The *denouement* often involves a character's recognition of his or her state of mind or moral condition. A well-known example of *denouement* is the last scene of the play *As You Like It* by William Shakespeare, in which couples are married, an evildoer repents, the identities of two disguised characters are revealed, and a ruler is restored to power. Also known as Falling Action.

**Description:** Descriptive writing is intended to allow a reader to picture the scene or setting in which the action of a story takes place. The form this description takes often evokes an intended emotional response—a dark, spooky graveyard will evoke fear, and a peaceful, sunny meadow will evoke calmness. An example of a descriptive story is Edgar Allan Poe's *Landor's Cottage,* which offers a detailed depiction of a New York country estate.

**Detective Story:** A narrative about the solution of a mystery or the identification of a criminal. The conventions of the detective story include the detective's scrupulous use of logic in solving the mystery; incompetent or ineffectual police; a suspect who appears guilty at first but is later proved innocent; and the detective's friend or confidant—often the narrator—whose slowness in interpreting clues emphasizes by contrast the detective's brilliance. Edgar Allan Poe's "Murders in the Rue Morgue" is commonly regarded as the earliest example of this type of story. With this work, Poe established many of the conventions of the detective story genre, which are still in practice. Other practitioners of this vast and extremely popular genre include Arthur Conan Doyle, Dashiell Hammett, and Agatha Christie.

**Deus ex machina:** A Latin term meaning "god out of a machine." In Greek drama, a god was often lowered onto the stage by a mechanism of some kind to rescue the hero or untangle the plot. By extension, the term refers to any artificial device or coincidence used to bring about a convenient and simple solution to a plot. This is a common device in melodramas and includes such fortunate circumstances as the sudden receipt of a legacy to save the family farm or a last-minute stay of execution. The *deus ex machina* invariably rewards the virtuous and punishes evildoers. Examples of *deus ex machina* include King Louis XIV in Jean-Baptiste Moliere's *Tartuffe* and Queen Victoria in *The Pirates of Penzance* by William Gilbert and Arthur Sullivan. Bertolt Brecht parodies the abuse of such devices in the conclusion of his *Threepenny Opera.*

**Dialogue:** In its widest sense, dialogue is simply conversation between people in a literary work; in its most restricted sense, it refers specifically to the speech of characters in a drama. As a specific literary genre, a "dialogue" is a composition in which characters debate an issue or idea. The Greek philosopher Plato frequently expounded his theories in the form of dialogues.

**Diction:** The selection and arrangement of words in a literary work. Either or both may vary depending on the desired effect. There are four general types of diction: "formal," used in scholarly or lofty writing; "informal," used in relaxed but educated conversation; "colloquial," used in everyday speech; and "slang," containing newly coined words and other terms not accepted in formal usage.

**Didactic:** A term used to describe works of literature that aim to teach some moral, religious, political, or practical lesson. Although didactic elements are often found in artistically pleasing works, the term "didactic" usually refers to literature in which the message is more important than the form. The term may also be used to criticize a work that the critic finds "overly didactic," that is, heavy-handed in its delivery of a lesson. Examples of didactic literature include John Bunyan's *Pilgrim's Progress,* Alexander Pope's *Essay on Criticism,* Jean-Jacques Rousseau's *Emile,* and Elizabeth Inchbald's *Simple Story.*

**Dimeter:** See *Meter*

**Dionysian:** See *Apollonian and Dionysian*

**Discordia concurs:** A Latin phrase meaning "discord in harmony." The term was coined by the eighteenth-century English writer Samuel Johnson to describe "a combination of dissimilar images or discovery of occult resemblances in things apparently unlike." Johnson created the expression by reversing a phrase by the Latin poet Horace. The metaphysical poetry of John Donne, Richard Crashaw, Abraham Cowley, George Herbert, and Edward Taylor among others, contains many examples of *discordia concurs*. In Donne's "A Valediction: Forbidding Mourning," the poet compares the union of himself with his lover to a draftsman's compass: If they be two, they are two so, As stiff twin compasses are two: Thy soul, the fixed foot, makes no show To move, but doth, if the other do; And though it in the center sit, Yet when the other far doth roam, It leans, and hearkens after it, And grows erect, as that comes home.

**Dissonance:** A combination of harsh or jarring sounds, especially in poetry. Although such combinations may be accidental, poets sometimes intentionally make them to achieve particular effects. Dissonance is also sometimes used to refer to close but not identical rhymes. When this is the case, the word functions as a synonym for consonance. Robert Browning, Gerard Manley Hopkins, and many other poets have made deliberate use of dissonance.

**Doppelganger:** A literary technique by which a character is duplicated (usually in the form of an alter ego, though sometimes as a ghostly counterpart) or divided into two distinct, usually opposite personalities. The use of this character device is widespread in nineteenth- and twentieth- century literature, and indicates a growing awareness among authors that the "self" is really a composite of many "selves." A well-known story containing a *doppelganger* character is Robert Louis Stevenson's *Dr. Jekyll and Mr. Hyde,* which dramatizes an internal struggle between good and evil. Also known as The Double.

**Double Entendre:** A corruption of a French phrase meaning "double meaning." The term is used to indicate a word or phrase that is deliberately ambiguous, especially when one of the meanings is risque or impro-

per. An example of a *double entendre* is the Elizabethan usage of the verb "die," which refers both to death and to orgasm.

**Double, The:** See *Doppelganger*

**Draft:** Any preliminary version of a written work. An author may write dozens of drafts which are revised to form the final work, or he or she may write only one, with few or no revisions. Dorothy Parker's observation that "I can't write five words but that I change seven" humorously indicates the purpose of the draft.

**Drama:** In its widest sense, a drama is any work designed to be presented by actors on a stage. Similarly, "drama" denotes a broad literary genre that includes a variety of forms, from pageant and spectacle to tragedy and comedy, as well as countless types and subtypes. More commonly in modern usage, however, a drama is a work that treats serious subjects and themes but does not aim at the grandeur of tragedy. This use of the term originated with the eighteenth-century French writer Denis Diderot, who used the word *drame* to designate his plays about middle- class life; thus "drama" typically features characters of a less exalted stature than those of tragedy. Examples of classical dramas include Menander's comedy *Dyscolus* and Sophocles' tragedy *Oedipus Rex.* Contemporary dramas include Eugene O'Neill's *The Iceman Cometh,* Lillian Hellman's *Little Foxes,* and August Wilson's *Ma Rainey's Black Bottom.*

**Dramatic Irony:** Occurs when the audience of a play or the reader of a work of literature knows something that a character in the work itself does not know. The irony is in the contrast between the intended meaning of the statements or actions of a character and the additional information understood by the audience. A celebrated example of dramatic irony is in Act V of William Shakespeare's *Romeo and Juliet,* where two young lovers meet their end as a result of a tragic misunderstanding. Here, the audience has full knowledge that Juliet's apparent "death" is merely temporary; she will regain her senses when the mysterious "sleeping potion" she has taken wears off. But Romeo, mistaking Juliet's drug-induced trance for true death, kills himself in grief. Upon awakening, Juliet discovers Romeo's corpse and, in despair, slays herself.

**Dramatic Monologue:** See *Monologue*

**Dramatic Poetry:** Any lyric work that employs elements of drama such as dialogue, conflict, or characterization, but excluding works that are intended for stage presentation. A monologue is a form of dramatic poetry.

**Dramatis Personae:** The characters in a work of literature, particularly a drama. The list of characters printed before the main text of a play or in the program is the *dramatis personae*.

**Dream Allegory:** See *Dream Vision*

**Dream Vision:** A literary convention, chiefly of the Middle Ages. In a dream vision a story is presented as a literal dream of the narrator. This device was commonly used to teach moral and religious lessons. Important works of this type are *The Divine Comedy* by Dante Alighieri, *Piers Plowman* by William Langland, and *The Pilgrim's Progress* by John Bunyan. Also known as Dream Allegory.

**Dystopia:** An imaginary place in a work of fiction where the characters lead dehumanized, fearful lives. Jack London's *The Iron Heel,* Yevgeny Zamyatin's *My,* Aldous Huxley's *Brave New World,* George Orwell's *Nineteen Eighty-four,* and Margaret Atwood's *Handmaid's Tale* portray versions of dystopia.

# E

**Eclogue:** In classical literature, a poem featuring rural themes and structured as a dialogue among shepherds. Eclogues often took specific poetic forms, such as elegies or love poems. Some were written as the soliloquy of a shepherd. In later centuries, "eclogue" came to refer to any poem that was in the pastoral tradition or that had a dialogue or monologue structure. A classical example of an eclogue is Virgil's *Eclogues,* also known as *Bucolics.* Giovanni Boccaccio, Edmund Spenser, Andrew Marvell, Jonathan Swift, and Louis MacNeice also wrote eclogues.

**Edwardian:** Describes cultural conventions identified with the period of the reign of Edward VII of England (1901-1910). Writers of the Edwardian Age typically displayed a strong reaction against the propriety and conservatism of the Victorian Age. Their work often exhibits distrust of authority in religion, politics, and art and expresses strong doubts about the soundness of conventional values.

Writers of this era include George Bernard Shaw, H. G. Wells, and Joseph Conrad.

**Edwardian Age:** See *Edwardian*

**Electra Complex:** A daughter's amorous obsession with her father. The term Electra complex comes from the plays of Euripides and Sophocles entitled *Electra,* in which the character Electra drives her brother Orestes to kill their mother and her lover in revenge for the murder of their father.

**Elegy:** A lyric poem that laments the death of a person or the eventual death of all people. In a conventional elegy, set in a classical world, the poet and subject are spoken of as shepherds. In modern criticism, the word elegy is often used to refer to a poem that is melancholy or mournfully contemplative. John Milton's "Lycidas" and Percy Bysshe Shelley's "Adonais" are two examples of this form.

**Elizabethan Age:** A period of great economic growth, religious controversy, and nationalism closely associated with the reign of Elizabeth I of England (1558-1603). The Elizabethan Age is considered a part of the general renaissance—that is, the flowering of arts and literature—that took place in Europe during the fourteenth through sixteenth centuries. The era is considered the golden age of English literature. The most important dramas in English and a great deal of lyric poetry were produced during this period, and modern English criticism began around this time. The notable authors of the period—Philip Sidney, Edmund Spenser, Christopher Marlowe, William Shakespeare, Ben Jonson, Francis Bacon, and John Donne—are among the best in all of English literature.

**Elizabethan Drama:** English comic and tragic plays produced during the Renaissance, or more narrowly, those plays written during the last years of and few years after Queen Elizabeth's reign. William Shakespeare is considered an Elizabethan dramatist in the broader sense, although most of his work was produced during the reign of James I. Examples of Elizabethan comedies include John Lyly's *The Woman in the Moone,* Thomas Dekker's *The Roaring Girl, or, Moll Cut Purse,* and William Shakespeare's *Twelfth Night.* Examples of Elizabethan tragedies include William Shakespeare's *Antony and Cleopatra,* Thomas Kyd's *The Spanish*

*Tragedy,* and John Webster's *The Tragedy of the Duchess of Malfi.*

**Empathy:** A sense of shared experience, including emotional and physical feelings, with someone or something other than oneself. Empathy is often used to describe the response of a reader to a literary character. An example of an empathic passage is William Shakespeare's description in his narrative poem *Venus and Adonis* of: the snail, whose tender horns being hit, Shrinks backward in his shelly cave with pain. Readers of Gerard Manley Hopkins's *The Windhover* may experience some of the physical sensations evoked in the description of the movement of the falcon.

**English Sonnet:** See *Sonnet*

**Enjambment:** The running over of the sense and structure of a line of verse or a couplet into the following verse or couplet. Andrew Marvell's "To His Coy Mistress" is structured as a series of enjambments, as in lines 11-12: "My vegetable love should grow/Vaster than empires and more slow."

**Enlightenment, The:** An eighteenth-century philosophical movement. It began in France but had a wide impact throughout Europe and America. Thinkers of the Enlightenment valued reason and believed that both the individual and society could achieve a state of perfection. Corresponding to this essentially humanist vision was a resistance to religious authority. Important figures of the Enlightenment were Denis Diderot and Voltaire in France, Edward Gibbon and David Hume in England, and Thomas Paine and Thomas Jefferson in the United States.

**Epic:** A long narrative poem about the adventures of a hero of great historic or legendary importance. The setting is vast and the action is often given cosmic significance through the intervention of supernatural forces such as gods, angels, or demons. Epics are typically written in a classical style of grand simplicity with elaborate metaphors and allusions that enhance the symbolic importance of a hero's adventures. Some well-known epics are Homer's *Iliad* and *Odyssey,* Virgil's *Aeneid,* and John Milton's *Paradise Lost.*

**Epic Simile:** See *Homeric Simile*

**Epic Theater:** A theory of theatrical presentation developed by twentieth-century German playwright Bertolt Brecht. Brecht created a type of drama that the audience could view with complete detachment. He used what he termed "alienation effects" to create an emotional distance between the audience and the action on stage. Among these effects are: short, self-contained scenes that keep the play from building to a cathartic climax; songs that comment on the action; and techniques of acting that prevent the actor from developing an emotional identity with his role. Besides the plays of Bertolt Brecht, other plays that utilize epic theater conventions include those of Georg Buchner, Frank Wedekind, Erwin Piscator, and Leopold Jessner.

**Epigram:** A saying that makes the speaker's point quickly and concisely. Samuel Taylor Coleridge wrote an epigram that neatly sums up the form: What is an Epigram? A Dwarfish whole, Its body brevity, and wit its soul.

**Epilogue:** A concluding statement or section of a literary work. In dramas, particularly those of the seventeenth and eighteenth centuries, the epilogue is a closing speech, often in verse, delivered by an actor at the end of a play and spoken directly to the audience. A famous epilogue is Puck's speech at the end of William Shakespeare's *A Midsummer Night's Dream.*

**Epiphany:** A sudden revelation of truth inspired by a seemingly trivial incident. The term was widely used by James Joyce in his critical writings, and the stories in Joyce's *Dubliners* are commonly called "epiphanies."

**Episode:** An incident that forms part of a story and is significantly related to it. Episodes may be either self-contained narratives or events that depend on a larger context for their sense and importance. Examples of episodes include the founding of Wilmington, Delaware in Charles Reade's *The Disinherited Heir* and the individual events comprising the picaresque novels and medieval romances.

**Episodic Plot:** See *Plot*

**Epitaph:** An inscription on a tomb or tombstone, or a verse written on the occasion of a person's death. Epitaphs may be serious or humorous. Dorothy Parker's epitaph reads, "I told you I was sick."

**Epithalamion:** A song or poem written to honor and commemorate a marriage ceremony. Famous examples include Edmund Spenser's "Epithalamion" and e. e. cummings's "Epithalamion." Also spelled Epithalamium.

**Epithalamium:** See *Epithalamion*

**Epithet:** A word or phrase, often disparaging or abusive, that expresses a character trait of someone or something. "The Napoleon of crime" is an epithet applied to Professor Moriarty, arch-rival of Sherlock Holmes in Arthur Conan Doyle's series of detective stories.

**Exempla:** See *Exemplum*

**Exemplum:** A tale with a moral message. This form of literary sermonizing flourished during the Middle Ages, when *exempla* appeared in collections known as "example-books." The works of Geoffrey Chaucer are full of *exempla*.

**Existentialism:** A predominantly twentieth-century philosophy concerned with the nature and perception of human existence. There are two major strains of existentialist thought: atheistic and Christian. Followers of atheistic existentialism believe that the individual is alone in a godless universe and that the basic human condition is one of suffering and loneliness. Nevertheless, because there are no fixed values, individuals can create their own characters—indeed, they can shape themselves—through the exercise of free will. The atheistic strain culminates in and is popularly associated with the works of Jean-Paul Sartre. The Christian existentialists, on the other hand, believe that only in God may people find freedom from life's anguish. The two strains hold certain beliefs in common: that existence cannot be fully understood or described through empirical effort; that anguish is a universal element of life; that individuals must bear responsibility for their actions; and that there is no common standard of behavior or perception for religious and ethical matters. Existentialist thought figures prominently in the works of such authors as Eugene Ionesco, Franz Kafka, Fyodor Dostoyevsky, Simone de Beauvoir, Samuel Beckett, and Albert Camus.

**Expatriates:** See *Expatriatism*

**Expatriatism:** The practice of leaving one's country to live for an extended period in another country. Literary expatriates include English poets Percy Bysshe Shelley and John Keats in Italy, Polish novelist Joseph Conrad in England, American writers Richard Wright, James Baldwin, Gertrude Stein, and Ernest Hemingway in France, and Trinidadian author Neil Bissondath in Canada.

**Exposition:** Writing intended to explain the nature of an idea, thing, or theme. Expository writing is often combined with description, narration, or argument. In dramatic writing, the exposition is the introductory material which presents the characters, setting, and tone of the play. An example of dramatic exposition occurs in many nineteenth-century drawing-room comedies in which the butler and the maid open the play with relevant talk about their master and mistress; in composition, exposition relays factual information, as in encyclopedia entries.

**Expressionism:** An indistinct literary term, originally used to describe an early twentieth-century school of German painting. The term applies to almost any mode of unconventional, highly subjective writing that distorts reality in some way. Advocates of Expressionism include dramatists George Kaiser, Ernst Toller, Luigi Pirandello, Federico Garcia Lorca, Eugene O'Neill, and Elmer Rice; poets George Heym, Ernst Stadler, August Stramm, Gottfried Benn, and Georg Trakl; and novelists Franz Kafka and James Joyce.

**Extended Monologue:** See *Monologue*

# F

**Fable:** A prose or verse narrative intended to convey a moral. Animals or inanimate objects with human characteristics often serve as characters in fables. A famous fable is Aesop's "The Tortoise and the Hare."

**Fairy Tales:** Short narratives featuring mythical beings such as fairies, elves, and sprites. These tales originally belonged to the folklore of a particular nation or region, such as those collected in Germany by Jacob and Wilhelm Grimm. Two other celebrated writers of fairy tales are Hans Christian Andersen and Rudyard Kipling.

**Falling Action:** See *Denouement*

**Fantasy:** A literary form related to mythology and folklore. Fantasy literature is typically set in non-existent realms and features supernatural beings. Notable examples of fantasy literature are *The Lord of the Rings* by J. R. R. Tolkien and the Gormenghast trilogy by Mervyn Peake.

**Farce:** A type of comedy characterized by broad humor, outlandish incidents, and often vulgar subject matter. Much of the "comedy" in film and television could more accurately be described as farce.

**Feet:** See *Foot*

**Feminine Rhyme:** See *Rhyme*

**Femme fatale:** A French phrase with the literal translation "fatal woman." A *femme fatale* is a sensuous, alluring woman who often leads men into danger or trouble. A classic example of the *femme fatale* is the nameless character in Billy Wilder's *The Seven Year Itch*, portrayed by Marilyn Monroe in the film adaptation.

**Fiction:** Any story that is the product of imagination rather than a documentation of fact. Characters and events in such narratives may be based in real life but their ultimate form and configuration is a creation of the author. Geoffrey Chaucer's *The Canterbury Tales*, Laurence Sterne's *Tristram Shandy*, and Margaret Mitchell's *Gone with the Wind* are examples of fiction.

**Figurative Language:** A technique in writing in which the author temporarily interrupts the order, construction, or meaning of the writing for a particular effect. This interruption takes the form of one or more figures of speech such as hyperbole, irony, or simile. Figurative language is the opposite of literal language, in which every word is truthful, accurate, and free of exaggeration or embellishment. Examples of figurative language are tropes such as metaphor and rhetorical figures such as apostrophe.

**Figures of Speech:** Writing that differs from customary conventions for construction, meaning, order, or significance for the purpose of a special meaning or effect. There are two major types of figures of speech: rhetorical figures, which do not make changes in the meaning of the words, and tropes, which do. Types of figures of speech include simile, hyperbole, alliteration, and pun, among many others.

**Fin de siecle:** A French term meaning "end of the century." The term is used to denote the last decade of the nineteenth century, a transition period when writers and other artists abandoned old conventions and looked for new techniques and objectives. Two writers commonly associated with the *fin de siecle* mindset are Oscar Wilde and George Bernard Shaw.

**First Person:** See *Point of View*

**Flashback:** A device used in literature to present action that occurred before the beginning of the story. Flashbacks are often introduced as the dreams or recollections of one or more characters. Flashback techniques are often used in films, where they are typically set off by a gradual changing of one picture to another.

**Foil:** A character in a work of literature whose physical or psychological qualities contrast strongly with, and therefore highlight, the corresponding qualities of another character. In his Sherlock Holmes stories, Arthur Conan Doyle portrayed Dr. Watson as a man of normal habits and intelligence, making him a foil for the eccentric and wonderfully perceptive Sherlock Holmes.

**Folk Ballad:** See *Ballad*

**Folklore:** Traditions and myths preserved in a culture or group of people. Typically, these are passed on by word of mouth in various forms—such as legends, songs, and proverbs—or preserved in customs and ceremonies. This term was first used by W. J. Thoms in 1846. Sir James Frazer's *The Golden Bough* is the record of English folklore; myths about the frontier and the Old South exemplify American folklore.

**Folktale:** A story originating in oral tradition. Folktales fall into a variety of categories, including legends, ghost stories, fairy tales, fables, and anecdotes based on historical figures and events. Examples of folktales include Giambattista Basile's *The Pentamerone*, which contains the tales of Puss in Boots, Rapunzel, Cinderella, and Beauty and the Beast, and Joel Chandler Harris's Uncle Remus stories, which represent transplanted African folktales and American tales about the characters Mike Fink, Johnny Appleseed, Paul Bunyan, and Pecos Bill.

**Foot:** The smallest unit of rhythm in a line of poetry. In English-language poetry, a foot is typically one accented syllable combined with one or two unaccented syllables. There are many different types of feet. When the accent is on the second syllable of a two syllable word (con-*tort*), the foot is an "iamb"; the reverse accentual pattern (*tor*-ture) is a "trochee." Other feet that commonly occur in poetry in English are "anapest," two unaccented syllables followed by an accented syllable as in in-ter-*cept*, and "dactyl," an accented syllable followed by two unaccented syllables as in *su*-i-cide.

**Foreshadowing:** A device used in literature to create expectation or to set up an explanation of later developments. In Charles Dickens's *Great Expectations,* the graveyard encounter at the beginning of the novel between Pip and the escaped convict Magwitch foreshadows the baleful atmosphere and events that comprise much of the narrative.

**Form:** The pattern or construction of a work which identifies its genre and distinguishes it from other genres. Examples of forms include the different genres, such as the lyric form or the short story form, and various patterns for poetry, such as the verse form or the stanza form.

**Formalism:** In literary criticism, the belief that literature should follow prescribed rules of construction, such as those that govern the sonnet form. Examples of formalism are found in the work of the New Critics and structuralists.

**Fourteener Meter:** See *Meter*

**Free Verse:** Poetry that lacks regular metrical and rhyme patterns but that tries to capture the cadences of everyday speech. The form allows a poet to exploit a variety of rhythmical effects within a single poem. Free-verse techniques have been widely used in the twentieth century by such writers as Ezra Pound, T. S. Eliot, Carl Sandburg, and William Carlos Williams. Also known as *Vers libre.*

**Futurism:** A flamboyant literary and artistic movement that developed in France, Italy, and Russia from 1908 through the 1920s. Futurist theater and poetry abandoned traditional literary forms. In their place, followers of the movement attempted to achieve total freedom of expression through bizarre imagery and deformed or newly invented words. The Futurists were self-consciously modern artists who attempted to incorporate the appearances and sounds of modern life into their work. Futurist writers include Filippo Tommaso Marinetti, Wyndham Lewis, Guillaume Apollinaire, Velimir Khlebnikov, and Vladimir Mayakovsky.

## G

**Genre:** A category of literary work. In critical theory, genre may refer to both the content of a given work—tragedy, comedy, pastoral—and to its form, such as poetry, novel, or drama. This term also refers to types of popular literature, as in the genres of science fiction or the detective story.

**Genteel Tradition:** A term coined by critic George Santayana to describe the literary practice of certain late nineteenth-century American writers, especially New Englanders. Followers of the Genteel Tradition emphasized conventionality in social, religious, moral, and literary standards. Some of the best-known writers of the Genteel Tradition are R. H. Stoddard and Bayard Taylor.

**Gilded Age:** A period in American history during the 1870s characterized by political corruption and materialism. A number of important novels of social and political criticism were written during this time. Examples of Gilded Age literature include Henry Adams's *Democracy* and F. Marion Crawford's *An American Politician.*

**Gothic:** See *Gothicism*

**Gothicism:** In literary criticism, works characterized by a taste for the medieval or morbidly attractive. A gothic novel prominently features elements of horror, the supernatural, gloom, and violence: clanking chains, terror, charnel houses, ghosts, medieval castles, and mysteriously slamming doors. The term "gothic novel" is also applied to novels that lack elements of the traditional Gothic setting but that create a similar atmosphere of terror or dread. Mary Shelley's *Frankenstein* is perhaps the best-known English work of this kind.

**Gothic Novel:** See *Gothicism*

**Great Chain of Being:** The belief that all things and creatures in nature are organized in a hierarchy from inanimate objects at the bottom to God at the top. This system of belief was popular in the seventeenth and eighteenth centuries. A summary of the concept of the great chain of being can be found in the first epistle of Alexander Pope's *An Essay on Man,* and more recently in Arthur O. Lovejoy's *The Great Chain of Being: A Study of the History of an Idea.*

**Grotesque:** In literary criticism, the subject matter of a work or a style of expression characterized by exaggeration, deformity, freakishness, and disorder. The grotesque often includes an element of comic absurdity. Early examples of literary grotesque include Francois Rabelais's *Pantagruel* and *Gargantua* and Thomas Nashe's *The Unfortunate Traveller,* while more recent examples can be found in the works of Edgar Allan Poe, Evelyn Waugh, Eudora Welty, Flannery O'Connor, Eugene Ionesco, Gunter Grass, Thomas Mann, Mervyn Peake, and Joseph Heller, among many others.

# H

**Haiku:** The shortest form of Japanese poetry, constructed in three lines of five, seven, and five syllables respectively. The message of a *haiku* poem usually centers on some aspect of spirituality and provokes an emotional response in the reader. Early masters of *haiku* include Basho, Buson, Kobayashi Issa, and Masaoka Shiki. English writers of *haiku* include the Imagists, notably Ezra Pound, H. D., Amy Lowell, Carl Sandburg, and William Carlos Williams. Also known as *Hokku.*

**Half Rhyme:** See *Consonance*

**Hamartia:** In tragedy, the event or act that leads to the hero's or heroine's downfall. This term is often incorrectly used as a synonym for tragic flaw. In Richard Wright's *Native Son,* the act that seals Bigger Thomas's fate is his first impulsive murder.

**Harlem Renaissance:** The Harlem Renaissance of the 1920s is generally considered the first significant movement of black writers and artists in the United States. During this period, new and established black writers published more fiction and poetry than ever before, the first influential black literary journals were established, and black authors and artists received their first widespread recognition and serious critical appraisal.

Among the major writers associated with this period are Claude McKay, Jean Toomer, Countee Cullen, Langston Hughes, Arna Bontemps, Nella Larsen, and Zora Neale Hurston. Works representative of the Harlem Renaissance include Arna Bontemps's poems "The Return" and "Golgotha Is a Mountain," Claude McKay's novel *Home to Harlem,* Nella Larsen's novel *Passing,* Langston Hughes's poem "The Negro Speaks of Rivers," and the journals *Crisis* and *Opportunity,* both founded during this period. Also known as Negro Renaissance and New Negro Movement.

**Harlequin:** A stock character of the *commedia dell'arte* who occasionally interrupted the action with silly antics. Harlequin first appeared on the English stage in John Day's *The Travailes of the Three English Brothers.* The San Francisco Mime Troupe is one of the few modern groups to adapt Harlequin to the needs of contemporary satire.

**Hellenism:** Imitation of ancient Greek thought or styles. Also, an approach to life that focuses on the growth and development of the intellect. "Hellenism" is sometimes used to refer to the belief that reason can be applied to examine all human experience. A cogent discussion of Hellenism can be found in Matthew Arnold's *Culture and Anarchy.*

**Heptameter:** See *Meter*

**Hero/Heroine:** The principal sympathetic character (male or female) in a literary work. Heroes and heroines typically exhibit admirable traits: idealism, courage, and integrity, for example. Famous heroes and heroines include Pip in Charles Dickens's *Great Expectations,* the anonymous narrator in Ralph Ellison's *Invisible Man,* and Sethe in Toni Morrison's *Beloved.*

**Heroic Couplet:** A rhyming couplet written in iambic pentameter (a verse with five iambic feet). The following lines by Alexander Pope are an example: "Truth guards the Poet, sanctifies the line,/ And makes Immortal, Verse as mean as mine."

**Heroic Line:** The meter and length of a line of verse in epic or heroic poetry. This varies by language and time period. For example, in English poetry, the heroic line is iambic pentameter (a verse with five iambic feet); in French, the alexandrine (a verse with six iambic feet); in classical literature, dactylic hexameter (a verse with six dactylic feet).

**Heroine:** See *Hero/Heroine*

**Hexameter:** See *Meter*

**Historical Criticism:** The study of a work based on its impact on the world of the time period in which it was written. Examples of post-modern historical criticism can be found in the work of Michel Foucault, Hayden White, Stephen Greenblatt, and Jonathan Goldberg.

**Hokku:** See *Haiku*

**Holocaust:** See *Holocaust Literature*

**Holocaust Literature:** Literature influenced by or written about the Holocaust of World War II. Such literature includes true stories of survival in concentration camps, escape, and life after the war, as well as fictional works and poetry. Representative works of Holocaust literature include Saul Bellow's *Mr. Sammler's Planet*, Anne Frank's *The Diary of a Young Girl*, Jerzy Kosinski's *The Painted Bird*, Arthur Miller's *Incident at Vichy*, Czeslaw Milosz's *Collected Poems*, William Styron's *Sophie's Choice*, and Art Spiegelman's *Maus*.

**Homeric Simile:** An elaborate, detailed comparison written as a simile many lines in length. An example of an epic simile from John Milton's *Paradise Lost* follows: Angel Forms, who lay entranced Thick as autumnal leaves that strow the brooks In Vallombrosa, where the Etrurian shades High over-arched embower; or scattered sedge Afloat, when with fierce winds Orion armed Hath vexed the Red-Sea coast, whose waves o'erthrew Busiris and his Memphian chivalry, While with perfidious hatred they pursued The sojourners of Goshen, who beheld From the safe shore their floating carcasses And broken chariot-wheels. Also known as Epic Simile.

**Horatian Satire:** See *Satire*

**Humanism:** A philosophy that places faith in the dignity of humankind and rejects the medieval perception of the individual as a weak, fallen creature. "Humanists" typically believe in the perfectibility of human nature and view reason and education as the means to that end. Humanist thought is represented in the works of Marsilio Ficino, Ludovico Castelvetro, Edmund Spenser, John Milton, Dean John Colet, Desiderius Erasmus, John Dryden, Alexander Pope, Matthew Arnold, and Irving Babbitt.

**Humors:** Mentions of the humors refer to the ancient Greek theory that a person's health and personality were determined by the balance of four basic fluids in the body: blood, phlegm, yellow bile, and black bile. A dominance of any fluid would cause extremes in behavior. An excess of blood created a sanguine person who was joyful, aggressive, and passionate; a phlegmatic person was shy, fearful, and sluggish; too much yellow bile led to a choleric temperament characterized by impatience, anger, bitterness, and stubbornness; and excessive black bile created melancholy, a state of laziness, gluttony, and lack of motivation. Literary treatment of the humors is exemplified by several characters in Ben Jonson's plays *Every Man in His Humour* and *Every Man out of His Humour*. Also spelled Humours.

**Humours:** See *Humors*

**Hyperbole:** In literary criticism, deliberate exaggeration used to achieve an effect. In William Shakespeare's *Macbeth*, Lady Macbeth hyperbolizes when she says, "All the perfumes of Arabia could not sweeten this little hand."

## I

**Iamb:** See *Foot*

**Idiom:** A word construction or verbal expression closely associated with a given language. For example, in colloquial English the construction "how come" can be used instead of "why" to introduce a question. Similarly, "a piece of cake" is sometimes used to describe a task that is easily done.

**Image:** A concrete representation of an object or sensory experience. Typically, such a representation helps evoke the feelings associated with the object or experience itself. Images are either "literal" or "figurative." Literal images are especially concrete and involve little or no extension of the obvious meaning of the words used to express them. Figurative images do not follow the literal meaning of the words exactly. Images in literature are usually visual, but the term "image" can also refer to the representation of any sensory experience. In his poem "The Shepherd's

Hour," Paul Verlaine presents the following image: "The Moon is red through horizon's fog;/ In a dancing mist the hazy meadow sleeps." The first line is broadly literal, while the second line involves turns of meaning associated with dancing and sleeping.

**Imagery:** The array of images in a literary work. Also, figurative language. William Butler Yeats's "The Second Coming" offers a powerful image of encroaching anarchy: Turning and turning in the widening gyre The falcon cannot hear the falconer; Things fall apart....

**Imagism:** An English and American poetry movement that flourished between 1908 and 1917. The Imagists used precise, clearly presented images in their works. They also used common, everyday speech and aimed for conciseness, concrete imagery, and the creation of new rhythms. Participants in the Imagist movement included Ezra Pound, H. D. (Hilda Doolittle), and Amy Lowell, among others.

**In medias res:** A Latin term meaning "in the middle of things." It refers to the technique of beginning a story at its midpoint and then using various flashback devices to reveal previous action. This technique originated in such epics as Virgil's *Aeneid*.

**Induction:** The process of reaching a conclusion by reasoning from specific premises to form a general premise. Also, an introductory portion of a work of literature, especially a play. Geoffrey Chaucer's "Prologue" to the *Canterbury Tales*, Thomas Sackville's "Induction" to *The Mirror of Magistrates*, and the opening scene in William Shakespeare's *The Taming of the Shrew* are examples of inductions to literary works.

**Intentional Fallacy:** The belief that judgments of a literary work based solely on an author's stated or implied intentions are false and misleading. Critics who believe in the concept of the intentional fallacy typically argue that the work itself is sufficient matter for interpretation, even though they may concede that an author's statement of purpose can be useful. Analysis of William Wordsworth's *Lyrical Ballads* based on the observations about poetry he makes in his "Preface" to the second edition of that work is an example of the intentional fallacy.

**Interior Monologue:** A narrative technique in which characters' thoughts are revealed in a way that appears to be uncontrolled by the author. The interior monologue typically aims to reveal the inner self of a character. It portrays emotional experiences as they occur at both a conscious and unconscious level. images are often used to represent sensations or emotions. One of the best-known interior monologues in English is the Molly Bloom section at the close of James Joyce's *Ulysses*. The interior monologue is also common in the works of Virginia Woolf.

**Internal Rhyme:** Rhyme that occurs within a single line of verse. An example is in the opening line of Edgar Allan Poe's "The Raven": "Once upon a midnight dreary, while I pondered weak and weary." Here, "dreary" and "weary" make an internal rhyme.

**Irish Literary Renaissance:** A late nineteenth- and early twentieth-century movement in Irish literature. Members of the movement aimed to reduce the influence of British culture in Ireland and create an Irish national literature. William Butler Yeats, George Moore, and Sean O'Casey are three of the best-known figures of the movement.

**Irony:** In literary criticism, the effect of language in which the intended meaning is the opposite of what is stated. The title of Jonathan Swift's "A Modest Proposal" is ironic because what Swift proposes in this essay is cannibalism—hardly "modest."

**Italian Sonnet:** See *Sonnet*

# J

**Jacobean Age:** The period of the reign of James I of England (1603-1625). The early literature of this period reflected the worldview of the Elizabethan Age, but a darker, more cynical attitude steadily grew in the art and literature of the Jacobean Age. This was an important time for English drama and poetry. Milestones include William Shakespeare's tragedies, tragi-comedies, and sonnets; Ben Jonson's various dramas; and John Donne's metaphysical poetry.

**Jargon:** Language that is used or understood only by a select group of people. Jargon may refer to terminology used in a certain profession, such as computer jargon, or it may refer to any nonsensical language that is not understood by most people. Literary examples of jargon are Francois Villon's *Ballades en jargon,* which is composed in the secret language of the *coquillards,* and Anthony Burgess's *A Clockwork Orange,* narrated in the fictional characters' language of "Nadsat."

**Juvenalian Satire:** See *Satire*

# K

**Knickerbocker Group:** A somewhat indistinct group of New York writers of the first half of the nineteenth century. Members of the group were linked only by location and a common theme: New York life. Two famous members of the Knickerbocker Group were Washington Irving and William Cullen Bryant. The group's name derives from Irving's *Knickerbocker's History of New York.*

# L

**Lais:** See *Lay*

**Lay:** A song or simple narrative poem. The form originated in medieval France. Early French *lais* were often based on the Celtic legends and other tales sung by Breton minstrels—thus the name of the "Breton lay." In fourteenth-century England, the term "lay" was used to describe short narratives written in imitation of the Breton lays. The most notable of these is Geoffrey Chaucer's "The Minstrel's Tale."

**Leitmotiv:** See *Motif*

**Literal Language:** An author uses literal language when he or she writes without exaggerating or embellishing the subject matter and without any tools of figurative language. To say "He ran very quickly down the street" is to use literal language, whereas to say "He ran like a hare down the street" would be using figurative language.

**Literary Ballad:** See *Ballad*

**Literature:** Literature is broadly defined as any written or spoken material, but the term most often refers to creative works. Literature includes poetry, drama, fiction, and many kinds of nonfiction writing, as well as oral, dramatic, and broadcast compositions not necessarily preserved in a written format, such as films and television programs.

**Lost Generation:** A term first used by Gertrude Stein to describe the post-World War I generation of American writers: men and women haunted by a sense of betrayal and emptiness brought about by the destructiveness of the war. The term is commonly applied to Hart Crane, Ernest Hemingway, F. Scott Fitzgerald, and others.

**Lyric Poetry:** A poem expressing the subjective feelings and personal emotions of the poet. Such poetry is melodic, since it was originally accompanied by a lyre in recitals. Most Western poetry in the twentieth century may be classified as lyrical. Examples of lyric poetry include A. E. Housman's elegy "To an Athlete Dying Young," the odes of Pindar and Horace, Thomas Gray and William Collins, the sonnets of Sir Thomas Wyatt and Sir Philip Sidney, Elizabeth Barrett Browning and Rainer Maria Rilke, and a host of other forms in the poetry of William Blake and Christina Rossetti, among many others.

# M

**Mannerism:** Exaggerated, artificial adherence to a literary manner or style. Also, a popular style of the visual arts of late sixteenth-century Europe that was marked by elongation of the human form and by intentional spatial distortion. Literary works that are self-consciously high-toned and artistic are often said to be "mannered." Authors of such works include Henry James and Gertrude Stein.

**Masculine Rhyme:** See *Rhyme*

**Masque:** A lavish and elaborate form of entertainment, often performed in royal courts, that emphasizes song, dance, and costumery. The Renaissance form of the masque grew out of the spectacles of masked figures common in medieval England and Europe. The masque reached its peak of popularity and development in seventeenth-century England, during the reigns of James I and, especially, of Charles I. Ben Jonson, the most significant masque writer, also created the "antimasque," which incorporates elements of humor and the grotesque into the traditional masque and achieved greater dramatic quality. Masque-like interludes appear in Edmund Spenser's *The Faerie Queene* and in William Shakespeare's *The Tempest.* One of the best-known English masques is John Milton's *Comus.*

**Measure:** The foot, verse, or time sequence used in a literary work, especially a poem. Measure is often used somewhat incorrectly as a synonym for meter.

**Melodrama:** A play in which the typical plot is a conflict between characters who personify extreme good and evil. Melodramas usually end happily and emphasize sensationalism. Other literary forms that use the same techniques are often labeled "melodramatic." The term was formerly used to describe a combination of drama and music; as such, it was synonymous with "opera." Augustin Daly's *Under the Gaslight* and Dion Boucicault's *The Octoroon, The Colleen Bawn,* and *The Poor of New York* are examples of melodramas. The most popular media for twentieth-century melodramas are motion pictures and television.

**Metaphor:** A figure of speech that expresses an idea through the image of another object. Metaphors suggest the essence of the first object by identifying it with certain qualities of the second object. An example is "But soft, what light through yonder window breaks?/ It is the east, and Juliet is the sun" in William Shakespeare's *Romeo and Juliet.* Here, Juliet, the first object, is identified with qualities of the second object, the sun.

**Metaphysical Conceit:** See *Conceit*

**Metaphysical Poetry:** The body of poetry produced by a group of seventeenth-century English writers called the "Metaphysical Poets." The group includes John Donne and Andrew Marvell. The Metaphysical Poets made use of everyday speech, intellectual analysis, and unique imagery. They aimed to portray the ordinary conflicts and contradictions of life. Their poems often took the form of an argument, and many of them emphasize physical and religious love as well as the fleeting nature of life. Elaborate conceits are typical in metaphysical poetry. Marvell's "To His Coy Mistress" is a well-known example of a metaphysical poem.

**Metaphysical Poets:** See *Metaphysical Poetry*

**Meter:** In literary criticism, the repetition of sound patterns that creates a rhythm in poetry. The patterns are based on the number of syllables and the presence and absence of accents. The unit of rhythm in a line is called a foot. Types of meter are classified according to the number of feet in a line. These are the standard English lines: Monometer, one foot; Dimeter, two feet; Trimeter, three feet; Tetrameter, four feet; Pentameter, five feet; Hexameter, six feet (also called the Alexandrine); Heptameter, seven feet (also called the "Fourteener" when the feet are iambic). The most common English meter is the iambic pentameter, in which each line contains ten syllables, or five iambic feet, which individually are composed of an unstressed syllable followed by an accented syllable. Both of the following lines from Alfred, Lord Tennyson's "Ulysses" are written in iambic pentameter: Made weak by time and fate, but strong in will To strive, to seek, to find, and not to yield.

**Mise en scene:** The costumes, scenery, and other properties of a drama. Herbert Beerbohm Tree was renowned for the elaborate *mises en scene* of his lavish Shakespearean productions at His Majesty's Theatre between 1897 and 1915.

**Modernism:** Modern literary practices. Also, the principles of a literary school that lasted from roughly the beginning of the twentieth century until the end of World War II. Modernism is defined by its rejection of the literary conventions of the nineteenth century and by its opposition to conventional morality, taste, traditions, and economic values. Many writers are associated with the concepts of Modernism, including Albert Camus, Marcel Proust, D. H. Lawrence, W. H. Auden, Ernest Hemingway, William Faulkner, William Butler Yeats, Thomas Mann, Tennessee Williams, Eugene O'Neill, and James Joyce.

**Monologue:** A composition, written or oral, by a single individual. More specifically, a speech given by a single individual in a drama or other public entertainment. It has no set length, although it is usually several or more lines long. An example of an "extended monologue"—that is, a monologue of great length and seriousness—occurs in the one-act, one-character play *The Stronger* by August Strindberg.

**Monometer:** See *Meter*

**Mood:** The prevailing emotions of a work or of the author in his or her creation of the work. The mood of a work is not always what might be expected based on its subject matter. The poem "Dover Beach" by Matthew Arnold offers examples of two different moods originating from the same experience: watching the ocean at night. The mood of the first three lines—The sea is calm tonight The tide is full, the moon lies fair Upon the straights.... is in sharp contrast to the mood of the last three lines— And we are here as on a darkling plain Swept with confused alarms of struggle and flight, Where ignorant armies clash by night.

**Motif:** A theme, character type, image, metaphor, or other verbal element that recurs throughout a single work of literature or occurs in a number of different works over a period of time. For example, the various manifestations of the color white in Herman Melville's *Moby Dick* is a "specific" *motif,* while the trials of star-crossed lovers is a "conventional" *motif* from the literature of all periods. Also known as *Motiv* or *Leitmotiv.*

**Motiv:** See *Motif*

**Muckrakers:** An early twentieth-century group of American writers. Typically, their works exposed the wrongdoings of big business and government in the United States. Upton Sinclair's *The Jungle* exemplifies the muckraking novel.

**Muses:** Nine Greek mythological goddesses, the daughters of Zeus and Mnemosyne (Memory). Each muse patronized a specific area of the liberal arts and sciences. Calliope presided over epic poetry, Clio over history, Erato over love poetry, Euterpe over music or lyric poetry, Melpomene over tragedy, Polyhymnia over hymns to the gods, Terpsichore over dance, Thalia over comedy, and Urania over astronomy. Poets and writers traditionally made appeals to the Muses for inspiration in their work. John Milton invokes the aid of a muse at the beginning of the first book of his *Paradise Lost:* Of Man's First disobedience, and the Fruit of the Forbidden Tree, whose mortal taste Brought Death into the World, and all our woe, With loss of Eden, till one greater Man Restore us, and regain the blissful Seat, Sing Heav'nly Muse, that on the secret top of Oreb, or of Sinai, didst inspire That Shepherd, who first taught the chosen Seed, In the Beginning how the Heav'ns and Earth Rose out of Chaos....

**Mystery:** See *Suspense*

**Myth:** An anonymous tale emerging from the traditional beliefs of a culture or social unit. Myths use supernatural explanations for natural phenomena. They may also explain cosmic issues like creation and death. Collections of myths, known as mythologies, are common to all cultures and nations, but the best-known myths belong to the Norse, Roman, and Greek mythologies. A famous myth is the story of Arachne, an arrogant young girl who challenged a goddess, Athena, to a weaving contest; when the girl won, Athena was enraged and turned Arachne into a spider, thus explaining the existence of spiders.

# N

**Narration:** The telling of a series of events, real or invented. A narration may be either a simple narrative, in which the events are recounted chronologically, or a narrative with a plot, in which the account is given in a style reflecting the author's artistic concept of the story. Narration is sometimes used as a synonym for "storyline." The recounting of scary stories around a campfire is a form of narration.

**Narrative:** A verse or prose accounting of an event or sequence of events, real or invented. The term is also used as an adjective in the sense "method of narration." For example, in literary criticism, the expression "narrative technique" usually refers to the way the author structures and presents his or her story. Narratives range from the shortest accounts of events, as in Julius Caesar's remark, "I came, I saw, I conquered," to the longest historical or biographical works, as in Edward Gibbon's *The Decline and Fall of the Roman Empire,* as well as diaries, travelogues, novels, ballads, epics, short stories, and other fictional forms.

**Narrative Poetry:** A nondramatic poem in which the author tells a story. Such poems may be of any length or level of complexity. Epics such as *Beowulf* and ballads are forms of narrative poetry.

**Narrator:** The teller of a story. The narrator may be the author or a character in the story through whom the author speaks. Huckleberry Finn is the narrator of Mark Twain's *The Adventures of Huckleberry Finn.*

**Naturalism:** A literary movement of the late nineteenth and early twentieth centuries. The movement's major theorist, French novelist Emile Zola, envisioned a type of fiction that would examine human life with the objectivity of scientific inquiry. The Naturalists typically viewed human beings as either the products of "biological determinism," ruled by hereditary instincts and engaged in an endless struggle for survival, or as the products of "socioeconomic determinism," ruled by social and economic forces beyond their control. In their works, the Naturalists generally ignored the highest levels of society and focused on degradation: poverty, alcoholism, prostitution, insanity, and disease. Naturalism influenced authors throughout the world, including Henrik Ibsen and Thomas Hardy. In the United States, in particular, Naturalism had a profound impact. Among the authors who embraced its principles are Theodore Dreiser, Eugene O'Neill, Stephen Crane, Jack London, and Frank Norris.

**Negritude:** A literary movement based on the concept of a shared cultural bond on the part of black Africans, wherever they may be in the world. It traces its origins to the former French colonies of Africa and the Caribbean. Negritude poets, novelists, and essayists generally stress four points in their writings: One, black alienation from traditional African culture can lead to feelings of inferiority. Two, European colonialism and Western education should be resisted. Three, black Africans should seek to affirm and define their own identity. Four, African culture can and should be reclaimed. Many Negritude writers also claim that blacks can make unique contributions to the world, based on a heightened appreciation of nature, rhythm, and human emotions—aspects of life they say are not so highly valued in the materialistic and rationalistic West. Examples of Negritude literature include the poetry of both Senegalese Leopold Senghor in *Hosties noires* and Martiniquais Aime-Fernand Cesaire in *Return to My Native Land.*

**Negro Renaissance:** See *Harlem Renaissance*

**Neoclassical Period:** See *Neoclassicism*

**Neoclassicism:** In literary criticism, this term refers to the revival of the attitudes and styles of expression of classical literature. It is generally used to describe a period in European history beginning in the late seventeenth century and lasting until about 1800. In its purest form, Neoclassicism marked a return to order, proportion, restraint, logic, accuracy, and decorum. In England, where Neoclassicism perhaps was most popular, it reflected the influence of seventeenth-century French writers, especially dramatists. Neoclassical writers typically reacted against the intensity and enthusiasm of the Renaissance period. They wrote works that appealed to the intellect, using elevated language and classical literary forms such as satire and the ode. Neoclassical works were often governed by the classical goal of instruction. English neoclassicists included Alexander Pope, Jonathan Swift, Joseph Addison, Sir Richard Steele, John Gay, and Matthew Prior; French neoclassicists included Pierre Corneille and Jean-Baptiste Moliere. Also known as Age of Reason.

**Neoclassicists:** See *Neoclassicism*

**New Criticism:** A movement in literary criticism, dating from the late 1920s, that stressed close textual analysis in the interpretation of works of literature. The New Critics saw little merit in historical and biographical analysis. Rather, they aimed to examine the text alone, free from the question of how external events—biographical or otherwise—may have helped shape it. This predominantly American school was named "New Criticism" by one of its practitioners, John Crowe Ransom. Other important New Critics included Allen Tate, R. P. Blackmur, Robert Penn Warren, and Cleanth Brooks.

**New Negro Movement:** See *Harlem Renaissance*

**Noble Savage:** The idea that primitive man is noble and good but becomes evil and corrupted as he becomes civilized. The concept of the noble savage originated in the Renaissance period but is more closely identified with such later writers as Jean-Jacques Rousseau and Aphra Behn. First described in John Dryden's play *The Conquest of Granada,* the noble savage is portrayed by the various Native Americans in James Fenimore Cooper's "Leatherstocking Tales," by Queequeg, Daggoo, and Tashtego in Herman Melville's *Moby Dick,* and by John the Savage in Aldous Huxley's *Brave New World.*

# O

**Objective Correlative:** An outward set of objects, a situation, or a chain of events corresponding to an inward experience and evoking this experience in the reader. The term frequently appears in modern criticism in discussions of authors' intended effects on the emotional responses of readers. This term was originally used by T. S. Eliot in his 1919 essay "Hamlet."

**Objectivity:** A quality in writing characterized by the absence of the author's opinion or feeling about the subject matter. Objectivity is an important factor in criticism. The novels of Henry James and, to a certain extent, the poems of John Larkin demonstrate objectivity, and it is central to John Keats's concept of "negative capability." Critical and journalistic writing usually are or attempt to be objective.

**Occasional Verse:** poetry written on the occasion of a significant historical or personal event. *Vers de societe* is sometimes called occasional verse although it is of a less serious nature. Famous examples of occasional verse include Andrew Marvell's "Horatian Ode upon Cromwell's Return from England," Walt Whitman's "When Lilacs Last in the Dooryard Bloom'd"—written upon the death of Abraham Lincoln—and Edmund Spenser's commemoration of his wedding, "Epithalamion."

**Octave:** A poem or stanza composed of eight lines. The term octave most often represents the first eight lines of a Petrarchan sonnet. An example of an octave is taken from a translation of a Petrarchan sonnet by Sir Thomas Wyatt: The pillar perisht is whereto I leant, The strongest stay of mine unquiet mind; The like of it no man again can find, From East to West Still seeking though he went. To mind unhap! for hap away hath rent Of all my joy the very bark and rind; And I, alas, by chance am thus assigned Daily to mourn till death do it relent.

**Ode:** Name given to an extended lyric poem characterized by exalted emotion and dignified style. An ode usually concerns a single, serious theme. Most odes, but not all, are addressed to an object or individual. Odes are distinguished from other lyric poetic forms by their complex rhythmic and stanzaic patterns. An example of this form is John Keats's "Ode to a Nightingale."

**Oedipus Complex:** A son's amorous obsession with his mother. The phrase is derived from the story of the ancient Theban hero Oedipus, who unknowingly killed his father and married his mother. Literary occurrences of the Oedipus complex include Andre Gide's *Oedipe* and Jean Cocteau's *La Machine infernale,* as well as the most famous, Sophocles' *Oedipus Rex.*

**Omniscience:** See *Point of View*

**Onomatopoeia:** The use of words whose sounds express or suggest their meaning. In its simplest sense, onomatopoeia may be represented by words that mimic the sounds they denote such as "hiss" or "meow." At a more subtle level, the pattern and rhythm of sounds and rhymes of a line or poem may be onomatopoeic. A celebrated example of onomatopoeia is the repetition of the word "bells" in Edgar Allan Poe's poem "The Bells."

**Opera:** A type of stage performance, usually a drama, in which the dialogue is sung. Classic examples of opera include Giuseppi Verdi's *La traviata,* Giacomo Puccini's *La Boheme,* and Richard Wagner's *Tristan und Isolde.* Major twentieth-century contributors to the form include Richard Strauss and Alban Berg.

**Operetta:** A usually romantic comic opera. John Gay's *The Beggar's Opera,* Richard Sheridan's *The Duenna,* and numerous works by William Gilbert and Arthur Sullivan are examples of operettas.

**Oral Tradition:** See *Oral Transmission*

**Oral Transmission:** A process by which songs, ballads, folklore, and other material are transmitted by word of mouth. The tradition of oral transmission predates the written record systems of literate society. Oral transmission preserves material sometimes over generations, although often with variations. Memory plays a large part in the recitation and preservation of orally transmitted material. Breton lays, French *fabliaux,* national epics (including the Anglo-Saxon *Beowulf,* the Spanish *El Cid,* and the Finnish *Kalevala*), Native American myths and legends, and African folktales told by plantation slaves are examples of orally transmitted literature.

**Oration:** Formal speaking intended to motivate the listeners to some action or feeling. Such public speaking was much more common before the development of timely printed communication such as newspapers. Famous examples of oration include Abraham Lincoln's "Gettysburg Address" and Dr. Martin Luther King Jr.'s "I Have a Dream" speech.

**Ottava Rima:** An eight-line stanza of poetry composed in iambic pentameter (a five-foot line in which each foot consists of an unaccented syllable followed by an accented syllable), following the abababcc rhyme scheme. This form has been prominently used by such important English writers as Lord Byron, Henry Wadsworth Longfellow, and W. B. Yeats.

**Oxymoron:** A phrase combining two contradictory terms. Oxymorons may be intentional or unintentional. The following speech from William Shakespeare's *Romeo and Juliet* uses several oxymorons: Why, then, O brawling love! O loving hate! O anything, of nothing first create! O heavy lightness! serious vanity! Mis-shapen chaos of well-seeming forms! Feather of lead, bright smoke, cold fire, sick health! This love feel I, that feel no love in this.

## P

**Pantheism:** The idea that all things are both a manifestation or revelation of God and a part of God at the same time. Pantheism was a common attitude in the early societies of Egypt, India, and Greece—the term derives from the Greek *pan* meaning "all" and *theos* meaning "deity." It later became a significant part of the Christian faith. William Wordsworth and Ralph Waldo Emerson are among the many writers who have expressed the pantheistic attitude in their works.

**Parable:** A story intended to teach a moral lesson or answer an ethical question. In the West, the best examples of parables are those of Jesus Christ in the New Testament, notably "The Prodigal Son," but parables also are used in Sufism, rabbinic literature, Hasidism, and Zen Buddhism.

**Paradox:** A statement that appears illogical or contradictory at first, but may actually point to an underlying truth. "Less is more" is an example of a paradox. Literary examples include Francis Bacon's statement, "The most corrected copies are commonly the least correct," and "All animals are equal, but some animals are more equal than others" from George Orwell's *Animal Farm.*

**Parallelism:** A method of comparison of two ideas in which each is developed in the same grammatical structure. Ralph Waldo Emerson's "Civilization" contains this example of parallelism: Raphael paints wisdom; Handel sings it, Phidias carves it, Shakespeare writes it, Wren builds it, Columbus sails it, Luther preaches it, Washington arms it, Watt mechanizes it.

**Parnassianism:** A mid nineteenth-century movement in French literature. Followers of the movement stressed adherence to well-defined artistic forms as a reaction against the often chaotic expression of the artist's ego that dominated the work of the Romantics. The Parnassians also rejected the moral, ethical, and social themes exhibited in the works of French Romantics such as Victor Hugo. The aesthetic doctrines of the Parnassians strongly influenced the later symbolist and decadent movements. Members of the Parnassian school include Leconte de Lisle, Sully Prudhomme, Albert Glatigny, Francois Coppee, and Theodore de Banville.

**Parody:** In literary criticism, this term refers to an imitation of a serious literary work or the signature style of a particular author in a ridiculous manner. A typical parody adopts the style of the original and applies it to an inappropriate subject for humorous effect. Parody is a form of satire and could be considered the literary equivalent of a caricature or cartoon. Henry Fielding's *Shamela* is a parody of Samuel Richardson's *Pamela.*

**Pastoral:** A term derived from the Latin word "pastor," meaning shepherd. A pastoral is a literary composition on a rural theme. The conventions of the pastoral were originated by the third-century Greek poet Theocritus, who wrote about the experiences, love affairs, and pastimes of Sicilian shepherds. In a pastoral, characters and language of a courtly nature are often placed in a simple setting. The term pastoral is also used to classify dramas, elegies, and lyrics that exhibit the use of country settings and shepherd characters. Percy Bysshe Shelley's "Adonais" and John Milton's "Lycidas" are two famous examples of pastorals.

**Pastorela:** The Spanish name for the shepherds play, a folk drama reenacted during the Christmas season. Examples of *pastorelas* include Gomez Manrique's *Representacion del nacimiento* and the dramas of Lucas Fernandez and Juan del Encina.

**Pathetic Fallacy:** A term coined by English critic John Ruskin to identify writing that falsely endows nonhuman things with human intentions and feelings, such as "angry clouds" and "sad trees." The pathetic fallacy is a required convention in the classical poetic form of the pastoral elegy, and it is used in the modern poetry of T. S. Eliot, Ezra Pound, and the Imagists. Also known as Poetic Fallacy.

**Pelado:** Literally the "skinned one" or shirtless one, he was the stock underdog, sharp-witted picaresque character of Mexican vaudeville and tent shows. The *pelado* is found in such works as Don Catarino's *Los effectos de la crisis* and *Regreso a mi tierra*.

**Pen Name:** See *Pseudonym*

**Pentameter:** See *Meter*

**Persona:** A Latin term meaning "mask." *Personae* are the characters in a fictional work of literature. The *persona* generally functions as a mask through which the author tells a story in a voice other than his or her own. A *persona* is usually either a character in a story who acts as a narrator or an "implied author," a voice created by the author to act as the narrator for himself or herself. *Personae* include the narrator of Geoffrey Chaucer's *Canterbury Tales* and Marlow in Joseph Conrad's *Heart of Darkness*.

**Personae:** See *Persona*

**Personal Point of View:** See *Point of View*

**Personification:** A figure of speech that gives human qualities to abstract ideas, animals, and inanimate objects. William Shakespeare used personification in *Romeo and Juliet* in the lines "Arise, fair sun, and kill the envious moon,/ Who is already sick and pale with grief." Here, the moon is portrayed as being envious, sick, and pale with grief—all markedly human qualities. Also known as *Prosopopoeia*.

**Petrarchan Sonnet:** See *Sonnet*

**Phenomenology:** A method of literary criticism based on the belief that things have no existence outside of human consciousness or awareness. Proponents of this theory believe that art is a process that takes place in the mind of the observer as he or she contemplates an object rather than a quality of the object itself. Among phenomenological critics are Edmund Husserl, George Poulet, Marcel Raymond, and Roman Ingarden.

**Picaresque Novel:** Episodic fiction depicting the adventures of a roguish central character ("picaro" is Spanish for "rogue"). The picaresque hero is commonly a low-born but clever individual who wanders into and out of various affairs of love, danger, and farcical intrigue. These involvements may take place at all social levels and typically present a humorous and wide-ranging satire of a given society. Prominent examples of the picaresque novel are *Don Quixote* by Miguel de Cervantes, *Tom Jones* by Henry Fielding, and *Moll Flanders* by Daniel Defoe.

**Plagiarism:** Claiming another person's written material as one's own. Plagiarism can take the form of direct, word-for-word copying or the theft of the substance or idea of the work. A student who copies an encyclopedia entry and turns it in as a report for school is guilty of plagiarism.

**Platonic Criticism:** A form of criticism that stresses an artistic work's usefulness as an agent of social engineering rather than any quality or value of the work itself. Platonic criticism takes as its starting point the ancient Greek philosopher Plato's comments on art in his *Republic*.

**Platonism:** The embracing of the doctrines of the philosopher Plato, popular among the poets of the Renaissance and the Romantic period. Platonism is more flexible than Aristotelian Criticism and places more emphasis on the supernatural and unknown aspects of life. Platonism is expressed in the love poetry of the Renaissance, the fourth book of Baldassare Castiglione's *The Book of the Courtier*, and the poetry of William Blake, William Wordsworth, Percy Bysshe Shelley, Friedrich Holderlin, William Butler Yeats, and Wallace Stevens.

**Play:** See *Drama*

**Plot:** In literary criticism, this term refers to the pattern of events in a narrative or drama. In its simplest sense, the plot guides the author in composing the work and helps the reader follow the work. Typically, plots exhibit causality and unity and have a beginning, a middle, and an end. Sometimes, however, a plot may consist of a series of disconnected events, in which case it is known as an "episodic plot." In his *Aspects of the Novel,* E. M. Forster distinguishes between a story, defined as a "narrative of events arranged in their time- sequence," and plot, which organizes the events to a "sense of causality." This definition closely mirrors Aristotle's discussion of plot in his *Poetics.*

**Poem:** In its broadest sense, a composition utilizing rhyme, meter, concrete detail, and expressive language to create a literary experience with emotional and aesthetic appeal. Typical poems include sonnets, odes, elegies, *haiku,* ballads, and free verse.

**Poet:** An author who writes poetry or verse. The term is also used to refer to an artist or writer who has an exceptional gift for expression, imagination, and energy in the making of art in any form. Well-known poets include Horace, Basho, Sir Philip Sidney, Sir Edmund Spenser, John Donne, Andrew Marvell, Alexander Pope, Jonathan Swift, George Gordon, Lord Byron, John Keats, Christina Rossetti, W. H. Auden, Stevie Smith, and Sylvia Plath.

**Poetic Fallacy:** See *Pathetic Fallacy*

**Poetic Justice:** An outcome in a literary work, not necessarily a poem, in which the good are rewarded and the evil are punished, especially in ways that particularly fit their virtues or crimes. For example, a murderer may himself be murdered, or a thief will find himself penniless.

**Poetic License:** Distortions of fact and literary convention made by a writer—not always a poet—for the sake of the effect gained. Poetic license is closely related to the concept of "artistic freedom." An author exercises poetic license by saying that a pile of money "reaches as high as a mountain" when the pile is actually only a foot or two high.

**Poetics:** This term has two closely related meanings. It denotes (1) an aesthetic theory in literary criticism about the essence of poetry or (2) rules prescribing the proper methods, content, style, or diction of poetry. The term poetics may also refer to theories about literature in general, not just poetry.

**Poetry:** In its broadest sense, writing that aims to present ideas and evoke an emotional experience in the reader through the use of meter, imagery, connotative and concrete words, and a carefully constructed structure based on rhythmic patterns. Poetry typically relies on words and expressions that have several layers of meaning. It also makes use of the effects of regular rhythm on the ear and may make a strong appeal to the senses through the use of imagery. Edgar Allan Poe's "Annabel Lee" and Walt Whitman's *Leaves of Grass* are famous examples of poetry.

**Point of View:** The narrative perspective from which a literary work is presented to the reader. There are four traditional points of view. The "third person omniscient" gives the reader a "godlike" perspective, unrestricted by time or place, from which to see actions and look into the minds of characters. This allows the author to comment openly on characters and events in the work. The "third person" point of view presents the events of the story from outside of any single character's perception, much like the omniscient point of view, but the reader must understand the action as it takes place and without any special insight into characters' minds or motivations. The "first person" or "personal" point of view relates events as they are perceived by a single character. The main character "tells" the story and may offer opinions about the action and characters which differ from those of the author. Much less common than omniscient, third person, and first person is the "second person" point of view, wherein the author tells the story as if it is happening to the reader. James Thurber employs the omniscient point of view in his short story "The Secret Life of Walter Mitty." Ernest Hemingway's "A Clean, Well-Lighted Place" is a short story told from the third person point of view. Mark Twain's novel *Huck Finn* is presented from the first person viewpoint. Jay McInerney's *Bright Lights, Big City* is an example of a novel which uses the second person point of view.

**Polemic:** A work in which the author takes a stand on a controversial subject, such as abortion or religion. Such works are often extremely argumentative or provocative. Classic examples of polemics include John Milton's *Aeropagitica* and Thomas Paine's *The American Crisis.*

**Pornography:** Writing intended to provoke feelings of lust in the reader. Such works are often condemned by critics and teachers, but those which can be shown to have literary value are viewed less harshly. Literary works that have been described as pornographic include Ovid's *The Art of Love,* Margaret of Angouleme's *Heptameron,* John Cleland's *Memoirs of a Woman of Pleasure; or, the Life of Fanny Hill,* the anonymous *My Secret Life,* D. H. Lawrence's *Lady Chatterley's Lover,* and Vladimir Nabokov's *Lolita.*

**Post-Aesthetic Movement:** An artistic response made by African Americans to the black aesthetic movement of the 1960s and early '70s. Writers since that time have adopted a somewhat different tone in their work, with less emphasis placed on the disparity between black and white in the United States. In the words of post-aesthetic authors such as Toni Morrison, John Edgar Wideman, and Kristin Hunter, African Americans are portrayed as looking inward for answers to their own questions, rather than always looking to the outside world. Two well-known examples of works produced as part of the post-aesthetic movement are the Pulitzer Prize-winning novels *The Color Purple* by Alice Walker and *Beloved* by Toni Morrison.

**Postmodernism:** Writing from the 1960s forward characterized by experimentation and continuing to apply some of the fundamentals of modernism, which included existentialism and alienation. Postmodernists have gone a step further in the rejection of tradition begun with the modernists by also rejecting traditional forms, preferring the anti-novel over the novel and the anti-hero over the hero. Postmodern writers include Alain Robbe-Grillet, Thomas Pynchon, Margaret Drabble, John Fowles, Adolfo Bioy-Casares, and Gabriel Garcia Marquez.

**Pre-Raphaelites:** A circle of writers and artists in mid nineteenth-century England. Valuing the pre-Renaissance artistic qualities of religious symbolism, lavish pictorialism, and natural sensuousness, the Pre-Raphaelites cultivated a sense of mystery and melancholy that influenced later writers associated with the Symbolist and Decadent movements. The major members of the group include Dante Gabriel Rossetti, Christina Rossetti, Algernon Swinburne, and Walter Pater.

**Primitivism:** The belief that primitive peoples were nobler and less flawed than civilized peoples because they had not been subjected to the tainting influence of society. Examples of literature espousing primitivism include Aphra Behn's *Oroonoko: Or, The History of the Royal Slave,* Jean-Jacques Rousseau's *Julie ou la Nouvelle Heloise,* Oliver Goldsmith's *The Deserted Village,* the poems of Robert Burns, Herman Melville's stories *Typee, Omoo,* and *Mardi,* many poems of William Butler Yeats and Robert Frost, and William Golding's novel *Lord of the Flies.*

**Projective Verse:** A form of free verse in which the poet's breathing pattern determines the lines of the poem. Poets who advocate projective verse are against all formal structures in writing, including meter and form. Besides its creators, Robert Creeley, Robert Duncan, and Charles Olson, two other well-known projective verse poets are Denise Levertov and LeRoi Jones (Amiri Baraka). Also known as Breath Verse.

**Prologue:** An introductory section of a literary work. It often contains information establishing the situation of the characters or presents information about the setting, time period, or action. In drama, the prologue is spoken by a chorus or by one of the principal characters. In the "General Prologue" of *The Canterbury Tales,* Geoffrey Chaucer describes the main characters and establishes the setting and purpose of the work.

**Prose:** A literary medium that attempts to mirror the language of everyday speech. It is distinguished from poetry by its use of unmetered, unrhymed language consisting of logically related sentences. Prose is usually grouped into paragraphs that form a cohesive whole such as an essay or a novel. Recognized masters of English prose writing include Sir Thomas Malory, William Caxton, Raphael Holinshed, Joseph Addison, Mark Twain, and Ernest Hemingway.

**Prosopopoeia:** See *Personification*

**Protagonist:** The central character of a story who serves as a focus for its themes and incidents and as the principal rationale for its development. The protagonist is sometimes referred to in discussions of modern literature as the hero or anti-hero. Well-known protagonists are Hamlet in William Shakespeare's *Hamlet* and Jay Gatsby in F. Scott Fitzgerald's *The Great Gatsby*.

**Protest Fiction:** Protest fiction has as its primary purpose the protesting of some social injustice, such as racism or discrimination. One example of protest fiction is a series of five novels by Chester Himes, beginning in 1945 with *If He Hollers Let Him Go* and ending in 1955 with *The Primitive*. These works depict the destructive effects of race and gender stereotyping in the context of interracial relationships. Another African American author whose works often revolve around themes of social protest is John Oliver Killens. James Baldwin's essay "Everybody's Protest Novel" generated controversy by attacking the authors of protest fiction.

**Proverb:** A brief, sage saying that expresses a truth about life in a striking manner. "They are not all cooks who carry long knives" is an example of a proverb.

**Pseudonym:** A name assumed by a writer, most often intended to prevent his or her identification as the author of a work. Two or more authors may work together under one pseudonym, or an author may use a different name for each genre he or she publishes in. Some publishing companies maintain "house pseudonyms," under which any number of authors may write installations in a series. Some authors also choose a pseudonym over their real names the way an actor may use a stage name. Examples of pseudonyms (with the author's real name in parentheses) include Voltaire (Francois-Marie Arouet), Novalis (Friedrich von Hardenberg), Currer Bell (Charlotte Bronte), Ellis Bell (Emily Bronte), George Eliot (Maryann Evans), Honorio Bustos Donmecq (Adolfo Bioy-Casares and Jorge Luis Borges), and Richard Bachman (Stephen King).

**Pun:** A play on words that have similar sounds but different meanings. A serious example of the pun is from John Donne's "A Hymne to God the Father": Sweare by thyself, that at my death thy sonne Shall shine as he shines now, and hereto fore; And, having done that, Thou haste done; I fear no more.

**Pure Poetry:** poetry written without instructional intent or moral purpose that aims only to please a reader by its imagery or musical flow. The term pure poetry is used as the antonym of the term "didacticism." The poetry of Edgar Allan Poe, Stephane Mallarme, Paul Verlaine, Paul Valery, Juan Ramoz Jimenez, and Jorge Guillen offer examples of pure poetry.

## Q

**Quatrain:** A four-line stanza of a poem or an entire poem consisting of four lines. The following quatrain is from Robert Herrick's "To Live Merrily, and to Trust to Good Verses": Round, round, the root do's run; And being ravisht thus, Come, I will drink a Tun To my *Propertius*.

## R

**Raisonneur:** A character in a drama who functions as a spokesperson for the dramatist's views. The *raisonneur* typically observes the play without becoming central to its action. *Raisonneurs* were very common in plays of the nineteenth century.

**Realism:** A nineteenth-century European literary movement that sought to portray familiar characters, situations, and settings in a realistic manner. This was done primarily by using an objective narrative point of view and through the buildup of accurate detail. The standard for success of any realistic work depends on how faithfully it transfers common experience into fictional forms. The realistic method may be altered or extended, as in stream of consciousness writing, to record highly subjective experience. Seminal authors in the tradition of Realism include Honore de Balzac, Gustave Flaubert, and Henry James.

**Refrain:** A phrase repeated at intervals throughout a poem. A refrain may appear at the end of each stanza or at less regular intervals. It may be altered slightly at each appearance. Some refrains are nonsense expressions—as with "Nevermore" in Edgar Allan Poe's "The Raven"—that seem to take on a different significance with each use.

**Renaissance:** The period in European history that marked the end of the Middle Ages. It began in Italy in the late fourteenth century. In broad terms, it is usually seen as spanning the fourteenth, fifteenth, and sixteenth centuries, although it did not reach Great Britain, for example, until the 1480s or so. The Renaissance saw an awakening in almost every sphere of human activity, especially science, philosophy, and the arts. The period is best defined by the emergence of a general philosophy that emphasized the importance of the intellect, the individual, and world affairs. It contrasts strongly with the medieval worldview, characterized by the dominant concerns of faith, the social collective, and spiritual salvation. Prominent writers during the Renaissance include Niccolo Machiavelli and Baldassare Castiglione in Italy, Miguel de Cervantes and Lope de Vega in Spain, Jean Froissart and Francois Rabelais in France, Sir Thomas More and Sir Philip Sidney in England, and Desiderius Erasmus in Holland.

**Repartee:** Conversation featuring snappy retorts and witticisms. Masters of *repartee* include Sydney Smith, Charles Lamb, and Oscar Wilde. An example is recorded in the meeting of "Beau" Nash and John Wesley: Nash said, "I never make way for a fool," to which Wesley responded, "Don't you? I always do," and stepped aside.

**Resolution:** The portion of a story following the climax, in which the conflict is resolved. The resolution of Jane Austen's *Northanger Abbey* is neatly summed up in the following sentence: "Henry and Catherine were married, the bells rang and every body smiled."

**Restoration:** See *Restoration Age*

**Restoration Age:** A period in English literature beginning with the crowning of Charles II in 1660 and running to about 1700. The era, which was characterized by a reaction against Puritanism, was the first great age of the comedy of manners. The finest literature of the era is typically witty and urbane, and often lewd. Prominent Restoration Age writers include William Congreve, Samuel Pepys, John Dryden, and John Milton.

**Revenge Tragedy:** A dramatic form popular during the Elizabethan Age, in which the protagonist, directed by the ghost of his murdered father or son, inflicts retaliation upon a powerful villain. Notable features of the revenge tragedy include violence, bizarre criminal acts, intrigue, insanity, a hesitant protagonist, and the use of soliloquy. Thomas Kyd's *Spanish Tragedy* is the first example of revenge tragedy in English, and William Shakespeare's *Hamlet* is perhaps the best. Extreme examples of revenge tragedy, such as John Webster's *The Duchess of Malfi*, are labeled "tragedies of blood." Also known as Tragedy of Blood.

**Revista:** The Spanish term for a vaudeville musical revue. Examples of *revistas* include Antonio Guzman Aguilera's *Mexico para los mexicanos*, Daniel Vanegas's *Maldito jazz*, and Don Catarino's *Whiskey, morfina y marihuana* and *El desterrado*.

**Rhetoric:** In literary criticism, this term denotes the art of ethical persuasion. In its strictest sense, rhetoric adheres to various principles developed since classical times for arranging facts and ideas in a clear, persuasive, appealing manner. The term is also used to refer to effective prose in general and theories of or methods for composing effective prose. Classical examples of rhetorics include *The Rhetoric of Aristotle*, Quintillian's *Institutio Oratoria*, and Cicero's *Ad Herennium*.

**Rhetorical Question:** A question intended to provoke thought, but not an expressed answer, in the reader. It is most commonly used in oratory and other persuasive genres. The following lines from Thomas Gray's "Elegy Written in a Country Churchyard" ask rhetorical questions: Can storied urn or animated bust Back to its mansion call the fleeting breath? Can Honour's voice provoke the silent dust, Or Flattery soothe the dull cold ear of Death?

**Rhyme:** When used as a noun in literary criticism, this term generally refers to a poem in which words sound identical or very similar and appear in parallel positions in two or more lines. Rhymes are classified into different types according to where they fall in a line or stanza or according to the degree of similarity they exhibit in their spellings and sounds. Some major types of rhyme are "masculine" rhyme, "feminine" rhyme, and "triple" rhyme. In a masculine rhyme, the rhyming sound falls in a single accented syllable, as with "heat" and "eat." Feminine rhyme is a rhyme of two syllables, one stressed and one unstressed, as with "merry" and "tarry." Triple rhyme matches the sound of the accented syllable and the two unaccented syllables that follow: "narrative" and "declarative." Robert Browning alternates feminine and masculine rhymes in his "Soliloquy of the Spanish Cloister": Gr-r-r—there go, my heart's abhorrence! Water your damned flower-pots, do! If hate killed men, Brother Lawrence, God's blood, would not mine kill you! What? Your myrtle-bush wants trimming? Oh, that rose has prior claims— Needs its leaden vase filled brimming? Hell dry you up with flames! Triple rhymes can be found in Thomas Hood's "Bridge of Sighs," George Gordon Byron's satirical verse, and Ogden Nash's comic poems.

**Rhyme Royal:** A stanza of seven lines composed in iambic pentameter and rhymed *ababbcc.* The name is said to be a tribute to King James I of Scotland, who made much use of the form in his poetry. Examples of rhyme royal include Geoffrey Chaucer's *The Parlement of Foules,* William Shakespeare's *The Rape of Lucrece,* William Morris's *The Early Paradise,* and John Masefield's *The Widow in the Bye Street.*

**Rhyme Scheme:** See *Rhyme*

**Rhythm:** A regular pattern of sound, time intervals, or events occurring in writing, most often and most discernably in poetry. Regular, reliable rhythm is known to be soothing to humans, while interrupted, unpredictable, or rapidly changing rhythm is disturbing. These effects are known to authors, who use them to produce a desired reaction in the reader. An example of a form of irregular rhythm is sprung rhythm poetry; quantitative verse, on the other hand, is very regular in its rhythm.

**Rising Action:** The part of a drama where the plot becomes increasingly complicated. Rising action leads up to the climax, or turning point, of a drama. The final "chase scene" of an action film is generally the rising action which culminates in the film's climax.

**Rococo:** A style of European architecture that flourished in the eighteenth century, especially in France. The most notable features of *rococo* are its extensive use of ornamentation and its themes of lightness, gaiety, and intimacy. In literary criticism, the term is often used disparagingly to refer to a decadent or over-ornamental style. Alexander Pope's "The Rape of the Lock" is an example of literary *rococo.*

**Roman à clef:** A French phrase meaning "novel with a key." It refers to a narrative in which real persons are portrayed under fictitious names. Jack Kerouac, for example, portrayed various real-life beat generation figures under fictitious names in his *On the Road.*

**Romance:** A broad term, usually denoting a narrative with exotic, exaggerated, often idealized characters, scenes, and themes. Nathaniel Hawthorne called his *The House of the Seven Gables* and *The Marble Faun* romances in order to distinguish them from clearly realistic works.

**Romantic Age:** See *Romanticism*

**Romanticism:** This term has two widely accepted meanings. In historical criticism, it refers to a European intellectual and artistic movement of the late eighteenth and early nineteenth centuries that sought greater freedom of personal expression than that allowed by the strict rules of literary form and logic of the eighteenth-century neoclassicists. The Romantics preferred emotional and imaginative expression to rational analysis. They considered the individual to be at the center of all experience and so placed him or her at the center of their art. The Romantics believed that the creative imagination reveals nobler truths—unique feelings and attitudes—than those that could be discovered by logic or by scientific examination. Both the natural world and the state of childhood were important sources for revelations of "eternal truths." "Romanticism" is also used as a general term to refer to a type of sensibility found in all periods of literary history and usually considered to be in opposition to the principles of classicism. In this sense, Romanticism signifies any work or philosophy in which the exotic or dreamlike figure strongly, or that is devoted to individualistic expression, self-analysis, or a pursuit of a higher realm of knowledge than can be discovered by human reason. Prominent Romantics include Jean-Jacques Rousseau, William Wordsworth, John Keats, Lord Byron, and Johann Wolfgang von Goethe.

**Romantics:** See *Romanticism*

**Russian Symbolism:** A Russian poetic movement, derived from French symbolism, that flourished between 1894 and 1910. While some Russian Symbolists continued in the French tradition, stressing aestheticism and the importance of suggestion above didactic intent, others saw their craft as a form of mystical worship, and themselves as mediators between the supernatural and the mundane. Russian symbolists include Aleksandr Blok, Vyacheslav Ivanovich Ivanov, Fyodor Sologub, Andrey Bely, Nikolay Gumilyov, and Vladimir Sergeyevich Solovyov.

## S

**Satire:** A work that uses ridicule, humor, and wit to criticize and provoke change in human nature and institutions. There are two major types of satire: "formal" or "direct" satire speaks directly to the reader or to a character in the work; "indirect" satire relies upon the ridiculous behavior of its characters to make its point. Formal satire is further divided into two manners: the "Horatian," which ridicules gently, and the "Juvenalian," which derides its subjects harshly and bitterly. Voltaire's novella *Candide* is an indirect satire. Jonathan Swift's essay "A Modest Proposal" is a Juvenalian satire.

**Scansion:** The analysis or "scanning" of a poem to determine its meter and often its rhyme scheme. The most common system of scansion uses accents (slanted lines drawn above syllables) to show stressed syllables, breves (curved lines drawn above syllables) to show unstressed syllables, and vertical lines to separate each foot. In the first line of John Keats's *Endymion,* "A thing of beauty is a joy forever:" the word "thing," the first syllable of "beauty," the word "joy," and the second syllable of "forever" are stressed, while the words "A" and "of," the second syllable of "beauty," the word "a," and the first and third syllables of "forever" are unstressed. In the second line: "Its loveliness increases; it will never" a pair of vertical lines separate the foot ending with "increases" and the one beginning with "it."

**Scene:** A subdivision of an act of a drama, consisting of continuous action taking place at a single time and in a single location. The beginnings and endings of scenes may be indicated by clearing the stage of actors and props or by the entrances and exits of important characters. The first act of William Shakespeare's *Winter's Tale* is comprised of two scenes.

**Science Fiction:** A type of narrative about or based upon real or imagined scientific theories and technology. Science fiction is often peopled with alien creatures and set on other planets or in different dimensions. Karel Capek's *R.U.R.* is a major work of science fiction.

**Second Person:** See *Point of View*

**Semiotics:** The study of how literary forms and conventions affect the meaning of language. Semioticians include Ferdinand de Saussure, Charles Sanders Pierce, Claude Levi-Strauss, Jacques Lacan, Michel Foucault, Jacques Derrida, Roland Barthes, and Julia Kristeva.

**Sestet:** Any six-line poem or stanza. Examples of the sestet include the last six lines of the Petrarchan sonnet form, the stanza form of Robert Burns's "A Poet's Welcome to his love-begotten Daughter," and the sestina form in W. H. Auden's "Paysage Moralise."

**Setting:** The time, place, and culture in which the action of a narrative takes place. The elements of setting may include geographic location, characters' physical and mental environments, prevailing cultural attitudes, or the historical time in which the action takes place. Examples of settings include the romanticized Scotland in Sir Walter Scott's "Waverley" novels, the French provincial setting in Gustave Flaubert's *Madame Bovary,* the fictional Wessex country of Thomas Hardy's novels, and the small towns of southern Ontario in Alice Munro's short stories.

**Shakespearean Sonnet:** See *Sonnet*

**Signifying Monkey:** A popular trickster figure in black folklore, with hundreds of tales about this character documented since the 19th century. Henry Louis Gates Jr. examines the history of the signifying monkey in *The Signifying Monkey: Towards a Theory of Afro-American Literary Criticism,* published in 1988.

**Simile:** A comparison, usually using "like" or "as," of two essentially dissimilar things, as in "coffee as cold as ice" or "He sounded like a broken record." The title of Ernest

Hemingway's "Hills Like White Elephants" contains a simile.

**Slang:** A type of informal verbal communication that is generally unacceptable for formal writing. Slang words and phrases are often colorful exaggerations used to emphasize the speaker's point; they may also be shortened versions of an often-used word or phrase. Examples of American slang from the 1990s include "yuppie" (an acronym for Young Urban Professional), "awesome" (for "excellent"), wired (for "nervous" or "excited"), and "chill out" (for relax).

**Slant Rhyme:** See *Consonance*

**Slave Narrative:** Autobiographical accounts of American slave life as told by escaped slaves. These works first appeared during the abolition movement of the 1830s through the 1850s. Olaudah Equiano's *The Interesting Narrative of Olaudah Equiano, or Gustavus Vassa, The African* and Harriet Ann Jacobs's *Incidents in the Life of a Slave Girl* are examples of the slave narrative.

**Social Realism:** See *Socialist Realism*

**Socialist Realism:** The Socialist Realism school of literary theory was proposed by Maxim Gorky and established as a dogma by the first Soviet Congress of Writers. It demanded adherence to a communist worldview in works of literature. Its doctrines required an objective viewpoint comprehensible to the working classes and themes of social struggle featuring strong proletarian heroes. A successful work of socialist realism is Nikolay Ostrovsky's *Kak zakalyalas stal* (*How the Steel Was Tempered*). Also known as Social Realism.

**Soliloquy:** A monologue in a drama used to give the audience information and to develop the speaker's character. It is typically a projection of the speaker's innermost thoughts. Usually delivered while the speaker is alone on stage, a soliloquy is intended to present an illusion of unspoken reflection. A celebrated soliloquy is Hamlet's "To be or not to be" speech in William Shakespeare's *Hamlet*.

**Sonnet:** A fourteen-line poem, usually composed in iambic pentameter, employing one of several rhyme schemes. There are three major types of sonnets, upon which all other variations of the form are based: the "Petrarchan" or "Italian" sonnet, the "Shakespearean" or "English" sonnet, and the "Spenserian" sonnet. A Petrarchan sonnet consists of an octave rhymed *abbaabba* and a "sestet" rhymed either *cdecde, cdccdc,* or *cdedce*. The octave poses a question or problem, relates a narrative, or puts forth a proposition; the sestet presents a solution to the problem, comments upon the narrative, or applies the proposition put forth in the octave. The Shakespearean sonnet is divided into three quatrains and a couplet rhymed *abab cdcd efef gg.* The couplet provides an epigrammatic comment on the narrative or problem put forth in the quatrains. The Spenserian sonnet uses three quatrains and a couplet like the Shakespearean, but links their three rhyme schemes in this way: *abab bcbc cdcd ee.* The Spenserian sonnet develops its theme in two parts like the Petrarchan, its final six lines resolving a problem, analyzing a narrative, or applying a proposition put forth in its first eight lines. Examples of sonnets can be found in Petrarch's *Canzoniere,* Edmund Spenser's *Amoretti,* Elizabeth Barrett Browning's *Sonnets from the Portuguese,* Rainer Maria Rilke's *Sonnets to Orpheus,* and Adrienne Rich's poem "The Insusceptibles."

**Spenserian Sonnet:** See *Sonnet*

**Spenserian Stanza:** A nine-line stanza having eight verses in iambic pentameter, its ninth verse in iambic hexameter, and the rhyme scheme ababbcbcc. This stanza form was first used by Edmund Spenser in his allegorical poem *The Faerie Queene.*

**Spondee:** In poetry meter, a foot consisting of two long or stressed syllables occurring together. This form is quite rare in English verse, and is usually composed of two monosyllabic words. The first foot in the following line from Robert Burns's "Green Grow the Rashes" is an example of a spondee: Green grow the rashes, O.

**Sprung Rhythm:** Versification using a specific number of accented syllables per line but disregarding the number of unaccented syllables that fall in each line, producing an irregular rhythm in the poem. Gerard Manley Hopkins, who coined the term "sprung rhythm," is the most notable practitioner of this technique.

**Stanza:** A subdivision of a poem consisting of lines grouped together, often in recurring patterns of rhyme, line length, and meter. Stanzas may also serve as units of thought in a poem much like paragraphs in prose. Examples of stanza forms include the quatrain, *terza rima, ottava rima,* Spenserian, and the so-called *In Memoriam* stanza from Alfred, Lord Tennyson's poem by that title. The following is an example of the latter form: Love is and was my lord and king, And in his presence I attend To hear the tidings of my friend, Which every hour his couriers bring.

**Stereotype:** A stereotype was originally the name for a duplication made during the printing process; this led to its modern definition as a person or thing that is (or is assumed to be) the same as all others of its type. Common stereotypical characters include the absent-minded professor, the nagging wife, the troublemaking teenager, and the kindhearted grandmother.

**Stream of Consciousness:** A narrative technique for rendering the inward experience of a character. This technique is designed to give the impression of an ever-changing series of thoughts, emotions, images, and memories in the spontaneous and seemingly illogical order that they occur in life. The textbook example of stream of consciousness is the last section of James Joyce's *Ulysses.*

**Structuralism:** A twentieth-century movement in literary criticism that examines how literary texts arrive at their meanings, rather than the meanings themselves. There are two major types of structuralist analysis: one examines the way patterns of linguistic structures unify a specific text and emphasize certain elements of that text, and the other interprets the way literary forms and conventions affect the meaning of language itself. Prominent structuralists include Michel Foucault, Roman Jakobson, and Roland Barthes.

**Structure:** The form taken by a piece of literature. The structure may be made obvious for ease of understanding, as in nonfiction works, or may obscured for artistic purposes, as in some poetry or seemingly "unstructured" prose. Examples of common literary structures include the plot of a narrative, the acts and scenes of a drama, and such poetic forms as the Shakespearean sonnet and the Pindaric ode.

**Sturm und Drang:** A German term meaning "storm and stress." It refers to a German literary movement of the 1770s and 1780s that reacted against the order and rationalism of the enlightenment, focusing instead on the intense experience of extraordinary individuals. Highly romantic, works of this movement, such as Johann Wolfgang von Goethe's *Gotz von Berlichingen,* are typified by realism, rebelliousness, and intense emotionalism.

**Style:** A writer's distinctive manner of arranging words to suit his or her ideas and purpose in writing. The unique imprint of the author's personality upon his or her writing, style is the product of an author's way of arranging ideas and his or her use of diction, different sentence structures, rhythm, figures of speech, rhetorical principles, and other elements of composition. Styles may be classified according to period (Metaphysical, Augustan, Georgian), individual authors (Chaucerian, Miltonic, Jamesian), level (grand, middle, low, plain), or language (scientific, expository, poetic, journalistic).

**Subject:** The person, event, or theme at the center of a work of literature. A work may have one or more subjects of each type, with shorter works tending to have fewer and longer works tending to have more. The subjects of James Baldwin's novel *Go Tell It on the Mountain* include the themes of father-son relationships, religious conversion, black life, and sexuality. The subjects of Anne Frank's *Diary of a Young Girl* include Anne and her family members as well as World War II, the Holocaust, and the themes of war, isolation, injustice, and racism.

**Subjectivity:** Writing that expresses the author's personal feelings about his subject, and which may or may not include factual information about the subject. Subjectivity is demonstrated in James Joyce's *Portrait of the Artist as a Young Man,* Samuel Butler's *The Way of All Flesh,* and Thomas Wolfe's *Look Homeward, Angel.*

**Subplot:** A secondary story in a narrative. A subplot may serve as a motivating or complicating force for the main plot of the work, or it may provide emphasis for, or relief from, the main plot. The conflict between the Capulets and the Montagues in William Shakespeare's *Romeo and Juliet* is an example of a subplot.

**Surrealism:** A term introduced to criticism by Guillaume Apollinaire and later adopted by Andre Breton. It refers to a French literary and artistic movement founded in the 1920s. The Surrealists sought to express unconscious thoughts and feelings in their works. The best-known technique used for achieving this aim was automatic writing— transcriptions of spontaneous outpourings from the unconscious. The Surrealists proposed to unify the contrary levels of conscious and unconscious, dream and reality, objectivity and subjectivity into a new level of "super-realism." Surrealism can be found in the poetry of Paul Eluard, Pierre Reverdy, and Louis Aragon, among others.

**Suspense:** A literary device in which the author maintains the audience's attention through the buildup of events, the outcome of which will soon be revealed. Suspense in William Shakespeare's *Hamlet* is sustained throughout by the question of whether or not the Prince will achieve what he has been instructed to do and of what he intends to do.

**Syllogism:** A method of presenting a logical argument. In its most basic form, the syllogism consists of a major premise, a minor premise, and a conclusion. An example of a syllogism is: Major premise: When it snows, the streets get wet. Minor premise: It is snowing. Conclusion: The streets are wet.

**Symbol:** Something that suggests or stands for something else without losing its original identity. In literature, symbols combine their literal meaning with the suggestion of an abstract concept. Literary symbols are of two types: those that carry complex associations of meaning no matter what their contexts, and those that derive their suggestive meaning from their functions in specific literary works. Examples of symbols are sunshine suggesting happiness, rain suggesting sorrow, and storm clouds suggesting despair.

**Symbolism:** This term has two widely accepted meanings. In historical criticism, it denotes an early modernist literary movement initiated in France during the nineteenth century that reacted against the prevailing standards of realism. Writers in this movement aimed to evoke, indirectly and symbolically, an order of being beyond the material world of the five senses. Poetic expression of personal emotion figured strongly in the movement, typically by means of a private set of symbols uniquely identifiable with the individual poet. The principal aim of the Symbolists was to express in words the highly complex feelings that grew out of everyday contact with the world. In a broader sense, the term "symbolism" refers to the use of one object to represent another. Early members of the Symbolist movement included the French authors Charles Baudelaire and Arthur Rimbaud; William Butler Yeats, James Joyce, and T. S. Eliot were influenced as the movement moved to Ireland, England, and the United States. Examples of the concept of symbolism include a flag that stands for a nation or movement, or an empty cupboard used to suggest hopelessness, poverty, and despair.

**Symbolist:** See *Symbolism*

**Symbolist Movement:** See *Symbolism*

**Sympathetic Fallacy:** See *Affective Fallacy*

# T

**Tale:** A story told by a narrator with a simple plot and little character development. Tales are usually relatively short and often carry a simple message. Examples of tales can be found in the work of Rudyard Kipling, Somerset Maugham, Saki, Anton Chekhov, Guy de Maupassant, and Armistead Maupin.

**Tall Tale:** A humorous tale told in a straightforward, credible tone but relating absolutely impossible events or feats of the characters. Such tales were commonly told of frontier adventures during the settlement of the west in the United States. Tall tales have been spun around such legendary heroes as Mike Fink, Paul Bunyan, Davy Crockett, Johnny Appleseed, and Captain Stormalong as well as the real-life William F. Cody and Annie Oakley. Literary use of tall tales can be found in Washington Irving's *History of New York*, Mark Twain's *Life on the Mississippi,* and in the German R. F. Raspe's *Baron Munchausen's Narratives of His Marvellous Travels and Campaigns in Russia.*

**Tanka:** A form of Japanese poetry similar to *haiku*. A *tanka* is five lines long, with the lines containing five, seven, five, seven, and seven syllables respectively. Skilled *tanka* authors include Ishikawa Takuboku, Masaoka Shiki, Amy Lowell, and Adelaide Crapsey.

**Teatro Grottesco:** See *Theater of the Grotesque*

**Terza Rima:** A three-line stanza form in poetry in which the rhymes are made on the last word of each line in the following manner: the first and third lines of the first stanza, then the second line of the first stanza and the first and third lines of the second stanza, and so on with the middle line of any stanza rhyming with the first and third lines of the following stanza. An example of *terza rima* is Percy Bysshe Shelley's "The Triumph of Love": As in that trance of wondrous thought I lay This was the tenour of my waking dream. Methought I sate beside a public way Thick strewn with summer dust, and a great stream Of people there was hurrying to and fro Numerous as gnats upon the evening gleam, . . .

**Tetrameter:** See *Meter*

**Textual Criticism:** A branch of literary criticism that seeks to establish the authoritative text of a literary work. Textual critics typically compare all known manuscripts or printings of a single work in order to assess the meanings of differences and revisions. This procedure allows them to arrive at a definitive version that (supposedly) corresponds to the author's original intention. Textual criticism was applied during the Renaissance to salvage the classical texts of Greece and Rome, and modern works have been studied, for instance, to undo deliberate correction or censorship, as in the case of novels by Stephen Crane and Theodore Dreiser.

**Theater of Cruelty:** Term used to denote a group of theatrical techniques designed to eliminate the psychological and emotional distance between actors and audience. This concept, introduced in the 1930s in France, was intended to inspire a more intense theatrical experience than conventional theater allowed. The "cruelty" of this dramatic theory signified not sadism but heightened actor/audience involvement in the dramatic event. The theater of cruelty was theorized by Antonin Artaud in his *Le Theatre et son double* (*The Theatre and Its Double*), and also appears in the work of Jerzy Grotowski, Jean Genet, Jean Vilar, and Arthur Adamov, among others.

**Theater of the Absurd:** A post-World War II dramatic trend characterized by radical theatrical innovations. In works influenced by the Theater of the Absurd, nontraditional, sometimes grotesque characterizations, plots, and stage sets reveal a meaningless universe in which human values are irrelevant. Existentialist themes of estrangement, absurdity, and futility link many of the works of this movement. The principal writers of the Theater of the Absurd are Samuel Beckett, Eugene Ionesco, Jean Genet, and Harold Pinter.

**Theater of the Grotesque:** An Italian theatrical movement characterized by plays written around the ironic and macabre aspects of daily life in the World War I era. Theater of the Grotesque was named after the play *The Mask and the Face* by Luigi Chiarelli, which was described as "a grotesque in three acts." The movement influenced the work of Italian dramatist Luigi Pirandello, author of *Right You Are, If You Think You Are*. Also known as *Teatro Grottesco*.

**Theme:** The main point of a work of literature. The term is used interchangeably with thesis. The theme of William Shakespeare's *Othello*—jealousy—is a common one.

**Thesis:** A thesis is both an essay and the point argued in the essay. Thesis novels and thesis plays share the quality of containing a thesis which is supported through the action of the story. A master's thesis and a doctoral dissertation are two theses required of graduate students.

**Thesis Play:** See *Thesis*

**Three Unities:** See *Unities*

**Tone:** The author's attitude toward his or her audience may be deduced from the tone of the work. A formal tone may create distance or convey politeness, while an informal tone may encourage a friendly, intimate, or intrusive feeling in the reader. The author's attitude toward his or her subject matter may also be deduced from the tone of the words he or she uses in discussing it. The tone of John F. Kennedy's speech which included the appeal to "ask not what your country can do for you" was intended to instill feelings of camaraderie and national pride in listeners.

**Tragedy:** A drama in prose or poetry about a noble, courageous hero of excellent character who, because of some tragic character flaw or *hamartia*, brings ruin upon him- or herself. Tragedy treats its subjects in a dignified and serious manner, using poetic language to help evoke pity and fear and bring about catharsis, a purging of these emotions. The tragic form was practiced extensively by the ancient Greeks. In the Middle Ages, when classical works were virtually unknown, tragedy came to denote any works about the fall of persons from exalted to low conditions due to any reason: fate, vice, weakness, etc. According to the classical definition of tragedy, such works present the "pathetic"—that which evokes pity—rather than the tragic. The classical form of tragedy was revived in the sixteenth century; it flourished especially on the Elizabethan stage. In modern times, dramatists have attempted to adapt the form to the needs of modern society by drawing their heroes from the ranks of ordinary men and women and defining the nobility of these heroes in terms of spirit rather than exalted social standing. The greatest classical example of tragedy is Sophocles' *Oedipus Rex*. The "pathetic" derivation is exemplified in "The Monk's Tale" in Geoffrey Chaucer's *Canterbury Tales*. Notable works produced during the sixteenth century revival include William Shakespeare's *Hamlet, Othello,* and *King Lear*. Modern dramatists working in the tragic tradition include Henrik Ibsen, Arthur Miller, and Eugene O'Neill.

**Tragedy of Blood:** See *Revenge Tragedy*

**Tragic Flaw:** In a tragedy, the quality within the hero or heroine which leads to his or her downfall. Examples of the tragic flaw include Othello's jealousy and Hamlet's indecisiveness, although most great tragedies defy such simple interpretation.

**Transcendentalism:** An American philosophical and religious movement, based in New England from around 1835 until the Civil War. Transcendentalism was a form of American romanticism that had its roots abroad in the works of Thomas Carlyle, Samuel Coleridge, and Johann Wolfgang von Goethe. The Transcendentalists stressed the importance of intuition and subjective experience in communication with God. They rejected religious dogma and texts in favor of mysticism and scientific naturalism. They pursued truths that lie beyond the "colorless"

realms perceived by reason and the senses and were active social reformers in public education, women's rights, and the abolition of slavery. Prominent members of the group include Ralph Waldo Emerson and Henry David Thoreau.

**Trickster:** A character or figure common in Native American and African literature who uses his ingenuity to defeat enemies and escape difficult situations. Tricksters are most often animals, such as the spider, hare, or coyote, although they may take the form of humans as well. Examples of trickster tales include Thomas King's *A Coyote Columbus Story*, Ashley F. Bryan's *The Dancing Granny* and Ishmael Reed's *The Last Days of Louisiana Red*.

**Trimeter:** See *Meter*

**Triple Rhyme:** See *Rhyme*

**Trochee:** See *Foot*

# U

**Understatement:** See *Irony*

**Unities:** Strict rules of dramatic structure, formulated by Italian and French critics of the Renaissance and based loosely on the principles of drama discussed by Aristotle in his *Poetics*. Foremost among these rules were the three unities of action, time, and place that compelled a dramatist to: (1) construct a single plot with a beginning, middle, and end that details the causal relationships of action and character; (2) restrict the action to the events of a single day; and (3) limit the scene to a single place or city. The unities were observed faithfully by continental European writers until the Romantic Age, but they were never regularly observed in English drama. Modern dramatists are typically more concerned with a unity of impression or emotional effect than with any of the classical unities. The unities are observed in Pierre Corneille's tragedy *Polyeuctes* and Jean-Baptiste Racine's *Phedre*. Also known as Three Unities.

**Urban Realism:** A branch of realist writing that attempts to accurately reflect the often harsh facts of modern urban existence. Some works by Stephen Crane, Theodore Dreiser, Charles Dickens, Fyodor Dostoyevsky, Emile Zola, Abraham Cahan, and Henry Fuller feature urban realism. Modern examples include

Claude Brown's *Manchild in the Promised Land* and Ron Milner's *What the Wine Sellers Buy.*

**Utopia:** A fictional perfect place, such as "paradise" or "heaven." Early literary utopias were included in Plato's *Republic* and Sir Thomas More's *Utopia,* while more modern utopias can be found in Samuel Butler's *Erewhon,* Theodor Herzka's *A Visit to Freeland,* and H. G. Wells' *A Modern Utopia.*

**Utopian:** See *Utopia*

**Utopianism:** See *Utopia*

# V

**Verisimilitude:** Literally, the appearance of truth. In literary criticism, the term refers to aspects of a work of literature that seem true to the reader. Verisimilitude is achieved in the work of Honore de Balzac, Gustave Flaubert, and Henry James, among other late nineteenth-century realist writers.

**Vers de societe:** See *Occasional Verse*

**Vers libre:** See *Free Verse*

**Verse:** A line of metered language, a line of a poem, or any work written in verse. The following line of verse is from the epic poem *Don Juan* by Lord Byron: "My way is to begin with the beginning."

**Versification:** The writing of verse. Versification may also refer to the meter, rhyme, and other mechanical components of a poem. Composition of a "Roses are red, violets are blue" poem to suit an occasion is a common form of versification practiced by students.

**Victorian:** Refers broadly to the reign of Queen Victoria of England (1837-1901) and to anything with qualities typical of that era. For example, the qualities of smug narrowmindedness, bourgeois materialism, faith in social progress, and priggish morality are often considered Victorian. This stereotype is contradicted by such dramatic intellectual developments as the theories of Charles Darwin, Karl Marx, and Sigmund Freud (which stirred strong debates in England) and the critical attitudes of serious Victorian writers like Charles Dickens and George Eliot. In literature, the Victorian Period

was the great age of the English novel, and the latter part of the era saw the rise of movements such as decadence and symbolism. Works of Victorian literature include the poetry of Robert Browning and Alfred, Lord Tennyson, the criticism of Matthew Arnold and John Ruskin, and the novels of Emily Bronte, William Makepeace Thackeray, and Thomas Hardy. Also known as Victorian Age and Victorian Period.

**Victorian Age:** See *Victorian*

**Victorian Period:** See *Victorian*

# W

**Weltanschauung:** A German term referring to a person's worldview or philosophy. Examples of *weltanschauung* include Thomas Hardy's view of the human being as the victim of fate, destiny, or impersonal forces and circumstances, and the disillusioned and laconic cynicism expressed by such poets of the 1930s as W. H. Auden, Sir Stephen Spender, and Sir William Empson.

**Weltschmerz:** A German term meaning "world pain." It describes a sense of anguish about the nature of existence, usually associated with a melancholy, pessimistic attitude. *Weltschmerz* was expressed in England by George Gordon, Lord Byron in his *Manfred* and *Childe Harold's Pilgrimage,* in France by Viscount de Chateaubriand, Alfred de Vigny, and Alfred de Musset, in Russia by Aleksandr Pushkin and Mikhail Lermontov, in Poland by Juliusz Slowacki, and in America by Nathaniel Hawthorne.

# Z

**Zarzuela:** A type of Spanish operetta. Writers of *zarzuelas* include Lope de Vega and Pedro Calderon.

**Zeitgeist:** A German term meaning "spirit of the time." It refers to the moral and intellectual trends of a given era. Examples of *zeitgeist* include the preoccupation with the more morbid aspects of dying and death in some Jacobean literature, especially in the works of dramatists Cyril Tourneur and John Webster, and the decadence of the French Symbolists.

# Cumulative Author/Title Index

# G

Gale, Zona
  *Miss Lulu Bett:* V17
García Lorca, Federico
  *Blood Wedding:* V10
  *The House of Bernarda Alba:* V4
Gardner, Herb
  *I'm Not Rappaport:* V18
  *A Thousand Clowns:* V20
Gems, Pam
  *Stanley:* V25
Genet, Jean
  *The Balcony:* V10
Gerstenberg, Alice
  *Overtones:* V17
*Getting Out* (Norman): V32
*The Ghost Sonata* (Strindberg): V9
*Ghosts* (Ibsen): V11
Gibson, William
  *The Miracle Worker:* V2
  *The Miracle Worker* (Motion
    picture): V28
Gilbert, Willie
  *How to Succeed in Business
    without Really Trying:* V31
Gilman, Rebecca
  *Blue Surge:* V23
Gilroy, Frank D.
  *The Subject Was Roses:* V17
*The Gin Game* (Coburn): V23
Ginzburg, Natalia
  *The Advertisement:* V14
Giraudoux, Jean
  *The Madwoman of Chaillot:* V28
Glaspell, Susan
  *Alison's House:* V24
  *Trifles:* V8
  *The Verge:* V18
*The Glass Menagerie* (Williams): V1
*Glengarry Glen Ross* (Mamet): V2
*Glengarry Glen Ross* (Motion
    picture): V34
*The God of Carnage* (Reza): V34
Gogol, Nikolai
  *The Government Inspector:* V12
*Golden Boy* (Odets): V17
Goldman, James
  *The Lion in Winter:* V20
Goldoni, Carlo
  *The Servant of Two Masters:* V27
Goldsmith, Oliver
  *She Stoops to Conquer:* V1
Gomolvilas, Prince
  *The Theory of Everything:* V34
*The Good Person of Szechwan*
    (Brecht): V9
*Goodnight Desdemona (Good
    Morning Juliet)* (MacDonald):
    V23
Goodrich, Frances
  *The Diary of Anne Frank:* V15

Gorki, Maxim
  *The Lower Depths:* V9
*The Gospel at Colonus* (Breuer): V35
*The Governess* (Simon): V27
*The Government Inspector* (Gogol):
    V12
*The Great God Brown* (O'Neill): V11
*The Great White Hope* (Sackler): V15
*The Green Pastures* (Connelly): V12
Greenberg, Richard
  *Take Me Out:* V24
  *Three Days of Rain:* V32
Gregg, Stephen
  *This Is a Test:* V28
Guare, John
  *A Free Man of Color:* V34
  *The House of Blue Leaves:* V8
  *Six Degrees of Separation:* V13
  *Six Degrees of Separation* (Motion
    Picture): V33
  *Guys and Dolls* (Burrows, Loesser,
    Swerling): V29

# H

*Habitat* (Thompson): V22
Hackett, Albert
  *The Diary of Anne Frank:* V15
*The Hairy Ape* (O'Neill): V4
Hammerstein, Oscar II
  *The King and I:* V1
Hanff, Helene
  *84, Charing Cross Road:* V17
Hansberry, Lorraine
  *A Raisin in the Sun:* V2
  *A Raisin in the Sun* (Motion
    picture): V29
Hare, David
  *Blue Room:* V7
  *Plenty:* V4
  *The Secret Rapture:* V16
Harris, Bill
  *Robert Johnson: Trick the Devil:*
    V27
Hart, Moss
  *Once in a Lifetime:* V10
  *You Can't Take It with You:* V1
*Harvey* (Chase): V11
Havel, Vaclav
  *The Memorandum:* V10
*Having Our Say: The Delany Sisters'
    First 100 Years* (Mann): V28
*Hay Fever* (Coward): V6
Hayes, Joseph
  *The Desperate Hours:* V20
*Heather Raffo's 9 Parts of Desire*
    (Raffo): V27
Hecht, Ben
  *The Front Page:* V9
*Hedda Gabler* (Ibsen): V6
Heggen, Thomas
  *Mister Roberts:* V20

*The Heidi Chronicles* (Wasserstein):
    V5
*Hell-Bent fer Heaven* (Hughes): V31
Hellman, Lillian
  *The Children's Hour:* V3
  *The Little Foxes:* V1
  *Watch on the Rhine:* V14
Henley, Beth
  *Crimes of the Heart:* V2
  *Impossible Marriage:* V26
  *The Miss Firecracker Contest:* V21
*Henrietta* (Jones Meadows): V27
Herzog, Amy
  *4,000 Miles:* V32
Highway, Tomson
  *The Rez Sisters:* V2
*Hippolytus* (Euripides): V25
*The Hitch-Hiker* (Fletcher): V34
Hollmann, Mark
  *Urinetown:* V27
Holmes, Rupert
  *The Mystery of Edwin Drood:* V28
*The Homecoming* (Pinter): V3
*The Hostage* (Behan): V7
*Hot L Baltimore* (Wilson): V9
*The House of Bernarda Alba*
    (GarcíaLorca, Federico): V4
*The House of Blue Leaves* (Guare):
    V8
*How I Learned to Drive* (Vogel): V14
*How to Succeed in Business without
    Really Trying* (Loesser,
    Burrows, Weinstock, Gilbert):
    V31
Howard, Sidney
  *They Knew What They Wanted:* V29
Howe, Tina
  *Coastal Disturbances:* V32
Hudes, Quiara Alegría
  *Water by the Spoonful:* V33
Hughes, Hatcher
  *Hell-Bent fer Heaven:* V31
Hughes, Langston
  *Black Nativity:* V32
  *Mulatto:* V18
  *Mule Bone:* V6
Hurston, Zora Neale
  *Mule Bone:* V6
  *Poker!:* V30
Hwang, David Henry
  *M. Butterfly:* V11
  *The Sound of a Voice:* V18
  *Trying to Find Chinatown:* V29

# I

*I Am My Own Wife* (Wright): V23
*I Hate Hamlet* (Rudnick): V22
*I Never Saw Another Butterfly*
    (Raspanti): V27
*I Remember Mama* (Van Druten):
    V30

*I, Too, Speak of the Rose*
   (Carballido): V4
Ibsen, Henrik
   *Brand:* V16
   *A Doll's House:* V1
   *An Enemy of the People:* V25
   *Ghosts:* V11
   *Hedda Gabler:* V6
   *The Master Builder:* V15
   *Peer Gynt:* V8
   *The Wild Duck:* V10
*The Iceman Cometh* (O'Neill): V5
*An Ideal Husband* (Wilde): V21
*Idiot's Delight* (Sherwood): V15
*Icebound* (Davis): V31
Iizuka, Naomi
   *36 Views:* V21
*Ile* (O'Neill): V26
*I'm Black When I'm Singing, I'm Blue*
   *When I Ain't* (Sanchez): V32
*I'm Not Rappaport* (Gardner): V18
*Imaginary Friends* (Ephron): V22
*The Imaginary Invalid* (Molière): V20
*The Importance of Being Earnest*
   (Wilde): V4
*The Importance of Being Earnest*
   (Motion picture): V31
*Impossible Marriage* (Henley): V26
*Inadmissible Evidence* (Osborne):
   V24
*India Song* (Duras): V21
*Indian Ink* (Stoppard): V11
*Indians* (Kopit): V24
*Indiscretions* (Cocteau): V24
Inge, William
   *Bus Stop:* V8
   *Come Back, Little Sheba:* V3
   *Picnic:* V5
*Inherit the Wind* (Lawrence and Lee):
   V2
*The Insect Play* (Capek): V11
*Into the Woods* (Sondheim and
   Lapine): V25
Ionesco, Eugène
   *The Bald Soprano:* V4
   *The Chairs:* V9
   *The Killer:* V35
   *Rhinoceros:* V25
*Iphigenia in Taurus* (Euripides): V4
Ives, David
   *Time Flies:* V29

**J**

*J. B.* (MacLeish): V15
Jarry, Alfred
   *Ubu Roi:* V8
Jensen, Erik
   *The Exonerated:* V24
*Jesus Christ Superstar* (Webber and
   Rice): V7
*The Jew of Malta* (Marlowe): V13

*Joe Turner's Come and Gone*
   (Wilson): V17
Jones, LeRoi
   *see* Baraka, Amiri
Jones Meadows, Karen
   *Henrietta:* V27
Jonson, Ben(jamin)
   *The Alchemist:* V4
   *Volpone:* V10

**K**

Kaufman, George S.
   *Once in a Lifetime:* V10
   *You Can't Take It with You:* V1
Kaufman, Moisés
   *The Laramie Project:* V22
Kennedy, Adam P.
   *Sleep Deprivation Chamber:* V28
Kennedy, Adrienne
   *Funnyhouse of a Negro:* V9
   *Sleep Deprivation Chamber:* V28
*The Kentucky Cycle* (Schenkkan):
   V10
Kesselring, Joseph
   *Arsenic and Old Lace:* V20
*The Killer* (Ionesco): V35
*The King and I* (Hammerstein and
   Rodgers): V1
Kingsley, Sidney
   *Detective Story:* V19
   *Men in White:* V14
Kopit, Arthur
   *Indians:* V24
   *Oh Dad, Poor Dad, Mamma's*
      *Hung You in the Closet and I'm*
      *Feelin' So Sad:* V7
   *Y2K:* V14
Kotis, Greg
   *Urinetown:* V27
Kramm, Joseph
   *The Shrike:* V15
Kron, Lisa
   *Well:* V30
*Krapp's Last Tape* (Beckett): V7
Kushner, Tony
   *Angels in America:* V5
Kyd, Thomas
   *The Spanish Tragedy:* V21

**L**

*Lady Windermere's Fan* (Wilde): V9
Lapine, James
   *Into the Woods:* V25
*The Laramie Project* (Kaufman):
   V22
Larson, Jonathan
   *Rent:* V23
   *Rent* (Motion picture): V32
*The Last Night of Ballyhoo* (Uhry):
   V15
*The Last White Class* (Piercy): V33

Laurents, Arthur
   *West Side Story:* V27
Lavery, Bryony
   *Frozen:* V25
Lawrence, Jerome
   *Inherit the Wind:* V2
   *The Night Thoreau Spent in Jail:*
      V16
*Le Cid* (Corneille): V21
*Lear* (Bond): V3
Lee, Robert E.
   *Inherit the Wind:* V2
   *The Night Thoreau Spent in Jail:*
      V16
Leight, Warren
   *Nine-Ten:* V31
   *Side Man:* V19
Leonard, Hugh
   *The Au Pair Man:* V24
   *Da:* V13
Lessing, Doris
   *Play with a Tiger:* V20
*A Lesson from Aloes* (Fugard): V24
Letts, Tracy
   *August: Osage County:* V33
Levin, Ira
   *Deathtrap:* V34
*The Life and Adventures of Nicholas*
   *Nickleby* (Edgar): V15
*A Life in the Theatre* (Mamet): V12
*Life Is a Dream* (Calderón de la
   Barca): V23
*Light Shining in Buckinghamshire*
   (Churchill): V27
Lindsay, Howard
   *State of the Union:* V19
Lindsay-Abaire, David
   *Rabbit Hole:* V31
*The Lion in Winter* (Goldman):
   V20
*The Little Foxes* (Hellman): V1
*The Little Shop of Horrors*
   (Ashman): V33
Loesser, Frank
   *Guys and Dolls:* V29
   *How to Succeed in Business*
      *without Really Trying:* V31
Lonergan, Kenneth
   *This Is Our Youth:* V23
*Long Day's Journey into Night*
   (O'Neill): V2
*Look Back in Anger* (Osborne): V4
*Look Homeward, Angel* (Frings):
   V29
López, Josefina
   *Real Women Have Curves:* V33
*Los Vendidos* (Valdez): V29
*Lost in Yonkers* (Simon): V18
*Love for Love* (Congreve): V14
*Love! Valour! Compassion!*
   (McNally): V19
*The Lower Depths* (Gorki): V9

# Cumulative Nationality/Ethnicity Index

Robbins, Jerome
  *West Side Story:* V27
Sherman, Martin
  *Bent:* V20
Simon, Neil
  *Biloxi Blues:* V12
  *Brighton Beach Memoirs:* V6
  *The Governess:* V27
  *Lost in Yonkers:* V18
  *The Odd Couple:* V2
  *The Prisoner of Second Avenue:* V24
Sondheim, Stephen
  *Into the Woods:* V25
  *Sunday in the Park with George:* V27
  *West Side Story:* V27
Uhry, Alfred
  *Driving Miss Daisy:* V11
  *Driving Miss Daisy* (Motion picture): V30
  *The Last Night of Ballyhoo:* V15

## Mexican

Carballido, Emilio
  *I, Too, Speak of the Rose:* V4
López, Josefina
  *Real Women Have Curves:* V33
Solórzano, Carlos
  *Crossroads:* V26
Soto, Gary
  *Novio Boy:* V26

## Native Canadian

Highway, Tomson
  *The Rez Sisters:* V2

## Nigerian

Clark, John Pepper
  *The Raft:* V13
Soyinka, Wole
  *Death and the King's Horseman:* V10
  *The Trials of Brother Jero:* V26

## Norwegian

Ibsen, Henrik
  *Brand:* V16
  *A Doll's House:* V1
  *An Enemy of the People:* V25
  *Ghosts:* V11
  *Hedda Gabler:* V6
  *The Master Builder:* V15
  *Peer Gynt:* V8
  *The Wild Duck:* V10

## Puerto Rican

Rivera, José
  *Tape:* V30

## Romanian

Ionesco, Eugène
  *The Bald Soprano:* V4
  *The Chairs:* V9
  *The Killer:* V35
  *Rhinoceros:* V25

## Russian

Chekhov, Anton
  *The Bear:* V26
  *The Cherry Orchard:* V1
  *The Seagull:* V12
  *The Three Sisters:* V10
  *Uncle Vanya:* V5
Gogol, Nikolai
  *The Government Inspector:* V12
Gorki, Maxim
  *The Lower Depths:* V9
Rand, Ayn
  *Night of January 16th:* V35
Swerling, Jo
  *Guys and Dolls:* V29
Turgenev, Ivan
  *A Month in the Country:* V6

## Scottish

Barrie, J(ames) M.
  *Peter Pan:* V7

## South African

Fugard, Athol
  *Boesman & Lena:* V6
  *A Lesson from Aloes:* V24
  *"Master Harold" . . . and the Boys:* V3
  *Sizwe Bansi is Dead:* V10

## Spanish

Buero Vallejo, Antonio
  *The Sleep of Reason:* V11
Calderón de la Barca, Pedro
  *Life Is a Dream:* V23
García Lorca, Federico
  *Blood Wedding:* V10
  *The House of Bernarda Alba:* V4

## Swedish

Strindberg, August
  *The Ghost Sonata:* V9
  *Miss Julie:* V4
  *The Stronger:* V29

## Swiss

Frisch, Max
  *The Firebugs:* V25

## Ukrainian

Chayefsky, Paddy
  *Marty:* V26

## Venezuelan

Kaufman, Moisés
  *The Laramie Project:* V22

# Subject/Theme Index

$167.00                              6/18